Beyond MIDI

Beyond MIDI

The Handbook of Musical Codes

Edited by
Eleanor Selfridge-Field

The MIT Press
Cambridge, Massachusetts
London, England

Library of Congress Cataloging-in-Publication Data

Beyond MIDI: the handbook of musical codes / edited by Eleanor Selfridge-Field.
    p. cm.
    Includes bibliographical references and index.
    ISBN 0-262-19394-9
    1. Music—Data processing. 2. Musical notation—Data processing. 3. MIDI (Standard) 4. Computer sound processing. I. Selfridge-Field, Eleanor.
ML74.B49 1997
780'.285'572—dc21   97-2596
                                                      CIP
                                                      MN

Printed and bound in the United States of America.

Finale is a registered trademark of Coda Music Technology.
MuseData is a registered trademark of the Center for Computer Assisted Research in the Humanities.
Nightingale is a registered trademark of Advanced Music Notation Systems.
NoteScan is a registered trademark of Grande Software.
SCORE is a registered trademark of San Andreas Press.
Windows and *Windows NT* are registered trademarks of Microsoft Corp.

Other product names mentioned in this text may also be protected.

Contents

§ Musical Notation Codes (2): Other ASCII Representations

§ **Codes for Data Management and Analysis (1):**
    Monophonic Representations

§ **Codes for Data Management and Analysis (2):**
    Polyphonic Representations

§ **Reflections**

Preface

The purpose of *Beyond MIDI: The Handbook of Musical Codes* is to provide a general description, with encoded examples, of numerous ways of representing music in the computer.

Hundreds of codes for music have been developed. Most are intentionally made invisible to users. Not so happily, documentation about many musical codes is extremely scarce. This scarcity impedes applications. It deprives many potential users from investigating the relative merits of different schemes for data representation. It thwarts discussion of generalized representation systems. Worst of all, it imprisons data sets within the confines of the specific applications for which they were created.

MIDI is a conspicuous exception. MIDI is widely used, well documented, and works on almost every personal-computer platform. However, MIDI is, among all the codes presented here, the most limited in terms of the number of aspects of music that it represents. It is also the most remote from the music itself, for although it is capable of generating quite life-like electronic performances, its origin in hardware protocols divorces it from the musical concepts that are integral parts of most other codes. Hence the title *Beyond MIDI*.

* * *

Musical codes can be used to support several application domains. Among them sound, notation, and analysis are the most common and the ones on which we concentrate. While the information sets needed in all three domains have some common features, each has unique attributes as well.

The codes selected for inclusion in the *Handbook* are either in the public domain or are otherwise available for use without restriction. Among them, we have favored those in most widespread use at the present time, those demonstrating the greatest potential for future use, and/or those providing the best models for emulation.

To give some taste of the range of purposes and systems that codes may serve, we have also included brief coverage of a few codes designed for special tasks and unusual platforms. Although many codes are specific to one platform, this collection of material relates to all operating systems in widespread use today—including DOS, *Windows (3.x* and *NT)*, OS2, Macintosh, *NeXTStep*, and UNIX—and some platforms that are better known abroad (e.g., Acorn and Atari) than in the U.S.

The emphasis of the *Handbook* is intended to be on practical concepts. While the *Handbook* cannot serve as a complete reference for any one code, it is designed to cover the basic features of pitch, duration, articulation, dynamics, timbre, and other defining features of music. It also describes the file organization for each code, existing applications, data archives (where relevant), existing file interchange provisions, published references, and sources of further information.

Since, apart from the *de facto* use of Standard MIDI Files, there is no widely accepted method for the interchange of musical information, either within one family of applications or across the applications spectrum, we are pleased to be able to offer an entire section on nascent standards (two of them newly available) for data exchange. The *Handbook* should be a valuable resource for those who wish to evaluate the issues involved.

Inevitably, some codes of which readers may seek a description are absent. We cannot describe codes that are proprietary.[1] We have not attempted to describe audio formats, which are covered in numerous other sources. We have not attempted to cover languages for sound synthesis, which have been well served for 20 years by the *Computer Music Journal*. Codes which were seminal in their time but are no longer in common use, such as *Music V* and *MUSTRAN*, are described briefly in the glossary.

* * *

Apart from supporting musical applications, the present collection of musical codes may offer useful insights to those interested in text/speech applications requiring coordination of the sound and graphics domains. Such aspects of speech as pitch, accentuation, pace, and inflection all have parallels in music; to date "talking text" software is not highly evolved and texts that speak electronically in local dialects or selected voices (capabilities for which electronic performances of music must provide

---

1. The most notable omission is the proprietary *Enigma Transportable File Format* used with the commercial scoring program *Finale*; permission to describe this code was not forthcoming from *Finale*'s owner, Coda Music Software.

the analogues) are unknown. This collection may also be of interest to those concerned with a broad range of other theoretical and practical questions outside the immediate confines of music applications. At its base, however, the *Handbook* is intended to be accessible to ordinary musicians. Wherever possible it takes *musical* (rather than technical) definitions of musical practice and theory as its primary bases.

* * *

Beyond MIDI originated as an initiative of the Study Group on Musical Data and Computer Applications of the International Musicological Society, which has been co-chaired since 1987 by Walter B. Hewlett and myself. Many of the society's members are interested in the possibility of searching large databases of musical information, in producing new editions from raw materials in machine-readable form, in using online scores for classroom teaching and assignments, in verification of theoretical models, in simulation of performance practice and of compositional techniques, in diverse methods of musical analysis, and simply in easy management of and online access to sources that traditionally have consumed miles of physical shelf space. The single greatest impediments to such activities are the general absence of such databases and lack of access to those that exist. The original goal of the group was to facilitate translation from one code to another so that such resources as already existed could be pooled. The contents of this book demonstrate why this is not an easily achieved goal. We continue to believe, however, that it is possible.

Those involved in the field of musical representation are at every turn gifted individuals committed to a difficult undertaking. I am greatly indebted to our authors (many of whom are members of the IMS Study Group) for their diligence and cooperation; to the ANSI Musical Information Processing Committee and the *NIFF* Task Force for their penetrating discussions of practical issues in the interchange of musical information; to the 80 or so notation software developers who have participated in the annual surveys of *Computing in Musicology* over the past ten years; and to my colleagues (also well represented among our contributors) for their insights.

Most of what I know about musical representation I have learned from my esteemed colleague Walter B. Hewlett. I am particularly indebted to Dr. Hewlett for his ability to explain complex matters in elegantly simple ways and eager that readers should recognize his valuable, though inconspicuous, participation in and support for this project. I am similarly indebted to Edmund Correia, Jr., a member of our staff at the Center for Computer Assisted Research in the Humanities (CCARH) since 1985. Mr. Correia is responsible not only for the bulk of the typesetting of this text but also for virtuoso proof-reading, sometimes resulting in needed corrections that had escaped the notice of both the author and the editor, and for tracking down much of the information included in the glossary. (Given its nature, there is no chance that this book is free of errors, but we have done our best to provide copy that is consistent in its presentation, accurate, and up-to-date. Readers who find errors are encouraged to report them to CCARH.)

We acknowledge with special gratitude the important graphical contributions of Donald Anthony, Nicholas P. Carter, Werner Icking, and William P. Mahrt, the comments of David Huron on the completed manuscript, the Braille typesetting of Bettye Krolick, the valued advice of Douglas Sery (MIT Press), and the diligent assistance of Frances Bennion and Steven Rasmussen. Lastly, I wish to thank my husband, Clive Field, and our son Brent for their patience, suggestions, and involvement.

Eleanor Selfridge-Field
CCARH, Stanford University
March 4, 1997

Introduction

1   Introduction: Describing Musical Information

Eleanor Selfridge-Field

1.1   What Is Musical Representation?

Musical codes have been used since man's earliest efforts to transcribe sounds. From the accents for tonal inflection in many of the world's languages, through the neumes representing chant in medieval monasteries, to the *solfegge* of musical pedagogy in recent centuries, codes for sound have always had the purpose of prescribing consistency of practice. Almost as often, the practice so defined has been a relatively local one.

1.1.1   Musical Codes in Common Use

Many musical codes are in common use, particularly in music pedagogy. Consider the singer's *solfegge*, for example. The overriding purpose of *solfegge* is to cultivate in the singer's mind a mental apparatus for relating each tone to its neighbors and thereby to provide a solid foundation for singing accurately at sight. *Solfegge* can convey, through its emphasis on pitch contours, the similarity (in a relative sense) of works built (in an absolute sense) of different components. That is, the syllables *do-re-mi* can represent the ascending pitch strings *C-D-E* and *G-A-B* equally well. Finger numbers in piano literature, the ideograms we call tablatures for the guitar and other fretted instruments, the shape notes (a graphic version of *solfegge*) of the American South, and many special symbols designed to convey particular ways of playing the drum, the harp, and other instruments are all codes of one kind or another.

The most comprehensive coded language in regular use for representing sound is the common musical notation (CMN) of the Western world. Western musical notation as it has evolved over many centuries is a system of symbols that is relatively, but not completely, self-consistent and relatively stable but still, like music itself, evolving.

It is an open-ended system that has survived over time partly because of its flexibility and extensibility.

The adaptability of common notation means that it is not a perfect guide to the reproduction of sound. The apparent continuity of graphic symbols over centuries does not guarantee the same degree of continuity in practice. Yesterday's dot of prolongation and today's dot of prolongation are known, for example, to have had different relative numerical values in eighteenth-century France and modern-day Europe and North America. Graphical context is, in fact, of considerable importance in evaluating many symbols used in musical notation. There is no easy substitute for a knowledge of the history of musical performance in determining how the "common" notation should be converted to sound.

At the same time, common musical notation is the cornerstone of all efforts to preserve a sense of the musical present for other and later performers and listeners. The large body of music we consider to constitute the "classics" or "standard repertory" owes its existence to a generally well understood system of graphic communication.

In the late nineteenth and early twentieth centuries a number of interests gave rise to a perceived need to be able to describe melodies in terms sufficiently abstract to facilitate their comparison. Hymnographers wanted to trace melodies to earlier models. Ethnomusicologists wanted to be able to group works into familial clusters. Music theorists wanted to inventory rhythmic and melodic patterns. Music historians wanted to identify examples of musical paraphrase. Many codes were invented to further these analytical aims.[1]

Prior to the invention of the player piano, whose punched paper scores (or "rolls") constituted a graphical code for musical performances, inventors were eager to devise mechanical methods of transcription from a piano. Their designs gave rise to bar- and line-graphs that are remarkably similar to the visual reductions of notation provided today by many sequencer programs.[2]

---

1. Among the hymnographers, the system used by James Love (*Scottish Church Music*, Edinburgh, 1889) is noteworthy for its quite effective extensions to *solfegge*. Early efforts to describe musical contour go back at least to the work of Frances Densmore (1918) on the music of the Sioux. Among theoretical writings, the encoding scheme for rhythmic patterns developed by Mauritz Hauptmann in his study of harmony and meter (1853) is especially noteworthy. The responsibility for recognizing musical paraphrase has fallen largely to music bibliographers, whose work is discussed in later portions of this publication.

2. See especially Alexander Rossignol's "apparatus for tracing music" (1872) as described in *A Dictionary of Music and Musicians*, ed. Sir George Grove (London: Macmillan, 1889), IV, 769f.

Since the representation of music is entirely independent of the use of computers, there is every reason to expect that codes designed for the representation of music in computer applications will eventually be (as many already are) entirely independent of both hardware configurations and software processes. Since many developments in the computer field are driven to some degree by practical exigencies, however, detachment is not guaranteed.

1.1.2   Musical Representations for Computer Applications

While musical codes are not circumscribed by computer applications, most that are devised for ordinary rather than machine communication are selective in what they represent: finger use, fretboard position, relative melodic interval sizes, thematic incipits, and so forth. Because of its power and memory, the computer offers an opulent possibility: the opportunity to represent entire musical works of considerable length with as many attributes of their identity as the interested party is willing to identify and encode.

The lure of "total" representations has now been pursued for roughly three decades. This volume gives considerable recognition to those systems which aim to provide the greatest degrees of completeness. Yet no one involved with the most competent of systems claims that any piece of music can be represented at the 100% level in all of its conceivable aspects. Every system makes sacrifices somewhere to optimize clarity of its preferred features.

Most systems are extensible, but all become cumbersome when they begin to seem like centipedes—with too little core to support a large array of extensions and too few links between extensions to provide an integrated logical foundation for understanding the music as music. Each new addition takes the representation further from the object it attempts to simulate and taxes programming effort as well.

The slight amount of available memory on computers that filled rooms as large as football fields and the exorbitant costs of processing data in jobs that sat in queues for hours, if not days, encouraged the first wave of music-code designers to make conciseness of data representation a top priority. Conciseness not only saved valuable memory; it also facilitated rapid input and processing. Systems in use today for music printing that attempt at some level to represent the music itself can be traced to the Sixties and reflect these early concerns.

These goals were gradually eclipsed in the Eighties by the advent of personal computers. For home users (who suddenly had access to more memory and faster processing than professionals of the Sixties) "friendliness" became a primary goal. The advent of desktop publishing encouraged greater sophistication in graphical presentation. New user interfaces brought with them the ability to edit graphical results. A concentration of interest in graphics served to diminish the logical representation of musical semantics and structure, since within the realm of graphical applications the concept of, let us say, lines and circles was more general than that of staves and noteheads.

The establishment of the Musical Instrument Digital Interface (MIDI) in the late Eighties gave easy access to tools for musical sound to home users, hobbyists, and millions of ordinary musicians. These users established a new constituency who could experiment with sound control in ways that previously had been possible only in research studios. MIDI is now the most prevalent representation of music, but what it represents is based on hardware control protocols for sound synthesis. Programs that support sound input for graphics output necessarily must span a gamut of representational categories. What is most likely to be lost is any sense of the musical work.

Practical users will undoubtedly ask whether any of this really matters. For applications in printing and sound it often does not matter. For applications in pedagogy, analysis, simulation, and music theory, however, the nature of the representation matters a great deal. Four "black circles" between two "vertical lines" do not have the same semantic meaning as four "quarter notes" between two "bar lines." MIDI key number 64 is always in the first instance interpreted with the note name E, denying it the possibility of being an F♭ or a D♯♯.

At the same time, practical considerations do remain essential. The amount of time required to implement really robust music applications is frequently longer than the shelf life of hardware models, operating systems, and software products. Music programmers have sometimes been faced with cruel choices, such as whether to rush to market with or abandon altogether half-finished products about to be made inoperable by the relentless "progress" of new systems. Some of the potential benefits of improvements in memory capacity and processing time have been offset by the uncertainty inflicted by platform and system wars between the DOS, Macintosh, Windows, and UNIX operating systems. Thus, universal solutions seem as remote as universal applications.

Overall, the redefinition of the computer as a consumer product has not accelerated the pace at which concepts of music representation evolve. Our infatuation with visual glitz, which serves cosmetically finished notation well and logically complete abstract representations badly, may even have retarded it somewhat. Given these factors, existing systems for representing music must be expected to expand and new systems to appear.

1.1.3   Reusable Codes

Since encoding music by any system is laborious, there naturally arises an interest in driving multiple applications from single data sets and in interchanging data sets between different commercial applications intended for a single purpose, such as music printing. The discussion of possible schemes to facilitate the interchange of musical data is one that has already been in progress for many years.

The road to platform- and system-independent music printing applications has been full of cul-de-sacs, and the road to analytical applications is still a dirt one, full of potholes. Only sound applications have thrived. MIDI succeeds as a lowest common denominator in the world of musical information. Thus much remains to be done.

1.2   Parameters of Musical Information

1.2.1   The Three Contexts

Musical information may describe music in any of its several contexts—the sound or phonological context, the notation or graphical context of notation, the rational context of analytical parameters, and the semantic context of musical perception and understanding. "Gestural" information, prescribing physical movements by a performer, is sometimes recognized as constituting a further context. The differences between these contexts are made manifestly clear in the topical outline of this work; we concentrate on the first three. Most codes described here are optimized for one of these three domains, but readers will want to bear in mind the broader relationships and the possibility of representing multiple contexts simultaneously.

Nothing seems to sum up the challenges posed by the sometimes contradictory natures of these contexts so well as some remarks made recently by the noted musicologist Margaret Bent in relation to the "dilemma" of editing early music. Bent wrote:

> In one sense, music exists only in sound, but paradoxically, sound is its least stable element. But also, visual presentation may be an important or essential ingredient, even to the extent of constituting part of the structure or at least of the aesthetic. And there are other senses in which the music exists in dimensions (e.g., numerical) that are not immediately audible.[3]

---

3. Margaret Bent, "Editing Early Music: The Dilemma of Translation," *Early Music* XXII/3 (1994), 392.

A fundamental question that users will want to consider in evaluating different systems is which of these three modes holds the dominant position. The coordination of sound and graphics is native to musicological applications, but the ultimate objective of representing both in relation to an entity at once more fundamental and more complete—the "logical" or "core" work—is the one that holds the highest interest as an ultimate objective. Schemes of representation that fall short of this requirement are often conducive to the use of different data sets for every application, and this of course is ultimately wasteful.

At the same time, there are many enquiries applications for which specialized sets of data may be of practical value. An interest in only one attribute, such as rhythm, or in an unusual repertory, such as lute music, may enable the user to fashion with impunity an economical system that is tailored to the objective. In this case, if the user were forced to represent every aspect of the music, the study might be impractical to conduct.

1.2.2   The Principal Attributes of Musical Information

Music, like speech, has several manifestations. The most familiar of these are sound and a visual representation. The sound dimension of music—its most basic manifestation—deserves the claim of a universal language, since interpretations of sound all begin from a common set of physically describable features. Common musical notation is widely read and understood in diverse cultures. Since notation begins as a representation of sound, it tends to introduce arbitrary elements into its scheme of description.

The attributes of a musical "event" are arbitrary in number. The sound phenomenon, the notated representation, and the underlying "logical core" of a musical work have some shared and some unique attributes. Some common attributes of a note are indicated in Figure 1.1.

Certain details of each of these attributes differ according to the context in which they are considered.

The phenomenon we call *pitch* exists in sound but not in notation. The notehead position that represents it on the page provides, in combination, three absolute elements of information:

- it confers a pitch name (A–G) by vertical staff position

- it implies an octave position (commonly 1–8), which may be inferred from a clef sign

- it allows for a chromatic inflection, which may be conferred globally in a key signature or locally by an accidental sharp (♯), flat (♭), or natural sign (♮)

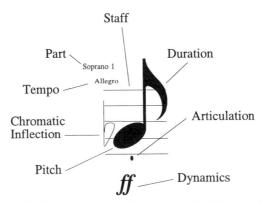

Figure 1.1 Some attributes of (or associated with) a single note.

The phenomenon we call *duration* exists only in sound and, in fact, only in the context of other sounds, since duration is conventionally represented as a relative value. The eighth note in Figure 1.1 nominally takes half the value of a quarter note, which takes half the value of a half note, and so forth. But the system of durational values is not always binary. In some metrical contexts three eighth notes would equal one quarter note. By notational convention any number of notes may be assigned to one value. For example, 14 (or 27 or 65, etc.) notes could be assigned to a quarter note as a run or cadenza. In the case of tuplets, as such arbitrary groupings are called, the actual amount of time consumed in the performance is itself variable, since musicians are not bound to equate exactly the displaced durational value.

In the graphical representation of duration, there are three possible components:

- notehead "color" (open or filled)
- the presence or absence of a stem
- the presence or absence of flags or, for groups of notes, beams
- the presence of augmentation dots

All four aspects differentiate longer from shorter notes in a complex hierarchy of values ranging from whole notes (value = 1) to 256th notes (value = 1/256). A fourth variable in the description of duration is notehead shape: square and rectangular noteheads represent note values greater than whole notes.[4] These physical characteristics are all irrelevant to sound except in helping to determine how the duration of the note should be determined. It is not possible to "perform" such visual elements as a flag or a stem or a beam; yet they are essential to the correct rhythmic interpretation of written scores.

In notation, rests represent only duration. Yet in many representation schemes their presence must be recorded as a "pitch" event to retain a pitch "marker" in a stream of events.

The *tempo* of a live performance is ultimately established by a user. The user may be guided by a verbal specification ("Allegro," "Largo," etc.), which is general and subject to interpretation. If a metronomic indication is provided ($\flat = 120$), then the number of beats per minute is explicit. Rallentandos and rubatos are necessarily arbitrary in their realization.

Dynamic level is relative, since "loud" (f) must be determined not only in relation to "soft" (p) but also in relation to a moderate dynamic level for the complex of performers involved and the dynamics of the room or hall. The "moderate" dynamic level of a 100-piece orchestra in a concert hall is necessarily much greater than that of a solo guitar in a small room.

Articulation as a class of interpretive features includes staccato (truncated) and legato (smooth) performance. The first is indicated by a dot under or over the notehead (Figure 1.1 includes an instance) and the second by a curved line over the affected group of notes. These kinds of articulations affect duration and often have implications for dynamics. For example, a plucked string will often sound louder than a bowed string. In sound, a staccato eighth note is necessarily shorter in duration than an ordinary eighth note. The attack times of two consecutive eighths will be the same, whether or not they are staccato. In notation it is the theoretical eighth-note value that is represented; in notational logic the staccato dot represents the subtraction of a variable proportion of the theoretical value to achieve the actual duration. This distinction causes a significant divide between representations that take sound as primary and those that take notation as primary. Sound-based representations will contain shorter relative durations, with intervening rests not given in a score, than notation-based representations, in which rests would be inappropriate for this purpose. Many other kinds of gestural information cause similar discontinuities between sound-based and notation-based representations.

---

4. Notehead shapes can also be used to differentiate percussion instruments and other variables that are independent of pitch.

In music for more than one performer, the *part* as a component of the whole is also a cause for considerable attention. The grouping aspects of this problem are discussed under "Processing Order," but in relation to performance it is sometimes the *timbral definition* that is most relevant. Parts do have distinctive timbral qualities in performance, and much of the work of electronic music research has been concerned with simulating "natural" sounding timbres. Timbre *per se* is largely irrelevant to the notation of music. For this reason, notation-based representations typically may lack an essential piece of information required in sound realizations.

Many conventions of Western notation require that one graphic element serve more than one purpose. Thus the stem that is involved in representing note duration can also be relevant, through its *orientation*, to the differentiation of two parts when notated on one staff. Very extensive but poorly codified rules governing stem orientation, slur rotation, and beam slant contribute to the precision required for the complete representation of notated music.

In general, a study of the representation of musical notation induces a profound respect for its ingeniousness. Graphical features have been used very cleverly to convey aspects of sound that must be accommodated in the realization of a single event.

1.2.3   Implicit Information

When the items constituting a series of "events" are grouped together in the representation of a complete musical work, issues of context play an increased role. The specific implications for representation vary according to whether the domain is spatial (as for printing) or temporal (as for sound).

Many elements of musical notation are contextually determined, and a fundamental question in the representation of notation is how to prioritize contextual or implicit information in relation to absolute or explicit information.

Given clef and key signature, for example, may one presume that only staff position must be encoded in order to derive a valid list of pitches represented in some abbreviated way? This is the kind of assumption that was made in many early schemes of notational representation. In some cases letter name might be absolute but octave number would be relative. Experience in using such systems quickly proved, however, that there were many pitfalls. Those of human error—such as failing to indicate the change of a clef, a key signature, or an octave number—rendered some early data sets useless.

One alternative is to make explicit the pitch name and octave register of every note. Then all possibility of ambiguity is removed. Another alternative is to add explicit information that is not provided by the notation because contextual assumptions underlie the grammar of written notation and simplify it.

Musical notation is highly dependent on oral tradition for its actual interpretation. The value attached to musical performance in Western culture is highly bound up with the differing suppositions that musicians make in the interpretation of a written score, and "schools" of performance that descend from one famous teacher abound in the annals of concert life of the past two hundred years. One pianist's "Allegro" tempo will be different from another's. One trumpeter may use a mute in alternative passages of a work without any cue from a written score. One group may perform a four-part work with strings and another group with trombones.

More significant from the point of view of representing music is the fact that some widely accepted conventions of notation require that the underlying logic of the performance contradict the logic of the written score. Music of the Baroque era (1600–1750) abounds in examples. Among the most frequently encountered are these:

- written single dots understood to be interpreted as double dots

- written dotted-eighth/sixteenth pattern (duple subdivision of beat) understood to be interpreted as eighth/sixteenth pattern (compound subdivision of beat)

- a vocal cadence staggered ahead of an accompaniment cadence understood to be performed in coincidence with it

An unwritten principle of some early encoding projects was to avoid "interpretation" of information at all costs. It is possible to encode ambiguity itself, if that is what one desires in a resulting file, but it is often more practical to decide at the outset what choices should be made, to make them consistently, and to document them well. In this way a later user is always free to reinterpret the information.

1.2.4   Issues of Processing Order

Software used to process musical information must make certain assumptions about the ordering of elements. The musical score is easily viewed as a two-dimensional array, but there is no natural processing order among its dimensions.

Figure 1.2 represents a hypothetical score. In a well-behaved example, all the parts would be active for the duration of the score and all would be represented individually. Individual parts are represented on the horizontal axis. The simultaneous activities of all of these would be represented on the vertical plane.

If the score involves many performers, let us say a conventional orchestra, then each system, representing the total complex, is likely to be subdivided into groups of similar timbre—strings, winds, brasses, and percussion instruments. Our model score contains only two subgroups—the top one of four voices or instruments and an underlying one. It does not indicate whether multiple performers (e.g., all first violinists) might play from one part.

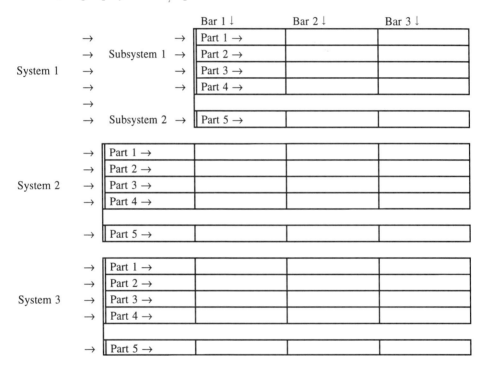

Figure 1.2 A hypothetical score viewed as a two-dimensional array.

Within the two-dimensional array there may be various splittings and joinings. If the underlying part in the hypothetical example were a piano accompaniment, it would be written on the so-called grand staff in which treble and bass staves are combined. If the highest part were for first violins in a concerto grosso, *solo* and *tutti* cues[5]

5. That is, verbal instructions without other notational expression.

would indicate where only the soloists would play and where all the first violinists would play together—from one part.

Part reinforcement complicates sound applications as well as graphic applications, for timbral specification only confers sound quality. It does not give any sense of the relative dynamic levels of parts within a whole.[6]

Common notation evolved with a view toward economy, but many conventions that save space or time in print complicate the operational instructions required to process musical information automatically. For example, in orchestral music of the eighteenth century, passages in which parts of different timbres play the same notes (e.g., violin and oboe) may be combined on one staff but they will be split into separate parts (*divisi*) when the content is no longer duplicated. In orchestral music of the nineteenth century, long passages of repeated notes on one pitch may be indicated by *tremolandi* signs (diagonal strokes).[7] In the preparation of parts, it is customary to represent long series of rests by an appropriate bar count over a broadened whole-note rest. Thus 36 bars of rests that occupy the appropriate horizontal track with 36 signs in a score may occupy only one bar's worth of horizontal space in a part.

These requirements, and myriad others like them, place a considerable burden on applications programs designed to manipulate musical information.

The optimum format for musical information is determined in part by assumptions of processing order. Thus, although musical information may be discussed in isolation from applications, all systems of representation have been devised with some particular application in mind and these intended applications have influenced fundamental design features.

1.2.5   Feature Selection and Definition

Assumptions concerning end use determine what elements of information are to be considered essential. Notation programs must produce stems, beams, and slurs but sound applications can function perfectly well without these elements of visual grammar. Systems designed in the Sixties and Seventies tended to make provision for the encoding of stem directions and beams, whereas systems designed in more recent years have allowed the software to make inferences, to use defaults, and to provide

---

6. At the present time few sequencer programs recognize the need to "double" unison parts in the electronic performance of orchestral scores.

7. For example, in the Finale of Beethoven's Fifth Symphony the use of *tremolandi* reduced the page count in one printing experiment from 80 to 50.

for overrides of undesirable results. Thus the number of visual objects encoded in one system may greatly exceed the number encoded in another.

These issues have been somewhat obscured by the popularity of input systems based on sound capture. A great many features that appear on the printed page are non-sounding. These include not only stems, beams, bar lines, and (arguably) slurs but also tempo and character indications and instructions with implications for the sequence of passages in actual performance: repeat marks, multiple endings, *da capo* and *dal segno* instructions, and the like.

Although ambidexterity between sound and notation applications is a venerable goal in the design of musical information systems, most systems are inevitably biased toward one or the other type of application. The MIDI interface was not designed with such discrepancies in mind, and MIDI software will not automatically play repeats that are symbolically implied in a written score. The software designer may solicit user input through an interactive dialogue, or the user may modify the files to be played with tools built into the software. The data provider can only optimize the information set within the limits of the potential methods of use that he or she envisions.

1.2.6   Problems Rooted in the Nature of Notation

Musical notation is not logically self-consistent. Its visual grammar is open-ended—far more so than any numerical system or formal grammar. The musical notation for a relatively complex work only provides reasonably common results from one group of performers to another because a vast amount of oral tradition stands behind it. Those preparing for a concert career still seek out particular teachers for the purpose of gaining insights into interpretation and technique that may be suggested by written signs to the trained eye but are not actually explicit.

1.2.7   Issues of Sequence Specification

Musical structures that are easily parsed usually include sections of material that are repeated. Varying sequences of repetition differentiate one musical form from another. Economy in music printing may substitute verbal or symbolic instructions for visual reiteration.

Let us take a predictable case. There is common agreement about the performing order (and therefore the processing order) of the double movement type of the minuet and trio. It is represented in Table 1.1.

The regularity of this procedure and the number of examples are both so great and so familiar that it is very tempting to assume that musical works could easily be encoded to assure an appropriate result in electronic performance.[8] It happens, however, that the number of ways in which this procedure is expressed by score markup is very large.

No.	Sequence of items in score	No.	Sequence of items in performance
1	Minuet section (A), Part a	1	Minuet section (A), Part a
		2	Minuet section (A), Part a
2	Minuet section (A), Part b	3	Minuet section (A), Part b
		4	Minuet section (A), Part b
3	Trio section (B), Part a	5	Trio section (B), Part a
		6	Trio section (B), Part a
4	Trio section (B), Part b	7	Trio section (B), Part b
		8	Trio section (B), Part b
		9	Minuet section (A), Part a
		10	Minuet section (A), Part b

Table 1.1 Differences of sectional sequence in the ordering of a score vs. the ordering of a performance of a "minuet and trio" movement.

A few years ago we conducted a survey of methods used to indicate the repeats found in such movements. We stopped counting after compiling a list of 25 different conventions.

Many cases are less predictable. In Baroque suites, for example, there are procedurally similar designs compounded by the execution of additional movements before the reprise of the original minuet or gavotte or bourrée movement. Some other complicating factors were these:

- Repeats do not always start with the original first bar.

---

8. The sections numbered 2, 4, 6, and 8 are repetitions of the sections that immediately precede them. Sections 9 and 10 and reiterations of sections 1 and 3. Such repetitions are exact in theory, but in practice multiple endings may differentiate one iteration from another.

- Last-beat and first-beat rhythms do not always make up a full bar's worth of beats.

- Multiple endings for movement sections that are sometimes but not always repeated require explicit instructions: for example, "select the first ending in the first execution of two but the second ending in the first execution of one."

In practice automatic sequencing will sometimes fail to produce the correct result for lack of recognizable cues.

1.2.8   Features with Context-Dependent Interpretations

Inevitably some elements of sound are more easily represented than others. The studies of performance practice that have occurred over recent decades have demonstrated over and over that some elements of notation that have remained fixed over long periods of time have nonetheless varied in their interpretation from century to century. Historical context may therefore bestow on performers the need to modify the sound, or, in the case of electronic applications, the sound output.

Tuning systems have varied with time and place, such that the A = 440 of modern times can be reinterpreted as A = 415 in historical performances of string music or A = 460 in brass music of Gabrieli's time or A = 392 in French music for the early oboe. Within the octave, however reconciled in hertz,[9] the tuning of the individual notes of the scale has also varied substantially over time. Timbres of specific instruments have changed subtly as the materials and mechanics of instrument manufacture have changed. The accommodation of these kinds of variables has been explored in many research environments, but easily available software that supports historical adaptation is not the norm. Synthesis hardware may provide some accommodation of tuning systems, however.[10]

Also related to pitch representation are the varying practices employed by transposing instruments as they have evolved over the past three hundred years. Sound-oriented programs will invariably represent sounding pitch, while notation-oriented programs will represent written pitch. Thus in a work for modern trumpet and orchestra in C Major, the part for B♭ trumpet will be written in D Major. Here, and

---

9. i.e., cycles per second.

10. The Roland electronic harpsichord models C-20 and C-50 that offered the choice of five historical temperaments (equal, mean-tone, just, "Kirnberger," and "Werckmeister 3") have been withdrawn from general circulation.

in numerous other instances, someone wishing to analyze music would prefer the sound representation, but the notational information is also useful documentation. In centuries past, most transposing instruments known today in only one size (and tuning) were known in multiple sizes (and tunings).

The most prevalent area of interpretive discrepancy is that of rhythm. Western notation is better suited to express binary than ternary subdivisions of the beat. When two eighth notes take the time of one quarter note they need only be presented to be correctly interpreted. When three eighth notes take the time of one quarter note, they are normally accompanied by the numeral "3" to indicate this less common grouping. There is no particular difficulty in representing these occurrences in either sound or notation data.

Difficulties arise when the examples become more complex. For example, the Baroque notational convention of writing a dotted eighth followed by a sixteenth (an implied quadruple subdivision of the beat) to imply a triple subdivision[11] prevents one representation from serving the dual purposes of sound and notation. Well trained performers will recognize the passages requiring reinterpretation, but the theoretical information that would need to be maintained to facilitate appropriate electronic performance is dauntingly great. A similar situation arises with *notes inégales*—those passages with long series of single-dotted notes that, it is generally believed, were performed as if they were double-dotted. Other contradictions between sight and intended sound arise in the realization of arpeggiated chords, the *style brisé*, grace notes, ornaments, basso continuo figuration, and cadenzas.

The interpretation of grace notes, which occur prolifically in Western music, is also dependent on historical context. In the eighteenth century[12] grace notes were normally executed on the beat, stealing time from succeeding notes. In the nineteenth century[13] the interpretation became the reverse: the succeeding note took its full value. Time was theoretically borrowed instead from the preceding note. In both cases the written notation was the same, and in both cases the beat count was complete without the grace notes.

The implementation of grace notes therefore diverges according to the intended application. In many notation-oriented systems of representation, grace notes have a time value of zero. In sound applications, however, grace notes must have a positive

11. The dotted eighth note takes two thirds of the time of the quarter note; the sixteenth note takes the remaining one third.

12. For example in the music of Haydn and Mozart.

13. For example in the music of Chopin and Mendelssohn.

time value in order to sound. The eighteenth-century model is easy to implement, but the nineteenth-century model is very difficult to implement in sound applications: real time already spent cannot be recaptured!

The implementation of arpeggiated chords, the arpeggiated *style brisé*,[14] and the realization of ornaments all belong to the same category of difficulties as the grace-note problem because all three are suggestive notations that necessarily take time values in actual performance that are different from those expressed in writing. All the notes of an arpeggiated chord are shown with identical rhythmic values, but each has a different attack time. The unmeasured notation of the *style brisé* usually aimed to produce something akin to an arpeggio, but the tones included could be scalar as well as chordal and the composite line was represented on the diagonal or horizontal rather than on the vertical plane of the arpeggio.[15]

The interpretation of ornaments is a heady subject on which consensus goes only so far. There is general agreement as to which tones relative to the principal note are involved in the execution of such common ornaments as trills, mordents, and turns. The amount of time each of these notes takes and how it is derived from the reduction in values of surrounding notes is subject to some of the same considerations as the interpretation of grace notes. In the domain of real-time execution, there is greater scope for rhythmic latitude in the interpretation of many ornaments. There is also widespread criticism of ornaments that sound "too mechanical." This has led some music systems developers to devise algorithms to subtly vary the sounding durations of logically equal values.

Inevitably there are many tradeoffs between representation and software. Some early notation programs required the encoding of stem directions, but today most stemming and beaming is done automatically by the software. Does this mean, however, that stem and beam information can be safely forgotten? Not necessarily, for stem information may denote the differentiation of rhythmically independent voices, and beam information may suggest intended phrasing or breathing or the delineation of voices in a polyphonic context.

Short cadenzas—the passages of virtuoso display that appear just before the final cadence of sonatas and concertos—are performed at the discretion of the soloist.

---

14. In which non-coincident decay times are often shown in notation. However, this visual representation may only attempt to express what is true of arpeggios in general—that the sooner the note is struck, the sooner it will decay.

15. One representation scheme that has dealt successfully with this problem of "diagonal texture" is that of the musicologist Etienne Darbellay. It is mentioned in the glossary under the software name WOLFGANG.

Maximum latitude is expressed by rhythmic values that are merely suggestive but, as written, consume many more beats than can be accommodated within the one theoretical bar in which they are shown. This presents a very great problem in the coordination of written and sounded information. Let us suppose that a cadenza containing 14 written beats is designated to occur within the time otherwise taken by one 4-beat bar. Adequately articulate software will reproduce the notation, but an analogous electronic performance will necessarily require the time normally taken by 3.5 bars. Thus ensuing bar numbers will diverge between the two data sets and the metrical stress (which admittedly exists only in the mind of the listener) will also be shifted.

File organization is predominantly determined by the presumed context of use. Many notation codes and one of the proposed interchange schemes we include are page-specific, while sound and analysis codes tend to be organized by voice and movement—that is by musical rather than physical units. Programmers like to claim that conversions from a page-dominant to a part-dominant format are easy to make, but successful examples do not abound. Sound files altogether lack the spacing information required for page layout; page files contain a great deal of information that is irrelevant to sound output. These are some of the principal issues that are illustrated in the passages of codes that are shown.

1.3   Purposes of This Handbook

This book has two main aims. One is to introduce the general subject of music representation, showing how intended applications influence the kinds of information that are encoded. The second aim is to present a broad range of representation schemes, illustrating a wide variety of approaches to music representation. We have grouped these approaches, somewhat arbitrarily, into ten categories and have provided at least two sample schemes within each category. In some categories dozens more might have been provided.

In order to facilitate comparison between representation schemes, each approach is illustrated using a common set of musical examples. Since the codes themselves are generally so different in what they aim to represent, it is almost impossible to compare them when unrelated works are shown by each author. Yet this is the normal state of available documentation.

In collecting such diverse codes within a single volume, we hope to encourage informed discussion about the interchange of data in diverse formats. In general data interchange is more practical within single-application domains, such as printing, than between application domains, such as sound *and* printing, or printing *and* analysis.[16] Ultimately, however, we leave the questions of feasibility to our readers. Our overriding goal is simply to provide materials that may be drawn upon in forming such judgments.

To accomplish these aims, we have attempted to organize each chapter according to a common outline. On account of the highly diverse nature of the codes, their content (ASCII, binary, hexadecimal, etc.), and their file organization, this has not always been fully possible.

The main topics, where relevant, are a general description of the history and intended purposes of the code, a description of the representation of the primary attributes of music (pitch, duration, accentuation, ornamentation, dynamics, and timbre), a description of the file organization, some mention of existing data in this format, reference to resources for further information, and at least one encoded example.

1.4   Musical Examples

The examples of musical code shown in this book are based on a common set of short notated examples which collectively illustrate some of the most common problems in musical encoding generally and which also tend to highlight the differences between sound-oriented approaches and notation-oriented ones. The number of examples set was left to the discretion of each contributor, and would inevitably be influenced by the purposes of the code, the current state of development, and the time available to the contributor.

---

16. Although programmers and statisticians would assume the output of analysis programs to be fundamentally numerical, there is no defined set of features constituting an analytical input domain. Among the most popular kinds of analysis currently practiced by music theorists and analysts, Schenkerian analysis is a reductionist system dependent on notation with output expressed graphically. Set theory is reductionist in its substitution of relative pitch classes for absolute octave numbers and exact pitch names (making it well suited to MIDI input), but its focus is primarily on transformations of order and its expression is typically in numerical series or tables. Types of analysis that require enharmonic pitch information, or are concerned with aspects of rhythm, or which concentrate on the coordinated study of features of pitch and/or rhythm and/or harmony and/or form, or which differentiate one style of composition from another for the purpose of generating new works have distinctly different, and widely varied, needs. No adequate discussion of the issues that arise can be presented here. The analysis domain (if one exists) must be understood to be a generalized one which in particular instances may overlap with any of the others.

Each example is presented and discussed below. The functional titles used are also retained in the chapter descriptions. Many contributors submitted output as well as code, but since the aesthetic merits of different systems are not our topic here, we have standardized the presentation: Examples 1.1, 1.2, 1.3, 1.4, 1.5B, and 1.6 were set by Nicholas P. Carter using *SCORE*; Werner Icking's setting of Example 1.5A is used in Chapter 17, where numerous special characters have also been produced using *MusiXTEX*; in this chapter Example 1.5A is scanned.

1.4.1   The Mozart Trio

This example, which is taken from the second trio section of Mozart's Clarinet Quintet, is musically very simple. Respondents were asked to set only the first twelve bars (up to the repeat sign).[17] Respondents for monophonic systems were asked only to encode the *Clarinet in A*.

The entry was intended to be simple. Each instrument occupies a different staff and plays single notes. The meter is regular, although there is a tuplet in Bar 8 of the clarinet part. The articulation marks include slurs and staccatos.

The most telling feature of this example is the transposing part of the *Clarinet in A*, which is notated in the key of C Major, three half steps higher than its sounding pitch of A Major. Although transposition is a simple matter on the computer, the vertical shifts in layout often require that notation users re-edit the graphic result. Although in Example 1.1 the space between staves is generous, it often happens that low notes on one staff will overwrite high ones on the staff below or dynamics signs between staves or, in vocal music, text underlay beneath the part.

The implementation of sound applications is not subject to such considerations. In sound applications, however, one may wish to consider the consequences of the repeat signs, for what is only 12 bars in print could, if these are acknowledged, become 24 in sound applications. If the example were of Baroque music, the software developer might wish to leave the option to repeat the passage up to the user by providing a switch of some kind, but repeats in Mozart minuets (of which this example is a part) are not regarded as optional.

---

17. Some encodings also necessarily capture the layout. The example was distributed in two different layouts—one with a system break after Bar 7 and the other with a system break after Bar 10.

Example 1.1 Second trio from the Mozart Clarinet Quintet, K. 581 ("Mozart trio").

1.4.2 The Mozart Piano Sonata

In the identification of staves and systems, piano parts are atypical. One "instrument" typically occupies two staves, and within the context of a work for multiple performers these two staves may function as one sub-system. This example exhibits some other complications: (a) mixed durations within single chords in the right hand, (b) grace notes preceding chords (right hand), and (c) arpeggiated grace notes (left hand).

Reconciling these arpeggiations with those of the right-hand chords in real time is a task that none of our contributors sought to explain.

Example 1.2 Excerpt from the Mozart piano sonata in A Major, K. 331.

1.4.3   The Saltarello

This anonymous dance piece from the early Renaissance is very simple musically. The complexity it represents is one of processing sequence, on account of its multiple endings. In this case a representation for printing only is significantly simpler than one designed for playback or structural analysis.

Example 1.3 Anonymous saltarello.

1.4.4   The Telemann Aria

This aria is scored for voice (Staff 1), an instrumental ensemble consisting of oboe, violin, and viola (Staff 2), and a basso continuo complement of cello or double bass and keyboard (Staff 3). The right-hand part for keyboard is not realized here.

The vocal part contains text underlay that includes the need for diacriticals (here the ö and ü) and special characters (German ß). The width requirements of the text syllables are extremely erratic, complicating text underlay.

Example 1.4 The Telemann aria "Liebe! Liebe! Was ist schöner als die Liebe?".

The information on Staff 2 is very complex. The oboe and violin generally share the same part (shown in full-size notes), although they split in accompanying the words "süsser" and "schöner." The viola part (shown with stems down) contains a mixture of single notes and double stops. In Bar 10, there are mixed durations (quarter and eighth notes) in the double stop on the second beat. The cue-size notes are editorial ones suggesting material that is missing in the original source.

These features make sound interpretation from a representation devised for printing particularly troublesome. The oboe and violin require separate sound tracks because of their very different timbres. In these separate tracks the notes will not be identical. The execution of the trill in Bar 10 also requires the output of sound in multiple tones in real time where a print file contains only a single symbol.

The basso continuo part (Staff 3) is more straightforward, but it also requires some differentiation of temporally different parts on a common staff.

If a sound representation is taken as primary, the task of achieving this visual grammar without significant amounts of hand-editing is daunting.

1.4.5   Unmeasured Chant

Two examples are given. "Alma Redemptoris Mater" (Style A) is shown in neumes on a four-line staff as it appears in the *Liber Usualis*.

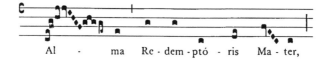

Al   -   ma   Re - dem - ptó - ris   Ma - ter,

Example 1.5A   Chant: "Alma Redemptoris Mater" written in neumes.

"Quem queritis" (Style B) is shown in modern notation that offers phrase markings but does not impose any rhythmic identity on the notes.

Angelus dicit:

Quem que _ ri _ tis in se _ pul _ _ chro, _____ o   Chri _ sti _ co _ lae?

Example 1.5B   Chant: "Quem queritis" written in modern notation.

Electronic-sound representations of chant are almost meaningless, since exact durational information was not precisely conveyed and the interpretation of relational durations remains a subject of debate.

1.4.6   The Binchois *Magnificat*

This three-voice work by the Renaissance composer Gilles Binchois illustrates some of the complexities of distinguishing original from editorial material in representations of modern editions of early music. On Staff 1 a single voice (the *Cantus*) is notated. On Staff 2, System 1 two voices (*Cantus 2* and *Tenor*) play a common instrumental part (stem directions are determined by proximity of the notehead to the middle line of the staff). On Staff 2, System 2 these instruments have separate parts (indicated by upward stems for *Cantus 2* and downward ones for the *Tenor*).

Magnificat secundi toni

Example 1.6 Binchois *Magnificat*.

The main complexities of this example are in the editorial markup. Editorial elements include (a) the incipit of *Cantus 1* in "colored" but unstemmed notes, (b) horizontal brackets showing where ligatures[18] were used, and (c) editorial accidentals (e.g., in Bar 6).[19]

1.4.7   Free Choices

Contributors were invited to submit additional examples to explain their treatment of contemporary music or other repertories outside the realm of "common music notation." There were very few contributions of this nature and no way of comparing them, as the range of printing aberrations is great. The concurrent use of multiple meters, unusual noteheads, beams unconnected to stems (and therefore to notes), wedge-shaped beams, and circular staves are some of the features that have marked contributions shown in recent issues of *Computing in Musicology*, particularly Vol. 9 (1993-94). Numerous special signs are also required in popular music repertories.

---

18. Contiguous or composite symbols representing two or more notes in the original source; such visual arrangements conveyed information about performance such as phrasing and, to a degree, duration.

19. In the Renaissance practice of *musica ficta*, some accidentals were implied by the hexachordal modes used in composition but they were not made explicit in notation. Modern editions tend to make them so. Not all editorial accidentals are accepted by performers, who therefore wish to know which accidentals are added and which are original.

1.5   Code Categories

The organization of this book reflects an overall tripartite categorization—codes for sound applications, codes for notational applications, and codes of analytical and/or more abstract applications. The influence of more specific aims, and sometimes of platform strength and weakness, causes the further differentiation found below. The *raison d'être* of the items to which whole chapters are devoted is explained briefly here. Many additional codes are cited briefly in the glossary.

1.5.1   Sound-Related Codes (1): MIDI

This first section gives a presentation of the Standard MIDI File Format and then presents several schemes for enriching MIDI. These extensions barely scratch the surface of a complex world of possibilities.

Since there is a wealth of detailed literature on MIDI, it is not our intention to provide a definitive resource here. Interested readers will want to consult the specialized literature, such as that given in the references section. MIDI is included here as much to show its deficiencies, in comparison with most of the other codes described, as its accomplishments. Our presentation does differ from most in giving plain ASCII text, organized in columns within which pitch information and duration information are grouped separately, as an alternative to the hexadecimal code (hex) shown in most MIDI manuals. For musical readers unfamiliar with hex, we also include an annotated hex file.

The proposals for MIDI extensions represented here are but a few of hundreds of adaptations that have been conceptualized and dozens that have been put into practice in proprietary applications software. All of these have been tested in working environments and all are in the public domain.

It is symptomatic of the larger issue of resolving the potentially conflicting needs of sound, notation, and analysis applications that even here, within the context of mere extensions of a code acknowledged to be based on sound, many separate tangents are being pursued.

In the course of the preparation of this book we asked some contributors whether they might consider adopting some of these other sets of extensions. Those we asked all preferred their own systems on the grounds of being better suited to their own applications.

There are good reasons for this failure to coalesce: all the intended applications are different.[20] The differences are suggested below:

- Kjell Nordli's *NoTAMIDI* suggested meta-events facilitate a more complete representation of attributes required for printing from data captured by synthesizer. That is, the input is a MIDI file, while the output is printed music.

- The *Expressive MIDI* parameters of David Cooper, Kia Ng, and Roger D. Boyle are designed to make data capture by optical recognition of the printed page more practical. That is, their input is a printed page, while their output is a MIDI file.

- Walter B. Hewlett's *MIDIPlus* extensions facilitate accurate conversion of MIDI note numbers in generating accurate enharmonic notation (a staple of tonal music) from a MIDI file. This more explicit encoding provides a solid foundation for harmonic analysis, which is otherwise lacking in MIDI file information.

- Max V. Mathews's *Augmented MIDI* extensions facilitate more articulate control of MIDI information in a real-time controller environment. The dot that creates a staccato in print does not give a precise specification of the duration. Many sequencer programs apply a simple algorithm that gives every staccato the same percentage of "off" time from the stated value of the related note. Here the aim is to allow the user to vary the degree of staccato as well as the degree of accentuation and other nuances from instance to instance.

1.5.2 Sound-Related Codes (2): Other Codes for Representation and Control

Most of the sound codes featured in this section are predominantly associated with specialized or research-related activities. Our coverage includes these systems for representing musical sound:

---

20. See also Peer Sitter's proposed "Extended Standard MIDI File Format" in the glossary. Too few details of these enhancements, intended to facilitate analytical and pedagogical applications, were available at press time to warrant a full chapter. In this system "dummy events" are created to remedy some of MIDI's deficiencies, such as its failure to represent rests.

- *Csound*, developed by Barry Vercoe at the Massachusetts Institute of Technology in the early Eighties, is probably the most widely used sound code apart from MIDI. Implementations exist on several platforms. The code has capabilities for handling speech as well as music. David Bainbridge is familiar with *Csound* through his efforts to create an optical recognition program that produces *Csound* files.

- *Music Macro Language* is widely used on the Japanese NEC computer platform, particularly for games software. Toshiaki Matsushima has enabled us to offer this description, the first ever in English.

- UNIX workstations have not been well suited to real-time processing, which conflicts with their fundamental approach to multitasking, so MIDI files have been less easily used on them. The NeXT operating system, a popular platform for the composition of electronic music, is an exception. The NeXT *ScoreFile* format, described here by David Jaffe, works with his widely implemented NeXT Music Kit on both NeXT and Silicon Graphics workstations and with the *NeXTStep* operating system available for PCs.

- While we cannot describe all the data formats designed to work with the many controllers in use today, Max V. Mathews provides a specification for one—his *Radio Baton Conductor* score file. The associated code exists in two iterations—as an independent code and as a track that can be added to a Standard MIDI File—and suggests the main attributes of performance that must be represented in some way if they are to be controlled. Note its debts to a seminal sound-related code, Mathews's *Music V*.[21]

1.5.3   Musical Notation Codes (1): *DARMS*

DARMS is the oldest comprehensive code for music still in use. Originally developed for mainframe computers, it is highly compact. *DARMS* does not describe "music" so much as it describes written symbols and their placement. Because of its relative antiquity, *DARMS* exists in several dialects. Many further extensions are conceivable.

- Canonical *DARMS*, described in Chapter 11, gives explicit and complete information but is rarely implemented in actual software. Its theoretical existence allows applications designers to select, abridge, and enhance those features that are relevant to their tasks.

---

21. Described in the glossary.

- The *Note-Processor DARMS* dialect, developed by J. Stephen Dydo in the early and middle Eighties, is known to the largest number of current users, since the *Note Processor* has been available for the PC for ten years.

- The *A-R DARMS* dialect, developed by Thomas Hall in the late Seventies, has produced the largest quantity of music (more than 100,000 pages), first from mainframe computers and in recent years on Sun Sparcstations at the offices of A-R Editions, Inc.

- The extensibility of *DARMS* is demonstrated by two specific applications—those of Frans Wiering for lute tablature and of Lynn M. Trowbridge for Renaissance notation.

1.5.4   Musical Notation Codes (2): Other ASCII Representations

Other ASCII representations of musical notation are quite numerous and we present only four of them here. These can be grouped into two sub-classes. The first two address particular typesetting contexts—*PostScript* in the first case and TeX in the second. However, the first is primarily designed to pipe electronic compositions to a printer, whereas the second is oriented towards the character encoding of material.

- *Common Music Notation*, a program still under development by Bill Schottstaedt, works with a sound-synthesis program (*Common Music* by Heinrich Taube) to produce *PostScript* files and is intended primarily for composers.

- The *M*TEX* family of programs produces musical examples for the *TEX* typesetting program used prevalently in scientific document production. Werner Icking enlightens us on the background and use of these programs, which have multiple authors. *M*TEX* is widely used in Germany, particu larly for typesetting musical examples in articles and books.

The second two systems are associated with specific operating systems—DOS (with pending implementation in *Windows*) and the system native to the Acorn microcomputer. In principle, either could be implemented on other systems. However, these and most other input codes for notation programs are converted to an intermediate code (not shown) that determines the final appearance of the page.

- *Philip's Music Scribe*, a notation program by Philip Hazel, is designed to run on Acorn computers.[22] The scheme of music representation, however, typifies what is required in producing notation—irrespective of the platform—and in this respect enables the reader better to understand the requirements of representations intended to support printing.

- *SCORE*, a program by Leland Smith that traces its roots back almost 25 years, and its data structures may constitute the system sustained longest by one individual. Originating on a mainframe and operating today on a PC, *SCORE* is celebrated for its superior graphical results and its facility in handling the extended and sometimes arbitrary notations of twentieth-century music. It is used as a professional publishing program for the complete works of many noted composers (among them Schumann, Verdi, Wagner, and Schoenberg) and for a great deal of popular music from such companies as the Hal Leonard Company.

1.5.5   Musical Notation Codes (3): Graphical-Object Descriptions

DARMS and *SCORE* typify the enormous effort expended in the Sixties and Seventies to describe the symbols used in music notation and their relative placement on the page. The arrival of the Macintosh platform, with its graphical user interface, in the early Eighties created a strange new environment for conceptualizing musical notation. Why represent the object at all? Why not simply draw it, store the image for future reference, and finalize the placement with a mouse?

The two systems we offer here have roots in mainframe notation programs of the early Seventies:

- *LIME*'s *Tilia* representation, developed by Lippold Haken and Dorothea Blostein, is oriented entirely towards the graphical image and is stored as binary code, assuming that the user has no requirement to "read" or comprehend the code. Its elegant predecessor, *OPAL*, was a highly transparent ASCII representation comparable in many ways with *Kern* and *MuseData*, but with more extensive integration of sound, notation, and "logical" representation.

- *Nightingale* is the Macintosh adaptation of Donald Byrd's extensive earlier work in providing a printing system for the *MUSTRAN* representation,

---

22. The Acorn computer is in use principally in the United Kingdom and in certain commonwealth countries (especially Canada, Australia, New Zealand, and South Africa).

which supported numerous research projects of the Seventies and early Eighties. Byrd has cleverly dealt with the problem of the loss of a meaningful representation of the music by creating a metacode (*Notelist*) for data transport to and from codes with an ASCII representation. Tim Crawford, a leading exponent of *Nightingale* in the U.K. and an expert on music representation, describes the code here.

1.5.6   Musical Notation Codes (4): Braille

Braille music code is a graphics-oriented one that substantially precedes in date of origin the use of computers to typeset music. Since its aim is to represent the sound and gestural elements of notated music, but not elements of layout or cosmetic refinements, some elements of its logic are unique.

The automatic generation of Braille scores from other codes for music is often cited as an intention of the developers. Music programmers sometimes overlook the interest of many Braille music code users in creating scores in common music notation for sighted associates.

The syntax of Braille musical notation has evolved into many national dialects, but a recently adopted international code should encourage greater standardization in the codes used.

- Roger Firman's overview (Chapter 22) considers concepts and organizational issues, mentions frequently used programs, and provides two annotated examples (in the "English" dialect) of its use.

- Bettye Krolick and Sile O'Modhrain explain the most commonly used symbols (Chapter 23), based on the newly published (1996) "standard" international version of the code.

1.5.7   Musical Data for Analysis (1): Monophonic Representations

Monophonic music is simpler to handle than polyphonic music, and for this reason its use in actual applications has been much greater. The codes cited in this section are used in a single field of relational databases. Combined access to text and music fields is valuable in the management of information about musical sources. These kinds of projects give the clearest idea of what kinds of analytical work may be possible in the future with polyphonic databases.

- The *Essen Associative Code* (*EsAC*), developed by Helmut Schaffrath, has been the backbone of a series of projects in the transcription and analysis of folksong repertories. More than 14,000 works have been encoded in a database framework with six basic fields that supports twelve basic search types aimed at identifying musical similarity.

- *Plaine and Easie Code*, developed in the Sixties by Barry Brook and Murray Gould, has been the basis of the musical incipit databases of the *Répertoire International des Sources Musicales* (*RISM*). Almost 300,000 incipits have now been transcribed in databases containing more than 100 fields. These materials are used both to catalogue works and to locate matching and derivative versions of works in multiple locations.

1.5.8   Musical Data for Analysis (2): Polyphonic Representations

Only since the Eighties have computer memory and processing speed made it feasible to think of processing large quantities of musical repertory. Of the two projects listed in this section, the first is intended principally for musical analysis, while the second is intended to provide a comprehensive representation scheme to support applications in sound, notation, and analysis.

- The *Kern* representation is one of several used with the *Humdrum Toolkit*, a set of UNIX tools for music applications developed by David Huron. Sixty analytical operations[23] are currently supported. Since analytical objectives may focus on only one or a few attributes of music, *Kern* permits the selective encoding of musical attributes.

- The *MuseData* representation, under development by Walter B. Hewlett since 1982, aims to facilitate applications in multiple domains. It supports the ongoing development of large corpora of standard repertory, exporting works to various formats associated with printing and sound applications. Few analytical applications have thus far been developed.

---

23. *Humdrum* supports particular tasks frequently carried out in tonal analysis, row analysis, thematic analysis, and in perceptual studies of music.

1.5.9   Representations of Musical Form and Process

The intricacies of musical representation have provided a fertile field for the attention of researchers in artificial intelligence. Where those concerned with notation see objects in spatial positions and those concerned with sound hear events and timbres, researchers in artificial intelligence and related disciplines[24] look for grouping mechanisms that place objects into semantic clusters. Of the many efforts at representation guided in this way, we cite two recent ones below. Note that in both cases, the result is less well suited to translation between data formats than more explicit representations.

- Some works are much more formulaic than others. Our Mozart trio example is characteristic of works in which large clusters of notes form one pattern. In Chapter 28, Ulf Berggren demonstrates an approach to encoding based on descriptions of these formulas.

- Segmentation is a favorite device of linguistics researchers for whom sound is the fundamental level of a work's identity. In Chapter 29, Andranick Tanguiane gives us a parallel example to model the train of changing perceptions that occur in the learning of a new musical work.

Such examples represent only a small portion of the literature on theoretical aspects of musical cognition and epistemology. Psychologists of music sometimes speak of the mental "encoding" that facilitates the perception and understanding of music. While this topic lies well beyond our scope here, a literature on it exists.[25]

1.5.10   Interchange Codes

No one questions the desirability of defining ways of interchanging data between applications. What this book clearly demonstrates is how treacherous the ground becomes when efforts are made to accommodate multiple domains (sound, graphics, analysis) in one representation scheme. Sound exists in time, notation exists in space, and analysis can be based on either or both, or on elements of the "logical" work not represented in either one, or even on implied information (such as accent) experienced in performance (the "gestural" domain of some commentaries).

24. Notably in quantitative and structural linguistics and in cognitive psychology.

25. See, for example, "The Values, Limitations, and Techniques of Encoding Low-Level Cognitive Structures in Melody," the final chapter of Eugene Narmour's *The Analysis and Cognition of Melodic Complexity: The Implication-Realization Model* (University of Chicago Press, 1992), pp. 330-360.

Our coverage here rests on the three interchange codes that have achieved some kind of presence. Each is introduced below.

- *HyTime* and *Standard Music Description Language (SMDL)* are offshoots of *Standard Generalized Markup Language (SGML)*, a set of document description tags intended to facilitate generic markup of texts and to simplify computerized typesetting of text among multiple systems and vendors. *SGML*, which for the first 15 or so years of its existence was used primarily in the printing of U.S. government documents, got its second wind from another offshoot—*HyperText Markup Language (HTML)*, the markup language currently dominant in World-Wide Web applications. *HyTime* was approved by the International Standards Organization (ISO) in 1992; *SMDL* was adopted by the ISO in 1996. The main uses of *HyTime*, a multimedia scheduling protocol, have been outside the field of music; *SMDL* has not yet been tested to a significant degree in music applications.

- The *Notation Interchange File Format (NIFF)* was still in beta-test stage in 1996. It was originally conceived as an aid to notation placement for the output of optical recognition programs. It was drafted to conform to the Microsoft *Resource Interface File Format (RIFF)* for multimedia applications running under *Windows*. Much of the recent development work has attempted to accommodate MIDI data. Whether a blend of these three needs makes for a practical standard will be determined once the format has been widely tested. Many notation and sequencer program developers have looked in on the *NIFF* effort but few have volunteered the kind of time required to make a robust standard.[26]

- *Standard Music Expression (SMX)* was the first effort at data interchange that was put into actual, effective use. Developed only to a provisional level in the mid-Eighties, *SMX* has been used to facilitate the sharing of data between printed scores, Braille notation, and musical robotics. *SMX* printing is optimized for the *Dai Nippon Music Processor*, a dedicated machine using hardware that evolved from the Danish *SCANNOTE* representation of the early Seventies.

Certain issues of relationships between codes, and between codes and hardware, are are touched upon in the five appendices, which are located at the ends of the sections to which they are relevant. A great many other codes—some very distinctive, some

---

26. Twelve Tone Systems announced in January 1996 the intention of implementing a *NIFF* conversion utility in some of its music software.

very venerable, some relatively new and little known, and some excluded from the main section only for lack of authority to describe them—are listed in the glossary.

1.6   Notes on Typography

To aid in the deciphering of the many codes presented, we have adopted the following usage:

- Code elements are given in Courier, e.g., `5RQ`, `11WJ1`, etc. Quotation marks in Courier are literal, not grammatical.

- Lines of composed code are given against a grey background.

- Bold-face type in such passages is added editorially to facilitate an understanding of file organization.

- Integer variables that must be supplied by the user are represented by an italicized letter *n*.

- A blank space is enclosed by double quotation marks, e.g., `" "`.

- Items in a series or range of values are represented by the first and last symbols and a two-dot ellipsis, e.g., `A..Z`.

References

Balaban, Mira. "Music Structures: A Temporal-Hierarchical Representation for Music," *Musikometrika* 2 (1990), 1–51.

Baroni, Mario and Laura Callegari (eds.). *Musical Grammars and Computer Analysis: Atti del Convegno (Modena 4–6 Ottobre 1982)*. Florence: Olschki, 1984.

Brinkman, Alexander R. "Representing Musical Scores for Computer Analysis," *Journal of Music Theory* 30 (1986)/2, 225–275.

Byrd, Donald. "Music Notation Software and Intelligence," *Computer Music Journal* 18/1 (1994), 17–20.

Dannenberg, Roger B. "Music Representation Issues, Techniques, and Systems," *Computer Music Journal* 17/3 (1993), 20–30.

Hewlett, Walter B. "The Representation of Musical Information in Machine-Readable Form," *Computing in Musicology* [as the *Directory of Computer Assisted Research in Musicology*] 3 (1987), 1–22.

Huron, David. "Design Principles in Computer-Based Music Representation" in *Computer Representations and Models in Music*, ed. Alan Marsden and Anthony Pople (London: Academic Press, 1992), 5–39.

Mikumo, Mariko. "Coding Strategies of Tonal and Atonal Melodies," *Proceedings of the First International Conference on Music Perception and Cognition (Oct. 1989)*, pp. 147–150.

Ó Maidín, Donncha. "Representation of Music Scores for Analysis" in *Computer Representations and Models in Music*, ed. Alan Marsden and Anthony Pople (London: Academic Press, 1992), 67–93.

Oura, Y. "Constructing a Melodic Representation: Transforming Melodic Segments into Reduced Pitch Patterns Instantiated by Modifiers" in *Proceedings of the First International Conference on Music Perception and Cognition (Oct. 1989)*, pp. 331–336.

Pope, Stephen. "Music Notation and the Representation of Musical Structure and Knowledge," *Perspectives of New Music* 24/2 (1986), 156–189.

Powers, Harold S. "Language Models and Computer Applications," *Ethnomusicology* 24 (1980), 1–60.

Roads, Curtis. "An Overview of Music Representation" in *Musical Grammars and Computer Analysis: Atti del convegno (Modena 4–6 ottobre 1982)*, ed. Mario Baroni and Laura Callegari (Florence: Leo S. Olschki Editore, 1984), 7–37.

Roads, Curtis. "Grammars as Representations for Music" in *Foundations of Computer Music*, ed. Curtis Roads and John Strawn (Cambridge: MIT Press, 1985), pp. 403–442.

Schnell, Christoph. *Die Eingabe musikalischer Information als Teil eines Arbeits-instrumentes.* Bern: Peter Lang, 1985.

Selfridge-Field, Eleanor. "Music Analysis by Computer: Approaches and Issues" in *Music Processing*, ed. Goffredo Haus (Madison, WI: A-R Editions, Inc., and Oxford: Clarendon Press, 1993), pp. 3–24.

Selfridge-Field, Eleanor. "The *MuseData* Universe: A System of Musical Information," *Computing in Musicology* 9 (1993-94), 11–29.

Sundberg, Johan, and Björn Lindblom. "Generative Theories for Describing Musical Structure" in *Representing Musical Structure*, ed. Peter Howell, Robert West, and Ian Cross (San Diego: Academic Press, 1991), pp. 245–272.

Wiggins, Geraint, Eduardo Miranda, Alan Smaill, and Mitch Harris. "A Framework for the Evaluation of Music Representation Systems," *Computer Music Journal* 17/3 (1993), 31–42.

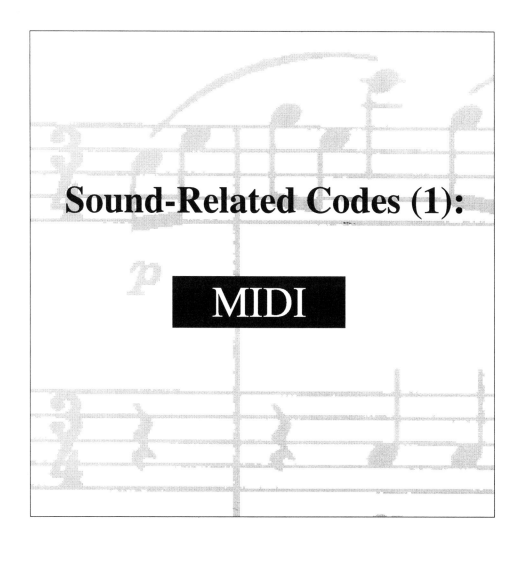

Sound-Related Codes (1):

MIDI

2   MIDI

Walter B. Hewlett and Eleanor Selfridge-Field
with David Cooper, Brent A. Field, Kia-Chuan Ng, and Peer Sitter[1]

2.1   What Is MIDI?

MIDI, an acronym for the Musical Instrument Digital Interface, has taken on multiple meanings. It may refer to a hardware interface, a file format, the data in a Standard MIDI File, or the instrumental simulation specifications of General MIDI. The ubiquity of the term is not necessarily matched by uniformity of operations, nor by interchangeability of data without some loss of information, nor by applications without some limitation of capabilities. A great many proprietary extensions have been developed by individual manufacturers. Defaults make it possible to use MIDI data on diverse machines, but they do not always produce results that are identical.

Since a large number of detailed manuals on MIDI are available, and since all of the principal documentation is in the public domain and easily available from numerous electronic archives, our efforts here are concentrated on giving some sense of why MIDI exists, what kinds of applications it is best suited to, and how it relates to other codes for the representation of music.

1. The first version of this chapter was drafted by Eleanor Selfridge-Field. It was expanded and revised by Walter H. Hewlett. Various parts of it have been corrected, elaborated, or newly drafted by David Cooper, Brent A. Field, Kia-Chuan Ng, and Peer Sitter. We are also grateful for the comments of various readers including Chris Chafe and David Huron.

2.1.1   MIDI: The Hardware Interface

MIDI originated as a real-time protocol to enable communication between separate hardware devices (e.g., between two electronic keyboards or between an electronic keyboard and a personal computer). Specifically the intent was to make sound-wave frequency and duration-of-depression information obtained from an electronic keyboard interpretable across devices. The first is captured by identifying the key that is pressed and the second by recording its "on" and "off" times. The protocol specification was published in 1988[2] and is available without cost on many electronic networks and in the appendices to many standard references on MIDI.

MIDI-enabled devices are easily coupled with each other and with all standard brands of personal computers. Boards that enable the use of the protocol now number into the dozens. MIDI applications are prevalent on the Macintosh, PowerPC, MS-DOS, and Windows platforms. They have also been used with great success on other PC platforms such as those of the Atari and Amiga. Because of its architecture, the UNIX operating system was originally unable to support MIDI.[3] Other, often more sophisticated, means of sound support have generally been pursued in the UNIX domain. One example is *Csound*, which is described separately.

As a hardware interface, MIDI is concerned with real-time processing. In the MIDI sense, music consists of a string of events. These events happen one at a time and from moment to moment. To process streams of these events, something must always be in motion. What is always in motion in MIDI hardware is a clock.

In contrast, the musical score (or recording) is a fixed object that wholly exists at one time. The work of the MIDI interface is to facilitate two-way traffic between such static objects and the dynamic processes controlled by hardware.

Since MIDI facilitates both input and output,[4] it supports two kinds of processes. As a recording (input) device, a MIDI keyboard captures key strokes and converts

---

2. The idea of a musical hardware interface was first discussed in 1982. The earliest commercial use of the MIDI hardware interface was in 1986.

3. Some manufacturers have addressed this problem. The NeXT operating system uses a special sound chip to facilitate sound/music applications. In many locales the original hardware is being replaced by *NextStep* software running on PCs. Silicon Graphics has developed proprietary hardware enhancements to support music applications of various kinds but also can use AIFF and NeXT sound files. The QUNIX dialect of UNIX supports real-time processing but has been little used in music applications. Newer sound chips may bring music capabilities to other UNIX workstations, but these lie outside the realm of this discussion of MIDI.

4. We exclude here a discussion of MIDI throughput (from one electronic instrument to another).

them into data that can be read by a computer. As a broadcast device, a MIDI file sends data one event at a time to an output device.

Traffic in both directions is regulated by the MIDI clock. Every hardware signal representing a musical event must be time-stamped by the clock, which is always moving. Once time-stamped, the data representing the event is recorded to a (static) disk.

The MIDI hardware byte remains one of eight bits. MIDI hardware codes are byte-oriented and are most conveniently represented in hexadecimal notation. These codes, which are organized from the machine (real-time) perspective rather than from the musician's perspective, are normally invisible to the user. MIDI files used with popular sequencer programs are usually stored in binary format.

Different meanings of the term MIDI are conferred by real-time devices, static files, and time stamps. The following section is intended for readers who do not have a secure understanding of the relationships among these variables. Those who do will want to pass on to the examples.

2.1.2   MIDI 1.0: The Standard File Format

The Standard MIDI File (SMF) 1.0 contains time-stamped data in a format specially designed to work with MIDI hardware devices. It is in understanding the file format that recognition of the differences between real-time processing and static objects becomes important.

From a software perspective, MIDI was designed exclusively for sound applications. From this beginning it has grown to facilitate applications in a wide variety of venues. MIDI software has gradually detached itself from some limitations of MIDI hardware. For example, byte combinations can exist in any size.

The Standard MIDI File described below represents a consensus agreement by hardware manufacturers.[5] MIDI is not an official standard adopted by an organization such as the American National Standards Institute (ANSI). Since the problems of interfacing MIDI with other codes for music are attributable largely to differences of underlying logic, the following commentary relies wherever possible on interpretations of MIDI data in ordinary English text and numbers (ASCII code).

---

5. The MIDI Manufacturers' Association.

2.1.3 MIDI: The General Instrument Specification

The General MIDI Instrument Specification, adopted in 1991 by the MIDI Manufacturers' Association, provides a common set of instrument-number assignments. General MIDI is organized as two lists of 128 assignments. The first 128 slots[6] are common to all General MIDI hardware and software. The second group of slots is reserved for proprietary use. Most manufacturers use only some of the slots in this second group, thus leaving many slots free for user-defined instruments.[7]

2.2 Organization of Standard MIDI Files

The representation of musical attributes via MIDI cannot be understood without an overview of the organization of Standard MIDI Files. There is no best order in which to describe the elements of such a file because the three main elements of organization—file types, chunk types, and event types—are somewhat interdependent.

2.2.1 File Types

The Standard MIDI File specification offers three ways of organizing multi-part (or -track) music. These are called Formats 0, 1, and 2.

- *Format 0* might be considered to be *vertically* one-dimensional. It is best used for monophonic music. If multiple voices are represented, they must be collapsed into one track in Format 0.

- *Format 1* is intended for music with multiple voices and is essential for music with tracks that are melodically independent. Each voice occupies one track. Collectively, the tracks are *vertically* one-dimensional, since they all conform to one time line.

---

6. Listed in Appendix 1, which immediately follows this chapter.

7. General MIDI's roster of instruments is somewhat deficient in offerings that would support a full complement of historically correct instruments for art music of the Renaissance, Baroque, Classical, and Romantic periods. Many low-order slots are taken up by simulations of folk instruments, by couplings of articulation and timbre (e.g., "pizzicato strings"), generic acoustical properties of instruments (e.g., "brightness"), purely arbitrary synthetic timbres with imaginative names, and with simulated noises that lack discrete pitch content (e.g., "seashore" and "gunshot").

- *Format 2* is *horizontally* one-dimensional. It accommodates music with tracks that are temporally independent.[8]

While it is possible to collapse multiple tracks into one track in Formats 1 and 2, this option is unattractive because combined tracks cannot have independent timbral assignments.

2.2.2 Chunk Types

A Standard MIDI File consists of a series of 8-bit bytes. Each file contains two kinds of sections or *chunks*: header chunks (MThd) and track chunks (MTrk). Each chunk has a 4-character ASCII type and a 32-bit length. The chunk concept and syntax are outgrowths of the Interchange File Format (IFF) architecture first offered by the company Electronic Arts. MIDI files can be converted to IFF files, but reverse conversion is not possible. MIDI files may also be integrated with other materials in multimedia applications using the Resource Interchange File Format (RIFF) offered by Microsoft.[9]

A. HEADER CHUNKS [**MThd**]

Information in the header chunk pertains to the entire MIDI file. The syntax of the header chunk is:

```
<HeaderChunk> = <ChunkType><HeaderLength><Format><Ntrks><Division>
```

The *chunk type* [Bytes 1–4] is MThd.

The *header length* [Bytes 5–8] is given as a 32-bit representation of the number of bytes of data that follow (type and length descriptions are excluded from the computation).

The MIDI *format* (also called a *file type* or simply a *type*) [Bytes 9–10] may be 0, 1, or 2.

Ntrks [Bytes 11–12] identifies the number of track chunks in the file.

- *Format 0* uses a header chunk followed by one track chunk.

---

8. See LINEAR DECOMPOSITION in the glossary and in the coverage of *DARMS*.

9. Further information on RIFF is included in the chapter on *NIFF*.

- *Formats 1 and 2* use a header chunk followed by one or (usually) more track chunks.

Division [Bytes 13–14] gives the meaning of the delta times.[10] It has two formats.

- In *Format 0* it specifies an ideal metrical time (expressed as the number of ticks per quarter note).

- In *Format 1* it specifies a time code based measure (expressed as the number of ticks per frame).

If the number is negative, then SMPTE[11] timing must be used.

B. TRACK CHUNKS [**MTrk**]

Sequential data (i.e., streams of musical events) are stored in track chunks. Events for as many as 16 channels may be stored in one track. The syntax of the *MTrk* (the chunk containing the data) is:

$$\mathit{<MTrk>} = [\mathit{<Delta\ Time>}\ \mathit{<Event>}]$$

Delta time, a fundamental concept in the structure of MIDI files, is considered in a later section of this chapter.

The syntax of track chunks is the same for Formats 0, 1, and 2:

```
<Track Chunk> = <Chunk Type> <Track Length> <MTrk Events>
```

The *chunk type* [Bytes 1–4] is `Mtrk`.
The *track length* is a 32-bit representation of the number of bytes of the track.

2.2.3   Event Types

Standard MIDI File track chunks provide for three types of events. These are

- *MIDI events*: `Note_On`/`Note_Off` events, Time Clock, Tuning Standard, Sample Dump Standard, File Dump, and many other options.

---

10. Explained in a later section.

11. SMPTE stands for the Society of Motion Picture and Television Engineers. SMPTE timing facilitates coordination of sound events with streams of images.

- *Meta-events*, such as track names, tempo indications, time-stamped lyrics, copyright notices, and so forth (i.e., global specifiers and parallel information sets).[12]

- *System-exclusive events*: hardware addresses that are often specific to one manufacturer.

A. MIDI EVENTS

Note events must contain five items of information: (1) a delta time, (2) note on/note off status, (3) a channel (track) number, (4) a note number (pitch), and (5) an attack velocity (dynamics). These parameters must be presented in this exact sequence.[13]

Independent headers must be given for the work and for each individual track.

B. META-EVENTS

Every meta-event starts with the code FF and may include these elements:

        FF <EventType> <EventLength> <Data Bytes>

The *event type* is an integer between 0 and 127 and is mandatory. Variable-length events require an *event length* specification (>0) referring to the number of succeeding data bytes. The actual data bytes are then given in order.

All currently accepted meta-events are listed in Table 2.1:

EVENT TYPE	DESIGNATION	VAR. LENGTH	DATA BYTES AND/OR THEIR CONTENT
Sequence Number	FF 00 02	no	Byte1 Byte2
Text Event	FF 01	yes	text
Copyright Notice	FF 02	yes	text
Sequence/Track Name	FF 03	yes	text
Instrument Name	FF 04	yes	text
Lyric	FF 05	yes	text
Marker	FF 06	yes	text
Cue Point	FF 07	yes	text
MIDI Channel Prefix	FF 20 01	no	Data Byte

12. Possible extensions to meta-events are discussed in Chapter 3 (*NoTAMIDI*).

13. We have altered the order of elements in our ASCII representations of MIDI files in order to cluster "pitch" and "duration" data.

End of Track	FF 2F 00	no	
Set Tempo[14]	FF 51 03	no	Byte1 Byte2 Byte3
SMPTE Offset	FF 54 05	no	hour min sec frame fractional-frames (100ths of a frame)
Time Signature	FF 58 04	no	numerator denominator cc bb
Key Signature	FF 59 02	no	sf mi
Sequencer-Specific	FF 7F	yes	Data Bytes

Table 2.1 Some common meta-events.

Generally, simultaneous meta-events may be stored in an arbitrary order. Sequence Number and Sequence/Track Name events occur at Time 0. End-of-Track events occur as the final event of the track.

C. SYSTEM-EXCLUSIVE EVENTS

The Standard MIDI File System-Exclusive (SysEx) event is used to convey a message that pertains to a particular hardware system. It is of variable length and can contain substantial amounts of code. An extensive amount of information about particular manufacturers' system-exclusive events is given in Braut's book.[15]

2.3   Time Parameters in Standard MIDI Files

2.3.1   Delta Time (Fixed Length)

Delta time indicates the time delay between the onsets of discrete MIDI events in a serial stream of data. Delta times are encoded either as pulses per quarter note (PPQN) or as SMPTE time code.

The delta-time format is made explicit in the file's header, as is the initial tempo, allowing for the calculation of the absolute inter-event delay. Subsequent tempo changes are encoded as meta-events either in the single track, if Type 0 MIDI files are used, or in a separate tempo-change track, if Type 1 MIDI files are being used.

If the pulses-per-quarter-note option is used, each delta time measures the number of uniform divisions (or *ticks*) of a quarter note consumed by the depressed MIDI key.

14. In microseconds/MIDI quarternote.

15. Christian Braut, *The Musician's Guide to MIDI*, tr. H. B. J. Clifford. Alameda, CA: Sybex, Inc., 1994.

Often these divisions are computed as multiples of 96 or 120 (we have used 96 in the examples in this chapter).

When SMPTE time code is used, each delta time is a multiple of the frame rate times the sub-frame rate. Two other parameters—the number of ticks and the number of quarter notes—are also required.

The delta-time format takes two bytes, the bits of which are numbered here from left to right as 1..16.[16]

If Bit 1 (B1) = 0, Bits 2–16 represent pulses-per-quarter-note.

If Bit 1 = 1, delta times are represented as SMPTE time code, corresponding to subdivisions of a second. Bits 2–8 hold the format number (-24, -25, -29, or -30 frames per second) in twos' complement form, and the second byte (Bits 9–16) represents the number of units into which the frame is divided.

To convert from pulses-per-quarter-note to the SMPTE frame rate, the smallest unit of time must be known. The unsigned value of the first byte should have 256 subtracted from it, and the positive (absolute) value taken, i.e.,

$$ABS(Unsigned\_Byte-Value1-256)$$

Each delta-time increment in seconds is:

$$\frac{1}{ABS(Unsigned...Byte...Value1-256)*FrameDivision}$$

2.3.2   Delta Time (Variable Length)

To optimize storage space, MIDI uses a variable-length format, using between one and four bytes to represent some of the values for delta-time measurement and the lengths of some meta-events. It would be less efficient to use a fixed-length format when many values may only require a single byte.

Commonly used data formats such as *char*, *integer*, or *long* use one, two, or four bytes respectively.

The variable-length representation splits the value into a stream of 7-bit numbers. Values of less than 0x80 (0..127) are represented by a single byte. For values greater than 127, the most significant bit (0x80) of all encoded bytes, except the lowest, is set. This scheme enables the decoding process to track the end of the current

---

16. These bits may also be numbered 0..15, 15..0, and 16..1.

variable-length value and thus allows the discrimination of the next MIDI status byte or meta-event component.

The following pseudo-code can be used to encode a given number into its variable-length representation.

```
Let InValue be the input number.
Let OutByte[n] be the encoded output byte (unsigned char) array.
Let & be the bitwise AND.

n := 0
OutByte[n] := InValue + 127
RightShift InValue by 7 bits
WHILE InValue > 0
BEGIN
    increase n by 1
    OutByte[n] := ((InValue + 127) + 128)
    RightShift InValue by 7 bits
END
```

After the above process, $n+1$ bytes are needed to represent the input number in the variable-length format. The OutByte[n] array containing the encoded version can be written to a file. For example:

```
FOR i := n to 0
BEGIN
    write_char(OutByte[i], out_file)
END
```

The following pseudo-code demonstrates a decoding method. After the process, the variable ActualValue, which must be 32 bits or more, i.e., a *long* integer, will contain the actual value.

```
tempByte := read_char(inputFile)
ActualValue := tempByte + 127
WHILE (tempByte + 128)
BEGIN
    tempByte := read_char(inputFile)
    ActualValue := (LeftShift ActualValue by 7 bits) + (tempByte
    + 127)
END
```

Key and meter signatures with variable-length delta-time values may be included in track chunks.

The above pseudo-codes are for illustration purposes only. More compact example routines to read and write variable-length value, written in the C language, are provided in the documentation for Standard MIDI Files 1.0.

2.4   Representation of Musical Attributes in a Standard MIDI File

The MIDI protocol is a message-oriented one. When a sound begins, a Note_On message is sent and executed. When a sound ends, a Note_Off message is sent and executed. The protocol itself is not concerned with duration.

In Standard MIDI Files, MIDI messages are identified by type in the first, or *status byte*. This information (hexadecimal 0..F) is concatenated with a track specification (0..F). Some of the most common status bytes are these:

Note_Off	80H
Note_On	90H
Key pressure	A0H
Control change	B0H
Program change	C0H
Aftertouch	D0H
Pitch bend	E0H
System exclusive	F0H

The 0 in each specification represents Channel 1 and is a variable. Note events can address 16 hardware channels (0..F). There are many methods by which more channels (up to 128) may be addressed. This presentation will not describe these methods nor the hardware features involved in the implementation of key pressure, control change, program change, aftertouch, pitch bend, or system-exclusive messages (A0H..FFH).

2.4.1   Note Events

Note events (80H..9FH) represent, in an indirect hardware-oriented way, the musical parameters of pitch (by key number), duration (by delta time), dynamics (by key velocity), voice part (by low-order track number), and event type (Note_On, Note_Off). They are controlled in real time. A time stamp precedes the command.

A. PITCH [kkkkkkk: note # <*n*>]

In the context of the MIDI protocol, pitch means frequency. In a Standard MIDI File, key numbers represent pitch. Middle C is assigned a key number (e.g., 60) on a scale from 0 to 127.[17] The 88 notes of the piano keyboard are encompassed between 21 and 108. All numbers that are a multiple of 12 within this range [24, 36, 48, ...] are Cs. The MIDI scale of 128 note numbers makes provision for 20 additional bass and 20 additional treble frequencies in half-tone increments.[18]

In MIDI output, the octave is divided into 12 tones, corresponding to those of the chromatic scale. The numerical codes that identify tones are incapable of expressing enharmonic discrimination of pitch, i.e., F♯ and G♭. The black notes of the piano are all described as sharps (C♯, D♯, F♯, G♯, A♯) only. Neither the white notes B♯ and E♯ nor any flat can be specified by name in a Standard MIDI File except by the use of special extensions.[19]

Where C4 represents Middle C, the key numbers and hexadecimal specifications for the Cs of the piano keyboard are these:

KEY	KEY NUMBER	HEX CODE
C-1	0	00
C0	12	0C
C1	24	18
C2	36	24
C3	48	30
C4	60	3C
C5	72	48
C6	84	54
C7	96	60
C8	108	6C

B. DURATION [**00:00:000** or **00:00:00:00**]

As a real-time system, the MIDI hardware interface has no need of durational information as used in conventional Western notation. Musical events are measured strictly by the clock.

---

17. In specific MIDI software applications, Middle C is variously represented as C3, C4, or C5. We have selected C4 here because it is the most common octave numbering system in general use. See the entry on PITCH NOMENCLATURE in the glossary.

18. There are two ways in which the tuning can be changed—through the use of the MIDI Tuning Standard and through the use of proprietary features (e.g., on the Yamaha DX7 keyboard) to create user-defined scales.

19. Some are described in the following chapters.

A *time-code address* indicates time already elapsed at the start of an event. This code may contain three elements—(1) bars, (2) beats, and (3) fractions of a beat [not a second] ("ticks")—or four (each expressed as a two-digit number)—(1) hours, (2) minutes, (3) seconds, and (4) frames.[20] Most sequencer and notation programs use the three-element scheme. In these the number of ticks is frequently 96 or 120; some programs handle 192 or 240 ticks per beat, and many other groupings are possible.

The delta time found in each note event indicates the amount of time in ticks that has elapsed since the start of the last event. There is no explicit representation of rests, since a Note_Off cannot be paired with another Note_Off.

C. DYNAMIC RANGE [vvvvvvv]

Dynamic range can be recorded from some electronic instruments by measuring what MIDI manuals call *key velocity*. On this logarithmic scale, $1 = $ ***ppp***, $64 = $ ***mp***, and $127 = $ ***fff***. The number 0 is reserved to signal a Note_Off condition. The number 64 is also an arbitrary default (48 and 72 are also commonly used) for instruments without "velocity" sensors.

Many MIDI files simply use a default value (e.g., 64) for all note events.

2.4.2   Meta-Events

Meta-events (i.e., non-temporal events) represent more general features of the music such as key, meter, tempo, and time signature that are not conceived in real time.

A. KEY SIGNATURE [sf] AND MODE [mi]

The key signature meta-event [sf] uses positive integers for sharps, negative integers for flats, e.g.,

0	C Major/A Minor
3	3 sharps
-6	6 flats

Naturals, which are only required in written notation, are not represented. Mode indicators [mi] are 0 for major and 1 for minor.

---

20. Frame information facilitates coordination of audio and video in multimedia applications.

B. METER AND TEMPO

The concept of meter has no real meaning in MIDI, since all beats have, in principle, a uniform emphasis. Meter is, however, such a fundamental aspect of the perception and understanding of music that most programs attempt to provide through the user interface some sense of the rhythmic grouping of notes.

Standard MIDI Files assume that a tempo and a time signature will be provided. The tempo is calibrated in micro-seconds. Each note-event message is executed as soon as it is received. The concept of bar numbers is foreign to MIDI and is not represented in Standard MIDI Files. In the absence of such information, the defaults of 120 beats per minute and the meter 4/4 are usually assumed.

The delta time of a meta-event is 0.

C. TIME SIGNATURES [**nn dd cc bb**]

The four indicators of the time signature meta-event represent the numerator [nn] and denominator [dd] of the time signature in written notation, the number of MIDI clocks in a metronome click [cc], and the number of 32nd notes in a MIDI quarter note [bb].[21] The denominator is n in the formula

$$\texttt{numerical name} = 2^n$$

An eighth note $= 2^3$ and dd $= 3$.

---

21. The intention of bb is to allow for the distinction between duple and triple subdivisions of the beat. Multiple mixed compounds (duple at one level, triple at the adjacent level) are possible. However, 32 is not a large enough number to handle multiple rhythms of any significant complexity. For example, in the duple subdivision of the quarter note, an eighth note would be equivalent to four 32nd notes; a sixteenth note would be equivalent to two 32nd notes, etc. For triple subdivisions of the quarter note, 48 and 96 are more convenient numbers to use, and in the classical repertory many instances are encountered in which still larger multiples (or, in other file formats, floating-point arithmetic) are required for clarity and accuracy.

2.5   Examples

The independent tracks of Format 1 are given in Example 2.1. They are interleaved, as in Format 0, in Example 2.2. In all cases only the first two tracks of the five required for the Mozart trio are encoded.

2.5.1   The Mozart Trio: Tracks 1 and 2 (Format 1—ASCII)

In Format 1 separate tracks for *Clarinet* and *Violino 1* are provided. The other three tracks are not shown on account of space limitations. In this example both tracks are encoded at *written* pitch.[22]

To aid understanding of the content, ASCII equivalents of hexadecimal notation are used in Examples 2.1 and 2.2.

Header Chunk Information:
      Chunk type: MThd
      Header length: 6
      MIDI format type: 1
      Number of tracks: 2 [*Clarinet* and *Violino 1*]
      Ticks per quarter note: 96

Header Information:
      Key signature: 0
      Time signature: 3 4
      Ticks per quarter note: 96
      Number of 32nds per quarter note: 8

Track Chunk Information:
      The order of parameters for a note event in a Standard MIDI File would be (1) delta time, (2) event type, (3) track number, (4) MIDI note number, and (5) attack velocity number. The arrangement used here groups related parameters (note name and key number; elapsed time and delta time) to facilitate comparison of the information represented with that contained in other file formats. (Only starred items are required in a Standard MIDI File.)

      All rests, which are not included in a Standard MIDI File, have been added editorially and are indicated in brackets.

---

22. At sounding pitch [used in Example 2.2], all key numbers in Track 1 (*Clarinet*) would be lower by 3; all note names (which are produced by software) would be a minor third lower.

Track 1

MIDI INFORMATION [FOR SOUND]		PITCH INFORMATION [FOR PRINTING]		DURATION INFORMATION		PERFORMANCE INFORMATION
Track No.*	Event Type*	Note Name	Key No.*	Delta Time*	Elapsed Time* (Bars:Beats:Ticks)	Dynamic Level* (Velocity)
1	Note on	C5	72	0	01:04:000	48
1	Note off	C5	72	48	01:04:048	48
1	Note on	E5	76	0	01:04:048	48
1	Note off	E5	76	48	01:04:096	48
1	Note on	G5	79	0	02:01:000	48
1	Note off	G5	79	48	02:01:048	48
1	Note on	E5	76	0	02:01:048	48
1	Note off	E5	76	48	02:01:096	48
1	Note on	C6	84	0	02:02:000	48
1	Note off	C6	84	96	02:02:096	48
1	Note on	G5	79	0	02:03:000	48
1	Note off	G5	79	48	02:03:048	48
1	Note on	E5	76	0	02:03:048	48
1	Note off	E5	76	48	02:03:096	48
1	Note on	D5	74	0	03:01:000	48
1	Note off	D5	74	48	03:01:048	48
1	Note on	F5	77	0	03:01:048	48
1	Note off	F5	77	48	03:01:096	48
1	Note on	A5	81	0	03:02:000	48
1	Note off	A5	81	96	03:02:096	48
1	Note on	F5	77	0	03:02:000	48
1	Note off	F5	77	48	03:03:048	48
1	Note on	D5	74	0	03:03:048	48
1	Note off	D5	74	48	03:03:096	48
1	Note on	C5	72	0	04:01:000	48
1	Note off	C5	72	48	04:01:048	48
1	Note on	B4	71	0	04:01:048	48
1	Note off	B4	71	48	04:01:096	48
1	Note on	E5	76	0	04:02:000	48
1	Note off	E5	76	48	04:02:048	48
1	Note on	D5	74	0	04:02:048	48
1	Note off	D5	74	48	04:02:096	48
1	Note on	G5	79	0	04:03:000	48
1	Note off	G5	79	48	04:03:048	48
1	Note on	F5	77	0	04:03:048	48
1	Note off	F5	77	48	04:03:096	48
1	Note on	D#5	75	0	05:01:000	48
1	Note off	D#5	75	96	05:01:096	48
1	Note on	E5	76	0	05:02:000	48
1	Note off	E5	76	96	05:02:096	48
1	Note on	C5	72	0	05:03:000	48
1	Note off	C5	72	48	05:03:048	48
1	Note on	E5	76	0	05:03:048	48
1	Note off	E5	76	48	05:03:096	48
1	Note on	G5	79	0	06:01:000	48
1	Note off	G5	79	48	06:01:048	48
1	Note on	E5	76	0	06:01:048	48
1	Note off	E5	76	48	06:01:096	48

1	Note on	C6	84	0	06:01:000	48
1	Note off	C6	84	96	06:02:096	48
1	Note on	G5	79	0	06:03:000	48
1	Note off	G5	79	48	06:03:048	48
1	Note on	E5	76	0	06:03:048	48
1	Note off	E5	76	48	06:03:096	48
1	Note on	D5	74	0	07:01:000	48
1	Note off	D5	74	48	07:01:048	48
1	Note on	F5	77	0	07:01:048	48
1	Note off	F5	77	48	07:01:096	48
1	Note on	A5	81	0	07:02:000	48
1	Note off	A5	81	96	07:02:096	48
	[Rest]				07:03:000	
	[Rest]				08:01:000	
	[Rest]				09:01:000	
	[Rest]				09:02:000	
1	Note on	D4	62	576	09:03:000	48
1	Note off	D4	62	32	09:03:032	48
1	Note on	A3	57	0	09:03:032	48
1	Note off	A3	57	32	09:03:064	48
1	Note on	F3	53	0	09:03:064	48
1	Note off	F3	53	32	09:03:096	48
1	Note on	A3	57	0	10:01:000	48
1	Note off	A3	57	48	10:01:048	48
1	Note on	D4	62	0	10:01:048	48
1	Note off	D4	62	24	10:01:072	48
1	Note on	F4	65	24	10:01:096	48
1	Note off	F4	65	24	10:02:024	48
1	Note on	A4	69	24	10:02:048	48
1	Note off	A4	69	24	10:02:072	48
1	Note on	D5	74	24	10:03:096	48
1	Note off	D5	74	24	10:03:024	48
1	Note on	F5	77	24	10:03:048	48
1	Note off	F5	77	24	10:03:072	48
1	Note on	A5	81	0	11:01:000	48
1	Note off	A5	81	48	11:01:048	48
1	Note on	G5	79	0	11:01:048	48
1	Note off	G5	79	48	11:01:096	48
1	Note on	F5	77	0	11:02:000	48
1	Note off	F5	77	48	11:02:048	48
1	Note on	E5	76	0	11:02:048	48
1	Note off	E5	76	48	11:02:096	48
1	Note on	F5	77	0	11:03:000	48
1	Note off	F5	77	48	11:03:048	48
1	Note on	D5	74	0	11:03:048	48
1	Note off	D5	74	48	11:03:096	48
1	Note on	C5	72	0	12:01:000	48
1	Note off	C5	72	192	12:02:096	48
1	Note on	E5	76	0	12:03:000	48
1	Note off	E5	76	48	12:03:048	48
1	Note on	D5	74	0	12:03:048	48
1	Note off	D5	74	48	12:03:096	48
1	Note on	C5	72	0	13:01:000	48
1	Note off	C5	72	96	13:01:096	48
	[Rest]				13:02:000	

Track 2

	[Rest]				01:03:000	
	[Rest]				02:01:000	
2	Note on	A4	69	192	02:02:000	48
2	Note off	A4	69	96	02:02:096	48
2	Note on	A4	69	0	02:03:000	48
2	Note off	A4	69	96	02:03:096	48
	[Rest]				03:01:000	
2	Note on	A4	69	96	03:02:000	48
2	Note off	A4	69	96	03:02:096	48
2	Note on	A4	69	0	03:03:000	48
2	Note off	A4	69	96	03:03:096	48
	[Rest]				04:01:000	
2	Note on	G#4	68	96	04:02:000	48
2	Note off	G#4	68	96	04:02:096	48
2	Note on	G#4	68	0	04:03:000	48
2	Note off	G#4	68	96	04:03:096	48
	[Rest]				05:01:000	
2	Note on	A4	69	96	05:02:000	48
2	Note off	A4	69	96	05:02:096	48
2	Note on	A4	69	0	05:03:000	48
2	Note off	A4	69	96	05:03:096	48
	[Rest]				06:01:000	
2	Note on	A4	69	96	06:02:000	48
2	Note off	A4	69	96	06:02:096	48
2	Note on	A4	69	0	06:03:000	48
2	Note off	A4	69	96	06:03:096	48
2	Note on	F#4	66	0	07:01:000	48
2	Note off	F#4	66	96	07:01:096	48
	[Rest]				07:02:000	
2	Note on	C#5	73	96	07:03:000	48
2	Note off	C#5	73	48	07:03:048	48
2	Note on	A#4	70	0	07:03:048	48
2	Note off	A#4	70	48	07:03:096	48
2	Note on	B4	71	0	08:01:000	48
2	Note off	B4	71	48	08:01:048	48
2	Note on	D5	74	0	08:01:048	48
2	Note off	D5	74	48	08:01:096	48
2	Note on	F#5	78	0	08:02:000	48
2	Note off	F#5	78	96	08:02:096	48
2	Note on	C#5	73	0	08:03:000	48
2	Note off	C#5	73	48	08:03:048	48
2	Note on	A#4	70	0	08:03:048	48
2	Note off	A#4	70	48	08:03:096	48
2	Note on	B4	71	0	09:01:000	48
2	Note off	B4	71	48	09:01:048	48
2	Note on	D5	74	0	09:01:048	48
2	Note off	D5	74	48	09:01:096	48
2	Note on	F#5	78	0	09:02:000	48
2	Note off	F#5	78	96	09:02:096	48
	[Rest]				09:03:000	
	[Rest]				10:01:000	
	[Rest]				11:01:000	
2	Note on	C#4	61	0	12:01:000	48
2	Note off	C#4	61	48	12:01:048	48
2	Note on	E4	64	0	12:01:048	48
2	Note off	E4	64	48	12:01:096	48

2	Note on	C#4	61	0	12:02:000	48
2	Note off	C#4	61	48	12:02:048	48
2	Note on	E4	64	0	12:02:048	48
2	Note off	E4	64	48	12:02:096	48
2	Note on	D4	62	0	12:03:000	48
2	Note off	D4	62	48	12:03:048	48
2	Note on	E4	64	0	12:03:048	48
2	Note off	E4	64	48	12:03:096	48
2	Note on	C#4	61	0	13:01:000	48
2	Note off	C#4	61	96	13:02:096	48
2	[Rest]					

Example 2.1 The Mozart trio, Tracks 1 and 2 in ASCII representation of Format 1.

2.5.2   The Mozart Trio: Tracks 1 and 2 (Format 0—ASCII)

In Format 0, Tracks 1 and 2 (*Clarinet* and *Violino 1*) are interleaved to create one time sequence. In this example, key numbers and note names for Track 1 (*Clarinet*) are represented at *sounding* pitch.[23]

Header Chunk Information:
    Chunk type: MThd
    Header length: 6
    MIDI format type: 0
    Number of tracks: 2 [*Clarinet* and *Violino 1*] collapsed into 1
    Ticks per quarter note: 96

Header Information:
    Key signature: 0
    Time signature: 3   4
    Ticks per quarter note: 96
    Number of 32nds per quarter note: 8

---

23. In this case a clarinet in A is required. At written pitch, its part is shown a minor third higher than it is sounded. Thus the written C5 is equivalent to the sounding A4. The violin is not a transposing instrument, so written and sounding pitches are always the same.

MIDI INFORMATION [FOR SOUND]		PITCH INFORMATION [FOR PRINTING]		DURATION INFORMATION		PERFORMANCE INFORMATION
Track No.*	Event Type*	Note Name	Key No.*	Delta Time*	Elapsed Time	Dynamic Level
1	Note on	A4	69	0	01:03:000	48
[2]	[Rest]				[01:03:000]	
1	Note off	A4	69	48	01:03:048	48
1	Note on	C#5	73	0	01:04:048	48
1	Note off	C#5	73	48	01:04:096	48
1	Note on	E5		0	02:01:000	48
[2]	[Rest]				[02:01:000]	
1	Note off	E5	76	48	02:01:048	48
1	Note on	C#5	73	0	02:01:048	48
1	Note off	C#5	73	48	02:01:096	48
1	Note on	A5	81	0	02:02:000	48
2	Note on	A4	69	192	02:02:000	48
1	Note off	A5	81	96	02:02:096	48
2	Note off	A4	69	96	02:02:096	48
1	Note on	E5	76	0	02:03:000	48
2	Note on	A4	69	0	02:03:000	48
1	Note off	E5	76	48	02:03:048	48
1	Note on	C#5	73	0	02:03:048	48
1	Note off	C#5	73	48	02:03:096	48
2	Note off	A4	69	96	02:03:096	48
1	Note on	B4	74	0	03:01:000	48
[2]	[Rest]				[03:01:000]	
1	Note off	B4	71	48	03:01:048	48
1	Note on	D5	74	0	03:01:048	48
1	Note off	D5	74	48	03:01:096	48
1	Note on	F#5	78	0	03:02:000	48
2	Note on	A4	69	96	03:02:000	48
1	Note off	F#5	78	96	03:02:096	48
2	Note off	A4	69	96	03:02:096	48
1	Note on	F#5	74	0	03:02:000	48
2	Note on	A4	69	0	03:03:000	48
1	Note off	D5	74	48	03:03:048	48
1	Note on	B4	71	0	03:03:048	48
1	Note off	B4	71	48	03:03:096	48
2	Note off	A4	69	96	03:03:096	48
1	Note on	A4	69	0	04:01:000	48
[2]	[Rest]				[04:01:000]	
1	Note off	A4	69	48	04:01:048	48
1	Note on	G#4	68	0	04:01:048	48
1	Note off	G#4	68	48	04:01:096	48
1	Note on	C#5	73	0	04:02:000	48
2	Note on	G#4	68	96	04:02:000	48
1	Note off	C#5	73	48	04:02:048	48
1	Note on	B4	71	0	04:02:048	48
1	Note off	B4	71	48	04:02:096	48
2	Note off	G#4	68	96	04:02:096	48
1	Note on	E5	76	0	04:03:000	48
2	Note on	G#4	68	0	04:03:000	48
1	Note off	E5	76	48	04:03:048	48
1	Note on	D5	74	0	04:03:048	48
1	Note off	D5	74	48	04:03:096	48
2	Note off	G#4	68	96	04:03:096	48
1	Note on	C5	72	0	05:01:000	48
[2]	[Rest]				[05:01:000]	

1	Note off	C5	72	96	05:01:096	48
1	Note on	C#5	73	0	05:02:000	48
2	Note on	A4	69	96	05:02:000	48
1	Note off	C#5	73	96	05:02:096	48
2	Note off	A4	69	96	05:02:096	48
1	Note on	A4	69	0	05:03:000	48
2	Note on	A4	69	0	05:03:000	48
1	Note off	A4	69	48	05:03:048	48
1	Note on	C#5	73	0	05:03:048	48
1	Note off	C#5	73	48	05:03:096	48
2	Note off	A4	69	96	05:03:096	48
1	Note on	E5	76	0	06:01:000	48
[2]	[Rest]				[06:01:000]	
1	Note off	E5	76	48	06:01:048	48
1	Note on	C#5	73	0	06:01:048	48
1	Note off	C#5	73	48	06:01:096	48
1	Note on	A5	81	0	06:01:000	48
2	Note on	A4	69	96	06:02:000	48
1	Note off	A5	81	96	06:02:096	48
2	Note off	A4	69	96	06:02:096	48
1	Note on	E5	76	0	06:03:000	48
2	Note on	A4	69	0	06:03:000	48
1	Note off	E5	76	48	06:03:048	48
1	Note on	C#5	73	0	06:03:048	48
1	Note off	C#5	73	48	06:03:096	48
2	Note off	A4	69	96	06:03:096	48
1	Note on	B4	71	0	07:01:000	48
2	Note on	F#4	66	0	07:01:000	48
1	Note off	B4	71	48	07:01:048	48
1	Note on	D5	74	0	07:01:048	48
1	Note off	D5	74	48	07:01:096	48
2	Note off	F#4	66	96	07:01:096	48
1	Note on	F#5	78	0	07:02:000	48
[2]	[Rest]				[07:02:000]	
1	Note off	F#5	78	96	07:02:096	48
[1]	[Rest]				[07:03:000]	
2	Note on	C#5	73	96	07:03:000	48
2	Note off	C#5	73	48	07:03:048	48
2	Note on	A#4	70	0	07:03:048	48
2	Note off	A#4	70	48	07:03:096	48
[1]	[Rest]				[08:01:000]	
2	Note on	B4	71	0	08:01:000	48
2	Note off	B4	71	48	08:01:048	48
2	Note on	D5	74	0	08:01:048	48
2	Note off	D5	74	48	08:01:096	48
2	Note on	F#5	78	0	08:02:000	48
2	Note off	F#5	78	96	08:02:096	48
2	Note on	C5	73	0	08:03:000	48
2	Note off	C5	73	48	08:03:048	48
2	Note on	A#4	70	0	08:03:048	48
2	Note off	A#4	70	48	08:03:096	48
[1]	[Rest]				[09:01:000]	
2	Note on	B4	71	0	09:01:000	48
2	Note off	B4	71	48	09:01:048	48
2	Note on	D5	74	0	09:01:048	48
2	Note off	D5	74	48	09:01:096	48
[1]	[Rest]				[09:02:000]	
2	Note on	F#5	78	0	09:02:000	48
2	Note off	F#5	78	96	09:02:096	48
1	Note on	B3	59	576	09:03:000	48
[2]	[Rest]				[09:03:000]	

1	Note off	B3	59	32	09:03:032	48
1	Note on	F#3	54	0	09:03:032	48
1	Note off	F#3	54	32	09:03:064	48
1	Note on	D3	50	0	09:03:064	48
1	Note off	D3	50	32	09:03:096	48
1	Note on	F#3	54	0	10:01:000	48
[2]	[Rest]				[10:01:000]	
1	Note off	F#3	54	48	10:01:048	48
1	Note on	B3	59	0	10:01:048	48
1	Note off	B3	59	24	10:01:072	48
1	Note on	D4	62	24	10:01:096	48
1	Note off	D4	62	24	10:02:024	48
1	Note on	F#4	66	24	10:02:048	48
1	Note off	F#4	66	24	10:02:072	48
1	Note on	B4	71	24	10:03:096	48
1	Note off	B4	71	24	10:03:024	48
1	Note on	D5	74	24	10:03:048	48
1	Note off	D5	74	24	10:03:072	48
1	Note on	F#5	78	0	11:01:000	48
[2]	[Rest]				[11:01:000]	
1	Note off	F#5	78	48	11:01:048	48
1	Note on	E5	76	0	11:01:048	48
1	Note off	E5	76	48	11:01:096	48
1	Note on	D5	74	0	11:02:000	48
1	Note off	D5	74	48	11:02:048	48
1	Note on	C#5	73	0	11:02:048	48
1	Note off	C#5	73	48	11:02:096	48
1	Note on	D5	74	0	11:03:000	48
1	Note off	D5	74	48	11:03:048	48
1	Note on	B4	71	0	11:03:048	48
1	Note off	B4	71	48	11:03:096	48
1	Note on	A4	69	0	12:01:000	48
2	Note on	C#4	61	672	12:01:000	48
2	Note off	C#4	61	48	12:01:048	48
2	Note on	E4	64	0	12:01:048	48
2	Note off	E4	64	48	12:01:096	48
2	Note on	C#4	61	0	12:02:000	48
2	Note off	C#4	61	48	12:02:048	48
2	Note on	E4	64	0	12:02:048	48
1	Note off	A4	69	192	12:02:096	48
2	Note off	E4	64	48	12:02:096	48
1	Note on	C#5	73	0	12:03:000	48
2	Note on	D4	62	0	12:03:000	48
1	Note off	C#5	73	48	12:03:048	48
1	Note on	B4	71	0	12:03:048	48
2	Note off	D4	62	48	12:03:048	48
2	Note on	E4	64	0	12:03:048	48
1	Note off	B4	71	48	12:03:096	48
2	Note off	E4	64	48	12:03:096	48
1	Note on	A4	69	0	13:01:000	48
2	Note on	C#4	61	0	13:01:000	48
1	Note off	A4	69	96	13:01:096	48
[1]	[Rest]				[13:02:000]	
2	Note off	C#4	61	96	13:02:096	48
[2]	[Rest]				[13:03:000]	

Example 2.2 The Mozart trio, Tracks 1 and 2 in Format 0.

2.5.3   The Mozart Trio: Tracks 1 and 2 (Format 1—Hexadecimal Code)

Here we see the MIDI data represented in Example 2.2 (with Track 1 at *sounding* pitch) in its hexadecimal format. An explanatory commentary in which each chunk is decoded follows this initial presentation.

BYTE NO.   MIDI DATA

0	4d54	6864	0000	0006	0001	0005	00f0	4d54	726b	0000
20	001c	00ff	5804	0302	1808	00ff	5103	0989	6800	ff54
40	0540	0000	005d	00ff	2f00	4d54	726b	0000	0016	00ff
60	030e	2843	2920	2620	2850	2920	3139	3935	7fff	2f00
80	4d54	726b	0000	0016	00ff	030e	4343	4152	482c	5374
100	616e	666f	7264	00ff	2f00	4d54	726b	0000	01a9	00ff
120	030d	436c	6172	696e	6574	2069	6e20	4100	c047	0090
140	455a	7480	4500	0490	495a	7480	4900	0490	4c5a	7480
160	4c00	0490	495a	7480	4900	0490	515a	816a	8051	0006
180	904c	5a74	804c	0004	9049	5a74	8049	0004	9047	5a74
200	8047	0004	904a	5a74	804a	0004	904e	5a81	6a80	4e00
220	0690	4a5a	7480	4a00	0490	475a	7480	4700	0490	455a
240	7480	4500	0490	445a	7480	4400	0490	495a	7480	4900
260	0490	475a	7480	4700	0490	4c5a	7480	4c00	0490	4a5a
280	7480	4a00	0490	485a	816a	8048	0006	9049	5a81	6a80
300	4900	0690	455a	7480	4500	0490	495a	7480	4900	0490
320	4c5a	7480	4c00	0490	495a	7480	4900	0490	515a	816a
340	8051	0006	904c	5a74	804c	0004	9049	5a74	8049	0004
360	9047	5a74	8047	0004	904a	5a74	804a	0004	904e	5a81
380	6a80	4e00	8b26	903b	5a4d	803b	0003	9036	5a4d	8036
400	0003	9032	5a4d	8032	0003	9036	5a74	8036	0004	903b
420	5a74	803b	0004	903e	5a74	803e	0004	9042	5a74	8042
440	0004	9047	5a74	8047	0004	904a	5a74	804a	0004	904e
460	5a74	804e	0004	904c	5a74	804c	0004	904a	5a74	804a
480	0004	9049	5a74	8049	0004	904a	5a74	804a	0004	9047
500	5a74	8047	0004	9045	5a83	5680	4500	0a90	495a	7480
520	4900	0490	475a	7480	4700	0490	455a	816a	8045	0000
540	ff2f	004d	5472	6b00	0001	0900	ff03	0956	696f	6c69
560	6e6f	2049	00c1	2883	6091	455a	816a	8145	0006	9145
580	5a81	6a81	4500	8176	9145	5a81	6a81	4500	0691	455a
600	816a	8145	0081	7691	445a	816a	8144	0006	9144	5a81
620	6a81	4400	8176	9145	5a81	6a81	4500	0691	455a	816a
640	8145	0081	7691	455a	816a	8145	0006	9145	5a81	6a81
660	4500	0691	425a	816a	8142	0081	7691	495a	7481	4900
680	0491	465a	7481	4600	0491	475a	7481	4700	0491	4a5a
700	7481	4a00	0491	4e5a	816a	814e	0006	9149	5a74	8149
720	0004	9146	5a74	8146	0004	9147	5a74	8147	0004	914a
740	5a74	814a	0004	914e	5a81	6a81	4e00	8d16	913d	5a74
760	813d	0004	9140	5a74	8140	0004	913d	5a74	813d	0004
780	9140	5a74	8140	0004	913e	5a74	813e	0004	9140	5a74
800	8140	0004	913d	5a81	6a81	3d00	00ff	2f00		

(816 bytes)

Example 2.3a The Mozart trio, tracks for *Clarinet* and *Violino 1*, Bars 1–12, in hexadecimal code.

2.5.4 The Mozart Trio: Commentary on Hexadecimal Codes

Using the byte numbers as a key, the elements of the file shown in Example 2.3a are explained here.

BYTE NO.   CODE   ANALYSIS

    0   4d54 6864 0000 0006 0001 0005 00f0 ....

Header chunk: 4d54 6864 0000 0006 0001 0005 00f0
Meaning: "Mthd"   ....6 ...1 ...5 .240

                    6   length of this chunk (in bytes)
                    1   MIDI Format (FileType) 1
                    5   five track chunks in this file
                  240   240 units (divisions) per quarter note

     0   .... 4d54 726b 0000
    20   001c 00ff 5804 0302 1808 00ff 5103 0989 6800 ff54
    40   0540 0000 0000 00ff 2f00 ....

Track chunk 1: 4d54 726b 0000 001c
Meaning: "Mtrk"   .... ..28 (decimal)   28 = length of this chunk
                                                                  (in bytes)

                                                                               NO. OF BYTES
      TIME ←(00) ff5804:   ff58 = time signature   04 = length   4
                 0302   3/4 time   2
                 1808   24 MIDI clocks per metronome tick;   2
                              8 32nd notes per quarter note.

      TIME ←(00) ff5103:   ff51 = tempo setting   03 = length   4
                 098968   625,000 u-secs per quarter note (q = 96.00)   3

      TIME ←(00) ff5405:   ff54 = SMPTE value   05 = length   4
                 4000000000   start track after 64 hours!   5

      TIME ←(00) ff2f00:   ff2f = end of track   00 = length   4

                              Total number of bytes in this chunk   28

    40   .... 4d54 726b 0000 0016 00ff
    60   030e 2843 2920 2620 2850 2920 3139 3935 7fff 2f00

Track chunk 2: 4d54 726b 0000 0016
                "Mtrk"   .... ..22 (decimal)   22 = length of this chunk

NO. OF BYTES

TIME ←(00) ff030e: ff03 = sequence or track name   0e = len   4
          2843 2920 2620 2850 2920 3139 3935   14
              14 bytes ASCII = " (C) & (P) 1995"

TIME ←(7f) ff2f00:   ff2f = end of track   00 = length   4

              Total number of bytes in this chunk   22

```
 80   4d54 726b 0000 0016 00ff 030e 4343 4152 482c 5374
100   616e 666f 7264 00ff 2f00 .... .... .... .... ....
```

Track chunk 3: 4d54 726b 0000 0016
          "Mtrk"   .... ..22 (decimal)   22 = length of this chunk

NO. OF BYTES

TIME ←(00) ff030e: ff03 = sequence or track name   0e = len   4
          4343 4152 482c 5374 616e 666f 7264   14
              14 bytes ASCII = "CCARH,Stanford"

TIME ←(00) ff2f00:   ff2f = end of track   00 = length   4

              Total number of bytes in this chunk   22

```
100   .... .... .... .... .... 4d54 726b 0000 01a9 00ff
120   030d 436c 6172 696e 6574 2069 6e20 4100 c047 ....
```

Track chunk 4: 4d54 726b 0000 01a9
          "Mtrk"   .... .425 (decimal)   425 = length of this chunk

NO. OF BYTES

TIME ←(00) ff030d: ff03 = sequence or track name   0d = len   4
          436c 6172 696e 6574 2069 6e20 41   13
              13 bytes ASCII = "Clarinet in A"

TIME ←(00) c047:   program change: 3
              channel 0 = instrument 72 (clarinet)

Note_On/Note_Off data for Track 1 (Clarinet):   401

```
120   .... .... .... .... .... .... .... .... 0090
140   455a 7480 4500 0490 495a 7480 4900 0490 4c5a 7480
160   4c00 0490 495a 7480 4900 0490 515a 816a 8051 0006
180   904c 5a74 804c 0004 9049 5a74 8049 0004 9047 5a74
200   8047 0004 904a 5a74 804a 0004 904e 5a81 6a80 4e00
220   0690 4a5a 7480 4a00 0490 475a 7480 4700 0490 455a
240   7480 4500 0490 445a 7480 4400 0490 495a 7480 4900
260   0490 475a 7480 4700 0490 4c5a 7480 4c00 0490 4a5a
```

```
280    7480 4a00 0490 485a 816a 8048 0006 9049 5a81 6a80
300    4900 0690 455a 7480 4500 0490 495a 7480 4900 0490
320    4c5a 7480 4c00 0490 495a 7480 4900 0490 515a 816a
340    8051 0006 904c 5a74 804c 0004 9049 5a74 8049 0004
360    9047 5a74 8047 0004 904a 5a74 804a 0004 904e 5a81
380    6a80 4e00 8b26 903b 5a4d 803b 0003 9036 5a4d 8036
400    0003 9032 5a4d 8032 0003 9036 5a74 8036 0004 903b
420    5a74 803b 0004 903e 5a74 803e 0004 9042 5a74 8042
440    0004 9047 5a74 8047 0004 904a 5a74 804a 0004 904e
460    5a74 804e 0004 904c 5a74 804c 0004 904a 5a74 804a
480    0004 9049 5a74 8049 0004 904a 5a74 804a 0004 9047
500    5a74 8047 0004 9045 5a83 5680 4500 0a90 495a 7480
520    4900 0490 475a 7480 4700 0490 455a 816a 8045 00..
```

The code shown above in bold-face type is as follows:

00	0	ticks of time
90		Note_On (Track 0)
45		= dec 69 (A4 pitch)
5a		= dec 90 (velocity)
74	116	ticks of time (later)
80		Note_Off (Track 0)
45		= dec 69 (A4 pitch)
00		= dec 0 (velocity)
04	4	ticks of time (later)
90		Note_On (Track 0)
49		= dec 69 (C#5 pitch)
5a		= dec 90 (velocity)
etc.		

```
520    .... .... .... .... .... .... .... .... .... ..00
540    ff2f 00.. .... .... .... .... .... .... .... ....
```

TIME ←(00) ff2f00:	ff2f = end of track	00 = length	4
	Total number of bytes in this chunk		425

```
540    .... ..4d 5472 6b00 0001 0900 ff03 0956 696f 6c69
560    6e6f 2049 00c1 28.. .... .... .... .... .... ....
```

Track chunk 5: 4d54 726b 0000 0109
             "Mtrk"   .... .265 (decimal)   265 = length of this chunk

NO. OF BYTES

TIME ←(00) ff0309:	ff03 = sequence or track name	09 = len	4
	5669 6f6c 696e 6f20 49		9
	9 bytes ASCII = "Violino I"		

```
TIME ←(00) c128:        program change:                          3
                        channel 1 = instrument 41 (violin)
```

Note_On/Note_Off data for Track 2 (*Violino 1*):   245

```
560   ....  ....  ....  ..83 6091 455a 816a 8145 0006 9145
580   5a81 6a81 4500 8176 9145 5a81 6a81 4500 0691 455a
600   816a 8145 0081 7691 445a 816a 8144 0006 9144 5a81
620   6a81 4400 8176 9145 5a81 6a81 4500 0691 455a 816a
640   8145 0081 7691 455a 816a 8145 0006 9145 5a81 6a81
660   4500 0691 425a 816a 8142 0081 7691 495a 7481 4900
680   0491 465a 7481 4600 0491 475a 7481 4700 0491 4a5a
700   7481 4a00 0491 4e5a 816a 814e 0006 9149 5a74 8149
720   0004 9146 5a74 8146 0004 9147 5a74 8147 0004 914a
740   5a74 814a 0004 914e 5a81 6a81 4e00 8d16 913d 5a74
760   813d 0004 9140 5a74 8140 0004 913d 5a74 813d 0004
780   9140 5a74 8140 0004 913e 5a74 813e 0004 9140 5a74
800   8140 0004 913d 5a81 6a81 3d00 ....  ....
```

The code shown in bold-face type above is as follows:

```
83    1_0000011 \ → 0000011 1100000 = hex 01e0 = dec 480
60    0_1100000 /    480 ticks of time (silence)
91         Note_On (Track 1)
45         = dec 69  (A4 pitch)
5a         = dec 90  (velocity)
81    1_0000001 \ → 0000001 1101010 = hex 00ea = dec 234
6a    0_1101010 /    234 ticks of time (later)
81         Note_Off (Track 1)
45         = dec 69  (A4 pitch)
00         = dec 0  (velocity)
06    6 ticks of time (later)
91         Note_On (Track 1)
45         = dec 69  (A4 pitch)
5a         = dec 90  (velocity)
etc.
```

```
800   ....  ....  ....  ....  ....  .... 00ff 2f00
```

```
TIME ←(00) ff2f00:      ff2f = end of track      00 = length      4
```

Total number of bytes in this chunk   265

Example 2.3b Annotated commentary on segmented code from Example 2.3a.

2.6   MIDI as an Interchange Language

2.6.1.   Standard MIDI Files

As a potential format for data interchange, Standard MIDI Files have the disadvantage that they represent relatively few attributes of music. Because there is no simple way to compensate for information that is simply not there, MIDI data sets provide a poor basis for translation to formats that support notation programs: many features that the software can implement require data that may not be present.

MIDI often falls short when it is adapted to uses other than those for which it was originally intended. For example, when MIDI data is used as input to commercial music printing programs, it is not able to record non-sounding information relevant to the printed page (e.g., rests), nor can it make enharmonic distinctions of pitch (e.g., D♯/E♭).[24]

Despite such shortcomings, MIDI's ability to inspire software developers and users has been phenomenal. For simple applications with short, uncomplicated pieces, MIDI files sometimes suffice. Some programs compensate for missing information with clever algorithms. Various proprietary extensions exist to enrich the code. However, proprietary extensions do not assist in efforts at data interchange.

2.6.2   General MIDI Specifications

General MIDI has provided a degree of uniformity in synthesizer applications. All manufacturers initially reserved Track 2 for copyright notices, Track 10 for drum tracks, and so forth. Here too, however, full compliance seems to exist for only a short period of time. A single user modification to a file may alter this record structure in some current applications.

General MIDI instrument specifications are poorly suited to the representation of printed orchestral music insofar as they combine specific performance techniques (e.g., acoustical oscillations) with timbral specifications (e.g., "violin") in a single *instrument number*. Tremolo strings and pizzicato strings, for example, are General MIDI "instruments" 45 and 46 respectively, while "violin" is 41. Such designations undermine both sound-to-print applications, where the result will be overly mechanical, and

---

24. These shortcomings may be selectively addressed through the use of SMF meta-events and bar information.

print-to-sound applications, where track assignments may need to be changed midstream.[25]

Vis-à-vis the classical repertory, a great many instruments have no standard specification under General MIDI. In the music of Bach, for example, there is no *viola da gamba*, nor any *oboe d'amore*. The timbres of many entire families of instruments lack an electronic definition. At the present time manufacturers and users may create their own timbres and store them in the 128 unallocated slots.

MIDI has enabled millions of users to experiment with synthesized sound and has stimulated the creation of many tools that are effective in the modification and control of sound. These tools have been enormously useful in teaching.

2.6.3   MIDI Extensions

As long as MIDI data remains in its own self-contained domain, it has great power. It has tentacles that reach out to most of the other codes described in this book. More codes have a translation capability to or from the Standard MIDI File Format than to any other format for music applications. For this reason, we believe that extensions such as those proposed in the following chapters (*NoTAMIDI*, *Expressive MIDI*, *MIDIPlus*, and *Augmented MIDI*) are well worth the study of those committed to the long-term use of MIDI data. These particular sets of extensions are all in the public domain.

They facilitate several different kinds of goals. The first three aim to improve the accuracy and completeness of the Standard MIDI File for describing music and producing notation. Among them, *NoTAMIDI* is generalized for varied notational applications, while *MIDIPlus*, although generalizable, is associated with one environment. *Expressive MIDI*, developed for a research program in the automatic recognition of music, is unusual in using a sound code to convey information from old printed sources to new ones.

Extended MIDI, mentioned in the glosssary, shares many of the goals of other contributors but intends them for a research and teaching environment. *Augmented MIDI* aims to provide support for performance nuances managed via MIDI for applications using a control device, the *Radio Baton*.

25. A violin part that contains pizzicato passages would necessarily, for sound applications under General MIDI, be divided into two parts. The same data would be inappropriate for the generation of musical notation.

2.6.4   Which MIDI?

MIDI is so well entrenched in the worlds of performing musicians and music software developers that it seems likely that it will remain in common use for many years and that any standard for the interchange of musical information will assume or include conversion to and from MIDI data.

The question is, Which MIDI? The obvious choice for general purposes may well be the version with the attribute set shared by the largest number of applications. Yet for specific applications, modifications and enhancements may be highly desirable.

Of the available choices, many enhancement remain proprietary and these are likely to remain so. If too many proprietary dialects come into use, then over time MIDI could become, with regard to interchange capabilities, a victim of its own success.

Among the public-domain enhancements presented in the following chapters, the points of departure and methods of implementation are all different, partly because the goals are not uniform. Attempts to make MIDI files comprehensive encounter the more fundamental problems of musical representation discussed at the start of this book.

While this diversity of proposed formats may bewilder the reader, it documents the enormous range of possible uses for musical data. Efforts to accommodate all conceivable uses in one system of representation inevitably lead to bloated data sets that are difficult to decode and manage. A collection of application-specific extensions, some proprietary and some in the public domain, seems likely to be the most visible "norm" for some time to come.

References

Braut, Christian. *The Musician's Guide to MIDI*, tr. H. B. J. Clifford. Alameda, CA: Sybex, Inc., 1994.

De Furia, Steve, and Joe Scacciaferro. *MIDI Programmer's Handbook*. Redwood City, CA: M&T Books, 1989.

Huber, David Miles. *The MIDI Manual*. Carmel, IN: SAMS, 1991.

Jungleib, Stanley. *General MIDI*. Madison, WI: A-R Editions, Inc., 1995.

Rothstein, Joseph. *MIDI: A Comprehensive Introduction*. 2nd edn. Madison: A-R Editions, Inc., 1994.

Standard MIDI Files 1.0. Los Angeles: International MIDI Association, 1988.

Appendix 1
The General MIDI Instrument Specification

Class: PIANO

1	Acoustic Grand Piano
2	Bright Acoustic Piano
3	Electric Grand Piano
4	Honky-Tonk Piano
5	Rhodes Piano
6	Chorused Piano
7	Harpsichord
8	Clavinet

Class: CHROMATIC PERCUSSION

9	Celesta
10	Glockenspiel
11	Music Box
12	Vibraphone
13	Marimba
14	Xylophone
15	Tubular Bells
16	Dulcimer

Class: ORGAN

17	Hammond Organ
18	Percussive Organ
19	Rock Organ
20	Church Organ
21	Reed Organ
22	Accordion
23	Harmonica
24	Tango Accordion

Class: GUITAR

25	Acoustic Nylon Guitar
26	Acoustic Steel Guitar
27	Electric Jazz Guitar
28	Electric Clean Guitar
29	Electric Muted Guitar
30	Overdriven Guitar
31	Distortion Guitar
32	Guitar Harmonics

Class: BASS

33	Acoustic Bass
34	Fingered Electric Bass
35	Plucked Electric Bass
36	Fretless Bass
37	Slap Bass 1
38	Slap Bass 2
39	Synth Bass 1
40	Synth Bass 2

Class: STRINGS

41	Violin
42	Viola
43	Cello
44	Contrabass
45	Tremolo Strings
46	Pizzicato Strings
47	Orchestral Harp
48	Timpani 1

Class: ENSEMBLE

49	String Ensemble 1
50	String Ensemble 2
51	Synth Strings 1
52	Synth Strings 2
53	Choir "Aah"s
54	Choir "Ooh"s
55	Synth Voice
56	Orchestral Hit

Class: BRASS

57	Trumpet
58	Trombone
59	Tuba
60	Muted Trumpet
61	French Horn
62	Brass Section
63	Synth Brass 1
64	Synth Brass 2

Class: REEDS
65   Soprano Sax
66   Alto Sax
67   Tenor Sax
68   Baritone Sax
69   Oboe
70   English Horn
71   Bassoon
72   Clarinet

Class: PIPES
73   Piccolo
74   Flute
75   Recorder
76   Pan Flute
77   Bottle Blow
78   Shakuhachi
79   Whistle
80   Ocarina

Class: SYNTH LEAD
81   Lead 1 (square)
82   Lead 2 (square tooth)
83   Lead 3 (calliope)
84   Lead 4 (chiff)
85   Lead 5 (charang)
86   Lead 6 (voice)
87   Lead 7 (fifths)
88   Lead 8 (bass + lead)

Class: SYNTH PAD
89   Pad 1 (new age)
90   Pad 2 (warm)
91   Pad 3 (polysynth)
92   Pad 4 (choir)
93   Pad 5 (bowed)
94   Pad 6 (metallic)
95   Pad 7 (halo)
96   Pad 8 (sweep)

Class: SYNTH EFFECTS
97   SFX 1 (rain)
98   SFX 2 (soundtrack)
99   SFX 3 (crystal)
100   SFX 4 (atmosphere)
101   SFX 5 (brightness)
102   SFX 6 (goblins)
103   SFX 7 (echoes)
104   SFX 8 (sci-fi)

Class: ETHNIC INSTRUMENTS
105   Sitar
106   Banjo
107   Shamisen
108   Koto
109   Kalimba
110   Bagpipe
111   Fiddle
112   Shanai

Class: PERCUSSION
113   Tinkle Bell
114   Agogo
115   Steel Drums
116   Woodblock
117   Taiko Drum
118   Melodic Tom
119   Synth Drum
120   Reverse Cymbal

Class: SOUND EFFECTS
121   Guitar Fret Noise
122   Breath Noise
123   Seashore
124   Bird Tweet
125   Telephone Ring
126   Helicopter
127   Applause
128   Gun Shot

3 MIDI Extensions for Musical Notation (1): *NoTAMIDI* Meta-Events[1]

Kjell E. Nordli

The information required to print music efficiently greatly exceeds what MIDI provides, both quantitatively and qualitatively. For accurate notation some fundamental parameters that must be accommodated are clef signs, enharmonic pitch specifications, dynamics indications, and accents. Other aspects of musical notation that would be useful are the availability of part-specific information from global variables, graduated dynamics, and slurs.

The file extensions described below, which were developed at Oslo University in the late 1980s as part of the MUSIKUS project,[2] aimed to address these issues. This project was supported by the Norwegian Council for Research.[3] These specifications were made available to the International MIDI Association and the MIDI Manufacturers' Association, by whom no action was taken. They are now in the public domain.

This implementation requires the introduction of new meta-event types and the extension of some existing meta-events. At this writing (1996) only 15 meta-events have universally accepted definitions.

Standard MIDI File meta-events all start with the three bytes FF xx len, where xx is the specific number for each event type (e.g., hex 58 = time signature) and is assigned by the MIDI File administrator. The variable len specifies the number of

---

1. Portions of this commentary, which was drafted in 1988-89, were previously published in *Computing in Musicology* 6 (1990), 51–53, and are used by permission.

2. See also the glossary entry for MUSIKODE, which was another part of the MUSIKUS project.

3. Other projects of the Council are described in files linked to its home page: *http://www.notam.uio.no/index-e.html.*

bytes of varilable-length data that will follow. In MIDI Format (Type) 1 files these meta-events are used in tracks other than the tempo track.

A number of situations can be rectified by introducing, after len, the variable mm, the MIDI channel (track) number. This is especially useful in cases in which local exceptions to such things as time and key signatures occur.

For example, when different voices or parts are assigned to different MIDI channels (Format 0) or tracks (Format 1), one could consider using the MIDI channel-prefix meta-event [hex 20] with the time-signature and key-signature meta-events when different signatures are wanted in different parts (e.g., 2/4 time in some parts and 6/8 in others). However, programs unaware of the MIDI-prefix meta-event would interpret the time- and/or key-signature meta-events as *global* meta-events (in Format 0 files), that is, not limited to the MIDI channel in question. Hence one needs separate meta-events for time and key signatures for separate MIDI channels.

3.1   The Time-Signature Meta-Event [*nn dd cc bb*]

In the channel time-signature meta-event [xx = hex 58]

$$\text{FF } xx \text{ 05 } mm \text{ } nn \text{ } dd \text{ } cc \text{ } bb$$

nn and dd are the numerator and denominator of the time signature. The other parameters, cc and bb, indicate the number of MIDI clock ticks in a metronome tick and the number of thirty-second notes in a MIDI quarter note. Here and in the cases that follow, all variables apart from mm follow standard practice.

3.2   The Key-Signature Meta-Event [*sf, mi*]

In the channel key-signature meta-event [xx = hex 59]

$$\text{FF } xx \text{ 03 } mm \text{ } sf \text{ } mi$$

sf indicates the number of sharps or flats and mi indicates the mode (0 = major, 1 = minor). The code mm is again the MIDI channel number.

Note that these signature meta-events are used only to convey notational information and will not change the global signature. A channel time-signature meta-event could specify one part notated in 4/4 time even if the composition as a whole is in 3/4 time. This will not change the sounding beat.

3.3   The Clef-Sign Meta-Event [*cl li oc*]

The clef-sign meta-event is a new event type. It has the following format:

$$\texttt{FF } xx \texttt{ 04 } mm \texttt{ } cl \texttt{ } li \texttt{ } oc$$

It requires three parameters: clef type (*cl*), clef position on the staff (*li*), and octave transposition (*oc*).

cl = 0	C clef	li = 1	bottom line	oc = 0	no transposition
cl = 1	G clef	li = 3	middle line	oc = -1	one octave down
cl = 2	F clef	li = 5	top line	oc = +2	two octaves up
cl = 3	percussion clef				

The combined use of these three parameters is suggested by the following examples:

treble clef	cl = 1, li = 2, oc = 0
ottava bassa transposition of the bass clef	cl = 2, li = 4, oc = -1

Clef *cl* is to be used in MIDI channel *mm* from this point onward.

3.4   The Verbal Dynamics Meta-Event [*dd*]

Although each MIDI Note_On event contains a velocity byte, one parameter cannot differentiate the subtleties of accent as opposed to the ordinary dynamic level in which the accent occurs, nor can it correlate transitions from one dynamic level to another with verbal specifications (e.g., from *mf* to *f*) or fully regulate onset and offset of crescendos and diminuendos.

In the proposed verbal dynamics meta-event

$$FF \; xx \; 02 \; mm \; dd$$

the variable mm is the MIDI channel (0–15) which will receive the dynamic level. If $mm > 15$, all channels in this track receive the same dynamic value. Some values for dd are as follows:

1 *mf*	2 *f*	3 *ff*	4 *fff*	5 *ffff*
-1 *mp*	-2 *p*	-3 *pp*	-4 *ppp*	-5 *pppp*

3.5   The Crescendo/Diminuendo Meta-Event [*cc*]

The proposed crescendo/diminuendo meta-event marks the beginning and ending points of these marks. The format of the crescendo/diminuendo meta-event is

$$FF \; xx \; 02 \; mm \; cc$$

where the code *cc* introduces the following dynamics meta-events:

0	start of crescendo
1	end of crescendo
2	start of decrescendo
3	end of decrescendo

3.6   The Accent Meta-Event [*aa*]

Music contains accents of two kinds—quantitative accents, which are achieved by lengthening of a note, and qualitative accents, which are achieved by dynamic emphasis of the note.[4] Some recent writers[5] further subdivide qualitative accents into percussive, or *attack accents*, and *pressure accents*. Read defines the former as being represented by the sign > and the latter by the sign ^, the latter being the stronger of

---

4. These distinctions can be traced to Greek poetry of antiquity.

5. e.g., Gardner Read, *Music Notation* (London: Victor Gollancz, 1985), pp. 260ff. This is one of the principal visual grammars of musical notation.

the two. A third percussive accent is the *staccatissimo*[6] represented by the sign ▾. Since > and ^ can be combined with tenuto, staccato, or staccatissimo accents, a multitude of possible combinations can result.

The proposed accent meta-event takes the format

$$\text{FF } xx \text{ 01 } aa$$

The code aa introduces such accents as the following (this list is incomplete):

1	tenuto	32	*sf*
2	staccato	35	*fz*
4	staccatissimo	38	*sfz*
8	>	41	*rf*
16	^	42	*rfz*

If $aa < 32$, a combination of accents [Nos. 1..16] may be represented. For example, the statement $aa = 10$ indicates the sign > [Code 8] combined with a staccato mark [Code 2]. If $aa \geq 32$, it is a code for an abbreviated term, such as *rf*. The accent applies to the note following the accent meta-event.

3.7   The Slur Meta-Event [*ss*]

The proposed slur meta-event is intended for phrasing, not as a means to describe legato playing (e.g., tonguing in woodwinds). Since slurs can be nested, a single on/off switch is not adequate. Further, a number for phrase-matching (ss) is required. Upon the completion of a phrase the number may then be recycled.

The format for the slur meta-event is

$$\text{FF } xx \text{ 01 } ss$$

The usage is as follows:

$ss < 128$	Slur_On (slur number is ss)
$ss \geq 128$	Slur_Off (slur number is $ss - 128$)

---

6. An exaggerated degree of staccato.

3.8   The Enharmonic Pitch Meta-Event [*sf*]

The proposed (optional) enharmonic specification meta-event is of value when the key number of the sounding note is ambiguous in a notational context. For example, Key Number 66 (a hardware specification) can be interpreted as F♯ or G♭, but in a specific tonal context, only one spelling is correct.

The format for the enharmonic pitch meta-event is:

$$FF\ xx\ 01\ sf$$

Where *sf* equals an enharmonic specification, the proposed codes are:

0	sharp sign
1	flat sign
2	double sharp sign
3	double flat sign
4	natural sign

The first note following the enharmonic pitch meta-event must have the accidental specified by *sf*. Examples follow:

KEY NUMBER	*sf* VALUE	CORRECT NOTE NAME
59	0	B
59	1	C♭
60	3	D♭♭
61	0	C♯
61	1	D♭
61	2	B♯♯

Musically impossible meta-events are ignored. For example, sf = 1 followed by Key Number 62 would be impossible: no note with a single sharp equals Key 62.

The program that reads the MIDI file should use the normal rules for assigning note names within a key signature, so that an F♯ in G Major would normally have no associated enharmonic pitch meta-event. The enharmonic pitch meta-event does not change the sounding note.

3.9   The Tempo-Name Meta-Event [*text*]

The proposed (optional) tempo-name meta-event precedes the set-tempo meta-event [xx = 51] and is used for verbal specifications such as "Adagio," "Allegro," etc. Its format is

```
FF xx len text
```

3.10   Summary

In summary, these are the proposed and modified meta-events:

`FF xx 05 mm nn dd cc bb`	Channel Time Signature
`FF xx 03 mm sf mi`	Channel Key Signature
`FF xx 04 mm cl li oc`	Clef Sign
`FF xx 02 mm dd`	Verbal Dynamics
`FF xx 02 mm cc`	Crescendo/Diminuendo
`FF xx 01 aa`	Accent
`FF xx 01 ss`	Slur
`FF xx 01 sf`	Enharmonic Pitch
`FF xx len text`	Tempo Name

4 MIDI Extensions for Musical Notation (2): *Expressive MIDI*

David Cooper, Kia-Chuan Ng, and Roger D. Boyle

The Musical Instrument Digitial Interface (MIDI) was originally intended for digital communication between electronic instruments, not as a page-description language for musical scores. However, it is often used by notation packages as a convenient means of transferring note data. Here we discuss a means whereby the standard MIDI specification can be extended so that it encompasses the range of articulation symbols, dynamics, clefs, expression marks, and so on, normally found in typeset music. This extension, which we call *Expressive MIDI* (*expMIDI*), is compatible with the Standard MIDI File specification of 1988.

Our interest in a MIDI extension was motivated by an optical music recognition (OMR) project undertaken at the University of Leeds.[1] The extended output is used by a post-processing subsystem of the recognition process in which higher-level analysis of the output of earlier stages is performed in order to regenerate accurately the musical components of a score in the final output of the program.

---

1. See coverage of the *Automatic Music Score Recogniser* in E. Selfridge-Field, "Optical Recognition: A Survey of Current Work," *Computing in Musicology* 9 (1993-4), 109–145, and Kia-Chuan Ng and Roger D. Boyle, "Segmentation of Music Primitives," *Proceedings of the British Machine Vision Conference 1992*, pp. 472–480.

4.1   The *expEvent* Message

The system-exclusive *expEvent* message is used as a means whereby musical symbols may be attached to "notes" in a MIDI file. This allows clarification of possible ambiguities in the representation of the score—such as note quantization, the presence of ties and rests, accidental type, and metrical organization—in a Standard MIDI File.

Symbols are divided into two categories: isolated symbols, such as staccato dots, and extensible symbols, such as crescendos and slurs. The grouping of notes by beams is also made explicit within the MIDI file.

The *expEvent* message is implemented as a MIDI System Exclusive (SysEx) message with the ID number 0x7D (decimal 125)[2] to insert the extra information into the MIDI file. This system-exclusive event is placed immediately before the Note_Off message of the related note (except for bar lines, clefs, and rest signs). It may encode a single symbol (e.g., a staccato dot) or a group of them (e.g., a staccato dot under a tenuto line). Bar lines, clefs, and rest signs may not be associated with a note event and can be included at any appropriate place.

The format for the extension takes the following form:

0xF0	Start of system-exclusive message (SOSysEx)
0x7D	Non-commercial system-exclusive message
<data bytes>	Two or more bytes of data [< 127 in value]
0xF7	End of system-exclusive message (EOSysEx)

Two bytes are required to encode a single symbol, so the minimum length of the message is five bytes. The two data bytes take the following form:

Data byte 1	0XXYYYYY
Data byte 2	0ZZZZZZZ

Here the variable XX is the encoding-table number, $YYYYY$ is a symbol-specific parameter, and $ZZZZZZZ$ is the symbol number (0–127).

At present we use three tables of codes, each of which allows up to 128 symbols. The first two contain what we call *isolated* symbols (the shapes of which are invariable). The third contains *extensible* symbols (the shapes of which are variable in extent).

---

2. This number is reserved for non-commercial use in educational research.

The symbol-specific parameter contains five bit-flags which indicate the orientation and position of a symbol relative to a note and other attributes. For example, it is important to know if a crescendo lies above or below a notehead and if it starts or ends on the note.

Consecutive symbols may be packed into one system-exclusive message:

```
0xF0                          Start of system-exclusive message (SOSysEx)
0x7D                          Non-commercial system-exclusive message
<data byte 1 for Symbol 1>
<data byte 2 for Symbol 1>
<data byte 1 for Symbol 2>
<data byte 2 for Symbol 2>
...etc...
0xF7                          End of system-exclusive message (EOSysEx)
```

4.2   Isolated Symbols (Encoding Tables 0 and 1)

For isolated symbols which are associated with a notehead, such as those illustrated in Encoding Tables 0 and 1 (shown here as Tables 4.2 and 4.3), two bytes per symbol are needed. The five lower bits of the first data byte are used as a set of bit-flags:

$$\text{Data byte 1} \qquad 0XXY_1Y_2Y_3Y_4Y_5$$

The parameters represented by these flags are explained in Table 4.1.

	0	1
Y_1	Above a symbol	Below a symbol
Y_2	On a symbol	After a symbol
Y_3	Isolated	Symbol attachment
Y_4	Normal	Miniature (grace)
Y_5	Normal	Crushed

Table 4.1 Bit-flags for Encoding Tables 0 and 1.

Depending on the related symbols, some of the above flags in Table 4.1 may not be relevant and will be ignored. Stems may be encoded to clarify the orientation of the note and associated beam codes. Rest signs are included as isolated symbols. It is not necessary to include stem information for all notes. In most cases a general rule applies: note heads above the middle staff have their related stem at the lower left and note heads below the middle staff have their related stem at the upper right. Stem information is needed when the above rule does not apply.

	0	1	2	3	4	5	6	7	8	9
0		/	//	♯	4/4	𝄋	𝄞	▴	(	)
10		+	,	–			0	1	2	3
20	4	5	6	7	8	9				
30	>	𝄢	⫽	(♭)	𝄡	¢	□	𝅘𝅥𝅮	*mf*	´
40	𝅗𝅥		𝄾	□	○		(♮)	◇	*mp*	♩
50	□	*sf*	∾	𝄐	𝄞 (8)	𝅜	𝅘𝅥𝅯	◡	*fz*	(♯)
60	| stem	(𝄪)	∧	—	□	(♯)	♭	𝄴	□	𝅘𝅥𝅮
70	*f*	𝄽	𝅗𝅥		𝄾	· dot	◿	𝆗	♮	○
80	*p*	♩	□	*s*	𝄢 (8)	◡·	V	o	𝅘𝅥𝅯	△
90	*z*	(♭)	◇	( )	~	□	□	(𝄪)	*sfp*	□
100	□	□	□	□	□	□	□	□	(𝄫)	*sffz*
110	‖	:‖	‖:	:‖:	| barline	∧ Legato Pedal	⌒ tie1	‿ tie2	□	□
120	𝅘𝅥𝅰	𝅘𝅥𝅰	𝅘𝅥𝅱	𝅘𝅥𝅱	□	□	□	□		

Table 4.2 Encoding Table 0: Isolated symbols (Set 1).

	0	1	2	3	4	5	6	7	8	9
0	𝄞							*sfz*	⁊	
10		□	Λ	▫	·	*pppp*		△	V	⊓
20	◇	⌇	*sfpp*	▬ (semibreve rest)	*ppp*	*pp*	♭♭			*m*
30	≋	∅	×		▫		*ff*	⁊	▽	⫽.
40	=			□	□	□	⟨	•	■	▲
50	(♮)	(♭♭)	⁒	/			□			15ᵐᵃ
60	⁒	∐	⊕		▼	◇	◆	▪	⅂	⁊
70	□	♭	⅋		*fp*	*ffff*	*fff*		▬ (minim rest)	□
80	♪	⁞		⁄	⁊	⌐	+	○		
90	𝅝	❱								

Table 4.3 Encoding Table 1: Isolated symbols (Set 2).

The delta time of all expression-event (*expEvent*) system-exclusive messages is set to zero. This provision includes rest signs. In Standard MIDI Files tied notes are represented by their combined duration. To clarify the presence of the tie sign, we represent it as an isolated symbol attached to the first note, since there is a Note_Off message only for the note that completes the tie.

Dot signs carry two possible meanings which are differentiated by their parameters. If a dot is beside a note ($Y_2 = 1$), it is a duration attribute. If it is above a note ($Y_2 = 0$), it is an articulation sign.

Tuplets are represented by means of the numeric symbols 2 to 9 of Encoding Table 0. If notes are beamed, the tuplet *expEvent* is prefixed to the first beam *expEvent*; if not, the tuplet *expEvent* is prefixed to each Note_Off message.

Note that bar lines are not packed with other symbols, as they are generally prefixed to a Note_On rather than a Note_Off. A Standard MIDI File does not distinguish grace notes and represents them with their appropriate note duration. Bit-flag Y_4 may be used to indicate a grace note with the appropriate note-type code from Encoding Table 0. Bit-flag Y_5 indicates whether the grace note is crushed (*acciaccatura*). Bit-flag Y_5 is also used to indicate inverted turns, mordents, and other crushed ornaments.

For ornaments such as turns, trills, and mordents, attached accidentals such as the two shown here ♭♯ are indicated by the bit-flag Y_3. Encoding of such multiple-part ornaments is as follows:

```
SOSysEx
0x7D
∞ code                                                        [2 bytes]
♭ code with Y₁ = 0, Y₃ = 1, (Y₂, Y₄ and Y₅ not used)          [2 bytes]
♯ code with Y₁ = 1, Y₃ = 1, (Y₂, Y₄ and Y₅ not used)          [2 bytes]
EOSysEx
```

C-clefs have their own bit-flags. These are shown in Table 4.4.

	0	1
Y_1	Not centered on Line 1	Centered on Line 1
Y_2	Not centered on Line 2	Centered on Line 2
Y_3	Not centered on Line 3	Centered on Line 3
Y_4	Not centered on Line 4	Centered on Line 4
Y_5	Not centered on Line 5 (top)	Centered on Line 5 (top)

Table 4.4 Bit-flags for C-clefs.

4.3   Extensible Symbols (Encoding Table 2)

This encoding table supports relatively "larger" symbols such as beams, slurs, crescendos, and decrescendos. These symbols may have more than one related notehead and may be represented in multiple parts.

In order to accommodate recursive beaming in which lower-note-value beamed groups are contained within higher-value groups (for example, two beamed sixteenths inside two beamed eighths), a first-in last-out methodology is adopted, by analogy with the loop structure found in computer-programming languages. Thus, in the example above, the first eighth and following sixteenth are encoded with begin-beam messages, and the second sixteenth and last eighth are encoded with end-beam messages. While this method is sufficient to deal with monophonic music, complex beaming within polyphonic single-staff parts may not be supported, though beam attributes and stem codes can provide most of the information required to properly reassemble beam groups.

The encoding for octavo signs, pedal signs, and trills is indicated in Table 4.5. This parameter table below is used in conjunction with Encoding Table 2 (shown here as Table 4.6).

The beginning and end points of these symbols are simply attached to the appropriate notes. If the "isolated" bit (Y_4) is flagged, no symbol-end message is expected.

	0	1
Y_1	Above notehead	Below notehead
Y_2	Dotted line	Solid line
Y_3	With postfix line (¬,)	Without postfix line
Y_4	Continuous	Isolated
Y_5	Start	End

Table 4.5 Bit-flags for *octavo* signs, pedal signs, and trills for Encoding Table 2.

	0	**1**	**2**	**3**	**4**
0	Slur00	Slur01	Slur02	Slur03	Slur04
5	Slur05	Slur06	Slur07	Slur08	Slur09
10	Slur10	Slur11	Slur12	Slur13	Slur14
15	Slur15	Slur16	Slur17	Slur18	Slur19
20	Beam				
25					
30	crescendi	decrescendi	line		
35	8va —	8vb —	Ped...	tr	

Table 4.6 Encoding Table 2: Extensible symbols.

Slurs present greater problems than either hairpins or beams. In some polyphonic music (particularly in keyboard music), they may overlap each other, and thus they must be given specific ID numbers to differentiate them. Twenty cells from Encoding Table 2 are allocated to provide ID numbers for slurs. The encoding for a slur will thus have the following format:

```
SOSysEx
0x7D
XX = 2, Y₁..Y₅ as appropriate          (Byte 1)
Slur ID number (0..19)                 (Byte 2)
EOSysEx
```

Bit-flag parameters for beams, hairpins, lines, and slurs for Encoding Table 2 (Table 6) are shown in Table 4.7.

	0	**1**
Y_1	Above notehead	Below notehead
Y_2	Upward	Downward
Y_3	Not used	Horizontal beam
Y_4	Continuous	Isolated
Y_5	Start	End

Table 4.7 Bit-flags for beams, hairpins, lines, and slurs for Encoding Table 2.

4.4   Example: The Mozart Trio

We present below an extract of the first twelve bars of the score of the second trio from Mozart's Clarinet Quintet K. 581 and a listing of the first two tracks of MIDI data illustrating the encoding method. This ASCII representation is based on Example 1 in Chapter 2. Thus only the *Clarinet* and *Violino 1* parts are represented. Boldface type is added to indicate the first appearance of each *expEvent* message type.

As in Chapter 2, the note names given here are those of *written* pitch. This is particularly appropriate in this instance, where the information is intended to support printing applications.

Track 1

```
        MIDI information  Pitch information Duration information Performance
                          [for printing]
        Track Event       Note  Key   Delta Elapsed Time*       Dynamic Level*
        No.*  type*       Name  Num.* Time* (Bars:Beats:Ticks)  (Velocity)

        1     Note on      C5    72    0     1:04:000                48
        1     <Begin expEvent>               1:04:000
              CodeTbl=2, Y1=0(Above), Y2=0(Upward), Y3=0, Y4=0(Con), Y5=0(Start)
              Slur00_Code
              CodeTbl=2, Y1=1(Below), Y2=0(Upward), Y3=0, Y4=0(Con), Y5=0(Start)
              Beam_Code
              CodeTbl=0, Y1=1(Below), Y2=0, Y3=0(Isolated), Y4=0(Normal), Y5=0(Normal)
              "p"_Code
        1     <End expEvent>
        1     Note off     C5    72    48    1:04:048                48
        1     Note on      E5    76    0     1:04:048                48
        1     <Begin expEvent>               1:04:048
              CodeTbl=2, Y1=1(Below), Y2=0(Upward), Y3=0, Y4=0(Con), Y5=1(End)
              Beam_Code
        1     <End expEvent>
        1     Note off     E5    76    48    1:04:096                48
        1     <Begin expEvent>               1:04:096
              CodeTbl=0, Y1=0, Y2=0, Y3=0(Isolated), Y4=0(Normal), Y5=0(Normal)
              BarLine_Code
```

```
1        <End expEvent>
1        Note on      G5    79    0     2:01:000              48
1        <Begin expEvent>                2:01:000
         CodeTbl=2, Y1=1(Below), Y2=1(Downward), Y3=0, Y4=0(Con), Y5=0(Start)
         Beam_Code
1        <End expEvent>
1        Note off     G5    79    48    2:01:048              48
1        Note on      E5    76    0     2:01:048              48
1        <Begin expEvent>                2:01:048
         CodeTbl=2, Y1=1(Below), Y2=1(Downward), Y3=0, Y4=0(Con), Y5=1(End)
         Beam_Code
1        <End expEvent>
1        Note off     E5    76    48    2:01:096              48
1        Note on      C6    84    0     2:02:000              48
1        <Begin expEvent>                2:02:000
         CodeTbl=2, Y1=0(Above), Y2=0(Upward), Y3=0, Y4=0(Con), Y5=1(End)
         Slur00_Code
1        <End expEvent>
1        Note off     C6    84    96    2:02:096              48
1        Note on      G5    79    0     2:03:000              48
1        <Begin expEvent>                2:03:000
         CodeTbl=2, Y1=0(Above), Y2=0(Upward), Y3=0, Y4=0(Con), Y5=0(Start)
         Slur00_Code
         CodeTbl=2, Y1=1(Below), Y2=1(Downward), Y3=0, Y4=0(Con), Y5=0(Start)
         Beam_Code
1        <End expEvent>
1        Note off     G5    79    48    2:03:048              48
1        Note on      E5    76    0     2:03:048              48
1        <Begin expEvent>                2:03:048
         CodeTbl=2, Y1=1(Below), Y2=1(Downward), Y3=0, Y4=0(Con), Y5=1(End)
         Beam_Code
1        <End expEvent>
1        Note off     E5    76    48    2:03:096              48
1        <Begin expEvent>                2:03:096
         CodeTbl=0, Y1=0, Y2=0, Y3=0(Isolated), Y4=0(Normal), Y5=0(Normal)
         BarLine_Code
1        <End expEvent>
1        Note on      D5    74    0     3:01:000              48
1        <Begin expEvent>                3:01:000
         CodeTbl=2, Y1=1(Below), Y2=0(Upward), Y3=0, Y4=0(Con), Y5=0(Start)
         Beam_Code
1        <End expEvent>
1        Note off     D5    74    48    3:01:048              48
1        Note on      F5    77    0     3:01:048              48
1        <Begin expEvent>                3:01:048
         CodeTbl=2, Y1=1(Below), Y2=0(Upward), Y3=0, Y4=0(Con), Y5=1(End)
         Beam_Code
1        <End expEvent>
1        Note off     F5    77    48    3:01:096              48
1        Note on      A5    81    0     3:02:000              48
1        <Begin expEvent>                3:02:000
         CodeTbl=2, Y1=0(Above), Y2=0(Upward), Y3=0, Y4=0(Con), Y5=1(End)
         Slur00_Code
1        <End expEvent>
1        Note off     A5    81    96    3:02:096              48
1        Note on      F5    77    0     3:02:000              48
1        <Begin expEvent>                3:02:000
         CodeTbl=2, Y1=0(Above), Y2=0(Upward), Y3=0, Y4=0(Con), Y5=0(Start)
         Slur00_Code
         CodeTbl=2, Y1=1(Below), Y2=1(Downward), Y3=0, Y4=0(Con), Y5=0(Start)
         Beam_Code
1        <End expEvent>
1        Note off     F5    77    48    3:03:048              48
1        Note on      D5    74    0     3:03:048              48
1        <Begin expEvent>                3:03:048
         CodeTbl=2, Y1=1(Below), Y2=1(Downward), Y3=0, Y4=0(Con), Y5=1(End)
         Beam_Code
```

```
1      <End expEvent>
1      Note off    D5    74    48    3:03:096              48
1      <Begin expEvent>              3:03:096
       CodeTbl=0, Y1=0, Y2=0, Y3=0(Isolated), Y4=0(Normal), Y5=0(Normal)
       BarLine_Code
1      <End expEvent>
1      Note on     C5    72    0     4:01:000              48
1      <Begin expEvent>              4:01:000
       CodeTbl=2, Y1=1(Below), Y2=0, Y3=1(Horizontal), Y4=0(Con), Y5=0(Start)
       Beam_Code
1      <End expEvent>
1      Note off    C5    72    48    4:01:048              48
1      Note on     B4    71    0     4:01:048              48
1      Note off    B4    71    48    4:01:096              48
1      Note on     E5    76    0     4:02:000              48
1      Note off    E5    76    48    4:02:048              48
1      Note on     D5    74    0     4:02:048              48
1      Note off    D5    74    48    4:02:096              48
1      Note on     G5    79    0     4:03:000              48
1      Note off    G5    79    48    4:03:048              48
1      Note on     F5    77    0     4:03:048              48
1      <Begin expEvent>              4:03:048
       CodeTbl=2, Y1=0(Above), Y2=0(Upward), Y3=0, Y4=0(Con), Y5=1(End)
       Slur00_Code
       CodeTbl=2, Y1=1(Below), Y2=0, Y3=1(Horizontal), Y4=0(Con), Y5=1(End)
       Beam_Code
1      <End expEvent>
1      Note off    F5    77    48    4:03:096              48
1      <Begin expEvent>              4:03:096
       CodeTbl=0, Y1=0, Y2=0, Y3=0(Isolated), Y4=0(Normal), Y5=0(Normal)
       BarLine_Code
1      <End expEvent>
1      Note on     D#5   75    0     5:01:000              48
1      <Begin expEvent>              5:01:000
       CodeTbl=2, Y1=0(Above), Y2=0(Upward), Y3=0, Y4=0(Con), Y5=0(Start)
       Slur00_Code
       CodeTbl=0, Y1=0, Y2=0, Y3=0(Isolated), Y4=0(Normal), Y5=0(Normal)
       Sharp_Code
1      <End expEvent>
1      Note off    D#5   75    96    5:01:096              48
1      Note on     E5    76    0     5:02:000              48
1      <Begin expEvent>              5:02:000
       CodeTbl=2, Y1=0(Above), Y2=0(Upward), Y3=0, Y4=0(Con), Y5=1(End)
       Slur00_Code
1      <End expEvent>
1      Note off    E5    76    96    5:02:096              48
1      Note on     C5    72    0     5:03:000              48
1      <Begin expEvent>              5:03:000
       CodeTbl=2, Y1=0(Above), Y2=0(Upward), Y3=0, Y4=0(Con), Y5=0(Start)
       Slur00_Code
       CodeTbl=2, Y1=1(Below), Y2=0(Upward), Y3=0, Y4=0(Con), Y5=0(Start)
       Beam_Code
1      <End expEvent>
1      Note off    C5    72    48    5:03:048              48
1      Note on     E5    76    0     5:03:048              48
1      <Begin expEvent>              5:03:048
       CodeTbl=2, Y1=1(Below), Y2=0(Upward), Y3=0, Y4=0(Con), Y5=1(End)
       Beam_Code
1      <End expEvent>
1      Note off    E5    76    48    5:03:096              48
1      <Begin expEvent>              5:03:096
       CodeTbl=0, Y1=0, Y2=0, Y3=0(Isolated), Y4=0(Normal), Y5=0(Normal)
       BarLine_Code
1      <End expEvent>
1      Note on     G5    79    0     6:01:000              48
1      <Begin expEvent>              6:01:000
       CodeTbl=2, Y1=1(Below), Y2=1(Downward), Y3=0, Y4=0(Con), Y5=0(Start)
```

```
         Beam_Code
1        <End expEvent>
1        Note off     G5     79     48     6:01:048                    48
1        Note on      E5     76     0      6:01:048                    48
1        <Begin expEvent>                  6:01:048
         CodeTbl=2, Y1=1(Below), Y2=1(Downward), Y3=0, Y4=0(Con), Y5=1(End)
         Beam_Code
1        <End expEvent>
1        Note off     E5     76     48     6:01:096                    48
1        Note on      C6     84     0      6:01:000                    48
1        <Begin expEvent>                  6:01:000
         CodeTbl=2, Y1=0(Above), Y2=0(Upward), Y3=0, Y4=0(Con), Y5=1(End)
         Slur00_Code
1        <End expEvent>
1        Note off     C6     84     96     6:02:096                    48
1        Note on      G5     79     0      6:03:000                    48
1        <Begin expEvent>                  6:03:000
         CodeTbl=2, Y1=0(Above), Y2=0(Upward), Y3=0, Y4=0(Con), Y5=0(Start)
         Slur00_Code
         CodeTbl=2, Y1=1(Below), Y2=1(Downward), Y3=0, Y4=0(Con), Y5=0(Start)
         Beam_Code
1        <End expEvent>
1        Note off     G5     79     48     6:03:048                    48
1        Note on      E5     76     0      6:03:048                    48
1        <Begin expEvent>                  6:03:048
         CodeTbl=2, Y1=1(Below), Y2=1(Downward), Y3=0, Y4=0(Con), Y5=1(End)
         Beam_Code
1        <End expEvent>
1        Note off     E5     76     48     6:03:096                    48
1        <Begin expEvent>                  6:03:096
         CodeTbl=0, Y1=0, Y2=0, Y3=0(Isolated), Y4=0(Normal), Y5=0(Normal)
         BarLine_Code
1        <End expEvent>
1        Note on      D5     74     0      7:01:000                    48
1        <Begin expEvent>                  7:01:000
         CodeTbl=2, Y1=1(Below), Y2=0(Upward), Y3=0, Y4=0(Con), Y5=0(Start)
         Beam_Code
         CodeTbl=0, Y1=0, Y2=0, Y3=0(Isolated), Y4=0(Normal), Y5=0(Normal)
         Natural_Code
1        <End expEvent>
1        Note off     D5     74     48     7:01:048                    48
1        Note on      F5     77     0      7:01:048                    48
1        <Begin expEvent>                  7:01:048
         CodeTbl=2, Y1=1(Below), Y2=0(Upward), Y3=0, Y4=0(Con), Y5=1(End)
         Beam_Code
1        <End expEvent>
1        Note off     F5     77     48     7:01:096                    48
1        Note on      A5     81     0      7:02:000                    48
1        <Begin expEvent>                  7:02:000
         CodeTbl=2, Y1=0(Above), Y2=0(Upward), Y3=0, Y4=0(Con), Y5=1(End)
         Slur00_Code
1        <End expEvent>
1        Note off     A5     81     96     7:02:096                    48
1        [Rest]                            7:02:096
1        <Begin expEvent>                  7:02:096
         CodeTbl=1, Y1=0, Y2=0, Y3=0(Isolated), Y4=0(Normal), Y5=0(Normal)
         CrotchetRest_Code
1        <End expEvent>
1        <Begin expEvent>                  7:02:096
         CodeTbl=0, Y1=0, Y2=0, Y3=0(Isolated), Y4=0(Normal), Y5=0(Normal)
         BarLine_Code
1        <End expEvent>
1        [Rest]                            7:02:096
1        <Begin expEvent>                  7:02:096
         CodeTbl=1, Y1=0, Y2=0, Y3=0(Isolated), Y4=0(Normal), Y5=0(Normal)
         SemibreveRest_Code
1        <End expEvent>
```

```
    1     <Begin expEvent>                    7:02:096
          CodeTbl=0, Y1=0, Y2=0, Y3=0(Isolated), Y4=0(Normal), Y5=0(Normal)
          BarLine_Code
    1     <End expEvent>
    1     [Rest]                              7:02:096
    1     <Begin expEvent>                    7:02:096
          CodeTbl=1, Y1=0, Y2=0, Y3=0(Isolated), Y4=0(Normal), Y5=0(Normal)
          CrotchetRest_Code
    1     <End expEvent>
    1     [Rest]                              7:02:096
    1     <Begin expEvent>                    7:02:096
          CodeTbl=1, Y1=0, Y2=0, Y3=0(Isolated), Y4=0(Normal), Y5=0(Normal)
          CrotchetRest_Code
    1     <End expEvent>
    1     Note on     D4    62    576   9:03:000                48
    1     <Begin expEvent>                    9:03:000
          CodeTbl=2, Y1=1(Below), Y2=1(Downward), Y3=0, Y4=0(Con), Y5=0(Start)
          Slur00_Code
          CodeTbl=0, Y1=1(Below), Y2=1(After), Y3=0(Attachment), Y4=0(Normal),
Y5=0(Normal)
          Triplet_Code
          CodeTbl=2, Y1=0(Above), Y2=1(Downward), Y3=0, Y4=0(Con), Y5=0(Start)
          Beam_Code
    1     <End expEvent>
    1     Note off    D4    62    32    9:03:032                48
    1     Note on     A3    57    0     9:03:032                48
    1     Note off    A3    57    32    9:03:064                48
    1     Note on     F3    53    0     9:03:064                48
    1     <Begin expEvent>                    9:03:064
          CodeTbl=2, Y1=0(Above), Y2=1(Downward), Y3=0, Y4=0(Con), Y5=1(End)
          Beam_Code
    1     <End expEvent>
    1     Note off    F3    53    32    9:03:096                48
    1     <Begin expEvent>                    9:03:096
          CodeTbl=0, Y1=0, Y2=0, Y3=0(Isolated), Y4=0(Normal), Y5=0(Normal)
          BarLine_Code
    1     <End expEvent>
    1     Note on     A3    57    0     10:01:000               48
    1     <Begin expEvent>                    10:01:000
          CodeTbl=2, Y1=1(Below), Y2=1(Downward), Y3=0, Y4=0(Con), Y5=1(End)
          Slur00_Code
          CodeTbl=2, Y1=0(Above), Y2=0(Upward), Y3=0, Y4=0(Con), Y5=0(Start)
          Beam_Code
    1     <End expEvent>
    1     Note off    A3    57    48    10:01:048               48
    1     Note on     D4    62    0     10:01:048               48
    1     <Begin expEvent>                    10:01:048
          CodeTbl=0, Y1=1(Below), Y2=0, Y3=0(Isolated), Y4=0(Normal), Y5=0(Normal)
          Dot_Code
    1     <End expEvent>
    1     Note off    D4    62    24    10:01:072               48
    1     Note on     F4    65    24    10:01:096               48
    1     <Begin expEvent>                    10:01:096
          CodeTbl=0, Y1=1(Below), Y2=0, Y3=0(Isolated), Y4=0(Normal), Y5=0(Normal)
          Dot_Code
    1     <End expEvent>
    1     Note off    F4    65    24    10:02:024               48
    1     Note on     A4    69    24    10:02:048               48
    1     <Begin expEvent>                    10:02:048
          CodeTbl=0, Y1=1(Below), Y2=0, Y3=0(Isolated), Y4=0(Normal), Y5=0(Normal)
          Dot_Code
    1     <End expEvent>
    1     Note off    A4    69    24    10:02:072               48
    1     Note on     D5    74    24    10:03:096               48
    1     <Begin expEvent>                    10:03:096
          CodeTbl=0, Y1=1(Below), Y2=0, Y3=0(Isolated), Y4=0(Normal), Y5=0(Normal)
          Dot_Code
```

```
1    <End expEvent>
1    Note off     D5    74    24    10:03:024              48
1    Note on      F5    77    24    10:03:048              48
1    <Begin expEvent>                 10:03:048
     CodeTbl=2, Y1=0(Above), Y2=0(Upward), Y3=0, Y4=0(Con), Y5=1(End)
     Beam_Code
     CodeTbl=0, Y1=1(Below), Y2=0, Y3=0(Isolated), Y4=0(Normal), Y5=0(Normal)
     Dot_Code
1    <End expEvent>
1    Note off     F5    77    24    10:03:072              48
1    <Begin expEvent>                 10:03:072
     CodeTbl=0, Y1=0, Y2=0, Y3=0(Isolated), Y4=0(Normal), Y5=0(Normal)
     BarLine_Code
1    <End expEvent>
1    Note on      A5    81    0     11:01:000              48
1    <Begin expEvent>                 11:01:000
     CodeTbl=2, Y1=0(Above), Y2=0(Upward), Y3=0, Y4=0(Con), Y5=0(Start)
     Slur00_Code
     CodeTbl=2, Y1=1(Below), Y2=1(Downward), Y3=0, Y4=0(Con), Y5=0(Start)
     Beam_Code
1    <End expEvent>
1    Note off     A5    81    48    11:01:048              48
1    Note on      G5    79    0     11:01:048              48
1    Note off     G5    79    48    11:01:096              48
1    Note on      F5    77    0     11:02:000              48
1    Note off     F5    77    48    11:02:048              48
1    Note on      E5    76    0     11:02:048              48
1    Note off     E5    76    48    11:02:096              48
1    Note on      F5    77    0     11:03:000              48
1    Note off     F5    77    48    11:03:048              48
1    Note on      D5    74    0     11:03:048              48
1    <Begin expEvent>                 11:03:048
     CodeTbl=2, Y1=0(Above), Y2=0(Upward), Y3=0, Y4=0(Con), Y5=1(End)
     Slur00_Code
     CodeTbl=2, Y1=1(Below), Y2=1(Downward), Y3=0, Y4=0(Con), Y5=1(End)
     Beam_Code
1    <End expEvent>
1    Note off     D5    74    48    11:03:096              48
1    <Begin expEvent>                 11:03:096
     CodeTbl=0, Y1=0, Y2=0, Y3=0(Isolated), Y4=0(Normal), Y5=0(Normal)
     BarLine_Code
1    <End expEvent>
1    Note on      C5    72    0     12:01:000              48
1    <Begin expEvent>                 12:01:000
     CodeTbl=2, Y1=0(Above), Y2=0(Upward), Y3=0, Y4=0(Con), Y5=0(Start)
     Slur00_Code
1    <End expEvent>
1    Note off     C5    72    192   12:02:096              48
1    Note on      E5    76    0     12:03:000              48
1    <Begin expEvent>                 12:03:000
     CodeTbl=2, Y1=1(Below), Y2=1(Downward), Y3=0, Y4=0(Con), Y5=0(Start)
     Beam_Code
1    <End expEvent>
1    Note off     E5    76    48    12:03:048              48
1    Note on      D5    74    0     12:03:048              48
1    <Begin expEvent>                 12:03:048
     CodeTbl=2, Y1=0(Above), Y2=0(Upward), Y3=0, Y4=0(Con), Y5=1(End)
     Slur00_Code
     CodeTbl=2, Y1=1(Below), Y2=1(Downward), Y3=0, Y4=0(Con), Y5=1(End)
     Beam_Code
1    <End expEvent>
1    Note off     D5    74    48    12:03:096              48
1    <Begin expEvent>                 12:03:096
     CodeTbl=0, Y1=0, Y2=0, Y3=0(Isolated), Y4=0(Normal), Y5=0(Normal)
     BarLine_Code
1    <End expEvent>
1    Note on      C5    72    0     13:01:000              48
```

```
1      Note off    C5    72    96    13:01:096              48
1      [Rest]                        13:01:096
1      <Begin expEvent>              13:01:096
       CodeTbl=1, Y1=0, Y2=0, Y3=0(Isolated), Y4=0(Normal), Y5=0(Normal)
       CrotchetRest_Code
1      <End expEvent>
1      <Begin expEvent>              13:01:096
       CodeTbl=0, Y1=0, Y2=0, Y3=0(Isolated), Y4=0(Normal), Y5=0(Normal)
       ":||:"_Code
1      <End expEvent>
```

Track 2

```
2      [Rest]                        00:00:000
2      <Begin expEvent>              00:00:000
       CodeTbl=1, Y1=0, Y2=0, Y3=0(Isolated), Y4=0(Normal), Y5=0(Normal)
       CrotchetRest_Code
2      <End expEvent>
2      <Begin expEvent>              00:00:000
       CodeTbl=0, Y1=0, Y2=0, Y3=0(Isolated), Y4=0(Normal), Y5=0(Normal)
       BarLine_Code
2      <End expEvent>
2      [Rest]                        00:00:000
2      <Begin expEvent>              00:00:000
       CodeTbl=1, Y1=0, Y2=0, Y3=0(Isolated), Y4=0(Normal), Y5=0(Normal)
       CrotchetRest_Code
2      <End expEvent>
2      Note on     A4    69    192   02:02:000              48
2      <Begin expEvent>              02:02:000
       CodeTbl=0, Y1=1(Below), Y2=0, Y3=0(Isolated), Y4=0(Normal), Y5=0(Normal)
       "p"_Code
2      <End expEvent>
2      Note off    A4    69    96    02:02:096              48
2      Note on     A4    69    0     02:03:000              48
2      Note off    A4    69    96    02:03:096              48
2      <Begin expEvent>              02:03:096
       CodeTbl=0, Y1=0, Y2=0, Y3=0(Isolated), Y4=0(Normal), Y5=0(Normal)
       BarLine_Code
2      <End expEvent>
2      [Rest]                        02:03:096
2      <Begin expEvent>              02:03:096
       CodeTbl=1, Y1=0, Y2=0, Y3=0(Isolated), Y4=0(Normal), Y5=0(Normal)
       CrotchetRest_Code
2      <End expEvent>
2      Note on     A4    69    96    03:02:000              48
2      Note off    A4    69    96    03:02:096              48
2      Note on     A4    69    0     03:03:000              48
2      Note off    A4    69    96    03:03:096              48
2      <Begin expEvent>              03:03:096
       CodeTbl=0, Y1=0, Y2=0, Y3=0(Isolated), Y4=0(Normal), Y5=0(Normal)
       BarLine_Code
2      <End expEvent>
2      [Rest]                        03:03:096
2      <Begin expEvent>              03:03:096
       CodeTbl=1, Y1=0, Y2=0, Y3=0(Isolated), Y4=0(Normal), Y5=0(Normal)
       CrotchetRest_Code
2      <End expEvent>
2      Note on     G#4   68    96    04:02:000              48
2      Note off    G#4   68    96    04:02:096              48
2      Note on     G#4   68    0     04:03:000              48
2      Note off    G#4   68    96    04:03:096              48
2      <Begin expEvent>              04:03:096
       CodeTbl=0, Y1=0, Y2=0, Y3=0(Isolated), Y4=0(Normal), Y5=0(Normal)
       BarLine_Code
```

```
2      <End expEvent>
2      [Rest]                           04:03:096
2      <Begin expEvent>                 04:03:096
       CodeTbl=1, Y1=0, Y2=0, Y3=0(Isolated), Y4=0(Normal), Y5=0(Normal)
       CrotchetRest_Code
2      <End expEvent>
2      Note on      A4     69    96    05:02:000            48
2      Note off     A4     69    96    05:02:096            48
2      Note on      A4     69    0     05:03:000            48
2      Note off     A4     69    96    05:03:096            48
2      <Begin expEvent>                 05:03:096
       CodeTbl=0, Y1=0, Y2=0, Y3=0(Isolated), Y4=0(Normal), Y5=0(Normal)
       BarLine_Code
2      <End expEvent>
2      [Rest]                           05:03:096
2      <Begin expEvent>                 05:03:096
       CodeTbl=1, Y1=0, Y2=0, Y3=0(Isolated), Y4=0(Normal), Y5=0(Normal)
       CrotchetRest_Code
2      <End expEvent>
2      Note on      A4     69    96    06:02:000            48
2      Note off     A4     69    96    06:02:096            48
2      Note on      A4     69    0     06:03:000            48
2      Note off     A4     69    96    06:03:096            48
2      <Begin expEvent>                 06:03:096
       CodeTbl=0, Y1=0, Y2=0, Y3=0(Isolated), Y4=0(Normal), Y5=0(Normal)
       BarLine_Code
2      <End expEvent>
2      Note on      F#4    66    0     07:01:000            48
2      Note off     F#4    66    96    07:01:096            48
2      [Rest]                           07:01:096
2      <Begin expEvent>                 07:01:096
       CodeTbl=1, Y1=0, Y2=0, Y3=0(Isolated), Y4=0(Normal), Y5=0(Normal)
       CrotchetRest_Code
2      <End expEvent>
2      Note on      C#5    73    96    07:03:000            48
2      <Begin expEvent>                 07:03:000
       CodeTbl=2, Y1=0(Above), Y2=0(Upward), Y3=0, Y4=0(Con), Y5=0(Start)
       Slur00_Code
       CodeTbl=2, Y1=1(Below), Y2=1(Downward), Y3=0, Y4=0(Con), Y5=0(Start)
       Beam_Code
2      <End expEvent>
2      Note off     C#5    73    4B    07:03:048            48
2      Note on      A#4    70    0     07:03:048            48
2      <Begin expEvent>                 07:03:048
       CodeTbl=2, Y1=1(Below), Y2=1(Downward), Y3=0, Y4=0(Con), Y5=1(End)
       Beam_Code
       CodeTbl=0, Y1=0, Y2=0, Y3=0(Isolated), Y4=0(Normal), Y5=0(Normal)
       Sharp_Code
2      <End expEvent>
2      Note off     A#4    70    48    07:03:096            48
2      <Begin expEvent>                 07:03:096
       CodeTbl=0, Y1=0, Y2=0, Y3=0(Isolated), Y4=0(Normal), Y5=0(Normal)
       BarLine_Code

2      <End expEvent>
2      Note on      B4     71    0     08:01:000            48
2      <Begin expEvent>                 08:01:000
       CodeTbl=2, Y1=1(Below), Y2=0, Y3=1(Horizontal), Y4=0(Con), Y5=0(Start)
       Beam_Code
2      <End expEvent>
2      Note off     B4     71    48    08:01:048            48
2      Note on      D5     74    0     08:01:048            48
2      <Begin expEvent>                 08:01:048
       CodeTbl=2, Y1=1(Below), Y2=0, Y3=1(Horizontal), Y4=0(Con), Y5=1(End)
       Beam_Code
2      <End expEvent>
2      Note off     D5     74    48    08:01:096            48
```

```
2      Note on      F#5    78     0     08:02:000              48
2      <Begin expEvent>                08:02:000
       CodeTbl=2, Y1=0(Above), Y2=0(Upward), Y3=0, Y4=0(Con), Y5=1(End)
       Slur00_Code
2      <End expEvent>
2      Note off     F#5    78     96    08:02:096              48
2      Note on      C#5    73     0     08:03:000              48
2      <Begin expEvent>                08:03:000
       CodeTbl=2, Y1=0(Above), Y2=0(Upward), Y3=0, Y4=0(Con), Y5=0(Start)
       Slur00_Code
       CodeTbl=2, Y1=1(Below), Y2=1(Downward), Y3=0, Y4=0(Con), Y5=0(Start)
       Beam_Code
2      <End expEvent>
2      Note off     C#5    73     48    08:03:048              48
2      Note on      A#4    70     0     08:03:048              48
2      <Begin expEvent>                08:03:048
       CodeTbl=2, Y1=1(Below), Y2=1(Downward), Y3=0, Y4=0(Con), Y5=1(End)
       Beam_Code
       CodeTbl=0, Y1=0, Y2=0, Y3=0(Isolated), Y4=0(Normal), Y5=0(Normal)
       Sharp_Code
2      <End expEvent>
2      Note off     A#4    70     48    08:03:096              48
2      <Begin expEvent>                08:03:096
       CodeTbl=0, Y1=0, Y2=0, Y3=0(Isolated), Y4=0(Normal), Y5=0(Normal)
       BarLine_Code
2      <End expEvent>
2      Note on      B4     71     0     09:01:000              48
2      <Begin expEvent>                09:01:000
       CodeTbl=2, Y1=1(Below), Y2=0(Upward), Y3=0, Y4=0(Con), Y5=0(Start)
       Beam_Code
2      <End expEvent>
2      Note off     B4     71     48    09:01:048              48
2      Note on      D5     74     0     09:01:048              48
2      <Begin expEvent>                09:01:048
       CodeTbl=2, Y1=1(Below), Y2=0(Upward), Y3=0, Y4=0(Con), Y5=1(End)
       Beam_Code
2      <End expEvent>
2      Note off     D5     74     48    09:01:096              48
2      Note on      F#5    78     0     09:02:000              48
2      <Begin expEvent>                09:02:000
       CodeTbl=2, Y1=0(Above), Y2=0(Upward), Y3=0, Y4=0(Con), Y5=1(End)
       Slur00_Code
2      <End expEvent>
2      Note off     F#5    78     96    09:02:096              48
2      [Rest]                          09:02:096
2      <Begin expEvent>                09:02:096
       CodeTbl=1, Y1=0, Y2=0, Y3=0(Isolated), Y4=0(Normal), Y5=0(Normal)
       CrotchetRest_Code
2      <End expEvent>
2      <Begin expEvent>                09:02:096
       CodeTbl=0, Y1=0, Y2=0, Y3=0(Isolated), Y4=0(Normal), Y5=0(Normal)
       BarLine_Code
2      <End expEvent>
2      [Rest]                          09:02:096
2      <Begin expEvent>                09:02:096
       CodeTbl=1, Y1=0, Y2=0, Y3=0(Isolated), Y4=0(Normal), Y5=0(Normal)
       SemibreveRest_Code
2      <End expEvent>
2      <Begin expEvent>                09:02:096
       CodeTbl=0, Y1=0, Y2=0, Y3=0(Isolated), Y4=0(Normal), Y5=0(Normal)
       BarLine_Code
2      <End expEvent>
2      [Rest]                          09:02:096
2      <Begin expEvent>                09:02:096
       CodeTbl=1, Y1=0, Y2=0, Y3=0(Isolated), Y4=0(Normal), Y5=0(Normal)
       SemibreveRest_Code
2      <End expEvent>
```

```
  2     <Begin expEvent>                    09:02:096
        CodeTbl=0, Y1=0, Y2=0, Y3=0(Isolated), Y4=0(Normal), Y5=0(Normal)
        BarLine_Code
  2     <End expEvent>
  2     Note on      C#4    61    672    12:01:000            48
  2     <Begin expEvent>                    12:01:000
        CodeTbl=2, Y1=1(Below), Y2=1(Downward), Y3=0, Y4=0(Con), Y5=0(Start)
        Slur00_Code
        CodeTbl=2, Y1=0(Above), Y2=0, Y3=1(Horizontal), Y4=0(Con), Y5=0(Start)
        Beam_Code
  2     <End expEvent>
  2     Note off     C#4    61    48     12:01:048            48
  2     Note on      E4     64    0      12:01:048            48
  2     Note off     E4     64    48     12:01:096            48
  2     Note on      C#4    61    0      12:02:000            48
  2     Note off     C#4    61    48     12:02:048            48
  2     Note on      E4     64    0      12:02:048            48
  2     Note off     E4     64    48     12:02:096            48
  2     Note on      D4     62    0      12:03:000            48
  2     Note off     D4     62    48     12:03:048            48
  2     Note on      E4     64    0      12:03:048            48
  2     <Begin expEvent>                    12:03:048
        CodeTbl=2, Y1=1(Below), Y2=1(Downward), Y3=0, Y4=0(Con), Y5=1(End)
        Slur00_Code
        CodeTbl=2, Y1=0(Above), Y2=0, Y3=1(Horizontal), Y4=0(Con), Y5=1(End)
        Beam_Code
  2     <End expEvent>
  2     Note off     E4     64    48     12:03:096            48
  2     <Begin expEvent>                    12:03:096
        CodeTbl=0, Y1=0, Y2=0, Y3=0(Isolated), Y4=0(Normal), Y5=0(Normal)
        BarLine_Code
  2     <End expEvent>
  2     Note on      C#4    61    0      13:01:000            48
  2     Note off     C#4    61    96     13:02:096            48
  2     [Rest]                              13:02:096
  2     <Begin expEvent>                    13:02:096
        CodeTbl=1, Y1=0, Y2=0, Y3=0(Isolated), Y4=0(Normal), Y5=0(Normal)
        CrotchetRest_Code
  2     <End expEvent>
  2     <Begin expEvent>                    13:02:096
        CodeTbl=0, Y1=0, Y2=0, Y3=0(Isolated), Y4=0(Normal), Y5=0(Normal)
        ":||:"_Code
  2     <End expEvent>
```

Example 4.1 The Mozart trio, Tracks 1 and 2, Format 1—ASCII representation with annotations for *Expressive MIDI*.

4.5   Further Comments

It should be noted that the use of system-exclusive ID 125 is for local development and is not appropriate for commercial use. If such a scheme were to be adopted by the MIDI Manufacturers' Association, either a system-exclusive manufacturer ID or a meta-event ID would need to be allocated. Technical terms such as *pizz.* or *legato*, instrument names, and other text events are indicated by standard meta-events.

There are many cells in the encoding tables which are still unused and available for future enhancements, such as special symbols and drawing objects. These tables are not fully comprehensive. To maintain a standard font mapping, the ordering of symbols is adapted from that used by a number of musical fonts.[3]

A viewer is currently under development by the Leeds Computer Music Group, Department of Music, The University of Leeds. Completion is expected early in 1997. The viewer will then be available by anonymous ftp from *scs.leeds.ac.uk*. The font is not required and will not be used in the viewer, although the mappping will be.

Updates about *Expressive MIDI* will be placed in */scs/doc/expMIDI.**.

---

3. e.g., the Petrucci font originally used with *Finale* and now distributed with a number of *Windows* programs for work-processing, graphics presentation, and musical notation.

5   MIDI Extensions for Musical Notation (3): *MIDIPlus*

Walter B. Hewlett

The Center for Computer Assisted Research is engaged in the compilation of full-text musical databases for general distribution. Since Standard MIDI Files have become a *de facto* vehicle for exchanging musical data, we anticipate that the primary means of distribution for this data will be in the MIDI format.

We believe that a major use of the data will be in music printing. Yet no practical method for communicating many non-sounding elements of information, such as the proper spelling of musical pitches, has been implemented. This limitation has crippled the standard as far as software for printing music of professional quality is concerned.

5.1   Enharmonic Notation

Most commercially available software programs for printing music accept MIDI data as a form of input. These programs convert the MIDI data to their own internal format, making guesses in the process about what the correct spelling should be. For example, the MIDI Key Number 61 can be the note C♯4 or the note D♭4. The first of these is printed on a line and the second is printed in a space between lines.

Since all of the attributes of musical information absent in Standard MIDI Files are included in the master set of data[1] from which we translate, we devised a scheme for retaining some of them in our translations. The scheme that we devised for the representation of enharmonic note names is also extensible for the representation of other non-sounding elements of notation, such as slurs.

1. Encoded in the *MuseData* format; see Chapter 27.

We include this pitch spelling information[2] in the two low-order bits of the MIDI Note_On velocity byte. We regard the inclusion of this information in our data files to be an integral part of the process of reconstruction, display, and printing of the original music. It can be ignored by commercial programs which interpret this data in the standard way. Yet this "hidden" information can be of great value to software programs which know about it.

5.1.1   Name Classes

Although enharmonic notes such as C♯ and D♭ are rendered by the same key of a MIDI instrument and although they sound at the same frequency, they have different functions in notation. This reflects historical developments: what we now call "half steps" were not uniform in size, in terms of the ratio of sound frequencies, for all musical scales and keys until the mid-eighteenth century.[3]

Notation of the eighteenth and nineteenth centuries may utilize compound sharps and flats, such as C♯♯ (Key No. 62) and D♭♭ (Key No. 59). Even triple and quadruple sharps and flats are hypothetically possible, although they are inordinately rare.

Such distinctions are irrelevant in a playback performance. C♯ and D♭ would both be "routed" to Key 61 on a MIDI playback device. However, the spelling of musical pitches is absolutely vital to music printing. Correct spelling is essential to analytical applications cognizant of tonal harmonic theory. Our method of communicating pitch spelling using the conventional MIDI standard involves degrading the communication of velocity information by a small amount.

For most musical applications we see today, it is sufficient to represent note spellings which fall in the range of two flats to two sharps (Table 5.1).[4] In any particular octave, these are specifically:

---

2. Sufficient to support the printing of single and double sharps and flats (or their cancellation).

3. In the even-tempered system employed since the eighteenth century, an octave is the interval between two pitches whose ratio is 2 to 1. The size of the half-step interval is the twelfth root of two, or approximately 1.059463 to 1.

4. The number of sharps or flats required to "spell" correctly a note name depends on the key signature. Double sharps or flats typically occur in modulatory passages, whre a new "local" key temporarily eclipses a "global" key decalred in the signature.

2	1	0	1	2
C♭♭	C♭	C	C♯	C♯♯
D♭♭	D♭	D	D♯	D♯♯
E♭♭	E♭	E	E♯	E♯♯
F♭♭	F♭	F	F♯	F♯♯
G♭♭	G♭	G	G♯	G♯♯
A♭♭	A♭	A	A♯	A♯♯
B♭♭	B♭	B	B♯	B♯♯

Table 5.1 Note spellings within the range of two sharps or flats.

In all there are 35 specifications within the range of 0, 1, or 2 sharps or flats.

For any MIDI number, there are three possible pitch spellings within the range of two flats to two sharps. These are listed in Table 5.2 for the octave range ascending from Middle C (Key No. 60 or C4) to the B above it (Key No. 71 or B4):

1		D♭♭		F♭♭		G♭		B♭♭
2	60	C	63	E♭	66	F♯	69	A
3		B♯		D♯		E♯♯		G♯♯
1		D♭		F♭		A♭♭		C♭♭
2	61	C♯	64	E	67	G	70	B♭
3		B♯♯		D♯♯		F♯♯		A♯
1		E♭♭		G♭♭		A♭		C♭
2	62	D	65	F	68	G♯	71	B
3		C♯♯		E♯		F♯♯♯[5]		A♯♯

Table 5.2 Enharmonic pitch names in relation to MIDI key numbers.

5.1.2   A Parametric Solution

The MIDI velocity parameter, which can vary from 1 to 127, is in general more sensitive than is really needed. We use the two low-order bits of this parameter to convey pitch spelling. Let v be the value of the two low-order bits of the velocity

---

5. B♭♭♭ is similarly possible.

parameter. The variable v can take on the values 0, 1, 2, or 3. Table 5.3 shows how this can be used to represent pitch spelling:

Value	Key Number/Pitch Value											
	60	61	62	63	64	65	66	67	68	69	70	71
0	pitch spelling undetermined											
1	D♭♭	D♭	E♭♭	F♭♭	F♭	G♭♭	G♭	A♭♭	A♭	B♭♭	C♭♭	C♭
2	C	C♯	D	E♭	E	F	F♯	G	G♯	A	B♭	B
3	B♯	B♯♯	C♯♯	D♯	D♯♯	E♯	E♯♯	F♯♯	F♯♯♯	G♯♯	A♯	A♯♯

Table 5.3 Enharmonic pitch values coupled with MIDI key numbers.

An advantage of this system is that the variation in the velocity parameter caused by specification of spelling is, in fact, minimal for any particular key. This is because most music in a key is notated in a consistent way. Let us take, for example, the key of E with four sharps. Table 5.4 shows the pitch spellings one would most likely find in this key. The most common ones are shown in bold type; the next most common are italicized.

Value	Notated Pitch											
1	D♭♭	D♭	E♭♭	F♭♭	F♭	G♭♭	G♭	A♭♭	A♭	B♭♭	C♭♭	C♭
2	*C*	**C♯**	D	E♭	**E**	*F*	**F♯**	G	**G♯**	**A**	B♭	**B**
3	**B♯**	B♯♯	C♯♯	**D♯**	*D♯♯*	E♯	E♯♯	**F♯♯**	F♯♯♯	*G♯♯*	A♯	A♯♯

Table 5.4 Most probable pitch spellings in the key of E Major.

As can be seen, all of these pitches have a value of 2 or 3. This means that if we, for example, want to use a velocity in the range of 90, we would be choosing between 90 and 91 virtually all of the time (very few users can detect an audible difference between a velocity of 90 and a velocity of 91).

In Table 5.5 we see a second case, namely the key of F:

Value	Notated Pitch											
1	D♭♭	D♭	E♭♭	F♭♭	F♭	G♭♭	G♭	A♭♭	A♭	B♭♭	C♭♭	C♭
2	C	C♯	D	E♭	E	F	F♯	G	G♯	A	B♭	B
3	B♯	B♯♯	C♯♯	D♯	D♯♯	E♯	E♯♯	F♯♯	F♯♯♯	G♯♯	A♯	A♯♯

Table 5.5 Most probable pitch spellings in the key of F Major.

In this key, the most common notes are distributed between all three rows, but significantly, all of the bold ones are in the $v = 2$ row. This means that 99% of the notes would have the same value. In our case above, almost all of the velocities would be 90, with a few 89s and a few 91s, a difference that listeners are unlikely to notice.

The velocity parameter applies to both Note_On and Note_Off events. Pitch spelling information need only be attached to Note_On events. The need to know pitch spelling comes at the time a note is turned on, not off. It can happen that a note is turned on several times and subsequently turned off the same number of times. In this case, there is no way to connect each Note_Off event with a specific Note_On event, so representing pitch spelling in Note_Off events might lead to confusing or erroneous results.

5.2   Slurs

Musical slurs are an indispensable part of music printing, yet the Standard MIDI File specification provides no means to represent them. The next four lowest bits of the velocity parameter can be used to represent Slur_On and Slur_Off information.

No cases where more than three slurs are operable at one time in one part have so far been found in our database work. Thus, the following scheme (Table 5.6) for representing slurs (and coincident slurs) can be used:

VALUE OF THE BITS   MEANING

    0000   No slur information attached to this note
    0001   Start slur A on this note
    0010   Start slur B   "
    0011   Start slur C   "
    0100   Stop slur A   "

0101	Stop slur A and re-start slur A on this note
0110	Stop slur A and start slur B on this note
0111	Stop slur A and start slur C on this note
1000	Stop slur B on this note
1001	Stop slur B and start slur A on this note
1010	Stop slur B and re-start slur B on this note
1011	Stop slur B and start slur C on this note
1100	Stop slur C on this note
1101	Stop slur C and start slur A on this note
1110	Stop slur C and start slur B on this note
1111	Stop slur C and re-start slur C on this note

Table 5.6 Representation scheme for multiple simulatenous slurs.

A, B, and C can be assigned to slurs as they occur. If more than three slurs are active at one time (unusual case), the excess over three would be ignored.

5.3   Other Potential Enhancements for Music Printing

The velocity byte of Note_Off events is ideal for setting general flags in the context of music printing. It could be used to signal stem directions, for example, or to signal to software how to make guesses about pitch spelling when the exact spelling is not provided in the Note_On velocity byte.

Such a method would be less intrusive on the Standard MIDI File format, since the Note_Off velocity byte is basically ignored by all applications. However, it would require a tighter coupling between the data and the printing software, since the "guessing" algorithm would have to be uniquely specified.

We call this whole range of options for MIDI extensions *MIDIPlus*.

References

Hewlett, Walter B. "A Base-40 Number-Line Representation of Musical Pitch Notation," *Musikometrika* 4 (1992), 1–14. [For a brief summary, see HEWLETT'S BASE-40 SYSTEM in the glossary.]

6   MIDI Extensions for Sound Control:
Augmented MIDI

Max V. Mathews

Augmented MIDI is a proposed plan of extensions intended to provide more flexible control of some expressive factors in live musical performances which use Standard MIDI Files as scores. The *Radio Baton*[1] is the specific instrument for which these extensions are intended, but the additional information could prove useful in other performance situations. These extensions are still under development and may be modified in the course of testing.

The basic idea is to add a few bits of information to the MIDI file which will be combined with the information obtained from gestures of the performer. For example, some notes may have an accent bit added. In the performance, the actual strength of the accent will be determined by a gesture such as the position of the performer's left hand.

It is not envisioned that enough information would be added to the MIDI file so that it could be played automatically in a musically expressive way. Only when the additional bits are combined with performer gestures will a "musical" performance result.

One may ask why the additional information should be put in a MIDI file. Why not let the performer's gestures do the entire expressive interpretation? Some important expressive factors such as accents occur suddenly and frequently. If the performer is directly controlling the strength of notes with a hand position, he or she will have to make many quick, almost violent, movements for the accented notes. It seems better that the performer's hand position should control the difference in strength between accented notes versus unaccented notes and the electronic score should designate

---

1. See also the chapter concerning the *Radio Baton Conductor* score file format.

which notes are to be accented. The two features most requiring some representation are accents and articulations.

6.1   Accents

It is proposed that one bit of information be added to each MIDI Note_On command to indicate accents as follows:

1	accented note
0	unaccented note

Is one bit sufficient? The strength of accents must vary for different notes. In addition, some strength variations can be associated with the meter of the music via strong beats and weak beats. The prosodic variation in strength occurs slowly and irregularly enough so that it can best be left completely under the control of the performer. Metric information is available from the measure markings in the score, which is accessible to the *Radio Baton Conductor* program, so no additional bits are required to tell the program about the strong and weak beats.

6.2   Articulations

In common music notation, notes can have various articular markings including staccatos, legatos, and so forth. Note articulation can also be affected by slurs. Thus the slur marking may interact with the staccato or legato marks.

In music generated by MIDI files, the strongest factor affecting articulation is the duty factor for a note, where *duty factor* means the ratio of the time between the MIDI Note_On and Note_Off messages to the time allotted to the complete note by the score. For example, a quarter note at a tempo of 60 beats per minute would have an allotted time of one second. At 100% duty factor, the time between Note_On and Note_Off messages would also be one second. At 25% duty factor, the time would be .25 seconds.

The MIDI convention of having separate Note_On and Note_Off messages makes it difficult to change expressively the duty factor of notes with a human performer's gesture in a live performance. The computer program reading a Standard MIDI File does not know when the Note_Off command will occur at the time it reads the Note_On command. In order to know the note duration at the start of a note, the program must look ahead in the electronic score and find the corresponding Note_Off command. Although the data stream ahead can be scanned, the procedure is inconvenient.

Although the details of a program to control duty factor by combining performer gestures with articulation markings are not fully worked out, the following elements of a prescription provide a foundation:

1. Write all notes in the score at 100% duty factor.

2. Assign two bits of information to the Note_On command to encode legato-staccato markings as follows:

0	no comment
1	most legato
2	intermediate termination
3	most staccato

3. Assign two bits of information to the Note_On command to encode slurs as follows:

0	no comment
1	slur starts on note
2	slur ends on note
3	old slurs ends and new slur begins

Further information on the development of this scheme is available from the author.

Appendix 2
Overview of MIDI Extensions

It may seem that one extension is as good as another. In fact, if we compare the four that are described on the preceding pages, it becomes clear that major differences reflect differences in intended use. *NoTAMIDI* was an effort to extend MIDI in order to make MIDI data more useful as input to notation programs. Thus it addressed basic hardware/sound-to-graphics issues. *ExpMIDI* has a similar intention but an added complication: it wanted MIDI to serve as the hub of print-to-print applications. *MIDIPlus* represented an effort (1) to reduce data loss in sound applications based on already encoded graphical information, thus facilitating new graphical applications, and (2) to enhance the musical content of MIDI files to more nearly represent the sound realizations intended by the musical signs. Resulting files in any of these three formats may provide advantages for some kinds of analytical applications, but this possibility has not yet been tested. *AugMIDI* is not preoccupied with what is in the files; its purpose is to give live interpreters of MIDI data more control of the features that give nuance to performance. Inevitably the optimum information sets required for these purposes will vary. The divergent aims of these extensions are expressed in the figure below.

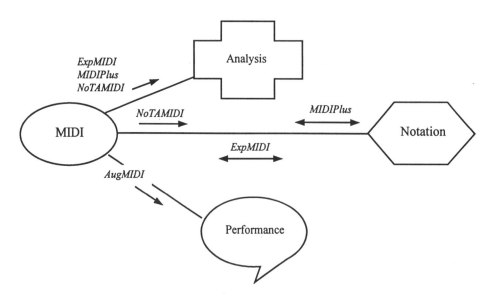

Figure A2.1 Goals of diverse MIDI extension sets.

Sound-Related Codes (2):

Other Codes for
Representation and Control

7   *Csound*

David Bainbridge

Csound is a sound-synthesis software product that facilitates the creation of musical performances from ASCII descriptions. It has been widely used in electronic music studios and is potentially of value as a sound-card protocol.

The *Csound* program was developed at the Massachusetts Institute of Technology in the early 1980s by Barry Vercoe. It builds on sound codes, such as *Music 5*, that were developed by Max Mathews and others at Bell Telephone Laboratories in Murray Hill, N.J., in the early 1960s. *Csound* was first released in 1991 and has an active project team extending its functionality. The package is "professional freeware"— software that is produced to professional standard, with controlled updates and comprehensive documentation, yet is freely available in source form. Instructions for obtaining *Csound* appear at the end of this chapter.

Csound is device-independent. However, it requires machine-specific audio hardware of some description. Originally it was developed for UNIX, but other ports now exist. The version released by M.I.T. can be directly installed on Vax/Dec, Sun, Silicon Graphics, NeXT, and Hewlett Packard workstations. In theory it is possible to install *Csound* on any machine running UNIX with a C compiler. M.I.T. provides a version of *Csound* for Macintosh computers.[1] A PC version of *Csound* is available from an electronic archive at the University of Bath, UK.

The musical attributes treated in *Csound* are pitch, duration, articulation, dynamics, and timbre. Audio output is created by merging information from two kinds of files:

---

1. A/UX is *not* required. The source code for this, which may be compiled using *ThinkC*, is available, but most users would only need the executable code, which is also provided.

- *orchestra* files, which contain definitions of individual *instrument* specifications (based on the attributes of timbre, articulation, and dynamics); and

- *score* files, which contain a time-based event-specification list (based on the attributes of pitch and duration).[2] Instrument coordination is also handled by *score* files. The *score* language is used primarily for representing new compositions but it can also be used for existing works.

Taken together, the *orchestra* and *score* files form a high-level, abstract description of the audio piece. *Csound* processes these two files to generate the audio output in much the same way as a compiler generates a machine-code executable file from a high-level description of a program. The ability to specify the quality of sound synthesis generated is different from that of a standard compiler. The finer the granularity, the greater the computation time required for processing the sound.

In basic orientation, *Csound* and MIDI have much in common. Both support the description of instrument sounds[3] and time-events. A *Csound score* file is analogous to the Standard MIDI File, and a *Csound orchestra* file to MIDI patch data or a General MIDI instrument implementation. *Csound* and MIDI can accomplish many identical tasks. *Csound* can in fact accept a Standard MIDI File (Type 0) in place of a *score* file, and workstations with advanced RISC architectures can take MIDI data directly from a musical keyboard or other MIDI hardware device.

The Standard MIDI and *Csound score* file formats are not directly interchangeable, however. *Csound score* files can handle musical articulation, such as slurring and staccato, at the symbolic level. MIDI can accommodate some kinds of text information, such as tempo indications. The most important difference between *Csound* and MIDI is that instruments in *Csound* are dynamic in nature, whereas MIDI timbres are static. A good example is provided by pizzicato (plucked) violins. *Csound* handles the instrument and the articulation as separate variables, while General MIDI combines them into one "instrument."

While *score* is the fundamental musical description language for *Csound*, the *scot* [= **sco**re **t**ranslator] file format is used for music generation. This format, providing a higher order of abstraction than the *score* format, was designed to preserve strong links with the layout of printed music. However, it is *not* aimed at the reproduction

---

2. Although the terminology—including such words as "instrument," "score," and "play"—seems musical, an *instrument* definition may specify random noise and the *score* a jumble of incoherent time-events.

3. *Patches* in MIDI parlance.

of graphical images of music (page layout and the like); it is simply a convenient style for describing music. To play a *scot* file, *Csound* must first translate the file to the *score* file format.

An overview of the component parts of *Csound* is presented in Table 7.1. These topics are then considered in turn.

Musical Attribute	How indicated			
	orchestra: definition of individual *instruments*	*scot*: representation of conventional notation	*score*: specification of time-based event list	Audio output: combined realization of *orchestra* and *score*
Pitch	———	by octave, note names	in cycles per second (*cps*)	generated in Hertz (*cps*)
Duration	———	in beats	in beats; may be modified by *t*-statement	generated in seconds
Articulation	initialized variables (*i*-statement)	in *instrument* definition	in *instrument* definition	generated through the *orchestra* definition
Dynamics	initialized variables (*i*-statement)	by extra parameters and macros	by extra parameters and macros	generated through the *orchestra* definition
Timbre	control signals (*k*-statement)	via *instrument* definition	via *instrument* definition	generated through the *orchestra* definition

Table 7.1 *Csound*'s component parts.

7.1 The *Orchestra*

Defining instruments in *Csound* is an art which cannot be described within the space available. A pipe organ simulation will be used as an arbitrary instrument specification in the examples provided.[4]

A timed event specifies onset time, duration, and instrumentation. It may also store additional data on such parameters as volume. Each instrument may be considered a concurrent entity existing in time and space. The *Csound* package manages time by using the timed events to notify the specified instrument at the specified time and by passing any extra data stored at the timed event. The instrument entity then generates its sound according to its definition and how the extra parameters affect it.

Instruments are designed using a special high-level language which offers many signal-processing techniques as simple function calls and facilitates the manipulation of audio signals. A sample *orchestra* file appears below.

```
sr = 8192    ; audio sampling rate is 8 kHz
kr = 256     ; control rate is 200 Hz
ksmps = 32   ; no of samples in a ctrl period (sr/kr)
nchnls = 1   ; no of channels of audio output

giclar      = 4000
giviolino   = 4000
giviola     = 4000
gicello     = 4000

gislur      = 2.0

; For this example each instrument defines the same pipe organ sound
; Normally each instrument would define a different sound
; Each instrument specification is further complicated by including staccato
; and slurring effects
        instr   1 ; clarinet in A
        ivol    = p6*giclar                      ; max vol of note
        islurs = (p4 <=1 ? 1 : 0)                ; slur start
        islure = ((p4==1) || (p4==3) ? 0 ; 1)    ; slur end
        idur = p3/p7                             ; audible dur
        islursd = islurs*idur/10                 ; slur start dur
        islured = islure*idur*3/10               ; slur end dur
kenvp   linen ivol,islursd,idur,islured          ; sound envelope plain
kenvs   linseg 0,islursd,ivol,idur-islursd-islured,ivol,islured,0,idur,0
kenv    = (p7==gislur ? kenvs : kenvp )
asig    oscil kenv, cpspch(p5), 1                ; audio oscillator f1
        out asig                                 ; send signal to chan 1
        endin
```

---

4. For a complete description of the *orchestra* language see F. Richard Moore, *Elements of Computer Music* (NY: Prentice Hall, 1990) and Charles D. Dodge and Thomas Jerse, *Computer Music Synthesis* (NY: Schirmer Books, 1985). The theoretical background to instrument design can be found in the *Csound* reference manual that comes with the source code.

```
        instr   10 ; clarinet in A incorporating transposition
        ivol  = p6*giclar                              ; max vol of note
        islurs = (p4 <=1 ? 1 : 0)                      ; slur start
        islure = ((p4==1) || (p4==3) ? 0 : 1)          ; slur end
        idur = p3/p7                                   ; audible dur
        islursd = islurs*idur/10                       ; slur start dur
        islured = islure*idur*3/10                     ; slur end dur
kenvp   linen ivol,islursd,idur,islured                ; sound envelope plain
kenvs   linseg 0,islursd,ivol,idur-islursd-islured,ivol,islured,0,idur,0
kenv    = (p7==gislur ? kenvs : kenvp )
        itrans = (p5-1.0)+0.09                         ; transpose pitch to A
asig    oscil kenv, cpspch(itrans), 1                  ; audio oscillator f1
        out asig                                       ; send signal to chan 1
        endin

        instr   2 ; violino
        ivol  = p6*giviolino                           ; max vol of note
        islurs = (p4 <=1 ? 1 : 0)                      ; slur start
        islure = ((p4==1) || (p4==3) ? 0 : 1)          ; slur end
        idur = p3/p7                                   ; audible dur
        islursd = islurs*idur/10                       ; slur start dur
        islured = islure*idur*3/10                     ; slur end dur
kenvp   linen ivol,islursd,idur,islured                ; sound envelope plain
kenvs   linseg 0,islursd,ivol,idur-islursd-islured,ivol,islured,0,idur,0
kenv    = (p7==gislur ? kenvs : kenvp )
asig    oscil kenv, cpspch(p5), 1                      ; audio oscillator f1
        out asig                                       ; send signal to chan 1
        endin

        instr   3 ; viola
        ivol  = p6*giviola                             ; max vol of note
        islurs = (p4 <=1 ? 1 : 0)                      ; slur start
        islure = ((p4==1) || (p4==3) ? 0 : 1)          ; slur end
        idur = p3/p7                                   ; audible dur
        islursd = islurs*idur/10                       ; slur start dur
        islured = islure*idur*3/10                     ; slur end dur
kenvp   linen ivol,islursd,idur,islured                ; sound envelope plain
kenvs   linseg 0,islursd,ivol,idur-islursd-islured,ivol,islured,0,idur,0
kenv    = (p7==gislur ? kenvs : kenvp )
asig    oscil kenv, cpspch(p5), 1                      ; audio oscillator f1
        out asig                                       ; send signal to chan 1
        endin

        instr   4 ; violoncello
        ivol  = p6*gicello                             ; max vol of note
        islurs = (p4 <=1 ? 1 : 0)                      ; slur start
        islure = ((p4==1) || (p4==3) ? 0 : 1)          ; slur end
        idur = p3/p7                                   ; audible dur
        islursd = islurs*idur/10                       ; slur start dur
        islured = islure*idur*3/10                     ; slur end dur
kenvp   linen ivol,islursd,idur,islured                ; sound envelope plain
kenvs   linseg 0,islursd,ivol,idur-islursd-islured,ivol,islured,0,idur,0
kenv    = (p7==gislur ? kenvs : kenvp )
asig    oscil kenv, cpspch(p5), 1                      ; audio oscillator f1
        out asig                                       ; send signal to chan 1
        endin
```

Example 7.1 A sample *orchestra* file. Features discussed in the text are shown in bold type. Instrument names and pitch variables are given in italics. The two violin parts constitute one "instrument" because they share one timbral specification.

The orchestra-definition language consists of a mixture of keywords and variables. A reader familiar with C will notice similarities in syntax. An instrument definition starts with the keyword `instr` and ends with `endin`, analogous to the `begin..` `..end` construct used in standard programming languages.

The language has many keywords for generating useful signals. In Example 7.1, the keyword `linen` is used to define a line envelope, whereas `linseg` is used to define a series of line segments. The keyword `oscil` generates an oscillator with the given attack envelope `kenv` at the specified pitch *p5*. It is the oscillator that gives the instrument its characteristic pipe organ sound. Comments are preceded by a semicolon.

The orchestra-definition language differs from the C programming language in that variable types are inferred rather than declared. The initial letter of a variable defines its type:

a indicates *audio* signals
k introduces *control* signals
i identifies ordinary *initialized* variables

Such variables are local to the instrument definition within which they appear. If the variable is additionally prefixed by the letter `g`, then it is a global version of that type of variable. This usage can be found throughout Example 7.1.

Data stored at a timed event are passed to the instrument as parameters *p1*, *p2*, etc. In Example 7.1 the parameter *p5* is used to specify pitch.

Instrument 10 in Example 7.1 differs slightly from the other instrument definitions because it represents a transposing instrument, the *Clarinet in A*. Here the pitch of the oscillator has deliberately been lowered by three semitones to simulate the appropriate transposition. The line in the orchestra file that achieves this is:

```
itrans = (p5-1.0)+0.09
```

Lowering the pitch by an octave (*p5*-1.0), then raising the pitch by nine semitones (+0.09) is equivalent to a drop in pitch of three semitones. This convoluted calculation is necessary because of the multiple pitch conventions explained below.

7.2   The *Csound Score* Language

Csound makes use of three types of numbers. *Rational*, or floating-point, numbers express fractional parts with decimal points and are the most commonly used numbers in a *score* file. *Integers* and *natural* numbers (non-negative integers) do not accommodate fractions.

Score provides two conversion functions for pitch representation. These are octave-point pitch-class (*pch*) and octave-point decimal (*oct*). Both specify pitch using a rational number. In each unit the whole part of the number represents the octave. Middle C = Octave 8. These specifications differ in the treatment of the fractional part:

- In *pch* an increase of 0.01 represents a semitone; 0.12 represents an octave.

- In *oct* the decimal part is used to define just one octave. An increase of .08333 represents a semitone; 1.0 represents an octave.

The A above Middle C can be represented as:

440	cycles per second	cps	hertz value
8.09	octave-point pitch	pch	octave . 1/100 pitch
8.75	octave-point decimal	oct	octave . 1/12 pitch

7.2.1 Example in *Csound Score*: The Mozart Trio

Example 7.2 shows one possible encoding of the Mozart trio. This example was processed using a formatter. Columns have been made to look homogeneous by adding verbose significant digits. The data were not entered as such.

The *score* format does not support the notion of a repeated section (other than a manual cut and paste of the text in an editor). For the encoding, the repeat marks were (incorrectly) ignored. Most of the basic constructs of the *score* language have been utilized in the example. However, some of the more sophisticated features have not been used. Ramping, for instance, would be useful if the piece had crescendos or diminuendos.

```
;Mozart: second trio from Clarinet Quintet
f1 0 256 10 1 ; wave table function
t0 100

; score for instrument 1
; inst     time       dur  slur  pitch  vol stac
i10.01   0.0000   0.500000     1   9.00  0.2  1.0 ; start of measure 1
i10.01       +    0.500000     3   9.04    .    .
i10.01       +    0.500000     .   9.07    .    .
i10.01       +    0.500000     .   9.04    .    .
i10.01       +    1.000000     .  10.00    .    .
i10.01       +    0.500000     .   9.07    .    . ; start of measure 2
```

```
i10.01      +       0.500000      .   9.04    .     .
i10.01      +       0.500000      .   9.02    .     .
i10.01      +       0.500000      .   9.05    .     .
i10.01      +       1.000000      2   9.09    .     .
i10.01      +       0.500000      1   9.05    .     . ; start of measure 3
i10.01      +       0.500000      3   9.02    .     .
i10.01      +       0.500000      .   9.00    .     .
i10.01      +       0.500000      .   8.11    .     .
i10.01      +       0.500000      .   9.04    .     .
i10.01      +       0.500000      .   9.02    .     .
i10.01      +       0.500000      .   9.07    .     . ; start of measure 4
i10.01      +       0.500000      2   9.05    .     .
i10.01      +       1.000000      1   9.03    .     .
i10.01      +       1.000000      2   9.04    .     .
i10.01      +       0.500000      1   9.00    .     . ; start of measure 5
i10.01      +       0.500000      3   9.04    .     .
i10.01      +       0.500000      .   9.07    .     .
i10.01      +       0.500000      .   9.04    .     .
i10.01      +       1.000000      2  10.00    .     .
i10.01      +       0.500000      1   9.07    .     . ; start of measure 6
i10.01      +       0.500000      3   9.04    .     .
i10.01      +       0.500000      .   9.02    .     .
i10.01      +       0.500000      .   9.05    .     .
i10.01      +       1.000000      2   9.09    .     .
i10.01   24.0000    0.333333      1   8.02    .     . ; start of measure 9
i10.01      +       0.333333      3   7.09    .     .
i10.01      +       0.333333      .   7.05    .     .
i10.01      +       0.500000      2   7.09    .     .
i10.01      +       0.500000      0   8.02    .    2.0
i10.01      +       0.500000      .   8.05    .     .
i10.01      +       0.500000      .   8.09    .     .
i10.01      +       0.500000      .   9.02    .     . ; start of measure 10
i10.01      +       0.500000      .   9.05    .     .
i10.01      +       0.500000      1   9.09    .    1.0
i10.01      +       0.500000      3   9.07    .     .
i10.01      +       0.500000      .   9.05    .     .
i10.01      +       0.500000      .   9.04    .     .
i10.01      +       0.500000      .   9.05    .     . ; start of measure 11
i10.01      +       0.500000      2   9.02    .     .
i10.01      +       2.000000      1   9.00    .     .
i10.01      +       0.500000      3   9.04    .     . ; start of measure 12
i10.01      +       0.500000      2   9.02    .     .
i10.01      +       1.000000      0   9.00    .     .
i10.01   48.0000    1.000000      .   9.07    .     . ; start of measure 17

; score for instrument 2
; inst    time       dur     slur  pitch  vol stac
i2.01    2.0000    1.000000      0   8.09   0.2 1.0
i2.01      +       1.000000      .   8.09    .     . ; start of measure 2
i2.01    5.0000    1.000000      .   8.09    .     .
i2.01      +       1.000000      .   8.09    .     . ; start of measure 3
i2.01    8.0000    1.000000      .   8.08    .     .
i2.01      +       1.000000      .   8.08    .     . ; start of measure 4
i2.01   11.0000    1.000000      .   8.09    .     .
i2.01      +       1.000000      .   8.09    .     . ; start of measure 5
i2.01   14.0000    1.000000      .   8.09    .     .
i2.01      +       1.000000      .   8.09    .     . ; start of measure 6
```

```
i2.01      +       1.000000      .    8.06    .    .
i2.01   18.0000    0.500000      1    9.01    .    .  ; start of measure 7
i2.01      +       0.500000      3    8.10    .    .
i2.01      +       0.500000      .    8.11    .    .
i2.01      +       0.500000      .    9.02    .    .
i2.01      +       1.000000      2    9.06    .    .
i2.01      +       0.500000      1    9.01    .    .  ; start of measure 8
i2.01      +       0.500000      3    8.10    .    .
i2.01      +       0.500000      .    8.11    .    .
i2.01      +       0.500000      .    9.02    .    .
i2.01      +       1.000000      2    9.06    .    .
i2.01   31.0000    0.500000      1    8.01    .    .
i2.01      +       0.500000      3    8.04    .    .
i2.01      +       0.500000      .    8.01    .    .
i2.01      +       0.500000      .    8.04    .    .
i2.01      +       0.500000      .    8.02    .    .  ; start of measure 12
i2.01      +       0.500000      2    8.04    .    .
i2.01      +       1.000000      0    8.01    .    .
i2.01   36.0000    0.500000      1    8.04    .    .  ; start of measure 13
i2.01      +       0.500000      3    8.08    .    .
i2.01      +       0.500000      .    8.11    .    .
i2.01      +       0.500000      .    8.08    .    .
i2.01      +       1.000000      2    9.04    .    .
i2.01      +       0.500000      1    8.04    .    .  ; start of measure 14
i2.01      +       0.500000      3    8.09    .    .
i2.01      +       0.500000      .    9.01    .    .
i2.01      +       0.500000      .    8.09    .    .
i2.01      +       1.000000      2    9.04    .    .
i2.01      +       0.500000      1    8.04    .    .  ; start of measure 15
i2.01      +       0.500000      3    8.11    .    .
i2.01      +       0.500000      .    9.02    .    .
i2.01      +       0.500000      .    8.11    .    .
i2.01      +       0.500000      .    9.04    .    .
i2.01      +       0.500000      .    9.02    .    .
i2.01      +       0.500000      .    9.01    .    .  ; start of measure 16
i2.01      +       0.500000      2    8.09    .    .
i2.01      +       0.500000      1    8.08    .    .
i2.01      +       0.500000      3    8.11    .    .
i2.01      +       1.000000      2    9.04    .    .
i2.01      +       0.500000      1    8.04    .    .  ; start of measure 17
i2.01      +       0.500000      2    8.08    .    .

; score for instrument 3
; inst    time       dur  slur  pitch  vol stac
i3.01   2.0000    1.000000      0    8.04   0.2  1.0
i3.01      +       1.000000      .    8.04    .    .  ; start of measure 2
i3.01   5.0000    1.000000      .    8.06    .    .
i3.01      +       1.000000      .    8.06    .    .  ; start of measure 3
i3.01   8.0000    1.000000      .    8.02    .    .
i3.01      +       1.000000      .    8.02    .    .  ; start of measure 4
i3.01   11.0000   1.000000      .    8.01    .    .
i3.01      +       1.000000      .    8.01    .    .  ; start of measure 5
i3.01   14.0000   1.000000      .    8.04    .    .
i3.01      +       1.000000      .    8.04    .    .  ; start of measure 6
i3.01      +       1.000000      .    8.02    .    .
i3.01   18.0000   1.000000      1    8.07    .    .  ; start of measure 7
i3.01      +       2.000000      3    8.06    .    .
```

```
i3.01     +        1.000000     .    8.07    .    .    ; start of measure 8
i3.01     +        2.000000     2    8.06    .    .
i3.01     31.0000  2.000000     1    7.09    .    .
i3.01     +        1.000000     2    7.08    .    .    ; start of measure 12
i3.01     +        1.000000     0    7.09    .    .
i3.01     37.0000  1.000000     .    7.11    .    .
i3.02     37.0000  1.000000     .    7.08    .    .
i3.01     +        1.000000     .    7.11    .    .
i3.02     38.0000  1.000000     .    7.08    .    .
i3.01     40.0000  1.000000     .    7.09    .    .
i3.02     40.0000  1.000000     .    7.09    .    .
i3.01     +        1.000000     .    7.09    .    .
i3.02     41.0000  1.000000     .    7.09    .    .
i3.01     43.0000  1.000000     .    8.08    .    .
i3.02     43.0000  1.000000     .    7.11    .    .
i3.01     +        1.000000     .    8.08    .    .
i3.02     44.0000  1.000000     .    7.11    .    .
i3.01     +        1.000000     .    8.09    .    .    ; start of measure 16
i3.02     45.0000  1.000000     .    8.01    .    .
i3.01     +        1.000000     .    8.08    .    .
i3.02     46.0000  1.000000     .    7.11    .    .
i3.01     +        1.000000     .    8.08    .    .
i3.02     47.0000  1.000000     .    7.11    .    .


; score for instrument 4
; inst     time       dur     slur  pitch  vol stac
i4.01     2.0000   1.000000     0    8.01   0.2  1.0
i4.01     +        1.000000     .    8.01    .    .    ; start of measure 2
i4.01     5.0000   1.000000     .    7.11    .    .
i4.01     +        1.000000     .    7.11    .    .    ; start of measure 3
i4.01     8.0000   1.000000     .    7.11    .    .
i4.01     +        1.000000     .    7.11    .    .    ; start of measure 4
i4.01     11.0000  1.000000     .    7.09    .    .
i4.01     +        1.000000     .    7.09    .    .    ; start of measure 5
i4.01     14.0000  1.000000     .    8.01    .    .
i4.01     +        1.000000     .    8.01    .    .    ; start of measure 6
i4.01     +        1.000000     .    7.11    .    .
i4.01     18.0000  1.000000     1    8.04    .    .    ; start of measure 7
i4.01     +        2.000000     3    8.02    .    .
i4.01     +        1.000000     .    8.04    .    .    ; start of measure 8
i4.01     +        2.000000     2    8.02    .    .
i4.01     31.0000  4.000000     0    7.04    .    .
i4.01     37.0000  1.000000     .    9.02    .    .
i4.02     37.0000  1.000000     .    8.04    .    .
i4.01     +        1.000000     .    9.02    .    .
i4.02     38.0000  1.000000     .    8.04    .    .
i4.01     40.0000  1.000000     .    9.01    .    .
i4.02     40.0000  1.000000     .    8.04    .    .
i4.01     +        1.000000     .    9.01    .    .
i4.02     41.0000  1.000000     .    8.04    .    .
i4.01     43.0000  1.000000     .    9.04    .    .
i4.01     +        1.000000     .    9.04    .    .
i4.01     +        1.000000     .    9.04    .    .    ; start of measure 16
i4.01     +        1.000000     .    9.04    .    .
i4.01     +        1.000000     .    9.04    .    .
```

```
; score for instrument 5
; inst      time       dur   slur  pitch  vol stac
i5.01    1.0000   1.000000     0   7.09  0.2 1.0
i5.01    4.0000   1.000000     .   7.02   .   .
i5.01    7.0000   1.000000     .   7.04   .   .
i5.01   10.0000   1.000000     .   7.06   .   .
i5.01   13.0000   1.000000     .   7.01   .   .
i5.01   16.0000   1.000000     .   7.02   .   .
i5.01   31.0000   1.000000     1   6.04   .  2.0
i5.01       +     1.000000     3   6.04   .   .
i5.01       +     1.000000     2   6.04   .   .  ; start of measure 12
i5.01       +     1.000000     0   6.09   .  1.0
i5.01   37.0000   1.000000     .   7.04   .   .
i5.01       +     1.000000     .   7.04   .   .
i5.01   40.0000   1.000000     .   7.04   .   .
i5.01       +     1.000000     .   7.04   .   .
i5.01   43.0000   1.000000     .   7.04   .   .
i5.01       +     1.000000     .   7.04   .   .
i5.01       +     1.000000     .   7.04   .   .  ; start of measure 16
i5.01       +     1.000000     .   7.04   .   .
i5.01       +     1.000000     .   6.04   .   .
e
```

Example 7.2 A *Csound score* file using seven parameters to represent the Mozart trio.

7.2.2 Backus-Naur Notation of the *Score* Language

· *Score* can be specified using Backus-Naur Notation (BNN), a grammar, or collection of rules, governing the syntax of the language over a set of letters (the alphabet). BNN, which is sometimes used in compiler construction, is employed here to clarify operations. *Terminals* are the letters of the language; a non-terminal represents a "black box" of unexpanded terminal letters. By convention, non-terminals are written in capitals.

The notation is reasonably self-explanatory to experienced programmers. In this case the *alphabet* consists of all printable characters. A *rule* consists of terminals and non-terminals. In BNN, a single non-terminal appears as the left-hand side of a rule and a mixture of terminals and non-terminals may appear on the right. In Example 7.3 the *score* file format is denoted using the Backus-Naur Form (BNF).

A non-terminal on the right-hand side of a rule can be replaced with the right-hand side of any rule whose left-hand side matches the original non-terminal. There is a special terminal symbol, epsilon (ε), which represents the empty transition, i.e., no terminal letter is needed. The vertical bar (|) is a shorthand notation for choice. A set of rules of the form:

$$STATS \rightarrow STAT\ STATS$$
$$STATS \rightarrow \varepsilon$$

can be written more concisely as:

$$\text{STATS} \quad \rightarrow \quad \text{STAT STATS} \mid \varepsilon$$

Score is the starting point for the grammar given in Example 7.3.[5]

SCORE	$\rightarrow$	STATS e | STATS
STATS	$\rightarrow$	STAT STATS | ε
STAT	$\rightarrow$	OPTSTAT OPTCOMMENT *newline*
OPTSTAT	$\rightarrow$	F| I | T | C | S | A| ε
F	$\rightarrow$	f *intnum ratnum natnum natnum* OPTNUMS
I	$\rightarrow$	i CNUM CPNUM CNUM OPTCRNPNUMS
T	$\rightarrow$	t NUMPAIR OPTNUMPAIRS
S	$\rightarrow$	s IGNORETEXT
A	$\rightarrow$	a *ratnum ratnum ratnum*
C	$\rightarrow$	c OPTTEXT
OPTCOMMENT	$\rightarrow$	; OPTTEXT | ε
OPTTEXT	$\rightarrow$	*text* | ε
IGNORETEXT	$\rightarrow$	*text* | ε
OPTNUMS	$\rightarrow$	*ratnum* OPTNUMS | ε
OPTCRNPNUMS	$\rightarrow$	CRNPNUM OPTCRNPNUMS | ε
OPTNUMPAIRS	$\rightarrow$	NUMPAIR OPTNUMPAIRS | ε
NUMPAIR	$\rightarrow$	*ratnum ratnum*
CNUM	$\rightarrow$	*ratnum* | .
CPNUM	$\rightarrow$	*ratnum* | . | +
CRNPNUM	$\rightarrow$	*ratnum* | . | < | np*ratnum*| pp*ratnum*

where *ratnum* represents a rational number
intnum represents an integer number
text represents a string of printable ASCII characters
newline represents carriage return

Example 7.3 Use of the Backus-Naur Form (BNF) to represent the *Csound score* language.

The bulk of this grammar is concerned with defining the overall structure of a *score* file. Informally a *score* file is a sequence of statements, one per line, with an optional comment at the end of it. Such comments start with a semicolon (;) and continue to the end of the line. A line may consist of a comment without a statement; alternatively, it may have neither a comment nor a statement. The significant rules in defining what sounds are generated are given by the non-terminals F, I, T, S, and A. The meaning of these rules is explained below.

5. Aho, Alfred V., Ravi Sethi, and Jeffrey D. Ullman, *Compilers: Principles, Techniques, and Tools* (Cambridge, MA: Addison Wesley Publishers, 1986).

7.2.3 Statement Types in *Score*

A. FUNCTION TABLES [**f** *p1 p2 p3 p4* . . .]

Where the parameters *p1* . . are numbers, the *f*-statement defines a stored function table, i.e., an array of floating-point numbers whose entries are determined by the specified generator function. The meaning of these parameters is explained in Table 7.2.

Parameter Name	Content	Restrictions
p1	table number	normally $1 \leq p1 \leq 200$
p2	time of creation	$p2 \geq 0$
p3	size of table	$p3 = 2^n$ or $p3 = 2^{(n+1)}$
p4	generator function	$p4 \geq 1$

Table 7.2 Parameters of the *f*-statement.

Additional arguments after *p4* are dependent on the generator function specified. A complete list of generator functions is given in the *Csound* reference manual.

For reasons of memory efficiency, it is possible to delete function tables. If the table number (*p1*) is negative, then the statement requests the deletion of the table at the time designated by *p2*.

Restrictions on the parameters are shown in Table 7.2. The symbol *n* denotes any natural number and serves to illustrate that *p3* is restricted to a power of 2 or a value one greater than a power of 2.

B. INSTRUMENT ACTIVATION [**i** *p1 p2 p3* . . .]

Where the parameters *p1* . . . are numbers, the *i*-statement specifies the activation of an instrument, also referred to as a timed event. The meaning of and restrictions on the parameters are shown in Table 7.3.

Parameter Name	Content	Restrictions
p1	instrument number	normally $1 \leq p1 \leq 200$
p2	starting time (in beats)	$p2 \geq 0$
p3	duration time (in beats)	normally $p3 > 0$

Table 7.3 Parameters for the *i*-statement.

Timed events are specified in (possibly fractional) beats. The number of beats per minute is controlled by the *t*-statement, discussed next. If the duration time (*p3*) is zero, then the instrument will be invoked, but only in an initialization capacity.

The *i*-statement carries out the same job as the Note_On and Note_Off constructs in MIDI. Here, however, it is accomplished by specifying a start time and duration. The style can be specified in the *i*-statement through the use of negative numbers. A negative duration signifies a Note_On condition. A negative value for an instrument number can be used to turn off a held note.

Instrument numbers in the *orchestra* file must be natural numbers. However, the *score* file format permits an instrument number to be a rational number. The fractional part of the number can be used to give the performance of a particular instrument at a particular time a unique tag. An instrument in a *score* file may play more than one note at once (even if that is impossible with the real instrument it is synthesizing). In this situation the fractional part of the number may be used to distinguish the individual events. It is not necessary to list the *instrument* activations in chronological order.

C. *SCORE* SECTIONS [**s** *anything*]

The *s*-statement designates the boundary of *score* sections. A *score* section is an independent block of time. At the start of a *score* section time is reset to zero. *Score* sections are performed in the order in which they are defined in the *score* file. Any text after the letter *s* is ignored.

D. TEMPO CHANGES [**t** *p1 p2 p3* . . .]

The *t*-command defines the tempo (number of beats per minute) throughout the current *score* section. The semantic meaning of the parameters is presented in Table 7.4.

Parameter Name	Content	Restrictions
p1	time of effect (in beats)	$p1 = 0$
p2	number of beats per minute	$p2 > 0$
p3	time of effect (in beats)	$p3 \geq p1$
p4	number of beats per minute	$p4 > 0$
p5 . . .	. . .	. . .

Table 7.4 Parameters for the *t*-statement.

The parameters *p1* and *p2* define the initial tempo. The default is 60 beats per minute, i.e., one beat/second. Later pairs of parameters specify how the tempo changes through the *score* section. The parameter pairs of the *t*-statement may be viewed as a tempo vs. time graph, in which time (the *y*-axis) is specified in beats rather than seconds. Thus the *x*-axis may not be linear: a flat section of the graph defines a period of the *score* with constant tempo; positive and negative gradients designate acceleration and retardation respectively; and a discontinuity marks an instantaneous change in tempo.

Only one *t*-statement may appear per *score* section and, like the *i*-statement, its location in the file is not determined by its chronological significance.

E. TIME ADVANCE [a *p1 p2 p3* . . .]

Where the parameters *p1*, etc. are numbers, the *a*-statement type causes time to jump from a specified departure point forward to an arrival point, omitting any audio performance that occurs during the intervening period. The parameters for the *a*-statement are defined in Table 7.5.

Parameter Name	Content	Restrictions
p1	nothing	usually 0
p2	time of effect (in beats)	$p2 \geq 0$
p3	duration of time to advance	$p3 > 0$

Table 7.5 Parameters for the *a*-statement.

Typical uses of the *a*-statement are to jump to a desired point in a *score* and to advance over an incomplete part of a *score*.

F. THE END STATEMENT [e *anything*]

The *e*-statement ends the *score*. Any instruments still held on are terminated. If no *e*-statement exists in the file, then the end of the file is taken to be the end of the score.

G. THE COMMENT STATEMENT [c *text*]

The *c*-statement is identical to a semicolon (;) comment that is on a line by itself.

7.2.4   Other *Score* Features

Some features of the *score* language are specially designed to reduce the burden of data entry by lowering the amount of typing required. There are three data-saving features for the *i*-statement: carry (.), addition (+) and ramping (<).

Any parameter value in an *i*-statement can be carried over to the next *i*-statement line by specifying a period (.) instead of repeating the numeric value. If an *i*-statement's parameter list finishes prematurely, *Csound* carries over the previous values of the remaining parameters.

A basic *score* file using *i*-statements is shown in Example 7.4. This can be replaced with the file shown in Example 7.5. Using the carry feature for the instrument-number parameter does not save typing, but it makes the data more flexible, because any change to an entry will automatically be carried over to subsequent entries.

```
i1  0  2  5.01  1000  1
i1  2  2  5     01    1200  1
i1  4  2  5.02  1400  1
i1  6  1  5.06  1600  1
i2  0  1  5.03  1000  1
```

Example 7.4 A basic *score* file illustrating the *i*-statement.

The carry feature works on unsorted files. This point is shown in Example 7.5, where the third parameter in the last line of the example has been carried over to Instrument 2 from Beat 6 of Instrument 1.

```
i1 0 2 5.01 1000 1
i. 2 .  .    1200
i. 4 . 5.02 1400
i. 6 1 5.06 1600
i2 0 . 5.03 1000
```

Example 7.5 The *score* i-statement using the carry feature.

Addition is only available for the *p2* parameter. It adds together the previous *p2* and *p3* values to generate the current *p2* parameter. Effectively it causes the next note to start as soon as the previous one finishes. The file shown in Example 7.5 can be further simplified to that shown in Example 7.6. The addition feature also works on an unordered file and may itself be carried.

```
i1 0 2 5.01 1000 1
i. + .  .    1200
i. + . 5.02 1400
i. + 1 5.06 1600
i2 0 . 5.03 1000
```

Example 7.6 The *score* i-statement using the addition feature.

A ramp runs from one specified number through a sequence of ramp symbols (<) to the next specified number. Its effect is to interpolate values from the start number to the end number. Using this technique, the file shown in Example 7.6 can equally be written as shown in Example 7.7.

```
i1 0 2 5.01 1000 1
i. + .  .      <
i. + . 5.02    <
i. + 1 5.06 1600
i2 0 . 5.03 1000
```

Example 7.7 The *score* i-statement using ramping.

Ramps can only be used on parameter *p4* or higher. Unlike the carry and addition features, ramping is calculated on the computer-generated time-sorted *score* file. A typical use of ramping would be to encode music that has crescendos and diminuendos.

The *next-p* and *previous-p* features available in the *score* language permit future/past substitution in one parameter field to be acquired from a different parameter field. It is a mechanism for providing contextual knowledge of the score.

Where *natnum* is a natural number, the next and previous statements have the syntax:

```
npnatnum
ppnatnum
```

If the file shown in Example 7.7 were changed to that shown in Example 7.8, then it would be equivalent to the file shown in Example 7.9, where all the parameter values are shown explicitly.

```
i1 0 2 5.01 1000   pp5
i. + .  .          <
i. + . 5.02        <
i. + 1 5.06 1600
i2 0 . 5.03 1000 1000
```

Example 7.8 The *score i*-statement using the *previous* parameter feature.

```
i1 0 2 5.01 1000      0
i1 2 2 5.01 1200 1000
i1 4 2 5.02 1400 1200
i1 6 1 5.06 1600 1400
i2 0 1 5.03 1000 1000
```

Example 7.9 The consequence of using the parameter feature shown in Fig. 7.8.

The next/previous feature may only appear in *p4* or higher fields; however, it may reference any parameter field. A reference may be recursive. A reference to a non-existent value will be given the value zero.

Like ramping, *next-p* and *previous-p* work on time-sorted scores to indicate the next or previous note played.

7.2.5   File Organization in *Score*

To generate an audio performance, *Csound* needs two files: an *orchestra* file and the timed events described in the *score* file format. The *score* language makes no requirement of the order of events. The basic organization may be part- (instrument-) oriented or score-oriented. Each timed event is specified in absolute beats from start to finish.

Score sections, delimited by the *s*-statement, correspond to movements in conventional notation. Decomposing a piece of music with numerous movements into *score* sections would be a natural step.

In a *score* file the parameters *p1*, *p2*, and *p3* have a fixed meaning for the *i*-statement. This is highlighted in the encoded *score* file shown in Example 7.2, where a comment is used to define the meaning of the various formatted columns. Parameters *p1–p3* define instrument number, activation time, and note duration respectively, but an instrument definition may use other parameters as it sees fit.

7.3   The *Csound Scot* Language

While the *score* language is designed for general sound generation, the *scot* language is designed specifically for encoding conventional music. Like a *score* file, a *scot* file is used in conjunction with an *orchestra* description to produce the desired musical performance.

How the *scot* language provides the basic concepts necessary for a musical file format is shown in Table 7.6.

Pitch	Specified as octave name and note name
Duration	Specified in beats
Articulation/ ornamentation	Specified in same way as in *score* format
Dynamics	Generally provided by extra parameters and macros. Similar to the *score* format, *scot* has a special *t*-command to alter the number of beats per minute.
Timbre	Specified in same way as in *score* format

Table 7.6 Fundamental musical concepts supported by *scot*.

Starting an octave specification with an equals sign (=) defines the starting point for octave definition to be Middle C. Each following comma (,) lowers the octave by one and an apostrophe (') raises the octave by one. Immediately following the octave definition is one of the pitch names: c, d, e, f, g, a, or b. A rest is specified by the letter r.

Pitch inflection is indicated by the following symbols:

n	natural
#	sharp
-	flat
##	double sharp
--	double flat

When the *scot* file is transformed into a *score* file, all this information is converted into *pch* units. All instruments that are to be used with a *scot* file must, therefore, convert *pch* to *cps* for the audio performance.

Only natural numbers are used to specify musical durations. Table 7.7 shows the relationship between number and musical duration.

American Term	British Term	*Scot* Value
whole note	semibreve	1
half note	minim	2
quarter note	crotchet	4
eighth note	quaver	8
sixteenth note	semiquaver	16

Table 7.7 Durations in *scot*.

Intermediate durations, such as a dotted quarter note, are represented by mirroring the musical interpretation of the durational dot. A period after the duration increases its length by 50%, two periods by 75%, and so on. Fractional durations, e.g., for triplets, can be expressed in *scot* using the *groupette* construct. This is more fully explained in a later section.

It might be argued that it is more intuitive to think of longer note durations as having a larger numeric value, but such an approach is restrictive. Using the inverse approach in *scot* (and other encoding systems), the shortest duration of a musical note is not resolution-dependent. If a duration longer than a whole note is required, it can be realized by tying notes together.

7.3.1   Example in *Csound Scot*: The Mozart Trio

The same sample piece of music encoded for the *score* format (Example 7.2) was entered using the *scot* language and is shown in Example 7.10. The *scot* language has the same inability to represent repeated sections; as with the *score* example, the repeat marks in the piece were ignored.

An example of a *scot* file is shown in Example 7.10.

```
; Mozart: second trio from Clarinet Quintet
orchestra { [ pp=0.1 p=0.2 mp=0.5 mf=1.0 f=1.5 ff=1.75
             plain=7:1.0 stac=7:2.0 ]
             clarinet=1 violino1=2 violino2=3 viola=4 violoncello=5 }
functions { f1 0 256 10 1 ; a sine wave function }
score {
$clarinet
!transpose ",a"
!time "3/4"
t100
8='c_[p plain] 8='e_ /                           ; measure  1
8=''g_ 8='e_ 4=''c_ 8=''g_ 8='e_ /              ; measure  2
8='d_ 8='f_ 4=''a  8='f_ 8='d_ /                ; measure  3
8='c_='b_='e_='d_=''g_='f /                     ; measure  4
4d#_e 8c_e_ /                                   ; measure  5
8g_e_ 4'c 8g_e_ /                               ; measure  6
8dn_f_ 4a 4r /                                  ; measure  7
2.r /                                           ; measure  8
; staff system 2
4rr {: 8=d_a_f_ : } /                           ; measure  9
8ad[stac]fadf /                                 ; measure 10
a_[plain]g_f_e_f_d /                            ; measure 11
2c_ 8e_d /                                      ; measure 12
4cr r /                                         ; measure 13
2.r /                                           ; measure 14
2.r /                                           ; measure 15
2.r /                                           ; measure 16
4rr'g /                                         ; measure 17

$violino1
; staff system 1
!key "#fcg"
!time "3/4"
4r /
4r ='a[p plain]a /                              ; measure  1
raa /                                           ; measure  2
rgg /                                           ; measure  3
raa /                                           ; measure  4
raa /                                           ; measure  5
fr 8'c_a#_ /                                    ; measure  6
b_d_ 4f 8c_a#_ /                                ; measure  7
; staff system 2                               ; measure  8
!ke "#fcg"
8b_d_ 4fr /                                     ; measure  9
2.r /                                           ; measure 10
2.r /                                           ; measure 11
8,c_e_c_e_d_e /                                 ; measure 12
4cr 8e_g_ /                                     ; measure 13
b_g_ 4'e 8,e_a_ /                              ; measure 14
c_a_ 4'e 8,e_ 'b_ /                            ; measure 15
d_b_e_d_c_a /                                   ; measure 16
g_b_ 4e 8,e_g /                                ; measure 17
```

```
$violino2
; staff system 1
!key "#fcg"
!time "3/4"
4r /                                          ; measure  1
4r =e[p plain]e /                             ; measure  2
rff /                                         ; measure  3
rdd /                                         ; measure  4
rcc /                                         ; measure  5
ree /                                         ; measure  6
drgn_ /                                       ; measure  7
2f_ 4gn_ /                                    ; measure  8
; staff system 2
!key "#fcg"
2f 4r /                                       ; measure  9
2.r /                                         ; measure 10
2.r /                                         ; measure 11
2,a_ 4g# /                                    ; measure 12
ar r /                                        ; measure 13
4=b[p]<g =b<g r /                             ; measure 14
=a<a  =a<a r /                                ; measure 15
='g<b g<b a<c /                               ; measure 16
g<b g<b r /                                   ; measure 17

$viola
; staff system 1
!key "#fcg"
!time "3/4"
4r /                                          ; measure  1
4r =c[p plain]c /                             ; measure  2
rbb /                                         ; measure  3
rbb /                                         ; measure  4
raa /                                         ; measure  5
rcc /                                         ; measure  6
bre_ /                                        ; measure  7
2d_ 4e_ /                                     ; measure  8
; staff system 2
!key "#fcg"
2d 4r /                                       ; measure  9
2.r /                                         ; measure 10
2.r /                                         ; measure 11
2.,e__ /                                      ; measure 12
4er r /                                       ; measure 13
4='d[p]<e d<e r /                             ; measure 14
c<e c<e r /                                   ; measure 15
eee /                                         ; measure 16
eer /                                         ; measure 17

$violoncello
; staff system 1
!key "#fcg"
!time "3/4"
4r /                                          ; measure  1
=a[p plain]rr /                               ; measure  2
,drr /                                        ; measure  3
err /                                         ; measure  4
frr /                                         ; measure  5
crr /                                         ; measure  6
drr /                                         ; measure  7
2.r /                                         ; measure  8
```

```
; staff system 2
!key "#fcg"
2.r /
2.r /                                             ; measure  9
2.r /                                             ; measure 10
4=,,e_[7:stac]e_e /                               ; measure 11
a[7:plain]r r /                                   ; measure 12
'e[p]er /                                          ; measure 13
eer /                                             ; measure 14
eee /                                             ; measure 15
e,er /                                            ; measure 16
}                                                 ; measure 17
```

Example 7.10 A sample *scot* file.

The *scot* language approximates to a graphical music description language, but it lacks certain elements, such as text. Dynamics markings in *scot* cannot be handled at the semantic level. It is possible to achieve the desired audio result by using extra parameters and macros, but this is not a standard interpretation of the file format.

7.3.2   Backus-Naur Notation of the *Scot* Language

The BNF for the *scot* language is shown in Example 7.11.

```
SCOT          →    ORCH FANDS
ORCH          →    OPTCOMS orchestra { OPTMACDEFS INSTDECS }
INSTDECS      →    INSTDEC OPTMACDEFS INSTDECS
                 | INSTDEC OPTMACDEFS
OPTMACDEFS    →    [ MACRODEFS ] | ε
MACRODEFS     →    MACRODEF MACRODEFS | MACRODEF
MACRODEF      →    text = OPTQTEXT
OPTQTEXT      →    text | "text"
INSTDEC       →    text = natnum
FANDS         →    FUNC FANDS | STSCORE FANDS | STSCORE
FUNC          →    OPTCOMS functions { SCORE }
STSCORE       →    score { INSTPARTS }
INSTPARTS     →    INSTPART INSTPARTS | ε
INSTPART      →    INSTNAME MEASURES
INSTNAME      →    $text
MEASURES      →    INMEASURE / MEASURES
INMEASURE     →    PCMD INMEASURE | TCMD INMEASURE
                   FIXDUR INMEASURE
                 | ε
PCMD          →    !time "natnum/natnum"
                   !key "ACC OCTPITCHES"
                   !accidentals ONOROFF
                   !octaves ONOROFF
                   !vertical ONOROFF
                   !transpose "OPTOCT OCTPITCH OPTACC"
                   !next PARAM"PARAM"
                   !previous PARAM"PARAM"
```

```
TCMD            →       tnatnum
ONOROFF         →       "on"  |  "off"
PARAM           →       pnattum
GROUPET         →       { natnum :natnum FIXDURS : }
                      | { natnum :: FIXDURS : }
                      | { : FIXDURS : }
FIXDURS         →       FIXDUR FIXDURS  |  FIXDUR
FIXDUR  →       OPTCHORD OPTDUR PITCHES
                      | OPTCHORD ( OPTDUR PITCHES )
                      | OPTCHORD GROUPET
OPTDUR  →       natnum OPTDOTS  |  ε
OPTDOTS         →       . OPTDOTS  |  ε
PITCHES         →       PITCH PITCHES  |  PITCH
PITCH           →       OPTOCT OCTPITCH OPTACC OPTSLUR OPTPAR
                      | OPTCHORD OPTOCT OCTPITCH OPTACC OPTTIE
                      | OPTOCT r
OPTCHORD        →       <  |  ε
OPTSLUR         →       _  |  ε
OPTTIE  →       __  |  ε
OPTOCT  →       OPTABSOCT OPTRELOCTS
OPTABSOCT       →       =  |  ε
OPTRELOCTS      →       DOWNOCTS  |  UPOCTS  |  ε
DOWNOCTS        →       , DOWNOCTS  |  ,
UPOCTS  →       ' UPOCTS  |  '
                →
OPPACC  →       ACC  |  ε
ACC             →       n  |  #  |  -  |  ##  |  --
OCTPITCHES      →       OCTPITCH OCTPITCHES  |  OCTPITCH
OCTPITCH        →       c  |  d  |  e  |  f  |  g  |  a  |  b
OPTPAR  →       [ MACROS ]
MACROS  →       CRMACRO MACROS  |  ε
CRMACRO         →       text  |  text: text  |  text: 'text  |  .  |  <
```
where the non-terminal SCORE is the start symbol for the *score* BNF.

Example 7.11 BNF for the *scot* language.

As with the *score* BNF, much of the *scot* BNF controls the overall structure of the file. Informally, a *scot* file is comprised of a series of *orchestra, function,* and *score* blocks. There can only be one *orchestra* block and this must be specified first. There are no restrictions on the number of *function* and *score* blocks.

The primary use of the *function* block is to define function tables. However, any *score*-language statement can appear within the curly braces ({. . .}) of a *function* block. This ability to include raw *score* code is useful in dealing with any unusual requirements or special effects.

A *score* block performs the same role as a *score* section in the *score* format. With the exception of the *function* block, a *scot* command can be spread over more than one line; more than one command can be given per line. Comments are defined as the *score* language.

7.3.3   The *Orchestra* Block in *Scot*

Each *instrument* in the *orchestra* file is identified by an arbitrary number. An *instrument* declaration takes the form:

$$text = natnum$$

The use of a particular instrument in a *score* block is initiated with the syntax:

$$\$text$$

Instruments in the *orchestra* file need not be bound to a name. More than one instrument name may be bound to the same instrument number.

Macros may be defined in the *orchestra* block. Macros serve many purposes. They may be used to introduce more meaningful names, reduce the quantity of text, or form a better abstraction of the music. More than one purpose can be served by a single macro. For example, instead of using the setting 1000 with all notes that are to be played loudly, the macro definition ff=1000 used in conjunction with the substitution ff for 1000 gives more control and makes it easy to change the value of "loud."

When the left-hand side of a macro definition appears in a *scot* file, *Csound* textually substitutes the right-hand side of the definition in its place. A macro definition may reference another macro, but it must never indirectly reference itself.

There are two types of macros. *Global* macros may be used by any instrument; a *local* macro may be used only by the instrument for which it was defined. A list of macro declarations has the syntax:

$$[\ text=text\ text=text\ \ldots\ ]$$

The global macro declaration list is placed before any instrument-name declarations. Macro definitions appearing immediately after an instrument declaration are local to that instrument.

Elements in the list are separated by white space. To distinguish this from a blank space in a text item, the text item may be placed in double quotes (" . . . ").

7.3.4   The *Score* Block in *Scot*

In addition to containing a list of notes to play, a *score* block will often include an instrument name ($*text*), a key signature (!*key*...), and a time signature (!*time*...).[6] Each time an instrument is invoked, time is "rewound" back to the start of that *score* block, and the new instrument plays concurrently with the other instruments named.

The performance of one note involves the execution of four variables: duration, octave position, note name, and pitch inflection. The duration and octave units are optional. If the duration field is omitted, then the previous value is assumed. If no octave information is given, the previous octave is assumed. Octave information that does not start with an equals sign (=) is interpreted as a move relative to the previous octave.

The computation of pitch is more complicated, both because relative and absolute specifications are acceptable and because the *scot* format employs octave folding.[7] When a relative pitch is specified, the note field binds to the note of the specified letter that falls within an augmented fourth (a half octave) of the previous note. Only then are any relative octaves (up or down) applied to the note's pitch to produce the final pitch. When an absolute pitch (introduced by =) is specified, the augmented fourth interval is based on Middle C and any additional octaves are applied. Octave folding may be controlled through the use of the !*octaves* command.

The end of a measure is notated by a forward slash (/). An accidental will be applied to all notes of the same name within the measure, as in traditional music notation. This default may be controlled by the !*accidentals* command.

The symbol for a slur is an underscore character (_). A tie is denoted using a double underscore (__). If a note is part of a slur, or tied to the next note, then the corresponding symbol is placed after the four-unit note specification. Only one of these may be present.

Slurring information in a *scot* file is translated to the *p4* parameter of an *i*-statement in the computer-generated *score* file. The meaning of the values is indicated in Table 7.8.

---

6. N.B. In this description italics represent the variable content of commands.

7. Also called "octave following." See the glossary.

4c d	no slur	$p4 = 0$
4c d_	slur after	$p4 = 1$
4c_d	slur before only	$p4 = 2$
4c_d_	slur before and after	$p4 = 3$

Table 7.8 Parameter values for slurs.

The three variations in syntax for a groupette are:

`{ dn ... :}`	d in the time of n
`{ d:: ... :}`	n will be the largest power of 2 less than d
`{ :    ... :}`	$d = 3$, $n = 2$ (normal triplets)

The curly braces (`{...}`) specify a region of the *score* block that temporarily works with different time units. Groupettes may be nested.

If a note is proceeded by a "less than" sign (<), then its time is not advanced, and it is stacked on top of the previous one. Thus a chord is formed. In most situations all the notes in the chord will have the same duration. Notes of mixed durations may be stacked in a *scot* file. *Csound* will schedule the start of the note following a chord at the end of the last note in the stack. Properties of stacks are controlled using the `!vertical` command.

A compound element may be formed by enclosing a sequence of notes in parentheses ((`"..."`)). Compound elements and groupettes may be stacked.

It has already been mentioned that the *score* file automatically generated from a *scot* file has predefined meanings for the parameters *p1–p5*. These definitions are:

p1	instrument number
p2	initialization time of instrument
p3	duration
p4	slur information
p5	pitch information in *pch* form

The user may assign meaning to the parameters *p6* and higher, which, if used, are specified in square brackets (`[...]`) after the note specification. Parameter values are in order, separated by white spaces. If a parameter has no specified value, or is specified as a period (`.`), it will carry over the previous value. This is analogous to the carry operator in the *score* format. The ramp operator (<) may also be specified as a parameter value. If a parameter value is preceded by an apostrophe ('), then that local *i*-statement is given the value, but the carry value that is stored for that parameter is unaltered.

A parameter can be specified directly using the syntax

```
natnum1:natnum2
```

where *natnum1* is the parameter number to be defined and *natnum2* is the value the parameter takes.

If the note is part of a slur, then the additional parameter list is placed after the underscore character (_). Because a group of tied notes in a *scot* file is converted into a single *i*-statement in the *score* file, it is not possible to change additional parameters partway through a tie.

Macro definitions may be used in the extra parameter list (indicated in Example 7.11).

A. PLING COMMANDS [! *anything*]

Pling commands roughly correspond to global specifiers—time signatures, key signatures, transposition, and so forth—in *DARMS*. The syntax of the *pling* commands, which are introduced by an exclamation mark (!), is straightforward. Time and key signatures are specified as:

```
!time "natnum1/natnum2"
!key "acc note ..."
```

where *acc* specifies an accidental and each *note* is drawn from the set [*a..g*]. All notes in the *score* block at those pitches will be appropriately modified. Accidentals may be modified locally with the syntax:

```
!accidentals <on> or <off>
```

Other *pling* commands that use the same syntax are:

```
!transpose pitch
!octaves <on> or <off>
!vertical <on> or <off>
```

The vertical command determines whether carry properties affect subsequent notes in the stack. All *pling* commands may be reduced to their first two letters, e.g., !tr.

B. DIRECT IMPORTS FROM THE *SCORE* FORMAT

The *next-p* and *previous-p* operators are available in *scot* in the form:

```
!next px py
!previous px py
```

The interpretation of the `!next` (or `!previous`) command is: "for the current instrument, px will contain the py value for the *next* (*previous*) note."

Tempo may be changed during a piece with the *t*-command:

```
tnatnum
```

At the musical point in time defined by the location of the *t*-command the tempo will be *natnum* beats per minute. Thus the *t*-command is a fragment of the *t*-statement, representing just one of the number pairs.

The *t*-command may appear in only one of the instruments in a *score* block.

7.3.5   File Organization in *Scot*

The file organization for *scot* is similar to that for *score* notation. An *orchestra* file defines instrument sounds and a *melody* file written in the *scot* language defines a tune.

In a *scot* file, instruments that play at the same time are placed into the same *score* block. Within the *score* block all the notes played by one instrument are entered before the next instrument's tune is given. The *score* block structure is an ideal construct for a piece in several movements.

In practice it is preferable to break a musical piece into sections smaller than a movement. These sections may be of arbitrary length. However, ties and slurs are not continued from one *score* block to the next, so care must be taken when choosing the section breaks.

7.4   General Comments

Csound provides a collection of utilities for analyzing the generated audio files, either to obtain user information or for resynthesis. The utility program *sndinfo* returns information for the user. It decodes the named audio file, printing out information concerning its file format, sample rate, etc. The utility programs *hetro*, *lpanal*, and *pvanal* respectively perform heterodyne filter, linear predictive, and Fourier analysis for resynthesis. They create new files that can be read by certain *Csound* generator functions.

It was stated at the beginning of the chapter that *Csound* produces audio files that are hardware dependent, to facilitate audio play back. *Csound* can alternatively be instructed to generate AIFF files, thus adding a degree of portability.[8]

A standard for the interchange of files containing musical information will probably want to consider the wider issue of a standard multimedia file format. Independent of this, some general observations are possible.

An evaluation of current full musical description file formats indicates that by today's standards of disk usage, the file size requirement to represent music is low. Clever techniques to reduce file size are therefore not a necessity. Graphics and audio hardware today are also readably available. This makes working with a standard musical file format through applications that graphically display and/or audibly play user operations a viable prospect. Consequently a text-readable format is not required and indeed a binary format seems the most appropriate.

Csound is certainly not up to the challenge of a standard, for it is only intended for audio output. However, it has many qualities worthy of emulation. Among these are the use of a *mixture* of block structures (*score* sections and groupettes) and delimiters (slurs and ties), whichever is the most appropriate, rather than opting entirely for one of the approaches. Some researchers believe that as chip processing speeds rise, *Csound* increasingly has the potential of becoming a software substitute for synthesizer hardware.

Since this chapter is intended to act as a filter for the information relevant to the interchange between different musical formats, emphasis has been given to describing the two audio file formats used by the *Csound* package, namely *score* and *scot*.

The *score* file format is based on raw timed events, with no imposed notion of musical structure. It is primarily an audio file format. There is a large overlap in common notions between the *score* format and other audio-file formats, particularly MIDI but also AIFF, MOD, etc. Developing translators between these formats should be straightforward.

The *scot* file format provides a much higher-level representation of musical structure, strongly reflecting the constructs found in graphical music. This link makes

---

8. An extremely useful utility program (unconnected with *Csound*) is called *sox*. It supports numerous hardware-dependent file formats as well as device-independent AIFF formats. Conversion between these conventions is possible as well as data manipulation, such as a changing the sample rate. It is available from numerous ftp sites.

the *scot* format a potential candidate for converting to and from a true graphical music description format (e.g., *Finale, DARMS,* etc.). As with the *score* format, there are strong similarities between the design of the *scot* language and the other file formats. This facilitates ease of translation. It is perhaps best to think of the *scot* format as a subset of the requirements of a graphical music description format.

If the subset property were to prove too much of a limitation, it should be remembered that *scot* is a flexible language and it is possible to represent practically any musical effect using the extra parameters. If the use of the extra parameters were more rigorously controlled (e.g., with *p6* for volume, etc.) as an extended version of the language (say *scot*-2), then the *scot* language could be an equal match for any graphical language. Required extensions would be:

- techniques such as bit-setting to represent note attenuation (staccato, etc.)
- enumerated types for mood or style-of-playing
- text management using ASCII strings as in Pascal

To expand upon the last point, a string could be represented in a *scot* file by using a consecutive block of parameters. The first parameter would represent the length of the string; subsequent parameters would represent each letter in the string.

7.5 Further Information

Csound can be obtained by ftp from various sites. The UNIX and Macintosh versions are available from the site *cecelia.media.mit.edu* in the directory */pub/Csound.* Further information can be obtained from *csound@media.mit.edu.*

The PC version is available by ftp from *ftp.bath.ac.uk* in the directories */pub/jpff* and */pub/dream.* These e-mail contacts are also available: *duprasm@ere.umontreal.ca* and *james@maths.exeter.ac.uk.*

There are two *Csound* mailing lists; both are called *csound-request.* The first is at *@media.mit.edu,* and the second is *@maths.ex.ac.uk.* In both cases, one may subscribe with this message:

```
subscribe <e-mail address>
```

Two collections of *Csound* example files (*orchestras, score-* and *scot*-formatted files) contributed by users are available by ftp. The first group of files is connected with the electronic discussion group mentioned above. Files can be found at the site *ftp.hmc.edu* in the directory */pub/csound/*. The second collection of files is provided by a company called Gravis. The file *cs_smpls.zip* contains a selection of *Csound* files. These can be found at the following sites:

LOCATION	SITE	DIRECTORY
N. America:	*archive.orst.edu*	*/pub/packages/gravis/util/dos/*
	uarchive.wustl.edu	*/systems/ibmpc/ultrasound/util/dos/*
Asia:	*nctuccca.edu.tw*	*/PC/ultrasound/util/dos/*
Europe:	*garbo.uwasa.fi*	*/mirror/ultrasound/util/dos/*

All *Csound* files used in this chapter are available from the ftp site *ftp.hmn.edu*. Based on the BNF grammars presented in this chapter and using the UNIX compiler tools *yacc* and *lex*, a simple parser for the *score* and *scot* file formats has been developed. The work provides a skeleton program that would be a useful starting point for anyone developing a translator from *Csound*. These files are available from the same ftp site.

A MIDI-to-*Csound* converter, supporting both *score* and *orchestra*, has recently been made available on the World-Wide Web[9] and may be obtained from the address *http://www.snafu.delrubo/songlab/midi2cs/midi2cs.zip*.

Cantor, a program for optical recognition developed as part of my thesis project at University of Canterbury (Christchurch, New Zealand), can produce *Csound* files and also has outputs to Standard MIDI Files and *LIME* binary files.

References

Dodge, Charles D., and Thomas Jerse. *Computer Music Synthesis*. New York: Schirmer Books, 1985.

Moore, Richard F. *Elements of Computer Music*. New York: Prentice Hall, 1990.

Vercoe, Barry. *Csound: A Manual for the Audio Processing System and Supporting Programs with Tutorials*. 2nd rev. edn. Cambridge, MA: Massachusetts Institute of Technology Media Lab, 1993.

9. Registration for this product and further information about it may be obtained from SongLab, Bonhöfferufer 13, D-10589 Berlin, Germany; *RuBo@Berlin.Snafu.De*.

8 *Music Macro Language*

Toshiaki Matsushima

Music Macro Language (*MML*) is a widely used music description language for applications running on NEC computers. Developed in the early Eighties, *MML* data may be embedded in procedural programming languages such as BASIC.[1] Yamaha was the first company to use *MML* in commercial products.

MML was originally designed to generate background music and sound effects for computer-game software. Although its syntax and semantics are simple, they suffice for these purposes. *MML* is especially widely used by Japanese computer-music hobbyists.

Like MIDI in relation to the kinds of PCs used in other parts of the world, *MML* can control sound-generator boards attached to NEC PCs. This operating environment offers a distinct advantage to users requiring simultaneous control of Japanese text and generated sound.

8.1   Code Description

MML supports the encoding of pitch, duration, and dynamics. Data is encoded as a string of ASCII characters.

Pitch is encoded as a single letter in the set A..G. Chromatic alterations use these signs:

+ or #	sharp
–	flat

---

1. Some functional analogues to *MML* are *SQL* (*Structured Query Language*) in the context of database software and *Linda* in process communication languages.

Since *MML* represents sound rather than notation, there is no provision for a natural sign.

Octave position is represented by two characters—the letter O (for *octave*) and a number in the range 1..8. For example, the expression O4 represents the fourth octave. Changes of octave can be represented by relational signifiers:

>   one octave up

<   one octave down

Duration is encoded as a numerical value in the range 1..64, where 1 represents a whole note and 64 a 64th note. Pitch and duration are always encoded as a pair of characters, e.g., C4 represents a quarter-note C. A note duration may be omitted by using the default code L.

A tie is represented by the character ^. The expression C8^8 would generate a quarter-note C.

Pitches of tuplets are enclosed within curly brackets. The expression {CCC4} represents three Cs played as triplets within the space of a quarter note.

Dynamics must be specified directly as a sound amplitude value. The range is from @V0 to @V127.

8.2 Example

The following example[2] shows the most complete version of the code:

```
O4A8A8R4R8A8>C8<B8G8G8R4R8G8B8G8E8E8R4E8E16E16F+8G8D8D8
R4G8D16D16F8E8
```

This code can be reduced to the following string:

```
O4L8AAR4RA>C<BGGR4RGBGEER4EE16E16F+GDDR4GD16D16FE
```

_____

2. From Act I, Scene 9, of Handel's opera *Ottone*.

Since the data sets are intended only for sound applications, the beams are not encoded.

8.3   Using *MML* Data

Data in the *MML* format may be attached, within double quotation marks, to individual commands in a program. Thus to use the reduced string above in a BASIC program, the complete command would be structured as follows:

```
PLAY "O4C4","O4E4","O4G4"
```

If the NEC PC has multiple channels for sound generation, the user may play polyphonic music by writing *PLAY* commands in parallel:

```
PLAY "O4L8AAR4RA>C<BGGR4RGBGEER4EE16E16F+GDDR4GD16D16FE"
```

8.4   Further Information

There is currently no documentation written in English or other European languages for *MML*. In fact, no stand-alone documentation for *MML* in Japanese is known. The specifications given here are based on the manual for NEC's Japanese BASIC.[3] Many informal extensions exist.

---

3. *N-88 Japanese BASIC(86).*

9   The NeXT *ScoreFile*

David Jaffe

The NeXT Music Kit *ScoreFile* is optimized for sound synthesis. Data in this format may be played with the Music Kit *ScorePlayer* or "playscore" programs and may be read by any Music Kit program. The file is in ASCII text. Complete documentation is found in the *ScoreFile Language Reference*.[1] The Music Kit is available via ftp from *ccrma-ftp.stanford.edu*.

The format is not appropriate for the representation of notation because it does not accept spatial placement commands.

9.1   File Organization

*ScoreFile*s are interpreted like computer programs and utilize Objective C processing calls. They contain headers and bodies that produce different results according to which operators and variables are invoked.

9.1.1   Statement Types

Header statements are of several kinds including:

- *Score Info* statements (to specify overall settings such as tempo, sampling rate, etc.)

- *Part* declarations

---

1. Chapter 4 of the *NeXT Reference Manual* (Redwood City, CA: Next, Inc., 1990).

- *Part Info* statements (may specify SynthPatch class, MIDI channel, etc., for a particular part)

- *tagRange* statements (used in mixing files)

Body statements are used primarily to give note information and current time [t] in beats. A note contains any number of parameters, a type (such as *noteOn*, *noteOff*, or *noteUpdate*), a tag used in phrase structure, and a *Part* name. Some other statements that may be used in the body are:

- *print*
- *tune*
- *comment*

9.1.2 Data Types

ScoreFiles offer seven data types for variables and parameter values:

double	*env*
int	*wave*
string	*object*
	var

The types *double* and *int* work as in C. The *string* data type takes ASCII data within quotation marks. The types *env*, *wave*, and *object* take envelope, wave table, and object values, while *var* can be used to store any type. Any number of envelopes may be used in a *ScoreFile* and each envelope may have any number of break points. *Include* statements may be used, as in C, to read and interpret another file while processing the current file.

Variables are declared as in the C programming language.

9.1.3 Operators

Operators that may be used in a *ScoreFile* are listed below in order of their decreasing priority:

OPERATOR	FUNCTION
( )	grouping
–	unary minus
dB	decibel computation (postfix)

^, ~	exponentiation, pitch transposition
*, /, %	multiplication, division, modulus
+, –	addition, subtraction
@	envelope lookup
&	string concatenation
=	assignment
,	sequence separator

There are also conditional and looping keywords: *if*, *else*, *repeat*, *while*, and *do*.

9.1.4   Predeclared Variables, Constants, and Special Symbols

Pitch variables, which are predefined by the *ScoreFile* language, represent frequencies, in hertz, over a ten-and-a-half-octave range. The format is

```
pitchLetter[sharpOrFlat]octave
```

The *pitchLetter* variables are a..g.

The *sharpOrFlat* variables are s (= sharp) and f (= flat). There is no support for double sharps, double flats, or natural signs.

The *octave* specifications range from 0, the lowest octave, to 9. Middle C is represented as c4.

Similarly, a set of key-number constants represents the number of a key on a hardware device, for example on a MIDI keyboard. These constants are of the form pitchLetter[sharpOrFlat]octaveK, e.g., C4K.

The special symbol *ran* is a random number (a *double* data type) between 0 and 1. A different series of numbers is generated every time the file is read.

9.1.5   Comments

As in the C programming language, comments are enclosed within the marks /* and */. White space is ignored by the compiler. Its use in Example 9.1 is to clarify the file structure. Another kind of comment begins with two slashes (//) and continues to the end of the line.

9.2   Example

In the following example, based on the opening bars of the second trio of the Mozart Clarinet Quintet, several editorial choices are made in the performance specifications to give details of synthesis.

```
                    /* Begin header */

info tempo:108;                 /* Global "parameter" settings. Here 108 bpm */
part vln1,vln2,vla,vlc,cl;      /* Declare parts */
part mark;                      /* For bar lines and such */

/* Assign suggested synthesis instruments ("SynthPatches") */
cl synthPatch:"Fm1i"            synthPatchCount:1;
vln1 synthPatch:"DBWave1vi"     synthPatchCount:2;
vln2 synthPatch:"DBWave1vi"     synthPatchCount:1;
vla synthPatch:"DBWave1vi"      synthPatchCount:1;
vlc synthPatch:"DBWave1vi"      synthPatchCount:1;

/* Create synthesis envelopes */
envelope legato         = [(0,0)(.1,1)(.2,.75)|(.5,0.0)];
// envelope detache     = [(0,0)(.07,1)(.2,.5)|(.3,0.0)];
envelope detache        = [(0,0)(.2,1,1.5)(.3,.8,1.5)(1,.8)(4,.5,2)|
                          (5.1,0.0,.25)];

/* Declare variables */
double ps = .2;                 /* Separation between phrases. Init to .2 */
int clp;                        /* Current clarinet phrase ("notetag") */
int vln1p,vln2p,vlap,vlcp;      /* Other instruments' phrase counters */
string timeSig = "3/4";         /* Can have string variables too */

double trp = 2^(-3/12.0);       /* Clarinet transposition */
double st = .7;                 /* Staccato multiplier */
double p = .08;                 /* Dynamic level of 'piano' */

BEGIN;          /* Begin body */

/* Give instruments some defaults */
cl    (noteUpdate)  amp:.13         ampAtt:0.3      ampRel:0.2 m1IndAtt:0.1
      m1IndRel:0.1  m1Ratio:2.001   m1Ind1:1.3      m1Ind0:0.1 svibAmp:0.009
      svibFreq:4    rvibAmp:0.005   bearing:-20     ampEnv:legato;
vln1  (noteUpdate)  waveform:"VNS"  ampEnv:detache  amp:p      bearing:-45
      svibAmp:.01   svibFreq:4.8    rvibAmp:.007;
vln2  (noteUpdate)  waveform:"VNS"  ampEnv:detache  amp:p*.8   /* Inner parts
                                                                  softer */
      svibAmp:.01   svibFreq:4.7    rvibAmp:.007    bearing:45;
vla   (noteUpdate)  waveform:"VNS"  ampEnv:detache  amp:p*.8   svibAmp:.01
      svibFreq:4.6  rvibAmp:.007    bearing:20;
vlc   (noteUpdate)  waveform:"VCS"  ampEnv:detache  amp:p*1.4  svibAmp:.01
      svibFreq:4.5  rvibAmp:.007    bearing:0;

/* Notes of type "mute" are used for timeSignature and such.
   We use strings here. Can also use MIDI file-format encoding. */
vla  (mute)     timeSignature:"3/4";
vln1 (mute)     keySignature:"3#"    timeSignature:timeSig;
vln2 (mute)     keySignature:"3#"    timeSignature:timeSig;
```

```
vla (mute)        keySignature:"3#"     timeSignature:timeSig;
vlc (mute)        keySignature:"3#"     timeSignature:timeSig;

repeat (2) {                                     /* Repeat what's in {}s twice */

clp = vln1p = vln2p = vlap = vlcp = 1;           /* Init phrase counters */
cl (.5,clp)          freq:c5*trp;                /* First note. Duration = .5 */
                                  t +.5;         /* Increment time */
cl (.5,clp)          freq:e5*trp;  t +.5;        /* Several statements can appear
                                                   on a line */

mark (mute) ms:1;                                /* Measure number */
cl (.5,clp)          freq:g5*trp;
vlc (1,vlcp)         freq:a3;      t +.5;
cl (.5,clp)          freq:e5*trp;  t +.5;
cl (1-ps,clp)        freq:c6*trp;

vln1 (.8,vln1p)      freq:a4;      t +ran*.01;  /* Add bit of separation for
                                                   chord */
vln2 (.8,vln2p)      freq:e4;
vla (.8,vlap)        freq:cs4;     t +1;
clp = clp + 1;                                   /* New clarinet phrase */
cl (.5,clp)          freq:g5*trp;

vln1 (.8,vln1p)      freq:a4;

vln2 (.8,vln2p)      freq:e4;

vla (.8,vlap)        freq:cs4;     t +.5;
cl (.5,clp)          freq:e5*trp;  t +.5;

mark (mute)          ms:2;
cl (.5,clp)          freq:d5*trp;

vlc (1,vlcp)         freq:d3;      t +.5;
cl (.5,clp)          freq:f5*trp;  t +.5;
cl (1-ps,clp)        freq:a5*trp;

vln1 (.8,vln1p)      freq:a4;

vln2 (.8,vln2p)      freq:fs4;
vla (.8,vlap)        freq:b3;      t +1;
clp = clp + 1;

cl (.5,clp)          freq:f5*trp;

vln1 (.8,vln1p)      freq:a4;

vln2 (.8,vln2p)      freq:fs4;
vla (.8,vlap)        freq:b3;      t +.5;
cl (.5,clp)          freq:d5*trp;  t +.5;

mark (mute) ms:3;
cl (.5,clp)          freq:c5*trp;
vlc (1,vlcp)         freq:e3;      t +.5;
cl (.5,clp)          freq:b4*trp;  t +.5;
cl (.5,clp)          freq:e5*trp;
vln1 (.8,vln1p)      freq:gs4;
vln2 (.8,vln2p)      freq:d4;
vla (.8,vlap)        freq:b3;      t +.5;
cl (.5,clp)          freq:d5*trp;  t +.5;
cl (.5,clp)          freq:g5*trp;
```

```
vln1 (.8,vln1p)        freq:gs4;
vln2 (.8,vln2p)        freq:d4;
vla (.8,vlap)          freq:b3;        t +.5;
cl (.5-ps,clp)         freq:f5*trp;    t +.5;

mark (mute) ms:4;
clp = clp + 1;
vlc (1,vlcp)           freq:fs3;
cl (1,clp)             freq:ds5*trp;   t +1;
cl (1-ps,clp)          freq:e5*trp;
vln1 (.8,vln1p)        freq:a4;
vln2 (.8,vln2p)        freq:cs4;
vla (.8,vlap)          freq:a3;        t +1;
clp = clp + 1;
cl (.5,clp)            freq:c5*trp;
vln1 (.8,vln1p)        freq:a4;
vln2 (.8,vln2p)        freq:cs4;
vla (.8,vlap)          freq:a3;        t +.5;
cl (.5,clp)            freq:e5*trp;    t +.5;

mark (mute) ms:5;
cl (.5,clp)            freq:g5*trp;
vlc (1,vlcp)           freq:cs3;       t +.5;
cl (.5,clp)            freq:e5*trp;    t +.5;
cl (1-ps,clp)          freq:c6*trp;
vln1 (.8,vln1p)        freq:a4;
vln2 (.8,vln2p)        freq:e4;
vla (.8,vlap)          freq:cs4;       t +1;
clp = clp + 1;
cl (.5,clp)            freq:g5*trp;
vln1 (.8,vln1p)        freq:a4;
vln2 (.8,vln2p)        freq:e4;
vla (.8,vlap)          freq:cs4;       t +.5;
cl (.5,clp)            freq:e5*trp;    t +.5;

mark (mute) ms:6;
cl (.5,clp)            freq:d5*trp;
vlc (1,vlcp)           freq:d3;
vln1 (.8,vln1p)        freq:fs4;
vln2 (.8,vln2p)        freq:d4;
vla (.8,vlap)          freq:b3;        t +.5;
cl (.5,clp)            freq:f5*trp;    t +.5;
cl (1,clp)             freq:a5*trp;    t +1;

mark (mute) ms:7;
vln1 (.5,vln1p)        freq:cs5;
vln2 (1,vln2p)         freq:g4;
vla (1,vlap)           freq:e4;        t +.5;
vln1 (.5,vln1p)        freq:as4;       t +.5;
vln1 (.5,vln1p)        freq:b4;
vln2 (2,vln2p)         freq:fs4;
vla (2,vlap)           freq:d4;        t +.5;
vln1 (.5,vln1p)        freq:d5;        t +.5;
vln1 (1-ps,vln1p)      freq:fs5;       t +1;
vln1p = vln1p + 1;
vln1 (.5,vln1p)        freq:cs5;
vln2 (1,vln2p)         freq:g4;
vla (1,vlap)           freq:e4;        t +.5;
vln1 (.5,vln1p)        freq:as4;       t +.5;
```

```
vln1 (.5,vln1p)      freq:b4;
vln2 (2,vln2p)       freq:fs3;
vla (2,vlap)         freq:d4;        t +.5;
vln1 (.5,vln1p)      freq:d5;        t +.5;
vln1 (1-ps,vln1p)    freq:fs5;       t +1;

mark (mute) ms:8;
vln1 (noteUpdate)    ampEnv:legato;
vln2 (noteUpdate)    ampEnv:legato;
vla (noteUpdate)     ampEnv:legato;
clp = clp + 1;
cl (.333,clp)        freq:d4*trp;    t +.333;
cl (.333,clp)        freq:a3*trp;    t +.333;
cl (.333,clp)        freq:f3*trp;    t +.333;

mark (mute) ms:9;
cl (.5,clp)          freq:a3*trp;    t +.5;
cl (.5*st)           freq:d4*trp;    t +.5;
cl (.5*st)           freq:f4*trp;    t +.5;
cl (.5*st)           freq:a4*trp;    t +.5;
cl (.5*st)           freq:d5*trp;    t +.5;
cl (.5*st)           freq:f5*trp;    t +.5;

mark (mute) ms:10;
cl (.5,clp)          freq:a5*trp;    t +.5;
cl (.5,clp)          freq:g5*trp;    t +.5;
cl (.5,clp)          freq:f5*trp;    t +.5;
cl (.5,clp)          req:e5*trp;     t +.5;
cl (.5,clp)          freq:f5*trp;    t +.5;
cl (.5-ps,clp)       freq:d5*trp;    t +.5;

mark (mute) ms:11;
clp = clp + 1;
cl (2,clp)           freq:c5*trp;
vln1 (.5,vln1p)      freq:cs4;
vln2 (2,vln2p)       freq:a3;
vla (4,vlap)         freq:e3;
vlc (1*st)           freq:e2;        t +.5;
vln1 (.5,vln1p)      freq:e4;        t +.5;
vln1 (.5,vln1p)      freq:cs4;
vlc (1*st)         ·  freq:e2;        t +.5;
vln1 (.5,vln1p)      freq:e4;        t +.5;
cl (.5,clp)          freq:e5*trp;
vln1 (.5,vln1p)      freq:d4;
vlc (1*st)           freq:e2;        t +.5;
cl (.5,clp)          freq:d5*trp;
vln1 (.5,vln1p)      freq:e4;        t +.5;

mark (mute) ms:12;
clp = clp + 1;
cl (1,clp)           freq:c5*trp;
vln1 (1)             freq:cs4;
vln2 (1)             freq:a3;
vlc (1,vlcp)         freq:a2;        t +2;

}                                        /* End of repeat block */
```

Example 9.1 The Mozart trio, Bars 1–12, in the NeXT *ScoreFile* format.

10 The *Radio Baton Conductor* Score File

Max V. Mathews

The *Radio Baton* is an electronic tool for expressive control of machine-readable data. It is currently in use as a composition, rehearsal, and research tool. The *Conductor* program feeds musical data from a computer to the *Baton* buffer, where it is available to the performer. Originally the *Conductor* program could accept only scores in a unique format (the format described here). A modified version of the program accepts scores in MIDI *Format (FileType) 0* notation.[1]

The score compiler, called *ns*, reads the input from a score stored in a file without an extension, e.g., *score*, and writes it to a file with the same name and the extension *.p* (e.g., *score.p*). The compiled score is then read and performed by the *Conductor* program, called *nc*.

If part of the score is saved as MIDI data, the file must contain the extension *.mid* (e.g., *score.mid*). The score can be divided between an input file and MIDI file, which can be read in alternation. Alternation is facilitated by the insertion of a *switch* instruction at the end of a section in a file.

---

1. The MIDI version of the program currently works with hardware which includes four knobs and four switches not included in the original design. The program also works with models that have embedded 80C186 processors. These batons communicate entirely via MIDI signals. Programs to control the embedded processors exist for both IBM PC-compatible and Apple Macintosh computers.

10.1   File Organization

10.1.1   Original Conductor Score Files

Original *Radio Baton Conductor* score files consist of a series of header records followed by a series of note records. All records are in ASCII. The header records identify the work, the key signature, and the default tempo. They give specifications for the instruments to be used.

The *Radio Baton* has two "drum sticks" that are used to control the performance of a score. Each may control designated parameters (e.g., velocity) or parts (e.g., cello). *Conductor* files implement these assignments, which may vary with the performance.

The *Conductor* program accommodates Voices 0 through 24. A number not preceded by an alphabetic character designates a voice, to which the following string of characters pertains. Voice 0 is the master timing voice. Each voice is defined in a header record. Such parameters as tuning, channel number, and baton stick assignment may be given. In note records, voices (including Voice 0) are grouped together, measure by measure.

Comments begin and end with an asterisk (*).

10.1.2   Compiled *Conductor* Score Files

Compiled *Conductor* score files consist of a string of characters. Each character is interpreted as an unsigned binary number in the range 0 to 127. The characters are grouped into records. Each record causes one event to happen at one time in the performance. Records are sorted into ascending times.

In the compiled score file, the first three characters in each record specify:

- the number of characters in the record
- an operation code for the record [OP CODE]
- the time interval

The remaining characters in the record depend on the specific OP CODE. In a voice specification record basic parameters are set. In a note record, the key numbers of the note or chord to be played are given.

10.2   Musical Attributes

10.2.1   Pitch [A..G, a..g]

Pitches are represented by the letter names A..G (or a..g). A sharp is represented by a the sign #, a flat by the sign @, and a natural by the sign $. Rests are indicated by the letters R or r. Key signatures can be set with the commands K*n*# and K*n*@, where *n* indicates the number of accidentals.

Each instrument specification contains a key number (preceded by the letter o), which must be known in order to decode the pitch specifications given in note records. In the Mozart trio example that follows, the two violins and viola are set to o60 (Middle C), while the cello is set to o48 (the C below it).

Octave numbers are not used. Relative to the key number given, upper-case letters designate the lower adjacent octave and lower-case letters the upper adjacent octave. The next lower octave is introduced by the character !; the next higher octave by the character ^.

Transposition (for example, of the clarinet part in the Mozart trio) can be accomplished by resetting the key number in the instrument specification. In this example the key number setting is o57 (the A to which the instrument is tuned). The pitch names will correspond to those of a written score, but the sounding pitch will be appropriate for performance.

10.2.2   Duration [. . .]

Beats in a score are normally specified by a sequence of dots (. . . .). The correspondence between a note of a given duration and a number of dots is selected by the composer to suit the accuracy with which events need to be specified in the particular composition being transcribed.

A comma (,) is used to specify fractional beats. One dot nominally equals 8 commas. The equivalence can be changed by writing an equation j*n*, in which j = one dot and *n* = the number of commas chosen by the user. The dot-comma equivalence can be changed at any point in the score by inserting a new value of j*n* in Voice 0.

A forward slash (/) is a trigger point in Voice 0. Two triggers per measure are normally used.

In contrast to Standard MIDI Files, in which each event involves a Note_On and a Note_Off message, the *Conductor* program scores contain only Note_On messages. All notes in a voice automatically terminate just before the beginning of the next note or an explicit rest. All notes in a chord contained within a single voice must terminate together.

Measure numbers are treated as comments: they are preceded and followed by a single asterisk.

10.2.3 Tempo [V*n*, v*n*]

Tempo control is a major component of the *Conductor* program. A fixed tempo can be specified by inserting the command V*n* or v*n* into the score. If V*n* is used, *n* = tempo in dots per minute. If v*n* is used, *n* = 30,000/tempo, where tempo is computed in dots per minute.

Normally tempo is computed by each baton beat as the time difference between the last two beats divided by the number of commas in the score between these two beats. This tempo is used until the next baton beat.

Several other modes of tempo control can be used. A fixed tempo can be written into the score just ahead of a baton beat and this tempo will be used instead of the baton tempo between the next two beats. Fixed tempo is indicated by writing either V*n* or v*n* into Track 0 of the score. In *no baton mode*, a continuous tempo written in the first line of the baton track will be used throughout the performance.

10.2.4 Articulation

Many elements of articulation are handled through specifications of duration or key velocity. The sustain function can be turned on or off with the command p.

Long sequences of legato and staccato notes are best handled by macros. Macro definitions take the form (*xxxx*) *z* where *xxxx* is the content and *z* is the macro name. In the Mozart example that follows, the second line of the file contains a macro called *a*. Its definition is (X..,,,,r,,,,)a.

A macro may be invoked by the command z*n*, where *z* is the macro name and *n* is the number of times it is to be used. If no number is given, the macro will be invoked once. The macro *a* (cited above) is invoked numerous times in the string parts of the Mozart example, often with the syntax [r *y* *y*]'a3, where *y* is a pitch name.

10.2.5 Dynamics [k]

MIDI key velocity, representing dynamics, is transmitted once for each Note_On message. The value of the key velocity can be obtained from any dimension of either baton and can be a constant. The key velocity for a given voice is specified by writing k*w*n in the voice score where *w* is a character and *n* is an integer. The command Z*n* changes key velocity by subtracting *n* from the velocity that would otherwise be used.

If a number 1 through 127 is written immediately after a pitch symbol in the score, it will be added to the key velocity as calculated from the expressive controls. This feature is useful for accenting notes.

10.2.6 Other Features

Miscellaneous characters, such as carriage returns and blanks, are ignored in the input file. This enables the use of carriage returns and blanks to arrange the input file for legibility.

MIDI control changes can be transmitted on control-change numbers 1 through 120 either by writing the control changes into the score or by coupling a dimension of one of the batons to a control-change number. The control changes are made by patch-chords q1 through q15.

Sections of a score can be created with standard sequencer programs. MIDI Channels 2 through 16 may be used; Channel 1 is reserved for the baton and control data. A Middle C (*keyno* = 60) is interpreted as a baton beat and is not played as a sounding note. The note Middle C♯ (*keyno* = 61) marks the end of a MIDI section and causes the next part of the score to be read from the *Conductor* program file. The command h*n* sets a MIDI channel to *n*.

In the *Conductor* program score, the character M causes the next part of the score to be read from a MIDI file. The note C♯ in Channel 1 terminates a MIDI section and causes the next section to be read from the *Conductor* program score.

Several additional programs supply utilities:

ps　　　prints the compiled *.p* file(s) for debugging purposes

calxy　　computes the baton calibration matrix *xycalib*. The data in this matrix are used to linearize and calibrate the signals from the baton receivers so that motion across the receiver box in the *x* or *y* directions will map onto the MIDI signal range 0 to 127.

ptxycal　prints the *xycalib* matrix data.

sdxyz　　prints the linearized and corrected *xyz* data for baton movements. This is useful to check the calibration data.

adtest　　prints the low-level *a*-to-*d* signals from the 16 *a*-to-*d* converters. Ten signals come from the baton antennae. Four signals come from the four ports [//]. Two signals come from the four switches.

10.3   A Sample *Conductor* Program File

The following *Conductor* file facilitates performance of the second trio of the Mozart Clarinet Quintet. In this example the repeat signified by the double bar in Measure 12 is actually performed. With the pickup bar numbered Bar 1, the sequence given here is for Bars 1–13 plus Bars 2–13. Slurs are not represented.[2] Staccatos are introduced as rests (Bar 10). Following the specifications kx1 and ky1, the string instruments control the *x*-axis and the clarinet the *y*-axis.

```
*Mozart: Second Trio from Clarinet Quintet*
(X...,,,,r,,,,)a
I
K3# v100
4   o57  h4   *t28*  ky1  *clarinet*     q0 h4   v90  c7    q0 h4   v0    c10
12  o60  h12  *t12*  kx1  *1st violin*   q0 h12  v100 c7    q0 h12  v0    c10
13  o60  h13  *t12*  kx1  *2nd violin*   q0 h13  v100 c7    q0 h13  v0    c10
14  o60  h14  *t12*  kx1  *viola*        q0 h14  v100 c7    q0 h14  v126  c10
15  o48  h15  *t12*  kx1  *cello*        q0 h15  v100 c7    q0 h15  v126  c10
*1*                                      4  K0# g..e..^c...,,,,r,,,,g..e..
0   /..../..../....                      12 K3# [r a a]'a3
4   K0# r........c..e..                  13 [r E E]'a3
*2*                                      14 [r C C]'a3
0   /..../..../....                      15 C....r
4   K0# g..e..^c...,,,,r,,,,g..e..       *7*
12  K3# [r a a]'a3                       0  /..../..../....
13  [r E E]'a3                           4  K0# d..f..^a....r
14  [r C C]'a3                           12 K3# F....r....c..#a..
15  a....r                               13 D....r....G
*3*                                      14 B....r....E
0   /..../..../....                      15 D....r
4   K0# d..f..^a...,,,,r,,,,f..d..       *8*
12  K3# [r a a]'a3                       0  /..../..../....
13  [r F F]'a3                           12 K3# b..d..f..,,,,r,,,,c..#a..
14  [r B B]'a3                           13 F........G
15  D....r                               14 D........E....
*4*                                      *9*
0   /..../..../....                      0  /..../..../....
4   K0# c..b..e..d..g..f.,,,,r,,,,       4  K0# r........D.,,A.,,!F
12  K3# [r G G]'a3                       12 K3# b..d..f....r
13  [r D D]'a3                           13 F........r
14  [r B B]                              14 D........r
15  E....r                               *10*
*5*                                      0  /..../..../....
0   /..../..../....                      4  K0#
4   K0# #d....e...,,,,r,,,,c..e..           A.,,,,r,,,,D.r.F.r.a.r.d.r.f.r.
12  K3# [r a a]'a3                       *11*
13  [r C C]'a3                           0  /..../..../....
14  [r A A]'a3                           4  K0# ^a..g..f..e..f..d.,,,,r,,,,
15  F....r                               *12*
*6*                                      0  /..../..../....
0   /..../..../....                      4  K0# c........e..d.,,,,r,,,,
```

2. Possibilities for their addition are discussed in the chapter on *Augmented MIDI*.

```
12 K3# C..E..C..E..D..E.,,,,r,,,,        12 K3# [r a a]'a3
13 A........#!G...,,,,r,,,,              13 [r E E]'a3
14 !E                                    14 [r C C]'a3
15 !E...r.!E...r.!E...r.                 15 C....r
*13*                                     *7r*
0  /..../..../....                       0  /..../..../....
4  K0# c....r....c..e..                  4  K0# d..f..^a....r
12 K3# C....r                            12 K3# F....r....c..#a..
13 A....r                                13 D....r....G
14 ....r                                 14 B....r....E ·
15 A....r                                15 D....r
*repeated bars start here*               *8r*
*2r*                                     0  /..../..../....
0  /..../..../....                       12 K3# b..d..f...,,,,r,,,,c..#a..
4  K0# g..e..^c...,,,,r,,,,g..e..        13 F........G
12 K3# [r a a]'a3                        14 D........E....
13 [r E E]'a3                            *9r*
14 [r C C]'a3                            0  /..../..../....
15 a....r                                4  K0# r........D.,,A.,,!F
*3r*                                     12 K3# b..d..f....r
0  /..../..../....                       13 F........r
4  K0# d..f..^a...,,,,r,,,,f..d..        14 D........r
12 K3# [r a a]'a3                        *10r*
13 [r F F]'a3                            0  /..../..../....
14 [r B B]'a3                            4  K0#
15 D....r                                   A.,,,,r,,,,D.r.F.r.a.r.d.r.f.r.
*4r*                                     *11r*
0  /..../..../....                       0  /..../..../....
4  K0# c..b..e..d..g..f.,,,,r,,,,        4  K0# ^a..g..f..e..f..d.,,,,r,,,,
12 K3# [r G G]'a3                        *12r*
13 [r D D]'a3                            0  /..../..../....
14 [r B B]                               4  K0# c........e..d.,,,,r,,,,
15 E....r                                12 K3# C..E..C..E..D..E.,,,,r,,,,
*5r*                                     13 A........#!G...,,,,r,,,,
0  /..../..../....                       14 !E
4  K0# #d....e...,,,,r,,,,c..e..         15 !E...r.!E...r.!E...r.
12 K3# [r a a]'a3                        *13r*
13 [r C C]'a3                            0  /..../..../....
14 [r A A]'a3                            4  K0# c....r
15 F....r                                12 K3# C....r
*6r*                                     13 A....r
0  /..../..../....                       14 ....r
4  K0# g..e..^c...,,,,r,,,,g..e..        15 A....r
                                         0
```

Figure 10.1 Second trio from the Mozart Clarinet Quintet.

Musical NotationCodes (1):

DARMS

11 *DARMS*, Its Dialects, and Its Uses

Eleanor Selfridge-Field

DARMS, an acronym for Digital Alternate Representation of Musical Scores, was
developed to provide a means for writing music with an ordinary computer keyboard.
The initial design of this language (or meta-language) was created by Stefan Bauer-
Mengelberg in 1963. The further elaboration of the design was done by a group of
people, including Raymond Erickson, who worked with Bauer-Mengelberg. *DARMS*
is now viewed by its developers and many of its users as the most mature and
complete digital representation of musical notation.

   DARMS is a relatively invisible encoding language. Its analytical uses are little
known outside academe, and its commercial use—to produce a substantial corpus of
scholarly editions of music in both common and unusual notations—has quietly gone
on for two decades with relatively little notice. *DARMS* is given a considerable spread
here for several reasons:

- *DARMS* is the earliest encoding language still in use.

- *DARMS* illustrates the orientation of print-oriented codes extremely well.

- *DARMS* offers a paradigm that is rarely present in the other codes discussed
  here: namely, that all files stored in *DARMS* code may be converted to an
  unambiguous "canonical" version.

   This last point is especially deserving of note. *DARMS*'s originators and early
developers intended programmers to have some latitude in the use of features and the
specific representation of them.

11.1   Canonical *DARMS* (1): An Introduction

Canonical *DARMS* is described at length in a typescript manual made by Erickson in 1976. Most implementations of *DARMS* have started out with the representation system described there as a foundation. Although we include coverage of several *DARMS* variants here, variants based on variants seem not to exist to any significant degree. Thus existing variants all have a first-generation relationship to the canonical language.

Canonical *DARMS* is intended to be unambiguous. No short-cuts are allowed. Every note is completely described; all positional information is explicit. "Smart" software that computes, let us say, beam placement in running eighth notes is unnecessary because all stem directions and beams will be explicitly encoded.

Conversely, however, software that determines when to suppress accidental signs within the bar is redundant for a different reason: canonical *DARMS* code indicates exactly what is to be on the page at the time of printing. Thus the determination was made at the time of encoding. "Pitch" specifications within *DARMS* are therefore not truly canonical in the same way as MIDI key numbers are, because *DARMS* is based entirely on relative spatial placement (and contexts imposed by global variables), not on sounding pitch.

The most significant difference between canonical *DARMS* and most dialects in current use concerns the *vertical space code* that identifies "pitches." On all five-line staves, the lowest line is encoded as 1 plus some multiple of 50; the four spaces take the intervening even numbers. Fifty positions (taking into account a wide range of possible leger lines) are reserved for each staff. On the topmost staff (normally the G clef), the lines from bottom to top are numbered 21, 23, 25, 27, and 29; the spaces are 22, 24, 26, and 28.

In a canonical *DARMS* encoding, a lower staff (presumably in the F clef) would have its lines number (from bottom to top) as 71, 73, 75, 77, and 79, etc. The lines of a pedal part in an organ score would be 121, 123, 125, 127, and 129.[1]

In most dialects of *DARMS*, space codes are related to the clef in current use. The lines, from bottom to top, are usually encoded simply as 1, 3, 5, 7, and 9, and the intervening spaces as 2, 4, 6, and 8. The number series continues in both directions

---

1. These codes pertain only to multiple staves treated within the context of one "instrument," e.g., piano or organ. In a string quartet, each instrument would normally use the codes given here for the "topmost" voice, since each instrument requires only one staff. However, it is possible in *DARMS* to encode the four voices of a string quartet as one instrument performing on four staves. This saves encoding time and file space but makes the data more awkward to use analytically.

to represent pitches above and below the clef. Thus, Middle C, if shown above the bass clef, would have the pitch code of 11^2; on the alto clef it would be 5 and on the treble clef it would be -1. Similarly, the D above Middle C would be 0 if shown below the treble clef, but 12 if shown above the bass clef.

Canonical *DARMS* does not resolve differences of enharmonic notation needing explicit representation for sound and analytical applications. The G above Middle C would be encoded as 3 if it were sounded as G, as well as if it were a sounding G♯ or G♭ whose accidental sign had been made redundant by a governing key signature. In effect, this requires some extra intelligence in the programming when *DARMS* data is converted to a sound code.

Canonical *DARMS* also permits text underlay to be treated in multiple ways, e.g., by attaching each syllable to the note on which it begins, or by attaching a whole line of text as a separate "voice" in a score.

The perceived purpose of canonical *DARMS* was to resolve differences between dialects when data was passed from one system or application to another. It has rarely been used for this purpose, since only a few printing implementations have been brought to sufficient competence over the almost 35 years of its existence to generate interest in encoding large quantities of data.[3]

Canonical *DARMS* has been important as a hypothetical construct, in particular for expressing ideas about possible data structures and data queries.[4] It has also been useful in certain analytical contexts, since it is easier to work with absolute representations than relative ones.

11.2 *DARMS* Dialects for Music Printing

While no statistics can be compiled on the subject, it is a reasonable supposition that between the late Sixties and the early Eighties, *DARMS* was the code most prevalently used for both music printing and musical analysis. The dialects discussed here are *Note-Processor DARMS*, *A-R DARMS*, and *COMUS DARMS*.

2. Unsigned numbers are positive.

3. Two examples of canonical *DARMS* appear here. One is Wiering's implementation of *Lute Code*, and the other is the chapter on *EsAC*, where the *DARMS* code shown has been generated from the Essen code.

4. See the work of McLean and Page.

.

11.2.1 *Note-Processor DARMS* and *A-R DARMS*

Although hypothetically it would seem preferable to give the fullest exposition to canonical *DARMS*, we have opted instead to offer substantial coverage of *Note-Processor DARMS*, which is the one implementation of *DARMS* code that is easily available. The *Note Processor* program, written in the mid-Eighties, runs on IBM PCs of various kinds and is the most visible tool based on *DARMS* code. Its developer, J. Stephen Dydo, has attempted to put a user-friendly front-end on code that is cryptically compact when first encountered. We also cover the A-R dialect, developed over the past 20 years by Thomas Hall; it has been optimized for production efficiencies. *DARMS*'s designers had the original intention of creating a code that could be put to use by people who did not read musical notation, and although A-R's staff of music encoders are musically literate, they more closely resemble the hypothetical future users imagined in the Sixties than do the MIDI aficionados using the *Note Processor* today. The A-R dialect of *DARMS* currently runs on Sun workstations.

A curious but telling similarity between these two dialects is that the authors first became involved with computer methods of music printing during their graduate student years at Columbia and Princeton Universities respectively. Columbia and Princeton, together with Bell Telephone Laboratories in Murray Hill, N.J., had been the cradles of electronic music in the late Fifties. Early efforts to support music printing were a seemingly natural outgrowth of the revolution taking place in the domain of computer-generated sound.

As a composer, Dydo's original motivation (like that of many other developers of notation software) was to develop an inexpensive method of producing scores of new music. *DARMS*'s ability to place symbols anywhere on the page lent it to this kind of application.[5]

As a scholar, Hall's early work was with a series of other codes developed at Princeton for the printing of modern editions of Renaissance polyphony, for the analysis of the multiple sources on which these were based, and for the study of compositional traits of particular repertories. Given this breadth of experience, it is a testimony to the durability and flexibility of *DARMS* that Hall opted to select it as his code of choice in developing a production-oriented system.

---

5. In most other notation programs available today, including the *Note Processor*, symbols can be easily moved with a mouse. Spacing is initially determined by the program, usually after some guidance from the user with regard to the basic layout desired.

11.2.2 *COMUS DARMS*[6]

COMUS Music Printing Software, developed by John Dunn in Staffordshire, UK, uses a subset of *DARMS* as its basic input. The subset follows the Erickson manual (1976) closely, including the retention of upper-case key-letters and @..$ delimiters for text strings where, however, lower case letters are valid. Space codes 00 through 50 are expected for all instruments regardless of score position. While space codes $50n+m$ are accepted, they have no meaning except for symbols of vertical extent which use the double space code. The rationale here is that instrument associations with specific staves in the composer's score should be recorded elsewhere than in the canonic file, and on final printing these associations are an editorial decision.

Strophic text is treated as a special type of *instrument* in its own right, as are percussion parts; these are indicated by attaching the suffix T or P to the instrument code. A *text instrument* consists of a series of syllables, each possessing a duration not necessarily in one-to-one correspondence with normal notes elsewhere.

For ease of data entry from a QWERTY keyboard, text delimiters have been dropped in this context. A possible fragment might look like:

```
I5T ... E,is Q,this Q,tre- / Q.,men- E,dous E,Stra- E,nger_ / RQ ...
```

Sensible hyphenation and underscoring are implemented by the drawing program. Rests, bar lines, and time signatures are, of course, not drawn in strophic text, but are used in the canonizer for checking.

Linear decomposition mode is the norm in *DARMS*. The meaning of the directive |& has been extended to allow "stacking" of this marker to enable repeated passes over a section of coding. This facilitates the coding of short sequences of complex structure, e.g., simultaneous beam systems can be encoded using this short form in two passes.

A canonizer directive !tn, in which n is an integer, has been added to facilitate the encoding of instruments with different concurrent time signatures such as 3:4 against 9:8.[7] The default duration value allocated to a quarter note by the canonizer is 240; !tn sets this to n.

---

6. Since the *COMUS* dialect of *DARMS* is not treated later in detail, a few of its innovations are cited here. This account is best read after the chapters on *N-P* and *A-R DARMS*. This description was provided by its developer, John Dunn. Further information may be obtained from Comus Music Printing, Armthorpe, Tixall, Stafford ST18 0XP, England, UK; tel. +44 1785/662520.

7. !Tn is retained as a crude but useful transposition directive.

Only the base-increment space code format has been retained for the encoding of chords. The various versions of push codes are not implemented.[8]

No problems have been encountered so far due to the lack of equate codes and similar macro-like constructs, or the push code. The null note and null symbols are generally useful and are implemented.

The odd-even numerical delimiters for symbols of horizontal extent have been applied to groupettes, so that groupette identifiers must be odd. This allows for easy and unambiguous identification of the end of a groupette.

For tremolos, square brackets ([..]) are used instead of parentheses as a simple note attribute, either in matched groups for single-note tremolos, or unmatched to indicate the beginning and end of a two-note tremolo. In the latter case, the tremolo is associated with a beam structure to establish the slope of the tremolo bars.

The long-form beam structure identifier may be used for this purpose, not necessarily associated with real beams. Thus:

5Q[[B3 6Q]]B4

The vocabulary of dictionary codes, ornaments, etc., covers only regularly used symbols. Fingering and figured bass codes are currently rudimentary, but follow Erickson. New dictionary codes, ornaments, and similar attributes and symbols are added to the software as the need arises, and generally follow Erickson; the software program structure was designed to allow this.

A general mechanism is in place to deal with horizontal structures (beams, slurs, hairpins, etc.) which extend past a system end. Unimplemented constructs are usually ignored in the drawing process; unimplemented attributes of an implemented basic event type are accepted without comment by the canonizer. Unimplemented basic constructs (e.g., the *push operator*) are rejected at the canonizer stage with a warning message.

The *COMUS* canonizer and drawing program also accept typesetting directives to facilitate entry of titles, but strictly speaking these are outside *DARMS*. They are easily recognizable as lines beginning with a right square bracket (]) character in the first position, before any *DARMS* constructs.

---

8. Linear decomposition, push codes, and other special features of *DARMS* are explained in the following chapter.

11.3   *DARMS* in Musical Analysis

11.3.1   Brinkman *DARMS*

DARMS has been used in musical analysis, particularly in the university environment, for almost three decades. The best introduction to this application is found in *Pascal Programming for Musical Research* by Alexander Brinkman (University of Chicago Press, 1990). Brinkman's coverage of *DARMS* (pp. 137–154) is especially useful in calling attention to multiple methods of encoding for the same situations. It shows appropriate grammars for attaching multiple ornaments to one event, discusses *skip codes*[9] in linear decomposition, and provides extensions for transposition[10] and for parts beginning on an anacrusis.[11] Brinkman has used *DARMS* in analytical research, in his case to study the use of chorale melodies in J. S. Bach's *Orgelbüchlein*.

Brinkman points out that *DARMS* "cannot be used for music analysis without a fair amount of interpretation" because *DARMS* is concerned with graphic objects rather than musical meaning and because the meaning of objects is context-sensitive.

Apart from some minor differences in the description of beams and flags, Brinkman *DARMS* is very largely the same as *Note-Processor DARMS*, and both remain very close to the 1976 rubric. Scanning software under development by William McGee outputs Brinkman *DARMS* files.[12]

11.3.2   Erickson (Canonical) *DARMS*

One of the earliest analytical applications of *DARMS* was by Erickson. In a Yale dissertation (1969), Erickson used *DARMS* to encode twelfth-century chant and analyze its rhythmic features. The most important consequences of this study were that the author later assembled the 1976 *DARMS* manual,[13] which has remained the only comprehensive description from that time to this, and that *DARMS* was informally

---

9. Introduced by the tilde [~].

10. Introduced by the directive !T.

11. Introduced by the directive !A.

12. See McGee's article "*MusicReader*: An Interactive Optical Music Recognition System," *Computing in Musicology* 9 (1993-94), 146–151.

13. The manual was prepared for a seminar for prospective *DARMS* users held at the State University of New York at Binghamton.

established as the encoding system of choice at Yale University, a strong base of music-theoretic and music-analytic studies.

Various studies related to music of the English Renaissance by John Morehen (Nottingham University, UK) have used canonical *DARMS*.

The extensive use of *DARMS* in the field of music bibliography has relied on the Erickson version; many such projects originated when there was no alternative. Harry Lincoln at SUNY Binghamton encoded and sorted 38,000 incipits of sixteenth-century madrigals, resulting in a 1988 publication, and then undertook a similar project concerned with motets. John Whenham (Birmingham University, UK) has used *DARMS* in a similar way in the study of seventeenth-century Italian cantatas.

An interrelated series of bibliographical databases that were designed in the mid-Eighties are managed at various locales in Italy. These include (1) the Fondazione Levi in Venice, which has produced a series of catalogues of musical sources in Venetian libraries; (2) the University of Ferrara, which has been developing a database of madrigal texts and musical sources;[14] and (3) the Conservatorio di Santa Cecilia in Rome, where various indices of secular cantata sources have been made since about 1990.

All of these bibliographical projects have involved the conversion of *DARMS* code to commercial or proprietary systems for music printing not otherwise mentioned in this book.

11.4   *DARMS* Extensions for Special Repertories

11.4.1   Trowbridge's *Linear Music Input Language*

Musical notation of the European Renaissance spanned an array of graphical procedures. The shapes of noteheads were angular rather than rounded. The computation of note duration operated on two levels—that of *tempus* (the metrical grouping of notes at the surface level of activity) and that of *prolation* (the metrical grouping of larger note values). The unit "3" was considered "perfect,"[15] while the unit "2" and its multiples were considered "imperfect." These divisions are implied by modern notational conventions: the time signature 12/8 could be said to have a tempus of 4

---

14. In this case, the choice of *DARMS* was made by the late Thomas Walker.

15. On account of its representation of the Holy Trinity of the Roman Catholic Church.

and a prolation of 3. The exact rhythmic interpretation of many symbols varied with the context.

Among the many kinds of notation that came and went, white mensural notation was particularly prevalent. Many vocal repertories are preserved in it. Noteheads could be either filled or void. Many results seem anomalous to the eye trained for modern notation. For example, whole notes could be filled (black), while eighth notes could be void (white). The invention of dots of prolongation in the early sixteenth century led to the gradual decline of mensural notation.

The encoding of mensural notation has attracted significant interest from such scholar/software authors as Thomas Hall[16] and Norbert Böker-Heil.[17] Although Lynn Trowbridge's extensions to *DARMS* for the encoding of mensural notation are not implemented in any currently available software product, the *Linear Music Input Language* (1980) that he devised is based on an underlying logic which could fruitfully be applied to the encoding of any repertory with the same kinds of rhythmic organization.

11.4.2 Wiering's *Lute Code*

Many methods of notating music for fretted instruments, such as the lute and guitar, have been invented. In all cases the intersection of fret and string is indicated, producing the graphic representation called a tablature. In tablature a formal note name is usually irrelevant. Many schemes for representing and reproducing this array of tablatures with computers have been developed.

In 1971 the Dutch musicologist Frans Wiering developed one that relies on extensions to *Note-Processor (N-P) DARMS. Lute Code* facilitates the printing of lute

---

16. The author of the chapter on the A-R dialect of *DARMS*, of which he is also the designer, Thomas Hall's earlier work with *FASTCODE* at Princeton University in the early 1970s supported the encoding of several hundred works by composers of the Renaissance. Hall was also the author of the most ambitious program, still not superseded, for the study of source filiation (the comparison of multiple sources for the purpose of establishing their order and relationship). An even earlier project at Princeton—to encode and analyze the works of the Renaissance composer Josquin—depended on the encoding system IML-MIR [see glossary].

17. Leader of the music research group at the Staatliches Institut für Musikforschung of the Stiftung Preussischer Kulturbesitz in (West) Berlin from the late 1970s until 1993, Norbert Böker-Heil was actively involved in many computer-assisted projects in sound generation and music printing as well as musical analysis programs. His work on the Renaissance *Tenorlied*, another repertory preserved in mensural notation, resulted in a three-volume publication (Kassel: Bärenreiter, 1979-86) of music. Böker-Heil was also instrumental in advancing the music-printing capabilities of the RISM project now based in Frankfurt (see John Howard's contribution on *Plaine and Easie Code*).

tablatures and produces a rough, chordal (i.e., non-polyphonic) transcription of the tablature. The code must be used in combination with a program that converts it into *NP DARMS* according to certain specifications (tuning of the lute, key signature) made by the user.

Lute Code is intended mainly for lute music from the sixteenth and seventeenth centuries preserved in Italian and French styles of tablature. Theoretically, it can thus encode almost everything that is possible in *N-P DARMS*. The principal musical attributes that are encoded are pitch and duration—so far as they are represented in the tablature.

More extensive details about these extensions appear in Chapter 14. It is undoubtedly the case that extensions for other special repertories could be developed for *DARMS*.

11.5   Canonical *DARMS* (2): A Synoptic View

Among the various dialects and extensions represented here some use common codes for diverse purposes. Individual contributors may be unaware of these overlaps, since each attended to his own application. Those wishing to achieve some kind of synthesis of *DARMS* dialects and extensions will rapidly become aware of them. As dialects and extensions multiply, the need for implementations of canonic *DARMS* does, as its inventors rightly foresaw, become more pressing. Below we cite a few of the major differences between Erickson *DARMS* (1976) and the specific implementations described in the following chapters.

Overall, canonical *DARMS* provides many descriptors for details provided in the *Note Processor* by *dictionary codes*—that is, calls for a particular symbol without reference to the exact context. These discrepancies demonstrate how even an intensely graphics-oriented code such as *DARMS* has been swept along in the tide of mouse-based graphics applications. For example, the canonical *DARMS* list of "attributes of notes and rests" includes such categories as tremolos (and *tremolandi*), fingerings, editorial accidentals, and figured bass[18] while omitting dynamics and extended character sets. In the *Note Processor* most of the symbols are identified with a

---

18. Canonical *DARMS* provides what may be the most precise and extensive treatment of figured bass. It allows for placement of figures above or below the bass line. It differentiates the "chord mnemonic" (i.e., "V" in the expression "V_7") from the numerical figures and accidental signs. It groups one numeral and any associated accidental together as one "element." Where multiple figures are to be combined vertically, the encoding order is from bottom to top.

dictionary code and placed with a mouse. Some can also be selected with the mouse, but in this case they will be omitted from the file containing the encoding and will be unavailable for analytical uses (and printing applications in other graphical contexts).

In meeting other needs, canonical *DARMS* differentiates between "special codes for conveying musical information" and "convenience codes." The former category includes the treatment of tuplets, ossias,[19] and font sizes. The latter includes staff transposition[20] and a list of phenomena whose meanings are not obvious: *doubling mode*,[21] *equate codes*,[22] *matrix codes, comment codes*, and *distribution codes*.[23]

Canonical *DARMS* treats bar lines, literals, repetition signs, and chord analysis symbols—in common with clefs, key signatures, and meter signatures—as musical symbols unallied with notes and rests. Pride of place in the 1976 manual is given to a detailed description of vertical and horizontal positions (absolute vs. relative, etc.) and their interrelationships.

Comments can be added anywhere within a *DARMS* encoding. Some examples show the use of comments to tag themes and other matter possibly useful for later extrapolation or analysis.

References

Bauer-Mengelberg, Stefan. "The Ford-Columbia Input Language" in Barry S. Brook, ed., *Musicology and the Computer* (New York: City University of New York, 1970), pp. 53–56.

Boody, Charles George. "Non-Compositional Applications of the Computer to Music." Ph.D. dissertation, University of Minnesota, 1975.

Brinkman, Alexander R. "A Data Structure for Computer Analysis of Musical Scores" in *Proceedings of the International Computer Music Conference (Paris, 1984)*, ed. William Buxton (ICMC, 1984), pp. 233–242.

19. i.e., alternative readings.

20. This code, used in the *Note Processor*, allows a reduction in the number of digits required to encode second and subsequent staves of multi-staved instruments, such as the piano or organ, by reducing the space code by a multiple of 50.

21. Used for multiple noteheads attached to the same stems, as in double stops for the violin.

22. Used to abbreviate the encoding process for repeated material.

23. Matrix and distribution codes were left undefined.

Brinkman, Alexander R. "Johann Sebastian Bach's *Orgelbüchlein*: A Computer-Assisted Study of the Melodic Influence of the Cantus Firmus on the Contrapuntal Voices." Ph.D. dissertation, Eastman School of Music, 1978.

Brinkman, Alexander R. *Pascal Programming for Musical Research.* Chicago: University of Chicago Press, 1990.

Brinkman, Alexander R. "Representing Musical Scores for Computer Analysis," *Journal of Music Theory* 30 (1986)/2, 225–275.

"Data Representation and Manipulation: The *DARMS* Code" in *Microcomputers and Music,* ed. Gary Wittlich, John W. Schaffer, and Larry R. Babb (Englewood Cliffs, NJ: Prentice-Hall, 1986), pp. 20–22.

Erickson, Raymond. "*DARMS*—A Reference Manual." Typescript. New York: Queen's College, 1976.

Erickson, Raymond, and Anthony B. Wolff. "The *DARMS* Project: Implementation of an Artificial Language for the Representation of Music" in *Computers and Language Research,* ed. Walter A. Sedelow, Jr., and Sally Yeates Sedelow (New York: Mouton Publishers, 1983), II, 171–219.

Forte, Allen. "A Program for the Analytical Reading of Scores," *Journal of Music Theory* 10 (1966), 330–364.

Lincoln, Harry B. *The Italian Madrigal and Related Repertories: Indexes to Printed Collections, 1500-1600.* New Haven: Yale University Press, 1988.

Lincoln, Harry B. *The Latin Motet: Indexes to Printed Collections, 1500-1600.* Montreal: Institute for Medieval Music, 1993.

McLean, Bruce. "The Representation of Musical Scores as Data for Applications in Musical Computing." Ph.D. dissertation, State University of New York at Binghamton, 1988.

Morehen, John. "Thematic Cataloguing by Computer," *Fontes Artis Musicae* XXXXI/1 (1984), 32–38.

Morehen, John. "Thematic Indexing by Plotter from *DARMS* Input," *Proceedings of the Second International Symposium on Computers and Musicology, Orsay 1981* (Paris: C.N.R.S., 1983), 31–42.

Page, Steven Dowland. "Computer Tools for Information Retrieval." D. Phil. thesis, Oxford University, 1988.

Rothgeb, John. "Harmonizing the Unfigured Bass: A Computational Study." Ph.D. dissertation, Yale University, 1968.

12 *DARMS*: The *Note-Processor* Dialect

J. Stephen Dydo

DARMS, in contrast to systems developed to utilize sound information from an electronic musical keyboard, represents all elements of musical notation alphanumerically. The efficiency of *DARMS* code is facilitated by a syntax that is highly sensitive to the order and function of individual elements. Codes that fail to appear in a prescribed position may be misinterpreted or ignored.

12.1 Global Specifiers [!]

DARMS codes are of three kinds—global specifiers, local codes, and comments. Attributes that are normally global include instrument numbers, clefs, key signatures, and time signatures. These items are introduced by the exclamation point (!) and terminated by a dollar sign ($).

Comments are introduced by the letter K and terminated by a dollar sign.

The delimiter for code elements that are horizontally segmented (e.g., key signatures, bar lines, and clusters of attributes pertaining to one note) is a blank space. The delimiter for elements that are vertically segmented (e.g., clef designations for treble and bass staves in a piano part) is a comma (,).

12.1.1 Instrument Numbers [!I*n*]

Every file must begin with an instrument number in the format !I*n*. Each instrument can later be printed as a stand-alone part and as a part in a score. If stand-alone parts are not required, it is possible to encode music for a number of instruments in the same file, so long as the encodings for each instrument begin with a unique instrument number.

12.1.2 Clef Specifications [!G, !F, !C]

The most common clef specifications are !G (G clef), !F (F clef), and !C (C clef). A separate clef specification is required for each line of music[1] common to a single *instrument*. Multiple clef indications must be separated by commas. Some examples of multiple staves within a common file are these:

a grand staff for the piano	!G, !F
a string quartet	!G, !G, !C, !F
a part for six solo violins	!G, !G, !G, !G, !G, !G

The complete header information for the three oboe parts of the first Brandenburg Concerto would be:

Oboe 1:	!I2	!G	!K1-	!MC
Oboe 2:	!I4	!G	!K1-	!MC
Oboe 3:	!I5	!G	!K1-	!MC

while the header information for all three parts combined into one file would be:

Oboes 1, 2, 3:   !I2 !G, !G, !G !K1- !MC

DARMS makes provision for a number of special staves. The code !T is used to produce a "tablature"—a staff without any clef sign; the code !P produces a percussion staff. Staves with unusual numbers of lines (1–25) may be produced by suffixing to the clef code the sign # and a number; e.g., !T#6 would produce a 6-line tablature staff; !P#1 would produce a 1-line drum staff.

12.1.3 Key Signatures [!K]

The key signature is specified by !K followed by the number of sharps, flats, or naturals. If no number is given, one accidental is assumed. Accidentals are indicated by the same symbols used for notes: sharps by #, flats by -, naturals by *. Cancellations (naturals) may be combined with the new signature; however, if one wishes to indicate a compound key signature, two separate key signatures must be specified. Thus:

!K2-	= 2 flats
!K#	= 1 sharp
!K4*1#	= 3 cancelled sharps

---

1. Up to a maximum of 12.

12.1.4 Time Signatures [!M]

All time signatures begin with !M followed by the upper part (number of beats), a colon, and the beat unit. Thus, !M4:4 indicates 4/4 time; !M12:8 indicates 12/8; and !M13:16 indicates 13/16. Two exceptions are !MC (common time) and !M¢ or !MC/ (cut time), where the correct character is printed and the 4/4 time signature is assumed.

The situation which occurs in Baroque music, where the signature is merely a "2" or a "3", must be handled by completing the implicit time signature (e.g., !M2:2, !M3:2, !M3:4) and revising the graphical situation with the screen editor.

12.2 Local Codes

A "note" often will require only one or two elements of information—typically a vertical space code and a duration code. When other parameters are needed, the codes for each must be presented in the following order:

A. vertical space code (for pitch)   F. tie code
B. pitch alteration code   G. stem code
C. notehead (rest) code   H. beam code
D. duration code   I. codes for performance: slurs,
E. horizontal space code   articulations, dynamics, extended
                                               character sets, etc.

No intervening spaces may separate these note attributes. These nine types and related topics are discussed below.

12.2.1 Vertical Space Codes [0..9]

As a language designed exclusively for music printing, *DARMS* uses space codes for controlling vertical and horizontal placement. Pitch is therefore represented not explicitly but instead as a vertical position relative to a staff, which is in turn controlled by a specified clef. *DARMS* also relies heavily on space codes to indicate positioning for rests, bar lines, articulation marks, ornaments, text underlay and other symbols that require exact placement relative to a musical staff, actual or imaginary. In general, 1 indicates the lowest line in the staff (or an equivalent vertical position), 0 the space below it, 9 the highest line, 10 the space above it, and so forth. In this context, Middle C would be represented as -1 on the G clef, as 11 on the F clef, and as 5 on the (alto) C clef.

Irrespective of the clef involved, odd numbers are always positions on lines and even numbers are positions in spaces:

A rest is represented by the character R in lieu of a space code. If vertical placement other than in the middle of the staff is desired, an appropriate space code may be prefixed to this character.

One may indicate a sequence of bars of rest (notated with whole rests) with code of the form RnW, where n is the number of bars of rest. Software commands determine whether these appear as physically separate bars:

R6W

or in the abbreviated format normally used for parts:

R6W

12.2.2 Staff Transposition

If one "instrument" involves multiple staves or if one part uses more than one staff, movement from one staff to another may be accomplished by *staff transposition*. Staff transpositions go in increments of 50, rather than 1.

- Global staff transposition is introduced by an exclamation point (!) concatenated with a number that is a multiple of 50. Its effect is to transpose all the music following it.

- Local staff transposition is written as an ordinary space code arithmetically added to the space code for the staff change (e.g., 51 indicates the lowest line of the staff above the present one). Local transposition affects only the character (with no intervening delimiters) immediately following. The following example shows both local (-40 [i.e., 10 on the -50 scale]) and global (!-50) space encoding:

A space code may be used (with implicit + or explicit –) to indicate relative positions of such non-pitch elements as tempo and dynamics indications and text underlay. While !C is a default indication for the alto clef, 5!C is a more explicit indication; 3!C would indicate the mezzo-soprano clef, 7!C the tenor clef, and so forth. The tenor G or guitar clef is indicated as !G-8 or 3!G-8.

12.2.3 Pitch Alteration Codes [#, –, *]

Single and double accidentals are supported. The complete list of accidental codes is:

#	sharp	*	natural
##	double sharp	*–	natural followed by flat
–	flat	*#	natural followed by sharp
––	double flat		

Since the aim of *DARMS* is to reproduce conventional musical notation, accidentals are not repeated within the bar nor are chromatic inflections implied by the key signature explicitly stated in the encoding.

Transposition by one (? ' = *8va*) or two (? " = *15ma*) octaves is handled by adding the appropriate sign for printing, while the space code remains unaltered. Transposition by key obviously requires a change in all space codes and may require a change in some stem directions. These changes are implemented by software. Transposing instruments are represented by *DARMS* at their written pitch.

12.2.4 Notehead Codes [N*n*]

DARMS makes provision for unconventional notehead types (e.g., asterisks for drum notation, diamonds for harmonics, and squares for chant). These are supported as numeric modifiers to the duration code, with an N (= notehead) preceding the number. A stemless notehead is indicated by the code 1; a stemless half is written N1H. Currently supported notehead types are these:

N0	notehead missing	N6	"X" notehead
N1	stem missing	N7	diamond notehead, stem centered
N2	double notehead	N8	diamond notehead, stem to side
N3	triangle notehead	NR	rest in place of notehead
N4	square notehead		

12.2.5 Duration Codes [W, H, Q, E, ...]

Duration codes are identical for notes and rests; the distinction between them is that an R must precede a rest's duration code. The following list gives the durations supported by *The Note Processor*:

WWW	long	S	sixteenth (semiquaver)
WW	breve	T	thirty-second (demisemiquaver)
W	whole (semibreve)	X	sixty-fourth (hemidemisemiquaver)
H	half (minim)	Y	128th
Q	quarter (crotchet)	Z	256th
E	eighth (quaver)	G	grace note

Any duration except that of a grace note (G) may be dotted by simply adding a period (.) to the duration code. Double and triple dots are supported. Thus, a dotted eighth is written E., a dotted eighth rest is RE., a triple-dotted half is H. . ., etc.

Tuplets are encoded by showing the rhythmic ratio which they produce. The ratio is written by first writing !R, then how many beats are written, then a colon, and finally how many beats of the basic tempo the first number of beats takes up. The table below shows the most common examples:

!R3:2	triplets	!R5:4	quintuplets
!R6:4	sextuplets (like triplets)	!R7:8	septuplets (usual)
!R2:3	duplets	!R7:4	septuplets (alternative)

All durations encoded after the tuplet indication will be interpreted as being within that ratio. The signal to return to normal durations is $R. If one is going from one tuplet directly to another, the $R is not necessary.

12.2.6 Horizontal Space Codes [}]

When it is necessary to override horizontal spacing defaults, for example in a song with some long syllables, the use of a special code for minimum horizontal space will prevent one syllable from being written over another. The code for minimum space is the right curly bracket (}) followed by a number indicating the amount of space. The unit of measure is the amount of space from one staff line to the next. This unit will be proportionally enlarged or compressed with larger and smaller staff sizes. An example of its use is shown below:

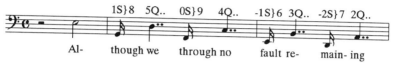

12.2.7 Ties [J]

Ties between two adjacent notes are indicated by the code J (= join) given after the duration of the note on which the tie begins. The tie will extend to the next note.

If a tie extends beyond the next note or rest, *identifiers* must be used to indicate the starting and ending note positions for the tie. The beginning of the tie may be indicated with any odd number less than 256. The end of the tie is indicated by the next higher even number. The example below connects the ties from the first two measures to the downbeat of the third:

        5RQ,11WJ1,1RH \Q,6H.J3 1HJ5D / 11WJ2,6J4,1J6 /

12.2.8 Stem Codes [U, D]

The stem direction is ordinarily calculated by *The Note Processor*, but one may override this by specifying U for an ascending stem and D for a descending stem.

It may be useful at times to adjust stem length. The stem-length specifier follows either U or D immediately and indicates the length of the stem in half-spaces. A stem is normally 7 half-spaces in length; flag placement or beam tilt may alter that length. The following example shows the effect of stem-length specifiers:

12.2.9 Beam Codes [(,)]

Beams are indicated by where they start and where they end. Parentheses are used to indicate both: " (" means "start a beam from this note," while ") " means "end a beam at this note." For instance, E(E) represents a pair of beamed eighths, while S((S S S)) produces four beamed sixteenths. Some examples of various beam groupings follow:

E(S(S)) E.(T((T))) S.((X((X))) E) S((T(T) T(T X(X) T)))

Short beams which are attached to only one note are specified by a semicolon [;] preceding the parenthesis. The parenthesis itself shows whether the short beam starts at the note (and thus goes off to the right) or ends at the note (and thus goes off to the left). All beams after the semicolon are interpreted as short beams. Therefore, if full and short beams are indicated at the same note, all of the full beams must precede all of the short ones. Some examples are:

S(;(E S);) E..(T);)) T;(((RS. T((;(S T));) S..((X;)) S.. X));))

12.2.10 Slurs [L]

Slurs are encoded almost identically to ties, except that they do not usually end at the same vertical position as that at which they started. To encode slurs between two adjacent notes place an L (= link) after the note where the slur begins; the slur will automatically extend to the next note. As with ties, if the slur extends beyond the next note or rest, the note at which the slur ends will also need an L following the other codes.

12.2.11 Articulation [>, ']

The types of articulations which are recognized without any other special symbol are:

> Accent
^ Sharp accent
_ Tenuto
' Staccato
" Staccatissimo

The following example gives instances of all of the above:

Although it is not possible to give a vertical space code for individual articulations, one may give a global space code for all articulations.

DARMS and its extensions provide a host of other articulation marks via special character combinations (introduced by a question mark [**?**]). These are some extensions used in *The Note Processor*:

?P	pedal	?D	down bow	?G	segno 1
?*	pedal up	?V	up bow	?%	segno 2
?U	organ heel	?O	harmonic circle	?/	stress sign
?<	organ toe	?Q	Bartók pizzicato	?-	unstressed sign

A global vertical position may be indicated by the code !A and cancelled by the code $A.

12.2.12 Dynamics [V]

Dynamics (*p*, *f*, *mf*, etc.) are indicated by the code V followed by the letter or letters of the dynamic, which may be any of the following: P, F, M, R, S, Z, or -. The actual dynamic may be of any length. A global vertical position may be introduced by the code !V and cancelled by the code $V.

12.2.13 Extended Character Sets [?]

DARMS makes provision for the creation of a dictionary of new symbols. These are indicated by ASCII characters which are attached to notes and rests and are treated in the same way as articulations for purposes of syntactical order. These codes are introduced by a question mark [?] and completed by a number from a table. The number assignments used by the *Note Processor* are given in Table 12.1. For example, the code 1Q?124 will produce a quarter note on the first line with a mordent below it. While some symbols can be produced by other means, these codes offer the best approach to encoding such performance information as ornamentation and basso continuo figuration, score mark-up such as rehearsal numbers, frames for ukelele and guitar chords, and grace notes.

NOTEHEADS:

34	●	quarter-note head
35	○	half-note head
36	○	whole-note head
37	⊟	breve head
38	◘	double-whole head
39	●	grace-note head (≤ quarter note)
40	○	grace-note head (≥ half note)
41	◇	white diamond (harmonic)
42	◆	black diamond (harmonic)

ACCIDENTAL SIGNS:

43	♯	sharp
44	♭	flat
45	♮	natural
46	×	double sharp
47	♯	small editorial sharp
48	♭	small editorial flat
49	♮	small editorial natural
50	×	small editorial double sharp
51			stem

CLEFS:

52	𝄞	G clef
53	𝄢	F clef
54	𝄡	C clef
55	‖	percussion clef
56	𝄞	small G clef
57	𝄢	small F clef
58	𝄡	small C clef
59	‖	small percussion clef

FLAGS:

60	♩	eighth-note flag up
61	♩	eighth-note flag down
62	♪	sixteenth-note flag up
63	♪	sixteenth-note flag down
64	♪	32nd-note flag up
65	♪	64th..256th-note flag up

66	♭	32nd-note flag down
67	♮	64th..256th-note flag down
68	♩	grace-note flag up
69	♩	grace-note flag down
70	♩	grace-note eighth flag up
71	♩	grace-note eighth flag down
72	♪	grace-note sixteenth flag up
73	♪	grace-note 32nd..256th flag up
74	♪	grace-note sixteenth flag down
75	♪	grace-note 32nd..256th flag down

RESTS:

76	▬	whole-note rest
77	▬	half-note rest
78	𝄽	quarter-note rest
79	♪	eighth-note rest
80	𝄾	sixteenth-note rest
81	𝄿	32nd-note rest
82	♪	64th..256th-note rest
83	.	dot of prolongation

METER NUMERALS:

84	**1**	1
85	**2**	2
86	**3**	3
87	**4**	4
88	**5**	5
89	**6**	6
90	**7**	7
91	**8**	8
92	**9**	9
93	**0**	0
94	**C**	common time

DYNAMICS:

95	*p*	p
96	*m*	m
97	*f*	f
98	*s*	s
99	*r*	r
100	*z*	z

ARTICULATION AND ORNAMENTATION MARKS:

101	>	accent
102	^	hard accent, up
103	v	hard accent, down
104	.	staccato
105	▾	*staccatissimo*, up
106	▴	*staccatissimo*, down
107	-	*tenuto*
108	’	breath mark
109	𝄐	fermata, up
110	𝄑	fermata, down
111	𝆖	trill
112	⌣	trill curl
113	⌇	arpeggio curl
114	𝄎	bar repeat
115	/	quarter repeat
116	//	half repeat
117	v	up bow
118	⊓	down bow
119	∪	heel (organ)
120	^	toe (organ)
121	*Ped.*	pedal depress (piano)
122	*	pedal release (piano)
123	°	harmonic
124	𝆘	mordent
125	𝆗	inverted mordent
126	⌒𝆗	mordent, variant
127	⌒𝆗	mordent, variant
128..160		[unassigned]
161	𝆗	mordent, variant
162	𝆙	turn
163	𝆚	inverted turn
164	S	vertical turn (arpeggio)
165	‹	*coule*
166	›	inverted *coule*

TUPLET NUMERALS:

167	*1*	1
168	*2*	2
169	*3*	3
170	*4*	4
171	*5*	5
172	*6*	6
173	*7*	7
174	*8*	8
175	*9*	9
176	*0*	0
177	*:*	colon for tuplet ratios

NOTES FOR METRONOME INDICATIONS:

178	𝅝	whole note
179	𝅗𝅥	half note
180	𝅘𝅥	quarter note
181	𝅘𝅥𝅮	eighth note
182	𝅘𝅥𝅯	sixteenth note
183	𝅘𝅥𝅰	32nd note

OCTAVE SPECIFIERS:

184	***8***	8va (1-octave transposition)
185	***15***	15ma (2-octave transposition)

FINGERING AND FIGURED BASS NUMERALS :

186	0	0
187	1	1
188	2	2
189	3	3
190	4	4
191	5	5
192	6	6
193	7	7
194	8	8
195	9	9
196	2+	2, altered
197	4+	4, altered
198	5+	5, altered
199	6+	6, altered
200	7+	7, altered

BAR LINES AND BRACES:

201	|	bar line
202	|	heavy bar line
203	⋮	dashed bar line
204	⋮	dotted bar line
205	⎧	straight brace, top
206	⎩	straight brace, bottom
207	⊏	rehearsal letter box, left
208	⊐	rehearsal letter box, right
209	⎧	curly brace, top
210	⎨	curly brace, middle
211	⎩	curly brace, bottom
212	⎪	curly brace, body
213	*8*	clef 8[va] sign
214	:	bar repeat dots
215	⁄	tremolando

OTHER LINES, SIGNS, AND SYMBOL COMPONENTS:

216	+	sign for time signatures
217	(	left parenthesis
218	)	right parenthesis
219	[	left bracket
220	]	right bracket
221	/	vertical slash
222	⁄	horizontal slash
223	´	stressed syllable
224	˘	unstressed syllable
225	┌	horizontal bracket, left
226	┐	horizontal bracket, right
227	-	bracket extender
228	H┐	*Hauptstimme*
229	N┐	*Nebenstimme*
230	♀	Bartok pizzicato
231	⊞	chord frame
232	⊞	chord-frame extension
233	↑	up arrow
234	↓	down arrow
235	←	left arrow
236	→	right arrow
237	O	perfect time (mensural notation)
238	C	imperfect time (mensural notation)
239	·	prolation dot for 237-8
240	-	dash for dynamics
241	⊕	*segno*, type 1
242	𝄋	*segno*, type 2

Table 12.1 Dictionary character assignments in *Note-Processor DARMS*. Positions 128–160 are not used for downloading characters.

12.2.14 Bar-Line Codes [/]

Bar lines are represented normally with a slash [/]. Many encoders prefer to allocate one line in a file to one measure in a part as an aid to proofreading the file. *DARMS* is actually indifferent to the arrangement of bars within a file.

Different types of bar lines require modifiers following or preceding the slash. Below are the symbols for various types of bar lines:

/	normal bar line	: / :	end one repeat, begin another
/ /	double (thin) bar line	/ .	dotted bar line
/ |	thin and thick bar line (end)	/ =	dashed bar line
/ :	beginning of repeat	/*	non-printing bar line
: /	end of repeat	/+	intermediate bar line

Below are examples of some of the bar-line types:

/   /:   /.   :/:   :/   //   /*   /|

Bar lines are automatically numbered by the *DARMS* interpreter, with the first bar numbered 1. If one does not wish the *DARMS* code to start at Bar 1, then when one encodes the first bar line in each line of music, one must follow the bar-line symbol immediately with the appropriate number for the bar following.

To specify a bar line which marks a metrical division within the bar, one follows the bar line with a +, to indicate that the full measure is the music following the previous bar line *plus* the music about to follow. Such intermediate bar lines are not used in calculating measure numbers; rather, they are given a measure number of −1. The *DARMS* interpreter will ignore them when figuring the number of beats in the full measure.

One may specify any kind of bar line as an intermediate bar line; the restrictions are that the total number of symbols to specify the bar line be no more than four, and that the + must be the last symbol. The following are all valid intermediate bar lines:

$$/+ \quad /:+ \quad :/:+ \quad /=+$$

The format for specifying bar-line position is ! /<*high*> | <*low*>, where <*high*> is the space code for the top of the bar line and <*low*> is the space code for the bottom. For example, ! /11 | −1 indicates that the bar lines are to start one full space above a five-line staff and end one full space below it.

12.3   Example

The encoding of the Mozart trio appears below. All five parts are encoded as one
"instrument"; alternatively, this passage could also have been encoded in five separate
files. The format, which places most measures on a seperate line, is purely stylistic.

Comments encoded between a K and a $ are comments that are ignored by the
DARMS compiler. Beam beginnings and endings are encoded here by left and right
parentheses, but in most instances they can be correctly generated automatically.
What might logically be represented as a tie (J) in Bars 11–12 of the viola part is here
represented as a slur (L) because of its slanted positioning.

```
!I1 !G,!G,!G,!C,!F
K Begin clarinet part $
!M3:4,15@Clarinet in A$ 6E(L1VP 8) /
10( 8) 13QL2 10E(L1 8) /
7( 9) 11QL2 9E(L1 7) /
6( 5 8 7 10 9)L2 /
7#QL1 8L2 6E(L1 8) /
10( 8) 13QL2 10E(L1 8) /
7*( 9) 11QL2 RQ / RW /
RQ RQ !R3 0E(L1 -3 -5) /
$R -3E(L2 0' 2' 4' 7' 9)' /
11(L1 10 9 8 9 7)L2 /
6HL1 8E( 7)L2 / 6Q RQ :/: !-50
K Begin first violin $
!K3# !M3:4,14@Violin I$ RQ /
RQ 4QVP Q /
RQ Q Q /
RQ 3 3 /
RQ 4 4 /
RQ 4 4 /
2 RQ 6E(L1 4#) /
5( 7) 9QL2 6E(L1 4#) /
5( 7) 9QL2 RQ / RW / RW /
-1E(L1 1 -1 1 0 1)L2 / -1Q RQ :/: !-50
K Begin second violin $
!K3# !M3:4,14@Violin II$ RQ /
RQ 1QVP Q /
RQ 2 2 /
RQ 0 0 /
RQ -1 -1 /
RQ 1 1 /
0 RQ 3*L1 /
2H 3*Q /
2HL2 RQ / RW / RW /
-3HL1 -4#QL2 / -3 RQ :/: !-50
```

```
K Begin viola $
!K3#  !M3:4,13@Viola$ RQ /
RQ 5VP 5 /
RQ 4 4 /
RQ 4 4 /
RQ 3 3 /
RQ 5 5 /
4 RQ 7L1 /
6H 7Q /
6HL2 RQ / RW / RW /
0H.L1 / QL2 RQ :/: !-50
K Begin cello $
!K3#  !M3:4,12@Violoncello$ RQ /
9QVP RQ RQ /
5 RQ RQ /
6 RQ RQ /
7 RQ RQ /
4 RQ RQ /
5 RQ RQ /
RW / RW / RW / RW /
-1L1' -1' -1L2' / 2 RQ :/:
```

Example 12.1. *N-P DARMS* encoding of the Mozart trio.

12.4   Special Features of *DARMS*

12.4.1 Repetitive Information Codes

DARMS has two provisions for reducing the encoding of repetitive information. These are the carry feature, which operates only within the bar and on only one attribute at a time, and the pattern repetition specification, which can facilitate the transcription of long passages of musical sequences.

A. THE CARRIED-SPACE CODE

The *carry feature* permits the encoder the liberty of not reiterating within the bar elements of information that remain constant. If a measure in common time contains 8 eighth notes, it is necessary to give the duration code (E) only once. Similarly, if the note on the second space occurs multiple times within a measure, its space code (4) may be given only once. If in a series of notes the pitch and duration parameters are identical, the encoding of either attribute (but not both simultaneously) may take advantage of the carry feature. The example below gives some examples of carried space codes:

The longer the passage, the greater the benefit of using the carry feature. Consider the following example from Bach:

B. THE PATTERN-REPETITION CODE [!X]

For phrases in which the same pattern of pitches and durations occurs over and over, the more formal repetition marker !X may be used. The format is !X*n* <*code*> $X, where *n* is a number specifying how many repeats are to be done and <*code*> is the *DARMS* code to be repeated. Everything up until the $X will be repeated *n* times. Any valid *DARMS* symbols may be repeated. Repeated measures will be incremented in the interpreted file. The following fragment is an example of a one-measure phrase repeated 12 times:

```
2Q. 3E / !X12 4E( 1 -1 1) / $X -3H. //
```

12.4.2 Text Underlay [a..$]

A text syllable to be appended to a note is introduced by the commercial @ sign and terminated by the dollar sign ($). A simple example of text, to be printed as lyrics, is:

```
-1Q@Do$ 0@re$ 1@mi$ 2@fa$ / 3H@sol$ 4Q@la$ 5@ti$ / 6W@do$ /
```

This will be printed as:

Text can be attached to any printable symbol, except for some global symbols (such as a clef or instrument number). When attaching text to a note no comma is used, since the text is regarded as a part of the note structure. However, for all other symbols, one must insert a comma between the symbol and the text. In *The Note*

Processor the default base line of the text syllable is -6. This may be altered by an explicit space code with global effect, e.g., -10!@.

12.4.3 Push Codes [\]

Push codes are non-printing rests indicated by the backslash (\). There is no carry feature for push codes, and pushing beyond a bar line is not allowed. One may attach other symbols to a push code, such as text or dynamics. The code \2H will push to a horizontal position two half notes to the right. (Note that this represents more space than a whole note.) Push codes provide one way to place symbols between notes. They can also be used to show unmeasured notation, as in this harmonic analysis:

```
!I1  !G  !K2#  0H(D,7N1Q  !N1  \E,1H,6Q  \E,5Q  \E,4H,8Q
\E,10Q  $N  0H)D,9N1Q  //
```

The printed copy is then:

12.4.4 Chordal Representation [,]

Chords are created by connecting a series of notes with each other by commas. All of the essential elements of each note (space code, accidental, duration, if needed) must be specified *before* the comma. In chords, things such as beams, dynamics, articulations, etc., will ordinarily be specified only once.

12.4.5 Linear Decomposition [!&..$&]

Linear decomposition, a method for representing multiple voices or strands of information on a single staff, addresses one of the significant difficulties encountered in the encoding of Western music. It is useful for such tasks as the following:

• the breaking up of polyphonic music into its individual lines;

• the breaking up of Baroque bass parts into the bass line notes and figured bass symbols;

• the separation of vocal music into the melody and its lyrics; and

• the differentiation in piano music of fingering information and the musical score.

Linear decomposition is initiated with the code ! & and terminated by the code $&.
Entrances of new voices are indicated with the code &. A simple case of two-part
counterpoint appears below:

This passage can be represented without linear decomposition, by using push codes
to create correct horizontal spacing, as the *DARMS* code below illustrates:

```
!I1 !G !K2# 3HU,0D 2QU,-2HD 5QU / 5HU,1H.D \Q,4Q. \E,-
3QD 3E / 2W;,-3 //
```

With linear decomposition, the same passage appears as:

```
!I1 !G !K2# !& !U 3H 2Q 5 / H 4Q. 3E / 2W; // & !D 0H
-2 / 1. -3Q / W // $&
```

Here decomposition often provides an easier or clearer way of representing the music.
In other instances, such as that shown below, decomposition may provide the only
way of representing the music:

```
!I2 !F !MC !& !U 11RE 11E( E 12) 13( 11 13 14) /
15Q 13 14 11E( 12) / 13 /*
& !D 1RE 9E( E 10) 13( 11 13 14) /
15( 6 9 8) 7Q 6E( 5) / \E,4H /* $&
```

The above example could not be input without linear decomposition, due to the fact
that it contains simultaneous beam systems.

12.4.6 Import and Export of Musical Examples

The Note Processor supports the export of music files to text and graphics documents
through utilities to create TIFF, EPS, and other graphics file formats. The optical
recognition program *MusicReader*[2] by William McGee and Paul Merkley creates *N-P
DARMS* as well as Standard MIDI Files.

---

2. Described in the glossary.

13   *DARMS*: The A-R Dialect

Thomas Hall

A-R Editions has been typesetting music electronically for its own publications and as a service to other music publishers since 1981. By the end of 1995, it and other users of its software had engraved well over 150,000 pages of music for publication, each of them first encoded in *DARMS*. *DARMS* has proven itself a remarkably well-conceived language and although we have always felt free to modify it for our own uses (we receive very little pre-encoded music), it has been our experience that most of the changes we at some point made to the actual syntax of the language were eventually regretted and discarded. With simple pre-processing to perform character/string substitutions, almost any standard *DARMS* file—with some implementation limitations noted below—can be transformed into the A-R dialect and parsed by our programs.

The A-R dialect evolved for several reasons:

1. *DARMS* was originally designed for the keypunch. Modern computer terminals have a different layout and an expanded character set. Because speed is of great importance in a production environment, we have substituted single keystrokes for many of the multi-character tokens, changed some codes to keys more readily accessible on the keyboard, and used the expanded character set to improve the mnemonics of the language.

2. The specification of the language is incomplete; instances of this are rare and relatively unimportant, however.

3. Music notation continues to evolve. We have had to expand the encoding capabilities to allow for such styles as rock guitar tablature, modern editions of medieval Greek chant, and various popular music "easy play" notations. Generally these expansions are done through the *DARMS* dictionary facility.

4. Some encoding can be avoided by using logic provided by software. We have added a number of operators to instruct the processing software to generate certain information automatically.

The following brief overview of the A-R dialect is not meant to be exhaustive of the differences between standard *DARMS* and A-R *DARMS*. It identifies some of the issues that should be involved in modernizing and standardizing *DARMS*.

13.1   Token Substitutions

Some simplifications of *DARMS* code are shown in Table 13.1.

Canonical *DARMS*	A-R *DARMS*	Meaning
!I	I or i	Instrument
!F	F	F clef
!G	G	G clef: The upper case distinguishes the G clef from the grace-note duration g
!C	C	C clef
!M	M	Meter signature
!K	K	Key signature
K...$	k...$	Comment
(	[	Using [and] for beams avoids the shift key needed for (and)
)	]	
¬[1]	\	The *push* operator
¢	~	Cut time

Table 13.1 A-R *DARMS* code substitutions.

1. The "logical not" operator found on keypunch machines.

Regarding *DARMS* input in general, an optical recognition program by Ichiro Fujinaga has been rigorously tested with *A-R DARMS* and is currently used under license by A-R Editions, Inc.

13.2 Example

The use of these substitutions is demonstrated in the A-R *DARMS* encoding of Bars 1–12 of the second trio from Mozart's Clarinet Quintet, which appears below.

```
i1 G M3:4,35@Trio II.$
[611,v(p) 8] / [30 8] 33q12 [3011 8] [7 9] 31q12 [911 7] [6 5 8 7 30
9]12 7#q1 8 [611 8] [30 8] 33q12 [3011 8] [7* 9] 31q12 rq
rw rqq [0e311 17e3s 15e3] [1712 0' 2' 4' 7' 9'] [3111 30 9 8 9 7]12
/ 6h11 [8 7]12 6q rq :/!/

i2 G K3# M3:4 rq / rq 4qvp q r q q r 3 3 r 4 4 r 4 4 2
r [611 4#] [5 7] 9q12 [611 4#] [5 7] 9q12 rq r2w / [1911 1 19 1 0
1]12 19q rq :/!/

i3 G K3# M3:4 rq / r 1qvp q r 2 2 r 0 0 r 19 q r 1 1 0 rq 3*q11 2h
3*q 2h12 rq r2w / 17h11 16#q12 17q rq :/!/

i4 C K3# M3:4 rq / r 5qvp 5 r 4 4 r 4 4 r 3 3 r 5 5 4 r 711 6h 7q
6h12 rq r2w / 3h.1 2q rq :/!/

i5 F K3# M3:4 rq / 9qvp r r 5 r r 6 r r 7 r r 4 r r 5 r r r4w /
19q'11 q' q'122 rq :/!/
```

Example 13.1 Start of the second trio from Mozart's Clarinet Quintet as encoded in A-R *DARMS*. In this example the lower-case letter l is distinguished from the number 1 by an underline, e.g., l.

13.3 New Tokens or Encodings

The codes described below have been newly introduced in A-R *DARMS*.

13.3.1 Chord [c..$]

The c functions syntactically as the @ does, but it signals that the following literal is to be formatted by the software as a chord title. The $ may be omitted if the chord title is followed by a space or comma delimiter.

13.3.2 Measure [m..$]

The m functions syntactically as the @ does, but it signals that the following literal is to be formatted by the software as a measure number. This number is also used to update the software's automatic measure numbering. The $ may be omitted if the measure number is followed by a space or comma delimiter.

13.3.3 Meter Code with Time-in-Measure Definition

The software automatically generates bar lines according to an internal table of meter signatures. If the time in a measure for a specific meter signature should be different from the default, the user may specify the time by an asterisk (*) followed by a floating-point number representing whole notes, e.g., Mo/*3.

13.3.4 Stem Code Suffixes [z, x, *et al.*]

Standard stem codes may be suffixed as follows:

z	for buzz roll on stem
x	code for X on stem
|n	to specify stem length, where *n* is the number of spaces
/	to indicate grace-note-like slash

An example is 3quz.

13.3.5 Bar-line Code Suffixes [ ), -]

New suffixes to bar-line codes are listed below:

)	to indicate mid-system bracket curls on thick bar line
–	to indicate a half bar line

13.4   New Operators

If the original plan for processing of *DARMS* were followed, most of the following operators would be handled by a canonizer. However, A-R *DARMS* is not translated into canonical *DARMS*. We have introduced the new operators listed below.

13.4.1 Text-Layer Linear Decomposition [!^ or !&^]

The input of lyrics using expressions embraced by the signs @ . . . $ is one of the most time-consuming aspects of *DARMS* encoding. We have developed a technique of typing a verse of lyrics as a single text block, interspersing numbers in the syllables to indicate melismas. The program then matches syllables to notes.

13.4.2 Space Codes [!+*n*, !-*n*]

Where *n* is the number of space codes to be added to, or subtracted from, space codes on all following notes: this is an extension of the !+50 staff-transposition operator. Here are some examples:

!+1	All notes are one space code higher than encoded.
!+50-1	All notes are in the lower staff and one space code lower than encoded.

These directives may be suffixed to linear decomposition codes, e.g., !&+3.

13.4.3 Style Properties [N*n* or !N*n*]

Where *n* is the number of a user-definable set of styling properties: this operator is used mainly for non-metric passages of notes, such as the incipits in Renaissance notation that precede each staff in an historical edition. These incipits are generally non-metrical and require special note spacing and styling.

Publishers have many differing ways of notating voice ranges. By placing the voice range within an N . . .N$ styling passage, the program can be instructed to style the music differently, perhaps omitting stems and automatically drawing a line between the noteheads.

13.4.4 Noteheads [!a*n*]

Where *n* is a notehead number: this code produces automatic noteheads. All noteheads following this operator are given a notehead code of *n*, until cancelled by !$.

13.4.5 Stems [!u, !d, !e, !h*n*, !l*n*]

These codes govern stem directions:

!u	All following stems go up
!d	All following stems go down
!e	Cancel automatic stemming direction

.

These operators override system stemming defaults. It is also permissible to suffix u, d, or e to a linear decomposition command, as in !&u,3q.

Two related variables are these:

!hn   Where *n* is a space code, the operator !h forces all stems to terminate at the specified space code. This is particularly useful in percussion parts on one- or two-line staves, where all beaming must be horizontal.

!|*n*   Where *n* is a stem length, in half-spaces, all stems on notes following the operator !| are of fixed length. This operator is cancelled by !$.

13.4.6 Leger Lines [!L or !l]

This operator cancels leger lines. All notes following will be notated without leger lines. The operator is cancelled by !$.

13.5   Syntactical Changes to Special Features

13.5.1 The Space Delimiter

In order to facilitate the reconstruction of the score in software, we make the following distinction among *DARMS* tokens:

- Only clefs, key signatures, meter signatures, bar lines, and notes may be delimited as horizontally distinct in the score.

- All other tokens are attributes of these and positioned in relation to them.

Thus, a code such as the following, indicating that a literal is positioned somewhere between two notes, is ambiguous in A-R *DARMS*:

```
3q 33@Tenor$ 4q
```

In A-R *DARMS* this would be encoded:

```
3q,\e,33@Tenor^$ 4q
```

That is, the literal must be an attribute of the note and positioned in relation to it. In cases such as this one, the encoder must make a decision about positioning the symbol.[2]

That only certain symbols command horizontal spacing in the score is a major departure from the *DARMS* specification, but one that has not limited the usefulness of the language to us. Not only is the processing software greatly simplified, but also the encoding process is conceptually simplified.

13.5.2 The Dictionary Facility [?]

We have found it necessary to expand the dictionary facility to allow greater control over the shaping of an object on an instance-by-instance basis. To do this, we allow any characters other than a comma (,) and a blank space to be suffixed to the dictionary code. If the dictionary code does not terminate with either delimiter, a $ must be used as a terminator. In the following example

```
3q,6,9,3|9?;h50$,@lyric$
```

the semicolon dictionary character (;) indicates a wavy-line arpeggio and the three characters that follow the semicolon indicate that the arpeggio should be drawn at 50% of its normal horizontal weight.

13.6   Features not Implemented in A-R *DARMS*

The following features of *DARMS* are not implemented in A-R *DARMS*:

- space-pattern format
- base-increment format
- chord structure definers and references
- equate codes

We found that encoding time was not significantly improved by the first three of these features and that their implementation and use were of such complexity that coding errors and training time were prohibitively increased.

Although originally implemented, our equate code facility has died from disuse, partly because errors made in equate passages tended to be obscure and difficult for

---

2. The carat (^) in the literal is a quad center command.

our coders and syntax-checking programs to handle, and partly because modern text editors make it easy to duplicate strings and to store frequently used strings under function keys.

13.7   Further Comments

For the purposes of music engraving in large volume and in a wide variety of styles, *DARMS* has been a remarkably effective tool for us at A-R Editions, Inc. Because almost all of our engraving work is done from manuscript, we do not expect scanning to replace coding in the near future. The only reason we might adapt to other encoding languages would be if our clients begin to submit pre-coded music in a volume sufficient to justify the programming costs. If such a time comes, it would be helpful to have to deal with a single standard interchange language. *DARMS*, with some simple modernization and standardization, would be ideal for such purposes.

However, it is not clear that an ASCII code such as *DARMS* is the proper focus of efforts at standardization. Most musical software applications follow the model:

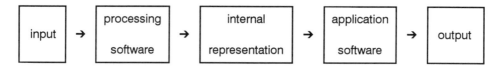

Input may be accomplished by a variety of means including encoding, keyboard performance, mousing, scanning, etc. Output will be in a variety of forms: notation, performance instructions (such as MIDI), analysis results, etc. Almost all applications that deal with notation will represent the score in some internal binary format. The internal representation is likely to have information added after the input process, either by the processing software or by human intervention through a software editor.

It is this data, not the input data, that needs to be made accessible to other applications. To translate this data back into a complex artificial language such as *DARMS* or *SGML* seems counterproductive; a formatted parametric representation of the score, in ASCII or binary, would be easier to devise and easier to process.

At the same time that this parametric representation is devised, a language for retrieving musical information should be written and implemented in a library of procedures—e.g., *Open_score* ( ), *Get_current_key* ( ), *Get_chord* ( ), etc. The format of the data then becomes irrelevant to the researcher. This approach greatly lessens the problem of varying dialects among the encoding languages.

14   *DARMS* Extensions for Lute Tablatures

Frans Wiering

Lute Code provides a way of representing tablature for the lute. It can be transcribed using a program called *LUTE* into both a *DARMS* representation of the tablature and a parallel transcription in common music notation (see Examples 14.1b and 14.2b). The code mainly represents pitch and duration as they are given in tablatures.

Lute tablature provides one line for each of the instrument's six strings. The neck of the instrument is fretted, and each fret is represented by either a letter or a number; no fretting is required to play an open string. The tablature gives the positions of the fingers on the neck of the instrument in much the same way as codes for conventional notation give *x* and *y* coordinates for placement on the staff. In the tablature, the durational values are indicated by headless stems and flags above the grid that represents the neck and gives the "pitch" values.

When *Lute Code* is used with the *Note Processor*, the program *LUTE* generates three *DARMS instruments*, which represent respectively the six-line tablature, the conventional notation on a two-stave grand staff, and a series of durational values. The canonical *DARMS* pitch values found in these files are reckoned from the treble of the grand staff.

There are two principal differences between *N-P DARMS* and *Lute Code*:

- Some control tokens, in particular !I1 at the beginning of a *DARMS* file, are superfluous, since by definition each file at input is concerned with only one instrument.

- The space code of each note token in *N-P DARMS* is replaced by a series of characters that represent the tablature chord. These chord codes consist of two parts: (1) the chord code *per se* and (2) a *DARMS* duration code.

14.1   Italian Tablature

Example 14.1 illustrates Italian-style tablature using Galilei's "Il Fronimo." Here the positions of the fingers on the neck of the lute are represented by numbers. The lowest (written) symbol of each chord is encoded first. Hyphens are used for strings that are not played; those following the highest written note can be left out. Durations are indicated by the usual *DARMS* codes; r represents a repeated chord, + a tied note. See, for example, Bar 6, represented on Line 7: here the + prolongs the 5 of the preceding chord. The input code is as follows:

```
K V. Galilei -- Ricercar 1 uit Fronimo $   --.
20-12Q,20@Ricercar del primo Tuono per h$ 40-2-0E 52-20E. /
rS 52-4-2E 42--4S ---4 -2-3E /
2-44-2 -2 -45 ---42 /
00---4 ----2 -2--0 -0-3-4 /
-2-4-2 2-4 -45 7----7 /
45-2 52-20 +-34-2S 4 2E /
--2-4S 2 12E 224--2 ---4 /
--01 -0 ---2-4 0 /
--3 -2---2 4-2 -----1 /
52-4-2 2-3 +-2-4 0-3 /
-3--2 --2 --3-4 -2--0 /
-0-2 0-2 -2320 5 /
+0-2-0 4 +30-2 2 /
-3 -0-0 2---42 --4 /
20-12- -0 --0 --22 /
--0 20-1 4+-2 -2 /
--34 2 --2-4 0-4 /
--5-2 -3 -2 -20-1 /
-3--2 --2 ----4 -23 /
-++-0S --2 -20E -0---4 ---3 /
-244-2 -35 ----2S -2 -30E /
0-3-4 --1 2-345 -3542 /
-355-3S -2 -0-0 ---2 2---42 0 -244E /
-4542;
/|
```

Example 14.1a *Lute Code* input for Italian tablature (Vincenzo Galilei, "Il Fronimo").

The music that this example generates appears below:

Example 14.1b Italian tablature and its transcription (Galilei's "Il Fronimo").

Three intermediate codes are generated by the input code shown in Example 14.1a. These are shown in Examples 14.1c, 14.1d, and 14.1e.

Example 14.1c contains the *DARMS* code for the six-line tablature which conveys pitch information by giving finger positions.

```
!I1
!T#6%200,!G,!F
!N0 !U
!/11|-50
K V. Galilei -- Ricercar 1 uit Fronimo $
12Q,0@ 2$,2@ 0$,6@ 1$,8@ 2$,20@Ricercar del primo Tuono per h$
```

```
12E,0@ 4$,2@ 0$,6@ 2$,10@ 0$
12E.,0@ 5$,2@ 2$,6@ 2$,8@ 0$
/
12S,0@ 5$,2@ 2$,6@ 2$,8@ 0$
12E,0@ 5$,2@ 2$,6@ 4$,10@ 2$
12S,0@ 4$,2@ 2$,8@ 4$
\S,6@ 4$
12E,2@ 2$,6@ 3$
/
\E,0@ 2$,4@ 4$,6@ 4$,10@ 2$
\E,2@ 2$
\E,2@ 4$,4@ 5$
\E,6@ 4$,8@ 2$

\E,0@ 0$,2@ 0$,10@ 4$
\E,8@ 2$
\E,2@ 2$,8@ 0$
\E,2@ 0$,6@ 3$,10@ 4$
/
\E,2@ 2$,6@ 4$,10@ 2$
\E,0@ 2$,4@ 4$
\E,2@ 4$,4@ 5$
\E,0@ 7$,10@ 7$
/
\E,0@ 4$,2@ 5$,6@ 2$
\E,0@ 5$,2@ 2$,6@ 2$,8@ 0$
12S,0@ +$,4@ 3$,6@ 4$,10@ 2$
\S,0@ 4$
12E,0@ 2$
/
```

```
12S,4@ 2$,8@ 4$
\S,0@ 2$
12E,0@ 1$,2@ 2$
\E,0@ 2$,2@ 2$,4@ 4$,10@ 2$
\E,6@ 4$
/
\E,4@ 0$,6@ 1$
\E,2@ 0$
\E,6@ 2$,10@ 4$
\E,0@ 0$
/
\E,4@ 3$
\E,2@ 2$,10@ 2$
\E,0@ 4$,4@ 2$
\E,10@ 1$
/
\E,0@ 5$,2@ 2$,6@ 4$,10@ 2$
\E,0@ 2$,4@ 3$
\E,0@ +$,4@ 2$,8@ 4$
\E,0@ 0$,4@ 3$
/
\E,2@ 3$,8@ 2$
\E,4@ 2$
\E,4@ 3$,8@ 4$
\E,2@ 2$,8@ 0$
/
\E,2@ 0$,6@ 2$
\E,0@ 0$,4@ 2$
\E,2@ 2$,4@ 3$,6@ 2$,8@ 0$
\E,0@ 5$
/
```

Example 14.1c *DARMS* code for the tablature finger positions ("pitch").

Example 14.1d contains the *DARMS* code for the transcription in conventional notation.

```
K V. Galilei -- Ricercar 1 uit Fronimo $
4Q,0Q,-43#Q,-45Q      3E,0E,-47E        -2S,-44S            6E,1E,-41E,-48E
5E,0E,-42E,-49E       -45E              4S                  4EJ,-1E
6E.,1E.,-42E.,-46E.   1E,-46E           3#E,1E              4E,-2E,-44E
/                     0E,-42#E,-47E      4E,1E,-1#E,-48E    3E,-1E
6S,1S,-42S,-46S       /                 -41E                /
6E,1E,-41E,-48E       1E,-41E,-48E       /                  2E,-45E
5S,1S,-44S            4E,-1#E           -41E,-43#E          -2E
-41S                  2#E,0E            0E                  -1E,-44E
1E,-42#E              7E,-45E           -42E,-47E           1E,-46E
/                     /                 3E                  /
4E,-1#E,-41E,-48E     5E,3E,-42E         /                  0E,-42E
1E                    6EJ,1E,-42E,-46E  -1E                 3E,-2E
2#E,0E                6S,-1S,-41S,-48S  1E,-48E             1E,-1E,-42E,-46E
-41E,-45E             5S                5E,-2E              6EJ
/                     4E                -49#E               /
                      /                 /
```

Example 14.1d *DARMS* code for the transcription in conventional notation.

The code for the durational values appears below in Example 14.1e. Its purpose is to fill the bass staff, which the *Note Processor* would otherwise consider to be empty, since all notes are encoded as if they appear in the treble staff. On this example each column represents one bar. Bars should be read from left to right.

```
K V. Galilei -- Ricercar 1 uit Fronimo $
\Q    \S    \E    \E    \E    \E    \S    \E    \E    \E    \E    \E
\E    \E    \E    \E    \E    \E    \S    \E    \E    \E    \E    \E
\E.   \S    \E    \E    \E    \S    \E    \E    \E    \E    \E    \E
/     \S    \E    \E    \E    \S    \E    \E    \E    \E    \E    \E
      \E    /     /     /     \E    \E    /     /     /     /     /
      /                       /     /
```

Example 14.1e *DARMS* code for tablature durations.

14.2 French Tablature

For French tablature, where fret numbers are replaced by fret letters, there is one other modification: the character r is eliminated for a repeated chord. The need for it seemed rarely to occur in this repertory.

In the next example, lower-case letters are employed instead of numbers. The colon (:) separates contrabass strings and ordinary strings. The verticule (|) is a symbol that indicates that notes should be played simultaneously. The input code for the piece called "La Dedicasse" by Gaultier (Example 14.2b) is shown in Example 14.2a.

```
K Denis Gaultier, La dedicasse (Apel, Notation, facs. 20)$
a---:-abaQ. ---aS --b ---aE e -cE. --cS / -abE a---:Q dE c --c ae --cS -e /
cE a: -a ---a ---c --b -cccE. ---eS / -e-|aE c -e --d a-:--eeQ ---eE ----a /
a----:--e-cQ -cE --c a---:--caaQ -abE -c /
-e-aaQ --dca --eeE ----c a--: --e /
--dcE -c --eeE. ----aS a--:--eccQ -cdE. ----aS / a-eeQ -cE --e --eecH :/:
----cQ aE ----e ----c --e --cc ---e /
ce--aQ a-:--|-aE ---a ----a a---: --b-a ----d /
--ccE a: -----c a c--|-c ----a -----c e /
-a--eE a---: -----e ----e -----g ----a -e--|eE. -----eS /
--c--cE -c ---c-c ---e -e-feQ --ccc / ce-|cQ ----aE -f a-ceQ -eE ----a /
a:|--ccE a--: ----c a-:--|-a a---:--c-aQ a-|eE --c /
a---:--b-aE -a -----e -c-|-c -e-aeQ --cceE. ----cS /
----eE a-: -e --f --feeH :/: ---eQ --eE --c -e-a -a ---c eS ---b /
---cE c ----a a-: a-----:--|-c --e ----e a---: /
a--:---|-cE ----c ----e a-: ---fe -----g -e-e-gE. -----fS /
----gE --g --e-e ----g -e-|-e ---f --cc-cE. -----eS /
--e-cE a -----e --c -e-|-e ----a --cc-cE. -----cS /
-c-|-cE e -a-aeQ a:-|-ce ----cE a--: / a-:--f-cQ -eg-a a:-e-c -c-cE ---c /
a-|eE --e ----c -c -e ----a ac-e ----aS ---e /
----aE a---: -a --b --baaH :/
```

Example 14.2a *Lute Code* input for French tablature (Denis Gaultier, "La Dedicasse").

The corresponding music appears below:

Example 14.2b French lute tablature and its transcription (Gaultier's "La Dedicasse").

The translations of the three parts of the display are generated as they were for the preceding example.

15   *DARMS* Extensions for Mensural Notation

Lynn M. Trowbridge

For the task of encoding a large repertory of fifteenth-century chansons, the *Linear Music Input Language* (1980), a modified subset of *DARMS* that facilitates dealing with the durational complexities of Renaissance music, was devised. The logic underlying this system could fruitfully be applied to the encoding of any repertory with the same rhythmic characteristics.

One general innovation is that in specifying the voice part being encoded, the total number of voices in the work is indicated. For reliable analytical results one must differentiate between a *Cantus Superius* in a two-voice texture, a *Cantus* in a three-voice texture, a *Cantus* in a four-voice texture, and a *Superius* in a five-voice work. Although this is irrelevant to representation *per se*, it has enviable strengths for analytical studies.

15.1   Pitch

Staff placement codes follow customary *DARMS* practice. The bottom line of any staff is in Vertical Space 1.

Following the original provisions of *DARMS*, codes for moveable clefs, preceded by an exclamation mark, are formed by coupling the line number with the sign C, F, or G (!3G, !7C).

In key codes, a flat is indicated by a minus (–) and a numeral indicates the number of pitch classes affected, as in other versions, but a sharp is represented by a plus (+). Thus, !K1+ introduces a work with one sharp.

15.2   Meter and Duration

Meter involves two variables—tempus and prolation. Perfect (triple) tempus was expressed by a circle O, imperfect (duple) tempus by a C (understood to be an incomplete circle). The numerals 3 and 2 are generally believed to have been used to indicate perfect (trripartite) and imperfect (bipartite) prolation respectively.

In the *Linear Music Input Language* (*LMIL*) the tempus and prolation variables are treated as if the music were in modern notation. The following meter codes are employed:

Mensural Sign	*DARMS* Meter Code
C	! M2 : 4
O	! M3 : 4
C2	! M2 : 2
₵	! M2 : 2
Ɔ	! M2 : 2
O2	! M3 : 2
Ⓞ	! M6 : 4
C3	! M6 : 4
O3	! M9 : 4
₵	! M6 : 8
⊙	! M9 : 8

The following tables, in which *DARMS* codes such as W (whole) and H (half) are substituted for the names of the original notes (*fusa, semiminim*, etc.), indicate how to interpret durations within these various metrical contexts.[1] Table 15.1 gives the code itself.

---

1. Those interested in the meaning of the terms used in Tables 15.1 and 15.2 may wish to consult specialized studies of Renaissance notation, such as Willi Apel, *The Notation of Polyphonic Music, 900-1600*, rev. 5th edn. (Cambridge: Harvard University Press, 1961).   Theories of rhythmic interpretation cointinue to evolve. See, for example, Margaret Bent, "The Use of the Sign Ⓞ," *Early Music* XXIV/2 (1996), 199-226.

Mensural Name	Note Shape	Modern Meter Signature							
		2/4	3/4	2/2	3/2	6/4	9/4	6/8	9/8
Fusa	♪	T	T	T	T	T	T	T	T
Semiminim	♪	S	S	S	S	S	S	S	S
Dotted semiminim	♪.	S.	S.	S.	S.	S.	S.	S.	S.
Colored minim	↓	&2/3 E*	E	&2/3 E*	&2/3 E*	E	E		
Colored minim (+ semibreve)	↓	S	S	S	S	S	S	S	S
Minim	↓	E	E	E	E	E	E	E	E
Dotted minim	↓.	E.	E.	E.	E.	E.	E.	E.	E.
Colored semibreve	◆	&2/3 Q*	Q	&2/3 Q*	&2/3 Q*	Q	Q	Q	Q
Colored semibreve (+ minim)	◆	E.	E.	E.	E.	E.	E.		
Imperfect	◇	Q	Q	Q	Q	Q	Q	Q	Q
Perfect semibreve	◇							Q	Q
Dotted semibreve	◇ •	Q.	Q.	Q.	Q.	Q.	Q.		
Colored breve	▬	&2/3 H*	H	&2/3 H*	&2/3 H*	H	H		H
Imperfect breve	⊟	H	H	H	H	H	H	H.	H.
Perfect breve	⊟		H.			H.	H.		WJE
Dotted breve	⊟•	H.		H.	H.				
Colored long	◥	&2/3	W	&2/3	W	W	W.		
Imperfect long	⊐	W	W.	W	W	W.	W.	W.	BJQ
Perfect long	⊐				W.		BJQ		
Dotted long	⊐˙	W.	BJQ	W.		BJQ		BJQ	B.JQJE
Imperfect maxima	⊐	B	B.	B	B.	B.	B.JWJH	B.	B.JWJH

Table 15.1 *DARMS-LMIL* rhythmic codes for mensural note values.

Mensural Name	Note Shape	Modern Meter Signature							
		2/4	3/4	2/2	3/2	6/4	9/4	6/8	9/8
Fusa	♪	3	3	3	3	3	3	3	3
Semiminim	♩	6	6	6	6	6	6	6	6
Dotted semiminim	♩.	9	9	9	9	9	9	9	9
Colored minim	↓	8	12	8	8	12	12		
Colored minim (+ semibreve)	↓	6	6	6	6	6	6	6	6
Minim	↓	12	12	12	12	12	12	12	12
Dotted minim	↓.	18	18	18	18	18	18	18	18
Colored semibreve	◆	16	24	16	16	24	24	24	24
Colored semibreve (+ minim)	◆	18	18	18	18	18	18		
Imperfect semibreve	◇	24	24	24	24	24	24	24	24
Perfect semibreve	◇							36	36
Dotted semibreve	◇·	36	36	36	36	36	36		
Colored breve	▬	32	48	32	32	48	48		72
Imperfect breve	⊟	48	48	48	48	48	48	72	72
Perfect breve	⊟		72			72	72		108
Dotted breve	⊟·	72		72	72				
Colored long	▮	64	96	64	96	96	14		
Imperfect long	⊓	96	14	96	96	14	14	14	216
Perfect long	⊓				14		21		
Dotted long	⊓·	14	21	14		21		21	324
Imperfect maxima	⊐	19	28	19	28	28	43	28	432

Table 15.2 Proportional representation of mensural note shapes in the principal mensurations.

LMIL code	Proportional representation	Note shapes			
		Perfect	Imperfect	Colored	Modern
T	3				
S	6				
&2/3 E*	8				
S.	9				
E	12				
&2/3 Q*	16				
E.	18				
Q	24				
&2/3 H*	32				
Q.	36				
H	48				
&2/3 W*	64				

Table 15.3 Note-shape equivalents in *DARMS-LMIL* code and proportional representation.

LMIL code	Proportional representation	Note shapes			
		Perfect	Imperfect	Colored	Modern
H.	72	♩	♩ ♩·	▰	♩.
W	96		♩	▰	o
WJE	108	♩			♩.♩.
W.	144	♩	♩ ♩·	▰	o.
B	192		♩		♩
BJQ	216	♩	♩ ♩·		o.♩.
B.	288		♩		♩·
B.JQJE	324		♩·		♩·♩.
B.JWJH	432		♩		♩·o·

Table 15.3, cont. Note-shape equivalents in *DARMS-LMIL* code and proportional representation.

By using three units to represent the smallest note encountered, fractional parts in the representation of colored (e.g., triplet) notes can be avoided. The numerical value of each note shape commonly encountered in the fifteenth century is shown in Table 15.2. In processing, the rhythmic portion of the internal representation (last three digits) is computed on the basis of 3 units per thirty-second note (*fusa*). Table 15.3 summarizes the information in Table 15.2, listing each possible numeric representation once. The use of 3 units to represent the smallest note encountered enables the user to avoid fractional parts in the representation of colored (e.g., triplet) notes. Had the *fusa* been assigned the value of 1 unit, for example, the colored minim would have had a value of 2.667.

One area of difficulty resolved in *LMIL* is the encoding of non-equivalent rhythmic groupings, such as triplets. Such groups are introduced by an ampersand (&). A reduced fraction is employed, in which the numerator indicates the number of rhythmic units actually occupied and the denominator the number of rhythmic units actually specified. The pitch and rhythm codes (disregarding coloration) are then given for each member of the group. An asterisk (*) closes the encoding. Some examples in black mensural notation (15.1a-h) follow.

Examples 15.1a–h Non-equivalent rhythmic groupings and their *DARMS-LMIL* encodings.

This system allows the exact rhythmic value of each member to be obtained by multiplication of the value of each unadjusted rhythmic symbol in the group by the reduced fraction described above.

The solutions to some common problems in white mensural notation are indicated in the following encodings (Examples 15.2a-e):

!3C !K1– !M3:47Q 7 9E. 8T 7 8Q 7E 6 5Q 4 RE 5 4 6E. 7S 8E 7 8 9Q

Example 15.2a Example in white mensural notation with its encoding.

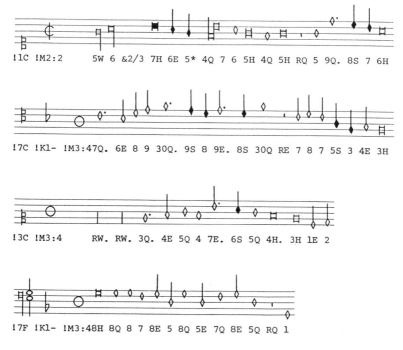

Examples 15.2b–e Passages in white mensural notation with their *DARMS-LMIL* encodings.

These examples are merely suggestive of the range of possibilities that such encodings can support. The underlying logic could obviously be used to extend any encoding system that is designed for polyphonic music.

References

Trowbridge, Lynn M. "The Burgundian Chanson: An Index and Analysis of Incipits by Application of Electronic Data Processing." Master's thesis, University of Illinois, 1971.

Trowbridge, Lynn M. *The Fifteenth-Century French Chanson: A Computer-Aided Study of Styles and Style Change.* Ph.D. dissertation: University of Illinois, 1982. The complete manual for the *Linear Music Input Language* is found on pp. 275–289.

Trowbridge, Lynn M. "Style Change in the Fifteenth-Century Chanson: A Comparative Study of Compositional Detail," *Journal of Musicology* IV/2 (1985-86), 146–170.

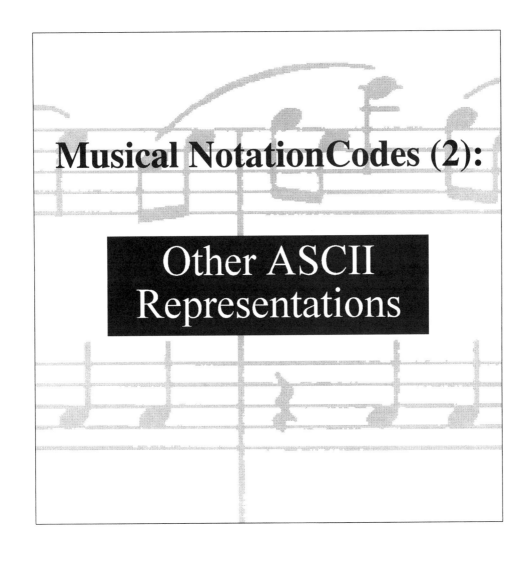

16 *Common Music Notation*

Bill Schottstaedt

Common Music Notation is a Lisp-based notation package available by anonymous file transfer protocol. It handles standard Western music notation. *CMN* was written to form one portion of the *Common Music* system developed by Heinrich Taube.[1] *Common Lisp Music* (*CLM*) is another member in this family. *Common Music Notation* is aimed primarily at composers, but scholars might find it useful to produce simple musical examples.

CMN input is intended to provide a readable (ASCII) text representation of the musical data present in the score. The notation is primarily what is represented. It takes the form of a Lisp expression using various standard musical names.

CMN runs on the NeXT, Macintosh, and Silicon Graphics Indigo (SGI) platforms, and on other machines running the *NeXTStep* operating system. *CMN* produces either *PostScript* or *Quickdraw* output currently. The Adobe *Sonata* font is used for clefs and other complicated symbols.

In conjunction with *Common Music*, *CMN* can turn its input into MIDI data, playable on a synthesizer. The reverse process—MIDI capture—is not supported. Similarly, the input data can be sent to *CLM* or *Csound* to produce a sound file.

1. Program in Composition and Theory, School of Music, University of Illinois, 1114 W. Nevada St., Urbana, IL 61801; *hkt@cmp-nxt.music.uiuc.edu.*

16.1   Musical Attributes

16.1.1 Pitch

Pitch is represented by names taken from *SCORE*:

c4	=	Middle C
cs4	=	Middle C♯
cf4	=	Middle C♭
cn4	=	Middle C♮

Octaves from 0 to 8 are built-in, but it is easy to add more.

16.1.2 Duration

Duration is represented using either the duration in quarter notes (e.g., the expression `duration 1.5` represents a dotted quarter note), or by various built-in rhythmic names such as e = eighth note, q = quarter, te = triplet eighth, etc.

Grace notes are handled by passing the musical data as the argument to the grace-note function, e.g.,

```
(cmn staff bass a-major a3 e (grace-note (slashed nil) a2
32nd c3 32nd e3 32nd))
```

for the start of the Mozart piano sonata (Example 1.2), bass staff. The 32nd indication is needed only because in this case *CMN*'s default is to use two beams.

Normally the first complete bar (measure[2]) is considered to be Measure 1. The Mozart trio example thus begins with Measure 0. The automatic bar numbers are indicated to be handled ":by-line", which means the number appears only on the first bar of each system ("line" in *CMN* jargon).

The repeat bar (shown in the Mozart trio and the saltarello) has no effect on measure numbering unless it is also a true bar line.

16.1.3 Articulation and Dynamics

Articulations and ornamentations are represented by their common (American) names: e.g., staccato. Trills are just another ornament.

For articulation marks that span several notes, there are switches such as begin-slur and end-slur.

2. "Bar" in *CMN* refers to a bar line.

Dynamics are given in a literal manner: f = forte, etc. Representative examples are also ff, fff, p, ppp, rfz, etc.

Timbre can be indicated by text (for example, sul pont) or by the instrument name present at the start of the staff.

16.1.4 Other Features

CMN supports printing on any *PostScript* printer. Text in any font, any size, at any orientation is handled through a call on the text function. There is also support for lyrics to make sure the various verses line up. The size of each score object can be determined by the user.

CMN provides support for part extraction, score/part transposition, and other operations involved in the creation of performance materials. Cues are not yet implemented.

Most twentieth-century percussion marks are supported.[3] It is relatively easy for a user to add his own graphical objects. *CMN* has support for feathered beams, proportional notation, unusual staff layouts, arrows, boxes, circles, all three piano pedals, harp diagrams, fancy rhythms, and so on *ad infinitum*. Most of the works encoded in *CMN* are composers' works in progress. At present there is no support for early music.

16.2 File Organization

CMN input files are calls on the *cmn* function. From the program's point of view, they are Lisp expressions input as ASCII text. The number of files is largely up to the user, since the input can be divided into sections either horizontally (i.e., one voice at a time) or vertically (i.e., by section) and glued together whenever it is convenient.

The parts can be combined in a single staff call, but this can lead to a lot of fussy typing. A simpler way is to have a separate virtual staff for each of the separate voices, then overlay them.

Sections and staves within sections occur in the order in which the user enters them in the *cmn* expression.

No sound or graphics conversions are supported directly. However, no technical problems that would hinder conversion to an interchange standard are currently

---

3. Examples include symbols for bass drum, cow bells, cymbals, gongs, maracas, hard and metal sticks, nail-pizzicatos, triangle and triangle stick, wire brush, and wood stick.

foreseen. If a standard is presented, translators for *CMN* would be provided, unless the resulting output were found to be aesthetically unbearable.

16.3   Example

The *CMN* encoding of the trio from the Mozart Clarinet Quintet is shown below:

```
(cmn (size 14)
     (automatic-measure-numbers :by-line)
     (always-show-staff-names nil)
     (first-measure-number 0)
     (staff-name-font "Times-Italic")
     (staff-name-font-scaler .6)
     (automatic-line-breaks nil)
     bracket
     (staff (staff-name "clarinet in A" (dx -.5)) treble (meter 3 4)
        c5 e begin-slur e5 e bar g5 e e5 e c6 q end-slur g5 e begin-slur e5 e bar
        d5 e f5 e a5 q end-slur f5 e begin-slur d5 e bar
        c5 e begin-beam b4 e e5 e d5 e g5 e f5 e end-slur end-beam bar
        ds5 q begin-slur e5 q end-slur c5 e begin-slur e5 e bar
        g5 e e5 e c6 q end-slur g5 e begin-slur e5 e bar
        dn5 e f5 e a5 q end-slur quarter-rest bar whole-rest bar line-break
        quarter-rest quarter-rest d4 te begin-slur a3 te f3 te bar
        a3 e end-slur begin-beam d4 e staccato f4 e staccato
        a4 e staccato d5 e staccato f5 e staccato end-beam bar
        a5 e begin-slur begin-beam g5 e f5 e e5 e f5 e d5 e end-slur end-beam bar
        c5 h begin-slur e5 e d5 e end-slur bar
        c5 q quarter-rest (begin-and-end-repeat-bar (fences '(.2 .3)))
        quarter-rest bar
        whole-rest bar whole-rest bar whole-rest bar
        quarter-rest quarter-rest g5 q (ring- (ring-length 1.5) unjustified) bar)
     (staff (staff-name "violino I" (dx -.5)) treble a-major (meter 3 4)
        quarter-rest bar quarter-rest a4 q p a4 q bar
        quarter-rest a4 q a4 q bar quarter-rest g4 q g4 q bar
        quarter-rest a4 q a4 q bar quarter-rest a4 q a4 q bar
        f4 q quarter-rest c5 e begin-slur as4 e bar
        b4 e d5 e f5 q end-slur c5 e begin-slur as4 e bar
        b4 e d5 e f5 q end-slur quarter-rest bar whole-rest bar whole-rest bar
        c4 e begin-slur begin-beam e4 e c4 e e4 e d4 e e4 e end-slur end-beam bar
        c4 q quarter-rest begin-and-end-repeat-bar e4 e begin-slur g4 e bar
        b4 e g4 e e5 q end-slur e4 e begin-slur a4 e bar
        c5 e a4 e e5 q end-slur e4 e begin-slur b4 e bar
        d5 e begin-beam b4 e e5 e d5 e c5 e a4 e end-slur end-beam bar
        g4 e begin-slur b4 e e5 q end-slur e4 e begin-slur g4 e end-slur bar)
     (staff (staff-name "violino II" (dx -.5)) treble a-major (meter 3 4)
        quarter-rest bar quarter-rest e4 q p e4 q bar
        quarter-rest f4 q f4 q bar quarter-rest d4 q d4 q bar
        quarter-rest c4 q c4 q bar quarter-rest e4 q e4 q bar
        d4 q quarter-rest gn4 begin-slur bar
        f4 h gn4 q bar
        f4 h end-slur quarter-rest bar whole-rest bar whole-rest bar
        a3 h begin-slur gs3 q end-slur bar
        a3 q quarter-rest begin-and-end-repeat-bar quarter-rest bar
        (chord (notes b3 g4) q
            (text "pizz." unjustified (font-scaler .5) (dy 1.5)) p)
```

```
(chord (notes b3 g4) q) quarter-rest bar
(chord (notes a3 a4) q) (chord (notes a3 a4) q) quarter-rest bar
(chord (notes g4 b4) q) (chord (notes g4 b4) q)
(chord (notes a4 c5) q stem-up) bar
(chord (notes g4 b4) q) (chord (notes g4 b4) q) quarter-rest bar)
(staff (staff-name "viola" (dx -.5)) alto a-major (meter 3 4)
quarter-rest bar quarter-rest c4 q p c4 q bar
quarter-rest b3 q b3 q bar quarter-rest b3 q b3 q bar
quarter-rest a3 q a3 q bar quarter-rest c4 q c4 q bar
b3 q quarter-rest e4 begin-slur bar
d4 h e4 q bar
d4 h end-slur quarter-rest bar whole-rest bar whole-rest bar
f3 h. begin-tie bar
f3 q end-tie quarter-rest begin-and-end-repeat-bar quarter-rest bar
(chord (notes d4 e4) q
     (text "pizz." unjustified (font-scaler .5) (dy .5)) (p (dy .25)))
(chord (notes d4 e4) q) quarter-rest bar
(chord (notes c4 e4) q) (chord (notes c4 e4) q) quarter-rest bar
e4 q e4 q e4 q bar e4 q e4 q quarter-rest bar)
(staff (staff-name "violoncello" (dx -.5)) bar bass a-major (meter 3 4)
quarter-rest bar a3 q p quarter-rest quarter-rest bar
d3 q quarter-rest quarter-rest bar
e3 q quarter-rest quarter-rest bar
f3 q quarter-rest quarter-rest bar
c3 q quarter-rest quarter-rest bar
d3 q quarter-rest quarter-rest bar whole-rest bar whole-rest bar
whole-rest bar whole-rest bar
e2 q begin-slur staccato e2 q staccato e2 q staccato end-slur bar
a2 q quarter-rest begin-and-end-repeat-bar quarter-rest bar
e3 q p (text "pizz." unjustified (font-scaler .5) (dy .5))
e3 q quarter-rest bar
e3 q e3 q quarter-rest bar
e3 q e3 q e3 q bar e3 q e2 q quarter-rest bar))
```

Example 16.1 Excerpt showing the first 16 bars (measures) of the Mozart trio in *CMN* input.

16.4   Further Information

CMN documentation exists in *WriteNow*, Rich Text, and ASCII formats. It comes with the *CMN* sources as *cmn.wn* (for example) in *cmn.tar.Z* available via anonymous ftp from *ccrma-ftp.stanford.edu:pub/Lisp/cmn.tar.Z*. The *CMN* tar file contains a variety of files (**.cmn*) showing more extended examples. *CMN* documentation is also available via the World-Wide Web from *http://ccrma-www.stanford.edu/CCRMA/ Software/cmn/cmn.html*.

17 *MuTEX, MusicTEX,* and *MusiXTEX*

Werner Icking

17.1 The *M*TEX* Family

MuTEX, MusicTEX, and *MusiXTEX* are public-domain sets of macros for music typography that operate with the *TEX* typesetting system developed by Donald Knuth. These packages can be used both for setting musical examples in text documents typeset with *TEX* and for setting musical scores and parts for a wide range of repertories. Various input codes work with these typesetting routines. The files that generate printed material are markup-intensive but provide full control over the shape and placement of a large number of musical symbols.

17.1.1 *MuTEX*

MuTEX, also called *MTEX,* was the first package to be developed. Written by Andrea Steinbach and Angelika Schofer as a master's thesis at Rheinische Friedrich-Wilhelms University in 1987, it is designed for setting monophonic music and can accommodate lyrics. Beams and slurs work well. In fact, this package has been used for highly varied tasks requiring typesetting of a professional quality. However, development of *MuTEX* has now lapsed.

17.1.2 *MusicTEX*

Although *MuTEX* provided the basis for *MusicTEX,* nearly nothing of *MuTEX* is retained in *MusicTEX. MusicTEX,* developed principally by Daniel Taupin, is intended for orchestral scores and polyphonic music. A full range of musical graphical symbols as well as beams and slurs are available and may be positioned at any place using a markup language which describes musical attributes such as pitch and duration.

In 1993, Ross Mitchell developed two add-ons to *MusicTEX* named *muflex* and *rmslur*. Because *TEX* is a typesetting facility for texts, it uses what it calls *glue* for margin justification. *Glue* is cumbersome in musical typesetting, so *muflex* introduces a three-pass processing routine to enable automatic line-breaking and page-filling without pasting bars together. *Rmslur* adds to *MusicTEX* the generation of slurs of nearly any slope or length.

17.1.3 *MusiXTEX*

These two packages were integrated into *MusicTEX* in 1994 by Andreas Egler, who in addition revised the code to accelerate the processing. This new system is named *MusiXTEX*. Two variants are available. The first, developed by Andreas Egler, is appropriate for users who are able and willing to work with (and on) a beta-test package. The other, maintained by Daniel Taupin, is recommended to those users who start typesetting music within *TEX*. It is now in a late beta-test stage. Daniel Taupin intends that the first official version will be fully compatible with the current version.

Because development of *MuTEX* has now lapsed and because in future *MusiXTEX* will be the successor of *MusicTEX*, the following description deals entirely with *MusiXTEX*.

17.2   Standard Features of *MusiXTEX*

Standard *MusiXTEX* supports scores of up to six *instruments*, where each one may occupy up to four staves. It is possible to increase this limit to either nine or twelve instruments so that, for example, the string section of an orchestra (*Violin 1, Violin 2, Viola, Cello*) may be handled as one instrument with four staves. Conversely, more than one voice may be typeset on one staff. For example, a choral score might consist of two voices sharing a treble-clef staff and two sharing a bass-clef staff.

Up to six beams or six slurs may be open concurrently,[1] but in many cases it is possible to process one beam or one slur after the other, because with *TEX* anything may be placed anywhere.

MusiXTEX provides two different font sizes: a default size of 20pt and a smaller one of 16pt. For both sizes a correspondingly smaller size may be used for grace notes, ornaments, suggested performance, excerpts from other voices, and so forth.

---

1. Using extensions under development.

Part of the *MusiXTeX* distribution consists of extensions for typesetting music for many special repertories including liturgical music, Gregorian chant, percussion scores, and chordal guitar accompaniment. Staves may have more or less than five lines. Special clefs may be used. Unconventional bar lines may be specified; alternatively they may be drawn in a score.

Because *MusiXTeX* is a macro package operating on top of *TeX*, it may be run on nearly any platform or base system.[2] Like *TeX*, *MusiXTeX* provides a device-independent output format. Many device drivers are available to send the output to a printer or to convert it to other graphics formats such as *PostScript*. Pre-generated fonts are available at 300 and 600 d.p.i.; for other resolutions fonts may easily be generated by processing the METAFONT sources which are part of the distribution.

17.3   Attribute Description in *MusiXTeX*

The code described here is that in which files are stored and from which prints are generated. Various input schemes are available.

All items are called by name. Similar items are grouped by class in the *MusiXTeX* documentation. Prospective users will want to download the graphics files that display the items named. Some of the file numbers containing these graphics are cited below.

Pitch names (online documentation chapter 2.1) are represented by letter either with the series A . . G or more continuous alphabets (A . . N ascending for two octaves to the G below Middle C; a . . z for pitches ascending for three-and-a-half octaves from the A below Middle C). This variability is reflected in octave indications:

PITCH	A . . G	A . . z
C1	`C	`C
C2	C	C
C3	'C	J
C4 (Middle C)	c	c
C5	'c	j
C6	''c	q
C7	'''c	x

All durational values (explained in the online documentation chapter 2.2) from a *maxima* through a sixty-fourth note (or rest) are supported, as are grace notes and a

---

2. *TeX* and its extensions utilize only lower-order ASCII characters.

range of unusual noteheads (see Example 17.1). Support is provided for accidentals through double sharps and double flats, as well as their editorial equivalents (shown at a smaller size within parentheses). Supported clefs are treble, alto, and bass as well as some more unusual ones— drum clef, Gregorian (i.e., four-line) C clef, Gregorian F clef, and an antique G clef.

Example 17.1 Partial roster of symbols, with their designations, available in *MusiXTeX*.

The above example also shows supported articulation marks, including staccato, legato, detached legato, martellato, up bows, and down bows. Ornamentation signs, pedal markings, a slide symbol, devices for editorial markup, repeat signs of several kinds are shown in Example 17.2, which also gives a menu of simple and compound meter signatures. (Further information on these can be found in the online documentation chapter 2.3.)

17.4   Examples

17.4.1a The Mozart Trio—Input

This example has been encoded using *PMX*, one of the *MusiXTEX* preprocessors. The part for *Clarinet in A* has been represented at its notated pitch (C Major), although *MusicTEX* and *MusiXTEX* offer transposition which includes automatic transposition of the accidentals. This is the *PMX* input for the first 13 bars:

```
\begin{verbatim}
% bars 0-4
r4   a43 r r  d- r r   e r r   f r r  /
r4   r4 c44 c   r b b   r b b   r a a  /
r4   r4 e44 e   r f f   r d d   r c c  /
r4   r4 a44 a   r a a   r g g   r a a  /
c85 s e g e c4+ s g8 s e   d f a4 s f8 s d   c b e d g f s   d4s s e s c8 s e /
% bars 5-8
c43 r r   d r r   r2d /
r4 c44 c   b r e s   d2 e4 /
r4 e44 e   d r gf s f2 g4f /
r4 a44 a   f r c8+ s as   b d f4 s c8 s as /
g85 e c4+ s g8 s e   dn f a4 s r4   r2d /
% bars 9-13
r2d  r2d   e42 s e e s   g r r /
d24 s r4   r2d   r2d   e2d- s   e4 s r r /
f24 s r4   r2d   r2d   a2- s g4n s   a4 r r /
b84 d f4   s r   r2d   r2d c8- s e c e d e s   c4 r e8 s g /
r4 r   d84 s a1f   a8 s d f a d f   a s g f e f d s   c2 s e8 d s c4 r r /
\end{verbatim}
```

Example 17.2a (1) *PMX* input code for the Mozart trio.

If the *Clarinet in A* had been notated at sounding pitch, its first eight bars would have been:

```
\begin{verbatim}
% bars 0-4
a84 s c e c a4+ s e8 s c   b d f4 s d8 s b   a g c b e d s   b4s s c s a8 s c /
% bars 5-8
e84 c e4+ s e8 s c   bn d f4 s r4   r2d /
\end{verbatim}
```

Example 17.2a (2) *PMX* input code for the *Clarinet in A* at sounding pitch.

During post-editing of the generated *MusiXTEX* source, the following code has to be added for the *Clarinet in A*:

```
\begin{verbatim}
\setsign50\def\Cla{\nextinstrument\transpose2}
\end{verbatim}
```

Example 17.2a (3) Additional input to support transposing instrument.

17.4.1b The Mozart Trio—Internal Code

The input code must be converted to actual *MusiXTEX*, an internal code. The following *MusiXTEX* definitions appear in the header section:

```
\begin{verbatim}
\geometricskipscale\smallmusicsize\parindent 27mm
\instrumentnumber 5\generalsignature 3\generalmeter{\meterfrac 3 4}
\setstaffs1 1\setclef1 \bass    \setname1{{Violoncello}}
\setstaffs2 1\setclef2 \alto    \setname2{Viola}
\setstaffs3 1\setclef3 \treble \setname3{Violino II}
\setstaffs4 1\setclef4 \treble \setname4{Violino I}
\setstaffs5 1\setclef5 \treble \setname5{Clarinet in A}\setsign50
\songbottom 1\songtop 5
\relativeaccid\interstaff{11}\beforeruleskip 0pt
\startbarno 0\startpiece\systemnumbers\addspace\afterruleskip
\end{verbatim}
```

Example 17.2b (1) Header definitions for *MusiXTEX* internal code.

The music itself is represented below:

```
\begin{music}
%\input musixtex
%\input pmx
%\input mymusix
 \edef\catcodeat{\the\catcode`\@}\catcode`\@=11
 \def\ek{\off{1\elemskip}}\def\eK{\off{-1\elemskip}}
 \def\Ek#1{\off{0.#1\elemskip}}\def\EK#1{\off{-0.#1\elemskip}}
 \newcount\nick@i
 \def\ttqb#1#2{\nick@i\transpose\tslur{#1}{#2}\transpose\nick@i\tqb{#1}{#2}}%
 \def\ttqh#1#2{\nick@i\transpose\tslur{#1}{#2}\transpose\nick@i\tqh{#1}{#2}}
 \catcode`\@=\catcodeat%
\font\sevenit=\fontid ti7
%\input mymusix
\geometricskipscale\smallmusicsize\parindent 27mm
\instrumentnumber 5\generalsignature 3\generalmeter{\meterfrac 3 4}
\setstaffs1 1\setclef1 \bass    \setname1{{Violoncello}}
\setstaffs2 1\setclef2 \alto    \setname2{Viola}
\setstaffs3 1\setclef3 \treble \setname3{Violino II}
\setstaffs4 1\setclef4 \treble \setname4{Violino I}
\setstaffs5 1\setclef5 \treble \setname5{Clarinet in A}\setsign50
\songbottom 1\songtop 5
\relativeaccid\interstaff{11}\beforeruleskip 0pt
```

```
\startbarno 0\startpiece\systemnumbers\addspace\afterruleskip
\NOtes\qp&\qp&\qp&\qp&\zcharnote{-5}{\ppff p}\ibl5{'c}5\isluru5c\qb5c\tqb5e\en
\bar% 1
\NOtes\zcharnote{-4}{\ppff p}\qa a&\qp&\qp&\qp&\ibl5{'g}{-5}\qb5g\tqb5e\en
\NOTes\qp&\zcharnote{-4}{\ppff p}\qa c&\zcharnote{-6}{\ppff p}\qa e%
   &\zcharnote{-4}{\ppff p}\qa{'a}&\tslur5{''c}\qa c\en
\NOtes\qp&\qa c&\qa e&\qa{'a}&\ibl5{'g}{-5}\isluru5g\qb5g\tqb5e\en
\bar% 2
\NOtes\qa{'d}&\qp&\qp&\qp&\ibl5{'d}5\qb5d\tqb5f\en
\NOtes\qp&\qa f&\qa{'a}&\tslur5{''a}\qa a\en
\NOtes\qp&\qa b&\qa f&\qa{'a}&\ibl5{'f}{-5}\isluru5f\qb5f\tqb5d\en
\bar% 3
\NOtes\qa{'e}\sk\qp\sk\qp&\qp\sk\qa b\sk\qa b&\qp\sk\qa d\sk\qa d%
   &\qp\sk\qa g\sk\qa g&\ibl5{'b}3\qb5c\qb5b\qb5e\qb5d\qb5g\ttqb5f\en
\bar% 4
\NOTes\ek\Ek2\qa{'f}\qp&\ek\Ek2\qp\qa a&\ek\Ek2\qp\qa c&\ek\Ek2\qp\qa{'a}%
   &\ek\Ek2\isluru5{'d}\qa{^d}\tslur5e\qa e\en
\NOtes\qp&\qa a&\qa c&\qa{'a}&\ibl5{'c}5\isluru5c\qb5c\tqb5e\en
\bar% 5
\NOtes\qa{'c}&\qp&\qp&\qp&\ibl5{'g}{-5}\qb5g\tqb5e\en
\NOTes\qp&\qa c&\qa e&\qa{'a}&\tslur5{''c}\qa c\en
\NOtes\qp&\qa c&\qa e&\qa{'a}&\ibl5{'g}{-5}\isluru5g\qb5g\tqb5e\en
\bar% 6
\NOtes\ek\Ek1\qa{'d}&\ek\Ek1\qa b&\ek\Ek1\qa d&\ek\Ek1\qa f%
   &\ek\Ek1\ibl5{'d}5\qb5{=d}\tqb5f\en
\NOtes\qp&\qp&\qp&\qp&\tslur5{''a}\qa a\en
\NOtes\qp&\isluru2e\qa e&\fl g\islurd3g\qa g%
   &\ibl4{'c}{-5}\isluru4c\qb4c\tqb4{^a}&\qp\en
\bar% 7
\NOtes&\ha d&\ha f&\ibl4{'b}5\qb4b\tqb4d&\en
\NOTes&&&\tslur4{'f}\qa f&\en
\NOtes&\qa e&\fl g\qa g&\ibl4{'c}{-5}\isluru4c\qb4c\tqb4{^a}&\en
\def\atnextbar{\znotes\centerpause&&&\centerpause\en}%
\def\atnextline{\Liftslur44}%
\bar% 8
\NOtes&\tslur2d\ha d&\tslur3f\ha f&\ibl4{'b}5\qb4b\tqb4d&\qp\en
\NOTes&&&\tslur4{'f}\qa f&\qp\en
\Notesp&\qp&\qp&\qp%
   &\ibu5d{-5}\islurd5{'g}\qb5{'d}\zcharnote{'d}{\sevenit 3}\qb5{'a}\tqh5{'f}
   \en
\def\atnextbar{\znotes\centerpause&&&\en}%
\bar% 9
\NOtes&&&\ibu5e5\tslur5{'f}\qb5{'a}\lpz d\qb5d\lpz f\qb5f%
                  \lpz{'a}\qb5a\lpz d\qb5d\lpz f\tqh5f\en
\def\atnextbar{\znotes\centerpause&\centerpause&\centerpause&\centerpause&\en}%
\bar% 10
\NOtes&&&\ibl5{'f}{-2}\isluru5{'a}\qb5{a'gfef}\ttqb5d\en
\def\atnextbar{\znotes\centerpause&\centerpause&\centerpause&\centerpause&\en}%
\bar% 11
\NOtes\islurd1{''d}\lpz e\qa e\sk\lpz e\qa e\sk\lpz e\tslur1d\qa e%
     &\islurd2{'e}\pt e\ha e&\islurd3a\ha a\sk\sk\sk\tslur3{'g}\qa{=g}%
     &\ibu4e0\islurd4c\qb4{ceced}\ttqh4e%
     &\isluru5{'c}\ha c\sk\sk\sk\ibl5e{-3}\qb5e\ttqb5d\en
\bar% 12
\NOTes\qa{''g}\qp&\tslur2{'e}\qa e\qp&\qa a\qp&\qa c\qp&\qa{'c}\qp\en
\advance\barno-1\leftrightrepeat
\NOtes\qp&\qp&\qp&\ibu4e3\roffset{0.3}{\isluru4{'e}}\qb4{'e}\tqh4g&\qp\en
\bar% 13
\NOtes\ek\Ek4\zcharnote{-4}{\ppff p}\zcharnote{10}{\smalltype pizz.}\qa{'e}%
     &\ek\Ek4\zcharnote{-4}{\ppff p}\zcharnote{10}{\smalltype pizz.}\lq d\qa e%
     &\ek\Ek4\zcharnote{-7}{\ppff p}\zcharnote{10}{\smalltype pizz.}\zq g\qa b%
     &\ek\Ek4\ibu4{'a}{-3}\qb4b\tqh4{'g}&\en
\NOTes\qa{'e}&\lq d\qa e&\zq g\qa b&\tslur4{'e}\qa e&\en
```

```
\NOtes\qp&\qp&\qp&\ibu4f4\roffset{0.3}{\isluru4{'e}}\qb4{'e}\tqh4{'a}&\en
\def\atnextbar{\znotes&&&\centerpause\en}%
\mulooseness=-3\endpiece
\songbottom\maxdimen\songtop 0\startbarno 1\parindent 0pt\setname1{}
\elemskip\oldelemskip\afterruleskip\oldafterruleskip\beforeruleskip\oldbefore
    ruleskip
\normalmusicsize
\end{music}
```

Example 17.2b (2) Main body of *MusiXTeX* code for the Mozart trio.

17.4.2 The Saltarello

Bar numbering may be handled in several ways. This example was set in three
different ways, but space limitations preclude reproducing the files here. All three
procedures relate to the presentation of printed bar numerals. The controlling
command is `Setvolta`.

17.4.3 The Telemann Aria

The Telemann example was not set, but the requisite capabilities—for the underlay of
text containing diacriticals and the presentation of multiple parts on one staff—exist
in *MusiXTeX*. A comparable example is given in the online documentation file 2.26.3.

17.4.4 Unmeasured Chant—Styles A and B

Since there is no need in *MusiXTeX* to specify any measure or to have any regular
number of notes in a bar, unmeasured chant is easily set. The encoding of invisible
bar lines in the "Alma Redemptoris" (Example 17.3a) allows automatic line breaks.

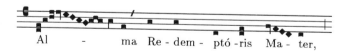

```
\parindent 40pt\setname1{Style A}
\shortbarrules\elemskip3pt
\def\word#1{\zcharnote{-6}{#1}}
\instrumentnumber1\setstaffs11\setlines14
\setclef 1{4000}\setaltoclefsymbol1\gregorianCclef
\startextract\transpose=-5
\notes\word{Al}\podatus ac\squ e\podatus fh\rsqu h\en
\notes\ynq{gfe}\word{-}\ynq d\torculus e f e\sk\sk\en
\NOtes\lsqu e\word{ma}\squ c\raise -1\Interligne\hbox{\caesura}\sk\en
\NOtes\word{Re -}\squ e\sk\word{dem -}\squ e\sk\sk\word{pt\'o -}\squ a\sk\en
\NOtes\word{ris}\podatus ac\sk\en
```

```
\notes\word{Ma -}\rsqu d\ynq{cba}\sk\en
\NOtes\word{ter,}\squ a\sk\en
\bar\notes\sk\en
\zendextract
\resetclefsymbols\transpose=0
\setclef2\treble
\setname1{}\setname2{}\setlines15\startrule\parindent0pt
\elemskip\oldelemskip\afterruleskip\oldafterruleskip\beforeruleskip\oldbefore
    ruleskip
\end{music}
```

Example 17.3a *MusiXTEX* code for unmeasured chant, Style A ("Alma Redemptoris Mater").

The modern transcription of "Quem queritis" is shown in Example 17.3b.

```
\begin{music}
\parindent 40pt\normalmusicsize\nobarnumbers\setname1{Style 1}
\instrumentnumber1\setstaffs11\setclef1\treble
\afterruleskip0pt\nostartrule
\startextract
\notes\zcharnote{10}{Angelus dicit:}\zcharnote{-7}{Quem\dots}%
    \slur gfd1\qu{gf}\slur ded2\qu{dfe}\slur ffd2\qu{fgf}\en
\Notes\qu{gf'a}\en
\notes\roffset{0.4}{\isluru0{'b}}\qa{acb}\tslur0a\qa a\en
\notes\slur{'c}fu3\qa{c'g'a'g}\caesura\en
\notes\slur g{'a}d1\qa{'g'a}\slur{'g}fd1\qa{gf}\en
\notes\roffset{0.4}{\isluru0{'a}}\qa a\tslur0c\zcharnote{-7}{\dots}\qa c\en
\Notes\zcharnote{-7}{co-}\qa{'a}\zcharnote{-7}{lae}\qa{'g}\en
\setdoublebar\bar\notes\sk\en
\zendextract

\edef\catcodeat{\the\catcode`\@}\catcode`\@=11
% separated short vrules over every staff (fits only for 1,2,3,5 Lines)
% adapted for exactly *4* lines
\def\rul@SEP#1{\n@loop\short@rule\repeat\addspace#1}
\def\short@rule{{\p@loop\y@\altportee\advance\y@\tw@\internote\raise\y@%\rlap
    {\raise
-1\internote\hbox{\vrule\@width\lthick\@height\f@ur\internote}}\count@portee\
    repeat}}
\def\shortbarrules{\let\writ@rule\rul@SEP }
\catcode`\@=\catcodeat
```

Example 17.3b *MusiXTEX* code for unmeasured chant, Style B ("Quem queritis").

17.4.5 The Binchois *Magnificat*

The Binchois example has not been set, but comparable features are exhibited in the *MusiXTEX* online documentation chapter 2.26.10.

17.4.6 Contemporary, Popular, and Other Special Repertories

MusiXTEX enables the user to define his or her own macros, symbols, and so forth, and to place anything anywhere. These capabilities are beneficial in setting contemporary music. A short example is given in chapter 2.21 of the online documentation. Many features of popular music are also supported. Divergent features may be arbitrarily combined.

17.5   Further Information

The base site for both *MusicTEX* and Taupin's version of *MusiXTEX* is *hprib.lps.u-psud.fr*, from which both packages may be obtained by anonymous ftp. The base site for Egler's *MusiXTEX* variant is *ftp.tex.ac.uk*. All three packages, as well as additional software, generated sheet music, and other materials are available by anonymous ftp from the server of the Forschungszentrum Informationstechnik GmbH in Sankt Augustin, Germany: *ftp.gmd.de*, which may be easily accessed via the World-Wide Web by starting at the URL *http://ftp.gmd.de/music/README.html*.[3] Especially for *MusicTEX* and *MusiXTEX* a user should verify his identity in order to retrieve a current version.[4]

The packages consist of all *TEX* sources, the font definitions, some examples, and the documentation. The documentation is available not only as *TEX* source code and a *TEX* dvi-file but also as data ready to be printed by *PostScript* and HPGL printers. The data is packed in both zipped archives (e.g., *musixtex.zip, musixexa.zip, musixpk.zip, musixdoc_ps.zip, \dots*) and as a compressed UNIX tar file (*musictex-516.tar.gz*). Small maintenance releases are provided by *ftp.gmd.de* in the directory *.../diff-files/...* .

Additional software packages which generate either *MusicTEX* or *MusiXTEX* input are available from many ftp servers and are collected at *ftp.gmd.de*. They have such names as *abc2mtex, midi2tex, mpp, PMTeX, PMX*, and so forth. A list of frequently asked questions (FAQs) is linked to *http://www.gmd.de/Mail/*.[5]

---

3. From this server the packages are mirrored by the UK sites, their mirrors, and many other sites. See also the files in *http://www.gmd.de/Misc/Music/*.

4. At this writing the current version of *MusicTEX* was 5.16 and the current version of *MusiXTEX* was T.42.

5. Further examples of the capabilities of *M*TEX* are shown in *Computing in Musicology* 10 (1995-96), 199-202.

18 *Philip's Music Scribe*

Philip Hazel

The program *Philip's Music Scribe* was designed for the purpose of typesetting music using conventional staff notation. The two main aims of its input code were to have a scheme that was easy for musicians to remember and to minimize the number of keystrokes required. Another aim was to provide a code with which many parameters could be defaulted, or left to the computer to choose, while retaining the possibility for the user to specify them if necessary. Above all, this is a practical code, intended for getting a job done.

The code has been used to set music in a wide range of musical styles, and from many periods.[1] A single input file is used to represent a piece; from this both a score and a set of individual parts (or composite parts) can be printed.

While the code itself is device-independent, the program which currently implements it runs under the RISC OS operating system on the range of computers made by the British company Acorn Computers Limited.[2] Output can be to any supported printer, or the program can generate its own *PostScript* files for export to high resolution printers or phototypesetters. In both cases, a font of music characters is used for printing the required glyphs.

---

1. Some representative examples of works typeset by *PMS* include instrumental and sacred vocal works by various English and South African composers such as Bax, Bayliss, Carletti, East, Gabrieli, Hind, Klatzow, Mendelssohn, Palestrina, Scheidt, Barry Smith, Tomkins, Van Dijk, Victoria, and Wilbye. Some works have been published by Oriel Library and JOED, London.

2. For information about Acorn computers, please contact the company at Acorn House, Vision Park, Histon, Cambridge CB4 4AE, England, UK; tel. +44 1223/254254; fax: +44 1223/254262; *postmaster@ acorn.co.uk*. The RISC OS operating system is unique to Acorn computers. The program described here does not run under MS DOS or *Windows* or any other operating system for IBM PC hardware.

18.1   Program Description

PMS encodes the pitch and duration of printed notes, together with accents, ornaments, ties, slurs, etc. It also supports several different kinds of text items. The encoding therefore represents a printed form of music rather than musical sounds. However, since the representation is in terms of absolute pitch and note length, it is possible to perform the music mechanically from this encoding. There is no support for encoding performance instructions other than for volume and tempo. MIDI output is supported.

Transposition of the music is supported. Once encoded, a piece can be printed out in any number of different keys, and individual parts can be independently transposed. There is special support for transposing music which uses the convention of one less accidental in the key signature than in the tonality.

There is a simple line-drawing capability for things which are not built into the program, but this is not a major feature. When generating *PostScript* files, users can specify their own *PostScript* fragments to be included in the output.

Although *PMS* is not designed for analysis, it reports, for each staff of input, the maximum and minimum pitch and also the average pitch; this latter gives an indication of the tessitura for vocal parts. If the piece consists of several movements, these data are given overall as well as for each movement separately.

18.2   Code Description

A *PMS* input file takes the form of a number of optional heading directives, followed by the encoded data for each staff. The heading directives come at the start of a movement and define heading texts, set up the layout of systems and staves, adjust various spacing and size parameters, define the text fonts and sizes required, and so on. Literals in *PMS* are enclosed in quotation marks.[3]

Each staff's data consists of notes and other items such as text strings, and there may also be *staff directives* which specify certain items and control how the music is printed (for example, changing the space between staves at a certain point in the piece). These are enclosed in square brackets to distinguish them from notes. *PMS* supports a large number of directives within staves; they are always enclosed in square brackets to distinguish them from note letters. Only a small number are covered in this document.

---

3. For this reason no quotation marks are used to enclose code in this commentary. All codes are shown in Courier type.

All dimensions specified in an input file are given in printers' points, of which there are 72 to an inch. Fractional values are permitted. *PMS* works internally in millipoints.

The references in this section are to the Mozart trio excerpt (Example 18.1).

18.2.1 Notes

The representation of a note has five parameters—accidental, pitch (or rest), duration, accent, and tie. Only pitch and duration need be present, and some of their coding is combined in the note letter.

A. ACCIDENTALS [#, $, %]

If the note is to be printed with an accidental, one of the characters # (sharp), $ (flat), or % (natural) precedes it. The second two characters are chosen because they lie alongside # on many computer keyboards. Double sharps and flats are encoded by doubling the accidental character.

B. PITCHES [a..g]

The pitch is represented by one of the note letters a..g. *PMS*'s octaves run from C to B, and the default octave is set by a directive within the music. Octave 1 starts at Middle C; octave numbers can be positive, zero, or negative. Notes outside the current default octave can be raised or lowered into other octaves by following them by one or more quote or grave accent characters, respectively. For example, consider Bar 8 of the *Clarinet*, with the default octave set to 1; the first, third, and fifth notes are in different octaves, and would therefore be encoded as a ' (one octave below the default), f (in the default octave), and d ' (one octave above the default), respectively.

Rests are encoded using the letters r or q, the difference between them being that q prints an invisible rest (that is, nothing at all). This is useful when printing keyboard music where there may be multiple voices that do not always fill each bar. When there is a succession of rest bars in all staves which are selected for printing, *PMS* automatically prints a long rest sign with a count above it.

C. DURATIONS [+, –]

The basic duration of a note is controlled by the case of the note letter. Upper-case letters (A..G) represent half notes, while lower-case letters represent quarter notes. For notes longer than a half note, the character + is used incrementally: A+ is a whole note, A++ is a double whole note. For notes shorter than a quarter note, tails are added in the form of the hyphen (–) or equals (=) characters: a– is an eighth note, a= is a sixteenth note, and so on. Dotted notes are encoded simply by adding one or two dots (see, for example, Bar 11 of the *Viola*).

The duration of rests is notated in the same way as that of pitches, with the addition of an extra code for whole bar rests: an exclamation mark. This can be seen in Bar 7 of the clarinet part.

Triplets are encoded by enclosing the set of notes in curly brackets (see Bar 8 of the *Clarinet*). For non-standard groupings of other lengths, a number is given after the opening bracket. For example, the expression {5 abcde} represents a quintuplet of five quarter notes.

PMS checks that the notes in a bar add up to the time signature, but the check can be disabled either for an individual bar or for the whole piece.

D. Articulations

This part of a note is used for accents, articulation marks, ornaments, and some other control features such as forcing the stem up or down. It consists of one or more code characters enclosed between back-slashes. The main facilities are:

.	staccato	o	harmonic (ring accent)
–	accent	sl<n>	extend stem length by <n> points
>	accent	sl<-n>	reduce stem length by <n> points
v	small closed vertical wedge	sp	spread sign (for two-note chords)
V	large open "circumflex" accent	su	stem up
~	inverted mordent	sd	stem down
~|	mordent (double also available)	sw	swap stem direction in beam
/	tremolo (double and triple also)	t	turn
ar	arpeggio (for chords)	tr	trill
d	string bow down	tr#	trill with sharp (also with flat and
g	grace note		natural)
g/	slashed grace note	u	string up bow
f	fermata		

For example, a\–\ is a quarter note with a single pressure accent. The first note of the third bar of the Telemann example would be encoded as c′=\tr\ to cause the *tr* sign to be printed for the trill. Ornaments can be moved in any direction. This is particularly relevant to turns, which must sometimes follow a note rather than lie above it.

Stem directions can be forced for sections of staves; the options here are for overriding the default for single notes. Defaults can also be set when the same accent applies to several notes (Bars 9 and 10 of the clarinet part).

E. TIES [_]

Ties are encoded by an underscore chracter (_) following the note (see Bar 11 of the *Viola*); if any accents or ornaments are present, these come first. The same notation is used for a short slur between two adjacent notes (Bar 4 of the *Clarinet*). Ties are normally drawn opposite the stems of the notes, but they can be forced to be upwards- or downwards-curving if necessary. For chords, the number of ties which curve in each direction can be set.

18.2.2 Chords

Any number of notes of the same duration can be printed as a chord by grouping them in round brackets. *PMS* automatically takes care of positioning the noteheads and any associated accidentals, though these can be explicitly positioned by the user if required. For example, the double-stopped chords in Bar 13 of the viola part would be encoded as (de).

18.2.3 Beaming

Notes that are shorter than a quarter note are automatically beamed together unless beam-separator characters are present in the input. A semicolon (;) specifies a complete break in a beam, while a comma (,) specifies a break of all but the primary beam. There are no examples of either in the Mozart, but if one wanted to print Bar 3 of the clarinet part as three pairs of beamed eighth notes, the input would be

                    c'-b-; e'-d'-; g'-f'-

Beams continue over sufficiently short rests unless explicitly broken. *PMS* also supports beaming over bar lines on request.

18.2.4 Bar Lines [|]

The vertical bar character (|) is used to indicate the ends of measures. Unless the feature is disabled, *PMS* checks that the correct number of notes have been entered, and this is a useful check against input errors. Double bar lines are encoded by two vertical bars (| |) and are automatically provided at key signature changes (though this can be suppressed). There is also an invisible bar line, encoded as | ?, which can be useful in very long measures as it indicates a place where *PMS* may break the line. A vertical bar followed by an equals sign (| =) indicates that a beam is to be continued over the bar line.

18.2.5 Dynamics [< >]

Crescendos and diminuendos are supported by using the characters < and > in the input to mark their beginnings and endings. They may be specified as printing above or below the staff, and their ends can be moved up, down, left or right independently, thus permitting sloping hairpins to be printed. Movement is specified by following < or > by one or more of the following:

    /u<n>   move up by <n> points
    /d<n>   move down by <n> points
    /l<n>   move left by <n> points
    /r<n>   move right by <n> points

There is no special provision for textual dynamic markings; they are handled in exactly the same way as other text items.

18.2.6 Staves

PMS supports traditional 5-line staves, single-line staves for percussion notation, and, for special effects, staves of 0, 2, 3, 4, and 6 lines.

18.2.7 Clefs

PMS supports the following clefs: treble, soprano, mezzo-soprano, alto, tenor, baritone, and bass. The percussion H-clef is also available. The figure 8 can be printed above or below a treble or bass clef. Music can also be printed without any clef, a feature useful for setting examination questions!

A clef is encoded by giving its name as a directive (e.g., [tenor]), optionally followed by an octave number, if a change of default octave is required. The artificial names *trebledescant*, *trebletenor*, *soprabass*, and *contrabass* have been invented for the forms with an 8 printed above or below.

18.2.8 Note Spacing

PMS maintains a table of the minimum amount of horizontal space that should follow each type of note duration. The initial values in the table can be set directly by the [notespacing] heading directive, but the most common use of this directive is to change all the values by a multiplicative factor. For example, the expression Notespacing *1.2 increases all the values by 20%. These values give the minimum spacing; when there is more than one staff, the notes on one staff may cause wider spacing than the minimum on another. Also, when systems are being right-justified (the normal case), additional space is inserted to align the end of the system with the right-hand margin.

The note spacing can be changed at any point in a piece by means of a staff directive, [notespacing]. Thus, individual bars can be printed more tightly or loosely if required. Adjustment of the notespacing parameter, both overall and for individual parts of a piece, is one means by which a piece can be fitted onto a given number of pages, once the magnification has been fixed.

18.2.9 Key Signatures

A key signature which applies to all staves may be given in the heading, but individual signatures may be given for each staff. In the Mozart example, the overall key is A Major, but the clarinet part has its key signature set to C Major, and the input notes are given in that key (e.g., the first note is given as c).

If it were required to print a score with the clarinet part in A Major, a downwards transposition of three semitones could be specified for the first staff simply by adding [transpose -3] at its start. Contrariwise, if the input manuscript had a clarinet part written at true pitch (i.e., in A Major), it could be input at that pitch and then transposed up to print in C.

A change of key signature is encoded using the [key] directive. Normally a cancellation key signature is not printed unless the new key is C Major or A Minor. However, multiple key directives can be given, so specifying C major followed by another key causes printing in the old style. *PMS* automatically prints warning key signatures at the ends of lines when there is a change at the start of the next line. These can be suppressed, either individually or overall.

18.2.10 Time Signatures

As well as time signatures consisting of numbers, *PMS* supports the time signatures for so-called common and *alla breve* time. In addition, code such as [time 2*C] specifies that the printed signature is to be the C of common time, but the music is to contain twice the normal number of notes per bar, that is, four half notes instead of four quarter notes.

The user may specify exactly what text string or pair of strings (one above the other) is to be printed for any given time signature. This makes it possible to print large single numbers if required, or to show signatures like 8/8 with, for example, the expression 3+3+2 as the numerator of the signature. *PMS* can print music where different staves have different time signatures, for example, 4/4 and 12/8.

The printing of time signatures can be completely suppressed (useful for hymn books), or just the initial one can be suppressed (useful for samples). *PMS* automatically prints warning time signatures at the ends of lines when there is a change at the start of the next line. These too can be suppressed, either individually or overall.

18.2.11 Slurs

Slurs between adjacent notes can be handled with an underscore character (_), as for ties. Longer slurs are encoded using directives.

The [slur] directive marks the start of a slur, and [endslur] marks the end (many examples in the clarinet part). The slur is drawn to cover the notes that lie between these two directives. A number of options are available for controlling the position and appearance of the slur; they are separated by slashes from the directive names. The main ones are as follows:

/a	draw slur above the notes (default)
/b	draw slur below the notes
/h	force slur to be "horizontal"
/w	draw a "wiggly" slur
/u<n>	move slur up <n> points
/d<n>	move slur down <n> points
/lu<n>	move the left end up <n> points
/ld<n>	move the left end down <n> points
/ll<n>	move the left end left <n> points
/lr<n>	move the left end right <n> points
/ru<n>	move the right end up <n> points
/rd<n>	move the right end down <n> points
/rl<n>	move the right end left <n> points
/rr<n>	move the right end right <n> points
/co<n>	pull the center out by <n> points
/ci<n>	push the center in by <n> points

A "horizontal" slur is one where the end-point level is the same as that of the starting point; that is, the pitch of the final note is ignored. This option is generally of more use for lines than slurs. "Wiggly" slurs are those where the direction of curvature changes in the middle. These are usually encountered in keyboard arrangements where a part is moving from one staff to the other.

The last two options adjust the control points which define the amount of curvature of the slur, which is drawn using Bezier curves. The two control points can also be individually moved, in order to create slurs of asymmetric shape. There are also options for controlling the different parts of a slur when it is split over one or more line ends.

Any number of slurs can be in existence simultaneously. Normally multiple slurs nest (that is, they are entirely contained within each other), but there are options for coping with exceptional cases where this does not hold.

18.2.12 Repeats

Repeated sections of music are encoded using the character sequences (: and :), which may occur at the end of a bar or in the middle (all parts, Bar 12). When a repeat is at the end of a bar, it is amalgamated with the bar line. Several different styles of repeat are available (with and without the thick bar line, with two or four dots).

18.2.13 Text

PMS allows any number of text strings to be associated with any one note. Options are available to specify whether any string should be printed above or below the staff; it can also be moved in any direction from its default position, or rotated to print at an angle. Bar 1 of the *Clarinet* has an example of a simple string, used for the dynamic *p*, printed in the bold italic font. A text string would also be used for "*pizz.*" in Bar 13 of the Mozart example.

The first of these would be encoded as "\bi\p" /b (where /b indicates that the text is to be printed below the staff), but since this is required in several places, in practice it would be defined as a macro.

A string can be specified as one of up to twelve different type sizes, set up by the user in the heading. The code /s<*n*> following a string (e.g., "abc"/s4) selects the size (in this example, size number 4). There are default sizes for normal text, underlay text, and figured bass text, but these can always be overridden.

Within a string, up to twelve different typefaces can be used; these are also selectable by the user. For example, in addition to the normal Roman font, bold, italic, and bold italic, sanserif or Greek could be used. Changes of typeface are encoded by escape sequences such as \rm\ for roman, \it\ for italic, and so on.

The *PMS* music font is available for use in text strings, appearing as just another typeface, thus enabling notes, clefs, accidentals, etc. to be printed at arbitrary positions if necessary. The most common use is for tempo indications such as "quarter note = 60". There are some escape sequences for common cases like this; the encoding would be *c\ = 60 where the asterisk selects the music font, and the c is a mnemonic for a crotchet (quarter note).

Text strings are also available at the start of staves for instrument names. These names can be changed anywhere in the piece. Naturally, there are also facilities for printing headings for pieces and for printing footings, page numbers, and so on. Footnotes are also supported, with *PMS* automatically breaking a paragraph into lines and justifying them.

Rehearsal letters are encoded as strings in square brackets, for example, ["A"]. By default, they are printed inside rectangular boxes, but there is a heading directive that can turn these off or request circular rings instead.

18.2.14 System Layout

Individual staves can be specified as printing smaller or larger relative to the other staves. In addition, the overall magnification can be set, making it possible to print staves of any desired size. As both the Acorn and *PostScript* fonts are held as outlines, there are no restrictions on the values that can be chosen for magnification. The standard gap between staff lines is four points.

The initial spacing between staves and systems can be set by heading directives. It can also be changed at any point by means of staff directives, either for an individual staff or system, or for all subsequent ones.

The joining signs (brackets and braces and a preliminary bar line) that appear at the left-hand edges of systems are also defined in the heading for the staves to which they apply. The spacing between systems can either be wholly controlled by the input file, or *PMS* can perform vertical justification so that the last system on all pages is at the same level.

By default, *PMS* assigns bars to systems and systems to pages using the simple rule of putting as many bars on a line and as many systems on a page as possible. Line breaks and page breaks can be forced at any point by means of the [newline] and [newpage] directives. To arrange for a piece to fill a certain number of pages exactly, the spacing between notes is adjusted. Alternatively, the [layout] heading directive can be used to specify at the start precisely where the line breaks and page breaks for the whole piece are to be.

18.2.15 Bar Numbering

Bar numbers can be printed either at the start of each system (except the first) or every so many bars (normally 5 or 10, but the user can choose). The size of bar numbers can be specified, and the numbers can be printed in square boxes or round rings.

A staff directive is available to force a bar number to be printed on a bar that otherwise would not get one, or to suppress a bar number that would otherwise appear. Individual bar numbers can be moved in any direction.

The staff directive [nocount] is used to cause a bar not to be counted for numbering purposes. Its most common use is at the start of pieces such as the Mozart, but it has other uses with first- and second-time bars (endings) and on occasions where a double bar line is required in the middle of a measure.

18.3   Example

The input for the first twelve bars of the second trio of the Mozart Clarinet Quintet is shown here. The notes below give some additional explanation to supplement the previous section.

```
@ Example for IMS Handbook of Musical Codes[4]
@ PMS input by Philip Hazel, September 1992

Heading "|Mozart: Second trio from Clarinet Quintet" 35[5]
```

---

4. The character @ introduces a comment which lasts until the end of the input line. It is very commonly used to keep track of bar numbers.

5. A vertical bar in a heading directive separates the left-aligned, centered, and right-aligned parts of a heading line. Any number of heading lines can be given. This one uses the default type size, but requests 35 points of space below it. Different heading and footing texts can be specified for the first page, the last page, and the in-between pages of a piece. There are facilities for conditionally printing text depending on whether the page number is odd or even, thus allowing alternating right and left page numbers to be printed.

```
*Define p "\bi\p"/b⁶

Barnumbers line 9⁷
Bracket 1-5⁸
Time 3/4
Key A
Unfinished⁹

[stave 1 "\it\clarinet in A" treble 2]¹⁰
[key C nocount nocheck] &p [slur] c-e- | @0¹¹
g-e-c' [endslur][slur] g-e- | @1
d-f-a [endslur][slur] f-d- | @2
c-b'-e-d-g-f- [endslur] | @3
#d_e [slur] c-e- | g-e-c' [endslur][slur] g-e- | @5
%d-f-a [endslur] r | R! | @7
rr [slur/b] {/b/n d'-a''-f''-} | @8
a''- [endslur] [\.\] d'-f'-a'-d-f- [\\] | @9
[slur] a-g-f-e-\.\f-\.\d- [endslur] | @10
[slur] Ce-d- [endslur] | cr :)(: r | @12
[endstave]

[stave 2 "\it\violino I" treble 1]
[nocheck] r | r &p aa | raa | rgg | [2] raa | @5
fr [slur] c'-#a- | b-d'-f' [endslur][slur] c'-#a- | @7
b-d'-f' [endslur] r | [2] R! | @10¹²
[slur/b] c-e-c-e-d-e- [endslur] | @11
cr :)(: [slur] e-g- | @12
[endstave]

[stave 3 "\it\violino II" treble 1]
[nocheck] r | r &p ee | rff | rdd | rcc | ree | @5
```

6. Lines starting with an asterisk are pre-processor lines. This one defines a macro called p which becomes a shorthand for the code to print a bold italic *p* below the staff. When the contents of a macro are required, its name is given after the character & anywhere below its definition.

7. This requests the printing of bar numbers at the start of every line, using a 9-point font.

8. This requests that staves 1–5 be joined by a bracket. In fact, the default is to join all staves with a bracket, so in this case the directive is superfluous.

9. The instruction Unfinished suppresses the solid bar line that would otherwise be printed at the end of the piece. It is useful for examples, sample pages, and the like.

10. Any number of staff directives may occur in a single pair of square brackets. The number after treble sets the octave.

11. The [nocount] directive causes the bar not to be counted; [nocheck] suppresses the check that the notes in the bar add up to the time signature. Checking can also be disabled completely by a heading directive.

12. The [2] in brackets causes the bar's data to be repeated. This is most often used with rest bars, but it is not restricted to them.

```
dr [slur/b] %g | F%g | F [endslur] r | [2] R! | @10
A'_#g' | a'r :)(: r | @12
[endstave]

[stave 4 "\it\viola" alto 1]
[nocheck] r | r &p cc | [2] rb'b' | ra'a' | rcc | @5
b'r [slur] e | De | D [endslur] r | [2] R! | @10
E'._ | e'r :)(: r | @12
[endstave]

[stave 5 "\it\violoncello" bass 0]
[nocheck] r | &p arr | drr | err | frr | crr | @5
drr | [4] R! | [slur/b] e'\.\e'\.\e'\.\ [endslur] | @11
a'r :)(: r | @12
[endstave]
```

Example 18.1 A *PMS* encoding of the Mozart trio, Bars 1–12.

18.4   File Organization

PMS requires only a single input file for any piece; in principle, a whole symphony could be encoded in one file. However, long pieces are usually more manageable when held in a series of separate files. For example, when a piece consists of several movements that each start on a new page, it is usual to keep each movement in a separate file and process it separately. This saves having to process the whole piece repeatedly and also reduces the amount of memory needed.

. *PMS* has a pre-processing directive *include, which makes it possible to include the contents of another file at any point in the input file. For a set of pieces (or movements) in similar (printing) style, the heading directives which set up the layout parameters, etc., can be kept in one file and simply brought into each piece's input file as required.

For the examples quoted in the guidelines, the input would typically (but not necessarily) be arranged as follows:

(a) One movement of a piano piece would be encoded as one file.

(b) Each movement of a string quartet would probably be encoded in a separate file, especially if only a score were to be printed. However, if a set of parts were also to be printed, and the movements were sufficiently short, the whole thing might be done in one file so that new movements in the parts could start in the middle of pages.

(c) A song for piano and voice would be encoded in one file. The underlay is included with the notes (see next section).

When a single file is being used for printing both a score and a set of parts, use is often made of the pre-processing directive *if, which allows certain parts of the file to be processed or skipped according to certain conditions. Typically one would want different headings for the score and parts, for example. Another common use is to arrange for rest bars to be printed in the score but cue bars in the parts, as in the following (artificial) example:

```
[stave 6 "Trumpet" treble 1]
[20] R! |
*if score
[2] R! |
*else
[cue] "(flute)"/a g'f'e' | [cue] C'. |
*fi
```

Example 18.2 The use of the [cue] directive.

The [cue] directive specifies that the remaining notes in the bar are to be printed at the cue-note size (which can be altered by the user).

18.5 Miscellaneous Features

18.5.1 First and Second Endings

First and second endings are encoded by the directives [1st], [2nd], and so on. More than one may be given to cope with multiple repeats.

In the saltarello example shown in Chapter 1, *PMS* would assign the numbers 7 and 9 to the first bar in each set of bars labelled I and II, by default, but the [nocount] directive could be used to stop it from counting two of them if required.

18.5.2 Separation and Combination of Parts on a Single Staff

Multiple parts on a single staff are achieved by specifying a vertical separation of zero between two staves; these then overprint. There are directives which can force all the stems of a part to be either up or down.

This scheme makes it possible to separate the parts again; in the Telemann example, separate *Oboe and Violin* and *Viola* parts could be printed. The [*if] directive could be used to ensure that the forcing of the stem direction applied only to the score and not to the separate parts.

The same approach is taken for keyboard parts which have stems in both directions; for complicated keyboard parts two pairs of overprinted staves are commonly used. Input for the first bar of the Mozart piano sonata example is as follows:

```
bracket                          @no system bracket
brace 1-3                        @brace staves 1-3
stavespacing 1/0                 @staves 1 & 2 overprint

[stave 1 treble 1 stems up]
c'' |
[endstave]

[stave 2 treble 1 stems down]
(c'\ar\e'a') q |                 @() for chord; \ar\ for arpeggio
[endstave]

[stave 3 bass 0]
[slur] a'=-\g\c=-\g\e=-\g\ a- [endslur] a-a-a- |
[endstave]
```

Example 18.3 The Mozart piano sonata excerpt.

Note the use of the invisible rest, encoded as q, in Staff 2 to fill out the bar. Grace notes are indicated by the code \g\ after the note; they are beamed like ordinary notes.

If a note in one staff would collide with one on the other staff, it must be manually repositioned by means of the [move] staff directive, as *PMS* is not clever enough to detect this for itself. There is an example of this in Bar 8 of the Telemann example where the first note with a downward-pointing stem would have to be moved.

In keyboard parts there are times when sets of beamed notes spread over both staves. *PMS* has a coupling facility whereby notes that are input with the data for one staff are automatically positioned on the staff above or below if their pitches are sufficiently high or low, respectively.

18.5.3 Text Underlay

Text that is specified as underlay (or overlay) is given with the staff data, immediately before the relevant notes. Any amount of text can be given at a time. *PMS* distributes the syllables to the notes which follow. Some users put the entire underlay for a piece at the start; others include it phrase by phrase.

The hyphen character [-] is used to indicate syllable boundaries, and the equals character [=] is used when a syllable is to be sung on more than one note (including tied notes). *PMS* automatically supplies hyphen strings or extender lines, as appropriate, in the output. Text can be marked as underlay by adding /ul after a string, or the default for the staff can be set to underlay, in which case non-underlay strings must be marked as such.

Within underlay, as within any *PMS* text string, the back-slash character (\) is used as an escape to encode changes of typeface and characters that are not on the keyboard. The common diacriticals of Western European languages are provided in this way. For example, Bars 18–21 of the vocal part of the Telemann example[13] are encoded thus:

```
"Was= ist ^sch\o.-==ner als ^die=== Lie-be,="/ul
d'-_a-; b- | [slur/b] f=.g==a-; [endslur] d- |
f'-; [slur] g'=f'=e'=d'= [endslur] | c'-.; b=a- |
```

Example 18.4 Excerpt from the vocal part of the Telemann aria.

The escape sequence \o. prints as ö. Normally, *PMS* prints underlay syllables centered on the first note to which each applies. However, if the circumflex (^) is encountered, only those characters that appear to the left of it are centered. If it appears at the start of a syllable, as here, that syllable begins at the note position and extends to the right.

There is also a hard space character, encoded as #, which is not recognized as ending a word but is counted for centering purposes and prints as a space. This can be used to move syllables small amounts to the left or right.

There is no limit to the number of verses that can be printed under one staff of music, though the staff spacing must be manually adjusted to accommodate them. Different verses can use different typefaces and be of different sizes.

By default, *PMS* takes note of the underlay when laying out a bar, and if necessary it puts additional space between notes in order to prevent the underlaid syllables from overlapping. Some users say that the note positioning should be a function of the music only, and that the underlay should be adjusted to fit, rather than vice versa. For this reason, there is a heading directive that disables the spreading of notes to suit the underlay. A good compromise is to set the default note spacing a little wider than normal when underlay is involved, especially if it is in a language with long syllables,

---

13. Note the semicolons to break the beaming.

but leave the automatic spreading on. Then most of the time the spacing is determined by the music, but extremely long syllables are prevented from overlapping.

18.5.4 Performance Cues

When suggested performance is shown as small notes, these can be printed using the [cue] directive. If there are many examples on a staff, a second overprinting staff would be used. If, on the other hand, there were not many, use could be made of the [reset] directive, which allows the current point to be reset to the start of the bar. Bar 30 of the vocal staff of the Telemann can be encoded like this:

```
"Ku\ss?" c'. [reset][cue][stems up] d'-_/a c' [stems auto] |
```

The effect of the cue directive is automatically cancelled at the end of the bar. The qualifier /a that follows the underscore signifying a slur between two notes causes the slur to be drawn above the noteheads.

18.5.5 Editorial Material

There are a number of different facilities for editorial markings:

- Accidentals can be printed in round or square brackets by following the accidental with a closing bracket of the appropriate type. For example, the last three notes of Bar 6 of the first staff of the Binchois example are encoded as #)c'-%)b=c'=.

- Accidentals can also be printed above or below notes by following the accidental with the letter o (over) or u (under).

- The [cue] directive can be used to print small notes.

- Whole staves can be printed at a size smaller than other staves by using a heading directive such as Stavesizes 4/0.8 , which causes Staff 4 to print at 0.8 times the normal size.

- Slurs can be printed in dashed form, or with a short stroke through their centers, by means of the qualifiers /i (intermittent) or /e (editorial).

18.5.6 Unmeasured Notation

Checking of bar lengths can be turned off, and invisible bar lines can be used to indicate to *PMS* where it may make line breaks. This makes it straightforward to print the unmeasured notation of Example 1.5B, the chant example.

Unmeasured notation as in Example 1.5A is not available. However, *PMS* can be instructed to print black noteheads without stems, which gives a third possibility.

18.5.7 Incipits

The first bar of the Binchois example uses a combination of different features and is encoded as follows:

```
startnotime                            @no time signature at start
startbracketbar 1                      @indent brackets by one bar
bracket                                @but we don't want brackets!

[stave 1 bass 0 text underlay]         @text is underlay by default
[key F]
"\rm\Chorus"/a                         @roman font, above stave
"Mag-ni-fi-=cat"                       @underlay by default
[nocheck nocount]
[noteheads only] c'd'c'_f'f' [noteheads normal] |
[bass 0 key F time 3/4]
"\rm\(C.)"/a/e "A-" rrf' |             @/e aligns text by its end
[endstave]

[stave 2 omitempty]
|                                      @empty first bar
"\rm\(C.T.)"/a/e
[bass 0 key F time 3/4]
[text underlay] "A-" rrf |
[endstave]
```

Example 18.5 *PMS* encoding of the incipit of the Binchois *Magnificat*.

The key features are the ability to indent the system bracket by one bar, and the use of [omitempty] on the second staff. This causes nothing at all to be printed for bars that have no data (without it, blank staff lines would be printed).

The [noteheads] directive can also be used to select diamond-shaped (harmonic) or cross-shaped noteheads, or to turn off the printing of noteheads altogether for the printing of rhythm indications using only stems and beams.

18.5.8 Hemiolas

Lines can be drawn above or below the staff, with or without vertical jogs on their ends, to mark hemiolas, or for other purposes. The [line] and [endline] directives are used for this, and they have options for additional control that are the same as for slurs. Such lines can be forced to be horizontal (/h) and can be printed as dashed lines (/i). Thus, the last bar of the first staff of the Binchois would be:

[line/a] e'f'. [endline] d'- |

18.5.9 Twentieth-Century Music

PMS does not contain any features specifically for twentieth-century music. There is a drawing facility which makes it possible to generate simple graphic shapes that are not otherwise available, and this might be useful in some cases. For example, if it were required to print a solid, upwards pointing triangle below a note, the heading of the file would contain the definition of the triangle as follows:

```
draw triangle
     3 -12 moveto          @move to apex
     -3 -6 rlineto         @line to bottom left
     6 0 rlineto           @horizontal line to bottom right
     -3 6 rlineto          @line back to apex
     fill                  @fill it in
enddraw
```

Example 18.6 Drawing routine to create a triangle in a musical score.

In the staff data, the directive [draw triangle] would appear immediately before each note where the triangle was wanted. Information about the pitch of the current note is available to the drawing routines, making it possible, for example, to draw rectangular boxes around notes by this means.

18.6   Further Remarks

18.6.1   Printing Issues

PMS does not contain any code for the rasterization of images, relying on supporting software (either in the operating system, or in a *PostScript* printer) for this.

The current version of *PMS* runs only under Acorn's RISC OS operating system. It makes use of the system's Outline Font Manager to display music and text on the screen and to print it via RISC OS printer drivers. Drivers are available for a wide variety of printers; many come with the system. Items such as slurs and lines are output using the system's drawing primitives.

Output pages can be converted into the standard graphic format for the RISC OS system, known as draw files. In this form they can be used as illustrations in the common desktop publishing packages. They can also be touched up by loading them into a drawing program. It is believed that software may exist to convert draw files into a more widely used standard form such as *TIFF*.

PMS can also generate *PostScript* directly, for printing on any *PostScript* printer that has had the *PostScript* version of its music font downloaded into it. *PostScript* is normally generated in the form of a complete document, but an option to produce individual pages in *.EPS* format is available.

PMS supports no sound mode conversions other than its ability to play the music either via the very limited RISC OS sound system or via MIDI.

18.6.2 Code Documentation, Conversion, and Interchange

A complete description of *Philip's Music Scribe* and its input code is given in the manual for the software, available from the author in printed form.

This code has not to date been converted to any other. It should be possible to write converters to and from an interchange standard, but information would probably be lost in one or both directions, unless the standard were very comprehensive.

18.6.3 Authorship and Copyright

Philip's Music Scribe was designed and implemented by the author. The program itself is copyrighted, and all rights are reserved. However, no copyright or other intellectual property claim is made for the input encoding scheme, though the author would appreciate a citation if any use is made of it.

19   *SCORE*

Leland Smith

SCORE is a commercial program running under DOS on IBM PC-compatible computers. The *SCORE* music printing system is intended to facilitate the creation of virtually any page of standard music notation with a final quality equal to that of true engraving. It originated on a mainframe computer, with plotter printout, in 1971. *SCORE* is written in FORTRAN. Output is designed for *PostScript* printers. In fact *SCORE* is a page-oriented language similar in organization to *PostScript*.

   SCORE has gained wide acceptance in the commercial printing of both classical and popular music on account of four features:

- its comprehensive approach to both conventional and unconventional notation

- its extensibility

- its precise control of symbol placement on the page

- the professional appearance of its output

SCORE is currently being used, for example, to produce professional quality scores of works by such composers as Berg, Buxtehude, Hindemith, Lully, Schumann, Verdi, and Wagner. It is also used to produce popular music with guitar chords and unusual graphic features.[1]

---

1. Among major users of *SCORE* are the publishers Ricordi, C. F. Peters, and Schotts Söhne for collected editions of classical music and the Hal Leonard Company for the production of popular music.

19.1 *SCORE* Input Code

An input language that is primarily alphabetic is used to initiate a music-page description. This may be created directly within the program or imported from files created by any computer text editor or word-processing program. The input code is converted to a parametric file format. Certain details of music description are normally entered only in the numeric parametric file format.

In the input file, musical attributes are separated into five parallel streams of information. These are pitch, duration, articulation, beams, and slurs. Each attribute stream (or input "pass"), whether or not it contains any data, is terminated by a semicolon (;).

19.1.1 Pitch [A..G]

Pitch name and octave number are designated using standard nomenclature; Middle C = C4, etc. Octave numbers are assumed to be repeated until explicitly changed.

Chromatic inflections are provided using the following codes:

F	flat (♭)	FF	double flat (♭♭)
S	sharp (♯)	SS	double sharp (♯♯)
N	natural (♮)		

Chromatic alterations suggested by *musica ficta* signs or introduced editorially (i.e., accidentals placed above the note) may be designated by these codes:

FIF	♭ above the note
FIS	♯ above the note
FIN	♮ above the note

However, they are treated as articulations (see later commentary).

Clefs may be designated by mnemonics or by number:

TR	or	0	treble clef
BA	or	1	bass clef
AL	or	2	alto clef
TE	or	3	tenor clef

Each pitch or rest assumes an ordinal number. These do not appear in the pitch stream but are required in the specification of articulation marks, ornamentation, dyanmics, beams, and slurs (in passes 3, 4, and 5) in order to establish the relationship of these "marks" to the original pitch stream.

19.1.2 Duration [W, H, Q, ...]

Durations may be handled by letter code or by numbers as divisions of a whole note. The most common letter codes are these:

W	whole	E	eighth
H	half	S	sixteenth
Q	quarter		

All durations have dotted versions (W., W.., etc.). Grace notes are designated by the code G. Rests are designated by the pitch code R followed by a duration code (e.g., H.). Tuplets are best handled by the numerical approach described below.

19.1.3 Articulation, Ornamentation, and Dynamics [TR, S, P, F, ...]

Ornaments may be represented by mnemonics and by numerals. Some common mnemonics are these:

S	staccato	TRS	trill with ♯
A	accent	TRF	trill with ♭
T	tenuto	TRN	trill with ♮
H	harmonic	FE	fermata
D	downbow	MO	mordent
U	upbow	IM	inverted mordent
TR	trill (*tr*)	P	piano
		F	forte

19.1.4 Beams and Slurs

The starting and ending event numbers, separated by a space and terminated by a slash (/), of each beam and slur constitute their description. The code 1 2/3 4 in the beam input would group notes 1 with 2 and 3 with 4. Some abbreviations are used to specify beaming patterns or overrides to them (e.g., the expression 2B tells the program to beam two notes by twos, etc.)

The code 1 4 in the slur input would place one slur over the first four notes. The "slur" pass in *SCORE* input captures information about curved lines; no actual distinction is made between ties and slurs.

19.2   Input File Organization

Since *SCORE* was originally designed solely for printing, information in a *SCORE* prametric file contains a vertical list of objects as they are encountered (or placed) from left to right on the page.

			Bar 1 ↓	Bar 2 ↓	Bar 3 ↓
System 1	→	→ Subsystem 1 →	Part 1 →		
	→	→	Part 2 →		
	→	→	Part 3 →		
	→	→	Part 4 →		
	→	→ Subsystem 2 →	Part 5 →		
System 2	→	Part 1 →			
	→	Part 2 →			
	→	Part 3 →			
	→	Part 4 →			
	→	Part 5 →			
System 3	→	Part 1 →			
	→	Part 2 →			
	→	Part 3 →			
	→	Part 4 →			
	→	Part 5 →			

Example 19.1 Hypothetical score of 11 bars (three on System 1 plus four each in Systems 2 and 3) with four principal parts (Parts 1-4) and an accompaniment (Part 5).

At input, each page of a musical score is described in a separate file in which systems and parts are numbered vertically from lowest to highest. Thus, in the hypothetical page of music for four parts plus accompaniment shown in Example 19.1, the staff described first in *SCORE* would contain Part 5 of System 3. Part 4 of System 3 would be next described, and so forth. After all the parts of System 3 are described, then System 2 would be addressed, beginning with Part 5. Finally, System 1 would be described, again from bottom to top. Within this arrangement, information is processed from left to right. In this example the bar order at input would be 8–11, 4–7, 1–3 [see Examples 19.2a and 19.2b]. The staff and system arrangement can be changed by editing the resulting parametric files, where the data are reordered.

19.3   Parametric-File Object Types and Codes[2]

SCORE's parameter structure consists of a sparse array whose contents describe the vertical and horizontal placement of all graphical objects as it identifies them. Each object is defined in a separate row. The parametric information, which varies with the object type, is given in columns. Some objects require more parameters than others; consequently some cells of the array are never filled. *SCORE*'s internal file format was originally derived from the sound file format developed for *Music V* and its predecessors.[3] It is the combination of the automatic features of the input mode and the parameter editing system which gives *SCORE* its greatest power.

The first four parameters have fixed functions and always identify the same elements of information: (1) object type, (2) the staff number concerned, (3) horizontal position, and (4) vertical position.

19.3.1   Object Types [Parameter 1]

The *SCORE* object-code types are as follows:

Code 1	notes		Code 4	lines
Code 2	rests		Code 5	slurs
Code 3	clefs		Code 6	beams

2. Many details are omitted here. See the *SCORE Reference Manual* for complete information.

3. See MUSIC V in the glossary.

Code 7	*tr, 8va, ped.* lines	Code 13	reserved
Code 8	staves	Code 14	bar lines
Code 9	symbol library	Code 15	added *PostScript* code
Code 10	numbers	Code 16	text and lyrics
Code 11	user-defined symbols	Code 17	key signatures
Code 12	geometric shapes, including guitar tablature	Code 18	meter numbers

Note that this system of object classification has more to do with graphic presentation than with musical logic. The "lines" category, for example, does not include staff lines or bar lines, which each occupy separate categories, but does include miscellaneous lines, such as those used to indicate crescendo and decrescendo.

19.3.2 Staff and Position Information [Parameters 2–4]

Every item is connected to a staff (Parameter 2), which determines its basic size and vertical position on the page. *SCORE* uses a fixed horizontal space unit (Parameter 3) wherein 200 units span the width of a 7.5" staff.[4] The vertical unit (Parameter 4) is a scale step determined by the staff size. The interpretation of Parameter 4 will vary according to the object-code numbers given in Parameter 1. Often the size factors will be found in Parameters 5 or 6. For some items which need two pairs of position numbers (horizontal and vertical), Parameters 3 and 4 represent the horizontal[5] and vertical[6] positions, while Parameters 5 and 6 represent the right vertical and horizontal positions.[7]

19.3.3 Variable Parameters [Parameters 5–18]

The object-type definition found in Parameter 1 (P1) determines the definition of Parameters 5 through 18. These variable meanings are described in detail in relation to each object code needed to interpret them. In the following commentary, numerous details concerning additional subcategories of parameters have, in the interest of space, been omitted.

---

4. Here a page size of 8.5 x 11 inches with .5 inch margins on all sides is assumed.

5. Measured from the left.

6. Measured from the top.

7. i.e., P3 and P6 are horizontal values, while P4 and P5 are vertical values.

IF OBJECT CODE = 1 [**NOTES**]

A common template is used to describe the variable meaning of the parameter codes from 5 onward. In this example, if the object code = 1, then Parameters 5..18 assume these meanings:

    P5   = note attributes, in the format $xy.z$ where
                x = stem direction
                  1 = up
                  2 = down
                y = accidental
                  0 = none
                  1 = ♭
                  2 = ♯
                  3 = ♮
                  4 = ♭♭
                z = horizontal offset of accidental

    P6   = note head type (sample settings)
                  0 = quarter note (oval note head)
                  1 = half note (oval note head)
                  2 = whole note (oval note head)
                  3 = breve (rectangular)
                  4 = half note (diamond note head)
                  6 = percussion "note" (x-shaped note head)

    P7   = note duration (sample settings)
                  1   = quarter
                  1.5 = dotted quarter
                  0.5 = eighth
                  0.25 = sixteenth
                  2   = half
                  4   = whole, etc.

    P8 = stem length: increments to be added to or subtracted from 7
    P9 = prolongation dots, flags, in the format $xy.z$
                x = number of dots of prolongation
                y = number of flags or tails
                z = offset of dots

   P10 = offset of note from given P3 position
                  10 = 1 note-width to right
                  20 = 1 note-width to left
                (Other values will give the exact offset.)

P11 = articulation marks, fingerings, etc.

These are drawn from a main symbol library which supplements the P9 library. Multiple P11 libraries may be created by the user. Some common examples follow:

5 = >   8 = ^
6 = ⁻   12 = ˅
7 = ·   13 = °

P12 = note in relation to staff
1 = put note on staff above
2 = put note on staff below

P13 = horizontal offset for marks and fingerings: set as in P11
P14 = vertical offset for marks and fingerings: set as in P11
P15 = overall size of note and attached elements:
0 + default = size 1, etc.

P16 = leger-line thickness control
P17 = extension of source of note stem
P18 = change size of attached marks from default: set as in P11

Grace notes (small notes with slashes) are produced by adding 100 to Parameter 4; P8 = 101.

Appoggiaturas (small notes without slashes) are producing by adding −100 to Parameter 4; P8 = 0.

IF OBJECT CODE = 2 [**RESTS**]

P5 = rest type
0 = quarter   −1 = half
1 = eighth   −2 = whole
2 = sixteenth   −3 = breve
3 = 32nd   −4 = passage repetition
4 = 64th   −5 = multibar rest
5 = 128th   −12 = 2-bar (Renaissance) rest

P6 = dots
P7 = duration [same as in Code 1/Notes]
P8 = numeral over rest or numbered bars of rest
−1 puts fermata over rest
P9 = centering of whole rest, etc.

P10 = offset of rest from given P3 position
P11 = vertical offset of number over rest
P12 = size of number over rest
P13 = instrument number for cues
P14 = type font for number over rest
P15 = size factor for rest
         Adding 100 or −100 to P4 produces a grace-note-sized rest.

IF OBJECT CODE = 3 [CLEFS]

P5   = clef type
         0 = treble   2 = C-clef (alto)
         1 = bass   3 = C-clef (tenor)

P6   = horizontal size (0 = default size 1)
P7   = vertical size (if 0, then same as P6)
P15 = horizontal offset from P3 position
         Adding 100 or −100 to P4 produces a small-sized clef.

IF OBJECT CODE = 4 [LINES]

P5   = vertical position of right end
P6   = horizontal position of right end
P7   = line type
         0 = ordinary line
       −1 = trill or arpeggio
        1 = dashes
       −2 = thin wiggle (for vibrato, etc.)

The slanted lines of crescendos and decrescendos are accommodated differently. Crescendo or decrescendo "hairpins" are made by setting P5 = 99. The decrescendo hairpin can also be made by setting P7 = −1.

P8   = width of dashes or wiggles
P9   = rotation, unless dashes or wiggle, otherwise space between dashes or height of wiggle
P10 = pixels to be added to line thickness
P11 = length of vertical line (up or down) at left for bracket

P12 = length of vertical line (up or down) at right for bracket
      Adding 100 to P11 or P12 produces a simple arrowhead to left (◄) or right (►).

P13 = rotation for dashes or wiggles

IF OBJECT CODE = 5 [**SLURS**]

P5 = vertical position of right end
P6 = horizontal position of right end
P7 = height of slur curve, in scale steps
P8 = various offsets for slur ends
          −1 = centered on note heads
          −2 = centered between note heads
          −3 = centered between dotted notes
          −4 = centered on vertical note stems
           1 = 1st ending bracket
           3 = triplet bracket

P9 = slur-flattening factor or, if P8 = 3, any other tuplet number
P10 = move tuplet number left or right of center
P11 = slur with discontinuous line
           1 = dashes or (if P8 = 3) continuous bracket with number inside
          −1 = dotted slur

P12 = partial slur
           1 = left half of slur only
           2 = right half only
          −1 = slur reverses direction in middle

P13 = slur thickness
           0 = thin
           1 = default

P14..P18 = provisions for broken slurs and numbers in broken slurs

IF OBJECT CODE = 6 [**BEAMS**]

P5 = vertical position of right end
P6 = horizontal position of right end

P7   = *xy*
      x = stem direction
         1 = up
         2 = down
      y = number of primary beams
         0 = tremolo beams
         1 = eighth-note beams

P8   = tuplet number over beam
P9   = complex horizontal offsets when some notes have stems going different directions
P10 = first secondary beam offset and number of beams
P11 = left end of first secondary beam
P12 = right end of first secondary beam
P13 = second secondary beam offset and number of beams
P14 = left end of second secondary beam
P15 = right end of second secondary beam
P16 = horizontal displacement of number over beam
P17 = beam thickness factor
P18 = beam size factor (used in conjunction with notes' P15)
P19 = vertical displacement of number over beam

IF OBJECT CODE = 7 [**ARTICULATION/ORNAMENTATION MARKS**]

Within the category of articulation and ornamentation marks, several parameters have a categorical meaning:

P5   = size, other features
P6   = right end of line, etc.
P7   = symbol type
P8   = various meanings
P9   = pedal or wiggle size
P15 = horizontal offset from P3

More precise meanings are specific to the particular type of sign. Some examples of the use of these parameters to create articulation marks are shown below.

For trills five parameters may be required:

P7   = ornament type
         0 = trill
P5   = size

P6 = right end of wiggle
      0 = no wiggle
P8 = associated accidental
      1 = flat
      2 = sharp
      3 = natural

P9 = wiggle size [if relevant]
      .75 = default

For octave transposition indications six parameters may be required:

P7 = transposition type
      8 = *8va (ottava alta)*
      -8 = *8ba (ottava bassa)*
      15 = *15ma (quindicesima)*

P5   = size
P6   = right end of dashed line
P8   = dash size
P9   = size of space between dashes
P12 = bracket orientation
      + = bracket up at end of dashes
      − = bracket down

For graphic harp pedal symbols five parameters may be required:

P7 = symbol type
      1 = harp pedal (where P8 = 123, P9 = 1232)

P5 = size
P6 = 0
P8 = left 3 pedals—a 3-digit number
P9 = right 4 pedals—a 4-digit number for P8, P9:
      1 = bottom pedal position
      2 = middle pedal position
      3 = top pedal position

As one example, if P8 = 111, then all left pedals are in the bottom position.
For graphic piano pedal symbols seven parameters may be required:

P7   = symbol type
   20 = piano pedal

P5   = pedal positions

P5 in this case is a 3-digit number indicating which of three pedals are to be depressed at any given time. If 1 = pedal down, and 0 = pedal up, then the following combinations can be represented:

   001 = right pedal down
   101 = both left and right pedals down
   010 = middle pedal down
   110 = left and middle pedals down

P6   = end point for line to right (P6 = P3, or = 0 = no line)
P8   = position of line extension to the left (only if P6 > 0)
P9   = pedal symbol size factor
P11 = left bracket
   + = bracket end on left side (using P8) (+100 = arrow)

P12 = right bracket
   + = bracket end on right (using P6) (+100 = arrow)

P7 and P8 can also be used to represent the overall shape of a piano pedal line. P7 gives the bump type and P8 the position of the bump.

IF OBJECT CODE = 8 [MUSICAL STAFF]

P5   = size of scale step
P6   = right end of staff
P7   = number of staff lines
   0 = 5 lines
   −1 = invisible lines

P8   = distance (in inches or centimeters) to next file
P9   = instrument ID number for part extraction
P10 = distance from Staff 1 (consecutive staves are calculated to be 18 staff-steps apart)
P11 = thickness of staff lines (used with *PostScript* only)

IF OBJECT CODE = 9 [**SYMBOL LIBRARY**]

The symbol library contains approximately 1000 symbols including not only objects regularly encountered in common musical notation but also special symbols found only in special contexts. Some examples include unusual time signatures and dynamics markings, signs for unusual ornaments, percussion notation symbols, and lute tablature symbols.

P5 = library order number. Some examples are:

       0 = 𝄞   52 = *pp*

       1 = 𝄢   169 = *ffp*

P6 = horizontal size factor (0 = 1)
P7 = vertical size (0 = same number as found in P6)
P8 = added thickness (for dot-matrix printers only)
P9 = degrees of clockwise rotation
P10 = line width additions in pixels (for laser printers only)
P15 = horizontal displacement from P3

IF OBJECT CODE = 10 [**NUMERALS**]

P5 = numeral required (upper limit = 999; 1000 = A, 1001 = B, etc.)
P6 = size factor (0 = 1)
P7 = text font type (selective listing)
       0 = Times Roman
       1 = Italic

P8 = enclosure types
       1 = numeral within circle
       2 = numeral within box

P10 = thickness of box/circle
P11 = horizontal box size
P12 = vertical box size
P13 = vertical displacement of box
P14 = change space between numbers
P15 = horizontal displacement from P3

IF OBJECT CODE = 11 [**USER-DEFINED SYMBOLS**]

If the Object Code = 11, then Parameters 5..15 assume the same values as with Code 9, except that P13 = 1 brings up the prompt for the name of the special library file (*.DRW*). *SCORE* supports drawing, and users may create and store their own images.

IF OBJECT CODE = 12 [**GEOMETRIC FIGURES**]

Some geometrical figures are already composed. These include:

    P5 = geometric type
            0   = rectangles, squares
            1   = circles
            −1..−5 = guitar chords
            2   = accordion

    P6 = bar thickness
    P7 = horizontal displacement from P3

For circles and polygons, five parameters may be required:

    P7 = vertical size (0 = same number as found in P6)
    P8 = added thickness
    P9 = degrees of clockwise rotation
    P10 = parallelogram offset (rectangles)
    P13 = fill pattern
            1 = fill area solid black

For circles only, two parameters may suffice:

    P10 = beginning point of arc (in degrees)
    P11 = end point of arc (in degrees)

Guitar-chord grids and other tablatures P7..P19 are used for automatic chord setups. Accordion notation was implemented in Version 3.1.

IF OBJECT CODE = 14 [**BAR LINES**]

    P4 = number of staves covered by bar lines
    P5 = bar-line type
            0 = normal bar line

                    1 = thin-thin bar-line pair
                    2 = thin-thick bar-line pair
                    3 = thin-thick bar-line pair preceded by repeat dots
                    7 = dashes

P6   = bar thickness
P7   = horizontal displacement
P8   = partial bracket (when P5 = 9) types:
                    0 = bracket with upper and lower curls
                    1 = bracket with upper curl
                    2 = bracket with lower curl
                    3 = bracket without curls

P8   = size of dash with dashed bar lines (when P5 = 7)
P9   = size of space with dashed bar lines (when P5 = 7)
P10 = alter bottom point of bar line
P11 = alter top point of bar line
P12 = switch for part extraction
                    1 = marker for part extraction in *PAGE*

IF OBJECT CODE = 15 [*POSTSCRIPT* LINK]

If the Object Code = 15 [*PostScript* Program Files], then *PostScript* language files may be inserted into the body of a *SCORE* file. See the *SCORE Reference Manual* for details on the use of this code.

IF OBJECT CODE = 16 [TEXT ELEMENTS]

Text elements include such information as titles, movement names, tempo designations, performance instructions, and lyrics. Commonly used parameters are these:

P5   = character space factor
P6   = horizontal size factor (0 = 1)
P7   = vertical size factor (0 = same factor as P6)
P8   = font override:
                    9..98 = *SCORE* fonts
                    1000..1034 = normal *PostScript* fonts

P9   = rotation of text string
P10 = add or subtract from size of the space character only
P11 = text offset from P3 setting
P12 = number of characters in the string

P13 = length of text in *SCORE* units; the actual text is stored as a string starting where P14 would normally be found. Within the string, type fonts are indicated by *_xy* where *xy* holds the font number. Some common font numbers are these:

_00   Times Roman
_04   Helvetica
_12   Palatino
_24   New Century Schoolbook
_29   Courier

IF OBJECT CODE = 17 [KEY SIGNATURES]

P5   = number of accidentals

$1 = 1\sharp$
$-1 = 1\flat$
$101 = 1\natural$ in position normally occupied by a $\sharp$
$-101 = 1\natural$ in position normally occupied by a $\flat$

P6   = clef number (determines positions of accidentals)
P7   = factor for spacing between accidentals
P14 = switch for "lineup" and "justify" routines

1 = make lineup and justify routines ignore this item

P15 = horizontal offset from P3 position[8]

IF OBJECT CODE = 18 [METER NUMBERS]

P5   = top number of meter

$98 = ¢$
$99 = C$

P6   = bottom number of meter
P7   = size factor
P8   = top number of second meter (for composite time signatures)
P9   = bottom number of second meter
P10, 11 = can alter spacing of composite meter

---

8. P8..P13 and P16 can be used in 3.1 and subsequent versions of *SCORE* to create irregular key signatures.

P12 = layout of polymeter numerals
      1 = suppress the "+" between the meters

P14 = switch for "lineup" and "justify" routines
      1 = make lineup and justify routines ignore this item

P15 = horizontal offset from P3 position

19.4   Output File Formats

Completed *SCORE* data may be saved in two forms. The normal procedure is to save the data in a binary file. However, it is also possible to save complete parameter data as an ASCII file. This latter form takes up more storage space, but it has the advantage that it may easily be edited or used as a data base for other programs. Because of their greater transparency to the reader, we consider parameter files in ASCII format first.

19.4.1   Parametric Files in ASCII Format

If the data is saved as an ASCII file, each line (or record) represents one *SCORE* item. Actually there are some exceptions to this. Text items (Code 16) and items which include an external file name will use two lines. It is from this data that the *SCORE* parameter structure may be most easily seen. The following list would produce a five-line staff, a treble clef, a quarter-note Middle C, and a bar line.

```
 8    1     0     0     0    200
 3    1     1     0     0
 1    1    10    10    10     0    1
14    1   200     1
```

These items are read line by line, from left to right. They describe a treble clef containing only a clef sign and a quarter-note Middle C. Four objects—a staff, a clef, a note, and a bar line—are described by the four lines of information, as follows:

Line 1 of code:

P1 (8)	=	OBJECT-TYPE = STAFF
P2 (1)	=	number of the staff concerned
P3 (0)	=	horizontal position of the left end of the staff
P4 (0)	=	vertical offset from page height
P5 (0)	=	size factor
P6 (200)	=	position of the right end of the staff

Line 2 of code:

P1 (3)	=	OBJECT-TYPE = CLEF
P2 (1)	=	number of the staff concerned
P3 (1)	=	horizontal position of clef
P4 (0)	=	vertical offset from page height
P5 (0)	=	clef symbol identifier (treble)

Line 3 of code:

P1 (1)	=	OBJECT-TYPE = NOTE
P2 (1)	=	number of staff concerned
P3 (10)	=	horizontal position of note
P4 (10)	=	vertical position of note
P5 (10)	=	stem direction (1 = up), associated accidental (0 = none)
P6 (0)	=	note-head type (0 = black)
P7 (1)	=	rhythmic value (1 = quarter note)

Line 4 of code:

P1 (14)	=	OBJECT-TYPE = BAR LINE
P2 (1)	=	number of staff concerned
P3 (200)	=	horizontal position of bar line
P4 (1)	=	number of staves covered by bar line

Example 19.4 contains parametric information in ASCII format for the Mozart trio.

19.4.2 Parametric Files in Binary Format

SCORE binary files contain the same data as in the ASCII format but they are necessarily more compact. The structure of a *SCORE* binary file is as follows:

$$word\ count - data - trailer$$

The basic word count is a two-byte integer which tells the total number of four-byte floating point words which will follow. This number includes the trailer data. In future releases of the program the word-count may be changed to a four-byte integer.

Each item in the data is made up of a word count, m, followed by m parameters. The very last word (word n) in the file contains −9999.0. The word before that is the word count (j) of the trailer. Thus the total count of the pertinent data is $n - (j + 1)$ words. A typical *read* routine in FORTRAN would appear as:

```
read(channel) n, (r(k), k=1,n); read the wordcount, then the
                                  main data
j = r(n - 1)        ; j is the trailer wordcount
knt = n - (j + 1)   ; knt is the actual count of the SCORE data
```

Now the local word count (*m*) for item 1 is set by $m = r(1)$, and the parameters for the item run from $r(2)$ to $r(m + 1)$. The word count for the next item is found at $r(m + 2)$, etc. The following routine would set up a pointer list (*iptr*) for all the items in the file.

```
   k = 1                  ; initialize the counters
   j = 0
99 j = j + 1              ; update the pointer list counter
   iptr(j) = k            ; points to the current item
   m = rn(k)              ; item's word count
   k = k + m + 1          ; point to the next item's word count
   if (k.lt.knt) go to 99 ; loop back until total word count is
                            exceeded
```

The total number of items is now found in *k*.

The file trailer is of variable size and will contain such information as the version and serial number of the program, whether inches or centimeters were the measuring units, and other kinds of information yet to be determined.

19.4.3 Print Files

SCORE creates standard *PostScript* graphics and type commands which can be sent directly to a *PostScript* printer or written to an *Encapsulated PostScript* file (*.EPS*). The *EPS* files can be transported later to a distant printer or be combined with the output of various standard word-processor or publishing programs. *PostScript* code is in ASCII (ordinary text) format. Most of the shapes used in music printing are found in the *SCORE* drawing library. Text items are usually handled by *PostScript* type fonts.

19.5 Examples

The input files for Bars 1–12 of the Mozart Clarinet Quintet are shown in Examples 19.2a and b. A corresponding parametric file in ASCII is shown as Example 19.4. These files are based on a layout in which the second system starts with Bar 11, and this is reflected in the encoding. Example 19.2a contains all five parts (from bottom to top) for the first system (Bars 1–11). Example 19.2b contains the parts for the second system up to the repeat sign in Bar 12.

```
IN 6 0 0 .6
sp 0 200 6
M5/BA/K3S/3 4/R/ M/A3/R// M/D/R// M/E/R// M/F/R// M/C/R//
M/D/R// M/RW/ M/RW/ M/RW/ M/RW/ M;
QX19/H.X4;
P 1;
;
;

IN 7 0 0 .6
sp=6
AL/K3S/3 4/R//C4/C/R/B3/B/R/B//R/A//R/C4/C/B3/R/E4/D/E/D/R/RW/;
QX19/H/Q/H/Q/H./H.;
P 1;
;
12 15;

IN 8 0 0 .6
sp=6
TR/K3S/3 4/R//E4/E/R/F//R/D//R/C//R/E//D/R/GN/F/GN/F/R/RW/;
QX19/H/Q/H/Q/H./;
P 1;
;
12 15;

IN 9 0 0 .6
sp=6
TR/K3S/3
4/R//A4/A/R/A//R/G//R/A//R/A//F/R/C5/AS4/B/D5/F/C/AS4/B/D5/F/R/RW/;
QX18/EX4/Q/EX4/Q//H./;
P 1;
2B;
12 16/17 21;

IN 10 0 0 .6
sp=6
TR/3
4/C5/E/G/E/C6/G5/E/D/F/A/F/D/C/B4/E5/D/G/F/DS/E/C/E/G/E/C6/G5/E/DN/F/A/R/
RW/R//D4/A3/F/A/D4/F/A/SU/D5/F/SO/A/G/F/E/F/D;
EX4/Q/EX4/Q/EX8/Q//EX4/Q/EX4/Q//H./Q//T///EX12;
S 35 36 37 38 39/P 1;
1 2/3 4/6 7/8 9/11 12/13 18/21 22/23 24/26 27/28 29/31 33/34 39/40 45;
1 5/6 10/11 18/19 20/21 25/26 30/31 34/40 45;
```

Example 19.2a *SCORE* input code for System 1 (Bars 1–10) of the second trio of the Mozart Clarinet Quintet. The parts are in the order "bass clef" (*Cello*), "alto clef" (*Viola*), "treble clef" (*Violino 2*), "treble clef" (*Violino 1*), and "treble clef" (transposing part for *Clarinet*). Staff numbers, clefs signs, and key-signature designations are in bold-face type here to clarify the input file organization.

```
IN 1 0 0 .6 50
0 50 1
M5/BA/K3S/E2/E// M/A/R/ ML;
QX5;
S 1 2 3;
;
1 3;

IN 2 0 0 .6 50
SP=1
AL/K3S/E3/E/R;
H./Q/;
P 1;
;
1 2;

IN 3 0 0 .6 50
SP=1
TR/K3S/A3/GS/A/R;
H/Q//;
;
;
1 2;

IN 4 0 0 .6 50
SP=1
TR/K3S/C4/E/C/E/D/E/C/R;
EX6/Q/;
;
6B;
1 6;

IN 5 0 0 .6 50
SP=1
TR/C5/E/D/C/R;
H/E//Q/;
;
2B;
1 3;
```

Example 19.2b *SCORE* input code for System 2 (Bars 11–12) of the second trio of the Mozart Clarinet Quintet. This file is marked in the same way as that shown in Example 19.2a.

In the corresponding parametric file that follows, Parameter 1 identifies the object being described and positioned.

Parameter 2 (the second column from the left) identifies the current staff. The ten staves used in this example are organized as follows:

Example 19.3 Mozart trio, Bars 1-12, in the exact layout reproduced by Examples 19.2a (upper-system encoding) and 19.2b (lower-system encoding), above, and Example 19.4 (parametric page file), below.

- Input codes 10, 9, 8, 7, 6 contain the System-1 parts for *Clarinet*, *Violino 1*, *Violino 2*, *Viola*, and *Cello*.

- Input codes 5, 4, 3, 2, and 1 contain the System-2 parts for the same parts.

That is, the first part described in 19.2b ("1") is the *Cello* from Bar 11 up to the repeat sign in Bar 12.

Note that within each system-staff Parameter 3 (the third column from the left) designates the horizontal position of each new object and gradually increases as each new staff is described.

8.	1.	.000	.00	.60	50.00	.000	.00	5.00		
14.	1.	.000	5.00							
3.	1.	1.200	.00	**1.00**						
17.	1.	5.901	.00	**3.00**	1.00					
1.	1.	12.561	1.00	10.00	.00	1.000	.00	.00	.0	7.0
5.	1.	12.561	-2.40	-2.40	28.05	-1.800	-1.00			
1.	1.	20.308	1.00	10.00	.00	1.000	.00	.00	.0	7.0
1.	1.	28.055	1.00	10.00	.00	1.000	.00	.00	.0	7.0
14.	1.	36.299	5.00							
1.	1.	38.200	4.00	10.00	.00	1.000				
2.	1.	43.563	.00	.00	.00	1.000	.00	-1.00		
14.	1.	50.000	5.00	3.00						
8.	2.	.000	-3.03	.60	50.00	.000	.00	4.00		
3.	2.	1.200	.00	**2.00**						
17.	2.	5.901	.00	**3.00**	2.00					
9.	2.	12.561	-3.00	53.00	1.00					
1.	2.	12.561	2.00	10.00	1.00	3.000	.00	10.00		
5.	2.	12.561	1.50	1.50	38.20	-1.882	-3.00			
1.	2.	38.200	2.00	10.00	.00	1.000				
2.	2.	43.563	.00	.00	.00	1.000	.00	-1.00		
8.	3.	.000	-6.65	.60	50.00	.000	.00	3.00		
3.	3.	1.200								
17.	3.	5.901	.00	**3.00**	.00					
1.	3.	12.561	-1.00	10.00	1.00	2.000	1.00			
5.	3.	12.561	-3.00	-4.00	28.05	-1.774	-1.00			
1.	3.	28.055	-2.00	12.00	.00	1.000	2.00			
1.	3.	38.200	-1.00	10.00	.00	1.000	1.00			
2.	3.	43.563	.00	.00	.00	1.000	.00	-1.00		
8.	4.	.000	-11.94	.60	50.00	.000	.00	2.00		
3.	4.	1.200								
17.	4.	5.901	.00	**3.00**	.00					
1.	4.	12.561	1.00	10.00	.00	.500	1.00	.00		
6.	4.	12.561	2.00	2.00	31.93	11.000				
5.	4.	12.561	-1.00	.60	31.93	-2.300	-1.00			
1.	4.	16.434	3.00	10.00	.00	.500	-1.00	.00		
1.	4.	20.308	1.00	10.00	.00	.500	1.00	.00		
1.	4.	24.181	3.00	10.00	.00	.500	-1.00	.00		
1.	4.	28.055	2.00	10.00	.00	.500				
1.	4.	31.928	3.00	10.00	.00	.500	-1.00	.00		
1.	4.	38.200	1.00	10.00	.00	1.000				
2.	4.	43.563	.00	.00	.00	1.000	.00	-1.00		
8.	5.	.000	-17.65	.60	50.00	.000	.00	1.00		
3.	5.	1.200								
1.	5.	12.561	8.00	20.00	1.00	2.000				
5.	5.	12.561	10.00	12.00	31.93	2.000	-1.00			
1.	5.	28.055	10.00	20.00	.00	.500	.01	.00		
6.	5.	28.055	10.00	9.00	31.93	21.000				
1.	5.	31.928	9.00	20.00	.00	.500	-.01	.00		
1.	5.	38.200	8.00	20.00	.00	1.000				
2.	5.	43.563	.00	.00	.00	1.000	.00	-1.00		
8.	6.	.000	-12.91	.60	200.00	.000	.00	5.00		
14.	6.	.000	5.00							
3.	6.	1.200	.00	**1.00**						
17.	6.	5.750	.00	**3.00**	1.00					
18.	6.	11.510	.00	3.00	4.00					
2.	6.	16.010	.00	.00	.00	1.000	.00	-1.00		
14.	6.	22.043	5.00							
1.	6.	23.642	11.00	20.00	.00	1.000				
9.	6.	23.642	-1.00	53.00	1.00					

2.	6.	29.108	.00	.00	.00	1.000	.00	-1.00
2.	6.	32.081	.00	.00	.00	1.000	.00	-1.00
14.	6.	38.113	5.00				
1.	6.	39.713	7.00	20.00	.00	1.000	
2.	6.	45.178	.00	.00	.00	1.000	.00	-1.00
2.	6.	48.152	.00	.00	.00	1.000	.00	-1.00
14.	6.	54.184	5.00				
1.	6.	55.784	8.00	20.00	.00	1.000	
2.	6.	61.249	.00	.00	.00	1.000	.00	-1.00
2.	6.	66.715	.00	.00	.00	1.000	.00	-1.00
14.	6.	72.747	5.00				
1.	6.	75.687	9.00	20.00	.00	1.000	
2.	6.	78.661	.00	.00	.00	1.000	.00	-1.00
2.	6.	82.284	.00	.00	.00	1.000	.00	-1.00
14.	6.	88.317	5.00				
1.	6.	89.917	6.00	10.00	.00	1.000	
2.	6.	95.382	.00	.00	.00	1.000	.00	-1.00
2.	6.	98.355	.00	.00	.00	1.000	.00	-1.00
14.	6.	104.388	5.00				
1.	6.	107.148	7.00	20.00	.00	1.000	
2.	6.	112.613	.00	.00	.00	1.000	.00	-1.00
2.	6.	116.637	.00	.00	.00	1.000	.00	-1.00
14.	6.	124.077	5.00				
2.	6.	125.677	.00	-2.00	.00	3.000	.00	131.98
14.	6.	141.555	5.00				
2.	6.	143.155	.00	-2.00	.00	3.000	.00	150.92
14.	6.	161.974	5.00				
2.	6.	163.573	.00	-2.00	.00	3.000	.00	170.87
14.	6.	181.437	5.00				
2.	6.	183.036	.00	-2.00	.00	3.000	.00	189.88
14.	6.	200.000	5.00				
8.	7.	.000	-17.11	.60	200.00	.000	.00	4.00
3.	7.	1.200	.00	2.00			
17.	7.	5.750	.00	3.00	2.00		
18.	7.	11.510	.00	3.00	4.00		
2.	7.	16.010	.00	.00	.00	1.000	.00	-1.00
2.	7.	23.642	.00	.00	.00	1.000	.00	-1.00
1.	7.	29.108	7.00	20.00	.00	1.000	
9.	7.	29.108	-3.40	53.00	1.00		
1.	7.	32.081	7.00	20.00	.00	1.000	
2.	7.	39.713	.00	.00	.00	1.000	.00	-1.00
1.	7.	45.178	6.00	10.00	.00	1.000	
1.	7.	48.152	6.00	10.00	.00	1.000	
2.	7.	55.784	.00	.00	.00	1.000	.00	-1.00
1.	7.	61.249	6.00	10.00	.00	1.000	
1.	7.	66.715	6.00	10.00	.00	1.000	
2.	7.	75.688	.00	.00	.00	1.000	.00	-1.00
1.	7.	78.661	5.00	10.00	.00	1.000	
1.	7.	82.284	5.00	10.00	.00	1.000	
2.	7.	89.917	.00	.00	.00	1.000	.00	-1.00
1.	7.	95.382	7.00	20.00	.00	1.000	
1.	7.	98.355	7.00	20.00	.00	1.000	
1.	7.	107.148	6.00	10.00	.00	1.000	
2.	7.	112.613	.00	.00	.00	1.000	.00	-1.00
1.	7.	116.637	9.00	20.00	.00	1.000	
5.	7.	116.637	12.00	10.00	143.16	2.147	-1.00
1.	7.	125.677	8.00	20.00	1.00	2.000	
1.	7.	134.115	9.00	20.00	.00	1.000	
1.	7.	143.155	8.00	20.00	1.00	2.000	

2.	7.	151.594	.00	.00	.00	1.000	.00	-1.00
2.	7.	163.573	.00	-2.00	.00	3.000	.00	170.87
2.	7.	183.036	.00	-2.00	.00	3.000	.00	189.88
8.	8.	.000	-22.71	.60	200.00	.000	.00	3.00
3.	8.	1.200						
17.	8.	5.750	.00	**3.00**	.00			
18.	8.	11.510	.00	3.00	4.00			
2.	8.	16.010	.00	.00	.00	1.000	.00	-1.00
2.	8.	23.642	.00	.00	.00	1.000	.00	-1.00
1.	8.	29.108	3.00	10.00	.00	1.000		
9.	8.	29.108	-2.00	53.00	1.00			
1.	8.	32.081	3.00	10.00	.00	1.000		
2.	8.	39.713	.00	.00	.00	1.000	.00	-1.00
1.	8.	45.178	4.00	10.00	.00	1.000		
1.	8.	48.152	4.00	10.00	.00	1.000		
2.	8.	55.784	.00	.00	.00	1.000	.00	-1.00
1.	8.	61.249	2.00	10.00	.00	1.000		
1.	8.	66.715	2.00	10.00	.00	1.000		
2.	8.	75.688	.00	.00	.00	1.000	.00	-1.00
1.	8.	78.661	1.00	10.00	.00	1.000		
1.	8.	82.284	1.00	10.00	.00	1.000		
2.	8.	89.917	.00	.00	.00	1.000	.00	-1.00
1.	8.	95.382	3.00	10.00	.00	1.000		
1.	8.	98.355	3.00	10.00	.00	1.000		
1.	8.	107.148	2.00	10.00	.00	1.000		
2.	8.	112.613	.00	.00	.00	1.000	.00	-1.00
1.	8.	116.637	5.00	13.00	.00	1.000		
5.	8.	116.637	2.00	2.00	143.16	-1.947	-1.00	
1.	8.	125.677	4.00	10.00	1.00	2.000		
1.	8.	134.115	5.00	13.00	.00	1.000		
1.	8.	143.155	4.00	10.00	1.00	2.000		
2.	8.	151.594	.00	.00	.00	1.000	.00	-1.00
2.	8.	163.573	.00	-2.00	.00	3.000	.00	170.87
2.	8.	183.036	.00	-2.00	.00	3.000	.00	189.88
8.	9.	.000	-28.42	.60	200.00	.000	.00	2.00
3.	9.	1.200						
17.	9.	5.750	.00	**3.00**	.00			
18.	9.	11.510	.00	3.00	4.00			
2.	9.	16.010	.00	.00	.00	1.000	.00	-1.00
2.	9.	23.642	.00	.00	.00	1.000	.00	-1.00
1.	9.	29.108	6.00	10.00	.00	1.000		
9.	9.	29.108	-1.00	53.00	1.00			
1.	9.	32.081	6.00	10.00	.00	1.000		
2.	9.	39.713	.00	.00	.00	1.000	.00	-1.00
1.	9.	45.178	6.00	10.00	.00	1.000		
1.	9.	48.152	6.00	10.00	.00	1.000		
2.	9.	55.784	.00	.00	.00	1.000	.00	-1.00
1.	9.	61.249	5.00	10.00	.00	1.000		
1.	9.	66.715	5.00	10.00	.00	1.000		
2.	9.	75.688	.00	.00	.00	1.000	.00	-1.00
1.	9.	78.661	6.00	10.00	.00	1.000		
1.	9.	82.284	6.00	10.00	.00	1.000		
2.	9.	89.917	.00	.00	.00	1.000	.00	-1.00
1.	9.	95.382	6.00	10.00	.00	1.000		
1.	9.	98.355	6.00	10.00	.00	1.000		
1.	9.	107.148	4.00	10.00	.00	1.000		
2.	9.	112.613	.00	.00	.00	1.000	.00	-1.00
1.	9.	116.637	8.00	20.00	.00	.500	1.01	.00
6.	9.	116.637	7.00	6.00	120.78	21.000		

5.	9.	116.637	10.00	13.00	131.14	1.723	-1.00	
1.	9.	120.777	6.00	22.00	.00	.500	-.01	.00
1.	9.	125.677	7.00	20.00	.00	.500	-.01	.00
6.	9.	125.677	7.00	8.00	128.41	21.000		
1.	9.	128.410	9.00	20.00	.00	.500	1.01	.00
1.	9.	131.142	11.00	20.00	.00	1.000		
1.	9.	134.115	8.00	20.00	.00	.500	1.01	.00
6.	9.	134.115	7.00	6.00	138.26	21.000		
5.	9.	134.115	10.00	13.00	148.62	1.723	-1.00	
1.	9.	138.255	6.00	22.00	.00	.500	-.01	.00
1.	9.	143.155	7.00	20.00	.00	.500	-.01	.00
6.	9.	143.155	7.00	8.00	145.89	21.000		
1.	9.	145.888	9.00	20.00	.00	.500	1.01	.00
1.	9.	148.620	11.00	20.00	.00	1.000		
2.	9.	151.594	.00	.00	.00	1.000	.00	-1.00
2.	9.	163.573	.00	-2.00	.00	3.000	.00	170.87
2.	9.	183.036	.00	-2.00	.00	3.000	.00	189.88
8.	10.	.000	-31.00	.60	200.00	.000	.00	1.00
3.	10.	1.200						
18.	10.	11.510	.00	3.00	4.00			
1.	10.	16.010	8.00	20.00	.00	.500	-.01	.00
9.	10.	16.010	-3.00	53.00	1.00			
6.	10.	16.010	8.00	9.00	18.74	21.000		
5.	10.	16.010	10.00	17.00	29.11	3.000	-1.00	
1.	10.	18.743	10.00	20.00	.00	.500	1.01	.00
1.	10.	23.642	12.00	20.00	.00	.500	1.01	.00
6.	10.	23.642	11.00	10.00	26.37	21.000		
1.	10.	26.375	10.00	20.00	.00	.500	-.01	.00
1.	10.	29.108	15.00	20.00	.00	1.000	1.00	
1.	10.	32.081	12.00	20.00	.00	.500	1.01	.00
6.	10.	32.081	11.00	10.00	34.81	21.000		
5.	10.	32.081	14.00	15.00	45.18	2.000	-1.00	
1.	10.	34.813	10.00	20.00	.00	.500	-.01	.00
1.	10.	39.713	9.00	20.00	.00	.500	-.01	.00
6.	10.	39.713	9.00	10.00	42.45	21.000		
1.	10.	42.446	11.00	20.00	.00	.500	1.01	.00
1.	10.	45.178	13.00	20.00	.00	1.000		
1.	10.	48.152	11.00	20.00	.00	.500	1.01	.00
6.	10.	48.152	10.00	9.00	50.88	21.000		
5.	10.	48.152	13.00	13.00	69.45	3.000	-1.00	
1.	10.	50.884	9.00	20.00	.00	.500	-.01	.00
1.	10.	55.784	8.00	20.00	.00	.500	.00	.00
6.	10.	55.784	8.00	8.00	69.45	21.000		
1.	10.	58.517	7.00	20.00	.00	.500	-1.00	.00
1.	10.	61.249	10.00	20.00	.00	.500	2.00	.00
1.	10.	63.982	9.00	20.00	.00	.500	1.00	.00
1.	10.	66.715	12.00	20.00	.00	.500	4.00	.00
1.	10.	69.447	11.00	20.00	.00	.500	3.00	.00
1.	10.	75.687	9.00	22.00	.00	1.000		
5.	10.	75.387	11.60	12.00	78.66	1.096	-1.00	
1.	10.	78.661	10.00	20.00	.00	1.000		
1.	10.	82.284	8.00	20.00	.00	.500	-.01	.00
6.	10.	82.284	8.00	9.00	85.02	21.000		
5.	10.	82.284	10.00	17.00	95.38	3.000	-1.00	
1.	10.	85.017	10.00	20.00	.00	.500	1.01	.00
1.	10.	89.917	12.00	20.00	.00	.500	1.01	.00
6.	10.	89.917	11.00	10.00	92.65	21.000		
1.	10.	92.649	10.00	20.00	.00	.500	-.01	.00
1.	10.	95.382	15.00	20.00	.00	1.000	1.00	

1.	10.	98.355	12.00	20.00	.00	.500	1.01	.00			
6.	10.	98.355	11.00	10.00	101.09	21.000					
5.	10.	98.355	14.00	15.00	112.61	2.000	-1.00				
1.	10.	101.088	10.00	20.00	.00	.500	-.01	.00			
1.	10.	107.148	9.00	23.00	.00	.500	-.01	.00			
6.	10.	107.148	9.00	10.00	109.88	21.000					
1.	10.	109.881	11.00	20.00	.00	.500	1.01	.00			
1.	10.	112.613	13.00	20.00	.00	1.000					
2.	10.	116.637	.00	.00	.00	1.000	.00	-1.00			
2.	10.	125.677	.00	-2.00	.00	3.000	.00	131.98			
2.	10.	143.155	.00	.00	.00	1.000	.00	-1.00			
2.	10.	148.620	.00	.00	.00	1.000	.00	-1.00			
5.	10.	151.287	-1.00	-3.00	163.57	-4.000	-1.00				
1.	10.	151.594	2.00	10.00	.00	.333	-.01	.00			
6.	10.	151.594	2.00	.50	157.77	11.000	3.00				
1.	10.	154.294	-1.00	10.00	.00	.333	2.25	.00			
1.	10.	157.774	-3.00	10.00	.00	.333	3.51	.00			
1.	10.	163.573	-1.00	10.00	.00	.500	9.50	.00			
6.	10.	163.573	8.50	10.00	177.24	11.000					
1.	10.	166.306	2.00	10.00	.00	.500	6.80	.00	.0	7.0	
1.	10.	169.039	4.00	10.00	.00	.500	5.10	.00	.0	7.0	
1.	10.	171.771	6.00	10.00	.00	.500	3.40	.00	.0	7.0	
1.	10.	174.504	9.00	10.00	.00	.500	.70	.00	.0	7.0	
1.	10.	177.237	11.00	10.00	.00	.500	-1.00	.00	.0	7.0	
1.	10.	183.036	13.00	20.00	.00	.500	2.00	.00			
6.	10.	183.036	11.00	10.00	196.70	21.000					
5.	10.	183.036	15.00	12.00	196.70	2.000	-1.00				
1.	10.	185.769	12.00	20.00	.00	.500	1.20	.00			
1.	10.	188.502	11.00	20.00	.00	.500	.40	.00			
1.	10.	191.235	10.00	20.00	.00	.500	-.40	.00			
1.	10.	193.967	11.00	20.00	.00	.500	.80	.00			
1.	10.	196.700	9.00	20.00	.00	.500	-1.00	.00			

Example 19.4 Parameter files in ASCII format for the Mozart trio, with layout as indicated in Examples 19.2a and 19.2b and shown in Example 19.3. Parameters for clef signs (Object-type 3) and key signatures (Object-type 17) are in bold-face type. Appropriately, no key signature is given for the *Clarinet*.

19.6   Observations and Further Information

Because of its extensive representation of the features of music from both the period of common practice and the twentieth century, *SCORE* is well suited to many kinds of analytical tasks. Its strongly graphical nature produces occasional obstacles to analysis. For example, the differentiation of ties and slurs (which are both described as curved lines) must be inferred from other information.

Translation programs to any other comprehensive music-description language can easily be written. While *SCORE* input files do not necessarily contain all the attributes of interest to the end-user of another printing program, *SCORE* parameter files are sufficiently comprehensive to preclude the absence of any standard data. Only custom-drawn symbols would lack a facility for translation.

Since, however, parameter files contain much information highly specific to printing, applications devised for sound output may fare better by translation from the input files. Because of its comprehensive nature, some attributes contained in the musical code are likely to be unaccommodated in translation. Thus those who require comprehensive encodings would probably fare better with the *SCORE* code itself than with translations.

Two commercial MIDI complements are available for *SCORE. MIDISCORE-WRITE* reads a MIDI (*.MID*) file created by a sequencer program, converts it to a *SCORE* input file, and produces a *SCORE .PMX* file. *MIDISCORE* concatenates a series of parametric page files produced by *SCORE* and reorganizes the material into MIDI files for playback on a synthesizer.[9] A program to translate *SCORE* binary files to the *Kern* format has recently been written by Andreas Kornstädt.[10]

A *SCORE* forum and ftp archive of preview files in binary format are maintained. To subscribe to the first, send the message SUBSCRIBE SCORE <Your Name> to *maiser@ace.acadiau.ca*. The ftp archive is at the same node, and details are available through the forum. There is also a mirror site at *ccrma-ftp.stanford.edu:/pub/score/*, which can be accessed as well through the World-Wide Web locator *http://ccrma-www.stanford.edu/CCRMA/Software/... .*

References

PostScript Language Reference Manual. Reading, MA: Addison-Wesley Publishing, Inc., 1985.

PostScript Language: Tutorial and Cookbook. Reading, MA: Addison-Wesley Publishing, Inc., 1985.

9. Both programs are available from New Notations, Unit 9, Down House, Broomhill Road, Wandsworth SW1B 4J0, England, UK.

10. See "*SCORE*-to-*Humdrum*: An Environment for Computer-Assisted Musical Analysis," forthcoming in *Computing in Musicology* 10 (1995-96).

Musical NotationCodes (3):

Graphical-object Descriptions

20   The *LIME Tilia* Representation

David Cottle and Lippold Haken

LIME is a graphically based notation program written by Lippold Haken and Dorothea Blostein.[1] Version 4.0 for the Macintosh, PowerMac, and *Windows* platforms was released early in 1996.

LIME is the successor to a group of programs developed by the Sound Group at the University of Illinois Computer-based Education Research Laboratory (CERL). CERL began developing programs for the management of musical information, with a primary emphasis on printing, in 1974. The music printing programs were originally written for the mainframe educational computer system (Plato) developed at CERL, and they are still actively used on that system. In this context an ASCII text-based system, *OPAL*, is used for music representation. *OPAL* is a score description language that holds much in common, in its overall organization and comprehensiveness, with the *Humdrum Kern* and *MuseData* systems of representation.

The *Tilia* representation used with *LIME* on the Macintosh and *Windows* platforms significantly departs from *OPAL*. It describes graphical objects in a linked-list data structure. This representation is never manipulated by the user; it is only manipulated through *LIME* and user-written programs. The *Tilia* representation is stored and processed in binary files.

1. Now in the Department of Computing and Information Science, Queen's University, Kingston, Ontario, Canada K7L 3N6; *blostein@qucis.queensu.ca*. The name *LIME* stands for *Lippold's Music Editor*.

LIME provides extensive capabilities for defining scores of Western classical music. It has also been used for the transcription of pre-tonal, experimental[2], and non-Western musics, as well as popular music, jazz, and microtonal music. *LIME* allows for MIDI input and playback, but sequencing is not a priority.

20.1 The *Tilia* Representation

Tilia is organized by *voice*. A separated linked list of nodes represents each voice. A voice often corresponds to a single instrument, for example, the clarinet in the Mozart example. Alternatively, several voices may be used to represent one instrument, as in the piano part (score reduction) of the Telemann example or the Mozart piano excerpt. The Mozart piano example also shows that a voice may contain chords, and that several voices may be printed together on one staff. Voices may start and stop printing at any point in the piece, and they may switch between staves.

20.1.1 Conceptual Elements

A. NODES[3]

Tilia's linked lists are heterogeneous. They contain many kinds of nodes, with each kind representing a different type of information.

The most common kind of node is the NOTE node. The order of NOTE nodes in the linked list matches the order in which notes are played. Other nodes, such as those containing ANNOTATIONS (dynamics markings, lyrics text, rehearsal marks, and other symbols added by the user), are located between NOTE nodes. An ANNOTATION precedes the NOTE node with which it is associated. This association allows for proper relocation of the ANNOTATION in case the associated note is moved to a new position on the page.

Other types of nodes related to visual musical objects include CLEF, KEYSIG, TIMESIG, BAR, BEAMING, PARAM, TEMPO, MIDI, TEXT, TPARAM, and LINE.

---

2. *LIME* represents all forms of written notation described in Kurt Stone's *Music Notation in the Twentieth Century* (New York: W. W. Norton, 1980) except predominantly graphic scores, such as Penderecki's *Threnody*. In such cases *LIME* may be used to generate musical examples which are imported into a graphics package for further visual editing.

3. In this chapter, which describes a hierarchical organization of data, node and record names are in capital letters; field names are in italics.

Node types related to layout include PRINT, ENDSYST, CMOVE, SMOVE, SPACE, and ZONE. The node VINFO is used for MIDI channel assignments.

B. CONTEXTS

Musical scores describe a variety of different performing situations. These have important consequences for the selection of parameters and visual representation on the page. *LIME* calls these variable conditions *contexts*. The same voice will have different graphical details in the visual contexts of a conducting score, an instrumental part, or a piano reduction.

C. TAGS

Every node in *Tilia* has a *visibility tag*. Visibility tags are used in support of notation contexts. They determine whether a node is "visible" to the formatter in the various notation contexts. A node which is not visible is simply ignored. The visibility variable, when applied to just a few nodes, produces a range of different notation contexts. The vast majority of nodes are shared between all notation contexts.

20.1.2 Standard and Special Features

Among the features *Tilia* covers are these:

A. PITCH

The NOTE node contains pitch and duration data. Aspects of pitch that may be defined include notated name, notated and sounding accidentals, clefs, note clusters, glissandi, harmonics, indeterminate pitches, user-defined microtones (up to 60[4]), transposition, tremolo, ligatures, grace notes, cue notes, etc.

In the two-byte pitch field, the first byte contains a MIDI note number. The second byte expresses pitch remainders in half-cent units. When this byte $\neq$ 0, the equal-tempered scale that MIDI relies on is superseded.

Notated pitch requires three fields: *mod7*, *acc*, and *accplot*. The first (*mod7*) assigns seven digits—one for each letter name—to each octave. Middle C and its chromatic alterations (C$\sharp$, C$\sharp\sharp$, C$\flat$, C$\flat\flat$) all take the integer 35. Middle D takes 36. The second field (*acc*) gives implicit accidentals. The third field (*accplot*) indicates whether the accidental must be written in the present context.

---

4. With playback.

B. DURATION

Tilia covers note values from the breve (or double whole note) to the 128th note. It supports irregular meters, mixed meters, user-defined beaming patterns, aperiodic meters, spatial (or proportional) notation, and time signatures of any combination.[5] Unusual user-defined time signatures (e.g., 5/32) are permitted.[6]

NOTE nodes support differentiation of written and playback durations. The "legal values" (*lgval*) for written durations are used:

0	whole note
1	half note
2	quarter note
3	eighth note
4	sixteenth note
5	thirty-second note
6	sixty-fourth note
7	triplet (or other tuplet)
8	cue note
9	grace note

Other fields related to duration are *dots* (for extension), *tupl* (for tuplets), and *intimeof*. The *intimeof* field will accept fractional bits.

Most beaming is done automatically in *LIME*; thus there is no explicit beam specification in *Tilia*. Tools for handling exceptional situations are provided.

C. ARTICULATION

Tilia supports a large array of articulations and allows user-defined playback definitions. It supports standard ornamentation, such as trills, mordents, and grace notes. It also distinguishes between slurred and non-slurred passages. Some commonly used codes are these:

*	slur
/	tie
=	marcato
Numlock	staccato

---

5. These are represented by number / division, e.g., (1–100) / (1–64).

6. *LIME* records input in real time with a fixed or user-defined metronome.

D. DYNAMICS

Tilia supports all standard dynamic markings and interprets them on playback.

E. TIMBRE

The VINFO node allows for voice assignment to a MIDI channel.

F. ADDITIONAL FEATURES

LIME's parameter menu gives the user control over hundreds of details. To take just one example, by changing the beam-separation parameter to 0, accelerando beams[7] can be created.

Unusual symbols or characters can be entered into the score by changing the default characters used to generate such ordinary items as noteheads and clefs.

Several details in *LIME*, such as the stacking of accidentals before chords and the placement of control points in ties and slurs, are done according to guidelines from Ohio State University.[8]

20.1.3 Editorial Markup

Tilia supports editorial markup, such as dotted ties and slurs, dotted bar lines, brackets around symbols, noteheads of different shapes and sizes, and various other symbols for indicating the editor's reading of a score.

20.1.4 Fonts

Two *PostScript Type 3* music fonts were specially developed for use with *LIME*. They are called *Marl* and *Tufa*. Paul Balga did much of the design on these fonts.

---

7. i.e., wedge-shaped beams used in contemporary music.

8. Dean K. Roush, "Music Formatting Guidelines" (OSU-CISRC-3/88-TR10), The Ohio State University (Computer and Information Science Research Center, 2036 Neil Avenue Mall, Columbus, OH 43210), 1988. A prior publication, OSU-CISCR-10/87-TR32, was also consulted.

20.2   File Organization

A *LIME* file is written in a binary (non-ASCII) format with the following components:

> header
> sequence of *LIME* nodes for the first voice
> sequence of *LIME* nodes for the second voice
> . . .
> sequence of *LIME* nodes for the last voice

The number of voices in the piece is defined in the header.

20.2.1   Header Section

In the Macintosh implementation the header section starts at Byte 0 of the data fork. The following information may be given:

version number for format of *LIME* nodes	2 bytes
H [number of header bytes]	2 bytes
page number	2 bytes
N [number of notation contexts]	2 bytes
current notation context	2 bytes
T [total number of bytes in N option records]	2 bytes
OPTIONS RECORD for N notation contexts	T bytes
R [number of bytes in performance record]	2 bytes
PERFORMANCE RECORD	R bytes
P [total number of bytes in N print records]	2 bytes
PRINT RECORDS for N notation contexts	P bytes
S [number of bytes in ncontext names record]	2 bytes
NOTATION CONTEXT NAMES RECORD	S bytes[9]

The OPTIONS RECORD sets up the logical page size and provides information about staves, systems, clefs, key signatures, etc.

The PERFORMANCE RECORD establishes many details of articulation including percentages of legal duration time to be used in the execution of staccatos, legatos, and slurs; scale tuning; and dynamics.

---

9. S/N bytes per name.

The NOTATION CONTEXT tells the program which voices are relevant and how they should be treated in the assembly of PRINT information.

20.2.2 Music Binary Section

In the Macintosh implementation this section begins at Byte (H+4). The order and length of items are as follows:

first LimeNode for first voice	24 bytes
second LimeNode for first voice	24 bytes
. . .	a multiple of 24 bytes
last LimeNode for first voice (if any)	24 bytes
first LimeNode for second voice (if any)	24 bytes
. . .	a multiple of 24 bytes
last LimeNode for second voice (if any)	24 bytes
first LimeNode for third voice (if any)	24 bytes
. . .	a multiple of 24 bytes
. . .	a multiple of 24 bytes
last LimeNode of last voice	24 bytes

20.3   Examples

Since *Tilia* files are in binary code, they are not generally comprehensible to the user. In lieu of samples of this code, *LIME*'s method of dealing with the various musical examples presented in Chapter 1 is to discuss them briefly below.

20.3.1 The Mozart Trio

For this example, the notes were entered in real time. Slurs, dynamics, and annotations were added later. As for the transposing part of the clarinet, the *LIME* key setup allows the user to specify the sounding pitch. If this is different from the written pitch, then notes will be transposed (from sounding to written) as they are entered and retransposed (from written to sounding) for playback.

20.3.2 The Mozart Piano Example

For this example the notes were entered by step (specifying pitch and duration). The grace notes were entered by giving their unique duration code.

20.3.3 The Saltarello

The BAR node in the linked-list data structure has bits to indicate whether or not a bar is numbered. Alternatively, this field can be used to restart numbering, which is useful in the case of multiple endings, such as those found in the saltarello example. This node can also suppress the printing of bar numbers.

There are a number of ways to handle first and second endings. The designators "1", "2", etc., can be given as annotations; the brackets can be generated from the tuplet feature. In this case the continuous line over the affected notes was generated by the *extend underline* feature.

20.3.4 The Telemann Example

This example, in which there are more than two different durations in one voice, was set up as one of six voices presented on four staves. The first four were allocated as follows:

Staff 1: the voice part
Staff 2: the stem-up and stem-down voices from the left hand of the piano part
Staff 3: the second stem-down voice in the right hand of the piano part
Staff 4: the stem-up and stem-down voices from the right hand of the piano part

The text was entered in *text annotation* mode.

20.3.5 The Chant Example

LIME provides two ways of entering non-measured music. One is to insert a measure in *n*/4 time and enter everything in quarter notes. The other is to create the requisite number of measures in 4/4 and then remove the bar lines. In this case one measure was entered in the meter 27/4 (with the signature suppressed).

20.3.6 The Binchois Example

This example was represented as three voices—one assigned to the top staff and two to the bottom staff. For Bars 1–7, the second and third voices were encoded for mixed stem directions. This allows the program to automatically suppress redundant rests. At Bar 8 the second voice became "stems-up" and the third "stems-down." This forces the printing of rests in both voices.

The cue notes for "Chorus" were entered in one bar in 5/4 meter with "no stem" selected. The lower staff of this portion was "drawn in white" to suppress its printing.

20.4 File Conversion

LIME accepts as input and produces as output both MIDI data and Standard MIDI Files. The optical recognition program called *Cantor*, by David Bainbridge, can produce *LIME* binary files. *LIME* necessarily converts from *OPAL* (an alphanumeric code) to its own binary code.[10] This conversion has facilitated the development of an extensive data archive. Entire blocks of a *LIME* score can be copied and pasted into word-processing and drawing programs.

LIME data can be converted to *Goodfeel*, the format used by Dancing Dots's *Braille Music Translator*.[11] Data from *LIME* can be directly interpreted by Symbolic Sound Corporation's *Kyma* audio-signal-processing environment.

In our first draft of this chapter we expressed the view that while a standard for interchange of music printing files in diverse codes and formats would be useful, it would be difficult to develop an interchange tool which would not be prohibitively difficult to use. However, we are now planning extensive support for *NIFF*.[12]

20.5 Further Information

LIME software for the Macintosh, Power Macintosh, *Windows95*, and *WindowsNT* operating systems is now distributed by Electronic Courseware Systems, Inc., 1210

---

10. Bill Walker wrote the program to translate files from the mainframe format to the new *LIME* format.

11. Further information on this topic is given in the glossary.

12. See Chapter 32.

Lancaster Drive, Champaign, IL 61821; tel. (800) 832-4965; fax: (217) 359-6578; *SoftEd@aol.com*.

A demonstration (of Macintosh Version 2.28) is available by ftp from */pub/lime* in *novamail.cerl.uiuc.edu* [IP 128.174.180.9]. This demo consists of a bin-hexed self-extracting archive. For a demo version of *Lime* for other operating systems, send a message to *Lime@uiuc.edu*.

References

Blostein, Dorothea, and Lippold Haken. "Justification of Printed Music," *Communications of the Association for Computing Machinery* 34/3 (1991), 88–99.

Blostein, Dorothea, and Lippold Haken. "Template Matching for Rhythmic Analysis of Music Keyboard Input," *Proceedings of the 10th International Conference on Pattern Recognition* (1990), 767–770.

Haken, Lippold, and Dorothea Blostein. "The *Tilia* Music Representation: Extensibility, Abstraction, and Notation Contexts for the *LIME* Music Editor," *Computer Music Journal* 17/3 (1993), 43–58.

Scaletti, Carla. "The CERL Music Project at the University of Illinois," *Computer Music Journal* 9/1 (1985), 45–58.

21 The *Nightingale® Notelist*

Tim Crawford[1]

The musical notation program *Nightingale®* was developed for the Apple Macintosh computer by a team led by Donald Byrd at Advanced Music Notation Systems. It makes the fullest use of the graphical user interface of the Macintosh operating system developed by Apple Computer, and in accordance with the ideals of this system, encoding methods for data input are avoided entirely. In the case of note entry, for example, the user chooses a symbol from an on-screen palette by means of the mouse pointer (or uses one of the user-configurable keyboard shortcuts), thus causing the cursor itself to change shape to that symbol. Symbols chosen in this way are then placed in the score by a simple mouse-click. Alternatively, a MIDI keyboard can be used for note entry in step- or real-time.

The symbols can be entered in more or less any order and any position on any page of the score (subject to certain logical restraints). They do not have to be entered in a temporal sequence, and one measure does not need to be filled before music can be entered into the next. By analogy with working with conventional manuscript paper and pencil, a score does not have to be "complete" at any stage. This has clear advantages for the working practice of composers or arrangers. It enables the production of music examples, which can later be incorporated into page-layout programs as *Encapsulated PostScript* (*EPS*) files. These may represent sketches, fragments, or otherwise incomplete musical extracts, as well as complete and logically consistent scores.

1. With Donald Byrd (*dbyrd@crocker.net*) and John Gibson (*jgg9c@darwin.clas.Virginia.edu*).

21.1   General Description

21.1.1   Data-Sharing Provisions of *Nightingale*

Nightingale has the ability, as have many other notation programs, to import and export Standard MIDI Files, but the well known limitations of MIDI mean that this is an unsatisfactory way of sharing musical data other than that required for performance on electronic instruments.

Another more useful facility for sharing the internally stored data is *Nightingale*'s *Notelist*, a human- and machine-readable ASCII file format which simply provides a listing of the essential musical contents of the score's data structure.

A complementary "Open *Notelist*" facility will be incorporated in a future release of *Nightingale*. This will allow the full two-way sharing of essential musical data between *Nightingale* and other programs whose files or data structures will allow conversion to or from *Notelist* format. A sample parser routine for *Nightingale Notelist* files, written in C by John Gibson and suitable for use in programs on non-Macintosh computers, is available on request from Musicware[2], the program's publisher.

Some uses for *Notelists* currently under development include a system for creating scores in Braille, a graphical "front-end" for the UNIX-based music research system *Humdrum*, and a means of automatically transcribing lute music written in tablature into normal notation.

21.1.2   *Notelist* and *Nightingale*'s Data Structure

Notelist can best be described as a snapshot of the structural features of a native *Nightingale* file. It does not, therefore, aim to represent fully the graphical appearance of the score (as is the avowed intention of codes such as *NIFF*) or simply the sequence of musical events within individual voices (as does a Format-1 MIDI file).

Musical events are listed as they occur in time. After an initial code letter identifying the type of musical event, the first parameter for most musical events in a score is the time at which that event occurs (measured from the beginning of the score). This time parameter is calculated from the logical notated durations of previously occurring objects, *not* from performance data. In this respect, a *Notelist* is unlike a MIDI file, which takes account of tempo fluctuations and ignores notational aspects altogether. Certain types of events, however, are not explicitly time-stamped,

---

2. Musicware/TAP Music Systems, PO Box 2882, Redmond, WA 98073; (800) 426-2673; fax (206) 462-1057; URL = *http://www.halcyon.com/musicware/...* . Enquiries may be directed to Michael Brockman (*brockman@u.washington.edu*).

and are simply inserted in their sequential position in the *Notelist*. Their temporal location must be inferred from the context. These include key and time signatures, tuplets, tempo markings, dynamics, and text strings.

Notes or rests belonging to a tuplet group are explicitly flagged as such in the *Notelist*. In a single tuplet group all notes and rests must belong to the same voice and part (or instrument), although the notes and rests may appear on different staves within the part. Each tuplet group is represented by a single "Tuplet" record, which must be inserted into the *Notelist* at some point before the first note or rest in the group. A bar line may not intervene between the tuplet record and the final note or rest in the tuplet group. (In other words, tuplets cannot extend over bar lines.)

Notelist does, however, incorporate the data necessary for performance of a score. As well as the timing data of a note's onset and its pitch (as the MIDI note number), it includes MIDI velocity and "play duration," which corresponds to the difference between Note_On and Note_Off times in a MIDI data stream.

Notelist, however, shares with its parent program the ability to cope with music written without bar lines or without time signatures.[3]

Alignment of music within measures is dependent on the timing information. If this information disagrees with the logical duration of the notes in the measure as given in the *Notelist*, the consequences may be unpredictable. As a general rule, if the logical duration (*ldur*) of a note implies an elapse of time less than the difference between that note's onset and that of the next event applying to the same voice as given by the timing data (*deltaT*), *Nightingale*'s data structure can accommodate a gap in that voice. If, however, *ldur* is greater than *deltaT* (implying events overlapping within a voice), an illegal situation has occurred. *Nightingale*'s "Open *Notelist*" routine would generate an error message and probably reject the file in such a situation.

Notelist also records the "play duration" of notes, allowing the incorporation of articulation or pedalization; this performance information, being concerned only with note-release time offsets, is independent of the logical duration and timing data, and is thus not restricted.

---

3. But see the caveat concerning invisible objects below.

21.1.3 Comments and Header Information

Comments can be added as records anywhere in a *Notelist*. They are identified by a percentage sign (%[4]) at the beginning of the line. For comments longer than a single line, a new percentage character must begin *each line*.

In order to simplify the task of parsing a *Notelist* file in order to recreate a score, it has been found necessary to add a simple structured-comment record type (as in *PostScript*) to the *Notelist* specification to carry important global data otherwise inferable only by scanning the entire file. At present, this is limited to the name of the file from which the *Notelist* was generated (by *Nightingale*, for example), and a listing of the basic structure of the score extract encoded. This concept may be extended in future.

21.1.4 Limitations and Caveats

A. LIMITS OF NOTATION

A *Notelist* file is restricted to the limits of normal musical notation as represented in the extensive capabilities of *Nightingale* itself. This fact should be borne in mind by those considering producing their own *Notelists* for import into *Nightingale*.

It is, for example, necessary that a score is fully quantized in the MIDI sense, and that highly complex or nested tuplet groups are avoided. For tuplets, the *Notelist* format merely records that a note forms part of a tuplet group; the parsing program must infer the structure of the tuplet from the timing data and the logical ("as notated") durations of its members.

B. TEXT AND OTHER GRAPHICS

In the interests of comprehensibility, the *Notelist* is restricted to the basic musical data most likely to be of use to musicologists and composers, rather than including graphical details of importance to publishers or engravers.

Purely graphical items (lines, boxes, circles, and graphics created by the use of non-standard font characters) are not recorded in the *Notelist*. It is unlikely that musical data recorded in graphical forms of notation can be meaningfully shared between programs in any case, without declaring the kind of standardized prescriptions for their use that such notations are designed to avoid.

---

4. ASCII character 37.

21.1.5 "Incomplete" *Notelists*

Nightingale allows the user to select either a contiguous region of a score (a "continuous" selection) or non-adjacent objects from anywhere in the score. A *Notelist* can be generated for any such selection regardless of the musical result. It is the responsibility of the parsing routine to test the timing data and sequence of logical durations in the *Notelist* for these conditions, and reject or accept it depending on the use to which the data is to be put.

21.1.6 Invisible Objects

A. BAR LINES

Bar lines in individual voices can be made invisible in *Nightingale*, thus enabling the user to "fake" the appearance of a score with different barrings in different voices, for example; within the data structure, however, each bar line's occurrence in time applies across the entire score and a bar line will be recorded in the *Notelist*.

B. NOTES

Noteheads, or entire notes or rests, can be made "invisible" in *Nightingale*. They exist in the data structure, but are not seen on the screen and they will not be printed (in the default situation, that is; a global command is provided which makes invisible objects visible on screen and in print). Invisible notes may or may not have performance implications, so they do carry MIDI information like any other notes. They thus appear in the *Notelist*, but with their appearance (`appear=`) parameter set to 0. It is the responsibility of the parsing program to decide whether or not to ignore them, or even make them invisible.

21.1.7 Unusual Notational Effects and Data Structure

A. MOVEABLE OBJECTS IN THE SCORE

One important aspect of *Nightingale*'s flexibility is the ability to move objects graphically some distance from their default positions. The *Notelist* only records their default or original entry position, not the visual displacement. This can have unforeseen consequences when, for example, slurs have been adjusted to extend over notes not included within the region of the score to which they were originally attached.

B. APPEARANCE AND PITCH

Just as notes may be made invisible within *Nightingale*, their appearance can be altered from the normal defaults. In some cases, this could lead to an apparent conflict with the musical intentions of the score. For example, in violin and guitar music, harmonics are often (but not universally) indicated by combining on a single stem a normal note representing the fingerboard position to be stopped with a diamond-shape note showing the harmonic node to be touched. Neither note has any real musical meaning: the actual sounding pitch is different from the written pitch, but the difference depends on the combination. *Nightingale* by default records the notated pitch of the notes but allows the user to change the pitch of any note as well as its appearance. The *Notelist* will reflect such changes, which may or may not indicate the sounding pitch.

C. OCTAVE TRANSPOSITION

Passages requiring transposition by one (*8va*) or two (*15ma*) octaves are recorded in a *Nightingale Notelist* at sounding pitch.

D. TRANSPOSING INSTRUMENTS

Transposing instruments are recorded in a *Nightingale Notelist* as they are notated in the score. It is the responsibility of the parsing program to recalculate pitches if necessary.

21.1.8 File Size

Since the *Notelist* format was designed to be readable by human beings as well as machines, it is not as economical in terms of file size as it might be were it intended only for machines. In the description that follows, it will be seen that there is much redundant repetition of field identifiers, each of which is followed by an "equals" sign (=). The field identifiers and the equals signs may be omitted from the *Notelist*; all parsing routines should ignore them.[5] This can considerably reduce the necessary disk space occupied by a *Notelist* file.

---

5. As does John Gibson's sample parser.

21.1.9 Plans for Further Development

This description, while it is as accurate as possible at the time of writing, does not constitute a final, binding definition of the *Notelist* format. There will possibly be some minor changes to the format in the future. The description should at least provide a sound working basis for the use of *Notelists*, and should be supplemented by reference to the documentation of *Nightingale* available from the publishers, Musicware.

21.2   Code Description

The *Nightingale Notelist* is an ASCII text file consisting of records delimited by return characters.[6] Each record, or line of the text file, relates to an individual musical event and thus to an object in a *Nightingale* score. Within each record, fields are delimited by space characters.[7]

For each object, the first field contains a single symbol to identify the type of object:

TIME-STAMPED		SEQUENTIALLY LOCATED	
N	note	%	comment
G	grace note	%%	structured comment/header info
R	rest	C	clef
/	bar line	K	key signature
		T	time signature
		P	tuplet
		M	tempo marking
		A	text string
		D	dynamic

For each object in the column headed "time-stamped," the second field gives the logical time ($t=n$) elapsed from the beginning of the score to the point at which the event occurs. *Logical time* refers to the sum of the time intervals between previous events as indicated in the notation alone, ignoring any effects due to expression marks or performance indications. The units are 480ths of a quarter note.

---

6. ASCII character 13.

7. ASCII character 32.

The remainder of the parameters in the *Notelist* are dependent on the object type. All numbers in *Notelists* are integers.

21.2.1 Notes [N]

Note records are initiated with the character N. The order of elements used in the specification of a note is as follows:

```
N  t=   v=   npt=   stf=   dur=   dots=   nn=   acc=   eAcc=   pDur=
vel=   ......  appear=  mods=
```

Each of these parameters is explained below.

A. TIME [t=]

The time in 480ths of a quarter note elapsed from the beginning of the score to the onset of the note (1..32000).

B. VOICE [v=]

The number of the polyphonic voice within a part, or instrument, to which the note is assigned (1..31[8]).

C. PART NUMBER [npt=]

The part (or instrument) number (1..64).

D. STAFF [stf=]

The number of the staff in the system on which the note occurs (1..64).

E. DURATION CODE [dur]

0	unknown duration [displayed as a stemless quarter note]
1	double whole note (breve)
2	whole note (semibreve)
3	half note (minim)

---

8. The ranges given for the voice, part number, and staff, when used with *Nightingale*, depend on the program's internal capacity. A system may contain from 1 to 64 staves, but no more than 16 staves per part. A score may contain as many as 100 voices, but no more than 31 per part. A score can contain as many as 64 parts, as long as the total number of staves in the score is 64 or less.

4   quarter (crotchet)
5   eighth (quaver)
6   sixteenth (semiquaver)
7   thirty-second (demisemiquaver)
8   sixty-fourth (hemidemisemiquaver)
9   one-hundred-twenty-eighth

F. NUMBER OF DOTS [**dots=**]

The number of augmentation dots associated with the note. The range depends on the duration of the note:

128ths	0
64ths	0..1
32nds	0..2
16ths	0..3
eighth	0..4
quarters	0..5
half notes	0..6
whole notes	0..7
breves	0..8

G. MIDI NOTE NUMBER [**nn=**]

The note's pitch expressed in semitones, with Middle C = 60, the C♯ above it = 61, etc. (0..127).

H. ACCIDENTAL CODE [**acc=**]

The explicit accidental sign displayed with the note (0..5). The codes are:

0	no accidental
1	double flat
2	flat
3	natural
4	sharp
5	double sharp

I. EFFECTIVE ACCIDENTAL CODE [**eAcc=**]

The implicit effective accidental applying to the note (1..5; values as for the acc field described above.)

J. PLAY DURATION [pDur=]

The actual duration (1..32000) for which the note should be sounded, regardless of the notation. This parameter is principally used for articulation and pedalling effects. In a *Nightingale Notelist*, this would usually be different from the logical (notated) duration, either by a default user-definable percentage or as the actual duration of the note as recorded over MIDI. Units are as for time (t=).

K. MIDI ON VELOCITY [vel=]

A numerical value (0..127) representing the downward velocity of the sounding keystroke on a synthesizer or other MIDI instrument. This parameter usually corresponds to audio volume. A MIDI velocity of 0 represents a non-sounding note, equivalent to a rest.

L. NOTE-ATTRIBUTE FLAGS [......]

A series of six characters (*not* separated by spaces, and *not* preceded by an equal sign [=]) representing certain attributes of a note. Each character can either be a period (default) or another character (CHAR. below) depending on its position (POS.) in the series:

POS.	CHAR.	MEANING
1	+	main note (carrying the stem) in a chord
1	–	other note in a chord
2	)	tied to the preceding note
3	(	tied to the following note
4	>	slurred to the preceding note
5	<	slurred to the following note
6	T	note is a member of a tuplet group[9]

M. APPEARANCE CODE [appear=]

A number code for the appearance of the note. This parameter usually applies only to the notehead, but it also allows "chord slashes" as used in jazz lead-sheets, etc., and invisible notes inserted for the convenience of the user but usually without any musical significance. Invisible notes can, however, carry MIDI data—e.g., for the realization of ornament signs—so they should be tested by the parsing routine.

---

9. See also Tuplets (21.2.10 below).

0	invisible notehead
1	normal appearance
2	x-shape notehead
3	"harmonic" notehead
4	hollow square notehead
5	filled square notehead
6	hollow diamond notehead
7	filled diamond notehead
8	half-note notehead
9	chord slash
10	note invisible (including stem and dots)

N. MODIFIER CODES [**mods=**]

A number code for various types of note-modifying symbols.

CODE	MEANING	SYMBOL
1	1 (finger number)	1
2	2 (finger number)	2
3	3 (finger number)	3
4	4 (finger number)	4
5	5 (finger number)	5
6..9	(unassigned)	
10	fermata	⌢
11	trill	*tr*
12	accent	>
13	heavy accent	∧
14	staccato	.
15	wedge	▼
16	tenuto	–
17	mordent	⤮
18	inverted mordent	∿
19	turn	∞
20	plus sign	+
21	circle	○
22	up-bow	∨
23	down-bow	⊓
24	tremolo (1 slash)	/
25	tremolo (2 slashes)	//
26	tremolo (3 slashes)	///
27	tremolo (4 slashes)	////

28	tremolo (5 slashes)	/////
29	tremolo (6 slashes)	//////
30	heavy accent with staccato	∧
31	long inverted mordent	⩘⩘

Multiple modifiers may be attached to a note by listing them separated by commas without spaces, e.g., `mods=22,14` (up-bow, staccato).

O. MODIFIER DATA VALUES

Any modifier may optionally carry an associated data value in the range −128 to +127. The data value follows the modifier code after a colon character without any spaces, e.g., `mods=22,14:54` (up-bow, staccato with data value of 54).

21.2.2 Grace Notes (G)

Grace-note records are introduced by the character G.[10] The number and order of elements used in the specification of a grace note are the same as those for ordinary notes, e.g.

```
G  t=  v=  npt=  stf=  dur=  dots=  nn=  acc=  eAcc=  pDur=
vel=  .....  appear=  mods=
```

except with respect to the codes for duration (`dur=`), dots (`dots=`), accidentals (`acc=`), and attributes (`......`). These parameters are explained below.

A. DURATION CODE [dur]

The following grace-note durational values are allowed:

4	quarter (crotchet)
5	eighth (quaver)
6	sixteenth (semiquaver)
7	thirty-second (demisemiquaver)

---

10. At the time of writing, grace-note timings were not implemented in *Nightingale*. Their interpretation by a *Notelist* parser routine is as yet undefined.

B. NUMBER OF DOTS [**dots=**]

The number of augmentation dots associated with the grace note.[11]

C. ACCIDENTAL CODE [**acc=**]

The following grace-note accidentals are allowed:

0	no accidental
1	double flat
2	flat
3	natural
4	sharp
5	double sharp

D. GRACE-NOTE ATTRIBUTE FLAG [......]

A series of six characters (*not* separated by spaces, and *not* preceded by "=") representing certain attributes of a grace note. Each character can either be a period (default) or another character depending on its position in the series:

POS.	CHAR.	MEANING
1	+	main note (carrying the stem) in a chord
1	–	other note in a chord
2*	)	tied to the preceding grace note[12]
3*	(	tied to the following grace note
4*	>	slurred to the preceding note or grace note
5*	<	slurred to the following note or grace note
6*	T	grace note is a member of a tuplet group

21.2.3 Rests (**R**)

Rest records are introduced by the character R. The order of elements in a rest specification is as follows:

```
R  t=  v=  npt=  stf=  dur=  dots=  ......  appear=  mods=
```

---

11. This number should always be 0.

12. At the time of writing, grace-note attributes for positions 2–6 (*) were not implemented in *Nightingale*. Their interpretation by a *Notelist* parser routine is as yet undefined.

Parameters for pitch and velocity are obviously irrelevant.

A. DURATION CODE [**dur=**]

−1	whole-measure rest (normally centered in the measure)
−2 to −127	multi-measure rests: number = number of measures[13]
1	double whole note (breve)
2	whole note (semibreve)
3	half note (minim)
4	quarter (crotchet)
5	eighth (quaver)
6	sixteenth (semiquaver)
7	thirty-second (demisemiquaver)
8	sixty-fourth (hemidemisemiquaver)
9	one-hundred-twenty-eighth

G. REST-ATTRIBUTE FLAGS [......]

A series of six characters (*not* separated by spaces nor preceded by an equal sign [=]) representing certain attributes of a rest. Each character can be either a period (default) or another character depending on its position in the series:

POS.	CHAR.	MEANING
1	.	[no meaning; always "."]
2	)	tied to the preceding note or rest
3	(	tied to the following note or rest
4	>	slurred to the preceding note or rest
5	<	slurred to the following note or rest
6	T	rest is a member of a tuplet group

21.2.4 Bar Lines [/]

Bar-line records are introduced by the forward slash (/). The order of elements in a bar-line specification is as follows:

$$/ \quad t= \quad type=$$

---

13. The actual duration is the total length, in measures, according to the prevailing time signature.

A. TIME [t=]

The time in 480ths of a quarter note elapsed from the beginning of the score to the logical end of the previous measure (1..32000).

B. BAR-LINE TYPE CODE [**type=**]

A number code for the appearance of the bar line (1..7).

1	normal bar line
2	double bar line
3	final double bar line
4	heavy double bar line
5	repeat-left double bar line (‖:)
6	repeat-right double bar line (:‖)
7	repeat-both double bar line (:‖:)

21.2.5 Comments [%]

A comment is introduced by the percentage sign (%). The order of elements in a comment specification is as follows:

```
%   <text>
```

Any amount of text can be put into a *Notelist* comment record following the percentage character (%), but it may not contain a return character.[14]

21.2.6 Header Information [%%]

A score header-data record begins with two percentage signs (%%). The order of elements in a header is as follows:

```
%%Score  file=  partstaves=
```

A. FILE NAME [**file=**]

The name of the file from which *Nightingale* (or another program) generated the *Notelist*. Up to 31 characters of ASCII text, enclosed within single quotation marks.[15]

14. ASCII character 13.

15. ASCII character 39.

B. PART INFORMATION [**partstaves=**]

The number of staves in each part, or instrument, in the score (numbered from the top of the page), separated by spaces, and terminated by the numeral 0.[16]

21.2.7 Clefs [C][17]

A clef record is introduced by the character C. The order of elements in a clef specification is as follows:

C   stf=   type=

A. STAFF [**stf=**]

The number of the staff on which the clef occurs (range as for Notes, above).

B. CLEF TYPE [**type=**]

A single character code for the type of clef:

1	treble clef with *8va* sign above
2	French violin clef (treble clef on bottom line)
3	treble clef
4	soprano clef (C clef on bottom line)
5	mezzo-soprano clef (C clef on 4th line from top)
6	alto clef
7	treble-tenor clef (treble clef with *8va* sign)
8	tenor clef (C clef on 2nd line from top)
9	baritone clef (C clef on top line)
10	bass clef
11	bass clef with *8va* sign below
12	percussion clef

16. The concept of structured-comment records may be extended in future versions of the *Nightingale Notelists*. Various types of comments may be identified by the word following the pair of percentage characters.

17. Clef records are optional. If clefs are not included at the beginning of a score's *Notelist*, it is the responsibility of the parsing program to supply reasonable defaults.

21.2.8 Key Signatures [K]

A key-signature record begins with the character K. The order of elements in a key signature is as follows:

$$K \quad stf= \quad KS=$$

A. STAFF [stf=]

The number of the staff (1..64) on which the key signature occurs.

B. KEY-SIGNATURE ITEMS [KS=]

Number and type of accidentals in the key signature in the form:

$$<number> \quad <accidental>[18]$$

The components are as follows:

<number>	integer in range 0..7[19]
<accidental>	represents sharps or flats:[20]
	#[21] sharp
	b[22] flat

21.2.9 Time Signatures [T]

A time-signature record is introduced by the character T. The order of elements in a time signature is as follows:

$$T \quad stf= \quad num= \quad denom= \quad displ=*$$

---

18. Separated by space character, ASCII character 32.

19. Where C Major = 7.

20. At the time of writing, *Nightingale* (and therefore any *Notelist* derived from it) supported only conventional key signatures.

21. ASCII character 35.

22. Lower-case letter b.

A. STAFF [stf=]

The number of the staff on which the time signature occurs (range as for Notes, above).

B. NUMERATOR [num=]

Numerator of the time signature (1..99).

C. DENOMINATOR [denom=]

Denominator of the time signature (powers of 2 from 1 to 64).

D. DISPLAY [displ=][23]

A numerical code indicating how the time signature is displayed:

1:	normal (i.e., numerator over denominator)
2:	C
3:	₵ ("cut time")
4:	numerator only

21.2.10 Tuplets [P]

A tuplet record is introduced by the character P. The order of elements in a tuplet specification is as follows:

```
P  v=  npt=  num=  denom=  appear=
```

The first two parameters are treated as in Note records.

A. TUPLET NUMERATOR [num=][24]

The numerator of the tuplet ratio. Frequently (e.g., in triplets) appears on its own. (See appear=, below.)

---

23. This field may be omitted if displ=1.

24. The *Notelist* tuplet record does not give the duration unit of the tuplet. It is the responsibility of the parsing program to infer the duration unit from the numerator, denominator, and the total duration of notes/rests in the tuplet.

B. TUPLET DENOMINATOR [denom=][26]

The denominator of the tuplet ratio. Usually not displayed, except in more complex cases (e.g., 5 : 6).

C. TUPLET APPEARANCE [appear=]

Appearance code for the tuplet numbers and the associated bracket: a three-digit number, where each digit can be 0 or 1, meaning "invisible" and "visible," respectively. The three digit positions represent the following options:

POSITION	OPTION	VISIBLE	INVISIBLE
1	numerator	1	0
2	denominator	1	0
3	tuplet bracket	1	0

21.2.11 Tempo Markings [M]

The tempo-marking record is introduced by the character M. The order of elements in a tempo specification is as follows:

```
M  stf=  <string>*  <note-value>*=<bpmstring>*
```

A. STAFF [stf=]

The number of the staff to which the tempo marking is attached. Its effect applies to the entire score.

B. TEXT STRING [*<string>*] (optional)

The text of the tempo marking (up to 63 characters), enclosed within single, non-typographical quotation marks.[25]

C. METRONOME NOTE-VALUE [*<note-value>*] (optional[26])

A single-character code for the note-value for a metronome marking:

---

25. ASCII character 39.

26. Either the text string or both metronome values may be omitted. In the latter case, the effect of the tempo marking is undefined.

b	double whole note (breve)
w	whole note (semibreve)
h	half note (minim)
q	quarter (crotchet)
e	eighth (quaver)
s	sixteenth (semiquaver)
r	thirty-second (demisemiquaver)
x	sixty-fourth (hemidemisemiquaver)
t	one-hundred-twenty-eighth

D. METRONOME BEATS PER MINUTE [<*bpmstring*>] (optional)

A text string, normally giving the number of <note-value> beats per minute, but allows ranges such as "96–108" and expressions such as "about 120" (up to 63 ASCII characters may be used).

21.2.12 Text Strings [A]

A text-string record is introduced by the character A. The order of elements in a text-string specification is as follows:

$$A \quad v= \quad npt= \quad stf= \quad S \text{ (or } L) \quad <string>$$

A. VOICE [v=]

The number of the polyphonic voice within a part, or instrument, to which the "owning" object of the text is assigned.[27]

B. PART NUMBER [npt=]

The part (or instrument) number of the "owning" object.

C. STAFF [stf=]

The number of the staff on which the "owning" object occurs.

---

27. Values of −2 for voice (v=), part number (npt=), and staff (stf=) indicate that the text is owned by the page. In *Nightingale*, if a graphic is attached to a bar line, clef, time signature, key signature, or a non-musical "spacer" object, then its staff (stf=) will be the same as the owning object's staff, but its voice number (v=) and part number (npt=) will both be set to −2.

D. TYPE CODE [**S** or **L**]

A letter code indicating the type of text:

S	a general text string
L	an item of lyric text

E. STRING

The text of the graphic (up to 255 characters), enclosed within single quotation marks.[28]

21.2.13 Dynamics [D]

A dynamics record is introduced by the character D. The order of elements in a dynamics specification is as follows:

$$D \quad stf= \quad dType=$$

A. STAFF [**stf=**]

The number of the staff to which the dynamic applies. A dynamic applies to all voices in a staff.

B. DYNAMIC CODE [**dType**]

A numerical code indicating the dynamic type:

1	*pppp*	14	*più forte*
2	*ppp*	15	*sf (sforzando)*
3	*pp (pianissimo)*	16	*fz*
4	*p (piano)*	17	*sfz*
5	*mp (mezzo piano)*	18	*rf (rinforzando)*
6	*mf (mezzo forte)*	19	*rfz*
7	*f (forte)*	20	*fp*
8	*ff (fortissimo)*	21	*sfp*
9	*fff*	22	hairpin (>) open at left
10	*ffff*		*(diminuendo)*
11	*più piano*	23	hairpin (<) open at right
12	*meno piano*		*(crescendo)*
13	*meno forte*		

28. ASCII character 39.

21.3   Example

```
%%Score file='Mozart clarinet quintet' partstaves=1 1 1 1 0
C stf=1 type=3
C stf=2 type=3
C stf=3 type=3
C stf=4 type=6
C stf=5 type=10
K stf=2 KS=3 #
K stf=3 KS=3 #
K stf=4 KS=3 #
K stf=5 KS=3 #
T stf=1 num=3 denom=4
T stf=2 num=3 denom=4
T stf=3 num=3 denom=4
T stf=4 num=3 denom=4
T stf=5 num=3 denom=4
D stf=1 dType=4
N t=0 v=1 npt=1 stf=1 dur=5 dots=0 nn=72 acc=0 eAcc=3 pDur=228 vel=35 ....<. appear=1
R t=0 v=1 npt=2 stf=2 dur=4 dots=0 ...... appear=1
R t=0 v=1 npt=3 stf=3 dur=4 dots=0 ...... appear=1
R t=0 v=1 npt=4 stf=4 dur=4 dots=0 ...... appear=1
R t=0 v=1 npt=5 stf=5 dur=4 dots=0 ...... appear=1
N t=240 v=1 npt=1 stf=1 dur=5 dots=0 nn=76 acc=0 eAcc=3 pDur=228 vel=35 ...... appear=1
/ t=480 type=1
D stf=5 dType=4
N t=480 v=1 npt=1 stf=1 dur=5 dots=0 nn=79 acc=0 eAcc=3 pDur=228 vel=35 ...... appear=1
R t=480 v=1 npt=2 stf=2 dur=4 dots=0 ...... appear=1
R t=480 v=1 npt=3 stf=3 dur=4 dots=0 ...... appear=1
R t=480 v=1 npt=4 stf=4 dur=4 dots=0 ...... appear=1
N t=480 v=1 npt=5 stf=5 dur=4 dots=0 nn=57 acc=0 eAcc=3 pDur=456 vel=35 ...... appear=1
N t=720 v=1 npt=1 stf=1 dur=5 dots=0 nn=76 acc=0 eAcc=3 pDur=228 vel=35 ...... appear=1
D stf=2 dType=4
D stf=3 dType=4
D stf=4 dType=4
N t=960 v=1 npt=3 stf=3 dur=4 dots=0 nn=64 acc=0 eAcc=3 pDur=456 vel=35 ...... appear=1
N t=960 v=1 npt=1 stf=1 dur=4 dots=0 nn=84 acc=0 eAcc=3 pDur=456 vel=35 ...>.. appear=1
N t=960 v=1 npt=2 stf=2 dur=4 dots=0 nn=69 acc=0 eAcc=3 pDur=456 vel=35 ...... appear=1
N t=960 v=1 npt=4 stf=4 dur=4 dots=0 nn=61 acc=0 eAcc=4 pDur=456 vel=35 ...... appear=1
R t=960 v=1 npt=5 stf=5 dur=4 dots=0 ...... appear=1
R t=1440 v=1 npt=5 stf=5 dur=4 dots=0 ...... appear=1
N t=1440 v=1 npt=1 stf=1 dur=5 dots=0 nn=79 acc=0 eAcc=3 pDur=228 vel=35 ....<. appear=1
N t=1440 v=1 npt=2 stf=2 dur=4 dots=0 nn=69 acc=0 eAcc=3 pDur=456 vel=35 ...... appear=1
N t=1440 v=1 npt=3 stf=3 dur=4 dots=0 nn=64 acc=0 eAcc=3 pDur=456 vel=35 ...... appear=1
N t=1440 v=1 npt=4 stf=4 dur=4 dots=0 nn=61 acc=0 eAcc=4 pDur=456 vel=35 ...... appear=1
N t=1680 v=1 npt=1 stf=1 dur=5 dots=0 nn=76 acc=0 eAcc=3 pDur=228 vel=35 ...... appear=1
/ t=1920 type=1
N t=1920 v=1 npt=1 stf=1 dur=5 dots=0 nn=74 acc=0 eAcc=3 pDur=228 vel=35 ...... appear=1
R t=1920 v=1 npt=2 stf=2 dur=4 dots=0 ...... appear=1
R t=1920 v=1 npt=3 stf=3 dur=4 dots=0 ...... appear=1
R t=1920 v=1 npt=4 stf=4 dur=4 dots=0 ...... appear=1
N t=1920 v=1 npt=5 stf=5 dur=4 dots=0 nn=50 acc=0 eAcc=3 pDur=456 vel=35 ...... appear=1
N t=2160 v=1 npt=1 stf=1 dur=5 dots=0 nn=77 acc=0 eAcc=3 pDur=228 vel=35 ...... appear=1
N t=2400 v=1 npt=1 stf=1 dur=5 dots=0 nn=81 acc=0 eAcc=3 pDur=456 vel=35 ...>.. appear=1
N t=2400 v=1 npt=2 stf=2 dur=4 dots=0 nn=69 acc=0 eAcc=3 pDur=456 vel=35 ...... appear=1
R t=2400 v=1 npt=5 stf=5 dur=4 dots=0 ...... appear=1
N t=2400 v=1 npt=4 stf=4 dur=4 dots=0 nn=59 acc=0 eAcc=3 pDur=456 vel=35 ...... appear=1
N t=2400 v=1 npt=3 stf=3 dur=4 dots=0 nn=66 acc=0 eAcc=4 pDur=456 vel=35 ...... appear=1
N t=2880 v=1 npt=1 stf=1 dur=5 dots=0 nn=77 acc=0 eAcc=3 pDur=228 vel=35 ....<. appear=1
N t=2880 v=1 npt=3 stf=3 dur=4 dots=0 nn=66 acc=0 eAcc=4 pDur=456 vel=35 ...... appear=1
N t=2880 v=1 npt=2 stf=2 dur=4 dots=0 nn=69 acc=0 eAcc=3 pDur=456 vel=35 ...... appear=1
R t=2880 v=1 npt=5 stf=5 dur=4 dots=0 ...... appear=1
N t=2880 v=1 npt=4 stf=4 dur=4 dots=0 nn=59 acc=0 eAcc=3 pDur=456 vel=35 ...... appear=1
N t=3120 v=1 npt=1 stf=1 dur=5 dots=0 nn=74 acc=0 eAcc=3 pDur=228 vel=35 ...... appear=1
/ t=3360 type=1
```

```
N t=3360 v=1 npt=1 stf=1 dur=5 dots=0 nn=72 acc=0 eAcc=3 pDur=228 vel=35 ...... appear=1
R t=3360 v=1 npt=2 stf=2 dur=4 dots=0 ...... appear=1
R t=3360 v=1 npt=3 stf=3 dur=4 dots=0 ...... appear=1
R t=3360 v=1 npt=4 stf=4 dur=4 dots=0 ...... appear=1
N t=3360 v=1 npt=5 stf=5 dur=4 dots=0 nn=52 acc=0 eAcc=3 pDur=456 vel=35 ...... appear=1
N t=3600 v=1 npt=1 stf=1 dur=5 dots=0 nn=71 acc=0 eAcc=3 pDur=228 vel=35 ...... appear=1
N t=3840 v=1 npt=1 stf=1 dur=5 dots=0 nn=76 acc=0 eAcc=3 pDur=228 vel=35 ...... appear=1
N t=3840 v=1 npt=2 stf=2 dur=4 dots=0 nn=68 acc=0 eAcc=4 pDur=456 vel=35 ...... appear=1
R t=3840 v=1 npt=5 stf=5 dur=4 dots=0 ...... appear=1
N t=3840 v=1 npt=4 stf=4 dur=4 dots=0 nn=59 acc=0 eAcc=3 pDur=456 vel=35 ...... appear=1
N t=3840 v=1 npt=3 stf=3 dur=4 dots=0 nn=62 acc=0 eAcc=3 pDur=456 vel=35 ...... appear=1
N t=4080 v=1 npt=1 stf=1 dur=5 dots=0 nn=74 acc=0 eAcc=3 pDur=228 vel=35 ...... appear=1
N t=4320 v=1 npt=1 stf=1 dur=5 dots=0 nn=79 acc=0 eAcc=3 pDur=228 vel=35 ...... appear=1
N t=4320 v=1 npt=3 stf=3 dur=4 dots=0 nn=62 acc=0 eAcc=3 pDur=456 vel=35 ...... appear=1
N t=4320 v=1 npt=2 stf=2 dur=4 dots=0 nn=68 acc=0 eAcc=4 pDur=456 vel=35 ...... appear=1
R t=4320 v=1 npt=5 stf=5 dur=4 dots=0 ...... appear=1
N t=4320 v=1 npt=4 stf=4 dur=4 dots=0 nn=59 acc=0 eAcc=3 pDur=456 vel=35 ...... appear=1
N t=4560 v=1 npt=1 stf=1 dur=5 dots=0 nn=77 acc=0 eAcc=3 pDur=228 vel=35 ...>.. appear=1
/ t=4800 type=1
N t=4800 v=1 npt=1 stf=1 dur=4 dots=0 nn=75 acc=4 eAcc=4 pDur=456 vel=35 ....<. appear=1
R t=4800 v=1 npt=2 stf=2 dur=4 dots=0 ...... appear=1
R t=4800 v=1 npt=3 stf=3 dur=4 dots=0 ...... appear=1
R t=4800 v=1 npt=4 stf=4 dur=4 dots=0 ...... appear=1
N t=4800 v=1 npt=5 stf=5 dur=4 dots=0 nn=54 acc=0 eAcc=4 pDur=456 vel=35 ...... appear=1
N t=5280 v=1 npt=1 stf=1 dur=4 dots=0 nn=76 acc=0 eAcc=3 pDur=456 vel=35 ...>.. appear=1
N t=5280 v=1 npt=2 stf=2 dur=4 dots=0 nn=69 acc=0 eAcc=3 pDur=456 vel=35 ...... appear=1
R t=5280 v=1 npt=5 stf=5 dur=4 dots=0 ...... appear=1
N t=5280 v=1 npt=4 stf=4 dur=4 dots=0 nn=57 acc=0 eAcc=3 pDur=456 vel=35 ...... appear=1
N t=5280 v=1 npt=3 stf=3 dur=4 dots=0 nn=61 acc=0 eAcc=4 pDur=456 vel=35 ...... appear=1
N t=5760 v=1 npt=1 stf=1 dur=5 dots=0 nn=72 acc=0 eAcc=3 pDur=228 vel=35 ....<. appear=1
N t=5760 v=1 npt=3 stf=3 dur=4 dots=0 nn=61 acc=0 eAcc=4 pDur=456 vel=35 ...... appear=1
N t=5760 v=1 npt=2 stf=2 dur=4 dots=0 nn=69 acc=0 eAcc=3 pDur=456 vel=35 ...... appear=1
R t=5760 v=1 npt=5 stf=5 dur=4 dots=0 ...... appear=1
N t=5760 v=1 npt=4 stf=4 dur=4 dots=0 nn=57 acc=0 eAcc=3 pDur=456 vel=35 ...... appear=1
N t=6000 v=1 npt=1 stf=1 dur=5 dots=0 nn=76 acc=0 eAcc=3 pDur=228 vel=35 ...... appear=1
/ t=6240 type=1
N t=6240 v=1 npt=1 stf=1 dur=5 dots=0 nn=79 acc=0 eAcc=3 pDur=228 vel=35 ...... appear=1
R t=6240 v=1 npt=2 stf=2 dur=4 dots=0 ...... appear=1
R t=6240 v=1 npt=3 stf=3 dur=4 dots=0 ...... appear=1
R t=6240 v=1 npt=4 stf=4 dur=4 dots=0 ...... appear=1
N t=6240 v=1 npt=5 stf=5 dur=4 dots=0 nn=49 acc=0 eAcc=4 pDur=456 vel=35 ...... appear=1
N t=6480 v=1 npt=1 stf=1 dur=5 dots=0 nn=76 acc=0 eAcc=3 pDur=228 vel=35 ...... appear=1
N t=6720 v=1 npt=3 stf=3 dur=4 dots=0 nn=61 acc=0 eAcc=4 pDur=456 vel=35 ...... appear=1
N t=6720 v=1 npt=2 stf=2 dur=4 dots=0 nn=69 acc=0 eAcc=3 pDur=456 vel=35 ...... appear=1
R t=6720 v=1 npt=5 stf=5 dur=4 dots=0 ...... appear=1
N t=6720 v=1 npt=1 stf=1 dur=4 dots=0 nn=84 acc=0 eAcc=3 pDur=456 vel=35 ...>.. appear=1
N t=6720 v=1 npt=4 stf=4 dur=4 dots=0 nn=57 acc=0 eAcc=3 pDur=456 vel=35 ...... appear=1
N t=7200 v=1 npt=4 stf=4 dur=4 dots=0 nn=57 acc=0 eAcc=3 pDur=456 vel=35 ...... appear=1
N t=7200 v=1 npt=3 stf=3 dur=4 dots=0 nn=61 acc=0 eAcc=4 pDur=456 vel=35 ...... appear=1
N t=7200 v=1 npt=2 stf=2 dur=4 dots=0 nn=69 acc=0 eAcc=3 pDur=456 vel=35 ...... appear=1
R t=7200 v=1 npt=5 stf=5 dur=4 dots=0 ...... appear=1
N t=7200 v=1 npt=1 stf=1 dur=5 dots=0 nn=79 acc=0 eAcc=3 pDur=228 vel=35 ....<. appear=1
N t=7440 v=1 npt=1 stf=1 dur=5 dots=0 nn=76 acc=0 eAcc=3 pDur=228 vel=35 ...... appear=1
/ t=7680 type=1
N t=7680 v=1 npt=1 stf=1 dur=5 dots=0 nn=74 acc=3 eAcc=3 pDur=228 vel=35 ...... appear=1
N t=7680 v=1 npt=2 stf=2 dur=4 dots=0 nn=66 acc=0 eAcc=4 pDur=456 vel=35 ...... appear=1
N t=7680 v=1 npt=3 stf=3 dur=4 dots=0 nn=62 acc=0 eAcc=3 pDur=456 vel=35 ...... appear=1
N t=7680 v=1 npt=4 stf=4 dur=4 dots=0 nn=59 acc=0 eAcc=3 pDur=456 vel=35 ...... appear=1
N t=7680 v=1 npt=5 stf=5 dur=4 dots=0 nn=50 acc=0 eAcc=3 pDur=456 vel=35 ...... appear=1
N t=7920 v=1 npt=1 stf=1 dur=5 dots=0 nn=77 acc=0 eAcc=3 pDur=228 vel=35 ...... appear=1
N t=8160 v=1 npt=1 stf=1 dur=4 dots=0 nn=81 acc=0 eAcc=3 pDur=456 vel=35 ...>.. appear=1
R t=8160 v=1 npt=2 stf=2 dur=4 dots=0 ...... appear=1
R t=8160 v=1 npt=3 stf=3 dur=4 dots=0 ...... appear=1
R t=8160 v=1 npt=4 stf=4 dur=4 dots=0 ...... appear=1
R t=8160 v=1 npt=5 stf=5 dur=4 dots=0 ...... appear=1
R t=8640 v=1 npt=1 stf=1 dur=4 dots=0 ...... appear=1
N t=8640 v=1 npt=2 stf=2 dur=5 dots=0 nn=73 acc=0 eAcc=4 pDur=228 vel=35 ....<. appear=1
```

```
N t=8640 v=1 npt=3 stf=3 dur=4 dots=0 nn=67 acc=3 eAcc=3 pDur=456 vel=35 ....<. appear=1
N t=8640 v=1 npt=4 stf=4 dur=4 dots=0 nn=64 acc=0 eAcc=3 pDur=456 vel=35 ....<. appear=1
R t=8640 v=1 npt=5 stf=5 dur=4 dots=0 ...... appear=1
N t=8880 v=1 npt=2 stf=2 dur=5 dots=0 nn=70 acc=4 eAcc=4 pDur=228 vel=35 ...... appear=1
/ t=9120 type=1
R t=9120 v=1 npt=1 stf=1 dur=-1 dots=0 ...... appear=1
N t=9120 v=1 npt=2 stf=2 dur=5 dots=0 nn=71 acc=0 eAcc=3 pDur=228 vel=35 ...... appear=1
N t=9120 v=1 npt=3 stf=3 dur=3 dots=0 nn=66 acc=0 eAcc=4 pDur=912 vel=35 ...... appear=1
N t=9120 v=1 npt=4 stf=4 dur=3 dots=0 nn=62 acc=0 eAcc=3 pDur=912 vel=35 ...... appear=1
R t=9120 v=1 npt=5 stf=5 dur=-1 dots=0 ...... appear=1
N t=9360 v=1 npt=2 stf=2 dur=5 dots=0 nn=74 acc=0 eAcc=3 pDur=228 vel=35 ...... appear=1
N t=9600 v=1 npt=2 stf=2 dur=4 dots=0 nn=78 acc=0 eAcc=4 pDur=456 vel=35 ...>.. appear=1
N t=10080 v=1 npt=2 stf=2 dur=5 dots=0 nn=73 acc=0 eAcc=4 pDur=228 vel=35 ....<. appear=1
N t=10080 v=1 npt=3 stf=3 dur=4 dots=0 nn=67 acc=3 eAcc=3 pDur=456 vel=35 ...... appear=1
N t=10080 v=1 npt=4 stf=4 dur=4 dots=0 nn=64 acc=0 eAcc=3 pDur=456 vel=35 ...... appear=1
N t=10320 v=1 npt=2 stf=2 dur=5 dots=0 nn=70 acc=4 eAcc=4 pDur=228 vel=35 ...... appear=1
/ t=10560 type=1
R t=10560 v=1 npt=1 stf=1 dur=4 dots=0 ...... appear=1
N t=10560 v=1 npt=2 stf=2 dur=5 dots=0 nn=71 acc=0 eAcc=3 pDur=228 vel=35 ...... appear=1
N t=10560 v=1 npt=3 stf=3 dur=3 dots=0 nn=66 acc=0 eAcc=4 pDur=912 vel=35 ...>.. appear=1
N t=10560 v=1 npt=4 stf=4 dur=3 dots=0 nn=62 acc=0 eAcc=3 pDur=912 vel=35 ...>.. appear=1
R t=10560 v=1 npt=5 stf=5 dur=-1 dots=0 ...... appear=1
N t=10800 v=1 npt=2 stf=2 dur=5 dots=0 nn=74 acc=0 eAcc=3 pDur=228 vel=35 ...... appear=1
R t=11040 v=1 npt=1 stf=1 dur=4 dots=0 ...... appear=1
N t=11040 v=1 npt=2 stf=2 dur=4 dots=0 nn=78 acc=0 eAcc=4 pDur=456 vel=35 ...>.. appear=1
P v=1 npt=1 num=3 denom=2 appear=100
N t=11520 v=1 npt=1 stf=1 dur=5 dots=0 nn=62 acc=0 eAcc=3 pDur=152 vel=35 .....T appear=1
R t=11520 v=1 npt=3 stf=3 dur=4 dots=0 ...... appear=1
R t=11520 v=1 npt=4 stf=4 dur=4 dots=0 ...... appear=1
N t=11680 v=1 npt=1 stf=1 dur=5 dots=0 nn=57 acc=0 eAcc=3 pDur=152 vel=35 .....T appear=1
N t=11840 v=1 npt=1 stf=1 dur=5 dots=0 nn=53 acc=0 eAcc=3 pDur=152 vel=35 .....T appear=1
/ t=12000 type=1
N t=12000 v=1 npt=1 stf=1 dur=5 dots=0 nn=57 acc=0 eAcc=3 pDur=228 vel=35 ...... appear=1
R t=12000 v=1 npt=2 stf=2 dur=-1 dots=0 ...... appear=1
R t=12000 v=1 npt=3 stf=3 dur=-1 dots=0 ...... appear=1
R t=12000 v=1 npt=4 stf=4 dur=-1 dots=0 ...... appear=1
R t=12000 v=1 npt=5 stf=5 dur=-1 dots=0 ...... appear=1
N t=12240 v=1 npt=1 stf=1 dur=5 dots=0 nn=62 acc=0 eAcc=3 pDur=228 vel=35 ...... appear=1
   mods=14
N t=12480 v=1 npt=1 stf=1 dur=5 dots=0 nn=65 acc=0 eAcc=3 pDur=228 vel=35 ...... appear=1
   mods=14
N t=12720 v=1 npt=1 stf=1 dur=5 dots=0 nn=69 acc=0 eAcc=3 pDur=228 vel=35 ...... appear=1
   mods=14
N t=12960 v=1 npt=1 stf=1 dur=5 dots=0 nn=74 acc=0 eAcc=3 pDur=228 vel=35 ...... appear=1
   mods=14
N t=13200 v=1 npt=1 stf=1 dur=5 dots=0 nn=77 acc=0 eAcc=3 pDur=228 vel=35 ...... appear=1
   mods=14
/ t=13440 type=1
N t=13440 v=1 npt=1 stf=1 dur=5 dots=0 nn=81 acc=0 eAcc=3 pDur=228 vel=35 ....<. appear=1
R t=13440 v=1 npt=2 stf=2 dur=-1 dots=0 ...... appear=1
R t=13440 v=1 npt=3 stf=3 dur=-1 dots=0 ...... appear=1
R t=13440 v=1 npt=4 stf=4 dur=-1 dots=0 ...... appear=1
R t=13440 v=1 npt=5 stf=5 dur=-1 dots=0 ...... appear=1
N t=13680 v=1 npt=1 stf=1 dur=5 dots=0 nn=79 acc=0 eAcc=3 pDur=228 vel=35 ...... appear=1
N t=13920 v=1 npt=1 stf=1 dur=5 dots=0 nn=77 acc=0 eAcc=3 pDur=228 vel=35 ...... appear=1
N t=14160 v=1 npt=1 stf=1 dur=5 dots=0 nn=76 acc=0 eAcc=3 pDur=228 vel=35 ...... appear=1
N t=14400 v=1 npt=1 stf=1 dur=5 dots=0 nn=77 acc=0 eAcc=3 pDur=228 vel=35 ...... appear=1
N t=14640 v=1 npt=1 stf=1 dur=5 dots=0 nn=74 acc=0 eAcc=3 pDur=228 vel=35 ...>.. appear=1
/ t=14880 type=1
N t=14880 v=1 npt=1 stf=1 dur=3 dots=0 nn=72 acc=0 eAcc=3 pDur=912 vel=35 ...... appear=1
N t=14880 v=1 npt=2 stf=2 dur=5 dots=0 nn=61 acc=0 eAcc=4 pDur=228 vel=35 ....<. appear=1
N t=14880 v=1 npt=3 stf=3 dur=3 dots=0 nn=57 acc=0 eAcc=3 pDur=912 vel=35 ....<. appear=1
N t=14880 v=1 npt=4 stf=4 dur=3 dots=1 nn=52 acc=0 eAcc=3 pDur=1368 vel=35 ..{... appear=1
N t=14880 v=1 npt=5 stf=5 dur=4 dots=0 nn=40 acc=0 eAcc=3 pDur=456 vel=35 ....<. appear=1
   mods=14
N t=15120 v=1 npt=2 stf=2 dur=5 dots=0 nn=64 acc=0 eAcc=3 pDur=228 vel=35 ...... appear=1
N t=15360 v=1 npt=2 stf=2 dur=5 dots=0 nn=61 acc=0 eAcc=4 pDur=228 vel=35 ...... appear=1
```

```
N t=15360 v=1 npt=5 stf=5 dur=4 dots=0 nn=40 acc=0 eAcc=3 pDur=456 vel=35 ...... appear=1
   mods=14
N t=15600 v=1 npt=2 stf=2 dur=5 dots=0 nn=64 acc=0 eAcc=3 pDur=228 vel=35 ..... appear=1
N t=15840 v=1 npt=1 stf=1 dur=5 dots=0 nn=76 acc=0 eAcc=3 pDur=228 vel=35 ..... appear=1
N t=15840 v=1 npt=2 stf=2 dur=5 dots=0 nn=62 acc=0 eAcc=3 pDur=228 vel=35 ..... appear=1
N t=15840 v=1 npt=3 stf=3 dur=4 dots=0 nn=56 acc=4 eAcc=4 pDur=456 vel=35 ...>.. appear=1
N t=15840 v=1 npt=5 stf=5 dur=4 dots=0 nn=40 acc=0 eAcc=3 pDur=456 vel=35 ...>.. appear=1
   mods=14
N t=16080 v=1 npt=1 stf=1 dur=5 dots=0 nn=74 acc=0 eAcc=3 pDur=228 vel=35 ..... appear=1
N t=16080 v=1 npt=2 stf=2 dur=5 dots=0 nn=64 acc=0 eAcc=3 pDur=228 vel=35 ...>.. appear=1
/ t=16320 type=1
N t=16320 v=1 npt=1 stf=1 dur=4 dots=0 nn=72 acc=0 eAcc=3 pDur=456 vel=35 ...... appear=1
N t=16320 v=1 npt=2 stf=2 dur=4 dots=0 nn=61 acc=0 eAcc=4 pDur=456 vel=35 ...... appear=1
N t=16320 v=1 npt=3 stf=3 dur=4 dots=0 nn=57 acc=0 eAcc=3 pDur=456 vel=35 ...... appear=1
N t=16320 v=1 npt=4 stf=4 dur=4 dots=0 nn=52 acc=0 eAcc=3 pDur=456 vel=35 .)... appear=1
N t=16320 v=1 npt=5 stf=5 dur=4 dots=0 nn=45 acc=0 eAcc=3 pDur=456 vel=35 ...... appear=1
R t=16800 v=1 npt=1 stf=1 dur=4 dots=0 ...... appear=1
R t=16800 v=1 npt=2 stf=2 dur=4 dots=0 ...... appear=1
R t=16800 v=1 npt=3 stf=3 dur=4 dots=0 ...... appear=1
R t=16800 v=1 npt=4 stf=4 dur=4 dots=0 ...... appear=1
R t=16800 v=1 npt=5 stf=5 dur=4 dots=0 ...... appear=1
/ t=17280 type=7
R t=17280 v=1 npt=1 stf=1 dur=4 dots=0 ...... appear=1
N t=17280 v=1 npt=2 stf=2 dur=5 dots=0 nn=64 acc=0 eAcc=3 pDur=228 vel=35 ....<. appear=1
R t=17280 v=1 npt=3 stf=3 dur=4 dots=0 ...... appear=1
R t=17280 v=1 npt=4 stf=4 dur=4 dots=0 ...... appear=1
R t=17280 v=1 npt=5 stf=5 dur=4 dots=0 ...... appear=1
N t=17520 v=1 npt=2 stf=2 dur=5 dots=0 nn=68 acc=0 eAcc=4 pDur=228 vel=35 ...... appear=1
/ t=17760 type=1
A v=1 npt=3 stf=3 S 'pizz.'
A v=1 npt=4 stf=4 S 'pizz.'
A v=1 npt=5 stf=5 S 'pizz.'
D stf=3 dType=4
D stf=4 dType=4
D stf=5 dType=4
D stf=2 dType=4
R t=17760 v=1 npt=1 stf=1 dur=-1 dots=0 ...... appear=1
N t=17760 v=1 npt=2 stf=2 dur=5 dots=0 nn=71 acc=0 eAcc=3 pDur=228 vel=35 ...... appear=1
N t=17760 v=1 npt=3 stf=3 dur=4 dots=0 nn=68 acc=0 eAcc=4 pDur=456 vel=35 -..... appear=1
N t=17760 v=1 npt=3 stf=3 dur=4 dots=0 nn=59 acc=0 eAcc=3 pDur=456 vel=35 +..... appear=1
N t=17760 v=1 npt=4 stf=4 dur=4 dots=0 nn=62 acc=0 eAcc=3 pDur=456 vel=35 -..... appear=1
N t=17760 v=1 npt=4 stf=4 dur=4 dots=0 nn=64 acc=0 eAcc=3 pDur=456 vel=35 +..... appear=1
N t=17760 v=1 npt=5 stf=5 dur=4 dots=0 nn=52 acc=0 eAcc=3 pDur=456 vel=35 ...... appear=1
N t=18000 v=1 npt=2 stf=2 dur=5 dots=0 nn=68 acc=0 eAcc=4 pDur=228 vel=35 ...... appear=1
N t=18240 v=1 npt=2 stf=2 dur=4 dots=0 nn=76 acc=0 eAcc=3 pDur=456 vel=35 ...>.. appear=1
N t=18240 v=1 npt=3 stf=3 dur=4 dots=0 nn=68 acc=0 eAcc=4 pDur=456 vel=35 ...>.. appear=1
N t=18240 v=1 npt=3 stf=3 dur=4 dots=0 nn=59 acc=0 eAcc=3 pDur=456 vel=35 +..... appear=1
N t=18240 v=1 npt=4 stf=4 dur=4 dots=0 nn=62 acc=0 eAcc=3 pDur=456 vel=35 -..... appear=1
N t=18240 v=1 npt=4 stf=4 dur=4 dots=0 nn=64 acc=0 eAcc=3 pDur=456 vel=35 +..... appear=1
N t=18240 v=1 npt=5 stf=5 dur=4 dots=0 nn=52 acc=0 eAcc=3 pDur=456 vel=35 ...... appear=1
N t=18720 v=1 npt=2 stf=2 dur=5 dots=0 nn=64 acc=0 eAcc=3 pDur=228 vel=35 ....<. appear=1
R t=18720 v=1 npt=3 stf=3 dur=4 dots=0 ...... appear=1
R t=18720 v=1 npt=4 stf=4 dur=4 dots=0 ...... appear=1
R t=18720 v=1 npt=5 stf=5 dur=4 dots=0 ...... appear=1
N t=18960 v=1 npt=2 stf=2 dur=5 dots=0 nn=69 acc=0 eAcc=3 pDur=228 vel=35 ...... appear=1
/ t=19200 type=1
R t=19200 v=1 npt=1 stf=1 dur=-1 dots=0 ...... appear=1
N t=19200 v=1 npt=2 stf=2 dur=5 dots=0 nn=73 acc=0 eAcc=4 pDur=228 vel=35 ...... appear=1
N t=19200 v=1 npt=3 stf=3 dur=4 dots=0 nn=69 acc=0 eAcc=3 pDur=456 vel=35 -..... appear=1
N t=19200 v=1 npt=3 stf=3 dur=4 dots=0 nn=57 acc=0 eAcc=3 pDur=456 vel=35 +..... appear=1
N t=19200 v=1 npt=4 stf=4 dur=4 dots=0 nn=61 acc=0 eAcc=4 pDur=456 vel=35 -..... appear=1
N t=19200 v=1 npt=4 stf=4 dur=4 dots=0 nn=64 acc=0 eAcc=3 pDur=456 vel=35 +..... appear=1
N t=19200 v=1 npt=5 stf=5 dur=4 dots=0 nn=52 acc=0 eAcc=3 pDur=456 vel=35 ...... appear=1
N t=19440 v=1 npt=2 stf=2 dur=5 dots=0 nn=69 acc=0 eAcc=3 pDur=228 vel=35 ...... appear=1
N t=19680 v=1 npt=2 stf=2 dur=4 dots=0 nn=76 acc=0 eAcc=3 pDur=456 vel=35 ...>.. appear=1
N t=19680 v=1 npt=3 stf=3 dur=4 dots=0 nn=69 acc=0 eAcc=3 pDur=456 vel=35 -..... appear=1
N t=19680 v=1 npt=3 stf=3 dur=4 dots=0 nn=57 acc=0 eAcc=3 pDur=456 vel=35 +..... appear=1
```

```
N t=19680 v=1 npt=4 stf=4 dur=4 dots=0 nn=61 acc=0 eAcc=4 pDur=456 vel=35 -..... appear=1
N t=19680 v=1 npt=4 stf=4 dur=4 dots=0 nn=64 acc=0 eAcc=3 pDur=456 vel=35 +..... appear=1
N t=19680 v=1 npt=5 stf=5 dur=4 dots=0 nn=52 acc=0 eAcc=3 pDur=456 vel=35 ...... appear=1
N t=20160 v=1 npt=2 stf=2 dur=5 dots=0 nn=64 acc=0 eAcc=3 pDur=228 vel=35 ....<. appear=1
R t=20160 v=1 npt=3 stf=3 dur=4 dots=0 ...... appear=1
R t=20160 v=1 npt=4 stf=4 dur=4 dots=0 ...... appear=1
R t=20160 v=1 npt=5 stf=5 dur=4 dots=0 ...... appear=1
N t=20400 v=1 npt=2 stf=2 dur=5 dots=0 nn=71 acc=0 eAcc=3 pDur=228 vel=35 ...... appear=1
/ t=20640 type=1
R t=20640 v=1 npt=1 stf=1 dur=-1 dots=0 ...... appear=1
N t=20640 v=1 npt=2 stf=2 dur=5 dots=0 nn=74 acc=0 eAcc=3 pDur=228 vel=35 ...... appear=1
N t=20640 v=1 npt=3 stf=3 dur=4 dots=0 nn=71 acc=0 eAcc=3 pDur=456 vel=35 -..... appear=1
N t=20640 v=1 npt=3 stf=3 dur=4 dots=0 nn=68 acc=0 eAcc=4 pDur=456 vel=35 +..... appear=1
N t=20640 v=1 npt=4 stf=4 dur=4 dots=0 nn=64 acc=0 eAcc=3 pDur=456 vel=35 ...... appear=1
N t=20640 v=1 npt=5 stf=5 dur=4 dots=0 nn=52 acc=0 eAcc=3 pDur=456 vel=35 ...... appear=1
N t=20880 v=1 npt=2 stf=2 dur=5 dots=0 nn=71 acc=0 eAcc=3 pDur=228 vel=35 ...... appear=1
N t=21120 v=1 npt=2 stf=2 dur=5 dots=0 nn=76 acc=0 eAcc=3 pDur=228 vel=35 ...... appear=1
N t=21120 v=1 npt=4 stf=4 dur=4 dots=0 nn=64 acc=0 eAcc=3 pDur=456 vel=35 ...... appear=1
N t=21120 v=1 npt=5 stf=5 dur=4 dots=0 nn=52 acc=0 eAcc=3 pDur=456 vel=35 ...... appear=1
N t=21120 v=1 npt=3 stf=3 dur=4 dots=0 nn=71 acc=0 eAcc=3 pDur=456 vel=35 -..... appear=1
N t=21120 v=1 npt=3 stf=3 dur=4 dots=0 nn=68 acc=0 eAcc=4 pDur=456 vel=35 +..... appear=1
N t=21360 v=1 npt=2 stf=2 dur=5 dots=0 nn=74 acc=0 eAcc=3 pDur=228 vel=35 ...... appear=1
N t=21600 v=1 npt=2 stf=2 dur=5 dots=0 nn=73 acc=0 eAcc=3 pDur=228 vel=35 ...... appear=1
N t=21600 v=1 npt=3 stf=3 dur=4 dots=0 nn=73 acc=0 eAcc=4 pDur=456 vel=35 +..... appear=1
N t=21600 v=1 npt=3 stf=3 dur=4 dots=0 nn=69 acc=0 eAcc=3 pDur=456 vel=35 -..... appear=1
N t=21600 v=1 npt=4 stf=4 dur=4 dots=0 nn=64 acc=0 eAcc=3 pDur=456 vel=35 ...... appear=1
N t=21600 v=1 npt=5 stf=5 dur=4 dots=0 nn=52 acc=0 eAcc=3 pDur=456 vel=35 ...... appear=1
N t=21840 v=1 npt=2 stf=2 dur=5 dots=0 nn=69 acc=0 eAcc=3 pDur=228 vel=35 ...>.. appear=1
/ t=22080 type=1
R t=22080 v=1 npt=1 stf=1 dur=4 dots=0 ...... appear=1
N t=22080 v=1 npt=2 stf=2 dur=5 dots=0 nn=68 acc=0 eAcc=4 pDur=228 vel=35 ....<. appear=1
N t=22080 v=1 npt=3 stf=3 dur=4 dots=0 nn=71 acc=0 eAcc=3 pDur=456 vel=35 -..... appear=1
N t=22080 v=1 npt=3 stf=3 dur=4 dots=0 nn=68 acc=0 eAcc=4 pDur=456 vel=35 +..... appear=1
N t=22080 v=1 npt=4 stf=4 dur=4 dots=0 nn=64 acc=0 eAcc=3 pDur=456 vel=35 ...... appear=1
N t=22080 v=1 npt=5 stf=5 dur=4 dots=0 nn=52 acc=0 eAcc=3 pDur=456 vel=35 ...... appear=1
N t=22320 v=1 npt=2 stf=2 dur=5 dots=0 nn=71 acc=0 eAcc=3 pDur=228 vel=35 ...... appear=1
R t=22560 v=1 npt=1 stf=1 dur=4 dots=0 ...... appear=1
N t=22560 v=1 npt=2 stf=2 dur=4 dots=0 nn=76 acc=0 eAcc=3 pDur=456 vel=35 ...>.. appear=1
N t=22560 v=1 npt=3 stf=3 dur=4 dots=0 nn=71 acc=0 eAcc=3 pDur=456 vel=35 -..... appear=1
N t=22560 v=1 npt=3 stf=3 dur=4 dots=0 nn=68 acc=0 eAcc=4 pDur=456 vel=35 +..... appear=1
N t=22560 v=1 npt=4 stf=4 dur=4 dots=0 nn=64 acc=0 eAcc=3 pDur=456 vel=35 ...... appear=1
N t=22560 v=1 npt=5 stf=5 dur=4 dots=0 nn=40 acc=0 eAcc=3 pDur=456 vel=35 ...... appear=1
N t=23040 v=1 npt=2 stf=2 dur=5 dots=0 nn=64 acc=0 eAcc=3 pDur=228 vel=35 ....<. appear=1
N t=23040 v=1 npt=1 stf=1 dur=4 dots=0 nn=79 acc=0 eAcc=3 pDur=456 vel=35 ....<. appear=1
R t=23040 v=1 npt=3 stf=3 dur=4 dots=0 ...... appear=1
R t=23040 v=1 npt=4 stf=4 dur=4 dots=0 ...... appear=1
R t=23040 v=1 npt=5 stf=5 dur=4 dots=0 ...... appear=1
N t=23280 v=1 npt=2 stf=2 dur=5 dots=0 nn=68 acc=0 eAcc=4 pDur=228 vel=35 ...... appear=1
/ t=23520 type=1
```

Example 21.1 *Nightingale Notelist* file for the Mozart Clarinet Quintet trio.

Musical NotationCodes (4):

Braille

22   Braille Musical Notation (1): An Overview

Roger Firman[1]

Louis Braille (1809–1852) introduced the concept of raised dot notation in a document published in 1829. As well as a Braille alphabet, this publication also proposed a system of Braille music. The code for music was revised by Braille himself during the next five years while other competing systems, based upon letters and numbers, were being developed. The big disadvantage of these alternative suggestions was that they could not be reproduced by visually impaired people. If these proposals were to be re-examined today, the situation would certainly be very different. Computer technology could be very easily used to make music available in situations where ease of access and non-specialist transcriptions are required.

Braille is based on a system of six raised dots contained within a cell—two dots on the top, middle, and bottom rows reading from left to right. Each dot is known by its number:

$$① \qquad ④$$
$$② \qquad ⑤$$
$$③ \qquad ⑥$$

The numeration of dots is invariable: top left = Dot 1; middle left = Dot 2; bottom left = Dot 3; upper right = Dot 4; middle right = Dot 5; bottom right = Dot 6. Within each of these six-dot cells it will be recognized that there are 64 possible combinations (one being no dots), many more than the 26 combinations required to form the letters of the English alphabet. The remaining formations and combinations of symbols with

---

1. I would like to thank two colleagues, Adam Ockelford and Sally Zimmerman, for their help while writing this chapter.

more than one cell are used for a contracted version of Braille known as Grade Two, where single letters as well as various groupings form words.

Braille music uses these same characters to convey musical meaning. Whereas print music is pictorial, Braille music is linear. Thus the need to print musical staves is redundant. It is important to note that the symbols used for the note name and its value are bound up within the one character and that separate signs are used to denote pitch. Other items are placed before or after the note, depending upon the symbol and situation. Beaming of eighth notes (quavers) is not reproduced in Braille. Neither are some aspects of music which are purely pictorial. Since there are both logical and tactile limitations to the cells, these must be vertically and horizontally self-referencing.

The available repertoire consists mainly of classically-based Western music for piano, organ, chorus and/or solo voices, flute, recorder, guitar, and other solo instruments. Some orchestral scores have been produced, but they are very bulky to use. Music for electronic keyboard and organ is also being transcribed, as is instrumental music from the folk music repertories of countries such as those of Eastern Europe.

The teaching of Braille music must be undertaken using a practical and musical approach. If not, the code will be learned with all the Braille literary connotations and be a purely theoretical exercise limiting any student to an incorrect understanding. The shapes produced in Braille must be related first to "sound," then to "symbol."

22.1   Musical Attributes

The aim of Braille music transcriptions is to convey the detail of the printed page. Thus there are signs for items such as articulation, intervals, fingering, arpeggios, slurs of various types, dynamics (including diverging and converging lines), bowing, strings, frets, ties, pauses, pedal (piano and organ), hand signs, and many more items.

22.1.1   Global Specifiers

The header of a Braille music file normally provides a tempo indication, metronome marking, key signature, and meter signature. The key signature will indicate only the number of sharps and flats, since there is no musical staff and therefore staff placement is an impossibility.

22.1.2   Pitch and Duration

Pitch is defined by octave and letter name. The lowest C on the piano is known as first-octave C and all the notes up to the B above are within the first octave. Middle C is known as fourth-octave C and so on. It is also possible to represent notes outside the customary seven octaves.

Note name and duration are given within a single cell. Dots 1, 2, 4, and 5 in combination give the note name. Dots 3 and 6 give the duration. Each duration has two possible meanings:

DOT 3	DOT 6	ALTERNATIVE MEANINGS
on	on	whole note or 16th note
on	off	half note or 32nd note
off	on	quarter note or 64th note
off	off	eighth note or 128th note

In most instances the musical context clarifies the duration. However, it is sometimes necessary to use a couple of signs to indicate whether the value is long or short.

22.1.3 Special Provisions

Braille music transcription makes use of several concepts designed to simplify encoding. Among these are the *doubling*, *interval*, *in-accord*, and *repeat* modes.

- *Doubling mode* is a system of transcription in which a sign remains in effect until it is specifically terminated.

- *Interval mode* is used, for instance, to indicate secondary notes of chords or two parts with similar rhythmic values. The highest or lowest note must be indicated by name. The associated notes are represented by their intervallic relation to this note.

- *In-accord mode* is used to show the difference between two rhythmically independent parts that are aligned vertically in print.[2]

- *Repeat mode* can be used to indicate the repetition of notes, beats, half-bars, and bars.

---

2. This is the condition referred to in *DARMS* as LINEAR DECOMPOSITION [see the glossary].

22.2   File Organization

Braille music may contain both textual material and musical code. Changes between these modes are indicated by a special sign. The music is written in horizontal lines consisting of Braille music characters; piano music may be represented by parallel lines ("bar-over-bar" format) terminated by a blank space.

The many methods used to organize notated scores inevitably cause Braille musical notation to exist in varied formats. For the purposes of this chapter we will confine the list and descriptions to those most often used.

22.2.1   Bar-Over-Bar Format

The bars in this layout are aligned vertically. Piano music would usually have two parallel lines, i.e., right-hand and left-hand.

22.2.2   Open-Score Format

This is a method of placing music and words close together, i.e., music beginning at the left-hand margin of one line, the words starting on the line below with an indentation of two spaces. This method is the nearest equivalent to sight-reading.

22.2.3   Short-Score Format

The parts of a choral work are combined to form a parallel approach, similar to that of the bar-over-bar format.

22.2.4   Section-By-Section Format

In this format, a composition is divided into sections with each part or hand being written in a separate paragraph.

22.2.5   Single-Line Format

The music is written for a single instrumental part using a new print line as a dividing point. These, with appropriate bar numbers, are indented two spaces on a free line. The music itself starts at the left-hand margin and continues for as many Braille lines as are necessary to complete it.

Key signatures reflect only the number of sharps or flats, not, as in print, the pitches.

22.3 Examples

22.3.1 The Mozart Trio

Bars 0–9 of the print-out of a Braille score file for the first 16 bars of the second trio of Mozart's Clarinet Quintet are shown in the accompanying example,[3] which is discussed below. The dots, shown here in black, would be raised in the production of an actual Braille score, which requires an impact printer.

The music is presented in bar-over-bar format, previously described, with bar numbers aligned above the music. Before this, the print name and Braille prefix designating the instrumentation are given, listing print names on the left-hand side with their Braille equivalents on the right.

Example 22.1 Bars 0–1 from an "English" Braille encoding of the Mozart trio. (This example continues on the next page.)

---

3. This example includes a few features specific to the English dialect of Braille musical notation. It may be compared with the "new international" transcription in the following chapter.

Example 22.1 (cont.) Bars 2–12 of the Mozart trio. Details are given in the text.

Note that there are six blocks of type in Example 22.1. The first block of type is in "literary" Braille. Full instrument names are given at the left. Abbreviated names are given at the right. The characters in the upper right-hand corner simply say "BRL [=Braille] PREFIX".

In the second block of type, a centered reference indicates "Line [=System] 1" of the printed score on Line 1.[4] The indications for "Bar 0" and "Bar 1" are found at appropriate points in Line 2 of this block. The next five lines of Block 2 form the first set of parallel parts. The *Clarinet*, *Violino I*, *Violino II*, *Viola*, and *Violoncello* parts are followed with the appropriate clef signs and key and time signatures. The clarinet part, being written in C Major, has a time signature but not a key signature.

Block 3 contains the encoding of Bars 2, 3, and 4; Block 4 contains Bars 5, 6, and 7; Block 5 contains Bars 8 and 9.[5] Block 6 contains Bars 10, 11, and the first part of 12. This example contains pitch signs in several octaves; use of these signs depends upon context. Every note does not require its own specific pitch sign. The durations require the representation of eighth notes, quarter notes, half notes, dotted half notes, quarter rests, and bar rests.

Other features of particular interest in this passage are:

BRACKETS: See Bars 0 and 1 of the *Clarinet* part. This is a device where groups of more than four notes are slurred. The beginning of the bracket slur or phrase (CELL 1: Dots 5, 6; CELL 2: Dots 2, 3) appears before the slurred note. The end of that slur (CELL 1: Dots 4, 5; CELL 2: Dots 2, 3) appears after the last note of that slur.[6]

DOTS WITH DOUBLE BAR: See first part of Bar 12.

TIES (CELL 1: Dot 4; CELL 2: Dots 1, 4): See Bar 11 and first part of Bar 12 in the *Viola* part.

22.3.2 The Mozart Piano Sonata

The five bars of the Mozart piano example demonstrate some other interesting features of the Braille music code.

---

4. The printed score for Example 22.1 as shown in the first chapter of this book.

5. The header says "Line [=System] 2" because in the original printed example System 2 began with Bar 8.

6. Note that in the Braille example a second slur begins immediately after the first and ends at the conclusion of Bar 3.

When bars are not numbered in a corresponding print, a note, written in parentheses, is included in the Braille. Bar numbers have been included in the Braille version except for Bar 100, which occupies the same lines as Bar 99. The example is transcribed in the customary bar-over-bar format with the line number given in the cell before the left-hand part of Bar 98.

Example 22.2a The Mozart piano sonata (Bars 98–102).

Example 22.2b Braille transcription of the Mozart piano sonata (22.2a). This example uses "bar-over-bar" format resulting in four tiers—Bar 98, Bars 99 and 100, Bar 101, and Bar 102. In each case the right- and left-hand parts are given in parallel.

Right- (Dots 4, 6) and left-hand (Dots 4, 5, 6) signs are written on each block and the parts are shown in parallel.

An arpeggio sign (CELL 1: Dots 3, 4, 5; CELL 2: Dots 1, 3) is used in Bar 98, right hand. A rest shows where the arpeggio lies; that is, the smaller note values of the "quarter notes" must be reconciled with the half note on top.

A number of other features are illustrated in this example:

- Bars 98 and 102, right hand, illustrate how the layout of the music in Braille necessitates use of the two-cell "in-accord" sign (CELL 1: Dots 1, 2, 6; CELL 2: Dots 3, 4, 5). Bar 102 has a dotted quarter note and an eighth note above the half-note chord and shows use of the sign previously mentioned.

- A device indicating that additional information has been included is found in Bar 98. In this case a quarter rest was inserted in the lower part of the right hand on the second beat, so that the beat count gives a correct result in Braille layout. The Dot 5 preceding the quarter rest is the indicator that the rest appears only in Braille, not in the corresponding print.

- Bar 98, left hand, demonstrates the use of small notes and small slurs (also see Bars 100 to 102, left hand).

- Bar 99, left hand, is an example of a whole bar repeated by use of a single sign (Dots 2, 3, 5, 6).

- Bar 99, right hand, uses a repeat sign showing that the first quarter-note beat, including the slur and staccato signs, is repeated.

- Bar 99, right hand, shows how it is possible to group sixteenth notes.[7]

- Bar 101 gives an example of using repeat signs for the second eighth notes and then a quarter-note repeat, these being separated by an appropriate dot. Use of Dot 3s following hand-signs can be seen by comparing Bars 98–99 with Bars 101–102. In its simplest form, Dot 3 is used where the following sign would use dots on the left side of the Braille cell, i.e., Dots 1, 2, or 3. It is also used for purposes of alignment.[8]

The encoding of music in Braille code requires a computer with a program which redefines the keys s, d, f, j, k, and l to act as input keys. This can be achieved by using a stand-alone software package such as *Megadots* from Raised Dot Computing, or *Edgar* from Duxbury Systems, or by transcribing with an adapted version of a word-processing package such as *Word Perfect*. Simulated dots appear on the screen. The user has complete control regarding layout, length of lines, and alignment, which is particularly important with this code. Prior to a Braille file's being embossed, it needs to be made ready in its ASCII version.

7. Note, however, that the rules governing this are complicated.

8. See the left hand of Bar 98 and right hand of Bar 99.

22.4 Comments

An enormous advantage of using this technology is storage and retrieval of the data. Because of developments and increasing use of music input programs, an obvious method for production of Braille music would be to take an already existing file and convert it to the appropriate structure and format. Needless to say, this would save hours of time because no initial input would be required.

Much research has been and is currently taking place into improving input methods, but the "six-keys" input method remains by far the most effective in terms of quality and accuracy.

Two programs that have been extensively used to originate Braille music codes are *SCORE* and *Finale*, each of which is highly regarded by those working in the field. As the concepts of print and Braille music are very different, the complexities in writing and adapting the software are not straightforward. The use of an intermediary file is being developed, and no doubt within the next few years more progress will be made.

As *Standard Music Description Language* (*SMDL*) becomes defined, this has the potential of solving many problems with current software by the very nature of the tasks each performs.[9]

22.5 Resources and References[10]

22.5.1 Works Transcribed in Braille Music Code

There is no single reference point for acquiring music notated in Braille code. Stocks of Braille music are preserved in various archives located in Australia, Austria, Belgium, Brazil, Canada, the Commonwealth of Independent States (C.I.S.), Denmark, Finland, France, Germany, Greece, Hungary, Iceland, Israel, Italy, Japan, Netherlands, Norway, Poland, South Africa, Spain, Sweden, Switzerland, the U.K., the U.S.A., and some formerly Yugoslav republics. Below are some useful contact points from which to start.

---

9. [Addendum by Eleanor Selfridge-Field: Perhaps because it has so often been a targeted by-product of notation software programs, and because most input methods presented in this section are tedious for the visually impaired, Braille music notation turns out to be in the vanguard of formats on which interchange standards will be tested. A case-in-point: the *Goodfeel* Braille Music Translator (see further description in the glossary) offered by Dancing Dots Braille Music Technology intends acceptance of MIDI input as well as files in *LIME*'s *Tilia* representation, with interchange to and from other codes via *NIFF*.]

10. Compiled by Roger Firman, with additions by Bettye Krolick and Eleanor Selfridge-Field.

Dutch Students' Library for the Blind
SVB
Molenpad 2
1016GM Amsterdam, Netherlands
Tel.: +31 20/626 6465
Fax: +31 20/620 8459

Royal National Institute for the Blind
Music Librarian
224 Great Portland Street
London W1N 6AA, UK
Tel.: +44 0171/388 1266, ext. 2437
Fax: +44 0171/388 2034

Library of Congress
National Library Service for the Blind
and Physically Handicapped
1291 Taylor Street N.W.
Washington, DC 20542, USA
Tel.: +1 202/707 9254
Fax: +1 202/707 0712

22.5.2 Practical Writings about Braille Music

Documentation for the Braille music code is available in numerous writings in both Braille and print. The most recent comprehensive source, which is available in both formats, is:

> *New International Manual of Braille Music Notation*, compiled by Bettye Krolick for the Braille Music Subcommittee, World Blind Union. 1996. ISBN 90-9009269-2.
>
> PRINT EDITION: Available from the Dutch Students' Library for the Blind, SVB, 1016 GM Amsterdam, Netherlands.
>
> BRAILLE EDITION: Available from SBS Braille Press, Zürich, 8047 Zürich, Switzerland.

This manual presents and explains the signs agreed to by 15 nations at a conference in Saanen, Switzerland, in February 1992. It includes examples of use, but it does not stress rules or locally used conventions.

Each country maintains its own manual and accepts international changes only through its own "Braille Authority." Thus some details may vary from one source to another. The current manual for the U.S. and Canada is:

> *Manual of Braille Music Notation American Edition, 1988.* American Printing House for the Blind, 1839 Frankfort Ave., Louisville, KY 40206-0085.

Numerous manuals exist in other languages.

Other useful resources in English include the following:

Braille Music Primer, Parts 1 and 2, compiled and ed. by David Bray. London: Royal National Institute for the Blind (RNIB), 1992 and 1994. ISBN 0-901797-79-0 and 1-85878-035-7. Further information is available from the Institute, Peterborough PE2 6WS, England, UK; tel. +44 01733/370777.

Burrows, Anne. *Music through Braille.* Alberta: MacNab Corp., 1987. ISBN 0-921889-00-3. Further information from the M. E. MacNab Corp., 10819–117th Street, Edmonton, Alberta T5H 3N4, Canada.

Krolick, Bettye. "Dictionary of Braille Music Signs" in *Braille Music in Brief* (Washington, DC: National Library for the Blind and Physically Handicapped, 1979), pp. 162–181.

Ockelford, Adam. "Music Notation for People with a Severe Visual Impairment." London: RNIB, 1992.

Watson, Edward. *A Guide to Braille Music Notation,* 2nd edn., rev. John Busbridge. London: RNIB, 1994. ISBN 1-85878-031-4.

22.5.3 Research Articles

Baptiste, Nadine. "Un système d'apprentissage assisté par ordinateur pour l'harmonie musicale pouvant être utilisé par des non voyants." Thesis, Paul Sabatier University (Toulouse, France), 1990.

Baptiste, Nadine, and Monique Truquet. "Harmony Program Learning for the Blind Person" in *Proceedings of the Sixth International Workshop on Computer Applications for the Visually Handicapped, Leuven* [Belgium]*, 19–21 Septembre 1990.*

Baptiste, Nadine, and Monique Truquet. "How to Help Visually Impaired Musicains: Automatic Braille Transcription" in *Proceedings of the First International Conference on Information Technology, Computerization, and Electronics in the Workplace for People with Disabilities, Washington, DC, December 1991.*

Frontin, J. "Un système interactif de transcription de partitions musicales universelles pour non voyants." Thesis, Paul Sabatier University, 1981.

"Music Software for the Visually Impaired" (compiled by Eleanor Selfridge-Field), *Computing in Musicology* 5 (1989), 25.

Ohteru, Sadamu, *et al.* "A Printed-Music-to-Braille Translation System" in *Proceedings of the Sixth International Workshop on Computer Applications for the Visually Handicapped, Leuven* [Belgium]*, 19–21 Septembre 1990.*

"Systems for the Visually Impaired" (compiled by Eleanor Selfridge-Field), *Computing in Musicology* 7 (1991), 102–106.

23   Braille Musical Notation (2): Common Signs

Bettye Krolick and Sile O'Modhrain

All of the symbols given here conform to the newly published manual of internationally adopted signs. This contribution is intended to complement the preceding one.

Note that in the composition of many Braille signs Dots 3 and 6 (shown in bold type in this chapter) are used as switches, so that particular configurations of Dots 1, 2, 4, and 5 form patterns which are differentiated only by the setting of these switches. Note also that some Braille signs consist of two cells.

Since many of the same dot combinations may occur in both textual and numerical contexts, Braille provides prefixes for distinguishing numbers from words:

Number sign ⠼

Word sign ⠠

Mixtures of textual and numeric symbols are very common in music because of the need to provide titles, instrument designations, tempo words, text underlay, and other verbal material.

Conversely, phenomena that use the same name in ordinary English, such as C the letter name and C the pitch name, do not necessarily use the same symbols in Braille. Braille necessarily has a logic of its own.

23.1   Letters of the English Alphabet

The method of representing the letters A..J constitutes a series of dot combinations that is reused to represent many other things:

LETTER	DOTS ON	CELL
A	1	
B	12	
C	1 4	
D	1 45	
E	1 5	
F	12 4	
G	12 45	
H	12 5	
I	2 4	
J	2 4	

For example, the letters K..T use the same dot combinations as the letters A..J but with the addition of Dot 3:

LETTER	DOTS ON	CELL
K	1 3	
L	123	
M	1 34	
N	1 345	
O	1 3 5	
P	1234	
Q	12345	
R	123 5	
S	234	
T	2345	

The dot combinations for the letters U, V, X, Y, and Z duplicate those for K, L, M, N, and O with the addition of Dot 6:

LETTER	DOTS ON	CELL
U	1 3 6	
V	123 6	
X	1 34 6	
Y	1 3456	
Z	1 3 56	

The letter W is the same as J with the addition of Dot 6:

W	2 45**6**	⠺

23.2 One-Cell Signs

23.2.1 Pitch and Duration

The dot combinations for the pitch names C..B duplicate those of the letters D..J:

PITCH NAME	DOTS ON	CELL
C	1 45	⠙
D	1 5	⠑
E	12 4	⠋
F	12 45	⠛
G	12 5	⠓
A	2 4	⠊
B	2 4	⠚
rest	1 **34 6**	⠭

Pitch and duration are combined in one cell. The values given above represent eighth notes. To create quarter notes Dot 6 must be switched on:

PITCH NAME	DOTS ON	CELL
C	1 45**6**	⠹
D	1 5**6**	⠱
E	12 4 **6**	⠫
F	12 45**6**	⠻
G	12 5**6**	⠳
A	2 4 **6**	⠪
B	2 45**6**	⠺
rest	12**3 6**	⠧

Dot 3 is added to create half notes:

PITCH NAME	DOTS ON	CELL
C	1 **3**45	⠝
D	1 **3** 5	⠕

E	1234	
F	12345	
G	123 5	
A	234	
B	2345	
rest	1 3 6	

For whole notes both Dots 3 and 6 are used.

PITCH NAME	DOTS ON	CELL
C	1 3456	
D	1 3 56	
E	1234 6	
F	123456	
G	123 56	
A	234 6	
B	23456	
rest	1 34	

Note that the eighth, quarter, half, and whole rests are equivalent to the letters X, V, U, and M.

23.2.2 Accidentals

Accidental signs are made from the codes for the letters A, B, and C with Dot 6 turned on:

SIGN	DOTS ON	CELL
♮	1 6	
♭	12 6	
♯	1 4 6	

Note that in the normal ordering of symbols, these precede the pitch names. Double sharps and double flats are created by reiterating the sign.

23.2.3 Numbers

Numbers duplicate letters A..J and can be distinguished from them by the number prefix.

NUMERAL	DOTS ON	CELL
1	1	⠁
2	12	⠃
3	1 4	⠉
4	1 45	⠙
5	1 5	⠑
6	12 4	⠋
7	12 45	⠛
8	12 5	⠓
9	2 4	⠊
0	2 45	⠚

A. OCTAVE NUMBERS

Octave numbers in Braille musical notation use only Dots 4, 5, and 6:

OCTAVE	DOTS ON	CELL
1	4	⠈
2	45	⠘
3	45**6**	⠸
4	5	⠐
5	4 **6**	⠨
6	5**6**	⠰
7	**6**	⠠

B. FINGER NUMBERS

In this way, Dots 1, 2, and 3 can be used simultaneously for finger numbers:

FINGER	DOTS ON	CELL
1	1	⠁
2	12	⠃
3	12**3**	⠇
4	2	⠂
5	1 **3**	⠅

23.3   Two- and Multiple-Cell Signs

Many features of Braille musical notation require the use of two or more cells.

23.3.1   Octave Numbers

A complete pitch definition in Braille consists of an octave number followed by a pitch name. The first pitch must always be preceded by an octave number. Octaves are numbered from C upward. Within the range of a fourth, the nearest note of the proper name is assumed; exceptions require clarification.

23.3.2   Clef and Hand Signs

A. PIANO AND VOCAL MUSIC

In the representation of piano music, two-cell signs are used for "left hand" (CELL 1: Dots 4, 5, 6; CELL 2: Dots 3, 4, 5) and "right hand" (CELL 1: Dots 4, 6; CELL 2: Dots 3, 4, 5). The hand signs are:

right hand

left hand

Clef signs are not indigenous to Braille musical notation. An octave sign combined with a (piano) hand sign serves the same purpose in that it establishes a starting position for piano music. In vocal music only the octave sign is used.

B. INSTRUMENTAL ENSEMBLE MUSIC

Clef signs for orchestral parts and scores require three cells:

Treble

Viola

Bass

23.3.3   Phrase Marks

The opening and closing signs of a phrase mark (taken to be equivalent to a slur) are mirror images of each other:

Open   Close

23.3.4 Bar Lines

A bar line is normally represented by a blank space, but a double bar line requires these two cells:

Double bar ⠶⠶

23.4 Example

Below we see the opening two bars of the Mozart trio, provided here to illustrate minor differences between the newly approved international Braille music code and the English dialect in which the Mozart trio is set in the preceding chapter. These differences include the clef signs and the overall alignment of symbols.

Example 23.1 Bars 0 and 1 of the Mozart trio in the new international Braille music code.

This example corresponds to Block 2 of Example 22.1 in the preceding chapter. The abbreviated instrument names are given, as before, in the first four columns. The next three (four) columns give the clef signs. Note the differences in usage.

After the first vertical break, the key signature is given (by three iterations of the sharp sign—Dots 1, 4, 6) except in the part for *Clarinet in A*, which does not require one. A number sign (Dots 3, 4, 5, 6) introduces a two-cell time signature of 3/4. The encoding of Bar 0 follows the next vertical break, and that of Bar 1 the break after that. The line number, bar numbers, and rests are handled as before, but in this case the space following the rests is not left blank. The clarinet and cello parts are flush-left with the start of each bar. This includes the "Letter P" dynamic marking in the cello part. In all other respects, these examples are the same.

Codes for Data Management and Analysis (1):

Monophonic Representations

24   The *Essen Associative Code*: A Code for Folksong Analysis

Helmut Schaffrath[†1]

The *Essen Associative Code* (*EsAC*) for monophonic music was developed in the early 1980s for folk-music research concerning repertories from Europe, Asia, and the Americas. A number of programs for input, display, analysis, and output of Essen data have been written. Initially all were for the PC, but some UNIX tools also now exist.

EsAC code consists entirely of ASCII characters and was designed to run on DOS machines. The code currently supports activities in ethnomusicology and music analysis as well as archives of recorded and printed music. As of 1994 more than 14,000 folksongs had been encoded in *EsAC*. The code was designed to occupy one field of a relational database.[2] This facilitates correlational studies of musical and contextual attributes.

The following field designators (based on German nomenclature) are used: CUT = title; TRD = source; MEL = the actual *EsAC* encoding; FKT = the social function of the music (religious, patriotic, etc.); BEM = remarks. The KEY field contains the database name code and item number (C0000 in the following example), the smallest rhythmic value (08), the key (C), and the meter (3 / 4).

1. Prof. Dr. Schaffrath, formerly of the Gesamthochschule für Musik, Essen University, was the developer of the code (and related databases) described in this chapter. Born in Aachen in 1942 and apprenticed in his youth to an organ-builder, Dr. Schaffrath completed his university education in Berlin. Devoting himself to folk-music research in the Seventies, he chaired the computer group of the International Council for Traditional Music and was a prolific author. An extended list of his writings is given in the References section. Six months before his untimely death in March 1994, Dr. Schaffrath prepared two possible contributions to this handbook. The present one, a conflation of the two, has been edited and updated by Eleanor Selfridge-Field, with the help of Ewa Dahlig and Ulrich Franzke.

2. The commercial program *AskSam*. This program is now scarce, but the ASCII database content as distributed is easily read by word-processing programs and can, with appropriate text delimiters, be readily imported into other database programs.

24.1 Means of Representation

24.1.1 Pitch

EsAC was intended to be so simple that users could sing at sight from it. The "associative" aspect of Essen code is that its simplicity would facilitate the association of sight-reading and sight-singing. Its pitch representation resembles *solfegge*, with scale-degree numbers replacing the moveable syllables *do, re, mi*, etc.:

do	1	tonic
re	2	supertonic
mi	3	mediant
fa	4	subdominant
sol	5	dominant
la	6	submediant
ti	7	leading tone

Chromatic alterations are represented in the following way:

+	sharp
b	flat

The principal octave (the one in which the largest number of notes fall) used in each encoding is unsigned. "Outer" octaves are signed in one of two ways:

–	if the pitch falls below principal octave
+	if the pitch falls above principal octave

Rests are represented by a zero.

24.1.2 Duration and Phrase Segmentation

EsAC is the only code in common use which requires phrases to be identified in the encoding process. The encoder decides how to divide melodies into musical or logical segments. Although this is an arguably interpretive gesture, such phrases often serve as the unit for parametric analysis (examples appear below).

Meter and phrase organization are indicated with the following symbols:

[blank]	measure boundary
[CR[3]]	phrase boundary
//	end of melody

Durations of the slightest value (e.g., a sixteenth note, if 16 is found in the KEY field) are assumed to be the default duration and are represented by a numeral without any extension. Notes of greater value assume the following extensions:

.	increases duration by 50%
_	increases duration by 100%
__	increases duration by 200%

24.1.3 Example: The Mozart Trio

Because *EsAC* is designed for monophonic music, only the clarinet part of the Mozart trio has been encoded for this contribution. It appears below in the MEL field.

```
CUT[Mozart: second trio from Clarinet Quintet: Clarinet Part]
TRD[Kopy CCARH]
KEY[C0000 08 C3/4]
MEL[+1+3 +5+3 ++1_+5+3 +2+4+6_+4+2 +17+3+2+5+4 +2#_+3_
    +1+3 +5+3++1_+5+3 +2+4+6_0_ 0___. 0_0_
    (2-6-4) -6246+2+4 +6+5+4+3+4+2 +1__+3+2 +1_0_//]
FKT[Art music]
BEM[nn]
```

Example 24.1a *EsAC* encoding of the clarinet part of the Mozart trio.

Note that this encoding treats the music as consisting of three phrases segmented as follows:

---

3. CR = carriage return, i.e., ASCII character 13..

Example 24.1b Phrase segmentation implied by encoding.

24.1.4 Other Attributes and Capabilities

EsAC does not support polyphonic notation, dynamic or timbral information for playback, or spatial information for desktop publishing. Various other elements of information may be added optionally.

A. GRAPHICAL FEATURES OF STAFF NOTATION (*ESTAFF*)

Some programs designed to be run with *EsAC* data, such as the display program *ESTAFF*, allow for the interpolation of graphic features such as beams, articulations, and ornaments as well as the extrapolation of pitch and duration attributes. Some of *ESTAFF*'s capabilities are suggested in Example 24.2.

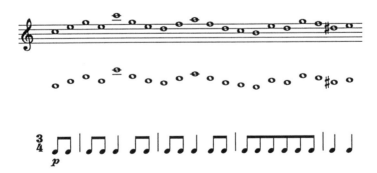

Example 24.2 Some *ESTAFF* displays of extracted data.

In Example 24.2 we see (1) extracted pitches shown on the staff, (2) extracted pitches with the staff removed ("contour"), and (3) extracted durations.[4]

B. LYRICS

Lyrics can be entered in a separate field (TXT) immediately following the MEL field. They may be given in phrase units or as syllables. The *ESTAFF* program reconciles alignment.

C. CODE RESTRICTIONS

EsAC's parsing depends on precise line formatting and assumes some maximum field lengths. These restrictions are explicit:

- The general length of 80 characters per line must not be exceeded.

- Melody lines in *EsAC* must not contain more than 40 note symbols.

- Unanalyzed documents are restricted to a length of 95 lines. The paragraphs preceding the melody are restricted to 17. The melody itself must not be longer than 59 lines. After the melody a maximum of 20 text lines may follow.

D. THE *JIANPU* NOTATION VARIANT

ESTAFF supports Chinese cipher (*Jianpu*) notation. This requires some substitutions for the codes given above. In the *Jianpu* variant vertical bars are used for bar lines. Octaves are identified by dots applied to the vertical plane of each pitch designator: a *subscript* dot indicates the first octave below the principal octave, while a *superscript* dot indicates the first octave above.

In the following example, which is a *Jianpu* encoding of Western music (the clarinet part from the Mozart trio), the default duration is the quarter note. Eighth notes are represented by an underlined pitch name, while half notes are indicated by a hyphen following the pitch name.

---

4. These may also be displayed on a five-line staff or without any staff lines.

Example 24.3 The Mozart trio clarinet part encoded in *Jianpu*.

24.2   The *EsAC* Framework for Musical Analysis

While it is generally beyond the scope of this book to describe the analytical procedures that may be used with musical data, *EsAC* provides such a clear example and such a well-developed set of tools that the course of future applications using codes for polyphonic music may be suggested by a brief glimpse of the kinds of routines that such basic information supports.

24.2.1   Basic Analysis Software (*ANA*)

At its simplest level, the analysis software provides numerous translations of *EsAC* code. These are reported in additional fields of the relational database structure. Among the results that may be reported are these:

- distribution of ascending intervals
- distribution of descending intervals
- distribution of durations
- distribution of pitches
- rhythmic patterns
- scale type and tessitura
- final tones of phrases
- melodic spine
- phrase repetition as determined by pitches
- phrase repetition as determined by durations
- pitch contour
- phrase initiation (on upbeat or downbeat)

All of these routines belong to one program, *ANA*.[5]

To illustrate how such derivative fields may be used in combination, we might consider the capability to reduce melodies to strings of pitches from which actual durations and repeated notes have been removed. These prototypes may then be used to represent melodic contours, that is, generalized representations.

In the following example the columns labelled FOT, FOR, and FOK report (1) the pattern of phrase repetitions conveyed by pitch alone, (2) the pattern of phrase repetitions conveyed by duration alone, and (3) a mnemonic for the pitch contour displayed to the right.

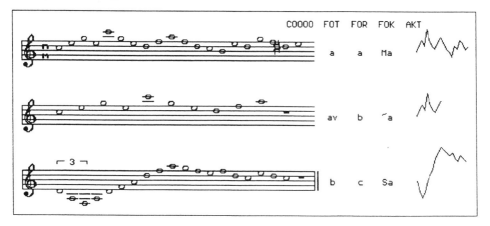

Example 24.4 *ANA* analyses of phrase patterns and contours in the Mozart trio.

The *melodic spine* (ACC), in contrast, reduces a melody to those pitches which occur on accented beats. The *final-tones-of-phrases* field (CAD) turns out to be useful in searching for similarities between songs because, although variants may contain different numbers of notes or melodic contours, they tend to retain underlying harmonic structures. No output to either of these fields is shown here.

24.2.2 Melodic Comparison

"Melodic comparison" is a phrase used loosely to describe a great range of different procedures. Here we consider searches based only on pitch information, searches based only on rhythmic information, and searches based on a combination of the two.

---

5. *ANA* was written in the late Eighties by Barbara Jesser, then a student at Essen University, to run on the DOS platform.

A. CORRESPONDING PITCH COMPONENTS

The dream of many music researchers is to use the computer as a tool for identifying closely related materials. For this contribution a database of 6,070 German folksongs was searched for the pitch incipit of the Mozart trio. Its pitch profile is 1353 +1. It was found to occur six times among all the folksongs, but in only three cases was it in 3/4 meter. Two examples—"Hoert Ihr Herrn und lasst euch sagen" [Item E1581] and "Trauer, Trauer, über Trauer" [Item K2208]—appear, following the original, below:

Example 24.5 Opening pitch strings matching that of the Mozart trio.

B. CORRESPONDING DURATION COMPONENTS

In a search for the rhythmic profile of the first phrase of the Mozart trio

60 examples containing the beginning durational profile xx xxx_xx in the first melodic phrase were found; 31 of these contained the next three notes (xxx_), but none contained the exact rhythm of the complete phrase through Bar 4.

Some examples in which the rhythmic pattern was preserved but the pitches were not are shown below. These examples come from the German "Willst du mich denn nicht mehr lieben" [Item E0699A] and one version of the Bohemian "Ufm bergli bin i gesaesse" [Item B0397].

Example 24.6 Nearest rhythmic approximations to the first five bars of the Mozart trio found in a database of 6070 folksongs.

C. COMBINED ATTRIBUTE MATCHES

The complete incipit with its pitch and duration correlates (13 53 +1_) appears only once among the 6,070 German folksongs, and in this case not in the first line but in the third. Interestingly, however, it occurs in another version of "Willst du mich denn nicht mehr lieben" [Item E0699]:

Example 24.7 "Willst du mich denn nicht mehr lieben": five-note sequence corresponding in pitch and duration to the opening notes of the Mozart trio.

These examples indicate in a modest way the central problem that one encounters in the comparison of simple melodies in a monophonic context: exact matches are few. The combinatorial explosion of coupled musical attributes can best be managed by fuzzy searching, but the most effective combinations of precise and imprecise elements remain to be determined. Preliminary work suggests that they are likely to vary from repertory to repertory and to depend on access to features that are not necessarily encoded in all systems. In the context of polyphonic repertories and codes which represent numerous other attributes of the music, the range of possible procedures is greater by many orders of magnitude.

24.2.3 Recombination

Because music is encoded phrase by phrase in *EsAC*, it is a fairly simple task to combine selected phrases from diverse pieces to produce "new" folksongs. For example, the pattern of durations in the first phrase of the Mozart quotation could serve as a controlling template for the selection of other phrases that would be combined in sequence. The first two lines of Example 24.6, for instance, could serve as antecedent and consequent phrases of a "new work." Recomposition obviously lies well beyond the scope of this book, but this example points to a fourth domain (after sound, notation, and analysis) for the use of musical data—simulation of musical repertories.[6]

24.3   The *EsAC* Program Library

The library of *EsAC* programs[7] *ca.* 1990 included the following items:

ANA   Carries out up to 12 analytical procedures on one-part
           melodies encoded in *EsAC*.

---

6. The most sustained research in this sphere has been carried out by David Cope, among whose many writings the most extensive description is found in *The Computer and Musical Style* (Madison: A-R Editions, Inc., 1993).

7. Some of these programs were written by Ulrich Franzke and Barbara Jesser, both former pupils of Dr. Schaffrath at Essen University.

ES 3   *ESTAFF*, Version 3. Provides Western staff-line and Asian cypher notation for screen display and printing. Also used for transposition and for display of rhythmic and pitch patterns generated by analyses.

MAPPET   A package of programs to encode, control, analyze, and play the melodies (via speaker or synthesizer).[8]

PAT   This program searches for user-defined patterns in *EsAC* melodies. Occurrences can be displayed in staff notation and played by the speaker.

STRIP   Five programs strip *EsAC* data of *ANA* results stored in various database fields. They can selectively omit pitches, repetitions, and/or data durations.

RIP   This utility program combines an editor that can switch between ASCII and graphics with a database-system specially designed for *EsAC* files.

24.4   Data Interchange

EsAC data has been translated to such codes as *DARMS*, *Kern*, MIDI, *MTEX*,[9] and *SCORE* as well as to some user-designed and proprietary commercial codes.

The following graph of the Mozart example may serve as a comparison between *EsAC* and five other codes—*Jianpu* notation, canonical *DARMS*, *Note-Processor DARMS*, *SCORE*, and *MTEX*.[10]

---

8. The octave can be subdivided into as many as 21 tones for speaker or MIDI output.

9. An *MTEX* encoding of a Chinese song is shown together with its transcription in Western notation (i.e., the *TEX* output) in Dr. Schaffrath's contribution in *Computing in Musicology* 9 (1993-4), 222–223.

10. Another translation program supported conversion to the MIDI code used by an early version of the commercial program *Personal Composer*. Software to convert *EsAC* files to the Humdrum *Kern* format was written by David Huron in 1995. The result for this example would match exactly the left-most column in the polyphonic example given in Chapter 26.

Example 24.8 *EsAC* data for the Mozart trio with five translations.

The *EsAC* regular and *Jianpu* encodings were shown earlier. None of the polyphonic encodings given elsewhere for *Note-Processor DARMS*, *SCORE*, and a successor to *MTEX* corresponds exactly to the content shown here. These discrepancies give some insight into the flexibility with which the more complex codes may be used. However, they also collectively demonstrate the considerable effect that the printed page exerts on codes such as these, in contrast to a sound-based code such as *EsAC*.

24.4.1 Canonical *DARMS*[11]

```
|1 !G !K* !M3:4,33@MOZART SECOND TRIO FROM CLARINET QUINTET: CLARINET PART$
26E 28E /
30E 28E 33Q 30E 28E /
27E 29E 31Q 29E 27E /
26E 25E 28E 27E 30E 29E /
27#Q 28Q 26E 28E /
30E 28E 33Q 30E 28E /
27E 29E 31Q RQ /
RH. /
RQ RQ !R3:2 20E 17E 15E $R /
17E 20E 22E 24E 27E 29E /
31E 30E 29E 28E 29E 27E /
26H 28E 27E /
26Q RQ /!/
```

Example 24.9a Canonical *DARMS* data converted from *EsAC*.

11. Canonical *DARMS* is described in Chapter 11. The conversion program *END* used to generate this example was written by Frans Wiering.

24.4.2 *Note-Processor DARMS*[12]

```
!|1 !G !K* !M3:4,13@Mozart: second trio from Clarinet Quintet: Clarinet Part$
6E 8E /
10E 8E 13Q 10E 8E /
7E 9E 11Q 9E 7E /
6E 5E 8E 7E 10E 9E /
7#Q 8Q 6E 8E /
10E 8E 13Q 10E 8E /
7E 9E 11Q RQ /
RH. /
RQ RQ !R3:2 0E -3E -5E $R /
-3E 0E 2E 4E 7E 9E /
11E 10E 9E 8E 9E 7E /
6H 8E 7E /
6Q RQ /|
```

Example 24.9b *Note-Processor DARMS* data converted from *EsAC*.

24.4.3 *SCORE*[13]

```
!NP
in18
0
tr/t3 4/
c5/e/m/g/e/c6/g5/e/m/d/f/a/f/d/m/c/b4/e5/d/g/f/m/ds/e;
ex4/q/ex4/q/ex8/qx2;
;
;
;
t 18 0.1 15
C0000 Mozart: second trio from Clarinet Quintet: Clarinet Part
t 18 0.1 -3 .8 .8
Key C

in17
0
tr/
c5/e/m/g/e/c6/g5/e/m/d/f/a/r/m/r/m/rx2;
ex4/q/ex4/qx2/h./qx2;
;
;
;
```

12. This output also comes from Wiering's *END* program. The beam and slur information included in the corresponding example of *Note-Processor DARMS* is absent here because it was not present in the *EsAC* code.

13. The conversion program *ESSCORE* by Nigel Nettheim converts *EsAC* code to *SCORE* input code. This example differs in numerous ways from the *SCORE* encoding of the full score. These differences are principally caused by differences of physical layout: the full score is represented by *SCORE* from bottom to top and consists of two systems. This example is converted from a shortened monophonic original without beams or slurs.

```
in16
0
tr/
d4/a3/f/m/a/d4/f/a/d5/f/m/a/g/f/e/f/d/m/c/e/d/m/c/r/mh;
tx3/ex12/h/ex2/qx2;
;
;
1 303;
j
 16 3
```

Example 24.9c *SCORE* data converted from *EsAC* data.

24.4.4 *MTEX*[14]

```
\parindent 0pt \hrule\bigskip\bigskip          \\\endsong%                        \_{}{\a{-4}}%
\input mtex                                     %                                  \_{}{\a{-1}}%
\title{Mozart: second trio from Clarinet Quintet: Clarinet Part}                   \_{}{\a{1}}%
\composer{C0000}                                \vskip -2.2 true cm                \_{}{\a{3}}%
\beginsong \vio\C%                              \beginsong \vio\C%                 \_{}{\a{6}}%
\meter{3}/{4}%                                  \_{}{\a{5}}%                        \_{}{\a{8}}%
\_{}{\a{5}}%                                    \_{}{\a{7}}%                        \|%
\_{}{\a{7}}%                                    \|%                                \_{}{\a{10}}%
\|%                                             \_{}{\a{9}}%                        \_{}{\a{9}}%
\_{}{\a{9}}%                                    \_{}{\a{7}}%                        \_{}{\a{8}}%
\_{}{\a{7}}%                                    \_{}{\v{12}}%                       \_{}{\a{7}}%
\_{}{\v{12}}%                                   \_{}{\a{9}}%                        \_{}{\a{8}}%
\_{}{\a{9}}%                                    \_{}{\a{7}}%                        \_{}{\a{6}}%
\_{}{\a{7}}%                                    \|%                                \|%
\|%                                             \_{}{\a{6}}%                        \_{}{\h{5}}%
\_{}{\a{6}}%                                    \_{}{\a{8}}%                        \_{}{\a{7}}%
\_{}{\a{8}}%                                    \_{}{\v{10}}%                       \_{}{\a{6}}%
\_{}{\v{10}}%                                   \|%                                \|%
\_{}{\a{8}}%                                    \|%                                \_{}{\v{5}}%
\_{}{\a{6}}%                                    \\\endsong%                        \\=\endsong%
\|%                                             %                                  %
\_{}{\a{5}}%                                    \vskip -2.2 true cm                \medskip
\_{}{\a{4}}%                                    \beginsong \vio\C%                 \vfill\hrule\eject
\_{}{\a{7}}%                                    \_{}{\a{-1}}%                       \bigskip \noindent
\_{}{\a{6}}%                                    \_{}{\a{-4}}%                       %
\_{}{\a{9}}%                                    \_{}{\a{-6}}%
\_{}{\a{8}}%                                    \|%
\|%
\_{}{\x{6}\v{6}}%
\_{}{\x{7}}%
```

Example 24.9d *MTEX* data converted from *EsAC* data.

---

14. This family of codes (*M*TEX*) is the subject of Chapter 17. This example was set by Ulrich Franzke.

24.5   Further Information

Shortly before his death in 1994, Professor Schaffrath had announced an ambitious plan to publish a series of encoded folksong collections under the collective title *Your Electronic Songbook* (*YES*).[15]

Efforts are now underway to publish these songbooks in two graphical environments—MS *Windows* and LINUX *XView*. The software is being developed by Franzke.[16] As currently planned, these items will be available from *ftp.musik.uni-essen.de* in the directories:

```
/pub/ESAC/program/WINDOWS
/pub/ESAC/program/LINUX
```

An alternative address for programs and code is *http://fb4.musik.uni-essen.de/sauger.html*.

Some of the original German and Chinese folksong collections are viewable at the World-Wide Web site *http://fb4.musik.uni-essen.de/blubber.html*.[17] The home page is called "Der Interaktive Liedbetrachter." Eventual support for *.GIF*, *.MID*, and *.PS* files is planned.

Among the first *YES* titles announced were these:

> *634 German Folk and Children's Songs*, ed. Helmut Schaffrath (5 vols.)
> *106 Asturian Songs*, ed. Helmut Schaffrath
> *565 Evangelical Church Songs*, ed. Christoph Kinke (4 vols.)
> *100 Catholic Church Songs*, ed. A. Becker
> *430 Bach Chorales after Riemenschneider*, ed. David Halperin
> *106 Australian Folksongs*, ed. W. Fahey
> *129 Polish Folksongs and Dances*, ed. Ewa Dahlig
> *300 Traditional Blues Melodies*, ed. W. Kueppers

---

15. Helmut Schaffrath, "The *EsAC* Electronic Songbooks," *Computing in Musicology* 9 (1993-4), 78.

16. Franzke's personal e-mail address, to which enquiries concerning licensing fees should be addressed, is *franzke@fb4.musik.uni-essen.de*. Ordinary mail may be sent to him at the following address: Univertität GH Essen, Fachbereich 4 (Musikpädagogik), Henri-Dunant-Str. 65, 45131 Essen, Germany; tel.: 201/183-4247; fax: 201/183-4228.

17. IP address 132.252.110.150.

Additional titles featuring songs from Bulgaria, Finland, the Republic of Georgia, Greece, Israel, Luxembourg, Romania, Russia, the Slovak Republic, Sweden, Switzerland, and Turkey were planned.

The ongoing development of the databases is now officially in the charge of Dr. Ewa Dahlig.[18] A substantial body of Polish materials has been encoded in the past two years. Dr. Dahlig has, in addition, assumed leadership of the Computer Study Group of the International Council of Traditional Music founded by Prof. Schaffrath.

The Center for Computer Assisted Research in the Humanities at Stanford University makes available the European folksong collection in both the *EsAC* and *Kern* formats with extensive supporting documentation (in English) and a composite list of titles (in the original languages).[19] These items are as follows:

- *The Essen Data Package*: The original *EsAC* encodings with the program *ANA* and a 25-page manual by Eleanor Selfridge-Field and a composite title list. 4 DOS-formatted diskettes. (1994)

- *The Essen Folksong Collection in the Humdrum Kern Format*: The same collection of materials in *Kern* format with a 36-page manual by David Huron and a composite title list. 4 DOS-formatted diskettes. (1995)

There is a modest charge for these items.[20] A conversion utility from *EsAC* to MIDI exists in *Kern*.

Tools for the analysis of *EsAC* data, on the model of *ANA*, were written at Stanford University for the UNIX platform (in Perl) in 1995 by Lincoln Myers. To achieve a more precise articulation of tonal information in analytical results, this adaptation utilizes Walter B. Hewlett's base-40 system[21] of intervallic representation. The base-40 system supports intervallic complementarity that mirrors intervallic complementarity in theories of tonal harmony. Later the same year, the 6,000 principal *EsAC* melodies were translated to *Kern*, making them available for analysis with the *Humdrum Toolkit*.

18. Helmut Schaffrath Laboratory of Computer Aided Research in Musicology, Istytut Sztuki PAN, ul. Długa 16/29, 00-950 Warszawa skr. 994, Poland; fax: +48 22/31-31/49; e-mail: *eda@plearn.edu.pl.*

19. Compiled by David Huron; title list edited by Olga Termini.

20. Enquiries regarding either item may be sent to CCARH, Braun Music Center #129, Stanford University, Stanford, CA 94305-3076; fax: (650) 725-9290; or by e-mail to *ccarh@ccrma.stanford.edu.*

21. "A Base-40 Number-Line Representation of Musical Pitch Notation," *Musikometrika* 4 (1992), 1–14. A brief description is given under the entry HEWLETT'S BASE-40 SYSTEM in the glossary.

24.6   Postscript

The development of other tools that work with *EsAC* data has been pursued in several places including Australia, China, Canada, Germany, Israel, New Zealand, Poland, and the U.S. Franzke claims that his program-in-progress, called *EsLa*, constitutes a "programming language for musicology." It is clear that the work at Essen University has provided an unprecedented stimulus to experiments in the use of musical data for analysis. That this attention is widely scattered around the globe testifies to Helmut Schaffrath's important role in establishing the field of computer analysis of musical data. [Postscript added by E. S.-F.]

References

Franzke, Ulrich. "Die 'Essener Software'," *Musikometrika* 4 (1992), 181–205.

Franzke, Ulrich. "Formale und enliche Melodiesprachen und das Problem der Musikdatenkodierung," *Musikometrika* 5 (1993), 107–149.

Han, Baoqiang. "Hanzu Minge Yinyü de Tezhang: On the Compass of Han Nationality Folksongs" [in Chinese]. Essen and Beijing, 1991.

Huang, Yunzchen. "Jisuanji zhongde 'Mengjiangnü'" [in Chinese]. Essen University, 1990.

Jesser, Barbara. *Interaktive Melodieanalyse. Methodik und Anwendung computer-gestützter Analyseverfahren in Musikethnologie und Volksliedforschung: typologische Untersuchung der Balladensammlung des DVA* (Studien zur Volksliedforschung, 12). [Thesis, Essen University, 1989.] Bern: Peter Lang, 1991.

Leppig, Manfred. "Musikuntersuchungen im Rechenautomaten," *Musica* 2 (1987), 140–150.

Nettheim, Nigel. "The Pulse in German Folksong: A Statistical Investigation," *Musikometrika* 5 (1993), 69–89.

Piemontese, M. "Sperimentazione del *MAPPET* per l'analisi computerizzata di un gruppo di melodie popolari siciliani." *Tesi di laurea*, Faculty of Ethnomusicology, University of Bologna, 1993.

Schaffrath, Helmut. "Automatic Retrieval and Analysis in Ethnomusicology: Some Relations between Performance, Encoding, and Analysis of Traditional Music" in *The Dynamic Text: 9th International Conference on Computers and the Humanities*. Toronto: University of Toronto, 1989.

Schaffrath, Helmut. "Computer Cataloging: [A] Database System for Ethnic Music at Essen University, West Germany" in *IASA Phonographic Bulletin*, 39 (July, 1984), 35–39.

Schaffrath, Helmut (ed). *Computer in der Musik: Über den Einsatz in Wissenschaft, Komposition und Pädagogik.* Stuttgart: J. B. Metzler, 1991.

Schaffrath, Helmut. "Computer-wozu?," *Musica* 2 (1987), 135–139.

Schaffrath, Helmut. "Datenbanksystem zur Dokumentation von Musik auf Tonträgern" in J. Dittmar (ed.), *Dokumentationsprobleme heutiger Volksmusikforschung (Studien zur Volksmusikforschung*, 2), (Bern: Peter Lang, 1987), 183–197.

Schaffrath, Helmut. "Datenbank zur Erfassung von Musik auf Tonträger ETNO" in *Universität- Gesamthochschule Essen: Zukunftstechnologie Neue Medien. Schriften und Berichte*, 9 (1986), 59–65.

Schaffrath, Helmut. "Der Umgang mit Information über Musik. Am Beispiel einer Datenbank ethnomusikologischer Schallplatten der Universität Essen," *Musikpädagogische Forschung*, 6 (1985), 253–263.

Schaffrath, Helmut. *Einhundert Chinesische Volkslieder: Eine Anthologie (Studien zur Volksliedforschung*, 14). Bern: Peter Lang, 1993.

Schaffrath, Helmut. "The *EsAC* Databases and MAPPET Software," *Computing in Musicology* 8 (1992), 66.

Schaffrath, Helmut. "The *EsAC* Electronic Songbooks," *Computing in Musicology* 9 (1993-94), 78.

Schaffrath, Helmut. *The Essen Folksong Collection in the KERN Format.* Computer database with supporting documentation by David Huron. Menlo Park: CCARH, 1995.

Schaffrath, Helmut. "How to Retrieve One-Part Melodies and their Variants. Ideas and Strategies for Computer-Aided Analysis at Essen, FRG" in *Computer Models and Representations in Music,* ed. Alan Marsden and Anthony Pople (London: Academic Press, 1992), pp. 95–110.

Schaffrath, Helmut. "MusicTeX," *Computing in Musicology* 9 (1993-94), 222–223.

Schaffrath, Helmut. "Musikalische Analyse und Wissenschaftssprache," *Musikometrika* 5 (1993), 91–105.

Schaffrath, Helmut. "Repräsentation einstimmiger Melodien: computerunterstützte Analyse und Musikdatenbanken" in *Neue Musiktechnologie*, ed. Bernd Enders and Stefan Hanheide (Mainz: B. Schotts Söhne, 1993), pp. 277–300.

Schaffrath, Helmut. "The Retrieval of Monophonic Melodies and their Variants: Concepts and Strategies for Computer-Aided Analysis" in Alan Marsden and Anthony Pople (eds.), *Computer Representations and Models in Music* (London: Academic Press, 1992), pp. 95–109.

Schaffrath, Helmut. "Zum Einsatz von Computern in Musikwissenschaft und -pädagogik" in Helmut Schaffrath (ed.), *Computer in der Musik* (Stuttgart: Metzler, 1991), pp. 8–26.

Wang Sen and Shou Haihong. "Scale-Tone Functions and Melodic Structure in Chinese Folk Music" in *Computer Representations and Models in Music,* ed. Alan Marsden and Anthony Pople (London: Academic Press, 1992), pp. 111–120.

Zhang, Zuozhi, and Helmut Schaffrath. "Über die Shange unter den chinesischen Volksliedern" (Essen, 1991) and as "China's 'Mountain Songs'" in *CHIME* (April 1991), 23–33.

Zhang, Zuozhi, and Helmut Schaffrath. "Über die Haozi unter den chinesischen Volksliedern" (Essen, 1991).

Zhang, Zuozhi. "Die chinesischen Tanzlieder unter den Xiaodiao." Essen, 1992.

25   *Plaine and Easie Code*: A Code for Music Bibliography

John Howard

The *Plaine and Easie Code System for Musicke* was developed by Barry S. Brook and Murray Gould as a means of representing musical notation with ordinary typewriter symbols for use in bibliographic applications.[1] In particular, the code was proposed as a standard for use in

- library card catalogues, providing quick and precise identification of a musical work by its coded incipit;

- union catalogues and indexes, thematic catalogues, RISM, dealers' and publishers' catalogues, alternate versions of themes in critical editions, *kritische Revisionsberichte*,[2] brief musical examples in books and articles, etc.; and

- research projects, assisting in search, fact-finding, organization, tabulation, identification of anonymous works, etc.[3]

---

1. See Barry S. Brook and Murray Gould, "Notating Music with Ordinary Typewriter Characters (A Plaine and Easie Code System for Musicke)," *Fontes Artis Musicae*, XI (1964), 142–155, and Barry S. Brook, "The Plaine and Easie Code System for Notating Music: A Proposal for International Adoption," *Fontes Artis Musicae*, XII (1965), 156–160; see also the discussion of the code system in Jan LaRue and Marian W. Cobin, "The Ruge-Seignelay Catalogue: An Exercise in Automated Entries," *Elektronische Datenverarbeitung in der Musikwissenschaft*, ed. Harald Heckmann (Regensburg: Gustav Bosse, 1967), 41–56, *passim*.

2. Critical reports citing all editorial deviations from the content of the sources on which the edition is based.

3. Brook and Gould, p. 142.

According to its authors, an encoding system designed for these tasks—namely, the *Plaine and Easie Code*—would possess the following attributes:[4]

- It [should] be speedy, simple, absolutely accurate as to pitch and rhythm. It should be as closely related mnemonically to musical notation as possible, so that it appears natural and right, avoiding arbitrary symbols. It should require only a single line of typewriter characters without the need for backspacing or for a second pass over the line. It should be usable by non-musicians with only a few minutes of instruction. It must be easily recognizable as music from the symbols alone and immediately retranslatable, without loss, into conventional notation.

- It [should] be applicable to all Western music from Gregorian chant to serial music.

- It [should] be universally understandable and internationally acceptable.

- It [should] be so devised as to be readily transferrable to electronic data-processing equipment for key transposition, fact-finding, tabulating, and other research.

The attributes described above must be qualified somewhat by describing briefly some limits of the code. Above all, the code is designed to represent melody in conventional staff notation. As a result, encoding of music written in white mensural notation or earlier notational systems, in tablature, etc., require the encoder to make editorial decisions that depend on a critical apparatus specific to a particular application. Similarly, the linearity of the code makes it less appropriate for repertories where melodic or contrapuntal conception is less relevant to musical identity than non-linear musical structure. It is also a limitation of the code that it does not enable one to associate precisely a musical line with an associated text. Given these considerations, the code is probably best suited for applications such as those described generally by its authors that involve musical repertories from the seventeenth through early nineteenth centuries, or tune repertories in general.

While the *Plaine and Easie Code* has not been adopted for broad general use in music bibliography, it has been selected by the Répertoire Internationale des Sources Musicales (RISM) as the basis for encoding musical incipits in a major bibliographic

---

4. *Ibid.*, p. 143.

project: *RISM Series A/II*, an automated, world-wide inventory of music manuscripts of the period *ca.* 1600–1800. RISM's implementation of the code adapts it to certain considerations of local systems design and introduces some minor changes to the encoding orthography and syntax; some elements of the original *Plaine and Easie* system are also not implemented. A general description of the encoding system as adapted by RISM has been published by Norbert Böker-Heil.[5]

25.1   Code Description

The summary of code elements and usage below is based on RISM's current implementation. In this version of the system, code elements are arranged into seven discrete data categories. In RISM's electronic implementation, each of these categories is represented by a data element key. For encoding purposes, however, each could be represented symbolically by a typographic symbol. The RISM data scheme and symbolic field identifiers (where assigned) are shown below:

numeric identification	[symbol unassigned]
verbal identification	[symbol unassigned]
clef	%
key signature	$
time signature	@
musical context	[symbol unassigned]
commentary	~ (followed by single-cipher codes)

Omitted from the RISM implementation is a category to specify metronomic tempo indications. The revised *Plaine and Easie Code* specifies that this category be implemented after the example MM 2 = 120 (e.g., one half note equals 120).[6]

---

5. Norbert Böker-Heil, "Erläuterungen zur Codierung der Musikincipits" in "Fürstlich-Hohenlohe-Langenburg'sche Schlossbibliothek: Katalog der Musikhandschriften," *Fontes Artis Musicae*, XXV (1978), 408–411.

6. Barry S. Brook, "The Simplified 'Plaine and Easie Code System'," p. 157.

25.1.1 Clefs

The C-, F-, and G-clef specifications are as follows:

25.1.2 Key Signatures

Key-signature specifications indicate the alteration type and the pitches to which the alteration is applied, as in these examples:

25.1.3 Time Signatures

The manner in which time signatures are represented is suggested by the examples below:

$$\frac{3}{4} \qquad \frac{12}{8} \qquad \frac{4}{2} \qquad \mathbf{C} \qquad \mathbf{\mathct}$$

3/4   12/8   4/2   c   c/

25.1.4 Pitch Names   ### 25.1.5 Octave Registers

Pitch-name and octave-register codes are as follows:

Specification of octave register precedes specification of duration, accidental, and pitch name, e.g., an eighth-note Middle C = ' 8C; an eighth-note Middle C♯ = ' 8xC.

25.1.6 Accidentals

Incidental pitch inflections in conflict with the key signature may be specified immediately before the pitch name using these signs:

♮	♭	♭♭	♯	*x*
n	b	bb	x	xx

25.1.7 Durations

Note equivalents for durations are shown on the upper staff, while corresponding rests are shown on the lower staff:

25.1.8 Repeats

Some common repeat signifiers are indicated as shown below:

: ‖	‖ :	: ‖ :
: / /	/ / :	: / / :

25.1.9 Other Symbols

A. RESTS

−	rest
=/	full measure rest, beginning of encoded value
/=/	full measure rest, internal
=n/	multiple measures of rest, n = number of measures, beginning of encoded value
/=n/	multiple measures of rest, n = number of measures, within an encoded value

B. GLOBAL VARIABLE CHANGES

*% n *	change clef, n = clef encoding, e.g., *%G-2*[7]
*$ n *	change key signature,where n = key signature encoding, e.g., *$xF*
*@ n *	change time signature, where n = time signature coding, e.g., *@3/4*

C. TIES, SLURS, BEAMS, AND MUSICAL FIGURES

+	tie (follows the pitch value it affects)
y . . . z	begin . . . end a slur (not implemented by RISM)
! . . . !	begin . . . end a repeated musical figure
(. . .)	begin . . . end triplet figure
i(. . . ;n)	begin . . . end other tuplet figure: i = combined duration of the tuplet figure; n = numeric value of the tuplet
{ . . . }	begin . . . end beaming (precedes . . . follows pitch and duration code elements)

D. GRACE AND CUE NOTES

g	unmeasured (slashed) grace note (precedes pitch and duration code elements)
q	measured grace note (*appoggiatura*) (precedes pitch and duration code elements)

---

7. The asterisk was originally used to initiate and terminate global variable changes. Recently the blank space has been substituted for the terminatation marker in the RISM implementation of *Plaine and Easie Code*.

qq ... r   begin . . . end a group of grace notes or cue-sized notes
                  (beaming of values of less than a quarter-note duration is
                  assumed)

E. ORNAMENTATION AND ARTICULATION SIGNS

s   turn, mordent, etc. (follows the pitch value it affects; not
                  implemented by RISM)
t   trill (follows the pitch value it affects)
w   tremolo (follows the pitch value it affects; not implemented by
                  RISM)
(x)   fermata, x = pitch value or rest
j   glissando (follows the pitch value it affects; not implemented
                  by RISM)

F. REPETITIONS

f   repeat a musical figure (within a measure only)
i   repeat the previous measure
nnn   rhythmic pattern, to be repeated until the next occurrence of a
                  duration code element, e.g., 8.68

25.2   Sample Encodings

The following examples employ the data scheme and data element mnemonics used
in the RISM implementation of the code. The indications at the left identify the record
numbers within the database that contain the parameters for the musical encoding
(112A . . E) and the incipit (112F).

25.2.1 The Mozart Trio

For the purposes of RISM, only the top voice (here the clarinet part of the second trio
of the Clarinet Quintet) would be encoded. The incipit and its representation in the
RISM database are shown in Examples 25.1a-b.

Example 25.1a The *Clarinet* incipit of the Mozart trio.

```
112A    1.1
112B    cl in A.
112C    G-2
112D    xFCG
112E    3/4
112F    y{''8CE}/{GE}'''4Czy{''8GE}/{DF}4Azy{FD}/{C'B''EDGF}
        z/y4xDEzy{8CE}/{GE}'''4Czy{8GE}/{nDF}4Az-/
```

Example 25.1b *Plaine and Easie* encoding of the *Clarinet* incipit of the Mozart trio.

The example illustrates some basic features of the encoding syntax:

- code elements indicating rhythm and pitch are declared in the following order: octave register, rhythm, accidental, note value or rest;

- the declared octave register and durational values remain in effect for successive note values or rests until a change in either value occurs;

- the symbols for the specifications of beaming precede/follow code elements for duration and pitch;

- the paired symbols for slurs (y and z) precede/follow code elements for duration and pitch.

25.2.2 The Mozart Piano Sonata

Here also only the incipit would be encoded. In this example the arpeggios preceding the half notes are excluded, but the grace notes preceding the eighth notes are included.

```
112A    1.1.1
112B    pf.
112C    G-2
112D    xFCG
112E    2/4
112F    '''2C/!{y6DCz''B'''C}!f/2D/q3D{8Cq3D8Cq3D8Cq3D8C}/y'
        '4.B'''8Ez/
```

Example 25.2 Encoding of the right-hand incipit of the Mozart piano sonata.

Example 25.2 illustrates the following additional characteristics of the code:

- Repeated figures can be marked by exclamation points, the repetitions by the lowercase letter f.

- While slurs can be specified, staccato articulations cannot.

- Chord structures on a single staff cannot be specified.

25.3   Associated Software (RISM)

The principal ongoing use of the *Plaine and Easie Code System* is for the recording of musical incipits for the RISM Series A/II project. Data encoded according to the system described above constitutes a data structure in the general bibliographic description of each musical work catalogued by RISM.

Implementations of the RISM version of the system have been made at the RISM Zentralredaktion at Frankfurt, Germany,[8] and at the U.S. RISM Office at Harvard University. The data-processing system at the RISM Zentralredaktion has been developed to accommodate data submitted by all countries participating in the project and has pursued specific related processing, research, and publishing goals. The system in the USA has been developed not only to enable the U.S. RISM group to submit data electronically to the RISM Zentralredaktion but also to pursue specific national data-processing objectives. The approaches taken by each to code processing for conversion to other encoding systems, music printing, and for research purposes are described briefly below.

25.4   Code Conversions

The *Plaine and Easie Code System* in the implementation of the RISM Zentral-redaktion represents the "external" aspect of the encoded musical excerpt—data are entered and updated from the *Plaine and Easie* encoding. Because the *Plaine and Easie Code* does not lend itself to sorting according to the usual criteria for the systematic arrangement of thematic data, and because its syntax is context-sensitive, a secondary or "internal" encoding is generated from the "external" encoding. This

8. RISM Zentralredaktion, Sophienstrasse 26, D-60487 Frankfurt am Main, Germany; tel. +49 069/ 706231; fax: +49 69/706026; e-mail (for Klaus Keil): *Keil@StUB.uni-frankfurt.d400.de*. Address information for the U.S. RISM office is given at the end of this chapter and in the Author List.

internal encoding (or "metacode"), generated from algorithms developed by Norbert Böker-Heil, serves as the basis for the RISM Zentralredaktion's thematic sort routines, proofreading, and printing functions.

Both the RISM Zentralredaktion and the U.S. RISM Office have developed means of converting encoded musical information to the ASCII input format supported by the *SCORE* music typography system (the RISM Zentralredaktion generates the *SCORE* input file from the metacode, U.S. RISM from the unprocessed *Plaine and Easie Code*). All elements of the encoding are convertible. The ASCII input files can be batch processed by *SCORE* to generate musical data in the proprietary *SCORE* file format; a separate batch job enables the generation of *EPS* graphics files for musical excerpts which can then be included in printed output.

A program for conversion of *Plaine and Easie* to *MuseData* has been developed by Brent Field at the Center for Computer Assisted Research in the Humanities.

25.5   Further Information

25.5.1   Usage and Accessibility

The RISM Series A/II Project has amassed a substantial database of melodic excerpts in the *Plaine and Easie* encoding. More than 250,000 musical incipits representing approximately 188,000 musical pieces had been encoded as of the end of 1995.

Until recently, access to this data has been limited to individuals able to visit the RISM Zentralredaktion at Frankfurt. In December 1995, however, RISM released a CD-ROM version of the database through the K. G. Saur Verlag of Munich. The *Windows* CD-ROM product provides the capability to browse or search an index of musical incipits in *Plaine and Easie Code*, and it is able to graphically display the incipits they represent in staff notation on the PC console. Annual releases of the CD-ROM are anticipated; approximately 20,000 new bibliographic records will be added to each new release.

Plans are also in place to make the RISM Series A/II data available on the Internet. The development prospectus calls for mounting the bibliographic and encoded musical information in USMARC data format (ANSI Z39.2) on an ANSI Z39.50-compliant database server. Musical incipits would be searchable as ASCII text in the *Plaine and Easie Encoding*. Data returned to the user would include the musical encoding as well as a URL specifying the location of image data corresponding to the encoded musical information. Access from the client end is expected to be made through a Z39.50/

World-Wide Web gateway in order that textual and image data representing musical manuscripts can be integrated on a user's display console.

25.5.2 Online Information about the *Plaine and Easie Code* and RISM

Documentation about RISM's projects, publications, resources, and the *Plaine and Easie Code* is available online from the organization's World-Wide Web site (*http://www.rism.harvard.edu/rism/Welcome.html*). This resource also provides addresses of the various RISM national working groups, bibliographies of thematic catalogues, and links to online databases containing data compiled through RISM-sponsored projects. Requests for other information can be submitted to the RISM Zentralredaktion via e-mail (*Keil@StUB.uni-frankfurt.d400.de*) or the U.S. RISM online help desk (*rismhelp@rism.harvard.edu*). A CD-ROM with search software for the entire database, including support for screen display and printing of melodic incipits, is available from the German firm K. G. Saur.[9]

9. K. G. Saur Verlag, Postfach 70 16 20, D-81316 München, Germany, tel. +49 89/769020; fax: +49 89/76902150.

Codes for Data Management and Analysis (2):

Polyphonic Representations

26   *Humdrum* and *Kern*: Selective Feature Encoding

David Huron

The purpose of *Humdrum* is to facilitate the posing and answering of research questions in the field of music. *Humdrum* allows researchers to encode, manipulate, and output a wide variety of musically pertinent representations. Theoretically, any type of sequential symbolic data may be accommodated, including Schenkerian graphs, performance kinematics, changes of emotional states, MIDI data, German lute tablatures, dance steps, etc.

Over the past decade, *Humdrum* has been used in innumerable musical studies. It has been used to study melodic accent in Gregorian chant, to measure the harmonic similarity between chorale harmonizations, to investigate motivic features in Brahms string quartets, and to identify dynamic asymmetries in Muzak. *Humdrum* has been used to measure the degree of performance idiomaticism in works for trumpet, to characterize the textures of Asian and African vocal and instrumental works, to compare the effect of tempo on harmonic flow in works by Haydn, and to investigate the conformity between compositional practice and theoretical rules proposed by Zarlino and Berardi. More than a dozen published musicological studies have relied on *Humdrum*.

Humdrum is especially helpful in music research environments where new and unforeseen goals arise. For many scholars, an attraction of *Humdrum* is that it permits new types of representations to be defined by the user and integrated with other *Humdrum* representations. *Humdrum* is not a representation scheme in the conventional sense; rather it embodies an unbounded class of representations.

Because *Humdrum* is a syntax rather than a program, it is device-independent. The *Humdrum* Toolkit, by contrast, contains a set of utilities written primarily in the AWK, C, and YACC programming languages (commonly associated with UNIX operating systems). PCs are the most commonly used platform for the *Humdrum* tools.

Humdrum is designed to represent sequential and/or concurrent time-dependent discrete symbolic data. Sequential events are arranged in vertical columns; concurrent attributes are arranged in horizontal rows:

```
                    sequential events
                          ↓
    concurrent attributes  →  x        x        x
                              x        x        x
                              x        x        x
```

In this schematic drawing, a single sequential *event* describes all voices that sound at the same time. That is, multiple voices are encoded in parallel columns (see Examples 26.1 and 26.3).

Highly complex static situations, such as the physical arrangement of musical instruments in a museum display, or dense photographic images (such as microform images of manuscripts), cannot be handled by *Humdrum*. *Humdrum* could be used to encode multi-channel digital sound recordings; however it would require significantly more storage than established methods.

Humdrum avoids trying to represent everything within a single scheme. Instead, it encourages the user to break up the representational problem into independent manageable schemes, which are then coordinated. Each specific representation scheme will establish its own limits. While several representation schemes are predefined in *Humdrum*, users are free to develop their own schemes, tailored to their specific needs.

All *Humdrum* files are standard ASCII files. Typically, one file is used to encode a single work or movement. Depending on the application, multiple works may be amalgamated into a single file or independent files generated for each part, group of parts, measures, etc. Different forms of information pertaining to a single work (e.g., harmonic analysis, lyrics, modulation scheme, Schenkerian graphs) can be either separated into individual files, or encoded within a single file, depending on the user's goal.

Humdrum permits the representation of works in either strophic or through-composed forms; mixed strophic/through-composed organization is also possible. Several different editions or variants of a work can be encoded concurrently within a single document, and tools are provided to select or expand the work or rendition according to user-selected criteria.

26.1   The *Kern* Code

The *Humdrum* representation called *kern*[1] permits the representation of the bare bones of traditional Western musical notation—pitch, duration, and voicing. The *kern* representation will be the main focus of this introduction to *Humdrum*. Examples of other *Humdrum* symbol-schemes will be noted occasionally to demonstrate how *kern* may be combined with other representation schemes within the *Humdrum* format. For example, musical dynamics, the visual layout of a score, sound synthesis information, and analytic information (e.g., functional harmony) are not accommodated in *kern,* but other *Humdrum* encoding schemes are provided for these and other purposes.

The *kern* representation supports the score-related signifiers listed below. Note that none of the following information is required: for example, a bona fide *kern* encoding might consist solely of phrase marks.

> PITCH: concert pitch (Western notation), accidentals, clefs, clef position, key signatures, key, unpitched events, harmonics, glissandi, multiple stops, arpeggiations, et al.;

> DURATION: canonic musical durations, rests, augmentation dots, n-tuplets, gruppetto designations, acciaccaturas, ties, tempo (beats per minute), meter signatures, indefinite or durationless events;

> ARTICULATION AND ORNAMENTATION: staccato, spiccato, tenuto, fermata, pizzicato, breath mark, attacca, accent mark, sforzando, generic articulation, trills (half-step), trills (whole-step), mordent, inverted mordent, turn, inverted (Wagnerian) turn, generic ornaments;

> TIMBRE: instrument name, instrument class;

> OTHER: phrase marks, slurs, elision markers, bar lines, double bar lines, dotted bar lines, partial bar lines, invisible bar lines, measure numbers, system/staff arrangement, up-bows, down-bows, beams, partial beams, stem directions;

> EDITORIAL: ossias, *sic*, editorial interpretation markers, editorial intervention markers, editorial footnotes, global comments, local comments, user-defined symbols.

---

1. Strictly, within the context of other *Humdrum* representations, the name is ``**kern``.

While *kern* is quite restricted in what it can represent, other *Humdrum* symbol-schemes permit the representation of additional types of information. For example, in the case of pitch-related representations, other schemes can be used to represent frequency (hertz), ANSI standard notation (e.g., A4), transposed pitch, French *solfége*, German *Tonhöhe*, tonic-*solfa* syllables, semits, pitch class, normal form, scale degree, frets, MIDI key number, and cents. Psychoacoustically pertinent pitch-related representations include *mels*, critical bandwidths, spectral centroid, and cochlear coordinates.[2] Similarly, other representations allow the user to represent pitch *intervals* such as diatonic and chromatic interval distances, melodic *semits*, melodic contour, durations in seconds (elapsed, absolute, or relative), metric position, spectral content, etc.

A notable limit of *kern* is its inability to represent musical dynamics, but several other *Humdrum* schemes permit the representation of dynamics, such as amplitude, relative decibel level (dB), sound pressure level (dB SPL), *phons*, *sones*, dynamic markings, loudness, changes of loudness, and MIDI key velocity.

Kern encodes a canonical score rather than a visual rendering. Several ensuing encodings employ the *kern* interpretation. The encoded music is read down the page, as if the score had been turned sideways. Hence bass-to-treble voicing typically follows a left-to-right format. Concurrent material is horizontally aligned. The specific details of the *kern* representation scheme and its system of file organization are illustrated in the encoding of the second trio from Mozart's Clarinet Quintet (Example 26.1) and in subsequent examples.

26.1.1 General Elements of Notation and Organization

A. STAFF LINING [*|.]

Staff lining can be explicitly encoded. Some sample designations include the following:

*|.||||	four-line staff
*|.|	one-line staff
*|.0	no staff lines
*|.||R|	four-line staff with third line (from bottom) colored red
*|.|X|	three-line staff with middle line invisible
*|.:::::|	five-line staff consisting of dotted lines

---

2. Definitions of specialized terms used on this page are given in the glossary.

In addition to black, line colors include red (*ruber*—R), green (*viridis*—V), and blue (*caeruleus*—C).

B. STAFF POSITION [*staff]

The order of staves within a system can be explicitly encoded by either absolute or relative position. Note these examples:

*staff1	top-most staff in the system
*staff12	twelfth staff from the top of the system
*staff$	bottom-most staff in the system
*staff$-1	staff just above the bottom staff

C. CLEFS [*clef]

Clef information is explicitly encoded. The following designations are available:

*clefG2	treble clef (G-clef located on second line)
*clefF4	bass clef (F-clef located on fourth line)
*clefC3	alto clef
*clefC4	tenor clef
*clefG1	soprano clef
*clefX	no clef
*clefGv2	treble clef; *8va bassa*

D. KEY SIGNATURES [*k]

Kern distinguishes keys from key signatures. Knowledge of the key signature facilitates reconstruction of the musical source; knowledge of the key facilitates analysis of the musical content. A key signature is encoded by the expression *k followed by a list of altered tones in brackets:

$$*k[f\#g\#c\#]$$

Flats are encoded as minus signs whereas naturals are encoded using the lower-case n. Double sharps and flats are represented by letter repetition. Unconventional situations involving mixtures of sharps and flats or negation of previously used accidentals can be readily accommodated. The following expressions are legitimate:

$$*k[f\#b-]$$
$$*k[bnen]$$

Key specifications are introduced by an asterisk and terminated with a colon. Upper-case letters designate major modes, lower-case letters minor modes:

*G:	G Major
*d:	D Minor
*e-:	E♭ Minor
*?:	unknown key
*X:	atonal passage (no key)

E. Comments [!]

In Example 26.1, each instrument is represented by a single column of data; this structure is typical, although not mandatory. Comments are records (lines) that begin with an exclamation mark: global comments [!!] pertain to the entire encoding, whereas local comments [!] pertain to a single column of data. Columns of data are delimited by a single tab character.

F. Auxiliary Interpretations [*]

Records beginning with asterisk characters denote *Humdrum* interpretations. Interpretations are used to indicate the type of data being represented and its context. Two types of interpretations are distinguished: exclusive interpretations [**] and tandem interpretations [*]. In Example 26.1, two types of exclusive interpretations are present. Each column of data must be headed by an exclusive interpretation. The **kern* interpretation specifies a core representation, useful for representing the basic pitch and duration structure of a logical period-of-common-practice score.

The **dyn* interpretation is used to represent dynamic markings. In this example, a single column of **dyn* information is sufficient for all instruments.

In Example 26.1 the instrumentation has been specified using both local comments and interpretations. The local comments indicate the precise terms given in the score (e.g., *violino II*). By contrast, the *Humdrum* interpretations (e.g., *Ivioln) are potentially executable statements. For example, in sound playback, these interpretations might be used to invoke specific patches on a MIDI synthesizer. Alternatively, these interpretations can be used in analytic applications to invoke the appropriate spectral content from sound analyses. Instrument classes are also distinguished, such as woodwinds, brass, strings, etc. (e.g., *ICstr).

Other tandem interpretations—indicating the system organization, staff assignment, clef type and clef placement, meter signature, key signature, and key—are present in this example. These interpretations are optional and their order is not important. Only the exclusive interpretation [**] is mandatory.

26.1.2 Pitch Representation

A. PITCH [A..G]

Pitches and durations are represented by letters and numbers respectively. *Kern* encodes absolute pitches. Pitch letter-names are encoded using the upper- and lower-case letters A to G. Pitches in the octave from C4 to B4 are represented by a single lower-case letter. Pitches from C5 to B5 are represented by two lower-case letters (e.g., dd for D5). A similar system applies to pitches below Middle C using upper-case letters. Sharps, flats, and naturals are encoded as #, -, and n respectively. Double alterations are indicated by double symbols: ##, --, nn. Rests are denoted by lower case r. Some examples follow:

c	Middle C
B	B immediately below Middle C
Bn	B immediately below Middle C, if written with explicit natural
C	octave below Middle C
cc	octave above Middle C
d#	D♯ above Middle C
e-	E♭ above Middle C
f##	F𝗑 above Middle C

In sum, all pitches above Middle C are indicated by lower-case letters, while all pitches below Middle C are indicated by upper-case letters. An unspecified note or rest may be indicated by the symbol X.

B. PITCH TRANSPOSITION [*Tr]

In **kern*, scores are always encoded at concert pitch. The operator *Tr encodes the transposition in terms of both diatonic letter names and chromatic half steps. Since many music-analytic applications require extracts of passages, **kern* maintains concert pitch renderings in order to facilitate sound playback, harmonic analysis, and other software applications. In Example 26.1, the clarinet part is encoded in transposition. The expression *Tr+2d+3c indicates that the original notation is transposed up by two diatonic letter names [A→C] and three chromatic semitones from the encoded version. In some circumstances the second indicator alone would provide adequate information, but in others both are required. For example, the expression *Tr+1d+1c would transpose a passage in C Major to D♭ Major, while the expression *Tr+0d+1c would transpose it to C♯ Major.

C. OCTAVE TRANSPOSITION [*8]

Octave transposition may be indicated in the following ways:

*8va	notes sound an octave higher
*8bassa	notes sound an octave lower

26.1.3 Representation of Duration and Accent

A. METER SIGNATURES [*M<n>/<n>]

Kern can represent both common and unusual meter signatures. These are introduced by the signifier *M. Conventional meters are specified by a numerator and denominator separated by a forward slash [e.g., 2/4]. More complex beat groupings may be specified by integers separated by a plus sign (+) in the numerator. Only integer values may be given. A representative selection of meter signatures follows:

SIGNATURE	TYPE	MEANING
*M2/4	simple duple	two quarters per bar
*M3/2	simple triple	three halves per bar
*M4/0	simple quadruple	four breves per bar
*M6/8	compound duple	six eighths per bar
*M9/16	compound triple	nine sixteenths per bar
*M12/4	compound quadruple	twelve quarters per bar
*M5/4	irregular quintuple	five quarters per bar
*M3+2/4	irregular quintuple	three plus two quarters per bar
*M21/8..	arbitrarily irregular	twenty-one double-dotted eighths per bar
*M?	meter unknown	
*MX	ametric passage	no meter

B. DURATION [2, 4, 8, ...]

Durations are represented using a reciprocal numerical notation:

0	breve	12	eighth-note triplet
1	whole	16	sixteenth
2	half	24	sixteenth-note triplet
3	half-note triplet	32	thirty-second
4	quarter	64	sixty-fourth
6	quarter-note triplet	128	one-hundred-twenty-eighth
8	eighth	.	augmentation dot

Note that the whole-note rests (hanging from the fourth staff line) in the Mozart trio are encoded canonically as dotted half rests since the meter signature is 3/4. Null-tokens (.) are used to ensure that the various parts remain coordinated.

C. BAR LINES [=]

Bar lines are denoted by the equals sign (=) followed by an optional measure number. A double bar line is represented by two successive equals signs (==).

At the end of a *Humdrum* file, each column of data is terminated with the expression *-.

D. TEMPO [*MM]

Metronomic values and ranges can be represented by the indicator *MM. This may be followed by a value expressing the number of quarter-durations per minute (e.g., *MM76) or by a range of such values (*MM55-58).

When the basic beat is not a quarter note, equivalent values must be determined. For example, given a meter of 6/8 with a dotted quarter equal to 60, the correct tempo definition would be expressed by the equivalent quarter=90. Alternatively, the **dur* interpretation might be used to represent the precise duration of events in elapsed time (seconds). However, this duration information cannot be encoded in the same spine as a **kern* interpretation.

E. TIES, SLURS, AND PHRASE MARKINGS [[..], (..), {..}]

Kern distinguishes ties, slurs, and phrase markings. (In a *Humdrum* representation of a visually-rendered notation, such as **scor*, no distinction is made between these lines.)

The left square bracket ([) indicates the first note of a tie; the right square bracket (]) indicates the last note of a tie.[3] Slurs are indicated in the same manner by

parentheses: (. .). The beginnings and ends of phrases are indicated by curly brackets
({ . . }). The presence of an elision marker (&) allows slurs or phrases to overlap, e.g.,
(. . . & (. . .) . . . &), or to be nested, e.g., (. . . & (. . . &) . . .).

26.1.4 Performance Information

A. ARTICULATION MARKS [', ", ', ~, ^, ,, s, z, I]

Eight articulation types are recognized by *kern*. A provision is also made for
specifying other kinds of articulation by a generic articulation marker. The signifiers
are given below:

'	staccato	,	breath mark
"	pizzicato	s	spiccato
`	attacca	z	sforzando
~	tenuto	I	generic articulation
^	accent		(unspecified)

B. ORNAMENTS [**T, t, M, m, W, w, S, $, R, o, O**]

Kern recognizes several types of ornaments and provides a generic ornament marker.
In six cases semitone and whole tone intervals are differentiated:

T	trill (whole tone)	S	turn
t	trill (semitone)	$	inverted (Wagnerian) turn
M	mordent (tone)	R	terminating turn
m	mordent (semitone)	o	harmonic
W	inverted mordent (tone)	O	generic ornament
w	inverted mordent (semitone)		(unspecified)

26.1.5 Visual Information

A. STEM DIRECTION [/, \ ]

Up-stems and down-stems may be encoded as follows: / = up-stem; \ = down-stem.

---

3. See Example 26.1, Bars 11–12.

B. Beaming [L, J, k, K]

Both full and partial beams can be explicitly represented in the *kern* representation.

L	open a beam
J	close a beam
LL	open two beams
JJJ	close three beams
k	partial beam extending leftward
K	partial beam extending rightward
kk	two partial beams extending leftward
kK	partial beams extending both rightward and leftward

C. Processing Order of Features

Kern requires that accidental codes immediately follow the pitch code and that dots of augmentation immediately follow duration codes. In all other respects, the order in which attributes are presented is left to the user. Binary comparison of two versions of the same work is facilitated by the following order of elements:

1. open phrase
2. open slur
3. open tie
4. duration
5. pitch
6. accidental
7. ornament
8. articulation
9. bowing
10. stem direction
11. beaming
12. user-defined marks
13. close tie
14. close slur
15. close phrase
16. breath mark
17. editorial marks

26.2   File Organization

Because *kern* is simply one kind of representation that can occur in the *Humdrum* domain, it is important to understand how each kind of information is designated. A *Humdrum* file may contain zero or more comments, data records and interpretations. Global comments may appear anywhere in the file. Local comments and data records can appear only following an exclusive interpretation. A *spine* is a column of information which may contain data records, local comments, and interpretations. A *Humdrum* file must contain a coherent spine organization. Within a file, spines are separated by tabs. Spines may be split or joined, added or terminated within a file, but such changes must be indicated with path designators. These designators are the following:

*+	start a new spine
*-	terminate a current spine
*^	split a spine into two
*v	join two or more spines into one
*x	exchange the position of two spines

Like staves, spine numbers can be designated in the format !Spine2.

26.3   Examples

26.3.1   The Mozart Trio

The second trio from the Mozart Clarinet Quintet demonstrates many basic features of *kern* including file organization using spines to represent individual parts.

```
!! Mozart: Trio II from Clarinet Quintet
**kern        **kern        **kern        **kern        **kern        **dyn
!violon-      !viola        !violino      !violino      !clarinet
!cello        !             !II           !I            !in A
!*Icello      *Iviola       *Ivioln       *Ivioln       *Iclarinet    *
*ICstr        *ICstr        *ICstr        *ICstr        *ICww         *
*sys1         *sys1         *sys1         *sys1         *sys1         *sys1
*staff5       *staff4       *staff3       *staff2       *staff1       *staff*
*clefF4       *clefC3       *clefG2       *clefG2       *clefG2       *
*M3/4         *M3/4         *M3/4         *M3/4         *M3/4         *
*k[f#c#g#]    *k[f#c#g#]    *k[f#c#g#]    *k[f#c#g#]    *k[f#c#g#]    *
*A:           *A:           *A:           *A:           *A:           *
*             *             *             *             *Tr+2d+3c     *
4r            4r            4r            4r            (8a\          p
.             .             .             .             8cc#\
=1            =1            =1            =1            =1            =1
4A\           4r            4r            4r            8ee\          .
.             .             .             .             8cc#\
4r            4c#\          4e/           4a/           4aa\)         .
4r            4c#\          4e/           4a/           (8ee\
.             .             .             .             8cc#\
=2            =2            =2            =2            =2            =2
4D\           4r            4r            4r            8b\           .
.             .             .             .             8dd\
4r            4B/           4f#/          4a/           4ff#\)        .
4r            4B/           4f#/          4a/           (8dd\
.             .             .             .             8b\          .
=3            =3            =3            =3            =3            =3
4E\           4r            4r            4r            8a\           .
.             .             .             .             8g#\
4r            4B/           4d/           4g#/          8cc#\        .
.             .             .             .             8b\
4r            4B/           4d/           4g#/          8ee\          .
.             .             .             .             8dd\)
```

```
=4          =4          =4          =4          =4          =4
4F#\        4r          4r          4r          (4b#\       .
4r          4A/         4c#/        4a/         4cc#\)      .
4r          4A/         4c#/        4a/         (8a\        .
.           .           .           .           8cc#\       .
=5          =5          =5          =5          =5\         =5
4C#/        4r          4r          4r          8ee\        .
.           .           .           .           8cc#\       .
4r          4c#/        4e          4a/         4aa\)       .
4r          4c#/        4e          4a/         (8ee\       .
.           .           .           .           8cc#\       .
=6          =6          =6          =6          =6          =6
4D\         4B/         4d/         4f#/        8bn\        .
.           .           .           .           8dd\        .
4r          4r          4r          4r          4ff#\)      .
4r          (4e\        (4gn/       (8cc#\      4r          .
.           .           .           8a#\        .           .
=7          =7          =7          =7          =7          =7
2.r         2d\         2f#/        8b\         2.r         .
.           .           .           8dd\        .           .
.           .           .           4ff#\)      .           .
.           4e\         4gn/        (8cc#\      .           .
.           .           .           8a#\        .           .
=8          =8          =8          =8          =8          =8
2.r         2d\)        2f#/)       8b\         4r          .
.           .           .           8dd\        .           .
.           .           .           4ff#\)      4r          .
.           4r          4r          4r          (12B/       .
.           .           .           .           12F#/       .
.           .           .           .           12D/        .
=9          =9          =9          =9          =9          =9
2.r         2.r         2.r         2.r         8F#/)       .
.           .           .           .           8B'/        .
.           .           .           .           8d'/        .
.           .           .           .           8f#'/       .
.           .           .           .           8b'/        .
.           .           .           .           8dd'/       .
=10         =10         =10         =10         =10         =10
2.r         2.r         2.r         2.r         (8ff#\      .
.           .           .           .           8ee\        .
.           .           .           .           8dd\        .
.           .           .           .           8cc#\       .
.           .           .           .           8dd\        .
.           .           .           .           8b\)        .
=11         =11         =11         =11         =11         =11
(4EE'/      [2.E/       (2A/        (8c#/       (2a\        .
.           .           .           8e/         .           .
4EE'/       .           .           8c#/        .           .
.           .           .           8e/         .           .
4EE'/)      .           4G#/)       8d/         8cc#\       .
.           .           .           8e/)        8b\)        .
=12         =12         =12         =12         =12         =12
4AA/        4E]/        4A/         4c#/        4a\         .
4r          4r          4r          4r          4r          .
*-          *-          *-          *-          *-          *-
```

Example 26.1 A **kern* representation of the second trio of Mozart's Clarinet Quintet.

Additional features and special capabilities of *Humdrum* are illustrated in subsequent examples.

26.3.2   The Saltarello

Humdrum provides extensive capabilities for encoding alternative renditions or editions of works, such as abbreviated and through-composed materials. The saltarello (encoded in Example 26.2b) provides an elementary illustration of *Humdrum* section labels and expansion lists. Each of six passages has been labelled:

- section one (1)
- the first ending for section one (1a)
- the second ending for section one (1b)
- the second section (2)
- its first ending (2a)
- its second ending (2b)

Example 26.2a   Saltarello.

The names assigned to these sections are arbitrarily assigned by the user. Near the beginning of the sample encoding are two *Humdrum* expansion lists that identify two different ways of expanding the encoding into a through-composed rendition. The first expansion list, *[1,1a,1,1b,2,2a,2,2b], expands the work with all of the repeats. The second expansion list, *>norep[1,1b,2,2b], omits the repetitions. Note also that the second expansion list has itself been given a name or a version label (norep). The *Humdrum* thru command expands encoded files according to a user-selected version. The norep version label allows the user to specify the generation of that particular rendition. There is no limit to the number of different versions that may be encoded in a single *Humdrum* file. In addition to section labels and expansion lists, *Humdrum* provides methods for representing alternative renderings (usually given in scores as "or" [*ossia*] readings), strophic material (such as verses in a song), editorial interventions (such as adding missing notes or realizing a figured bass), editorial interpretations (such as marking *ficta* accidentals[4]), and editorial footnotes (where lengthy commentaries can be affixed to particular points in the encoding). These other mechanisms will not be illustrated here.

```
!! Saltarello
**kern                          **dyn                                   8B          .
*>[1,1a,1,1b,2,2a,2,2b]         *>[1,1a,1,1b,2,2a,2,2b]                 8c          .
*>norep[1,1b,2,2b]              *>norep[1,1b,2,2b]                      (4          .
*>1                             *>1                                     8e          .
*clefC3                         *                                       =8a         =8a
*M6/8                           *                                       8A'         .
=1-                             =1-                                     8e'         .
8c                              (f)                                     8e'         .
8B                              .                                       4.A         .
8A                              .                                       *>1b        *>1b
8G                              .                                       !! Second ending.
8A                              .                                       =7b         =7b
8B                              .                                       8c          (f)
=2                              =2                                      8B          .
8c                              .                                       8c          .
8d                              .                                       8A          .
8B                              .                                       8B          .
(4c                             .                                       8c          .
8G)                             .                                       =8b         =8b
=3                              =3                                      (16d        .
8A                              .                                       16c         .
8B                              .                                       8d)         .
8c                              .                                       8B          .
8A                              .                                       4.c         .
8B                              .                                       *>2         *>2
8G                              .                                       =9          =9
=4                              =4                                      8e          .
8c                              .                                       8d          .
8B                              .                                       8c          .
8c                              .                                       (4B         .
(4d                             .                                       8A)         .
8e)                             .                                       =10         =10
=5                              =5                                      (4c         .
8c                              .                                       8d)         .
8g                              .                                       (4e         .
8f                              .                                       8d)         .
(4e                             .                                       =11         =11
8d)                             .                                       8c          .
=6                              =6                                      8B          .
8c                              (p)                                     8c          .
8g                              .                                       (4A         .
8f                              .                                       8B)         .
(4e                             .                                       =12         =12
8d)                             .                                       8G          .
*>1a                            *>1a                                    8A          .
!! First ending.                                                        8B          .
=7a                             =7a                                     (4c         .
8c                              (f)                                     8G)         .
                                                                        =13         =13
```

4. Such accidentals, which express an editor's interpretation rather than an author's explicit intentions, are shown above, rather than before, the notes to which they pertain.

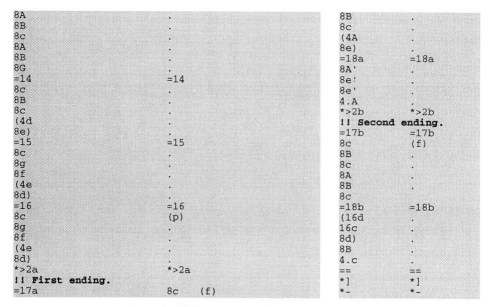

Example 26.2b *Kern* encoding of the Saltarello.

26.3.3 The Telemann Aria

Humdrum permits text to be interpreted in several different ways, such as alphabetic underlay or overlay. However, in this example we have chosen to interpret the underlay explicitly as lyrics, hence the exclusive interpretation **text in the seventh data column. Notice that a tandem interpretation (*LDeutsch) has been added in order to specify tht the language of the lyrics is German. As a demonstration of the extensibility of *Humdrum* representations, a further representation of the lyrics has been encoded using the International Phonetic Alphabet (IPA) in the right-most data column. This permits a phonetic representation of the lyrics that might prove valuable in some applications. For example, if two different English translations of the lyrics were provided, a researcher might use the corresponding phonetic representations to determine which of the two translations best preserves the vowel coloration of the original German lyrics.

Notice in Bars 29-30 that one of the voices is encoded as splitting into two (using a split interpretation *^) and subsequently rejoined (using two join interpretations *v). *Humdrum* provides operators to terminate, start, add, delete, exchange, split, and join data-paths. In addition, *Humdrum* provides a multiple-stop mechanism, which is illustrated in Bar 7 (third column), Bars 15–16 (fourth column), and Bar 26 (third column). Two or more note tokens may be encoded in a single data-column when separated by the space delimiter (rather than the tab). This mechanism is especially suitable for encoding homophonic music, such as piano scores that are highly chordal in nature.

Kern requires the user to interpret the implied voicing (or lack of voicing) in a score. Software tools are provided that allow the user to rearrange or reinterpret the voicings of already encoded works according to the analytic goal. Since many tasks (such as determining melodic intervals) presuppose an understanding of voicing, it is preferable to force the user to interpret the voicing rather than trying to build musically omniscient programs.

Example 26.3a Telemann aria.

Notice the encoding in Example 26.3b of the semitone trill (t) in Bar 10 of the music above. Whole-tone trills are encoded with an upper-case T.

In Bar 23, the presence of the square brackets around the accidental (G♯) has been tagged using the **kern question mark.

**kern	**kern	**kern	**kern	**kern	**kern	**text	**IPA
!! Telemann aria							
*	*	*	*	*	*	*LDeutsch	*LDeutsch
!BC	!BC cue	!Viola	!Violin	!Oboe	!voice	!lyrics	!phonetics
*Icembalo	*Icembalo	*Iviola	*Iviolin	*Ioboe	*Isoprano	*	*
*IC	*IC	*ICstr	*ICstr	*ICww	*ICvox	*	*
*sys1	*sys1	*sys1	*sys1	*sys1	*sys1	*sys1	*
*staff3	*staff3	*staff2	*staff2	*staff2	*staff1	*staff1	*
*clefF4	*clefF4	*clefG2	*clefG2	*clefG2	*clefG2	*	*
*M3/8	*M3/8	*M3/8	*M3/8	*M3/8	*M3/8	*M3/8	*
*D:	*D:	*D:	*D:	*D:	*D:	*	*
=1-	=1-	=1-	=1-	=1-	=1-	=1-	.
4.r	4.r	(8d	.	(8dd	4.r	.	.
.	.	8f#	.	8a)	.	.	.
.	.	8g)	.	8b	.	.	.
=2	=2	=2	=2	=2	=2	=2	.
4.r	4.r	4d	.	(16.f#	4.r	.	.
.	.	.	.	32g	.	.	.
.	.	.	.	8a)	.	.	.
.	.	8r	.	8d	.	.	.
=3	=3	=3	=3	=3	=3	=3	.
8D	8d	8a	8ff#	4.r	4.r	.	.
8C#	8e	8a	(16gg	.	.	.	.
.	.	.	16ff#)	.	.	.	.
8D	8d	16g	(16ee	.	.	.	.
.	.	16f#	16dd)	.	.	.	.
=4	=4	=4	=4	=4	=4	=4	.
4AA	4A	4e	(16.cc#	4.r	4.r	.	.
.	.	.	32dd	.	.	.	.
.	.	.	8ee)	.	.	.	.
8r	8r	8c#	8a	.	.	.	.
=5	=5	=5	=5	=5	=5	=5	.
4.r	4.r	4f#	4.r	(8dd	4.r	.	.
.	.	.	.	8a)	.	.	.
.	.	8g	.	8b	.	.	.
=6	=6	=6	=6	=6	=6	=6	.
4.r	4.r	4d	4.r	(16.f#	4.r	.	.
.	.	.	.	32g	.	.	.
.	.	.	.	8a)	.	.	.
.	.	8r	.	8d	.	.	.
=7	=7	=7	=7	=7	=7	=7	.
8G	4.r	8e 8b	8.ee	8.ee	4.r	.	.
8A	.	4e 8a	.	.	.	.	.
.	.	.	16cc#	16cc#	.	.	.
8AA	.	8g	8dd	8dd	.	.	.
!! voicing not clear here.							
=8	=8	=8	=8	=8	=8	=8	.
4D	4.r	4d 4f#	4dd	8dd	4.r	.	.
.	.	.	.	8a	.	.	.
8r	.	8g	8r	8b	.	.	.
=9	=9	=9	=9	=9	=9	=9	.

```
4.r        4.r        4d         4r         (16.f#     4.r        .          .
.          .          .          .          32g        .          .          .
.          .          8r         8r         8a)        .          .          .
!! voicing not clear here.                   8d         .          .          .
=10        =10        =10        =10        =10        =10        =10        .
8D         4.r        8B 8f#     8b         8b         4.r        .          .
8E         .          4B 8e      8.g#t      8.g#t      .          .          .
8EE        .          8d         .          .          .          .          .
.          .          .          16a        16a        .          .          .
=11        =11        =11        =11        =11        =11        =11        .
4.AA       4.r        4.A 4.c#   4.a        4.a        4.r        .          .
=12        =12        =12        =12        =12        =12        =12        .
4.r        4.r        4.r        4.r        4.r        4ee        Lie-       'li_
.          .          .          .          .          8a         -be!       _b@
=13        =13        =13        =13        =13        =13        =13        .
4.r        8A         8cc#       4.r        (8aa       4.r        .          .
.          8c#        8a         .          8ee)       .          .          .
.          8d         8a         .          8ff#       .          .          .
=14        =14        =14        =14        =14        =14        =14        .
4.r        4A         4e 4a      4.r        (16.cc#    4.r        .          .
.          .          .          .          32dd       .          .          .
.          .          .          .          8ee)       .          .          .
.          8r         8c#        .          8a         .          .          .
=15        =15        =15        =15        =15        =15        =15        .
4.r        4.r        4.r        4.r        4.r        (16.cc#    Lie-       'li_
.          .          .          .          .          32dd       .          .
.          .          .          .          .          8ee)       .          .
.          .          .          .          .          8a         -be!       _b@
=16        =16        =16        =16        =16        =16        =16        .
4.r        4A         4e 4cc#    4.r        (8aa       4.r        .          .
.          .          .          .          8ee)       .          .          .
.          8r         8r         .          8ff#       .          .          .
=17        =17        =17        =17        =17        =17        =17        .
4.r        4.r        4.a        4.r        (16.cc#    4.r        .          .
.          .          .          .          32dd       .          .          .
.          .          .          .          8ee)       .          .          .
.          .          .          .          8a         .          .          .
=18        =18        =18        =18        =18        =18        =18        .
4F#        4.r        4d 4a      4.r        4.r        (8dd       Was        v&s
.          .          .          .          .          8a)        .          .
8G         .          8d 8g 8b   .          .          8b         ist        Ist
=19        =19        =19        =19        =19        =19        =19        .
4.D        4.r        4.d 4.f#   4.r        4.r        (16.f#     schö-      'So_
                      4.a
.          .          .          .          .          32g        .          .
.          .          .          .          .          8a)        .          .
.          .          .          .          .          8d         -ner       _n@r
=20        =20        =20        =20        =20        =20        =20        .
8d         8d         8a         4.r        8ff#       8ff#       als        &ls
8c#        4e         8a         .          (16gg      (16gg      die        di
.          .          .          .          16ff#)     16ff#      .          .
8B         .          8g#        .          (16ee      16ee       .          .
.          .          .          .          16dd)      16dd)      .          .
=21        =21        =21        =21        =21        =21        =21        .
4A         4e         4.a        4.r        8.cc#      8.cc#      Lie-       'li_
.          .          .          .          16b        16b        -be,       _b@
8r         8c#.       .          .          8a         8a         .          .
=22        =22        =22        =22        =22        =22        =22        .
```

```
4F#        4.r        4d 4a      4.r        4r         8r         .          .
.          .          .          .          .          8dd        was        v&s
8r         .          8r         .          8r         8dd        schmeckt   SmEkt
=23        =23        =23        =23        =23        =23        =23        .
8r         4.r        8r         8r         8r         4dd        sü-        'zy_
8G         .          8d         8g         8b         .          .          .
8D         .          8d         8f#        8a         8dd        -sser      _s@r
=24        =24        =24        =24        =24        =24        =24        .
4GG        4.r        4d         4g         4b         8r         .          .
.          .          .          .          .          8b         was        v&s
8r         .          8r         8r         8r         8ee        schmeckt   SmEkt
=25        =25        =25        =25        =25        =25        =25        .
8r         4.r        8r         8r         8r         [4.ee      sü-        'zy_
8A         .          8e         8a         8cc#       .          .          .
8E         .          8e         8g#        8b         .          .          .
=26        =26        =26        =26        =26        =26        =26        .
4AA        4.r        4e         (16.a      (16.cc#    4.ee_      .          .
.          .          .          32b        32dd       .          .          .
.          .          .          8cc#)      8ee)       .          .          .
8r         .          8e         8g#        8b         .          .          .
=27        =27        =27        =27        =27        =27        =27        .
4r         4.r        4A         (16.a      (16cc#     4.ee_      .          .
.          .          .          32b        32dd       .          .          .
.          .          .          8cc#)      8ee)       .          .          .
8r         .          8e         8g#        8b         .          .          .
=28        =28        =28        =28        =28        =28        =28        .
4AA        4.r        4e         4a         4cc#       8ee]       .          .
.          .          .          .          .          (16dd      -sser      _s@r
.          .          .          .          .          16cc#      .          .
8D         .          8f# 8b     8r         8r         16b        .          .
.          .          .          .          .          16a)       .          .
=29        =29        =29        =29        =29        =29        =29        .
4.BB       4.r        4.d 4.g#   4r         4r         8r         .          .
.          .          .          .          .          8g#        als        &ls
.          .          .          8r         8r         8dd        ein        &In
*          *          *          *          *          *^         *          *

!          !          !          !          !          !          !suggest.  !          !
=30        =30        =30        =30        =30        =30        =30        =30        .
4.AA       4.r        4.c# 4.a   4.a        4.ee       4.cc#      8dd        Kuss?      kUs
.          .          .          .          .          .          4cc#       .          .
*          *          *          *          *          *v         *v         *          *

**kern     **kern     **kern     **kern     **kern     **kern     **text     **IPA
=31        =31        =31        =31        =31        =31        =31        =31
4.r        4.r        4f#        4.r        4.r        (8dd       Was        v&s
.          .          .          .          .          8a)        .          .
.          .          8g         .          .          8b         ist        Ist
=32        =32        =32        =32        =32        =32        =32        .
4.r        4.r        4.d        4.r        4.r        (16.f#     schö-      'So_
.          .          .          .          .          32g        .          .
.          .          .          .          .          8a)        .          .
.          .          .          .          .          8d         -ner,      _n@r
=33        =33        =33        =33        =33        =33        =33        .
8D         8d         4.r        8a         8ff#       4.r        .          .
4GG        4B         .          (16b       (16gg      .          .          .
.          .          .          16a)       16ff#)     .          .          .
.          .          .          (16g       (16ee      .          .          .
.          .          .          16f#)      16dd)      .          .          .
=34        =34        =34        =34        =34        =34        =34        .
```

4.AA	4e	4.e	(16.cc#	(16.cc#	4.r	.	.
.	.	.	32dd	32dd	.	.	.
.	.	.	8ee)	8ee)	.	.	.
.	8c#	.	8a	8a	.	.	.
=35	=35	=35	=35	=35	=35	=35	.
4.r	4.r	4f#	4.4	4.r	(8dd	was	v&s
.	.	.	.	.	8a)	.	.
.	.	8g	.	.	8b	schmeckt	SmEkt
=36	=36	=36	=36	=36	=36	=36	.
*-	*-	*-	*-	*-	*-	*-	*-

Example 26.3b *Kern* encoding of the Telemann aria.

26.3.4 Unmeasured Chant

Another property of the **kern* representation is that it does not require that the user
encode information (such as duration) that is immaterial to the problem. For example,
a file containing just phrase marks and bar lines is a sufficient and syntactically
correct representation. This is evident in the following encoding of the unmeasured
chant "Quem queritis."

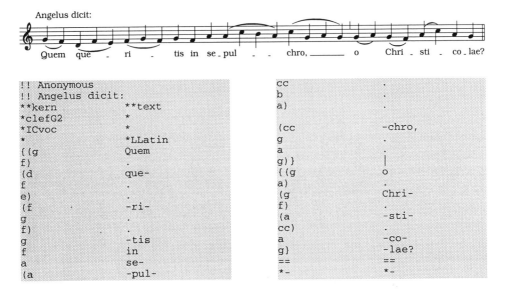

`!! Anonymous`		`cc`	`.`
`!! Angelus dicit:`		`b`	`.`
`**kern`	`**text`	`a)`	`.`
`*clefG2`	`*`		
`*ICvoc`	`*`	`(cc`	`-chro,`
`*`	`*LLatin`	`g`	`.`
`{(g`	`Quem`	`a`	`.`
`f)`	`.`	`g)}`	`.`
`(d`	`que-`	`{(g`	`.`
`f`	`.`	`a)`	`.`
`e)`	`.`	`(g`	`Chri-`
`(f`	`-ri-`	`f)`	`.`
`g`	`.`	`(a`	`-sti-`
`f)`	`.`	`cc)`	`.`
`g`	`-tis`	`a`	`-co-`
`f`	`in-`	`g}`	`-lae?`
`a`	`se-`	`==`	`==`
`(a`	`-pul-`	`*-`	`*-`

Examples 26.4a and 26.4b The unmeasured chant "Quem queritis" and a minimal **kern*
representation.

26.3.5 The Binchois *Magnificat*

Humdrum provides the opportunity to represent square and mensural notations directly, without resorting to transcriptions using modern notation. Nevertheless, for illustration purposes Example 26.5b (by Binchois) is again rendered using the **kern* representation. Measure numbers are optional. They have been added here in order to aid readability.

Magnificat secundi toni

Example 26.5a Beginning of the Binchois *Magnificat*.

Some of the syllabifications in subsequent measures (not shown) are incomplete in the printed source (e.g., notated *respe-xit* rather than *re-spe-xit*; *humili-* rather than *hu-mi-li-*). Whether or not these syllabifications should be expanded in the corresponding *Humdrum* representation would depend on the analytic goal of the user.

In the **kern* representation there is no reserved method for representing ligatures (as denoted by horizontal square brackets in the printed score). However, each *Humdrum* representation scheme provides unassigned signifiers that may be used at the discretion of the user. In the following example, the letters V and Z are used to signify the start and end of horizontal square brackets within a voice or part. If the user wanted to identify whether the brackets are above or below the staff the user could distinguish four signifiers rather than just two.

There is no special way of placing accidentals in parentheses. Here the user has chosen to represent parentheses using a free signifier, upper-case U.

```
!! Binchois, "Magnificat secundi toni."        4E            .             8c#U          .
!! Chorus                                       .             .             16BnU         .
!! Number 1                                     .             .             16c#U         .
!! duo                                          =7            =7            =7            =7
**kern        **text                            2.D           -num.         2.d           -num.
*             *LLatin                           ==8           ==8           ==8           ==8
*clefF4       *                                 *-            *-            *-            *-
*k[b-]        *                                 !! Number 2
c             Mag-                              **kern        **kern        **kern        **text
d             -ni-                              *staff2       *staff2       *staff1       *staff1
(c            -fi-                              *             *             *             *unter
f)            .                                 ! T.          ! CT.         ! (C.)        ! (C.)
f             -cat                              *             *             *             *LLatin
*-            *-                                *ICinstr      *ICinstr      *ICvox        *ICvox
**kern   **text   **kern   **text              *Iinstr       *Iinstr       *Itenor       *Itenor
*ICvox   *        *ICvox   *                    *clefF4       *clefF4       *clefF4       *
*        *LLatin  *        *LLatin              *[M3/4]       *[M3/4]       *[M3/4]       *[M3/4]
! (CT.)  ! (CT.)  ! (C.)   ! (C.)               =9            =9            =9            =9
*staff2  *staff2  *staff1  *staff1              4D            4.A           4d            Et
*        *unter   *        *unter               8F            .             8c            .
*clefF4  *        *clefF4  *                     8A            8F            8f            .
*k[b-]   *        *k[b-]   *                     4G            4B-           8e            .
*M3/4    *M3/4    *M3/4    *M3/4                 .             .             8d            .
=1-      =1-      =1-      =1-                   =10           =10           =10           =10
4r       .        4r       .                     4F            4c            4f            ex-
4r       .        4r       .                     8F            8A            4f            -ul-
4F       A-       4f       A-                     8F            8G            .             .
=2       =2       =2       =2                     4D            4B-           4f            -ta-
8D       -ni-     8f       -ni-                   =11           =11           =11           =11
8C       .        4g       -ma                    4D            4B-           V4f           -vit
4E       -ma      .        .                      2C;           8c            Z4e;          .
.        .        8e       .                      .             8B-           .             .
8F       me-      8.d      me-                     .             4G;           4r            .
8G       .        .        .                      =12           =12           =12           =12
.        .        16c      .                      4.G           2C            4.e           spi-
=3       =3       =3       =3                      8F            .             8d            .
4A       .        4c       -a                      4D            4BB-          8f            -ri-
8F       -a       4r       .                       .             .             8e            .
4A       do-      .        .                       =13           =13           =13           =13
.        .        8F       do-                      V4E           V4AA          8c            .
8F       .        [8A      .                        .             .             16B-          .
=4       =4       =4       =4                       .             .             16c           .
8c       .        8A]      .                        Z2D           Z4.A          4.d           -tus
8A       .        8F       .                        .             8F            8c            .
4F       .        8c       .                        =14           =14           =14           =14
.        .        8A       .                        V2D           4F            V4A           me-
8r       .        V4G      .                        .             4r            Z4.B-         .
8B-      .        .        .                        [4C           8E            8A            .
=5       =5       =5       =5                        .             [8E           8E            .
8A       .        Z4F      .                         =15           =15           =15           =15
4c       .        .        .                         4C]           8E]           4.A           .
.        .        8r       .                         .             8F            .             .
8A       .        8f       .                         Z2BB-         8D            8G            .
4G       .        8.e      .                         .             4D            8G            .
.        .        16d      .                         .             .             8F            .
=6       =6       =6       =6                         =16           =16           =16           =16
8F       .        8f       .                          2AA;          2E;           2A;           -us
8C       -mi-     [8e      .                          4r            4r            4r            .
8D       .        16e]     .                          =-
.        .        16d      .
8F       .        8d       -mi-
```

Example 26.5b *Kern* encoding of the Binchois *Magnificat.*

26.4   User Support

26.4.1   Associated Software and Data

Humdrum may be regarded as consisting of two parts: (1) the *Humdrum* syntax is a framework within which arbitrary representation schemes can be defined; (2) the *Humdrum Toolkit* is a set of 70-odd software tools for manipulating data conforming to the *Humdrum* syntax.

Current *Humdrum* software tools permit a wide variety of special-purpose and generalized operations. Musical passages may be accessed according to measure, phrase, metric position, instrumentation, or musical context (e.g., chord types, cadences, lyrics, dynamics, ornamentation, etc.). General-purpose tools permit either pre-defined or user-defined data to be transformed, classified, coordinated, transferred, edited, restructured, contextualized, and otherwise manipulated.

Sophisticated pattern searches may be made, cuing on any type of encoded or derived information, and according to horizontal, vertical, diagonal (e.g., *Klangfarbenmelodie*), or any combination of pattern orientations. For example, a user might search for specific finger-fret combinations in a work for Indian sitar. Or one might look for particular patterns of open and closed vowels in vocal lyrics that are associated with a certain melodic contour, and are also anchored to a specified metrical context. *Humdrum* is also able to characterize the similarity between various types of information according to user-defined criteria of similarity.

A set of measurement tools is provided, including tools for characterizing syncopation (Johnson-Laird), melodic accent (Thomassen), sensory dissonance (Kameoka and Kuriyagawa), information flow (Shannon), structural tonality (Krumhansl), pitch (Terhardt), and psychoacoustic harmony (Parncutt). *Humdrum* is able to represent and manipulate non-musical information (such as EEG, heart-rate and gesture data) as easily as pitch intervals, harmonic analyses, and ethnomusicological notations.

Tools are provided that allow MIDI data to be imported to *Humdrum* or exported from *Humdrum*. High quality *PostScript* musical notation can be generated from **kern* data using the *Humdrum* ms command in conjunction with *Mup*—a PC- and UNIX-based music publishing program produced by Arkkra Enterprises (*http://www.arkkra.com*). *Humdrum* utilities are also available for translating *Plaine and Easie Code* (used in the RISM documentation project) and *MuseData* (used in the CCARH musical databases) into the **kern* representation. In addition, a *SCORE*-to-*Humdrum* conversion program is available from Andreas Kornstädt at the University of Hamburg (*1kornsta@informatik.uni-hamburg.de*).

A graphical user interface for *Humdrum* has been designed and implemented by Michael Taylor (*wmt@bfs.Unibol.com*) of the Music Technology program at Queen's University of Belfast (Taylor, 1996). Taylor's interface runs under *Windows, Windows 95*, and *Windows/NT*. Another more specialized interface using the X-Window System is under development by Andreas Kornstädt. Several specialized musical applications software make use of *Humdrum* as the underlying processing engine.

Approximately 9,000 musical works are encoded in the Humdrum format—the majority in the **kern representation. In addition, roughly 10,000 musical incipits have been encoded. Most of these works are distributed by the Center for Computer Assisted Research in the Humanities at Stanford University.

Humdrum was explicitly designed to be upwardly compatible with the international Unicode 16-bit character representation (see Appendix E). As future operating systems and utilities begin to support Unicode, *Humdrum* will allow users to take full advantage of Unicode's native representations for remote scripts such as Tibetan, Gujarati, etc. Ethnomusicologists, for example, would be able to search and manipulate data that is encoded directly in a non-Western script. If the Unicode standard is extended to include musical symbols, the *Humdrum* software tools will permit immediate use of these extensions.

26.4.2 Documentation and Other Resources

The *Humdrum Toolkit* software is available free of charge via ftp or and at slight cost on diskettes with a 600-page manual from CCARH. Further details are available in a lengthy list of frequently asked questions (FAQs), and their answers, for *Humdrum*. On the Internet, this file may be retrieved and printed using the following commands:

```
unix> ftp archive.uwaterloo.ca
Login Name: anonymous
Password: [your e-mail address]
ftp> binary
ftp> cd uw-data/humdrum
ftp> get faq
fpt> quit
unix> lpr faq
[etc.]
```

A printed 550-page *Humdrum* reference manual is available. This manual includes an introduction to *Humdrum* and complete documentation for the software tools and existing predefined representations. On-line manual pages are available for all of the software tools. An electronic newsletter for *Humdrum* users is distributed periodically on the Internet. On the World-Wide Web, further information regarding *Humdrum* may be found at the University of Virginia's Digital Media Music Center (*http://www.lib.virginia.edu/dmmc/Music/Humdrum/index.html*).

References

Hewlett, Walter B., and Eleanor Selfridge-Field (eds.). "*Humdrum*: Music Tools for UNIX Systems," *Computing in Musicology* 7 (1991), 66–67.

Huron, David. "Error Categories, Detection and Reduction in a Musical Database," *Computers and the Humanities* 22/4 (1988), 253–264.

Huron, David. "Music Representation Reconsidered," paper presented at the Computers in Music Research Conference, Centre for Research into the Applications of Computers to Music, University of Lancaster, 1988. Conference Prospectus, pp. 43–44.

Huron, David. "Characterizing Musical Textures," *Proceedings of the 1989 International Computer Music Conference*. San Francisco: Computer Music Association, 1989, pp. 131–134.

Huron, David. "Tonal Consonance versus Tonal Fusion in Polyphonic Sonorities," *Music Perception* 9/2 (1991), 135–154.

Huron, David. "Design Principles in Computer-Based Music Representation" in Alan Marsden and Anthony Pople (eds.), *Computer Representations and Models in Music*, London: Academic Press, 1992, pp. 5–39.

Huron, David. "Chordal-Tone Doubling and the Enhancement of Key Perception," *Psychomusicology* 12 (1993), 73–83.

Huron, David. *UNIX Software Tools for Music Research; The Humdrum Toolkit Reference Manual*. Menlo Park, CA: Center for Computer Assisted Research in the Humanities, 1995.

Huron, David, and Richard Parncutt. "An Improved Model of Tonality Perception Incorporating Pitch Salience and Echoic Memory," *Psychomusicology* 12 (1993), 152–169.

Huron, David, and Peter Sellmer. "Critical Bands and the Spelling of Vertical Sonorities," *Music Perception* 10/2 (1992), 129–149.

Kameoka, A., and M. Kuriyagawa. "Consonance Theory, Part I: Consonance of Dyads," *Journal of the Acoustical Society of America* 45/6 (1969), 1451–1459.

Kameoka, A., and M. Kuriyagawa. "Consonance Theory, Part II: Consonance of Complex Tones and its Computation Method," *Journal of the Acoustical Society of America* 45/6 (1969), 1460–1469.

Kornstädt, Andreas. "*SCORE*-to-*Humdrum*: An Environment for Computer-Assisted Musicological Analysis," *Computing in Musicology* 10 (in press).

Krumhansl, Carol L. *The Cognitive Foundations of Musical Pitch*. Oxford: Oxford University Press, 1990.

Orpen, Keith S., and David Huron. "The Measurement of Similarity in Music: A Quantitative Approach for Non-Parametric Representations," *Computers in Music Research* 4 (1992), 1–44.

Parncutt, Richard. *Harmony: A Psychoacoustical Approach*. Berlin: Springer-Verlag, 1989.

Schaffrath, Helmut. *The Essen Folksong Collection in Kern Format* [computer database], D. Huron (ed.). Menlo Park, CA: Center for Computer Assisted Research in the Humanities, 1995.

Shannon, C. E., and W. Weaver. *The Mathematical Theory of Communication*. Urbana: University of Illinois Press, 1949.

Simpson, Jasba. *Cochlear Modeling of Sensory Dissonance and Chord Roots*. Master's thesis, Systems Design Engineering, University of Waterloo, 1994.

Simpson, Jasba, and David Huron. "The Perception of Rhythmic Similarity: A Test of a Modified Version of Johnson-Laird's Theory," *Canadian Acoustics* 21/3 (1993), 89–90.

Taylor, William Michael. "*Humdrum* Graphical User Interface." M.A. thesis, Music Technology program, Queen's University of Belfast, 1996.

Terhardt, Ernst. "Calculating Virtual Pitch," *Hearing Research* 1 (1979), 155–182.

Terhardt, Ernst, G. Stoll, and M. Seewann. "Algorithm for Extraction of Pitch and Pitch Salience from Complex Tonal Signals," *Journal of the Acoustical Society of America* 71 (1982), 679–688.

Thomassen, Joseph. "Melodic Accent: Experiments and a Tentative Model," *Journal of the Acoustical Society of America* 71 (1982), 1596–1605. See also, Thomassen, J. (1983) Erratum. *Journal of the Acoustical Society of America* 73 (1983), 373.

Thompson, William Forde, and Murray Stainton. "Using *Humdrum* to Analyze Melodic Structure: An Assessment of Narmour's Implication-realization Model," *Computing in Musicology* 10 (1995-6), 24-33.

27   *MuseData*: Multipurpose Representation

Walter B. Hewlett

The purpose of *MuseData* code is to represent the logical content of musical scores in a software-neutral fashion. The code is currently being used in the construction of full-text databases of music for several composers, including J. S. Bach, Beethoven, Corelli, Handel, Haydn, Mozart, Telemann, and Vivaldi. It is intended that these full-text databases be used for music printing, music analysis, and production of electronic sound files.

Although *MuseData* code is intended to be generic, we have developed software of various kinds in order to test its effectiveness. *MuseData* programs print scores and parts which have been used by professional performing groups and music publishers. They compile Standard MIDI Files which may be used with standard sequencer software. They facilitate high-speed searches of the data for specific rhythmic, melodic, and harmonic patterns.

To further demonstrate the software neutrality of the system, we have developed programs to generate *SCORE* parameter files and *DARMS* input files from the data. *MuseData* files have been successfully converted to the Humdrum *Kern* format[1] and used as a basis for analytical research projects. Work is in progress on programs to convert to other representations as well. All software currently runs on *x*86 architectures running the DOS operating system.

MuseData code is designed to represent both notational and sound information, but in both cases the representation is not intended to be fully complete. It is envisioned that *MuseData* files would serve as *source files* for generating page-specific graphics

---

1. See Chapter #26.

files and MIDI sound files, which might then be further edited as the user sees fit. The reasons for this position are two-fold:

(1) When we encode a musical work, what we are encoding is not the score itself but the logical content of the score. To encode the score would mean encoding the exact position of every note on the page; but our view is that such an encoding would actually contain more information than the composer intended to convey.[2]

(2) We cannot anticipate all of the uses to which this data might be put, but we can be fairly sure that each user will have his or her own special needs and preferences. It does not make sense, therefore, to try to encode detailed information about how a graphic realization of the data should look or how a sound realization of the data should sound.

On the other hand, it sometimes can be helpful to make suggestions about how the graphics and the sound should be realized. The important thing is to identify *suggestions* as a separate data type, which can easily be ignored by application software or stripped entirely from the data. Our own software makes use of these print and sound suggestions in the process of generating *SCORE* parameter files and MIDI sound files.

27.1 Composite File Organization

The organization of *MuseData* files is an integral part of the *MuseData* representation. Each *MuseData* file represents the encoding of one musical part from a movement of piece. In the following scheme one file would contain the information required for Part 1, Bars 1–11[3], another Part 2 (Bars 1–11), another Part 3 (Bars 1–11), and so forth.

---

2. When Bach made a fair copy of one of his works, he may have reproduced all of the notes in their proper order, but he surely did not put them in exactly the same place on the page as they had occupied in the composing copy. What we seek to encode, then, is the same information that Bach would have transferred from a composing copy to a fair copy, and that his copyists would have transferred to various instrumental parts from the score.

3. Of the last bar of the movement, if the score continued on successive pages.

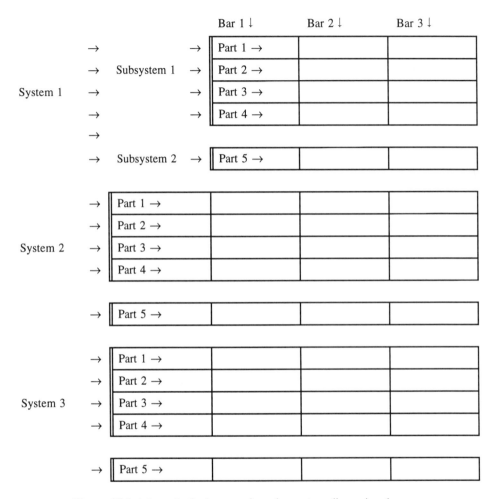

Figure 27.1 A hypothetical score viewed as a two-dimensional array.

The arrangement of parts into systems and subsystems and the layout of system breaks and page breaks is irrelevant to the encoding of *MuseData*. However, a musical part may be notated as one line or more of music. For example, if a movement has two oboe parts, *Oboe I* and *Oboe II*, these may be encoded as separate parts, or they may be combined on one staff and encoded as a single musical part, namely *Oboes I & II* (e.g., Parts 1 and 2 above). In the latter case, verbal cues and directions would be used to differentiate the two parts.

In the *MuseData* system, they may be encoded both ways, since a score might call for both oboes on one staff, but the players might want to play from separate parts. Music on the grand staff[4] may be encoded as one or two parts.[5] If musical notation or symbols cross between the staves of the grand staff, then the music on the grand staff must be treated as one musical part.

27.1.1 File Relationships within the Database

Our database currently consists of more than 7,000 *MuseData* files. When complete, the database could exceed 100,000 files. We currently use a hierarchical directory tree structure to organize these files, which is briefly outlined below. In this outline, you must imagine real composer names for *COMPOSER1*, *COMPOSER2*; real source names for *SOURCE1*, *SOURCE2*; and real work titles for *WORK1*, *WORK2*.

Stage-1 files contain data for pitch and duration only (i.e., note and rest records) and support sound applications. Stage-2 files contain a great deal of additional information to support printing and interpretive applications.

Stage-1 files are all of the same type, while Stage-2 files may belong to one or more of the following data-file types:

- *sound*   used to compile MIDI sound files
- *score*   used to print scores
- *parts*   used to print parts
- *short*   used to print short scores
- *tracks*   used for analysis
- *midi*   data specifically used to compile MIDI files (e.g., channel assignments and instrument assignments)
- *data*   anything and everything

---

4. i.e., the two-stave system used for piano music.

5. It may also be encoded as more than two parts. For example, in the encoding of a four-voice fugue for keyboard, each fugal part may be represented as a separate part.

```
MuseData/
        COMPOSER1/
        COMPOSER2/
        . . .
        COMPOSERn/
                INDEX
                SOURCE1/
                SOURCE2/
                . . .
                SOURCEn/
                        WORK1/
                        WORK2/
                        . . .
                        WORKn/
                                STAGE1/
                                        MVT1/
                                        MVT2/
                                        . . .
                                        MVTn/
                                STAGE2/
                                        MVT1/
                                        MVT2/
                                        . . .
                                        MVTn/
```

Figure 27.2 Hierarchy of file relationships within database.

27.1.2 Organization of Single Files

MuseData files consist of a set of time-ordered, variable length ASCII records. The order of the records is essential to the representation. Single *MuseData* files have four essential components—header records, a musical attributes record, a series of regular note records, and an end-of-file marker.

All records are organized as a series of 80-character columns. The first character in each record is called the *control key*, and this key determines the nature and function of the record.

A. HEADER RECORDS

The format and contents of the header records are as follows:

Record 1:   free
Record 2:   free
Record 3:   free
Record 4:   *<date> <name of encoder>*
Record 5:   WK*n*:*<work number>* MV*n*:*<movement number>*
Record 6:   *<source>*
Record 7:   *<work title>*
Record 8:   *<movement title>*
Record 9:   *<name of part>*
Record 10:   miscellaneous designations (e.g., *<mode>*,
             <movement type>, and *<voice>*)
Record 11:   group memberships *<name1> <name2>* . . .
Record 12:   *<name1>*: part *<x>* of *<number in group>*
Record 13:   . . .
. . .   (as needed)

Additional header records may be used, but those shown above are always used or, if not pertinent to the file at hand, reserved.

Files that are distributed contain copyright and other identifying information in Records 1–3.

B. GROUP MEMBERSHIPS [**Record 11**]

The concept of group membership for parts facilitates flexibility in the creation of diverse kinds of scores and parts and in other uses of the data. Record 11 contains a list of names, which are the application groups to which this file belongs. The group names can be anything the encoder wishes them to be.

In our data files, we use names that have an obvious connection to their associated application: e.g., score, parts, sound, tracks, shortscore, data, etc. For each name listed in Record 11, there is a record that starts with that name and specifies the order or ranking in the group to which it belongs. The idea is that all files for a particular movement should be placed in the same directory. This way, a program designed to compile a score would simply check every file in the directory and identify for use those belonging to the group called *score*.

The order in the group would determine the top-to-bottom order in the score. A program designed to compile MIDI sound files would identify for use those belonging to the group called *sound*. The same method would apply for other applications such as printing parts, printing short scores, and compiling track data for melodic and harmonic analysis.

C. THE MUSICAL ATTRIBUTES RECORD [$]

A musical attributes record immediately follows the last header record. In the above example it would constitute Record 13. This record identifies such attributes, usually pertaining throughout the file, as key signatures, time signatures, clef signs, etc.

Musical attribute records always begin with a dollar sign ($) in Column 1. Their format is as follows:

Column	1:	$
Column	2:	level number (optional)
Column	3:	footnote column
Columns	4–80:	attribute fields

The record may contain one or more fields; fields are initiated by the field identifier and terminated by a blank. In the case of clefs and directives, the field identifier may contain a number, which is the staff (1 or 2 at the moment) to which the clef or directive belongs. The absence of a number indicates Staff 1.

FIELD TYPE	FIELD IDENTIFIER	FIELD DATA TYPE
key	K:	integer (positive or negative)
divisions per quarter note	Q:	integer (positive only)
time designation	T:	two integers (positive only)
clef	C:	integer (positive only)
clef	Cn:	integer
transposing part	X:	integer (positive or negative)
number of staves for part	S:	integer (positive only; default = 1)
number of instruments represented	I:	integer (positive only; default = 1)
directive (last field on line)	D:	ASCII string
directive (last field on line)	Dn:	ASCII string

Here is one example of a musical attributes record:

```
K:-2  Q:8  T:3/8  C:4  C2:22  D:Allegro ma non troppo
```

Explanations of the parameters for the less self-evident data types represented in this record follow.

1. Clef Code [**C:**] The standard clefs are represented by a positive integer between 1 and 85. The tens digit of the code specifies the clef sign and the ones digit specifies the staff line to which the clef sign refers. The clef-sign codes are as follows:

0	G-clef
1	C-clef
2	F-clef
3	G-clef transposed down
4	C-clef transposed down
5	F-clef transposed down
6	G-clef transposed up
7	C-clef transposed up
8	F-clef transposed up

The line-number designations are as follows:

1	highest line
5	lowest line

Some examples of clef codes are these:

4	treble clef
13	alto clef
22	bass clef
34	treble clef for tenors

2. Transposing Part [**X:**] This integer (positive or negative) indicates a transposing interval (if one exists) and/or a doubling of the part an octave lower. The base-40 system[6] is used. 23 means the music sounds a fifth higher than it is written; −23 means the music sounds a fifth lower than it is written. Adding 1000 to the number indicates a doubling of the part an octave lower (e.g., violoncello and bass on the same part or 8' and 16' sound on an organ pedal line). In the base-40 system, the minor second has a value of 5 and the major second has a value of 6. All other interval sizes can be computed from these numbers.

3. Number of Instruments Represented [**I:**] This integer (1 or more) indicates the number of independent instruments represented in the file. If this number is more than one, these printing conventions will hold:

---

6. See the glossary for an explanation of Hewlett's base-40 system (1992).

- Notes with the same stem direction will be combined into one chord.

- If more than one voice is represented in a measure on a staff, then each voice will follow its own set of accidentals within the measure.

27.2   Organization of Data Records

MuseData utilizes character spacing of data within each line, since the meaning of many elements of the system are inferred from column placement. An 80-column row is assumed.

The first character in each record uses a control key to identify the record type. There are currently 23 valid control keys.[7] In alphabetical order they are:

A	regular note record	a	append to previous line
B	regular note record	b	backspace in time
C	regular note record	c	cue size note
D	regular note record	f	figured harmony
E	regular note record	g	grace note
F	regular note record	i	invisible rest
G	regular note record	m	bar line
P	print suggestions	r	regular rest
S	sound directions	$	musical attribute record
" "	extra note in chord	&	comment mode toggle switch
/	end of music or end of file	@	single line comment
		*	musical directions

27.2.1   Regular Note Records: Sound Information [A..G, r]

The most common type of record is the *regular note* or *rest record*. This is really the heart of the representation. This type of record can be identified by one of the seven key names—A, B, C, D, E, F, G—or the letter r (for rest) in Column 1. Complete sound information for pitch and duration is provided in Columns 1–9. Information pertaining to printing and interpretation is stored in Columns 13–80. Columns 10–12 are always left blank.

---

7. There are 96 available spaces. Thus there are currently 73 vacancies for adding new types of records to the representation, which is a significant factor in the system's ability to expand.

A. Pitch Information [**Columns 1–4**]

Pitch notation requires three parameters—pitch name (A . . G), chromatic inflection (♯,♭,♮), and octave number. The first and third parameters are given explicitly for every note in *MuseData*. Chromatic (or enharmonic) inflection is also explicit for every note,[8] because this facilitates accurate conversion to sound information. The complete pitch specification given in Columns 1–4 is thus of variable length, taking only two columns if there is no altered chromatic inflection.

Pitch name is specified in Column 1 by the relevant capital letter (A. .G) or an r for a rest.

Chromatic inflection is indicated in Columns 2–3. The codes are # (sharp), ## (double sharp), f (flat), and ff (double flat). Naturals are never indicated here; when graphically necessary, they are signalled by a flag in Column 19 (actual notated accidental).

An octave number in the range 0..9 is given in Column 2, 3, or 4 as the final element of the pitch specification. Middle C initiates Octave 4, the next higher octave is Octave 5, and the next lower octave is Octave 3. Thus Middle C = C4, while Bf3 (A#3) is the whole step below it. The whole step above it may be designated as D4 (also as C##4 and Eff4). The maximum range in current use extends from Cff0 to B##9.

Column 5 is left blank.

B. Duration Information [**Columns 6–9**]

Duration is specified in units called divisions. The number of divisions per quarter note is specified initially in a musical attribute record. The number of these divisions pertaining to the note or rest is specified, with right justification, in Columns 6–8. If a quarter note has four divisions, a sixteenth note will have one division. Column 9 is reserved for a tie flag (–), which is appended to the initiating note.

Duration means the complete logical duration of a pitch as opposed to the shortened or articulated duration that might be appropriate in a sound file. When the

---

8. Most notation-oriented representation systems and many MIDI sequencer programs rely on global specifications for correct interpretation of chromatic inflection. If the key signature provides a B♭, the encoded pitch will be given as B and, in fact, if the explicit pitch B♭ is given in the file, the associated *MuseData* programs will violate the visual grammar of musical notation by producing redundant flat signs.

notated duration of a pitch is different from the intended duration,[9] it is the intended duration that is represented. This favors appropriate results in the conversion to a sound file.

From the data in Columns 1 to 9 it is possible to construct sound output of the musical part. Here is the score for a common children's folk song ("Three Blind Mice"), in which each quarter note has two divisions:

```
measure 1                        measure 3
E4      2                        G4      2
D4      2                        F4      1
C4      2                        F4      1
rest    2                        E4      4
measure 2                        measure 4
E4      2                        G4      2
D4      2                        F4      1
C4      2                        F4      1
rest    2                        E4      4
```

Figure 27.3 Sample file for openings measures of "Three Blind Mice."

C. CHORDS ["   "]

A regular note may be followed by additional chord tones. A chord is thus made up of one regular note and one or more extra chord notes. The control key for an extra chord note is a blank space ("   "). The format for this type of record is as follows:

Column 1:	blank
Columns 2–5:	pitch (for content, see 27.2.1.A)
Columns 6–8:	duration or blanks (see 27.2.1.B)
Column 9:	tie flag
Columns 10–42:	same as for regular note

If the duration field (Columns 6–8) is blank, it is understood that the extra chord note has the same duration as the regular note. The duration of the extra notes need not be the same as that of the regular note, but must not exceed that of the regular note.[10] If all durations in the chord are the same, the pitches may be encoded in any order; any of the pitches may be encoded as the regular note. For purposes of analysis, it is possible to assign different notes of a chord to different tracks (Column 15).

9. Bach, for example, often notated a long-short triplet pattern with a dotted eighth and sixteenth note. The intended duration in this case would be the long-short triplet pattern.

10. The situation of different durations arises sometimes with string double stops.

D. Cue Notes and Grace Notes [c, g]

There are three types of small-size notes: small-size regular notes (treated as explained above), cue notes, and grace notes. Small-size regular notes and cue notes line up timewise with regular notes in a score, whereas grace notes have space of their own and are attached to a following regular note or to the end of a measure. Small size regular notes should be used to represent accompaniments and other musical material which is intended to be played. Cue notes should be used to represent notes that show in one part what is going on in another part or to represent a variant to regular notes.

An instrumental cadenza, expressed as small notes in a score and executed essentially in free time, would probably be represented with grace notes. If, on the other hand, the cadenza extended for several measures and were executed basically in measured time, it would probably be represented with regular notes, at either small or full size.

The control keys for grace notes and cue notes are g and c respectively. The formats for these records are as follows:

Column 1:	g (grace note) OR
	c (cue note[11])
Columns 2–5:	pitch/rest identification
Columns 6–7:	blank
Column 8:	note type
	0 eighth note with slash
	1 256th note
	2 128th note
	3 64th note
	4 32nd note
	5 16th note
	6 8th note
	7 quarter note
	8 half note
	9 whole note
	A breve
Column 9:	blank
Columns 10–80:	same as regular notes

Grace notes and cue notes may include extra chord tones. In this case the same keys g and c are used as control keys but the records have the following formats:

---

11. Same size as a grace note but written in time.

Column 1:	g or c (same as for single notes)
Column 2:	blank
Columns 3–6:	pitch (see regular note)
Column 7:	blank
Column 8:	note type (same as for single notes)
Column 9:	blank
Columns 10–80:	same as other grace and cue notes

27.2.2 Regular Note Records: Graphic and Interpretive Information

All remaining columns (13–80) are related to information pertinent to printing and data interpretation. A blank in any column reserved for a specific purpose means that no information is required. Columns 10–12 are also left blank.

A. FOOTNOTE, LEVEL, AND TRACK INFORMATION [Columns 13–15]

These columns are used as follows:

Column 13:	footnote flag (" " = none)	toggle
Column 14:	level number (optional)	integer
Column 15:	track number (optional)	integer

Where more than one musical line is represented in a printed part, it is essential for purposes of analysis to know for each note (or chord) the musical line or track to which the note belongs. In some cases this is interpretive information, provided as a service by the encoder in Column 15. Column 16 is left blank. Columns 17 to 43 extend the information given in Columns 1–9 with details about the *notation* of the pitch and duration. Occasionally this information will conflict with the information in Columns 1 to 9, since it is concerned with attributes related to correct printing, analysis, and interpretation.

B. GRAPHIC NOTE TYPE [Column 17]

The graphic note types, ranging from a long (*longa*) to a 256th note, and their full- and cue-size codes, are shown in the following listing:

NOTE TYPE	FULL-SIZE	CUE-SIZE
long	L	B
breve	b	A
whole	w	9
half	h	8
quarter	q	7
eighth	e	6
sixteenth	s	5
32nd	t	4
64th	x	3
128th	y	2
256th	z	1

C. DOTS OF PROLONGATION [**Column 18**]

Column 18 is reserved for a dot flag (.). A double dot is represented as a colon (:). If this column is unfilled, there is no dot.

D. ACTUAL NOTATED ACCIDENTALS [**Column 19**]

Although all pitches are given explicitly in Columns 1–4, accidentals are signalled by a flag in Column 19. The codes are these:

#	sharp (♯)		X	sharp-sharp (♯♯)
n	natural (♮)		&	flat-flat (♭♭)
f	flat (♭)		S	natural-sharp (♮♯)
x	double sharp (**x**)		F	natural-flat (♮♭)

E. TIME MODIFICATION [**Columns 20–22**]

Two digits, separated by a colon (:), are used to indicate unusual durational relationships. For standard cases, such as triplets (3 : 2), the colon and the second digit are usually omitted. The numbers 10–35 are represented by the letters A–Z.

F. STEM DIRECTION AND STAFF ASSIGNMENT [**Columns 23–24**]

Stem direction is indicated explicitly in Column 23 for every note with the following codes:

d	down
u	up
" "	no stem

For parts requiring one staff, Column 24 is left blank. For music on the grand staff, Column 24 indicates on which of the two staves a note should be placed. Column 25 is left blank.

G. BEAM CODES [**Columns 26–31**]

Codes for as many as six concurrent beams (through the 256th-note level) can be represented by concatenating the follow codes:

[	start beam
=	continue beam
]	end beam
/	forward hook
\	backward hook

Codes for eighth-note beams are placed in Column 26, those for sixteenth-note beams in Column 27, and so forth.

H. ADDITIONAL NOTATIONS [**Columns 32–43**]

Discrepancies between content originating with a composer and that provided by an editor or encoder can be differentiated in the encoding scheme through the use of a wide range of codes in Columns 32–43. The character & in any of these columns, followed by a digit (1..9, A..Z), is used to indicate a specified editorial level.[12] All codes to the left of the first & belong to the lowest (least edited) editorial level.

The following codes, which have been chosen for representing common elements of musical notation for Western music from the sixteenth through the nineteenth centuries, are somewhat arbitrary, since the encoding scheme is not complete and may be augmented and/or altered to meet the special requirements of the music being encoded.

1. Ties, Slurs, and Tuplets. The following codes extend the representation of ties, slurs, and tuplets:

–	tie	)	close slur1
(	open slur1	[	open slur2

---

12. Levels may be defined by the user to suit the circumstances. A note that is definitely wrong in the source represents a level approaching certainty, while a slur that ends between two notes and can be interpreted as having two possible lengths might occupy a different editorial category.

]	close slur2	z	open slur4
{	open slur3	x	close slur4
}	close slur3	*	start tuplet
		!	stop tuplet

The designations `slur1`, `slur2`, `slur3`, and `slur4` are arbitrary. It is possible for slurs to overlap timewise in a part (e.g., in piano music) and therefore necessary to have several open-slur, close-slur pairs available. Tuple numbers are not printed unless specified by an asterisk (*) in the first record of the group and an exclamation point (!) in the last record of the group.

2. Ornaments. The following codes are used for ornaments:

t	tr	~	wavy line (trill)
r	turn	c	continue wavy line
k	delayed turn	M	mordent
w	shake	j	slide

3. Technical Indications. Performance information for string and keyboard instruments is represented as follows:

v	up bow
n	down bow
o	harmonic
0	open string
Q	thumb position
1,2,3,4,5	fingering
:	next fingering is a substitution

4. Articulations and Accents. The following codes are used for articulations and accents:

A	vertical accent up (∧)
V	vertical accent down (∨)
>	horizontal accent (>)
.	staccato (·)
_	tenuto or marcato (–)
=	detached legato (÷)
i	spiccato (ǀ)
,	breath mark (')

Accidentals on ornaments, for which the codes are listed below, must follow directly after the ornament code:

s	sharp
ss	double sharp
h	natural
b	flat
bb	double flat
u	next accidental is below rather than above ornament

5. Other Indications and Codes.

S	arpeggiate (chords)	Z	*sfz*	
F	upright fermata	Zp	*sfp*	
E	inverted fermata	R	*rfz*	
p	piano (*p*, *pp*, etc.)	^	editorial accidental written above note	
f	forte (*f*, *ff*, *fp*, etc.)	+	cautionary/written out accidental	
m	mezzo (*mp*, *mf*)			

I. TEXT UNDERLAY [Columns 44–80]

In Columns 44–80 multiple lines of text may be set off by the verticule (|) character. For the carol "Deck the Halls with Boughs of Holly," which has three verses, the text for the first note would be indicated as Deck|See|Fast.

J. INFORMATION NOT REPRESENTED

It is instructive to point out the types of information not represented in the regular note or rest record.

In the case of ties and slurs, nothing is specified about their orientation (tips up vs. tips down) or their placement. The arrangement of basic beam components is fully described, but nothing is said about the orientation of the beam (length of stems, etc.). No provision is made for describing repeated notes or repeated note pairs under beams (repeaters).

No information concerning the horizontal distance between successive notes is given; in fact, no horizontal information of any kind is specified. The position of a note within a measure is implied by its position in the file, i.e., by the sum of previous durations within the measure. There is also no explicit information on vertical placement. The vertical position of noteheads relative to staff lines can be inferred from note pitch and from the controlling clef (specified earlier in a $-type record), but the vertical position of rests is completely unspecified.

The position of ornaments, technical indications, articulations and accents, and other indications and codes attached to notes is also unspecified.

All graphical information described in preceding sections can be represented in *MuseData* using print suggestion records, which are discussed in a later section. In most cases, however, this is not necessary. Intelligent software can deduce this type of information correctly most of the time. Print suggestions are generally reserved for those cases where software might not place graphical elements correctly.

The representation of ornaments and other symbols attached to notes (codes for Columns 32 to 43) is very incomplete at the present time. 53 character codes have been defined thus far, leaving room for 42 additional definitions. Rather than try to assign these codes now, we have chosen to leave them available for future uses.

Other than specifying basic pitch and duration, regular note records contain no specific sound information. Dynamics (*ff*, *pp*, etc.) are encoded but not quantified. Ornaments are specified, but their execution is not. Articulation information is present in the form of slurs, dots, etc., but no quantitative information is given. *MuseData* does provide a means for including specific information for sound realization, but this information takes the form of suggestions and is not considered part of the primary data (see section on *sound records* below).

27.2.3 Other Record Types

The creation of scores from parts inevitably involves the coordination of parts at every turn. Certain situations involve an additional level of interdependency. For example, in the figuration of a basso continuo part (represented by a stream of numbers that represent possible harmonic realizations), each figure relates to a particular note but not necessarily in a 1:1 manner. One harmony may extend over several notes; several harmonies may occur in conjunction with one note; some tones within the realization may be sustained while others are changed, and so forth. A similar degree of complexity can pertain to parts that are sometimes combined and sometimes divided, e.g., the *Oboe I/Oboe II* situations discussed in preceding sections.

A. Basso Continuo Figuration [f]

The *MuseData* system supports the representation of numerals and other cyphers for basso continuo figuration with a record that uses the control key f. The format is as follows:

Column 1:	f
Column 2:	number of figure fields
Columns 3–5:	blanks
Columns 6–8:	figure division pointer advancement

Figures take their position from the first regular note that follows the figure record(s). In the case where the figures change during the duration of a note, the advancing parameter (Columns 6–8) is used to indicate the elapsed time between changes. In the case where a figure appears after a note has sounded, the blank space is used as a place holder to advance the figure division pointer.

Columns 9–12:	blanks
Columns 13–15:	footnote and level information
	Column 13: footnote flag (" " = none)
	Column 14: level number (optional)
	Column 15: blank
Column 16:	blank
Columns 17–:	figure fields

The figure fields are set off by one or more blanks. Figure numbers may extend from 1 to 19. They may be prefixed by the characters #, n, f, and x. They may be followed by the suffixes #, n, f, +, \, and x. The #, n, f, and x signs may stand alone as figures. A b indicates a blank figure. This is used as a place holder in a list and also to start a continuation line with no figure. The first figure field is for the top of the figure list. For example, in the figure list #4, the 6 would be represented in the first field.

The figures, signs, and modifiers are these:

1..19	figure numbers
#	sharp
n	natural
f	flat
x	double sharp
+	augment (used with figure nos. 2, 4, and 5)
\	augment (used with figure nos. 6 and 7)
-	short line in
_	long line from previous figure
b	blank

B. COMBINED/DIVIDED PARTS [b, i]

In order to represent two musical parts simultaneously on one staff, and also to represent music on the grand staff (keyboard music) in a single data file (i.e., as a single musical part), it is necessary for the representation to have a *backup command*. This command essentially subtracts a specified number of divisions from the division counter in a measure, thereby allowing simultaneous musical tracks to be represented.

If it is possible to decrease the division counter by means of the backup command, then we must also have a means for increasing it without printing a rest. This is accommodated with an *invisible rest* record type. The control keys for these commands are b and i respectively. The format is as follows:

Columns 1–5:	back	backspace
	irest	forward space (invisible rest)
Columns 6–8:	duration to skip forward or back up	
Columns 9–12:	blanks	
Columns 13–15:	footnote and level information	
	Column 13:	footnote flag (" " = none)
	Column 14:	level number (optional)
	Column 15:	blank
Column 16:	blank	
Column 17:	pass number (optional)[13]	

The final length of a measure (in divisions) is given by the furthest extent of the division counter. It is good encoding practice to advance the division counter to the end of the measure, if it is not already there when the final note in the measure has been encoded.[14]

C. MEASURE LINES [m]

Measure breaks (also measure lines or bar lines) have their own record type in *MuseData*. The control key is m, and the format is as follows:

Column 1:	m	
Columns 2–7:	easure	regular bar line
	dotted	dotted bar line
	double	(light) double bar line

---

13. This feature can be used to express parallel action in the same part (e.g., keyboard music).

14. Our own software requires this.

`heavy1`	heavy bar line
`heavy2`	light-heavy double bar
`heavy3`	heavy-light double bar
`heavy4`	heavy-heavy double bar

Column 8:	empty
Columns 9–12:	optional bar number for this bar (left justified)
Columns 13–15:	footnote and level information
	Column 13: footnote flag (" " = none)
	Column 14: level number (optional)
	Column 15: blank
Column 16:	blank
Columns 17–80:	flags:

*	non-controlling bar line
~	continue wavy line trill across bar line
A	*segno* sign at bar
F	fermata sign over bar line
E	fermata sign under bar line
`start-end`*n*	start ending *n*
`stop-end`*n*	stop ending *n*
`disc-end`*n*	discontinue ending *n* line
: |	repeat backward
| :	repeat forward

Bar lines are divided into two types—controlling and non-controlling. These are defined as follows:

- *Controlling bar lines* are lines which run vertically through an entire score. They mark the beginning of a new global measure.

- *Non-controlling bar lines* need not have this property. Non-controlling bar lines may not serve for line breaks or page breaks.

The designation of a bar line as non-controlling is to some extent left to the discretion of the encoder.[15]

---

15. A double bar in the middle of a normal measure could be controlling or non-controlling. However, in a case such as the minuet from Mozart's opera *Don Giovanni*, where diverse parts in the score use three different meters simultaneously, the non-aligned bar lines must be designated as non-controlling.

D. GENERALIZED MUSICAL DIRECTIONS [*]

Musical directions which are not attached to specific notes—such things as rehearsal numbers, text instructions, crescendos and diminuendos, dynamics, piano pedal indications, and octave transpositions—have their own record type. The control key is *, and the format is as follows:

Column   1:   *
Columns 2–5:   blank
Columns 6–8:   optional forward offset, measured in units of duration and right justified in the field. Use of this field allows the encoder to place a musical direction at a division that does not otherwise contain a musical record.
Columns 9–12:   blank
Columns 13–15:   footnote and level information
                     Column 13:   footnote flag (" " = none)
                     Column 14:   level number (optional)
                     Column 15:   track number (necessary if there are two or more wedges, sets of dashes, 8va transpositions, etc.)
Column 16:   blank
Columns 17–18:   type of direction [see explanation after Column 25]
Column 19:   location flag (optional)
                     " " indication below line
                     +   indication above line (may be used by types A, B, C, D, E, F, G, H)
Column 20:   blank
Columns 21–23:   numerical parameter (optional)
                     for types E and F: wedge spread[16]
                     for types U and V: shift size (when not 8va)
                     for types A, B, C, D, G: optional font designator[17]
Column 24:   staff number[18] (" " = 1)
Columns 25–:   ASCII word string (used in A, B, C, D, and G)

---

16. Wedge spread is measured in tenths of staff line space. 10 units = space between two staff lines.

17. The inclusion of a font designator in this record actually runs counter to the philosophy of the representation. We no longer use this feature, but use a print suggestion record instead to specify a font. For the moment, however, several hundred existing data files still include this feature.

18. Used in the case of music represented on more than one staff.

EXAMPLE 1.   cresc. - - - - - - - - *ff*
        Starting record: DH   cresc.
        Ending record: JG   ff

EXAMPLE 2.   *f* <decreasing wedge> *p*
        Starting record: GE   15   f
        Ending record: FG   0   p

EXAMPLE 3.   <increasing wedge> *p*
        Starting record: E   0
        Ending record: FG   15   p

Direction types (Columns 17–18) are specified by a one- or two-letter code. Currently used direction types are these:

1. rehearsal numbers/letters
    A   *segno* sign
2. directions expressed in words
    B   right justified ASCII string
    C   centered ASCII string
    D   left justified ASCII string (may be combined with types E, F, G, H, J)
3. wedges
    E   begin wedge
    F   end wedge (may be combined with types B, C, D, G)
4. letter dynamics
    G   letter dynamics (given as ASCII string; may be combined with types B, C, D, E, F, H, J)
5. dashes (- - - - -)
    H   begin dashes (after words)
    J   end dashes (may be combined with types B, C, D, G)
6. pedal (pianoforte)
    P   begin pedal [*Ped.*]
    Q   release pedal [*]
7. octave shifts (in the printing process)
    U   shift notes up (usually by *8va*)[19]
    V   shift notes down (usually by *8va*)[20]
    W   stop octave shift

---

19. Pitches, usually in the bass clef, that are difficult to notate because they are very low are shifted up.

20. Pitches, usually in the treble clef, that are difficult to notate because they are very high are shifted down.

E. MIXED FONTS AND TEXT DIACRITICAL MARKS

In the verbal markings of a musical score or part it is occasionally necessary to change a font in the middle of an ASCII string. For example, the direction *più f* might call for the word più to be in italics and the sign *f* to be the *forte* character from the music font.[21]

This example also illustrates the necessity of being able to represent accents and other diacritical marks over letters. Since the ASCII character set is reliable only for seven-bit values in the range of 32 to 127, we must use an escape sequence to represent these other characters. We use the backslash character to initiate the sequence. This is followed by a number, and then by the letter being affected. The table below shows the escape sequences for various letter/diacritical mark combinations. All combinations except \2s also apply to capital letters.

\1n = ñ	\2c = ç	\4a = å	\5s = š
\1o = õ	\2o = ø		
	\2s = ß		
\3a = ä	\7a = á	\8a = à	\9a = â
\3e = ë	\7e = é	\8e = è	\9e = ê
\3i = ï	\7i = í	\8i = ì	\9i = î
\3o = ö	\7o = ó	\8o = ò	\9o = ô
\3u = ü	\7u = ú	\8u = ù	

Figure 27.4 Escape codes for diacritical marks.

Because it is sometimes hard to remember whether the number or the letter comes first after the back-slash escape character (\), we have defined the sequences both ways: \1n = \n1; \1o = \o1; \2s = \s2; etc. The back-slash character itself is represented by two back-slashes (\\).

---

21. We indicate a font change in a string with an exclamation mark, followed by a number. By convention, the number 1 is reserved for the music font. In this case the ASCII string would read pi\8u !1f.

F. COMMENTS [@, &]

There are two ways to include comments in a *MuseData* file. They are (1) with a single line comment, initiated by the control key @, or (2) with the comment toggle switch, indicated by the control key &.

G. RECORD LENGTH EXTENDER [a]

Although the normal maximum length of a *MuseData* record is 80 columns, if more columns are needed, these may be added with a *continuation record*, whose control key is a. This means to append the current line to the previous line.

H. THE END-OF-FILE RECORD [/]

The end of musical data and the end of a file are specified by an *end-type record*, whose control key is /. The format is as follows:

Column 1:	/	
Columns 2–5:	FINE	end of musical data
	END	end of file

Following the end of music data (i.e., the /FINE record), it is possible to include footnote data. In the case where there is no footnote section, the /FINE record may be omitted.

I. PRINT SUGGESTION RECORDS [P]

Suggestions for printing that may be ignored by the user without jeopardizing the logical coherence of the music are called *print suggestion records*. Print suggestions concern such matters as positioning of beams and slurs, orientation of ties, local positioning of notes to avoid collisions with other objects, and other matters requiring prioritization or accommodation in a particular graphic context. The control key is P and the various formats are explained below.

Column 1:   P

A print suggestion record can follow any record that contributes to the printed output of the music. This includes musical directions, bar lines, regular notes and rests, extra notes in a regular chord, grace notes and cue notes, extra grace/cue notes in a chord, and figured harmony.

Print suggestions use a multiple-field system. Each field is introduced by a capital C, followed immediately by a number and a colon, e.g., C8: or C23:. The data following this designation (all columns up to the next field or to the end of the record) will apply to the item in the specified column of the previous (non-sound) record.[22] A print suggestion which has a code C0: is a general suggestion and is not related to any specific column in a previous record.

At the present time, we can offer print suggestions in the following situations:

1. Position of slurs

    Field designator: C32: to C43: (depends on location of the slur)

    Data elements: o   place slur over the note in question

                      u   place slur under the note in question

These suggestions are needed only when the standard algorithms fail to place the slur properly, as sometimes happens with multiple parts on a staff or with double stops in the strings.

2. Orientation of ties

    Field designator: C32: to C43: (depends on location of the tie)

    Data elements: o   overhand tie (tips down)

                      u   underhand tie (tips up)

These suggestions are needed only when the standard algorithms fail to place the tie properly, as sometime happens with multiple parts on a staff or with double stops in the strings.

3. Suggestions modifying the printing of note, rest and figure objects

    Field designator: C1:

    Data elements: x$<n>$ shift default x position[23]

                                  $n > 0$: to the right

                                  $n < 0$: to the left

                    y$<n>$ shift default y position

                                  $n > 0$: down

                                  $n < 0$: up

22. For example, if the previous record were a note, and there were a slur starting on that note indicated by a left parenthesis (( ) in Column 33 of that record, then C33: would start a field containing one or more suggestions on how that slur should be printed.

23. All units in this section are calibrated in tenths of the interline distance.

X<*n*>	*x* position relative to default position
Y<*n*>	*y* position relative to top staff line
p<*n*>	printout modifier

> *n* = 0: (default)
> Suggestions for not printing the note:
> > *n* = 1: leave space, do not print object
> > *n* = 2: leave space, print a dot
>
> Suggestions extending note length:
> > *n* = 3: print object, no dot
> > *n* = 4: print object, add extension dot
> > *n* = 5: double note length, no dot
> > *n* = 6: double note length, print dot
> > *n* = 7: quadruple note length, no dot

4. Suggestions for location of notations attached to notes

Field designator: C32: to C43: (depends on column location of the notation)

Data elements:

x<*n*>	shift default *x* position
	n > 0: to the right
	n < 0: to the left
y<*n*>	shift default *y* position
	n > 0: down
	n < 0: up
X<*n*>	*x* position relative to note
Y<*n*>	*y* position relative to note
a	place notation above note (i.e., override default)
b	place notation below note (i.e., override default)

5. Suggestions for representing beamed notes with repeaters

Field designator: C26: or C27:

Data elements:

a	use repeater for next beam only
A	use repeaters for all beams which follow
b	return to normal beaming (used to cancel A)

Print suggestions for beams normally precede the beginning of beams. If the field designator is C26:, this indicates that the maximum use of repeaters is desired; if the field designator is C27:, then the top beam should not be represented as a repeater.

6. Suggestions for musical directions

Field designator: C17: or C18: (depends on location of the musical direction)

Data elements: f<*n*>   font number, for musical direction types A, B, C, D, G

The use of this suggestion will remove the need to place the font number in the numerical parameter field (Columns 21–23) of the musical direction, thus freeing this field for the exclusive use of wedges and transpositions.

x<*n*>	shift default *x* position
	n > 0: right →
	n < 0: left ←
y<*n*>	shift default *y* position
	n > 0: down
	n < 0: up
X<*n*>	*x* position relative to default position
Y<*n*>	*y* position relative to top staff line

7. General print suggestions
   Field designator: C0:
   Suggestion codes: p<*n*>   minimum distance between notes (expressed as percentage of the default)

   q<*n*>   duration which is assigned the minimum distance
          0   recompute default from this point onward
          1   whole notes
         . . .
          8   eighth notes
        16   sixteenth notes, etc.

   s<*n*>   space between grand staffs measured in multiples of staff lines times 10; e.g., 100 = 10 staff lines

   t<*n*>   global tuplet placement
        n = 0: use default
        n = 1: place tuplets near note heads
        n = 2: place tuplets near note stems (beams)
        n = 3: place all tuplets above notes
        n = 4: place all tuplets below notes

J. Sound Records [S]

Sound records are used for communicating suggestions for compiling sound (MIDI) files. The control key is S and the various formats are explained below.

Column 1:   S

A sound record can follow any record that produces a sound or influences time in some way. This includes regular notes and rests, extra notes in a regular chord, grace notes and cue notes, extra grace/cue notes in a chord, and figured harmony.

Sound information can be given for a variety of attributes connected with a note. Since sound directions may apply to a wide variety of musical attributes, e.g., the attack and dynamic envelope of a note, the time of attack and length of a note (or rest), and directions for performing ornaments, it makes sense to use a multiple-field system, similar to the one used for print suggestions.

To illustrate this with an example, suppose in the previous note record there were a trill indicated by a t in Column 33. In this case we would use C33: in a sound record to introduce information on how that trill should be executed in a sound file. Of course, each ornament or pitch or duration will have a different set of needs regarding its sound specification.

At the present time, sound information can be provided for the following situations:

1. Onset and length of grace notes
   Field designator: C1:
   Data elements: p   steal time from previous note
                       f   steal time from following note (default)
                       m   don't steal time; make time (free cadenzas, etc.)
                       t<n>
                                 CASE 1: stealing time
                                     where n = percentage (0 to 100) of time to
                                     steal for this note.
                                 CASE 2: making time
                                     where n = number of real-time divisions for
                                     this note.

2. Onset and length of trills, turns, shakes, and wavy lines
   Field designator: C32: to C43: (depends on where the ornament is indicated)
   Data elements: u   start on upper note (default)
                       m   start on main note
                       w   whole-step trill (default)
                       h   half-step trill
                       j   unison trill
                       e   include a two-note turn at the end of the trill
                                 (whole step)
                       f   include a two-note turn at the end of the trill
                                 (half step)
                       a   accelerate trill slightly
                       n<n>   number of beats (minimum = 2, default = 4)
                       s<n>   percentage point for landing on second beat of
                                 trill (default = 25)

t<*n*>   percentage point for landing on last beat of trill
(default = 75)

EXAMPLE: The default trill uwn4s25t75 is a four-note trill starting on the upper whole step and having four equal beats.

3. Onset and length of (inverted) mordents

Field designator:	C32: to C43: (depends on where the ornament is indicated)
Data elements:	m	start on main note (default)
	b	start on note below main note
	w	whole-step mordent (default)
	h	half-step mordent
	a	accelerate mordent slightly
	n<*n*>	number of beats (minimum = 2, default = 3)
	s<*n*>	percentage point for landing on second beat of mordent (default = 12)
	t<*n*>	percentage point for landing on last beat of mordent (default = 24)

EXAMPLE: The default mordent mwn3s12t24 is a three-note snap starting on the main note and going down a whole step.

4. Alternating sound (e.g., string *pizzicato*)

Field designator:	C2: (to distinguish it from grace note information)
Data elements:	a	*pizzicato* for this note (this designation must be contained in a sound record which follows directly after the note in question)
	A	*pizzicato* for this note and every regular note that follows in the file, until cancelled
	b	*arco* (used to cancel A)

5. *Da capo* direction, *segno* sign, and implied repeat (| :)

| Field designator: | C0:[24] |
| Data elements: | d | *da capo* to beginning of movement or to *segno* sign. Normally this record would directly precede the /END or /FINE record |

---

24. A zero coupled with C indicates that this does not relate to a column number.

S<*n*>   *segno* sign: *da capo* to this point in the file
                              n = divisions per quarter (information for sound
                              and MIDI generating programs)

|>   implied forward repeat dots (usually follows a
       bar line)

6. *Fine* signs (written or implied)
     Field designator: C8:
     Data elements: F<*n*>   *Fine* sign (written or implied)

This record should follow any final note or rest in a movement which has a *da capo* direction. The variable represented by the sign *n* indicates the actual duration of the final note or rest. This is needed because some *fine*s are indicated only by a fermata, and these can occur simultaneously over notes of different durations in different parts! In the case where there is more than one active track in the measure with the *Fine* (i.e., there is a backspace command in the measure), all final notes must have their durations specified by a *Fine* sound record. In the case of chords, the *Fine* sound record should follow the last chord tone record.

7. Tempo changes
     Field designator: C0:
     Data elements: W<*n*>   new tempo in quarter notes per minute. If
                                       parameter <*n*> = 0, the sound-generating
                                       programs must ask the user for a value at the
                                       time of compiling a sound (MIDI) file.

8. Changes in dynamics
     Field designator: C0:
     Data elements: V<*n*>   dynamic level (velocity) measured as a
                                       percentage of the default (which is *forte*).[25]

27.3   Examples

27.3.1   The Mozart Trio

The five *MuseData* files which comprise the encoding of the first 12 bars of the second trio from Mozart's Clarinet Quintet, K. 581, are displayed in Examples 27.1b-f.

---

25. Normally our programs to construct MIDI performance files assign a flat value of 90 to the velocity byte. Occasionally we may want to change this value either to bring out a part or to suppress a part.

Note that each of these files belongs to two groups: sound and score. Note also that the clarinet part is encoded at notated pitch, not sounding pitch. The fact that the part is a transposing part is indicated in the X: field of the first $-type record. A value of −11 means that all pitches in this part must be transposed down a minor third when compiling sound files.

Example 27.1a The Mozart trio.

```
04/16/93 E. Correia              C6      6       q    d            )
WK#:581        MV#:3c            G5      3       e    d    [       (
Breitkopf & Härtel, Vol. 13     E5      3       e    d    ]
Clarinet Quintet                measure 6
Trio II                         D5      3       e  n d    [       +
Clarinet in A                   F5      3       e    d    ]
1 0                             A5      6       q    d            )
Group memberships: sound, score rest    6       q
sound: part 1 of 5             measure 7
score: part 1 of 5             rest    18
$   K:0   Q:6   T:3/4  X:-11 C:4 measure 8
C5      3       e    d    [    (&0p rest   6       q
E5      3       e    d    ]     rest    6       q
measure 1                       D4      2       e  3 u    [       (*
G5      3       e    d    [     A3      2       e  3 u    =
E5      3       e    d    ]     F3      2       e  3 u    ]       !
C6      6       q    d         ) measure 9
G5      3       e    d    [    ( A3     3       e    u    [       )
E5      3       e    d    ]     D4      3       e    u    =       .
measure 2                       F4      3       e    u    =       .
D5      3       e    d    [     A4      3       e    u    =
F5      3       e    d    ]
A5      6       q    d         ) D5     3       e    u    =       .
F5      3       e    d    [    ( F5     3       e    u    ]       .
D5      3       e    d    ]     measure 10
measure 3                       A5      3       e    d    [       (
C5      3       e    d    [     G5      3       e    d    =
B4      3       e    d    =     F5      3       e    d    =
E5      3       e    d    =     E5      3       e    d    =
D5      3       e    d    =     F5      3       e    d    =
G5      3       e    d    =     D5      3       e    d    ]       )
F5      3       e    d    ]    ) measure 11
measure 4                       C5      12      h    d            (
D#5     6       q  # d         ( E5     3       e    d    [
E5      6       q    d         ) D5     3       e    d    ]       )
C5      3       e    d    [    ( measure 12
E5      3       e    d    ]     C5      6       q    d
measure 5                       rest    6       q
G5      3       e    d    [     mheavy4         :||:
E5      3       e    d    ]    /END
```

Example 27.1b *MuseData*: Mozart Clarinet Quintet (trio section), up to double bar. First part (clarinet) of five; the string parts are shown below. All encoded attributes (here pitch name, chromatic inflection, octave number, duration in time, duration name, stem direction, beam and slur information, and articulation) are indicated explicitly for each event.

```
04/16/93 E. Correia              $   K:3   Q:2   T:3/4   C:4
WK#:581        MV#:3c            rest    2       q
Breitkopf & Härtel, Vol. 13     measure 1
Clarinet Quintet                rest    2       q
Trio II                         A4      2       q    u            p
Violino I                       A4      2       q    u
1 0                             measure 2
Group memberships: sound, score rest    2       q
sound: part 2 of 5             A4      2       q    u
score: part 2 of 5             A4      2       q    u
```

```
measure 3                        A#4     1         e #  d    ]
rest    2         q               measure 8
G#4     2         q    u          B4      1         e    d    [
G#4     2         q    u          D5      1         e    d    ]
measure 4                         F#5     2         q    d              )
rest    2         q               rest    2         q
A4      2         q    u          measure 9
A4      2         q    u          rest    6
measure 5                         measure 10
rest    2         q               rest    6
A4      2         q    u          measure 11
A4      2         q    u          C#4     1         e    u    [         (
measure 6                         E4      1         e    u    =
F#4     2         q    u          C#4     1         e    u    =
rest    2         q               E4      1         e    u    =
C#5     1         e    d    [    ( D4     1         e    u    =
A#4     1         e #  d    ]      E4      1         e    u    ]         )
measure 7                         measure 12
B4      1         e    d    [      C#4     2         q    u
D5      1         e    d    ]      rest    2         q
F#5     2         q    d        )  mheavy4           :||:
C#5     1         e    d    [    ( /END
```

Example 27.1c *MuseData*: First violin part from the Mozart Clarinet Quintet.

```
04/16/93 E. Correia              C#4     2         q    u
WK#:581        MV#:3c            measure 5
Breitkopf & Härtel, Vol. 13     rest    2         q
Clarinet Quintet                 E4      2         q    u
Trio II                          E4      2         q    u
Violino II                       measure 6
1 0                              D4      2         q    u
Group memberships: sound, score  rest    2         q
sound: part 3 of 5               G4      2         q n  u              (
score: part 3 of 5               measure 7
$  K:3   Q:2   T:3/4   C:4       F#4     4         h    u
rest    2         q               G4      2         q n  u
measure 1                        measure 8
rest    2         q               F#4     4         h    u              )
E4      2         q    u        p rest    2         q
E4      2         q    u          measure 9
measure 2                        rest    6
rest    2         q               measure 10
F#4     2         q    u          rest    6
F#4     2         q    u          measure 11
measure 3                        A3      4         h    u              (
rest    2         q               G#3     2         q #  u              )+
D4      2         q    u          measure 12
D4      2         q    u          A3      2         q    u
measure 4                        rest    2         q
rest    2         q               mheavy4           :||:
C#4     2         q    u          /END
```

Example 27.1d *MuseData*: Second violin part from the Mozart Clarinet Quintet.

```
04/16/93 E. Correia              A3      2         q    u
WK#:581        MV#:3c            measure 5
Breitkopf & H\3artel, vol. 13    rest    2         q
Clarinet Quintet                 C#4     2         q    d
Trio II                          C#4     2         q    d
Viola                            measure 6
1 0                              B3      2         q    u
Group memberships: sound, score  rest    2         q
sound: part 4 of 5               E4      2         q    d         (
score: part 4 of 5               measure 7
$  K:3   Q:2   T:3/4   C:13      D4      4         h    d
rest    2         q              E4      2         q    d
measure 1                        measure 8
rest    2         q              D4      4         h    d         )
C#4     2         q    d    p    rest    2         q
C#4     2         q    d         measure 9
measure 2                        rest    6
rest    2         q              measure 10
B3      2         q    u         rest    6
B3      2         q    u         measure 11
measure 3                        E3      6-        h.   u         -
rest    2         q              measure 12
B3      2         q    u         E3      2         q    u
B3      2         q    u         rest    2         q
measure 4                        mheavy4           :||:
rest    2         q              /END
A3      2         q    u
```

Example 27.1e *MuseData*: Viola part from the Mozart Clarinet Quintet.

```
04/16/93 E. Correia              rest    2         q
WK#:581        MV#:3c            measure 5
Breitkopf & H\3artel, Vol. 13    C#3     2         q    u
Clarinet Quintet                 rest    2         q
Trio II                          rest    2         q
Violoncello                      measure 6
1 0                              D3      2         q    d
Group memberships: sound, score  rest    2         q
sound: part 5 of 5               rest    2         q
score: part 5 of 5               measure 7
$  K:3   Q:2   T:3/4   C:22      rest    6
rest    2         q              measure 8
measure 1                        rest    6
A3      2         q    d    p    measure 9
rest    2         q              rest    6
rest    2         q              measure 10
measure 2                        rest    6
D3      2         q    d         measure 11
rest    2         q              E2      2         q    u         (.
rest    2         q              E2      2         q    u         .
measure 3                        E2      2         q    u         ).
E3      2         q    d         measure 12
rest    2         q              A2      2         q    u
rest    2         q              rest    2         q
measure 4                        mheavy4           :||:
F#3     2         q    d         /END
rest    2         q
```

Example 27.1f *MuseData*: Violoncello part from the Mozart Clarinet Quintet.

27.3.2 The Mozart Piano Sonata

The second example (Example 27.2b), an encoding of the Mozart piano example, illustrates several features of the *MuseData* representation. The music is encoded into one file with two staves. The backup command (back) is used to encode simultaneous musical tracks. Print suggestion records are used to shift the orientation of the slurs in the lower staff; the program default placed them under rather than over the notes. The chord arpeggiation is encoded, but our printing software cannot yet typeset this symbol.

Example 27.2a The Mozart piano sonata.

```
06/23/94 W. Hewlett              C#6      1         s      d1 ]]        .
WK#:331        MV#:3             back     8
Breitkopf & H\3artel            gA2      4         t      u2 [[[       [
Piano Sonata                    P    C33:o
                                gC#3     4         t      u2 ===
1 0                             gE3      4         t      u2 ]]]
Group memberships: sound, score A3       2         e      d2 [         ]
sound: part 1 of 1              A3       2         e      d2 =
score: part 1 of 1             A3       2         e      d2 =
&                               A3       2         e      d2 ]
Initial conversion from stage 1 to measure 3
stage 2                         D6       8         h      d1
&                                A5      8         h      d1
$   K:3  Q:4  T:2/4  C1:4  C2:22 F#5     8         h      d1
C#6      8         h      u1      S  back     8
back     8                  1       gD2      4         t      u2 [[[       [
A5       4         q      d1      P    C33:o
E5       4         q      d1      gF#2     4         t      u2 ===
C#5      4         q      d1      gA2      4         t      u2 ]]]
back     4                       D3       2         e      d2 [         ]
gA2      4         t      u2 [[[  [ D3       2         e      d2 =
P    C33:o                       D3       2         e      d2 =
gC#3     4         t      u2 ===  D3       2         e      d2 ]
gE3      4         t      u2 ]]]  measure 4
A3       2         e      d2 [    ] gD6      4         t      u1            (
A3       2         e      d2 =    C#6      2         e      d1 [           )
A3       2         e      d2 =    A5       2         e      d1
A3       2         e      d2 ]    E5       2         e      d1
measure 2                        gD6      4         t      u1            (
D6       1         s      d1 [[   ( C#6      2         e      d1 =         )
C#6      1         s      d1 ==   ) A5       2         e      d1
B5       1         s      d1 ==   . E5       2         e      d1
C#6      1         s      d1 ]]   . gD6      4         t      u1            (
D6       1         s      d1 [[   ( C#6      2         e      d1 =         )
C#6      1         s      d1 ==   ) A5       2         e      d1
B5       1         s      d1 ==   . E5       2         e      d1
```

```
gD6       4           t      u1              (
C#6       2           e      d1 ]            )
 A5       2           e      d1
 E5       2           e      d1
back      8
gA2       4           t      u2 [[[          [
P     C33:o
gC#3      4           t      u2 ===
gE3       4           t      u2 ]]]
A3        2           e      d2 [            ]
A3        2           e      d2 =
A3        2           e      d2 =
A3        2           e      d2 ]
measure 5
B5        6           q.     u1              (
```

```
E6        2           e      u1              )
back      8
G#5       8           h      d1
 E5       8           h      d1
back      8
gE2       4           t      u2 [[[          [
P     C33:o
gG#2      4           t      u2 ===
gB2       4           t      u2 ]]]
E3        2           e      d2 [            ]
E3        2           e      d2 =
E3        2           e      d2 =
E3        2           e      d2 ]
measure 6
/END
```

Example 27.2b *MuseData* input code for the Mozart piano sonata excerpt.

27.3.3 The Telemann Aria

The Telemann aria illustrates the handling of text underlay, the encoding of small size regular notes and cue notes, and the use of print suggestions. It also shows the degree to which musical typesetting can be done directly from the representation without further human intervention. The typeset example is not perfect, nor does it place simultaneous notes in exactly the same order as in the original, but it is a very good approximation of the original and would need only a small amount of manual editing to correct these minor defects. This example is encoded in two files: one (27.3b, interrupted for reasons of layout by the music, 27.3a) represents the vocal part and the other (27.3c) a reduction of the instrumental score on two staves.

```
06/24/94 W. Hewlett
WK#:           MV#:
Unknown
Telemann aria

1 0 T
Group memberships: sound, score
sound: part 1 of 2
score: part 1 of 2
$   K:2   Q:8   T:3/8   C:4
rest  12
measure 2
rest  12
measure 3
rest  12
measure 4
rest  12
measure 5
rest  12
measure 6
rest  12
```

Example 27.3a The Telemann aria.

```
measure 7
rest   12
measure 8
rest   12
measure 9
rest   12
measure 10
rest   12
measure 11
rest   12
measure 12
E5     8         q    d                   Lie-
A4     4         e    u                   be!
measure 13
rest   12
measure 14
rest   12
measure 15
C#5    3         s.   d    [[      (      Lie-
D5     1         t    d    =]\             -
E5     4         e    d    ]       )       -
```

```
A4       4        e    u                        be!
measure 16
rest   12
measure 17
rest   12
measure 18
D5       4        e    d    [         (         Was_
A4       4        e    d    ]         )         ‾
B4       4        e    d                        ist
measure 19
F#4      3        s.   u    [[        (         sch\o3-
G4       1        t    u    =]\                 -
A4       4        e    u    ]         )         -
D4       4        e    u                        ner
measure 20
F#5      4        e    d                        als
G5       2        s    d    [[        (         die_
F#5      2        s    d    ==                  ‾
E5       2        s    d    ==                  ‾
D5       2        s    d    ]]        )         ‾
measure 21
C#5      6        e.   d                        Lie-
B4       2        s    u    [/                  be,_
A4       4        e    u    ]                    ‾
measure 22
rest     4        e
D5       4        e    d                        was
D5       4        e    d                        schmeckt
measure 23
D5       8        q    d                        s\u3-
D5       4        e    d                        \s2er,
measure 24
rest     4        e
B4       4        e    d                        was
D5       4        e    d                        schmeckt
measure 25
E5      12-       q.   d              -         s\u3-
measure 26
E5      12-       q.   d              -         -
measure 27
E5      12-       q.   d              -         -
measure 28
E5       4        e    d                        -
D5       2        s    d    [[        (         \s2er_
C#5      2        s    d    ==                  ‾
B4       2        s    d    ==                  ‾
A4       2        s    d    ]]        )         ‾
measure 29
rest     4        e
G#4      4        e    u                        als
D5       4        e    d                        ein
measure 30
cD5      6        e    u              (
P      C33:o
cC#5     7        q    u              )
C#5     12        q.   d                        Ku\s2?
measure 31
D5       4        e    d    [         (         Was_
A4       4        e    d    ]         )         ‾
B4       4        e    d                        ist
measure 32
```

```
F#4      3          s.    u    [[              (        sch\o3-
G4       1          t     u    =]\                      -
A4       4          e     u    ]              )         -
D4       4          e     u                             ner,
measure 33
rest  12
measure 34
rest  12
measure 35
D5       4          e     d    [              (         was_
A4       4          e     d    ]              )         
B4       4          e     d                             schmeckt
measure
/END
```

Example 27.3b Telemann aria: *MuseData* input for vocal part.

```
06/24/94 W. Hewlett              F#5      4        e    u1 [
WK#:            MV#:             G5       2        s    u1 =[          (
Unknown                         F#5      2        s    u1 ==          )
Telemann aria                   E5       2        s    u1 ==          (
                                D5       2        s    u1 ]]          )
                                back  12
1 0                             A4       4        6    d1 [
Group memberships: sound, score A4       4        6    d1 =
sound: part 2 of 2             G4       2        5    d1 =[
score: part 2 of 2             F#4      2        5    d1 ]]
P   C0:s125                     back  12
$   K:2  Q:8  T:3/8  C1:4  C2:22 D4      4        6    u2 [
*               D  +     10b.    E4      4        6    u2 =
P   C17:y-7                      D4      4        6    u2 ]
*               B  +     10b. Viol.  back  12
D5       4          e    u1 [           (   D3   4        e    d2 [
A4       4          e    u1 =           )   C#3  4        e    d2 =
B4       4          e    u1 ]               D3   4        e    d2 ]
back  12                                measure 4
*               B        1Viola         C#5      3        s.   u1 [[         (t
P   C17:y-15                             D5       1        t    u1 =]\
D4       4          e    d1 [       [    E5       4        e    u1 =          )
F#4      4          e    d1 =       ]    A4       4        e    u1 ]
G4       4          e    d1 ]            back  12
back  12                                 E4       8        7    d1
*               C        2Bc (u.         C#4      4        6    d1
                        Cemb.)          back  12
P   C17:y-15                             A3       8        7    u2
rest  12                 2              back  8
measure 2                               A2       8        q    d2
F#4      3          s.    u1 [[     (    rest     4        e    2
G4       1          s     u1 =]\         measure 5
A4       4          e     u1 =      )    *               D  +     10b.
D4       4          e     u1 ]           P   C17:y-7
back  12                                 D5       4        e    u1 [          (
D4       8          q     d1             A4       4        e    u1 =          )
rest     4          e     1             B4       4        e    u1 ]
back  12                                 back  12
rest  12                 2              F#4      8        q    d1
measure 3                               G4       4        e    d1
*               C  +     1Viol.          back  12
P   C17:y-15                             rest  12                 2
```

```
measure 6
F#4    3      s.    u1 [[      (
G4     1      s     u1 =]\
A4     4      e     u1 =        )
D4     4      e     u1 ]
back   12
D4     8      q     d1
rest   4      e     1
back   12
rest   12            2
measure 7
*            D +    1Viol.u.Ob.
P  C17:y-8
E5     6      e.    u1 [
C#5    2      s     u1 =\
D5     4      e     u1 ]
back   12
B4     4      6     d1
E4     4      6     d1
E4     8      7     d1
back   8
A4     4      6     d1 [
G4     4      6     d1 ]
back   12
G3     4      e     d2 [
A3     4      e     d2 =
A2     4      e     d2 ]
measure 8
D5     8      q     u1
rest   4      e     1
back   12
D5     4      e     d1 [      (
P  C33:o
A4     4      e     d1 =       )
B4     4      e     d1 ]
back   12
F#4    8      q     d1
G4     4      e     d1
back   12
D4     8      7     d1
back   8
D3     8      q     d2
rest   4      e     2
measure 9
rest   8      q     1
rest   4      e     1
back   12
F#4    3      s.    d1 [[      (
P  C33:o
G4     1      t     d1 =]\
A4     4      e     d1 =        )
D4     4      e     d1 ]
back   12
D4     8      q     d1
rest   4      e     1
back   12
rest   12            2
measure 10
*            C +    1(a 2.)
B4     4      e     u1 [
G#4    6      e.    u1 =        t

A4     2      s     u1 ]\
back   12
F#4    4      6     d1
B3     4      6     d1
B3     8      7     d1
back   8
E4     4      6     d1 [
D4     4      6     d1 ]
back   12
D3     4      e     u2 [
E3     4      e     u2 =
E2     4      e     u2 ]
measure 11
A4     12     q.    u1
back   12
C#4    12     7.    d1
A3     12     7.    d1
back   12
A2     12     q.    u2
measure 12
rest   12            1
back   12
rest   12            2
measure 13
*            D +    1Ob.
P  C17:y-26
A5     4      e     u1 [        (
E5     4      e     u1 =        )
F#5    4      e     u1 ]
back   12
C#5    4      6     d1 [
A4     4      6     d1 =
A4     4      6     d1 ]
back   12
A3     4      e     u2 [
C#4    4      e     u2 =
D4     4      e     u2 ]
back   12
rest   12            2
measure 14
C#5    3      s.    u1 [[      (
D5     1      t     u1 =]\
E5     4      e     u1 =        )
A4     4      e     u1 ]
back   12
A4     8      7     d1
E4     8      7     d1
C#4    4      6     d1
back   12
A3     8      q     u2
rest   4      e     2
back   12
rest   12            2
measure 15
rest   12            1
back   12
rest   12            2
measure 16
*            D +    1Ob.
P  C17:y-26
A5     4      e     u1 [        (
```

```
E5      4       e    u1 =         )
F#5     4       e    u1 ]
back    12
C#5     8       7    d1
 E4     8       7    d1
rest    4       6    1
back    12
A3      8       q    u2
rest    4       e    2
back    12
rest    12           2
measure 17
C#5     3       s.   u1 [[        (
D5      1       t    u1 =]\
E5      4       e    u1 =         )
A4      4       e    u1 ]
back    12
A4      12      q.   d1
back    12
rest    12           2
measure 18
rest    12           1
back    12
A4      8       7    d1
 D4     8       7    d1
B4      4       6    d1
 G4     4       6    d1
 D4     4       6    d1
back    12
F#3     8       q    d2
G3      4       e    d2
measure 19
rest    12           1
back    12
A4      12      7.   d1
 F#4    12      7.   d1
 D4     12      7.   d1
back    12
D3      12      q.   d2
measure 20
F#5     4       e    u1 [
G5      2       s    u1 =[        (
F#5     2       s    u1 ==        )
E5      2       s    u1 ==_       (
D5      2       s    u1 ]]        )
back    12
A4      4       6    d1 [
A4      4       6    d1 =
G#4     4       6    d1 ]
back    12
D4      4       6    u2
E4      8       7    u2
back    12
D4      4       e    d2 [
C#4     4       e    d2 =
B3      4       e    d2 ]
measure 21
C#5     6       e.   u1 [
B4      2       s    u1 =\
A4      4       e    u1 ]
back    12

A4      12      7.   d1
back    12
E4      8       7    u2
C#4     4       6    u2
back    12
A3      8       q    d2
rest    4       e    2
measure 22
rest    8       q    1
rest    4       e    1
back    12
A4      8       7    d1
D4      8       7    d1
rest    4       6    1
back    12
F#3     8       q    d2
rest    4       e    2
measure 23
rest    4       e    1
B4      4       e    u1 [
G4      4       e    u1
A4      4       e    u1 ]
 F#4    4       e    u1
back    8
D4      4       6    d1 [
D4      4       6    d1 ]
back    12
rest    4       e    2
G3      4       e    d2 [
D3      4       e    d2 ]
measure 24
B4      8       q    u1
 G4     8       q    u1
rest    4       e    1
back    12
D4      8       7    d1
back    8
G2      8       q    u2
rest    4       e    2
measure 25
rest    4       e    1
C#5     4       e    u1 [
 A4     4       e    u1
B4      4       e    u1 ]
 G#4    4       e    u1
back    8
E4      4       6    d1 [
E4      4       6    d1 ]
back    12
rest    4       e    2
A3      4       e    d2 [
E3      4       e    d2 ]
measure 26
C#5     3       s.   u1 [[        (
 A4     3       s.   u1
D5      1       t    u1 =]\
 B4     1       t    u1
E5      4       e    u1 =         )
 C#5    4       e    u1
B4      4       e    u1 ]
 G#4    4       e    u1
```

```
back    12
E4      8       7    d1
E4      4       6    d1
back    12
A2      8       q    u2
rest    4       e    2
measure 27
C#5     3       s.   u1 [[      (
 A4     3       s.   u1
D5      1       t    u1 =]\
 B4     1       t    u1
E5      4       e    u1 =       )
 C#5    4       e    u1
B4      4       e    u1 ]
 G#4    4       e    u1
back    12
A3      8       7    d1
E4      4       6    d1
back    12
rest    8       q    2
rest    4       e    2
measure 28
C#5     8       q    u1
 A4     8       q    u1
rest    4       e    1
back    12
E4      8       7    d1
B4      4       6    d1
 F#4    4       6    d1
back    12
A2      8       q    u2
D3      4       e    d2
measure 29
rest    8       q    1
rest    4       e    1
back    12
G#4     12      7.   d1
 D4     12      7.   d1
back    12
B2      12      q.   u2
measure 30
E5      12      q.   u1
 A4     12      q.   u1
back    12
A4      12      7.   d1
 C#4    12      7.   d1
back    12
A2      12      q.   u2
measure 31
rest    12            1
back    12

F#4     8       q    d1
G4      4       e    d1
back    12 rest  12                2
measure 32
rest    12            1
back    12
D4      12      q.   d1
back    12
rest    12            2
measure 33
*               C +  1Ob.
P  C17:x-15y+10
*               D    1Viol.
P  C17:y-15
F#5     4       e    u1 [
 A4     4       e    u1
G5      2       s    u1 =[      (
 B4     2       s    u1
F#5     2       s    u1 ==      )
 A4     2       s    u1
E5      2       s    u1 ==      (
 G4     2       s    u1
D5      2       s    u1 ]]      )
 F#4    2       s    u1
back    12
D4      4       6    u2
B3      8       7    u2
back    12
D3      4       e    d2
G2      8       q    d2
measure 34
C#5     3       s.   u1 [[      (
D5      1       t    u1 =]\
E5      4       e    u1 =
A4      4       e    u1 ]       )
back    12
E4      12      q.   d1
back    12
E4      8       7    u2
C#4     4       6    u2
back    12
A2      12      q.   d2
measure 35
rest    12            1
back    12
F#4     8       q    d1
G4      4       e    d1
back    12
rest    12            2
measure
/END
```

Example 27.7c Telemann aria—*MuseData* input code for score reduction.

27.3.4 Examples Not Set

The principal question raised by the saltarello, which we have not set, is the treatment of bar numbers in first and second endings. Our view of bar numberings is that these are an editorial addition and are somewhat arbitrary. As a matter of convention, we begin numbering bars at the first full measure. Initial pickup beats fall into an unmarked measure 0. Bar numbers under a first ending are given the suffix a, under the second ending b, etc. If an ending has no termination, e.g., if it means "perform the second ending and then continue," no suffixes are used. Bar numbers for sub-movements of movements (e.g., trios of minuets) might or might not restart at "1". Ending numbers are encoded as 1, 2, 3, etc., but the software that prints the music might use other notations.

The unmeasured chant example and the Binchois *Magnificat* contain notations (ligatures and incipits) which are outside the current range of *MuseData* specifications.

27.4   Comments

Our system of representation is optimized for data entry and storage, not for user applications. The various elements of our system of representation have been tested with software we have developed for practicality and completeness. As part of this testing process, we have used *MuseData* code in its raw form as a source for producing performance materials and analytical searches; in translation we have used it for sound files and printing on other systems.[26]

---

26. Among the works for which scores and parts have been produced are seven major works (operas and oratorios) by Handel, two by Telemann, five cantatas by Bach, and the twelve concertos of Vivaldi's Op. 8. The typesetting system is well illustrated by the score for this set of concertos published by Dover Publications, Inc. (as ISBN 0-486-28638-X) in 1995.

Our software is written in a non-standard language called *Ibex*[27] in an environment called *TenX*.[28] All data is in ASCII characters and can be used on any platform. For sound applications, *Ibex* supports direct communication to Roland-compatible MIDI cards. The *Ibex* language and the *TenX* environment are ideal for our purposes in developing database applications in music. As with any specialized environment, however, there is a steep learning curve, which is more arduous than most casual users would care to attempt.[29] Our working solution to the need for data interchange is to write our own translation programs and to offer data in formats intended for diverse applications—MIDI for sound output, *SCORE* for printing, and *Kern* for analysis.[30] Other formats may be supported in the future.

From our experiences with translation programs we can report a 99% or better data interchange rate with *SCORE* parameter files, i.e., almost everything that we represent is represented in *SCORE*, so data loss occurs only at an insignificant and relatively inconsequential level. Our interchange rate to *Kern* is almost as good, but because *Kern* does not currently support printed output there is no way to see the result and compare it with the original source. Interchange to MIDI filters out an enormous amount of detailed print data and can distort quite simple things, such as rests, grace notes, and unisons between parts. Plans to offer data in the *DARMS* format have been postponed because early experiments in translating to *DARMS* revealed that despite

27. The original version of *Ibex* was developed by David Woodley Packard for use in the study of ancient languages and classics. *Ibex* is implemented on the *x*86 architecture. Programs written in *Ibex* can directly address the entire high memory of the machine.

28. The *TenX* research environment developed by Walter B. Hewlett is similar to Microsoft *Windows* in that it runs on top of DOS and implements 32-bit, protected mode, programming. The native display mode of *TenX* is character mode (not graphics, as is the case for MS *Windows*), but the *Ibex* language includes commands that switch to graphics mode and can display bitmaps of any size. At present, *TenX* supports video graphics up to 1200 x 1048 in size. A version running on *Windows NT* is currently under development.

29. Adding to this problem is a paucity of good documentation for both *Ibex* and *TenX*. Rather than promote the environment as it currently exists, we believe a better approach would be to develop conversion programs. For our own research, however, we will continue to use the *TenX* environment, and we would recommend the same for anyone willing to invest the time it takes to learn to use it.

30. On the rationale for these choices please see Selfridge-Field (1994). The translators to MIDI and *SCORE* were written by Walter B. Hewlett. The translator to *Kern* was written by David Huron.

DARMS' professed orientation towards printing applications, there were significant lapses.[31]

Our current view is that a standard for interchange of musical information is not likely to thrive if it is developed in isolation from major applications and data sets. Pending schemes leave several problems unresolved, and this owes partly to limited manpower and the lack of robust testing.[32] This could be remedied by a standards effort supported by a large group of users.

Listings of data made available by CCARH are linked to the World-Wide Web home page *http://ccrma-www.stanford.edu/CCARH*.

References

Hewlett, Walter B. "A Base-40 Number-Line Representation of Musical Pitch Notation," *Musikometrika* 4 (1992), 1–14.

Hewlett, Walter B., and Edmund Correia, Jr. *DataBases of Musical Information from the Center for Computer Assisted Research in the Humanities*. 3rd draft. Menlo Park: CCARH, 1995.

Hewlett, Walter B. "The Representation of Musical Information in Machine-Readable Format," *Directory of Computer Assisted Research in Musicology* 3 (1987), 1–22.

Selfridge-Field, Eleanor. "The *MuseData* Universe: A System of Musical Information," *Computing in Musicology* 9 (1993-94), 9–30.

31. In testing a provisional translation program to *DARMS* written by Brent Field (1992), we found numerous features of fairly simple music that could not be fully translated into the *Note Processor* dialect, which is the only generally available *DARMS* printing implementation. These lapses occurred especially where the program relies on mouse-driven changes of a cosmetic nature rather than stored code (e.g., for grace notes [as in the Mozart piano sonata], multiple endings [as in the saltarello], and so forth). This means that the data sets produced are unsuitable for many analytical and most sound applications; more particularly, they may produce very incomplete printed scores. We would expect to encounter similar difficulties in translating to other codes that rely heavily on graphical information and post-editing, as opposed to information that attempts to represent the full musical syntax at the outset.

32. Effective beta testing of interchange codes is difficult, since when those items that are not yet represented are absent from data sets, many programs will be unable to do anything useful with what there is.

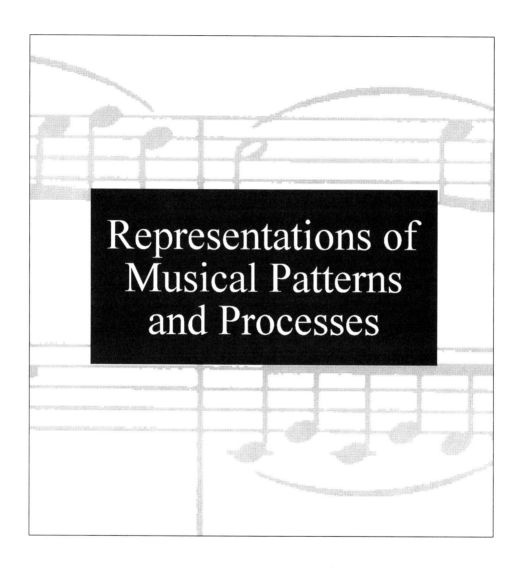

Representations of
Musical Patterns
and Processes

28 Encoding of Compositional Units

Ulf Berggren

An encoding system that is organized on the representation of phrases and their sub-units forms the basis of a project concerned with the simulation of compositional styles. Compositional structure is used as the basis for generating new compositions in the modelled style. The core material used in the design of the modelling part of this project consists of Mozart piano movements, specifically those in sonata form. It is assumed that much other classical music is organized by phrase.

The concept of building phrases from smaller components is important for the generation of surface-level activity. The surface is considered to consist of phrases (usually of one or two bars), and the phrases of indivisible units consisting of one or more notes. Previously stored compositional rules operate on the code during the generation of new movements. The same code is used, through data transformation, for printing.[1] The notation program generates MIDI codes for playback.

28.1 Code Description

Information is encoded into chunks which are called *compositional units*.[2] These units contain information about notes occurring in succession within one voice only. The length of a unit is defined to be one, two, or (occasionally) four beats. Some successive units (e.g., an Alberti bass in eighths and some other melodic- and accompaniment-figural types) may be paired.

1. Using the *Bella M* notation program.

2. *Formel* in Swedish.

In the following example (the first two bars of the Mozart piano sonata K. 545), each unit is marked by a circle. Paired units are connected:

Example 28.1 Opening of the Mozart piano sonata K. 545.

Each unit is associated with a set of parameters. The number of parameters is flexible, and depends on the application. In the present state of the model, the variables associated with each unit and having an influence on the notated score are the following: (1) duration, (2) pitch class, (3) octave number, (4) harmonic function, (5) voice type, and (6) texture type.

Global variables influencing all units in the piece include the following:

KEY:	major:	c, f, g, etc;
	minor:	am, dm, em, etc.
TIME:	2, 3, 4	e.g., 2/4; 3/4; 4/4

Structural relationships between units are of great importance in the simulation stage. Because units normally occur in several voices simultaneously, these relationships may be vertical as well as horizontal. Thus, units are connected in two dimensions.

28.1.1 Note Durations within a Unit

Note_value is a numerical data type. The note values used in the simulation programs are the following:

3	thirty-second note	24	quarter note
6	sixteenth note	30	quarter note tied to a sixteenth note
8	triplet eighth note		
12	eighth note	36	dotted quarter note
16	triplet quarter note	42	double-dotted quarter note
18	dotted eighth note	48	half note
21	double-dotted eighth note	96	whole note

These values describe rests:

203	thirty-second rest
206	sixteenth rest
208	triplet eighth rest
212	eighth rest
224	quarter rest

Rests longer than a quarter note (i.e., values higher than 224) are expressed in terms of two or more of these values.

Note_values are grouped into *duration lists*, so that the total length of the notes within a group add up to the length of the unit. Most groups have the length of a quarter note. These are some examples of duration groups:

[24]   the duration associated with a unit having only one note, a quarter note;

[48]   the duration associated with a unit having only one note, a half note;

[12,12]   the durations associated with a unit having two eighth notes;

[30,6,6,6]   the durations associated with a unit having a quarter note tied to a sixteenth note followed by three sixteenth notes.

28.1.2 Pitch-Class Numbers of Notes within a Unit

Each pitch within the unit is represented by pitch class name and octave number. The actual "spelling" of notes is dependent on information about harmonic functions.

PITCH CLASS: 1,2,3..12 where 1 = C, 2 = C♯/D♭, etc.

EXAMPLE: [1,5,8]   INTERPRETATION: the pitch classes of a three-note unit (corresponding to the tones C, E, G in C Major)

28.1.3 Octave Numbers of Notes within a Unit

OCTAVE: $[1,2,3,4,5,6]^3$

EXAMPLE: $[3,3]$ INTERPRETATION: the octaves of a two-note unit (both notes in the octave beneath the middle octave)

28.1.4 Harmonic Function

Each unit is associated with a harmonic function. All units occurring simultaneously refer to the same harmonic function. The harmonic function is essential to notation, in that it determines the enharmonic spelling of notes. For example, the fourth pitch class is notated as an E♭ in C Minor, a D♯ in E major.

Values for harmonic functions include the codes t, s, d, d7, s6, d64, tp, and so forth:

t	=	tonic
s	=	subdominant
tp	=	tonic parallel

28.1.5 Voice Type

In most cases the grouping of notes in notation follows the extension of units.
Some common voice types are these:

```
triad
scale in sixteenths
scale in eighths
Alberti bass in sixteenths
Alberti bass in eighths
```

Beams in notation sometimes extend from one unit to another, particularly in paired units. In such cases information about the grouping of notes is derived from the voice type associated with the unit. For example, the units having the voice type Alberti bass in eighths are paired. This will lead to notes grouped four at a time in the notation.

Another kind of unit that is paired is scale in eighths (also written four at a time). In units having other voice types, such as scale in sixteenths, the grouping of notes will not extend over the boundaries of the individual units.

---

3. The octave number of Middle C is 4; A4 = 440 Hz.

28.1.6 Texture Type

Vertical connections between voices are defined as consequences of the value of the variable texture type. For example, a texture having notes paired in thirds in the right hand will govern a specific relation connecting the two highest voices.

Some of the texture types used are these:

```
solo
treble-and-bass
thirds-and-bass
treble-and-thirds
chords-and-bass
parallel sixth chords
```

28.2   Example

Although the purpose of the code is not to be a means for musical notation, an analytical representation of the Mozart trio example is given below.

```
General parameters
Time = 3 (that is, 3/4)
Key = c (that is, C major)

Bar 0

Duration: [12,12]
Pitch classes: [1,5]
Octaves: [5,5]

Harmony: [t]
Voice type: [triad]
Texture: solo

Bar 1

Durations: [12,12], [24], [12,12]
Pitch classes: [8,5], [1], [8,5]
Octaves: [5,5], [6], [5,5]

Harmony: [t], [t], [t]
Voice types: [triad], [triad], [triad]
Texture: solo plus four-part writing

Bar 2

Durations: [12,12], [24], [12,12]
Pitch classes: [3,6], [10], [6,3]
Octaves: [5,5], [5], [5,5]

Harmony: [s6], [s6], [s6]
Voice types: [triad], [triad], [triad]
Texture: solo plus four-part writing
```

```
Bar 3

Durations: [12,12], [12,12], [12,12]
Pitch classes: [1,12], [5,3], [8,6]
Octaves: [5,4], [5,5], [5,5]

Harmony: [d7], [d7], [d7]
Voice types: [climbing], [climbing], [climbing]
Texture: solo plus four-part writing

Comment: "Climbing" means a melodic movement: step down/
leap up/step down, etc.

Bar 4

Durations: [24], [24], [12,12]
Pitch classes: [4], [5], [1,5]
Octaves: [5], [5], [5,5]

Harmony: [tp], [tp], [tp]
voice types: [scale], [scale], [triad]
Texture: solo plus four-part writing

Bar 5

Durations: [12,12], [24], [12,12]
Pitch classes: [8,5], [1], [8,5]
Octaves: [5,5], [6], [5,5]

Harmony: [t], [t], [t]
Voice types: [triad], [triad], [triad]
Texture: solo plus four-part writing

Comment: the position of chords is not specified by the
code.

Bar 6

Durations: [12,12], [24], [224]
Pitch classes: [3,6], [10], [10]
Octaves: [5,5], [5], [5]

Harmony: [s6], [s6], [dims6]
Voice types: [triad], [triad], [triad]
Texture: solo plus four part writing

Comment: "dims6" means a diminished chord directed at
the s6 function.

Bar 7

Durations: 224], [224], [224]
Pitch classes: [10], [10], [10]
Octaves: [5], [5], [5]

Harmony: [s6], [s6], [s6]
Voice types: [triad], [triad], [triad]
Texture: three parts
```

```
Bar 8

Durations: [224], [224], [8,8,8]
Pitch classes: [10], [10], [3,10,6]
Octaves: [5], [5], [4,3,3]

Harmony: [s6], [s6], [s6]
Voice types: [triad], [triad], [triad]
Texture: solo plus three parts

Bar 9

Durations: [12,12], [12,12], [12,12]
Pitch classes: [10,3], [6,10], [3,6]
Octaves: [3,4], [4,4], [5,5]

Harmony: [s6], [s6], [s6]
Voice types: [triad], [triad], [triad]
Texture: solo

Bar 10

Durations: [12,12], [12,12], [12,12]
Pitch classes: [10,8], [6,5], [6,3]
Octaves: [5,5], [5,5], [5,5]

Harmony: [s6], [s6], [s6]
Voice types: [scale], [scale], [triad]
Texture: solo

Bar 11

Duration: [48], [12,12]
Pitch classes: [1], [5,3]
Octaves: [5], [5,5]

Harmony: [d64], [d7]
Voice types: [scale], [scale]
Texture: solo plus four-part writing

Bar 12

Durations: [24], [224]
Pitch classes: [1], [1]
Octaves: [5], [5]

Harmony: [t], [t]
Voice types: [scale], [scale]
Texture: solo plus four-part writing
```

Example 28.2 Encoding of compositional units.

28.3   Comments

This example requires some further comments:

- The programs can compose in different keys (primarily in major keys such as C, F, B♭, G, and D major, but also in minor keys) and transpose music in tonal and real sequences (in the latter case a transposition is made to a new key). However, there are no explicit routines for dealing with transposing instruments.

- Information is grouped into units. The parametric values for each unit are written within brackets. To identify units will in this case be an *analytic* undertaking, while in the simulations in Mozart style the grouping is part of the structure built up by the programs.

- The labels for the voice types are simplified in the code.

- Pitch and octave numbers are specified for rests, but are not displayed on screen. See Bar 6.

- The textures specified above are evidently not those used in the modeling of the piano sonatas. However, the extension of the code required to match such textures is not a big one.

References

Berggren, Ulf. *ARS COMBINATORIA: Algorithmic Construction of Sonata Movements by Means of Building Blocks Derived from W. A. Mozart's Piano Sonatas.* Uppsala University: Department of Musicology, 1995.

Berggren [=Larnestam], Ulf. "Kodsekvenser i musik: En på semiotisk och informations-teoretisk metodik grundad klassifikation av musikalisk informations-överföring" [in Swedish]. Uppsala University: Department of Musicology, 1983.

Berggren [=Larnestam], Ulf. "Simulation of Keyboard Sonata Movements in the Style of Mozart," *Computing in Musicology* 8 (1992), 103–106.

29 A Score-Segmentation Approach to Music Representation

Andranick Tanguiane

Common Western notation does not explicitly reflect musical structure. Nevertheless, musicians recognize the structure while reading and thus overcome the lapses and imperfections of notation. While designing a system for music representation, the dynamic psychological aspects of music reading might be taken into account.

Two important factors that differentiate musical notation from musical meaning are the lack of phrase delimiters in and the variable redundancy of notation.

In notation, the bar line is visually perceived as a delimiter, and it is used as a potential boundary for line- and page-breaks. Especially in vocal music, bar lines may not coincide with the ends of musical phrases. Thus line breaks, being dependent on them, may impose inconsistencies on the sense of an underlaid text. Multiple musical endings make for some extreme cases. For example, the last syllable of a new verse can appear on a new page, with the next verse beginning under the *prima volta*, and being continued two pages back at the repeat symbol. In the dynamic of musical performance, however, the bar line has an important non-visual function: it indicates the subsequent metrical accent.

As for the variable redundancy of notation, every musician knows that a score which looks complex may prove to be easily read, while one that seems transparent may prove difficult in execution. A busy accompaniment may be easily read because of a repetitive pattern, for example. In this case some of the notation is redundant. An apparently simple polyphonic piece may be difficult to read because of the independence of individual voices. In this case the notation is not redundant.

Redundancy occurs mainly through various kinds of quasi-repetition. In a notated score, repeated material may look as complex as in its exposition, but through repeated performance symmetrical motives, transpositions, and other recurring phenomena become more apparent. Each time familiar material is repeated, our mental representations of it need be less fully encoded.

29.1   Score Segmentation and Data Reduction

Certain aspects of the relationship between musical notation and its perception lend themselves to the formulation of two principles.

First, music reading (the human decoding of written notation) is neither exclusively vertical nor exclusively horizontal but rather a mixture of the two. It is based on recognizing *meaningful* patterns and segments among the many symbols on the page. These patterns constitute, in a psychological sense, an *ecological* representation of music. This sets the psychological process of "encoding" scores distinctly apart from event-based time-ordered files for sound and the traditional "part" orientation of notation.

Second, the ability to recognize patterns of repetition (whether melodic, harmonic, textural, or rhythmical) is one of the keystones of fluent music reading. Such repetitions may be constituent parts of macro- or micro-forms of music.

In computer applications, these two principles may be reformulated as follows:

- A computer representation of music can operate with segments rather than with single notes, vertical cuts, or horizontal parts. The representations should be organized as a series of score segments.

- Data reduction can be aimed at eliminating repetitiveness, e.g., a pattern should be coded only once and then be recalled by reference. Such representations save memory storage, contain fewer printing errors, and are better suited for editing and computer analysis.

Concepts of abbreviated notations have an extensive history in early and traditional repertories (e.g., tablatures for fretted instruments, figured bass, Armenian *khazes*, Indian *ragas*, etc.). Modern notation even gives some hints about how to achieve more compact representations. For example, there are abbreviations for various fixed patterns (such as grace notes), and signs for predefined patterns (such as ·/. for repeated note-groups).

In the context of common music notation, the list of abbreviations might be extended to include designated arpeggio- and scale-segment types and by representing a piece with predefined generative patterns. The overall goal is to obtain the least complex representations based on meaningful score segments.[1]

29.2 Representation Streams for Rhythm and Pitch

The number of relative durations (e.g., quarters, eighths, sixteenths, and thirty-seconds) in a single melody is typically about three or four, whereas the number of pitches is usually somewhat greater. Correspondingly, the variety of rhythmic patterns is theoretically much more limited than that of pitch patterns.

Pitch data can be also reduced from a string of isolated events to a (sometimes much shorter) string of specific pitch sets. These sets are defined by patterns of repetition. Their number is limited by the fact that many melodic progressions can be represented by arpeggios and scale patterns. It is actually in segments that are short and heterogeneous that score-segment encoding may be more complex than direct coding.

29.3 Example

Below we construct a representation of the first 12 bars from the second trio of Mozart's Clarinet Quintet using the score-segmentation approach. This is accomplished one passage at a time. First, we model the process of music reading step-by-step. The reading is conventionally divided into two steps. The first reading assumes no knowledge about the piece, and relations are established only to the elements which are already met, e.g., a motive can be recognized as a derivative from the theme.

Next, we recognize generative patterns and use them for the representation. Since a comprehensible interpretation requires more than establishing relations to preceding elements, we attempt the second reading. Its goal is to reveal global relationships throughout the whole piece.

---

1. Formally, the complexity of a representation can be defined in the sense of Kolmogorov (1965) as the amount of memory storage required for the algorithm of the data generation; see also Calude (1988). In this sense, representations with little or no redundancy are most simple.

29.3.1 The First Reading

At the first glance, a texturally homogeneous section (Bars 1–6) can be singled out. The cues are that the instrument set is invariable and that the functions of the instruments are constant: the clarinet plays the melody and the strings provide the accompaniment. While reading, a section is not necessarily scanned to the very end. It suffices that the player estimate the homogeneity of the texture and look ahead in order to foresee its changes. However, in our model of music reading we consider whole sections.

The accompaniment, as a rhythmic and harmonic grid, is evaluated first. Typically an accompaniment is not read note-by-note. After a pattern has been identified, only the harmony is essential. According to this observation, we encode the string parts by the repetitive waltz pattern V (with a concluding chord in Bar 6) and a harmonic sequence in View 1 (Figure 29.1):

$$
V = \left\{
\begin{array}{l}
\text{V-no I} \\
\text{V-no II} \\
\text{V-la} \\
\text{Cello}
\end{array}
\right.
\quad
\begin{array}{|c|c|c|c|c|c|}
a_1 & a_1 & g\sharp_1 & a_1 & a_1 & f\sharp_1 \\
e_1 & f\sharp_1 & d_1 & c\sharp_1 & e_1 & d_1 \\
c\sharp_1 & b & b & a & c\sharp_1 & b \\
a & d & e & f\sharp & c\sharp & d
\end{array}
$$

Figure 29.1 First reading, View 1.

Note that such a representation resembles a figured bass.

A melody is usually read by short motives which are segmented primarily with respect to rhythmic cues.[2] The segments in Figure 29.1 are separated by double bars. Note that this scheme of segmentation corresponds more closely to the slurs of the original than to the bar lines.

The recognition of repeated material facilitates music reading. Here, the first two motives, which have the common rhythmic pattern ♫ | ♫ ♩, are repeated in Bars 4–6. In order to obtain the reduced representation of the melody shown in View 2 (Figure 29.2), we note that several pitch lines are set to the same rhythm:

$$B = $$
$$1.3.\,a_1c\sharp_2 \quad e_2c\sharp_2a_2 \qquad d_2b_1 \quad a_1g\sharp_1c\sharp_2b_1e_2d_2 \quad b\sharp_1c\sharp_2$$
$$2.4.\,e_2c\sharp_2 \quad b_1d_2 \; f\sharp_2$$

Figure 29.2 First reading, View 2.

---

2. Details on rules of musical segmentation can be found in Tanguiane (1992) and Tanguiane (1993).

Thus the first section is represented as melody and accompaniment. In this case, we do not use arpeggio and scale patterns because they would not reduce the representation.

The next texturally homogeneous section is a string trio in Bars 6–8. Here the melody is given by the *Violino 1*, while the *Violino 2* and *Viola* provide a harmonic pedal. Now the tasks are to evaluate the accompanying pedal part (with the rhythmic figure ♩ | ♩), setting it up, as in View 1, to produce View 3 (Figure 29.3):

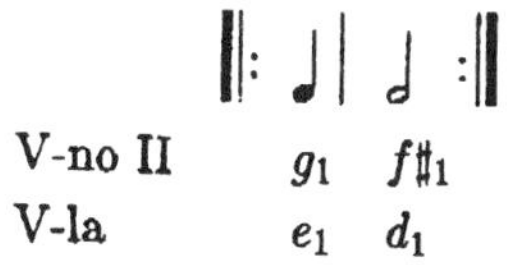

$$\|: \; \downarrow | \; \downarrow \; :\|$$

V-no II g_1 $f\sharp_1$
V-la e_1 d_1

Figure 29.3 First reading, View 3.

and to evaluate the melody, which falls into two identical motives as segmented by the formal rhythmic rules cited; this produces View 4 (Figure 29.4):

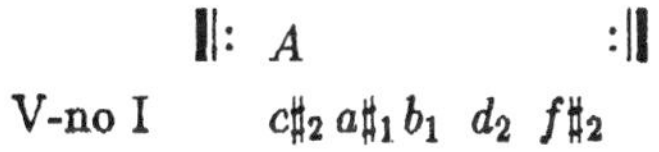

$$\|: \; A \qquad\qquad :\|$$

V-no I $c\sharp_2 \; a\sharp_1 \, b_1 \quad d_2 \; f\sharp_2$

Figure 29.4 First reading, View 4.

The third section consists of the clarinet solo in Bars 8–10. According to the rhythmic rules, the clarinet solo constitutes a single segment concluding with the half note A[3] in Bar 11. In this solo, one can easily recognize the arpeggio (b_m) and descending scale. The encoding of the clarinet solo is shown in View 5 (Figure 29.5):

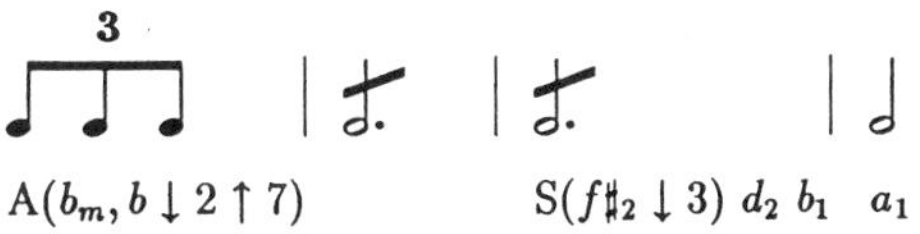

$$\overset{3}{\sqcap} \quad | \; \downarrow \quad | \; \downarrow \qquad | \; \downarrow$$

$A(b_m, b \downarrow 2 \uparrow 7)$ $S(f\sharp_2 \downarrow 3) \; d_2 \; b_1 \quad a_1$

Figure 29.5 First reading, View 5.

Note the abbreviation for repeated eighths, which corresponds to the reading of the rhythmic sequence as equal durations filling in two measures.

3. Written as C5.

The cadence section is comprised of Bars 11 and 12. Since this section is quite short, direct encoding may be simpler than a representation by generative patterns, although the common harmonic progression $V_{6/4}$—V_7—I is immediately recognized while reading.

The momentum of the clarinet solo is continued here by the *Violino 1*. According to the rhythmic rules cited, this means that the cadence is inseparable from the clarinet solo. Therefore, the clarinet motive from the fourth section should be joined to the preceding solo segment.

29.3.2 The Second Reading

The purpose of the second reading is to understand relationships between elements. Here we create generative patterns which unify and simplify the representation of a piece. From the first reading we know that the melody uses the rhythmic patterns A, B, and C (Figure 29.6):

Figure 29.6 Rhythmic patterns A, B, and C.

These may be regarded as derivatives of simpler root patterns. Omitting the details of finding them,[4] we may construct a hierarchy of elaborations of the pattern P (Figure 29.7):

Figure 29.7 A hierarchy of elaborations of the pattern P.

4. For these, see Tanguiane (1993).

where EP denotes the elaboration of P, E_3P the triplet elaboration, E^2P the elaboration of elaboration, etc. Hence, patterns can be expressed in terms of *sums* (denoted by the symbol +) and *junctions* (denoted by the letter J) of elaborations of the root pattern P:

```
A = E₃P
B = J(E²P + E²P)                    = J(2E²P)
C = J(E₃P + EP + EP) + EP  = J(E₃P + 2EP) + EP
```

The rhythmic structure of the melody can now be expressed by reference to the previously identified segments and repeat signs as shown in View 6 (Figure 29.8):

$$\text{||: } A \text{ :|| } B \text{ :||: } A \text{ :|| } C$$

with first ending ⌐1.⌐ and second ending ⌐2.⌐

Figure 29.8 Second reading, View 6.

By assuming the root patterns into this structure, we can obtain View 7, the most compact representation (Figure 29.9):

$$\text{||: } E^3P \quad \text{:|| } J(2E^2P) \quad \text{:||: } E^3P \quad \text{:|| } J(E_3P + 2EP) + EP$$

Figure 29.9 Second reading, View 7.

Now the rhythm of the melody must be united with the rhythm of accompaniment. The accompaniment contains the waltz pattern with a concluding V chord, a pedal based on Pattern P, a tacet, and a cadence (the only section encoded fully). The rhythm of the excerpt may be represented as shown in View 8 (Figure 29.10):

	⌐1.⌐	⌐2.⌐		
Cl. E^3P	$J(2E^2P)$.	V-no I E^3P	Cl. $J(E_3P + 2EP)+EP$	
Strings V		V-no II & V-la P	Tacet	Strings Cadence

Figure 29.10 Second reading, View 8.

By putting the pitch data (Views 1, 2, 3, 4, 5) into correspondence with this representation (View 8), we obtain a reduced representation of the 12-bar score. Thus the second reading models the understanding of a piece by describing it as being generated by irreducible patterns. Here we have constructed a unifying rhythmic structure, corresponding to the "rhythmic feel" of musical form which is usually acquired by multiple readings.

29.4 Comments

The main principles of an ecological representation involve the grouping of notes into meaningful segments, data reduction based on eliminating various forms of repetition, separate representation of rhythm and pitch data, a scheme of references to recurrent patterns of each, and a scheme of references to algorithms which may be said to generate a piece (via elaboration, sum, junction, etc.) from a few predefined patterns.

Data reduction requires the elucidation of semantic relationships. In this sense, the construction of compact representations is a step toward understanding music. Such representations contain information about the hierarchical organization of a piece and relationships between its segments.

In the realm of computer applications, a segmented score can be used to facilitate an expressive computer playback, computer analysis of scores, and pedagogy. In each case ecological representations support flexibility and creativity that exceed that of more literal representations.

References

Calude, C. *Theories of Computational Complexity,* Amsterdam: North-Holland, 1988.

Kolmogorov, A. N. "Three Approaches to Defining the Notion 'Quantity of Information'," *Problemy Peredatchi Informatsii,* [in Russian] 1/1 (1965), 3–11. Reprinted in: A. N. Kolmogorov, *Theory of Information and Theory of Algorithms* [in Russian] (Moscow: Kauka, 1987), 213–223.

Laske, Otto. "On Problems of a Performance Model for Music." Technical report, Institute of Sonology, University of Utrecht, 1972.

Smoliar, Stephen. "A Parallel Processing Model of Musical Structures." Technical report, Artificial Intelligence Laboratory, M.I.T., 1971.

Smoliar, Stephen. "Music Programs: An Approach to Music Theory through Computational Linguistics," *Journal of Music Theory* 20/1 (1976), 105–132.

Smoliar, Stephen. "Process Structuring and Music Theory," *Journal of Music Theory* 18/2 (1974), 308–337.

Tanguiane, Andranick S. "A Binary System for Classification of Rhythmic Patterns," *Computing in Musicology* 8 (1992), 75–81.

Tanguiane, Andranick S. *Artificial Perception and Music Recognition* (Lecture Notes in Artificial Intelligence, 746). Berlin: Springer-Verlag, 1993.

Interchange Codes

30 *HyTime* and *Standard Music Description Language*: A Document-Description Approach

Donald Sloan[1]

Hypermedia/Time-Based Structuring Language (*HyTime*) is an application of a well-established document interchange standard, *Standard Generalized Markup Language* (*SGML*).[2] *HyTime* extends *SGML*'s document representation facilities to a concept of documents including not simply words and still pictures but also to video, motion pictures, and sound. *HyTime* allows information to be represented in any structure and set of relationships that may be useful to an author or end-user.

Standard Music Description Language (*SMDL*) is, in turn, an application of *HyTime*. It uses many of *HyTime*'s facilities, as well as a special set of constructs meaningful to music representation. These schemes of document representation are device-independent and in the public domain. *HyTime/SMDL* may serve as a representation language in its own right. It is intended that it should be usable as an interchange format for other representation codes, thus offering a means for translation into and out of existing codes, as well as those codes not yet devised. In this sense, these standards are enabling, not constraining standards, presenting a set of tools that can be used to fashion a wide variety of software.

---

1. Stephen R. Newcomb is the author of the Additional Comments on *HyTime* (30.6).

2. International Standards Organization (ISO) document 8879. *HyTime*, assigned the ISO/IEC document number 10744, was drafted as part of a public standards project initiated in 1986 by the American National Standards Institute (ANSI), as a member of the ISO, for a standard means of representation of information in hypermedia in general, and musical information in particular.

    SMDL carries the ISO document number 10743. The history and description of these standards have been described in past issues of *Computing in Musicology* and other journals; the reader may find more detailed technical information in these sources. This article will focus on the issues of musical encoding as set forth by the examples under discussion.

HyTime/SMDL can represent sound, notation in any graphical form, and processes of each that can be described by any mathematical formula. The standards are not intended as a set of tools for musical composition, nor do they impose one standard form of representation on any kind of music, modern or otherwise. That information whose representation and interchange is of any use may be captured by *HyTime/SMDL*, without requiring that all aspects of a piece be captured in a standard way. It is possible, for example, to label a chunk of data without explaining how to interpret it. Thus, no standardization is enforced. However, it is made available insofar as it is useful to someone. The intent is to provide a means for representing and interchanging musical information without constraints in any way on creative activity.

HyTime contains, among other things, facilities for addressing data, structuring data into any arbitrary set of hierarchies, linking between objects, and—most important for musicians—a means for representing the temporal aspects of position and duration (called *scheduling* and *extent* in *HyTime*) both in the static means of a score and in the projection of this static information, as, for example, through performance. *SMDL* has all of these facilities available by virtue of inheritance; *HyTime* uses a kind of object-oriented structure called an architectural form.

30.1   *SMDL* Domains

SMDL organizes musical information into several domains. Of primary importance is the *logical domain*, called the *cantus*. The *cantus* contains that information which is not exclusively part of a score or a performance but rather part of both. For example, a quarter-note Middle C is a singular concept, although it can be represented several different ways on a score, or performed numerous ways. By separating the logical information into one domain, it allows many score representations or performances based on one piece of music.

Any musical score could be represented in the *visual domain* by using a set of visual symbols defined by an *SMDL* user. This means that a *DARMS*-encoded score could itself serve as the basis for the visual domain of an *SMDL* document. *HyTime* provides measurement and addressing facilities for linking each musical symbol to its logical construct in the *cantus*.

Similarly, the *gestural domain* captures the representation of actual sound performances, whether they be MIDI files or digital recording bitstreams, by allowing linking to objects in the *cantus*. In such a manner, one can get from performance to visual representation or vice versa by means of a mediator, the logical set of information.

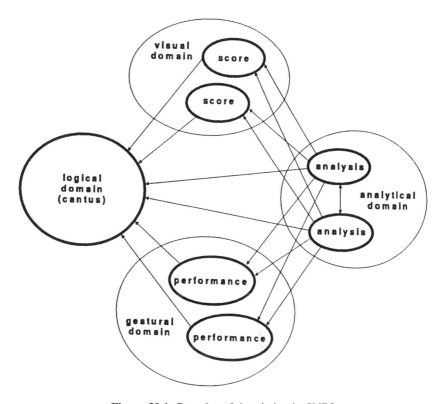

Figure 30.1 Domains of description in *SMDL*.

The fourth and final domain is an *analytic domain*, which allows analysis and commentary about the work in question, linking information to that of the logical domain if meaningful. Bibliographic information, such as composer names, work titles, themes, and so forth may be represented in any of the four domains.

For present purposes the main focus will be on the logical domain or *cantus*, since that is where the fundamental representation issues occur. Since the visual or gestural domains may consist of any existing or future data-content notation and may be linked to any piece of logical information in the *cantus*, it should be clear that a description of the *cantus* of *SMDL* is of primary concern. The following discussion will describe in brief how the various elements[3] of music may be represented in an *SMDL cantus*.

30.2 Basic Elements of Music in the Logical Domain

30.2.1 Pitch

Pitch may be represented as either a specific frequency, a function of a reference frequency (as in just intonation), or by means of a gamut, or lookup table, which names notes within the span of an octave. The *SMDL* gamut would be the means for representing pitch in most Western music notation.

30.2.2 Duration

Duration may be specified in either real time (seconds, minutes) or in virtual time, in which the units have a relationship to each other but need not be translated into real time until an actual performance occurs. Common music notation is a virtual-time system, since, for example, the length of a quarter note is determined by variables such as meter, tempo, and even the performance style and whims of a given performer. *HyTime*'s virtual-time system was developed specifically to handle such objects.

In *HyTime*, a duration is an extent or length on a coordinate axis, with the axis being measured in real or virtual units. Durations can be defined in their own right or by reference to the duration of another object.

30.2.3 Articulation and Ornamentation

It is difficult to represent these in a fully logical sense, since the interpretation of any given articulation is so highly dependent on context. It seems more prudent for *SMDL* merely to allow a description of any articulation or ornamentation, either by a lookup table or separately. Thus, a visual representation may be the actual symbol in the score or the word that names it, e.g., > or `accent`. The gestural representation is related to the way in which the sound is modified from the "unornamented" note and is difficult

---

3. In other chapters of this book the word "attributes" has been used to describe particular properties of notes, such as pitch and duration. In this chapter the words "elements" and "attributes" have exclusive and separate meanings to which the same words in other chapters cannot necessarily be equated.

to separate. Rather, the user may define a style sheet that can describe how a sound is to be modified in the case of particular articulations or ornaments.

30.2.4 Dynamics

Dynamics are understood in a manner similar to articulation and ornamentation. One can label dynamics by symbol or name, leaving the interpretation of this information to a performer.

30.2.5 Timbre

The notes in the *cantus* can be separated into different *threads*, or voices. Each thread can be given a label stating what instrument is supposed to play the notes in the thread. In situations in which the timbre results from digital or analog sound processing, the formula for such modification can be contained in an element called a *wand*.[4] In general, this area is treated much like articulations or dynamics, where in the absence of a complete understanding of how to represent such things compactly, the short description or musical symbol itself can be represented directly.

30.3 *SGML* Markup

HyTime/SMDL, like their parent standard, *SGML*, structures information by means of start (<) and end (/ . .>) tags. These tags will be familiar to users of the World-Wide Web markup language *HTML* (*HyperText Markup Language*).

The three basic tools are these:

- *entities*, which store information and user-definable structures
- *elements*, which define each object in the structure
- *attributes*, which assign various properties to elements

In *HyTime/SMDL* syntax, the first token after the < bracket is the *element type*. Any additional information before the next > bracket assigns values to various *attributes* of this element.

---

4. The *wand* contains any information that modifies an object, not just timbral information.

Following the *start tag* are the actual data. In proper syntax, the data are followed by an *end tag*, which takes the form `</element>`, where the element type is substituted for the word "element."

In cases in which a flat or a non-interlocking hierarchy is used, the end tags may usually be omitted. In such cases the start of the next element effectively ends the previous one. For example:

```
<note>t -1 c</note>
<note>t -1 d</note>
```

could be shortened to:

```
<note>t -1 c
<note>t -1 d
```

Comments are preceded and followed by two hyphens (--).

The initial records in *SGML*-style documents are concerned with document type definitions (DTD).

30.4   Examples

30.4.1 The Mozart Trio

Lines 1–61 of the code for the document containing the Mozart trio (Example 30.1) set up a document type definition. This *SMDL* DTD specifies which facilities will be used from *HyTime*, how virtual-time and real-time units will be measured, and how the coordinate axes for scheduling events will be set up; it also gives bibliographic information concerning this work.

Some of the entities described in this file (Lines 18–46) are time axes, lookup tables, musical event types (notes, rests, and chords), intonation scheme, and header information. Pitch and duration specifications are given in Lines 65–135. *Threads* that clarify relationships between elements and attributes are defined in Lines 138–148. Actual data are given, part by part, in Lines 153–366. The specific content is discussed following the example.

In this case, since the trio is the only section being encoded here, none of the rest of the piece is described. If the entire quintet were being encoded, the various movements, and possibly sections within movements (such as the trio section of the minuet), could be compartmentalized into work segments. The encoder decides what constitutes a work and how to segment it. The labels should make it clear to a user how this has been accomplished.

```
 1  <!DOCTYPE work SYSTEM "smdl.dtd" [
 2  <?HyTime VERSION "ISO/IEC 10744:1992" HYQCNT=32 >
 3  <?HyTime MODULE base
 4     desctxt dvlist lextype refctl >
 5  <?HyTime MODULE measure
 6     axismdu dimref fcsmdu HyFunk HyOp markfun >
 7  <?HyTime MODULE sched
 8     grpdex >
 9  <?HyTime MODULE rend
10     modify patch profun project >
11  <!NOTATION virtime PUBLIC -- virtual time --
12     "+//ISO/IEC 10744//NOTATION Virtual Time Unit//EN" >
13  <!ENTITY tactvtu -- number of vtus per tactus (beat) -- "80640" >
14  <!ENTITY % e.canti -- generic identifiers of canti; only one is defined
15  for this example:
16                      Trio II -- "Trio II">
17
18  <!ENTITY % av.wxdm  --  dimension of wfaxis -- "4294967295">
19  <!ENTITY % av.wxfm  --  mdu def for workfcs -- "'SIsecond 1 1000'" >
20  <!ENTITY % av.wxbg  --  basegran of wfaxis -- "msec" >
21  <!ENTITY % av.wxgh  --  gran2hmu of wfaxis -- "'1 1'" >
22  <!ENTITY % av.wxpg  --  pls2gran of wfaxis -- "'1 1'" >
23
24  <!ENTITY % av.cxdm  --  dimension of mustime axis -- "4294967295">
25  <!ENTITY % av.cxbg  --  basegran of mustime axis; -- "vtu" >
26  <!ENTITY % av.cxgh  --  gran2hmu of mustime axis -- "'1 1'" >
27  <!ENTITY % av.cxpg  --  pls2gran of mustime axis -- "'1 &tactvtu;'" >
28  <!ENTITY % av.cxfm  --  mdu def for mustime axis -- "'virtime 1 1'" >
29
30  <!ENTITY % e.rsrc   --Resources: lookup tables and definitions--
31                  "strestem|chordgam|pitchgam|mudef">
32
33  <!ENTITY % e.music  --Music events: notes, chords, rests--
34                  "note | chordchg | rest" >
35  <!ENTITY % m.ceg    "(%e.music; | ceg)+" >
36
37  <!ENTITY % m.np  --Content model: just intonation not supported--
38                  "(gampitch | freqspec)" >
39
40  <!ENTITY % e.intji "arbintvl" --Just intonation interval not supported-->
41
42  <!ENTITY % e.bib "title|author|date|issuer|descript|copr|status|role|
43  numclass">
44  <!ENTITY % d.bib "<!ELEMENT (%e.bib;) - O (#PCDATA)>"> %d.bib;
45  <!ENTITY % m.bib "(%e.bib; | theme)*">
46  <!ENTITY % a.theme "">
47  ]>
48
49  <work>
50  <bibdata>
51    <title>Clarinet Quintet
52  <author>W.A.Mozart
53  <descript>chamber music
54  </bibdata>
55
56  <workfcs>
```

```
 57 <workschd>
 58     <workseg>
 59         <bibdata>
 60             <title>Trio II
 61         </bibdata>
 62
 63 --The resources go here.--
 64
 65 --The pitch gamut defines the usual note names and distances between them.--
 66 <pitchgam id=pitchgm0
 67 gamutdes="conventional 12-tone equal temperament"
 68 highstep=11
 69 octratio=2 1
 70 >
 71 <genfreq> -- sets gamstep 9 (='a') to be 440 Hz --
 72 <gamstep>9</gamstep>
 73 <freqspec><hertz>440</hertz></freqspec>
 74 </genfreq>
 75 <namestep><pitchdef><pitchnm>c</pitchnm><gamstep>0</gamstep></pitchdef>
 76 </namestep>
 77 <namestep><pitchdef><pitchnm>d</pitchnm><gamstep>2</gamstep></pitchdef>
 78 </namestep>
 79 <namestep><pitchdef><pitchnm>e</pitchnm><gamstep>4</gamstep></pitchdef>
 80 </namestep>
 81 <namestep><pitchdef><pitchnm>f</pitchnm><gamstep>5</gamstep></pitchdef>
 82 </namestep>
 83 <namestep><pitchdef><pitchnm>g</pitchnm><gamstep>7</gamstep></pitchdef>
 84 </namestep>
 85 <namestep><pitchdef><pitchnm>a</pitchnm><gamstep>9</gamstep></pitchdef>
 86 </namestep>
 87 <namestep><pitchdef><pitchnm>b</pitchnm><gamstep>11</gamstep></pitchdef>
 88 </namestep>
 89
 90 </pitchgam>
 91
 92 --The ficta gamut adjusts the pitch gamut to reflect the key signature.--
 93 <fictagam  id=3sharps  idref=pitchgm0>
 94 <pitchnm>c</pitchnm> <fictadj>+1</fictadj>
 95 <pitchnm>f</pitchnm> <fictadj>+1</fictadj>
 96 <pitchnm>g</pitchnm> <fictadj>+1</fictadj>
 97 </fictagam>
 98
 99   --This code defines a macro for the music durations.--
100 <notedurs HyTime=desctab id=mydurs
101 <durname HyTime=desctxt>t</durname>
102 <durval HyTime=descdef><marklist>&tactvtu;</marklist></durval>
103 <durname HyTime=desctxt>t4</durname>
104 <durval HyTime=descdef>
105     <marklist>
106         <HyOp opname=div>
107             <marklist desctab=mydurs desctxt=t>
108             <marklist>4
109         </HyOp>
110     </marklist>
111 </durval>
112 </notedurs>
113
114 <ce HyTime=event exspec=myextlist2>
115 <extlist HyTime=extlist id=myextlist2>
116     <marklist HyTime=marklist desctxt="t4" desctab=mydurs>
117 </extlist>
```

```
118  </ce>
119  <ce HyTime=event exspec=myextlist>
120  <extlist HyTime=extlist id=myextlist>
121      <dimref HyTime=dimref elemref=dur1231 selcomp=last>
122      <marklist HyTime=marklist desctxt="t4" desctab=mydurs>
123  </extlist>
124  </ce>
125
126    --This code defines the meter of this example--
127  <strestem id=simptrip pointcnt=3>
128  <pointnum>1</pointnum>
129  <stresval><strestxt>┬downbeat╙</strestxt><stresval>
130  <strestem id=simpsub pointcnt=2>
131      <pointnum>1</pointnum>
132  </strestem>
133  </strestem>
134
135  <stresuse id=tsig1 idr=simptrip strespt=3>
136
137  <Trio II>
138    --The various threads are now defined.--
139  <thread id=thd1 nominst="Clarinet in A">
140  </thread>
141  <thread id=thd2 nominst="Violin 1">
142  </thread>
143  <thread id=thd3 nominst="Violin 2">
144  </thread>
145  <thread id=thd4 nominst="Viola">
146  </thread>
147  <thread id=thd5 nominst="Violoncello">
148  </thread>
149
150  <baton id=bat1>
151  </baton>
152
153  <start thd1> --Clarinet in A, but in concert pitch in the logical domain
154  here.--
155      <ceg id=clarline>
156          <note>t2 0 a
157          <note>t2 1 c
158          <note>t2 1 e
159          <note>t2 1 c
160          <note>t 1 a
161          <note>t2 1 e
162          <note>t2 1 c
163          <note>t2 0 b
164          <note>t2 1 d
165          <note>t 1 f
166          <note>t2 1 d
167          <note>t2 0 b
168          <note>t2 0 a
169          <note>t2 0 g
170          <note>t2 1 c
171          <note>t2 0 b
172          <note>t2 1 e
173          <note>t2 1 d
174          <note>t 0 b +1
175          <note>t 1 c
176          <note>t2 0 a
177          <note>t2 1 c
178          <note>t2 1 e
```

```
179          <note>t2 1 c
180          <note>t 1 a
181          <note>t2 1 e
182          <note>t2 1 c
183          <note>t2 0 b
184          <note>t2 1 d
185          <note>t 1 f
186          <rest>t rest
187          <rest>3t rest
188          <rest>2t rest
189          <note>t3 -1 b
190          <note>t3 -1 f
191          <note>t3 -1 d
192          <note>t2 -1 f
193          <note>t2 -1 b
194          <note>t2 0 d
195          <note>t2 0 f
196          <note>t2 0 b
197          <note>t2 -1 d
198          <note>t2 1 f
199          <note>t2 1 e
200          <note>t2 1 d
201          <note>t2 1 c
202          <note>t2 1 d
203          <note>t2 0 b
204          <note>2t 0 a
205          <note>t2 1 c
206          <note>t2 0 b
207          <note>t 0 a
208          <rest>t
209      </ceg>
210  --This group repeats previous material via reference to it.--
211      <ceg id=rpt1 conloc=clarline>
212      </ceg>
213
214 <end thd1>
215
216 <start thd2> --Violin 1--
217      <ceg id=vn1line>
218          <rest>t
219          <rest>t
220          <note>t 0 a
221          <note>t 0 a
222          <rest>t
223          <note>t 0 a
224          <note>t 0 a
225          <rest>t
226          <note>t 0 g
227          <note>t 0 g
228          <rest>t
229          <note>t 0 a
230          <note>t 0 a
231          <rest>t
232          <note>t 0 a
233          <note>t 0 a
234          <note>t 0 f
235          <rest>t
236          <note>t2 1 c
237          <note>t2 0 a +1
238          <note>t2 0 b
239          <note>t2 1 d
```

```
240        <note>t 1 f
241        <note>t2 1 c
242        <note>t2 0 a +1
243        <note>t2 0 b
244        <note>t2 1 d
245        <note>t 1 f
246        <rest>t
247        <rest>3t
248        <rest>3t
249        <note>t2 0 c
250        <note>t2 0 e
251        <note>t2 0 c
252        <note>t2 0 e
253        <note>t2 0 d
254        <note>t2 0 e
255        <note>t 0 c
256        <rest>t
257    </ceg>
258
259  --Repeat, as before.--
260    <ceg id=rpt2 conloc=vn1line>
261    </ceg>
262
263 <end thd2>
264
265 <start thd3>   --violin 2--
266    <ceg id=vn2line>
267        <rest>t
268        <rest>t
269        <note>t 0 e
270        <note>t 0 e
271        <rest>t
272        <note>t 0 f
273        <note>t 0 f
274        <rest>t
275        <note>t 0 d
276        <note>t 0 d
277        <rest>t
278        <note>t 0 c
279        <note>t 0 c
280        <rest>t
281        <note>t 0 e
282        <note>t 0 e
283        <note>t 0 d
284        <rest>t
285        <note>t 0 g -1
286        <note>2t 0 f
287        <note>t 0 g -1
288        <note>2t 0f
289        <rest>t
290        <rest>3t
291        <rest>3t
292        <note>2t -1 a
293        <note>t -1 g
294        <note>t -1 a
295        <rest>t
296    </ceg>
297
298  --Repeat, as before.--
299    <ceg id=rpt3 conloc=vn2line>
300    </ceg>
```

```
301 <end thd3>
302
303 <start thd4>   --viola--
304     <ceg id=vlaline>
305         <rest>t
306         <rest>t
307         <note>t 0 c
308         <note>t 0 c
309         <rest>t
310         <note>t -1 b
311         <note>t -1 b
312         <rest>t
313         <note>t -1 b
314         <note>t -1 b
315         <rest>t
316         <note>t -1 a
317         <note>t -1 a
318         <rest>t
319         <note>t 0 c
320         <note>t 0 c
321         <note>t -1 b
322         <rest>t
323         <note>t 0 e
324         <note>2t 0 d
325         <note>t 0 e
326         <note>2t 0 d
327         <rest>t
328         <rest>3t
329         <rest>3t
330         <note tie>3t -1 e
331         <note>t -1 e
332         <rest>t
333     </ceg>
334
335  --Repeat, as before.--
336     <ceg id=rpt4 conloc=vlaline>
337     </ceg>
338
339 <end thd4>
340
341 <start thd5>   --violoncello--
342     <ceg id=vcline>
343         <rest>t
344         <note>t -1 a
345         <rest>2t
346         <note>t -1 d
347         <rest>2t
348         <note>t -1 e
349         <rest>2t
350         <note>t -1 f
351         <rest>2t
352         <note>t -1 c
353         <rest>2t
354         <note>t -1 d
355         <rest>2t
356         <rest>3t
357         <rest>3t
358         <rest>3t
359         <rest>3t
360         <note>t -2 e
361         <note>t -2 e
```

```
362          <note>t -2 e
363          <note>t -2 a
364          <rest>t
365      </ceg>
366
367  --Repeat, as before.--
368      <ceg id=rpt5 conloc=vcline>
369      </ceg>
370 <end thd5>
```

Example 30.1 *SMDL* code for the Mozart trio.

Since the Mozart trio uses common music notation, the resources in Lines 65–135 will define pitch and duration in terms familiar to trained musicians. The note names are defined in the *pitch gamut*,[5] which names notes within an octave span and delineates the number of steps in an octave, as well as the distance between neighboring notes in the gamut (Lines 65–90). A *ficta*[6] *gamut* makes chromatic adjustments to notes in the *pitch gamut*. In this case (Lines 92–97), the *ficta gamut* gives a key signature of three sharps. Thus, as with a key signature, when one encounters the note g, one now reads this as g♯ unless otherwise altered.

The durations are defined in Lines 99–124 in terms of the *tactus*, or pulse. Briefly, the letter t is one pulse; a number immediately preceding is a *multiplier*, while a number immediately following is a *divisor*. This allows description of music duration in terms of the tactus. In this *cantus*, there is no information that explicitly defines the tactus as a quarter-note; this is a visual issue, as any editor or early musician could attest. In this case, it might be absurd to publish an edition of this trio in 3/8 instead of 3/4 time, but nevertheless, it is in the visual domain where one identifies the beat unit, perhaps with bibliographic information stating the authority of such a claim.

The last of the resources listed here (Lines 126–135) defines the meter. Here, a template outlines a triple meter, with 2 subdivisions of the tactus nested within it;

---

5. Not to be confused with the gamut of medieval music theory, in which the six names of hexachordal positions were conjugated with the range of tones spanning the pitches from *G* to *e″*.

6. In Renaissance music there was often a discrepancy between pitches as written and as performed. Unwritten accidentals, the need for which was based on the hexachord system, were inflected in performance.

Here "ficta" refers to written alterations, either by key signature or by unique accidentals. The logical domain of *SMDL* contains information that is used by both the written and the gestural (performance) domains. Thus, the ficta gamut here could affect a performance even if a score did not exist. This gamut permits a single pitch gamut to have multiple ficta gamuts, rather than necessitating the creation of a new pitch gamut for every key signature.

hence a simple triple meter. Line 135, the `stresuse` element, calls for this meter, and starts on the third pulse of the pattern. This takes care of the anacrusis in this example.

The various instruments are each given their own threads in Lines 138–148. Each thread names the instrument that is intended. This is the only timbral direction given in this entire example.

The *baton* that follows (Lines 150–151) directs the tempo. None is given in the score, but when called for, tempo can be described by a virtual-time-to-real-time ratio (as in "120 beats per minute"), by text ("Allegro non troppo"), or by reference to another baton defined elsewhere in the document.

The remainder of this example contains the actual notes within each thread. In the *cantus*, the clarinet is notated at concert pitch, since those are the notes intended to be heard. The responsibility for creating written-pitch data rests with the visual domain. *SMDL* will have facilities for automatic transposition in such an instance. Here, the designation of `Clarinet in A` in the *cantus* is advisory; it would be possible to publish a clarinet part for a clarinet in B♭, for example.

Events within the threads are organized into *cantus event groups* (`ceg`). These groups may be sequential, as is the default here, or simultaneous, as with chords. The events depicted within these groups are notes and rests. The notes contain a duration, described in terms of the tactus, as outlined above; an octave number, with the octave described in the pitch gamut given a designation of 0; and a note name, as defined in the pitch gamut. Chromatic alterations, if any, follow the note name with a signed integer. Thus, Line 174 shows a quarter-note B♯ in the *Clarinet*, while Lines 285 and 287 show a G♮ in the *Violino 2* part. At the end of each thread, a new *cantus* event group calls for the content of the group identified earlier in the thread. This has the effect of creating the specified repeat of the material.

There are several things still missing from the code of this example. As the code for the *cantus* only, such purely visual phenomena as the beat unit, the clef, and the actual layout of the score are not represented here. These would instead be part of the visual domain, with reference to appropriate objects here in the *cantus*.

Articulations are not represented here because they are not yet implemented in the *SMDL* draft; the planned design is described above. There is also no gestural information here. A user could devise a style sheet to be applied to this *cantus*, which would have the effect of imposing a performance style onto the logical information, such as how short staccato notes should be, how to interpret appoggiaturas, and so forth.

As noted, this file was set up to handle just the trio from this quintet. It would be equally possible to make this trio simply a section of the entire quintet. Thus, the issue of how many files are necessary depends on the intended use and who is doing the encoding. If, after this trio is encoded, someone wished to do the entire quintet, the vast majority of code here could be lifted without need for revision and put into a larger file. Similarly, code from a larger file could be excerpted, as might be the case for creating examples for a textbook by using scores encoded in a large database.

HyTime has its own data querying facilities, so a search for themes, incipits, or other identifying material is native to its functions. Thus, the question of external file organization and order is entirely flexible and up to the encoder to design. This flexibility in defining structure is one of the main features of *SGML* and *HyTime/SMDL*.

30.4.2 The Mozart Piano Sonata

Example 30.2 shows how the grace notes of the Mozart piano sonata might be encoded. The approach would be for a group of notes to be labeled as grace notes, given a nominal duration or extent, then be followed by the principal note, whose extent is the length of the entire grouping. It would be up to a performer to interpret this, but logically it is clear: the grace notes have a nominal duration, as does the principal note, but only the principal note marks distance on the coordinate axis, or in other words, only the time of the principal note is counted when counting beats.

```
<ceg grpdex=40320> --defines duration of entire grouping--
    <ceg grace> --these are grace notes--
        <note><extlist>2570<nompitch>-2 a
        <note><extlist>2570<nompitch>-1 c
        <note><extlist>2570<nompitch>-2 e
    </ceg>
    <ceg nograce> --this is the following note--
        <note><extlist>40230<nompitch>-1 a
    </ceg>
</ceg>
```

Example 30.2 Encoding of grace notes in the Mozart piano sonata.

Example 30.3 shows how *SMDL* handles several staves for one instrument, as in the piano excerpt. One simply creates a different thread for each staff. Cross-beaming and slurring are visual issues but they can be aided by the ability to create links from notes in one thread to notes in another.

```
<thread id=rhthd nominst="piano top staff">
</thread>
<thread id=lhthd nominst="piano bottom staff">
</thread>
```

Example 30.3 Encoding of multiple staves in the Mozart piano sonata.

30.4.3 The Saltarello

Example 30.4 demonstrates the ability to handle first and second endings, as called for in the saltarello. The *cantus* event group has the ability to choose one or all of its constituents. Here, each ending is put in a nested group, with the top level of the hierarchy indicating which to choose. In logical structure, first and second endings are similar to *ossia*[7] designations. In the former case, one chooses by criteria of placement in the piece, while in the latter, choices are made by other criteria; in both cases it forms an either/or branch. It may also be possible to create first and second endings entirely within separate groupings. That is, the material preceding the endings may be stated in its own group, putting the first ending as a separate group at the end of the first "occurrence" and the second ending after the *cantus* event group that repeats the original material (the second "occurrence"). This method is not demonstrated here.

```
<ceg choice=one>
    <ceg id=firstend>
    --notes and rests of first ending go here.--
    </ceg>
    <ceg id=secndend>
    --notes and rests of second ending go here.--
    </ceg>
</ceg>
```

Example 30.4 Handling of first and second endings in the saltarello.

30.4.4 The Telemann Aria

Example 30.5 shows a method for associating lyrics with musical notes in *SMDL*. Taking the first part of the Telemann example, a thread (Lines 5–14) contains the notes of the soprano line for the first 15 measures. A separate element called a *lyric* uses the previously defined thread as a reference. As events, however, it uses not notes and rests but rather syllables and rests (Lines 18–27). Ties in the lyric element have

---

7. That is, an alternative line for a phrase, as, for example, in a concerto, where a slightly easier passage may be suggested as a substitute for a difficult phrase. Other alternative readings might suggest how to execute an embellishment or give variant readings in manuscript sources.

the effect of extending the syllable over several notes. The separation of threads and lyrics allows easy application of strophic verse.

```
 1    --Lyrics with a vocal line. (Example 4)--
 2    --As before, showing only the code dealing directly
 3    with features in question.--
 4    --Here are the soprano notes.--
 5    <thread id=soprthd nominst="soprano">
 6        <rest>33t
 7        <note>2t 1 e
 8        <note>t 0 a
 9        <rest>6t
10        <note>3t4 1 c
11        <note>t4 1 d
12        <note>t 1 e
13        <note>t 0 a
14    </thread>
15
16    --Here are the words, linked to the notes above.--
17
18    <lyric id=soprtxt thread=soprthd>
19        <rest>33t
20        <syllable>Lie-
21        <syllable>be!
22        <rest>6t
23        <syllable tie>Lie-
24        <syllable tie>
25        <syllable>
26        <syllable>be!
27    </lyric>
```

Example 30.5 Linking of lyrics with notes in the Telemann example.

30.5 Additional Comments on *SMDL*

Several questions posed to contributors are not covered above. The question of measure numbering is not explicitly described in *HyTime/SMDL*. Instead it is given to the counting facilities in *HyTime*; creating such a function is implicit. The creator of the document would define issues like numbering for an upbeat or for first and second endings. As long as events may be properly referenced in the *cantus* of an *SMDL* document, it does not matter logically what numbers they are given. Thus, this is an issue for the visual domain to resolve.

The matter of differentiation of original and editorial material, as in the Telemann example, is strictly one of labels. In the *cantus*, each line may be in a separate thread, one perhaps labeled as editorial in origin. There is no restriction against combining several threads onto one staff for visual presentation. Therefore the proper separation of such material at the thread level would allow a score formatter to make the appropriate differentiation in presentation.

The question of early-music representation is often one of visual presentation. The logical information (pitches, durations, and words associated with them) would not be represented in the *cantus* in essentially different ways from post-Renaissance music. The visual appearance of neumes and ligatures[8] could be represented visually in any way that the encoder sees fit. If a ligature should represent several different pitches, these pitches could form a separate *cantus* event group to which the ligature would be linked. Since *SMDL* does not enforce measuring of music, unmeasured music creates no additional problem.

Likewise, modern notation should not pose problems of representation in *SMDL*. Whatever a particular symbol or glyph may represent, if it has meaning in terms of pitch or duration, it can be linked to *cantus* events as described above. For symbols that describe timbral change, they may be described as a formula that is part of a wand. These wands modify existing events in a manner defined by the user. For example, if the composer indicated a transition between open and closed sounds with a trumpet player's Harmon mute, the wand describing this may be a function over time of the percentage of the mute which is closed, or even just moments when open, moments when closed, and transitions in between, leaving the interpretation to a performer. Wands have durations, just as notes do, and they therefore can be given as specific a temporal indication, in real time or music time, as may be required.

It should be clear from the above discussion that *HyTime/SMDL* is well suited as a representation standard for virtually any other coding scheme. Even for those codes that represent things that are not explicitly represented in *HyTime/SMDL*, it is at least possible to label the chunk of data so that a machine encountering it would know what it was. While this is already accomplished by such things as file formats, *HyTime* has further facilities for internally labeling parts of the data and linking them arbitrarily to other constructs both within that particular chunk and outside it. For example, even if one does not have a program to interpret *DARMS* code, it may be useful to be able to mark and link each symbol to logical information in an *SMDL cantus*. In such a manner, translators can be built between the various existing codes.

If every code is to be able to be translated to any other, it is much more convenient to have a "mediator" language. To illustrate why, if ten different coding schemes were in regular use, one would need 90 translators to convert from any one to any other one. With a mediator such as *SMDL*, one would need only 20 translators—one for each specific code to and from *SMDL*. *SMDL* is ideal for this task because it provides

---

8. Neumes are icons used in the Middle Ages to represent musical pitches. Ligatures are groups of contiguous neumes read as a unit.

a means of representing or, at minimum, storing and identifying any item in any other code, whether it be for score or performance needs. No other code at this time can make this claim.

HyTime/SMDL code was not devised to be easily and quickly read by end-users; it is intended for machine use. While making some attempts through mnemonics and macro facilities to allow easier understanding by people, there is no requirement of easy legibility. It is not anticipated that end-users will need to be able to read *SMDL*; rather, it is up to software developers to create an interface that allows musicians to enter and view musical information in a format that is already familiar and convenient. *HyTime* and *SMDL* should work behind the scenes, in a manner transparent to the user. Indeed, its success as a potential standard is dependent on developers achieving this transparency.

HyTime/SMDL code in its pure form can be somewhat verbose, although there are several ways to make the representation more concise by what is called "markup minimization." Unfortunately, human legibility, full functionality, and compact representation are mutually antagonistic, and complete satisfaction in all of these areas is not feasible.

It should also be noted again that while *HyTime* has already been approved as an ISO standard, *SMDL* is still in draft form. The bulk of the work on *SMDL* has been in the areas of pitch and duration; while the other areas are designed in theory as described above, the actual coding is still often sketchy, and thus cannot necessarily be given specific lines of code in the examples. The reader is asked to accept on faith that if there is a piece of information that a musician wishes to be captured, there will be a way of representing it in *HyTime/SMDL*.

HyTime and *SMDL* do not themselves contain translators, style sheets, or other applications. These must be written by software developers. The future is now being passed from those who designed the standard to those who will ultimately either use or reject it.

30.6   Additional Comments on *HyTime*[9]

SMDL aims to provide a standard way to represent "locations" within files in established digital music notations, rather than to represent specific details of particular

---

9. Section 30.6, as well as Figures 30.1 and 30.2, have been provided by Steven R. Newcomb, Vice Chair of the ANSI committee that drafted *HyTime* and *SMDL*. He can be reached at TechnoTeacher, PO Box 23795, Rochester, NY 14692-3795; tel. +1 716/389-0964; fax: +1 716/389-0960; *srn@techno.com*.

editions or performances. Thus, *SMDL* can be used with music encoded in *DARMS*, *MUSTRAN*, *SCORE*, *Finale*, and the Standard MIDI File Format, as well as purely graphical formats such as *PostScript*. *HyTime*'s document location addressing facilities are ideally suited to the purpose of identifying specific subsets of data in such documents, and they can be used in concert with *HyTime* hyperlinks to make all useful relationships between performances and editions explicit. Such an address might be expressed as some number of quanta starting at some quantum number, where quanta are bytes, tokens, or tree nodes, or it might be expressed semantically in some user-specifiable query language, e.g., "the fourth sonority from the beginning of the recapitulation."

SMDL regards music as a combination of groups of events. The events occur in schedules in a finite coordinate space of one dimension (time). Each event has a position (start) and extent (duration) on the one-coordinate axis of the schedule (Figure 30.2). Both position and extent may be specified by explicit addresses on the axis and/or by reference to the start or duration of some other event. Specification by reference to some absolute time is also possible.

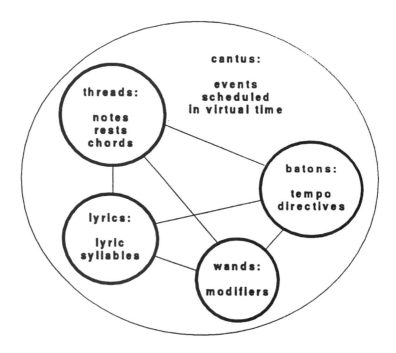

Figure 30.2 Structure of the logical domain (or *cantus*) of an *SMDL* document.

The ability to define events in terms of each other provides an economy of notation especially evident in cases in which schedules or portions of schedules can be represented merely by reference. Defining events relatively also means that proportionality can be maintained regardless of variations in the rate at which scheduled time is rendered.

In *SMDL* the beat rate is controlled by a *HyTime* construct called a *baton*. *Batons* are special schedules in the *cantus*, whose events may be thought of as tempo directives. Each tempo directive has a start time and a duration specified in the *baton* which associates it with those events scheduled in the *cantus* for which it will establish the tempo (or beat rate).

The variety of musical performing directions used to modify the character of musical events defies categorization. An instruction to depress the piano's damper pedal, for example, not only affects the perceived durations of the notes it governs; it also adds the sounds made by the sympathetic vibrations of all the undampened strings in the instrument, even if they were not struck. Some performing directions affect only the timbre of sustained tones, while others affect articulations, and still others change only the sound of the start of each note. All such user-defined semantics are handled in the *HyTime* scheduler called a *wand*. Only the means of expressing the *extent* of each modifier's effect is defined by the *SMDL* standard.

30.7   Further Information

Additional information on *HyTime* is available from the special interest group devoted to it. Enquiries may be addressed to John Chisholm, Registrar, SGML SIGhyper, 6610 Byrnes Drive, McLean, VA 22101.

Additional information on *SGML* is available in various archives of the Usenet discussion file *comp.text.sgml*. For information on access and holdings send a message to *enag@ifi.uio.no*.

Transcripts of the *HyTime* and *SMDL* draft (DIS) and formal IS) standards, adopted in the summer of 1996, may be obtained from the American National Standards Institute, 13th Floor, 11 W. 42nd St., New York, NY 10036-8002; tel. +1 212/642-4900; fax +1 212/398-0023, and by ftp from appropriately named files in the directory *ftp://ftp.ornl.gov/pub/smgl/WG8/* . . . .

References

Goldfarb, Charles F. *"HyTime*: A Standard for Structured Hypermedia Interchange," *IEEE Computer*, 24/8 (August, 1991), 81–84.

Goldfarb, Charles F. *The SGML Handbook*. New York: Oxford University Press, 1990.

Newcomb, Steven R., Neill A. Kipp, Victoria T. Newcomb, "The *HyTime* Hypermedia/ Time-Based Document Structuring Language," *Communications of the Association for Computing Machinery* (November, 1991), 67–83.

Sloan, Donald. "Aspects of Music Representation in *HyTime/SMDL*," *Computer Music Journal* 17/4 (Winter, 1993), 51–59.

31   The *Notation Interchange File Format*: A *Windows*-Compliant Approach

Cindy Grande

NIFF[1] is a file format designed to allow the interchange of music notation data between and among music notation editing and publishing programs and music scanning programs. Its design is a result of combined input from many commercial music software developers, music publishers, and experienced music software users.[2]

31.1   Goals and Context

The lack of an accepted standard format for music notation has for years been a source of great frustration for computer musicians, engravers and publishers. Numerous attempts have been made in the past to create a standard format. The effort resulting in *NIFF* is different for several reasons:

---

1. This summary was prepared just prior to the completion of *NIFF* Version 6a (June 1995), which was in trial implementation at press time (June 1996). Although the structural framework of the format had been settled, some details, such as exactly which ornaments were to be included, remained unfinished. Details presented in this introduction should not be considered final.

2. The financial sponsors of the *NIFF* design project include Passport Designs, Mark of the Unicorn, Opcode Systems, Musicware (previously known as TAP Music Systems), Twelve Tone Systems, Musitek, San Andreas Press, and Grande Software. Twelve Tone Systems announced in January 1996 its intention to support the *NIFF* method of data interchange.

    Cindy Grande, President of Grande Software, Inc., is Technical Coordinator; Chris Newell, President of Musitek Music Recognition Technologies, Inc., (410 Bryant Circle, Ste. K, Ojai, CA 93023-4209) is Administrative Coordinator. Special thanks for technical help is due to Alan Belkin of the University of Montreal, Dave Abrahams of Mark of the Unicorn, Norman Reid of San Francisco, CA, and Mark Walsen of Bellevue, WA.

- Many of the major forces in the commercial music software industry and several of the largest music publishers have shown a remarkable willingness to cooperate in the design of *NIFF*.

- Commercial music scanning programs are a recent addition to the software market. They require a common language with notation programs to avoid the enormous loss of detail that occurs when translating through MIDI files.

Music notation is a complex language. Like a natural language, it is always changing, it is at times ambiguous and/or redundant, and can be used in many different ways by different people for different purposes. Because of these qualities, it is impossible to create a perfect computer model for music notation.

The original sponsors of the *NIFF* project recognized these limitations, and set a more reasonable goal: to create a practical, useable format in a short time frame. *NIFF* project participants have agreed that a solid, workable solution, even if it excludes some unusual situations, is preferable to no solution.

The *NIFF* planners considered adopting as the standard an existing published format such as *DARMS* or *SCORE*, but decided against it. The designers of *DARMS* had somewhat different goals from *NIFF*'s. *SCORE*, although extremely comprehensive and appropriate in scope, was somewhat unwieldy due to its age and development history. Another possibility considered was the ISO/ANSI standard *HyTime* and its associated music standard known as *SMDL*, but *SMDL* was not yet complete at the time the *NIFF* project got underway.

A general strategy was chosen as follows: model *NIFF*'s feature set on *SCORE*'s, organize the data as systematically as possible, and use the most current file format conventions. During the development of the format, additional more specific goals have been established. Some useful functional features of *DARMS* have been incorporated as well.

The *NIFF* structure can accommodate full music publishing systems, simpler music display systems, logical-definition languages like *DARMS*, and music scanning programs. It allows representation of the most common situations occurring in conventional music notation, while making provision for software developers to define their own extensions to handle the more unusual situations. It allows inclusion of embedded *PostScript* files and fonts to allow interchange of features not otherwise defined in the format.

31.1.1 Extensibility, Flexibility, and Compactness

Extensibility is an important goal. The *NIFF* specification is not an attempt at an exhaustive catalog of music notation features. A high priority has thus been given to structuring the data in ways that minimize the pain of future enhancements.

NIFF is also designed to be flexible, in order to accommodate the differences between the programs and users it will serve.

An effort has been made to keep files as compact as possible, since *NIFF* files will likely be transmitted electronically over low-bandwidth lines.

31.1.2 Logical, Graphical, and MIDI Performance Data

Researchers have found that the computer representation of music notation has three distinct components only partially related to each other: logical, graphical, and performance (MIDI) information. *NIFF* designers have found it useful to further subdivide the graphical information into page-layout and non-page-layout information.

The only information that *NIFF* absolutely requires is the logical kind. *NIFF* is structured as a page-ordered format, but can accommodate writing programs without access to page-layout information and systems like *DARMS* which allow even non-page-layout graphical information such as stem directions to be absent.

When complete graphical information is present in a *NIFF* file, the reading program can decide between observing the page layout and other positioning information, ignoring this graphical information in favor of its own defaults, or some intelligent combination. When any graphical information is absent from a *NIFF* file, the reading program is expected to provide its own intelligent defaults.

It is recommended that the user of the *NIFF* writing and reading programs be given as much control as possible. The user should decide the level of detail stored in the file by the writing program, and the degree of freedom used in interpretation by the reading program.

NIFF also allows thorough linking of MIDI data and notation.

31.1.3 Illegal Notation Elements

There is no such thing as an "illegal notation element" in *NIFF*. That is, there is no requirement for the data in a *NIFF* file to "make sense." A reading program should expect occasionally to find data that is not compatible with its own range of acceptable usage. When an unknown or unacceptable element is encountered, the program should either ignore it or do the best it can with it, in order to create a valid file in its own internal format.

31.1.4 The Resource Interchange File Format (RIFF)

The *NIFF* format follows the design rules of the Resource Interchange File Format (RIFF) structure from Microsoft. In RIFF files, related data items are grouped into *chunks*, and related chunks can be combined into *lists*. Chunks and lists include their own length within their structure. RIFF files are designed to be upwardly compatible, that is, amenable to future enhancements.

A RIFF file and each of its lists and chunks can be variable in length. A logical definition is required for each RIFF format, to identify which elements are required or optional at each level and the order in which the elements may appear.

An additional type of data item known as a *tag* has been defined as an integral part of *NIFF*. Tags are used for adding optional elements to the required part of a chunk. Although not part of the standard RIFF design, tags can be described within RIFF's logical definition language.

Detailed rules on reading and writing RIFF files are published in the *Microsoft Windows Multimedia Programmer's Reference*.

31.1.5 Platform Independence

The *NIFF* format definition applies to both Intel (IBM-compatible) and Motorola (Macintosh) computers, although the integer byte order will differ on the two machines. The first four bytes of the file indicate which one is used. The designation RIFF indicates Intel byte order; RIFX indicates Motorola byte order. *NIFF* reading programs should expect to find either type of file, and be prepared to translate the data into their own machine's format.

31.2 Logical Structures

There are some terms commonly found in discussions of music notation which most musicians intuitively understand. This section defines these terms to help the reader understand their specific usage in *NIFF*.

31.2.1 Score

Each *NIFF* file contains one score. A score could hold anything from a one-bar music example, to a song, a piano sonata movement, or a scene from an opera in full score. A work in more than one movement would normally be stored with each movement in its own *NIFF* file.

31.2.2 Part

A stream of musical events and associated symbols, text and graphics which can be extracted and printed on a part score for an individual performer. A part may contain music to be played sequentially on different related instruments by the same performer (e.g., oboe/English horn). The maximum number of staves used for display is defined for each part.

31.2.3 Voice

A rhythmically independent stream of musical events within a part, and its associated symbols, text and graphics. Voices can appear and disappear at any time within a part.

31.2.4 System

The visual framework of a group of staves on a page, where symbols representing simultaneous events in the various parts are vertically aligned. All parts of the score are logically present in every system although some may be hidden.

31.2.5 Staff

A sort of vessel within a system into which musical symbols can be poured. It contains music symbols belonging to one or more parts.

31.2.6 Time-Slice

The mechanism by which a specific point in time is identified in the score. Musical symbols representing simultaneous events in the various parts are logically grouped within the same time-slice. The music symbols in a *NIFF* file are physically grouped by page and staff, so symbols belonging to a common logical time-slice may be physically separated in the file. A horizontal position within the measure can optionally be defined for a time-slice. There are three types of time-slice: bar-line, event, and non-event. A bar-line time-slice represents the start time of a measure, contrary to the traditional use of a bar line as the end of a measure, but more useful representationally. It is usually accompanied by one or more graphical bar-line symbols. A non-event time-slice is used strictly for defining a sequential position within a measure. It represents no specific start time, but may be assigned a horizontal position.

The logical part and staff structures were designed to handle situations like those described below.

A. EXAMPLE 1

In a Mahler symphony score there are three trumpet parts. The trumpets appear in one system all together on one staff, called "Tpts. 1, 2, 3", because they are playing monorhythmically. They are written as chords, with three notes on one stem. In another system the trumpets appear on three separate staves (labelled "Tpt. 1", "Tpt. 2", "Tpt. 3") because they are playing a complex canon. In the logical view, the notes played by the trumpets belong to three separate parts. In the physical view of the canonic system, each trumpet part is assigned to its own staff. Each staff name defaults to the name defined for the part.

In the physical view of the homophonic system, the three parts are combined together onto a single staff. Since there is a conflict in the names of the three parts, the default name is overridden for this staff to specify "Tpts. 1, 2, 3". The simultaneous notes of each chord played by the three trumpet parts appear together associated with a single stem within each time-slice. Each note indicates the part to which it belongs.

B. EXAMPLE 2

Consider a score with *divisi* writing where the first violin part is temporarily divided into groups. The first violin part is split onto two separate staves in one system, and three separate staves in another system. There are a variety of ways this could be represented in *NIFF*. The choice depends on the desired result when the parts are to be extracted and printed for individual players:

If the first violin part score is to show all the *divisi* parts, the first violin should be defined as a single part with a maximum number of staves of three. The notes of this part would be distributed among the one, two or three staves active for the part in each system. Three separate voices would be assigned, each voice appearing on its own staff.

If separate part scores are to be printed for different first violin players, more than one first violin part should be defined in the *NIFF* file, each one associated with the musical symbols that would be printed on a particular part score. If the same passage is to appear on two different part scores, both parts should be indicated for each individual symbol within the passage. A shorthand method allows the part or parts to be assigned in the staff header, when all symbols on a system's staff belong to the same part(s).

31.3   Physical Structures

A *NIFF* file is divided into two sections—the *setup section*, containing part definitions, defaults, and other header information, and the *data section*, containing the music symbols.

Most chunks in the setup section are used only for overriding defaults. For example, part definitions are only required when there is a need to define part name, abbreviation, default MIDI channel and cable numbers, transposition on playback, or a feature such as small font size.

The music symbols in the data section are stored in page-ordered format. The format has a hierarchical structure, in which pages contain systems, systems contain staves, and staves contain time-slices and individual music symbols. Within each level, data are supplied generally in a left-to-right, top-to-bottom order. Text and graphics can be included at any level of the hierarchy, according to the type of object to which they logically belong.

A special case of this hierarchical data structure is known as *simulated part ordering*. In this structure, all musical symbols are placed in one system on an indefinitely wide page, with one staff for each part. This special type of *NIFF* file is indicated by a page with zero width and length. This structure is compatible with programs which keep each part's data separate.

31.3.1 Measurement Units and Coordinate System

A. ABSOLUTE UNITS AND STAFF STEPS

NIFF uses two different measurement systems—absolute units and staff steps.

Absolute units are the writing program's own choice of units, declared in the Setup Section. The choice of absolute units is expressed as two field values: the *standard unit* (inches, centimeters, or points), and the number of *absolute units* per standard unit. For example, if the resolution used by the writing program were 4000 dots per inch, the writing program would choose a standard unit of inches and the number of absolute units per standard unit would be 4000.

The placement of a symbol whose meaning depends on its vertical position on a staff line or space is given as a *staff step*. The origin of the staff-step system is the bottom line, which is given the value zero. Step numbers increase by one for each successive line or space in an upward direction from the origin. Negative numbers are used for the lines and spaces below the origin.

B. TIMING REPRESENTATION

NIFF allows timing information to be stored for two kinds of playback: (1) logically precise playback derived from the notation, and (2) the nuanced rubato of a recorded performance.

For each playback event, there are two pieces of timing information: (1) start time, when the event is to occur, and (2) duration, how long it lasts.

For *logical playback*, both start time and duration are represented by rational numbers (fractions) which describe the relationship between a note value and a standard unit of time—the whole note. The rational number consists of two integers, a numerator and a denominator. A half note is 1/2 of a whole note; thus its numerator is 1 and its denominator is 2. A quarter note is 1/4. Infinitely smaller note types can be invented by increasing the denominator to any power of 2. The start time of a note or rest is the sum of all the durations of the preceding notes and rests in the measure in the same voice. The start time of a measure is the sum of all the durations of the preceding notes and rests in the score.

For a tuplet, an additional chunk is stored, containing a transformation ratio to be applied to each note in the tuplet, and graphical information about the appearance of the tuplet such as the presence of numbers and/or brackets.

Logical gaps can be represented by the addition of invisible place-holding bar lines or rests, or by adding extra value to the start time of the event following the gap to compensate for the missing time.

For *performance playback*, MIDI clocks are used to record start time and duration. The performance start time and duration are given as offsets (+/−) from the logical start time and duration of the event. MIDI channel and velocity can also be stored for each note.

The note and stem chunks contain graphical features such as number of flags and notehead shape. However, in *NIFF* these graphical features have no timing implications. It is the logical duration field stored on the note chunk that defines the timing. In practice, any combination of a note's graphical features, or even an invisible note on a zero-length stem, could be used to represent any time value.

The logical start time and duration are required fields; the performance start time and duration are optional. If not present, it is assumed that the performance values are equivalent to the logical values.

NIFF does not require logical adherence to time signatures. Any number of beats can occur in a measure.

A grace note is indicated by the addition of a grace-note tag to a note chunk. It is included in the same event time-slice as the note it graces. The grace-note tag gives the note's logical start-time offset from the time-slice start time (negative, zero or positive, depending on the chosen interpretation of grace notes and the note's position within a series of grace notes). The performance start time (in the note's performance tag) is given as an offset in MIDI clocks from the grace note's logical start time. Other optional information that might appear on a grace-note chunk are small size, horizontal offset (negative) from the time-slice, and slashed stem. Grace notes can be beamed and slurred like any other notes.

31.3.2 Symbol Relationships

The *NIFF* system of symbol relationships has been carefully designed for logical rigor, flexibility, and efficiency. It plays a major role in both file syntax and symbol placement.

A. SYMBOL ID'S AND UNIQUENESS CONTEXT

Each chunk is assigned an identification number (ID) either by default or explicitly. The ID for each chunk type is unique within a certain context such as the score or the staff/measure. ID numbers start with zero and increase sequentially within the uniqueness context, in the order in which the chunks are stored in the file.

B. DEPENDENT SYMBOLS AND THEIR ANCHORS

A symbol whose placement depends on one or more other symbols is called a *dependent symbol*, and the symbol or other chunk type on which its placement depends is called its *anchor*. For each symbol chunk type, a default anchor chunk type is defined. The anchor override tag can be used on a dependent symbol chunk to indicate a non-default anchor type.

The most important rule of file syntax is that the dependent symbol should physically appear in the file as soon as possible after its anchor. File syntax and anchor overrides allow for representation of complex dependencies, such as a slur between two fingering numbers dependent on a note, parentheses surrounding the staccatos over a series of notes, or a small sharp sign above a trill ornament over a note.

Beams, slurs, ties, and hairpins are examples of *multi-node symbols*—symbols which are normally dependent on more than one anchor. Multi-node symbols are decomposed into *node chunks*, each one corresponding to one of its anchor chunks. For example, each beam node indicates the number of beam parts to the left and right of its note stem. Each beam-node chunk physically appears in the file immediately after its corresponding stem chunk.

Cross-staff beams and chords, and symbols such as slurs that cross system and page boundaries can all be represented, using various multi-node symbol tags.

31.4   Musical Features

31.4.1   Articulation and Ornamentation

The details for handling articulation marks and ornamentation signs are not yet finalized. They may evolve during trial implementation. A separate chunk is defined for each symbol type with a different musical function, such as articulation, ornament, fingering, parenthesis.

The *articulation chunk* currently defines the following objects: strong accent (up-wedge), strong accent (▾), medium accent (>), light accent or tenuto (–), staccato, down-bow, up-bow, harmonic (○), fermata, arsis sign, thesis sign, and plus sign. These symbols can be combined using file syntax and optional placement tags.

The ornament table currently includes various trills, mordents, and turns, and an arpeggio that is dependent on two note anchors, on the same stem or on different staves.

31.4.2   Dynamics

Dynamics are represented in their text form by the dynamic chunk, with values *pppp* through *ffff*, *sp*, *sf*, *sfz*, *fz*, *fp*, *cresc.*, *crescendo*, *dim.*, and *diminuendo*. This list may be extended. Hairpins are represented with a multi-node chunk type, anchored to time-slices at each end by default.

31.4.3   Timbre

MIDI channel and cable numbers can be assigned to parts and/or notes, and other MIDI information affecting timbre can be included in MIDI data-stream chunks.

31.5   Graphic Anomalies

The four-line staff in Example 1.5A (unmeasured chant) can be described by overriding the default number of staff lines in the staff header. The non-standard clef sign can be described by a custom-shape tag on the *clef chunk*, its placement given as its staff step. The short vertical lines could be described with a *line chunk* with its termination points described by their staff step.

31.5.1   Early Music

NIFF is capable of representing all attributes of early music shown in the examples distributed. However, as one stretches *NIFF*'s capabilities, more creativity is required by the author of the writing program, and fewer reading programs will be designed to interpret the results correctly. In any case, here are some possibilities:

A. UNMEASURED NOTATION

The notation shown in Example 1.5B (the unmeasured chant "Quem queritis") is not a problem. Adherence to time signatures is not required. A measure can have any number of beats.

B. LIGATURES

NIFF is not designed specifically to handle early-music ligatures as shown in Example 1.5A (the unmeasured chant "Alma Redemptoris Mater"). However, it would be possible to represent successfully both the notation and the sound in a *NIFF* file, using the custom font feature and MIDI file embedding.

C. NEUMES

A character of any font may be specified as the shape for a note by appending a custom-shape tag to the note chunk. The whole font can be stored in the *NIFF* file, if desired, in *PostScript* format. There are several techniques that could be used to make the stem invisible; these include adding an *invisible tag*, adding a *height tag* of zero, or setting its endpoint to the same staff step as the note.

The most interesting challenge in Example 1.5A is that when a series of pitches is represented by a single neume, the sound cannot be represented by a single note chunk. Probably the best solution for this would be to anchor a MIDI data-stream chunk to the note chunk. The MIDI data-stream chunk is the way to embed a stream of MIDI events that correspond to a particular symbol in the notation.

D. INCIPITS

The most outstanding feature of the incipit shown in the Binchois *Magnificat* (Example 1.6) is the appearance of only one staff in the first measure. In addition, in the top staff, the clef sign and key signature appear in the second measure as well as the first measure, and the time signature appears only in the second measure. There are stemless notes. Finally, there appears to be an unusually shaped notehead for the last note, and a stem on the "wrong" side of the notehead. All of these features can be represented in *NIFF*.

The staff header for the second staff can be assigned a horizontal offset tag indicating that this staff starts about an inch to the right of the start of the system. The second staff's first bar-line time-slice should contain a start time equal to the start time on the first staff's second bar-line time-slice, probably 5/4.

The clef sign, key signature, and time signature can each be stored with a single chunk anywhere on a staff, any number of times. The techniques for making a stem invisible and using a non-standard notehead are described above for ligatures. For putting the stem on the wrong side of the notehead, a symbol-placement tag should be used, specifying that the dependent note is to the left of the stem.

E. HEMIOLAS

The hemiolas shown in Example 1.6 raise a performance issue, not a notation issue. There is nothing unusual about a *NIFF* file that represents this example.

31.5.2 Twentieth-Century Music

One of the challenges in designing *NIFF* has been to decide where to draw the line when defining features. Many twentieth-century innovations have been left for the category of system-exclusive extensions, whereby *NIFF* writing programs can define their own chunks and tags, each with its own function. The most useful of these are likely to become *de facto* additions to the *NIFF* standard. In addition, *NIFF*'s flexibility can be used creatively to handle a range of unusual situations, not all of them unique to the twentieth century. A few possibilities are discussed below:

A. THE CUSTOM-SHAPE SYMBOL CHUNK

In addition to the custom font shapes that can be assigned to notes and other defined symbols, there is a custom-shape *symbol chunk* that can be used when a custom graphic is to be placed anywhere on the page with no musical function or sound. A MIDI data-stream chunk might be anchored to it to describe its sound.

Straight lines, arrows, and wavy, dashed and dotted lines of various thicknesses starting and ending anywhere in the score can be described.

B. UNUSUAL CLEF AND METER SIGNS

When two clef signs appear simultaneously on one staff, one or more voice ID tags can be assigned to each clef and to a subset of the notes on the staff, to associate each clef with its corresponding notes.

Time signatures are allowed to contain any numbers, of any size, placed anywhere on, above or below the staff, with or without parentheses or plus signs.

Simultaneous meters can be present in a score. However, special care must be taken to ensure that the simultaneity of events in the different parts can be recognized by the reading program. For this to occur, the logical durations of events must be manipulated.

For example, consider two parts, where the same duration is to be notated as a quarter note in one part and a dotted quarter in the other, such as in 2/4 vs. 6/8 time. This can be accomplished by assigning the same logical duration of 1/4 to the notes in both parts, even though an augmentation dot appears next to the note in the second part. The augmentation dot, even in a score without simultaneous meters, is represented by a dot chunk with only graphical significance anchored to the note chunk. In a score without the simultaneous meter issue, a quarter note would be assigned a logical duration of 3/8 if it were to appear with an augmentation dot.

C. OMITTED STAFF LINES

Cutouts are a feature in contemporary scores where the staff lines are missing in all measures except those containing notes. This could be represented by using an invisible tag on a series of bar-line time-slices, which is defined to mean that the staff itself is invisible for the length of those measures.

31.6   File Organization

31.6.1   Processing Order

NIFF maintains a score-dominant as opposed to a part-dominant orientation toward the relevant materials. The nomenclature used is as follows:

31.6.2   Number of Files

The consequences of this system of organization in terms of the number of files produced is briefly represented by the following examples:

- ONE MOVEMENT OF A PIANO PIECE: Describe in one *NIFF* file containing one part, possibly with many voices.

- A STRING QUARTET IN FOUR MOVEMENTS: Describe in four *NIFF* files, each containing four parts. The data would be structured hierarchically by page, system, and staff, or simulated part ordering could be used, with each complete part stored in sequence.

- A STROPHIC SONG FOR PIANO AND SOLO VOICE WITH THREE VERSES: Describe in one *NIFF* file, with separate parts for piano and voice. Time-slices within the voice part would have three *lyric chunks* attached, with each lyric chunk representing a word or syllable belonging to one verse.

31.6.3   Combination/Separation/Recombination of Parts

The following example in pseudo-code, based on the Telemann aria (Example 1.4), gives the flavor of how a *NIFF* file would represent multiple parts on one staff, with one part shown in a small note size.

Simultaneous beams are also shown. In this score, since the part names appear scattered throughout the score rather than in the standard place to the left of the appropriate system, data-section text chunks should be used for part names. Two parts are explicitly defined in the Setup Section chunks to assign a small font size.

```
[Setup Section:]

Part, ID=3, small size
Part, ID=4, small size

[System 1, staff 2, measure 7:]
```

```
Time-slice, type=barline, start-time=18/3
Barline, type=thin line
Time-slice, type=event, start-time=0/8
Stem, staff step=13, part ID=2
Note, staff step=7, logical duration=3/16
Augmentation dot
Beam, ID=8, number of nodes=3, parts to left=0, parts to right=1
Stem, part ID=3, part ID=4, staff step=-4, flags=1
Note, staff step=0, logical duration=1/8
Note, staff step=4, logical duration=1/8
Time-slice, start-time=1/8
Stem, part ID=3, staff step=-3
Note, staff step=0, logical duration=1/4
Stem, part ID=4, staff step=-1,
    horizontal logical placement=to right [of time-slice]
Note, staff step=3, logical duration=1/8
Beam, ID=9, number of nodes=2, parts to left=0, parts to right=1
Time-slice, type=event, start time=3/16
Stem, part ID=2, staff step=12
Note, staff step=5, logical duration=1/16
Beam, ID=8, parts to left=2, parts to right=1

(etc.)
```

Example 31.1 *NIFF* handling of combined violin and oboe parts on one staff (see System 1, Staff 2, Bar 7 of the Telemann aria).

31.6.4 Bar Numbering

There is no logical significance to bar numbering, except as described below for repeated passages and multiple endings.

31.6.5 Repeated Passages and Multiple Endings

There is an *alternative-ending tag* applied to all bar-line time-slices of alternative endings, validating the otherwise logically inconsistent duplication of measure start times. The alternative-ending tag contains the sequence number of the ending to which the measure belongs. There would normally also be an alternative-ending graphical-symbol chunk which indicates the appearance of the alternative ending, at least on the topmost staff.

A repeated section of a score appears in the *NIFF* file only once. One or more graphical bar-line symbols follow the final time-slice of the repeated section. Each one describes the shape of one physical object: thick line, thin line, repeat dots, etc. To indicate the start and end of a section functionally, repeat indicator chunks should be used.

The following pseudo-code example gives the flavor of how a *NIFF* file would handle bar numbering, repeats, and alternative endings. Each line, except those in parentheses, represents one chunk in the following example (based on the saltarello, Example 1.3):

```
[Staff 1:]
Time-slice, type=barline, start-time=0/8
Time-slice, type=non-event
Clef
Time-slice, type=non-event
Time signature
Repeat indicator, code=start of section
Time-slice, type=non-event
Text, value="1.", anchor=repeat indicator, logical placement=above
    [staff]

[6 measures later:]
Time-slice, type=barline, start time=36/8, alternative ending=1
Barline, type=thin line
Alternative ending graphic, ID=1, number of nodes=2,
    shape=down jog at beginning + down jog at end
Text='I.', anchor=alternative ending graphic
(stems, notes, beams, etc.)
Time-slice, type=barline, start time=42/8, alternative ending=1
Barline, type=thin line
(stems, notes, beams, etc.)
Repeat indicator, code=end of section
Time-slice, type=non-event
Barline, type=repeat dots
Barline, type=thin line
Barline, type=thick line
Alternative ending graphic, ID=1, anchor=barline

[Staff 2:]
Time-slice, type=barline, start-time=36/8, alternative ending=2
Time-slice, type=non-event
Clef
Time-slice, type=non-event
Alternative ending graphic, ID=2, number of nodes=2,
    shape=down jog at beginning + down jog at end
Text='II.', anchor=alternative ending graphic

[2 measures later:]
Repeat indicator, code=end of section
Time-slice, type=barline, start-time=48/8
Barline, type=thin line
Alternative ending graphic, ID=2, anchor=barline
Barline, type=thick line
Barline, type=repeat dots
Repeat indicator, code=start of section
Text, value="2.", anchor=repeat indicator, logical placement= above
    [staff]
(more symbols ...)
```

Example 31.2 *NIFF* handling of selected details (repeats and multiple endings) in the saltarello.

31.6.6 Differentiation of Original and Editorially Realized Material

To differentiate editorially realized from original material a separate part ID could be defined, and its appearance made distinctive with graphical information such as size and location of symbols and text. For suggested performance such as in Bar 30 of the Telemann aria, a separate voice might be assigned to the small size notes, with the note in the first voice given the *silent* tag.

31.6.7 Editorial Accidentals

There is a parenthesis chunk that can be used to specify various shapes of parentheses—with different codes for left, right and both—as found in Bar 6 of the Binchois piece (Example 1.6). Shown in pseudo-code, this would be stored as follows:

```
Note
Accidental, shape=sharp sign
Parenthesis, shape="(", anchor=accidental, code=left, logical
    placement=left
Parenthesis, shape="(", anchor=accidental, code=right, logical
    placement=right
```

Example 31.3 *NIFF* treatment of editorial accidentals in the Binchois *Magnificat*.

31.7 Example

How these features interact can be seen in the following example based on the opening bars of the second trio from the Mozart Clarinet Quintet.[3]

ACTUAL DATA VALUES	DESCRIPTION AND COMMENTS
'RIFF' < length >	RIFF file
'NIFF' < length >	NIFF form
'LIST' 'ssec' < length >	**Setup Section** list chunk
'ninf' < length >	NIFF information chunk
'6a'	NIFF version
x01	writing program type = engraving program
x01	**standard units** = inches

---

3. The design of the chunks and tags shown has not been finalized at the time of this writing: some changes will likely have occurred in the course of *NIFF*'s further development.

```
          x012C                        absolute units per standard unit = 300
                                       (300 units per inch)
          x18                          MIDI clocks per quarter = 24

          'chlt' < length >            Chunk Length Table

          'cdte' x0000 'chlt' xFFFF 'dflt' xFFFF 'font' xFFFF 'grup' x0005
          'ninf' x000F
          'part' x0009 'pghd' x000C  etc.

'LIST'    'INFO' < length >            RIFF Information list
                                       (standard items defined in RIFF
                                       documentation)

          'IART' < length >            artist—the composer of the score
          "Mozart"Z                    RIFF notation for a null terminated ASCII
                                       string

          'ICOP' < length >            copyright
          "copyright CCARH 1994"Z                                ---.

          'ICRD' < length >            file creation date
          "May 7, 1995"Z

          'INAM' < length >            name—name of score
          "Mozart: Second Trio from Clarinet Quintet"Z

          etc.                         Many more standard RIFF INFO chunks could
                                       be added

'LIST'    'SSOC' < length >            Setup Section Optional Chunks list
                                       this list can optionally contain:
                                       String Table—compact storage of file's
                                       text strings
                                       Defaults—including music font, lyrics
                                       font, etc.
                                       Parts—including part names &
                                       abbreviations, number of staves, MIDI
                                       channel and cable numbers, number of
                                       steps to transpose for playback, and
                                       other features

          'strt' < length >            String Table

          "clarinet in A"Z
          "violino I"Z
          "violino II"Z
          "viola"Z
          "violoncello"Z

          'part' < length >            Part definition—part ID = 0
          x0000                        pointer to name "clarinet in A" in string
                                       table
          x0000                        pointer to name abbreviation (same as
                                       part name)
          x01                          number of staves for this part = 1
          x00                          MIDI channel = 1
          x00                          MIDI cable number = 1
          xFD                          transpose down 3 halfsteps for playback

          'part' < length >            Part definition—part ID = 1
```

```
          x000D  x000D  x01  x01  x00  x00

          'part' < length >              Part definition—part ID = 2
          x0017  x0017  x01  x02  x00  x00

          'part' < length >              Part definition—part ID = 3
          x0022  x0022  x01  x03  x00  x00

          'part' < length >              Part definition—part ID = 4
          x0028  x0028  x01  x04  x00  x00

                                         The Custom Data Table is not shown, but
                                         would be here if a unique font or any
                                         special graphics were required

'LIST'  'dsec' < length >               Data Section list chunk

'LIST'  'page' < length >               first page

        'pghd' < length >               page header
        x09F6                           page width = 8.5 inches, at 300 units per
                                        inch
        x0CE4                           page depth = 11 inches, at 300 units per
                                        inch

'LIST'  'syst' < length >               first system

        'syhd' < length >               system header
        x02A3                           horizontal placement = 2.25 inches from
                                        page left
        x02A3                           vertical placement = 2.25 inches from
                                        page top

        'grup' < length >               grouping ID = 0
        x04                             grouping type = bracket at left of system
        x0000                           first system staff in grouping: staff ID
                                        = 0
        x0004                           last system staff in grouping: staff ID =
                                        4

        'grup' < length >               grouping ID = 1
        x01                             grouping type = barline at left of system
        x0000                           first: staff ID = 0
        x0004                           last: staff ID = 4

        'grup' < length >               grouping ID = 2
        x02                             grouping type = measure barlines extend
                                        thru staves
        x0000                           first: staff ID = 0
        x0004                           last: staff ID = 4

'LIST'  'staf' < length >               first staff

        'sthd' < length >               staff header
        x0000                           horizontal placement = 0 abs units from
                                        system left
        x0000                           vertical placement = 0 abs units from
                                        system top
        x05DC                           staff width = 5 inches (1500 abs units)
        x000B                           space height = 11 absolute units (0.036
                                        inches)
```

```
x05                          lines per staff = 5
x00                          part ID = 0 (clarinet)
                             N.B.  If other parts were present on this
                             staff, they would be indicated by the
                             addition of a part ID tag for each one.

'tmsl' < length >            time-slice
x03                          type = barline
x00000025                    horizontal placement = 0 units from
                             previous barline time-slice
x0000   x0000                zero beats from start of score

'tmsl' < length >            time-slice
x03                          type = non-event
x00000025                    horizontal placement = 25 units from
                             barline time-slice
x0000   x0000                start time always zero for non-event
                             time-slices

'clef' < length >            clef symbol
x01                          shape = G clef
x02                          staff step = 2 for hot spot of this clef
                             symbol

'tmsl' < length >            time-slice
x03                          type = non-event
x000000E1                    horizontal placement = 225 from barline
                             time-slice
x0000   x0000                start time always zero for non-event
                             time-slices

'tmsg' < length >            standard time signature symbol
x03                          top number = 3
x04                          bottom number = 4
                             N.B.  A non-standard time signature chunk
                             should be used for more complex time
                             signatures.

'tmsl' < length >            time-slice
x02                          type = event
x00000012C                   horizontal placement = 300 units from
                             barline time-slice
x0000   x0008                start time = 0/8 from barline time-slice

'stem' < length >            stem symbol

'note' < length >            note symbol
x04                          shape = filled (solid) notehead
x05                          staff step = 5
x0001   x0008                logical duration = eighth note (1/8)

'beam' < length >            beam node
x0000                        beam ID = 0
x0002                        number of nodes = 2
x00                          beam parts to left: 0
x01                          beam parts to right: 1

'slur' < length >            slur node
x000                         slur ID = 0
x002                         number of nodes = 2
```

```
'VL'                          TAG "logical vertical placement"
                              (optional—placement of slur in relation
                              to stem)
x01                           above (another possible value would be
                              x04: note-side)

'dynm' < length >            dynamic symbol
                              (default anchor is part/time-slice)
x0004                         symbol = "p"

'tmsl' < length >            time-slice
x02                          type = event
x00000177                     horizontal offset from barline time-slice
x0001  x0008                  start time = 1/8 after barline time-slice

'stem' < length >            stem symbol

'note' < length >            note symbol
x04  x07  x0001  x0008

'beam' < length >            beam node
x0000                         beam ID = 0
x01                           beam parts to left: 1
x00                           beam parts to right: 0

'tmsl' < length >            time-slice
x01                          type = barline
x000001C2                     horizontal offset from previous
                              time-slice
x0001  x0004                  cumulative start time = 1/4 after start
                              of score

'tmsl' < length >            time-slice
x02                          type = event
x00000177                     horizontal offset from barline time-slice
x0000  x0008                  start time = 0/8 after barline time-slice

'stem' < length >            stem symbol

'note' < length >            note symbol
x04  x09  x0001  x0008

'beam' < length >            beam node
x0001  x00  x01
```

et cetera

Example 31.4 *NIFF* (Version 6a) representation of notation for the clarinet part (first three notes and all related markings in Bars 0 and 1) of the Mozart trio.

31.8 Comments and Further Information

The goal of the *NIFF* project is to provide a standard for interchange of files containing musical information. Judging by the high level of enthusiasm and participation from many commercial software developers, *NIFF*'s prospects of accomplishing its goal appear to be good. Nonetheless a few caveats are in order:

- Software and hardware are not a part of *NIFF*. Many companies plan to implement interfaces to *NIFF* in their own software, allowing interchange of data between programs. Each program's developers will choose what level of support to provide to the various features of the format.

- An implementable version of the specification has not yet been released at the time of this writing. It is expected that the *NIFF* 6 specification will continue to be refined during the course of implementation. At this writing no complete musical works have been encoded.

Because of the rapid evolution of *NIFF*, prospective users should contact the project directly.

The Center for Advanced Research Technology in the Arts and Humanities (CARTAH) at the University of Washington is currently making its ftp site—*ftp://blackbox.cartah.washington.edu*—available to the *NIFF* project. The most recent version of the specification and ongoing discussions are stored there.

Requests for electronic or printed copies of the specification may also be made to either Cindy Grande, the NIFF Technical Coordinator (for contact information, see Contributors), or Chris Newell, NIFF Administrator Coordinator (see Note 2).

References

Byrd, Donald. "Music Notation by Computer." Ph.D. dissertation, Indiana University, 1984. [UMI #DA8506091]

Grande, Cindy, and Alan Belkin. "The Development of the Notation Interchange File Format," *Computer Music Journal* 20/4 (1996), 33-43.

Ornstein, Severo M., and John Turner Maxwell III. *Mockingbird: A Composer's Amanuensis*. Palo Alto: Xerox Palo Alto Research Center, 1983. CSL-83-2 [P83-00002].

Microsoft Windows Multimedia Programmer's Reference. Redmond, WA: Microsoft Press, 1991. [ISBN#1-55615-389-9]

Read, Gardner. *Music Notation—A Manual of Modern Practice*, 2nd edn. New York: Taplinger Publishing Company, 1969/1979.

Ross, Ted. *The Art of Music Engraving and Processing*. Miami Beach: Hansen Books, 1970.

32 *Standard Music eXpression*:
Interchange of Common and Braille Notation

Toshiaki Matsushima

Standard Music eXpression (*SMX*) is a music-notation-based data interchange language which was mainly developed by Prof. Sadamu Ohteru and Toshiaki Matsushima of Waseda University, Tokyo, and Mr. Kentaro Oka of Dai Nippon Printing Co. Ltd., also in Tokyo, in 1988-1989.[1] *SMX* was designed to facilitate data interchange between three different music information processing systems:[2] (1) a system for producing Braille music notation, (2) a system for printing of common music notation (using the *Dai Nippon Music Processor*, or *DMP*), and (3) an optical recognition system for music notation. This code was used for practical experiments in Braille music production.

SMX was originally designed to cover standard Western music notation, especially piano music, and particularly to cover the capabilities of each of the music processing systems mentioned above. Some symbols that rarely appeared in piano notation or vocal texts were eliminated. While the development of *SMX* is currently halted, it is recognized that further improvement is still required.

---

1. See the *SMX Manual*, Version 1 (Ohteru Laboratory, Waseda University, February 25, 1989) and Toshiaki Matsushima, Kuniaki Naoi, Sadamu Ohteru, Shuji Hashimoto, Kentaro Oka, Y. Ishii, H. Ueno, and T. Hashimasa, "A Musical Data Expression for Integrated Music Information Processing System: SMX, 3K-3" in the *Proceedings of the 36th Annual Information Processing System (IPS) Convention* (Japan, March 1988). Both sources are in Japanese.

2. Matsushima, Toshiaki, Sadamu Ohteru, and Shuji Hashimoto, "An Integrated Music Information Processing System: PSB-er," *Proceedings of the International Computer Music Conference 1989*, 191–198.

The main characteristics of *SMX* are these:

- For portability and readability, *SMX* uses only the standard ASCII character set.

- Information contained and represented by *SMX* is restricted to objective notational symbols, that is, to symbols which are visible in the score. Subjective information, such as analytical results, is not coded.

- *SMX* describes the hierarchical order that pertains to the graphic presentation of musical notation.

- Coordinate positions of notation symbols can be specified in *SMX*.

- Hidden (or imaginary) symbols which are not printed in the score can also be encoded in *SMX*.

32.1   Order of Description of Elements

Scores are described in *SMX* in four levels of hierarchy—the *score*, the *measure*, the *bar*, and the *voice*. The top level is called the *score*. The *score* is assumed to be composed of series of *measure*s, which are divided by bar lines. Each *measure* contains several staves which relate to the different parts of music for piano or other instruments. In *SMX*, these segments of the staff are named *bars*. Each melody line in a single staff is named *voice* and is described separately. Notes and other major music symbols are basically described in this lowest *voice* level.

The level is identified by the symbol $ plus the name of the level.

$$\begin{array}{ll} \texttt{\$score} & \text{highest level} \\ \texttt{\$measure} & \\ \texttt{\$bar} & \\ \texttt{\$voice} & \text{lowest level} \end{array}$$

Identifiers of the level take a parameter to specify its number. Contents of each level consist of level attributes, notation symbols, and lower level descriptions. The description of each level ends when the same or a higher level identifier appears. The $score level ends with the identifier $end. Identifiers of level attributes are represented by the symbol @ with the name of the attributes. Values of attributes are described immediately after the attribute identifier (Table 32.1).

Level Id.	Attribute Id.	Attribute Value	Meaning
$score			
	@title	string	title of music
	@size	sheet type	size of sheet
	@meter	dot or mm	a measure of length
	@staff_width	decimal number	staff width
	@staff_len	decimal number	staff length
	@staff_location	list of coordinates	staff location
$measure			
	@bar	decimal number	number of bars
	@position	{left_end|right_end}	location in the section
$bar			
	@voice	decimal number	number of voices
$voice			
	no attributes		

Table 32.1 Level ($) and attribute (@) identifiers in *SMX*.

32.2   Description of Symbols

Notation symbols other than bar lines are described in the $voice level. Bar lines are described in the $bar level. Identifiers of notation symbols are introduced by the symbols ! or ? followed by the symbols' names. Identifiers introduced by ! indicate symbols which really exist in the score, while identifiers introduced by ? indicate ones which are not printed in the score. Symbols encoded with the ? identifier may be used for two purposes:

- to get complete local note information from the clef, the key, and the time signatures at the beginning of each voice level;

- to keep the beat consistent for partially present melodic lines by inserting unprinted rests.[3]

---

3. This usage is analogous to the textural situation for which *DARMS* would employ linear decomposition.

32.2.1 Symbol Identifiers

Symbol identifiers are given in Table 32.2.

IDENTIFIER	NOTATION SYMBOLS
!note	notes
!rest	rests
!clef	clefs
!key	key signatures
!time	time signatures
!front_bar	left side bar lines
!rear_bar	right side bar lines
!dynamics	dynamics
!tempo	tempos
!grace	grace notes

Table 32.2 Symbol (!) identifiers in *SMX*.

Attributes of symbols are introduced by the symbol # followed by the attribute names. They can take some parameters, including the coordinates (printed location specifications) of the symbols. The pitch of notes is represented by the combination of octave indicator, an accidental name, and a note name.

32.2.2 Octave Specification

The necessary number of superscript strokes (') is added for upper octaves; multiples of the subscript stroke (,) are used for lower octaves. Octave specification differs for the G clef and F clef: the one-line octave (c'-b') is used for the G clef, while the small octave (c-b) is used for the F clef.

32.2.3 Specification of Accidentals

The single characters s, f, and n are used for the accidentals of sharp, flat, and natural respectively.

32.2.4 Note Names

Note names are given by alphabetic letter.

Symbol Id.	Attribute Id.	Values
!note		
	#pitch	[{'|,}]*[{s|f|n}]*{C|D|E|F|G|A|B} [(x,y)]
	#duration	{1|2|4|8|16|32|64|128|2+|4+}[.]*
	#expr	{staccato|tenuto|accent|staccatissimo|fermata} [{up|down}]
	#tie	[{up|down}] {begin|end} [(x,y)]
	#slur	[{up|down}] {begin|cont|end} [(x,y)]
	#stem	{up|down} [(x,y)]
	#beam	NumberOfLeftBeams NumberOfRightBeams
	#tuplet	NumberOfTuplets [{up|down}] {begin|cont|end} [(x,y)]
	#octave	{8va|15va} {alto|basso} {begin|end}
	#ornament	{trill|turn|mordent} {up|down|between}
!rest		
	#duration	{1|2|4|8|16|32|64|128|2+|4+}[.]*
!clef		
	#type	{F|G}
!key		
	#type	{sharp|flat|natural} NumberOfAccidentals
!time		
	#type	{C|C+|N/N}
!front_bar		
	#type	{normal_bar|return_bar|return_to|double_bar|end_bar}
	#mark	{segno|ds|dscoda|coda|tocoda|dc|fine|returnN}
	#long	
!rear_bar		The same as !front_bar.
!bracket		
	#type	{middle | large}
	#bar	NumberOfStartStaff-NumberOfEndStaff [(x,y)]
!dynamics		
	#type	{cres|decres|[{m|f|p|s}]{f|p}} [(x,y)-(x,y)]
!grace		The same as !note.

Table 32.3 Symbol attribute identifiers (#) used in *SMX*.

32.2.5 Durations

Durations are specified as the denominator of the whole note's duration. Notes of a double-whole or greater value are indicated by a + after the multiple number. A chord is encoded as multiple `#pitch` attributes.

32.2.6 Symbol Attributes

Attributes of symbols are given Table 32.2. Here *x* and *y* refer to coordinate positions of symbols. Square brackets ([ ]) enclose optional information. Curly brackets ({ }) enclose a set from which a selection must be made in processing. Sets may be nested within sets. An asterisk (*) indicates a number of repetitions and requires a non-negative integer for processing. These attributes are shown in context in the following example.

32.3 Examples

32.3.1 The Mozart Trio

We show the encoding of the first 12 bars of the second trio from Mozart's Clarinet Quintet in Example 32.1. Since each incomplete bar is counted as one complete bar in *SMX*, the numbering of $measure starts at 1 and ends at 14.

SMX code is produced by the following procedure. First, music notation is input to (or drawn on) the computer using the *Dai Nippon Music Processor (DMP)*. In this step, the original notation is segmented into sections. In this example the first and second sections have four bars each and the third (last) section has six bars. Because *SMX* does not make a provision for the C clef, the viola part is given here in F-clef notation. The version of the *DMP* used for this encoding is a special version, with restricted capabilities, for the field testing of a Braille music production system, so the dynamics are not added at this stage. Next, the *SMX* data are produced from the notation data of the *DMP* by the conversion program. Last, the symbols (such as the dynamics) that have been thus far ignored are added to the *SMX* file manually using the text editor.

```
$score
          @title           "Mozart: second trio from Clarinet Quintet"
          @size            A4
          @meter           dot
          @format          p5*d3
          @staff_width     32
          @staff_len       720
          @staff_location     (48,54)  (48,110) (48,171) (48,226) (48,284)
                              (48,364) (48,420) (48,481) (48,548) (48,594)
                              (50,674) (50,730) (50,791) (50,846) (50,904)
$measure 1
          @bar 5
          @positon left_end
          !bracket         #type large
                           #bar 1-5 (-8,)
$bar 1
          @voice 1
```

```
                !front_bar      #type normal_bar (0,)
                                #long
$voice 1
                !clef           #type G (18,)
                !time           #type 3/4 (70,)
                !dynamics       #type p
                !note           #pitch 'C (118,)
                                #duration 8
                                #stem down ((113,12),(113,40))
                                #beam 0 1 (113,36)
                                #slur up begin (118,-10)
                !note           #pitch 'E (148,)
                                #duration 8
                                #stem down ((143,4),(143,32))
                                #beam 1 0 (143,28)
                                #slur up cont
$bar 2
                @voice 1
                !front_bar      #type normal_bar (0,)
                                #long
$voice 1
                !clef           #type G (17,)
                !key            #type sharp 3 (35,)
                !time           #type 3/4 (70,)
                !rest           #duration 4 (131,)
$bar 3
                @voice 1
                !front_bar      #type normal_bar (0,)
                                #long
$voice 1
                !clef           #type G (19,)
                !key            #type sharp 3 (35,)
                !time           #type 3/4 (70,)
                !rest           #duration 4 (131,)
$bar 4
                @voice 1
                !front_bar      #type normal_bar (0,)
                                #long
$voice 1
                !clef           #type F (17,)
                !key            #type sharp 3 (35,)
                !time           #type 3/4 (70,)
                !rest           #duration 4 (131,)
$bar 5
                @voice 1
                !front_bar      #type normal_bar (0,)
$voice 1
                !clef           #type F (20,)
                !key            #type sharp 3 (38,)
                !time           #type 3/4 (70,)
                !rest           #duration 4 (131,)
$measure 2
                @bar 5
$bar 1
                @voice 1
                !front_bar      #type normal_bar (187,)
$voice 1
                ?clef           #type G
                ?time           #type 3/4
                !note           #pitch 'G (204,)
                                #duration 8
```

```
                              #stem down ((199,-4),(199,24))
                              #beam 0 1 (199,20)
                              #slur up cont
            !note             #pitch 'E (240,)
                              #duration 8
                              #stem down ((235,4),(235,32))
                              #beam 1 0 (235,28)
                              #slur up cont
            !note             #pitch ''C (264,)
                              #duration 4
                              #stem down ((259,-16),(259,16))
            !note             #pitch 'G (306,)
                              #duration 8
                              #stem down ((301,-4),(301,24))
                              #beam 0 1 (301,20)
                              #slur up begin (304,-14)
            !note             #pitch 'E (336,)
                              #duration 8
                              #stem down ((331,4),(331,32))
                              #beam 1 0 (331,28)
                              #slur up cont
$bar 2
            @voice 1
            !front_bar        #type normal_bar (187,)
$voice 1
            ?clef             #type G
            ?key              #type sharp 3
            ?time             #type 3/4
            !rest             #duration 4 (220,)
            !dynamics         #type p
            !note             #pitch A (280,)
                              #duration 4
                              #stem up ((285,-8),(285,20))
            !note             #pitch A (320,)
                              #duration 4
                              #stem up ((325,-8),(325,20))
$bar 3
            @voice 1
            !front_bar        #type normal_bar (187,)
$voice 1
            ?clef             #type G
            ?key              #type sharp 3
            ?time             #type 3/4
            !rest             #duration 4 (218,)
            !dynamics         #type p
            !note             #pitch E (284,)
                              #duration 4
                              #stem up ((289,4),(289,32))
            !note             #pitch E (320,)
                              #duration 4
                              #stem up ((325,4),(325,32))
$bar 4
            @voice 1
            !front_bar        #type normal_bar (187,)
$voice 1
            ?clef             #type F
            ?key              #type sharp 3
            ?time             #type 3/4
            !rest             #duration 4 (220,)
            !dynamics         #type p
            !note             #pitch 'C (284,)
```

```
                                #duration 4
                                #stem down ((279,-8),(279,20))
            !note               #pitch 'C (324,)
                                #duration 4
                                #stem down ((319,-8),(319,20))
$bar 5
            @voice 1
            !front_bar          #type normal_bar (187,)
$voice 1
            ?clef               #type F
            ?key                #type sharp 3
            ?time               #type 3/4
            !dynamics           #type p
            !note               #pitch A (220,)
                                #duration 4
                                #stem down ((215,0),(215,28))
            !rest               #duration 4 (280,)
            !rest               #duration 4 (318,)
$measure 3
            @bar 5
$bar 1
            @voice 1
            !front_bar          #type normal_bar (363,)
$voice 1
            ?clef               #type G
            ?time               #type 3/4
            !note               #pitch 'D (384,)
                                #duration 8
                                #stem down ((379,8),(379,36))
                                #beam 0 1 (379,32)
                                #slur up cont
            !note               #pitch 'F (412,)
                                #duration 8
                                #stem down ((407,0),(407,28))
                                #beam 1 0 (407,24)
                                #slur up cont
            !note               #pitch 'A (440,)
                                #duration 4
                                #stem down ((435,-8),(435,20))
                                #slur up end (437,-19)
            !note               #pitch 'F (490,)
                                #duration 8
                                #stem down ((485,0),(485,28))
                                #beam 0 1 (485,24)
                                #slur up begin (488,-10)
            !note               #pitch 'D (520,)
                                #duration 8
                                #stem down ((515,8),(515,36))
                                #beam 1 0 (515,32)
                                #slur up cont
$bar 2
            @voice 1
            !front_bar          #type normal_bar (363,)
$voice 1
            ?clef               #type G
            ?key                #type sharp 3
            ?time               #type 3/4
            !rest               #duration 4 (382,)
            !note               #pitch A (444,)
                                #duration 4
                                #stem up ((449,-8),(449,20))
```

```
            !note              #pitch A (488,)
                               #duration 4
                               #stem up ((493,-8),(493,20))
$bar 3
            @voice 1
            !front_bar         #type normal_bar (363,)
$voice 1
            ?clef              #type G
            ?key               #type sharp 3
            ?time              #type 3/4
            !rest              #duration 4 (382,)
            !note              #pitch F (446,)
                               #duration 4
                               #stem up ((451,0),(451,28))
            !note              #pitch F (492,)
                               #duration 4
                               #stem up ((497,0),(497,28))
$bar 4
            @voice 1
            !front_bar         #type normal_bar (363,)
$voice 1
            ?clef              #type F
            ?key               #type sharp 3
            ?time              #type 3/4
            !rest              #duration 4 (384,)
            !note              #pitch B (450,)
                               #duration 4
                               #stem down ((445,-4),(445,24))
            !note              #pitch B (496,)
                               #duration 4
                               #stem down ((491,-4),(491,24))
$bar 5
            @voice 1
            !front_bar         #type normal_bar (363,)
$voice 1
            ?clef              #type F
            ?key               #type sharp 3
            ?time              #type 3/4
            !note              #pitch D (384,)
                               #duration 4
                               #stem down ((379,16),(379,44))
            !rest              #duration 4 (454,)
            !rest              #duration 4 (500,)
$measure 4
            @bar 5
            @postion right_end
$bar 1
            @voice 1
            !front_bar         #type normal_bar (547,)
            !rear_bar          #type normal_bar (720,)
$voice 1
            ?clef              #type G
            ?time              #type 3/4
            !note              #pitch 'C (568,)
                               #duration 8
                               #stem down ((563,12),(563,42))
                               #beam 0 1 (563,38)
                               #slur up cont
            !note              #pitch B (592,)
                               #duration 8
                               #stem down ((587,16),(587,40))
```

```
                                    #beam 1 1 (689,29) (563,38)
                                    #slur up cont
                    !note           #pitch 'E (620,)
                                    #duration 8
                                    #stem down ((615,4),(615,38))
                                    #beam 1 1 (689,29) (563,38)
                                    #slur up cont
                    !note           #pitch 'D (646,)
                                    #duration 8
                                    #stem down ((641,8),(641,36))
                                    #beam 1 1 (689,29) (563,38)
                                    #slur up cont
                    !note           #pitch 'G (668,)
                                    #duration 8
                                    #stem down ((663,-4),(663,34))
                                    #beam 1 1 (689,29) (563,38)
                                    #slur up cont
                    !note           #pitch 'F (694,)
                                    #duration 8
                                    #stem down ((689,0),(689,33))
                                    #beam 1 0 (689,29)
                                    #slur up end    (692,-13)
$bar 2
                    @voice 1
                    !front_bar      #type normal_bar (547,)
                    !rear_bar       #type normal_bar (720,)
$voice 1
                    ?clef           #type G
                    ?key            #type sharp 3
                    ?time           #type 3/4
                    !rest           #duration 4 (566,)
                    !note           #pitch G (620,)
                                    #duration 4
                                    #stem up ((625,-4),(625,24))
                    !note           #pitch G (668,)
                                    #duration 4
                                    #stem up ((673,-4),(673,24))
$bar 3
                    @voice 1
                    !front_bar      #type normal_bar (547,)
                    !rear_bar       #type normal_bar (720,)
$voice 1
                    ?clef           #type G
                    ?key            #type sharp 3
                    ?time           #type 3/4
                    !rest           #duration 4 (564,)
                    !note           #pitch D (624,)
                                    #duration 4
                                    #stem up ((629,8),(629,36))
                    !note           #pitch D (670,)
                                    #duration 4
                                    #stem up ((675,8),(675,36))
$bar 4
                    @voice 1
                    !front_bar      #type normal_bar (547,)
                    !rear_bar       #type normal_bar (720,)
$voice 1
                    ?clef           #type F
                    ?key            #type sharp 3
                    ?time           #type 3/4
                    !rest           #duration 4 (570,)
```

```
          !note              #pitch B (628,)
                             #duration 4
                             #stem down ((623,-4),(623,24))
          !note              #pitch B (674,)
                             #duration 4
                             #stem down ((669,-4),(669,24))
$bar 5
          @voice 1
          !front_bar         #type normal_bar (547,)
          !rear_bar          #type normal_bar (720,)
$voice 1
          ?clef              #type F
          ?key               #type sharp 3
          ?time              #type 3/4
          !note              #pitch E (570,)
                             #duration 4
                             #stem down ((565,12),(565,40))
          !rest              #duration 4 (634,)
          !rest              #duration 4 (674,)
$measure 5
          @bar 5
          @positon left_end
          !bracket           #type large
                             #bar 1-5 (-8,)
$bar 1
          @voice 1
          !front_bar         #type normal_bar (0,)
                             #long
$voice 1
          !clef              #type G
          ?time              #type 3/4
          !note              #pitch 'sD (86,)
                             #duration 4
                             #stem down ((81,8),(81,36))
                             #slur up begin (82,-5)
          !note              #pitch 'E (122,)
                             #duration 4
                             #stem down ((117,4),(117,32))
                             #slur up end   (119,-6)
          !note              #pitch 'C (150,)
                             #duration 8
                             #stem down ((145,12),(145,40))
                             #beam 0 1 (145,36)
                             #slur up begin (148,2)
          !note              #pitch 'E (172,)
                             #duration 8
                             #stem down ((167,4),(167,32))
                             #beam 1 0 (167,29)
                             #slur up cont
$bar 2
          @voice 1
          !front_bar         #type normal_bar (0,)
                             #long
$voice 1
          !clef              #type G
          !key               #type sharp 3
          ?time              #type 3/4
          !rest              #duration 4 (80,)
          !note              #pitch A (124,)
                             #duration 4
                             #stem up ((129,-8),(129,20))
```

```
            !note            #pitch A (160,)
                             #duration 4
                             #stem up ((165,-8),(165,20))
$bar 3
            @voice 1
            !front_bar       #type normal_bar (0,)
                             #long
$voice 1
            !clef            #type G
            !key             #type sharp 3
            ?time            #type 3/4
            !rest            #duration 4 (80,)
            !note            #pitch C (162,)
                             #duration 4
                             #stem up ((167,12),(167,40))
            !note            #pitch C (126,)
                             #duration 4
                             #stem up ((131,12),(131,40))
$bar 4
            @voice 1
            !front_bar       #type normal_bar (0,)
                             #long
$voice 1
            !clef            #type F
            !key             #type sharp 3
            ?time            #type 3/4
            !rest            #duration 4 (80,)
            !note            #pitch A (124,)
                             #duration 4
                             #stem down ((119,0),(119,28))
            !note            #pitch A (160,)
                             #duration 4
                             #stem down ((155,0),(155,28))
$bar 5
            @voice 1
            !front_bar       #type normal_bar (0,)
$voice 1
            !clef            #type F
            !key             #type sharp 3
            ?time            #type 3/4
            !rest            #duration 4 (132,)
            !rest            #duration 4 (160,)
            !note            #pitch F (84,)
                             #duration 2
                             #stem down ((79,8),(79,36))
$measure 6
            @bar 5
$bar 1
            @voice 1
            !front_bar       #type normal_bar (187,)
$voice 1
            ?clef            #type G
            ?time            #type 3/4
            !note            #pitch 'G (210,)
                             #duration 8
                             #stem down ((205,-4),(205,24))
                             #beam 0 1 (205,20)
                             #slur up cont
            !note            #pitch 'E (238,)
                             #duration 8
                             #stem down ((233,4),(233,32))
```

```
                                   #beam 1 0 (233,28)
                                   #slur up cont
              !note                #pitch ''C (278,)
                                   #duration 4
                                   #stem down ((273,-16),(273,16))
                                   #slur up end   (276,-24)
              !note                #pitch 'G (312,)
                                   #duration 8
                                   #stem down ((307,-4),(307,24))
                                   #beam 0 1 (307,20)
                                   #slur up begin (310,-14)
              !note                #pitch 'E (338,)
                                   #duration 8
                                   #stem down ((333,4),(333,32))
                                   #beam 1 0 (333,28)
                                   #slur up cont
$bar 2
              @voice 1
              !front_bar           #type normal_bar (187,)
$voice 1
              ?clef                #type G
              ?key                 #type sharp 3
              ?time                #type 3/4
              !rest                #duration 4 (208,)
              !note                #pitch A (268,)
                                   #duration 4
                                   #stem up ((273,-8),(273,20))
              !note                #pitch A (303,)
                                   #duration 4
                                   #stem up ((313,-8),(313,20))
$bar 3
              @voice 1
              !front_bar           #type normal_bar (187,)
$voice 1
              ?clef                #type G
              ?key                 #type sharp 3
              ?time                #type 3/4
              !rest                #duration 4 (212,)
              !note                #pitch E (270,)
                                   #duration 4
                                   #stem up ((275,4),(275,32))
              !note                #pitch E (310,)
                                   #duration 4
                                   #stem up ((315,4),(315,32))
$bar 4
              @voice 1
              !front_bar           #type normal_bar (187,)
$voice 1
              ?clef                #type F
              ?key                 #type sharp 3
              ?time                #type 3/4
              !rest                #duration 4 (214,)
              !note                #pitch 'C (268,)
                                   #duration 4
                                   #stem down ((263,-8),(263,20))
              !note                #pitch 'C (312,)
                                   #duration 4
                                   #stem down ((307,-8),(307,20))
$bar 5
              @voice 1
              !front_bar           #type normal_bar (187,)
```

```
$voice 1
            ?clef           #type F
            ?key            #type sharp 3
            ?time           #type 3/4
            !rest           #duration 4 (274,)
            !rest           #duration 4 (316,)
$measure 7
            @bar 5
$bar 1
            @voice 1
            !front_bar      #type normal_bar (363,)
$voice 1
            ?clef           #type G
            ?time           #type 3/4
            !note           #pitch 'nD (388,)
                            #duration 8
                            #stem down ((383,8),(383,36))
                            #beam 0 1 (383,32)
                            #slur up cont
            !note           #pitch 'F (416,)
                            #duration 8
                            #stem down ((411,0),(411,28))
                            #beam 1 0 (411,24)
                            #slur up cont
            !note           #pitch 'A (448,)
                            #duration 4
                            #stem down ((443,-8),(443,20))
                            #slur up end   (447,-17)
            !rest           #duration 4 (494,)
$bar 2
            @voice 1
            !front_bar      #type normal_bar (363,)
$voice 1
            ?clef           #type G
            ?key            #type sharp 3
            ?time           #type 3/4
            !rest           #duration 4 (436,)
            !note           #pitch F (396,)
                            #duration 4
                            #stem up ((401,0),(401,28))
            !note           #pitch 'C (484,)
                            #duration 8
                            #stem down ((479,12),(479,44))
                            #beam 0 1 (479,40)
                            #slur up begin (484,2)
            !note           #pitch sA (510,)
                            #duration 8
                            #stem down ((505,20),(505,44))
                            #beam 1 0 (505,40)
                            #slur up cont
$bar 3
            @voice 1
            !front_bar      #type normal_bar (363,)
$voice 1
            ?clef           #type G
            ?key            #type sharp 3
            ?time           #type 3/4
            !rest           #duration 4 (440,)
            !note           #pitch D (396,)
                            #duration 4
                            #stem up ((401,8),(401,36))
```

```
                    !note          #pitch nG (498,)
                                   #duration 4
                                   #stem up ((503,-4),(503,24))
                                   #slur up begin (497,44)
                                   #slur down begin (499,30)
$bar 4
                    @voice 1
                    !front_bar     #type normal_bar (363,)
$voice 1
                    ?clef          #type F
                    ?key           #type sharp 3
                    ?time          #type 3/4
                    !rest          #duration 4 (440,)
                    !note          #pitch B (398,)
                                   #duration 4
                                   #stem down ((393,-4),(393,24))
                    !note          #pitch 'E (498,)
                                   #duration 4
                                   #stem down ((493,-16),(493,16))
$bar 5
                    @voice 1
                    !front_bar     #type normal_bar (363,)
$voice 1
                    ?clef          #type F
                    ?key           #type sharp 3
                    ?time          #type 3/4
                    !rest          #duration 4 (444,)
                    !rest          #duration 4 (496,)
$measure 8
                    @bar 5
                    @postion right_end
$bar 1
                    @voice 1
                    !front_bar     #type normal_bar (547,)
                    !rear_bar      #type normal_bar (720,)
$voice 1
                    ?clef          #type G
                    ?time          #type 3/4
                    !rest          #duration 1 (632,)
$bar 2
                    @voice 1
                    !front_bar     #type normal_bar (547,)
                    !rear_bar      #type normal_bar (720,)
$voice 1
                    ?clef          #type G
                    ?key           #type sharp 3
                    ?time          #type 3/4
                    !note          #pitch B (574,)
                                   #duration 8
                                   #stem down ((569,16),(569,44))
                                   #beam 0 1 (569,40)
                                   #slur up cont
                    !note          #pitch 'D (598,)
                                   #duration 8
                                   #stem down ((593,8),(593,36))
                                   #beam 1 0 (593,32)
                                   #slur up cont
                    !note          #pitch 'F (632,)
                                   #duration 4
                                   #stem down ((627,0),(627,28))
                                   #slur up end   (630,-8)
```

```
                !note        #pitch 'sC (672,)
                             #duration 8
                             #stem down ((667,12),(667,44))
                             #beam 0 1 (667,40)
                             #slur up begin (671,2)
                !note        #pitch sA (698,)
                             #duration 8
                             #stem down ((693,20),(693,44))
                             #beam 1 0 (693,40)
                             #slur up cont
$bar 3
                @voice 1
                !front_bar   #type normal_bar (547,)
                !rear_bar    #type normal_bar (720,)
$voice 1
                ?clef        #type G
                ?key         #type sharp 3
                ?time        #type 3/4
                !note        #pitch F (578,)
                             #duration 2
                             #stem up ((584,0),(584,28))
                             #slur up cont
                             #slur down cont
                !note        #pitch nG (656,)
                             #duration 2
                             #stem up ((662,-4),(662,24))
                             #slur up cont
                             #slur down cont
$bar 4
                @voice 1
                !front_bar   #type normal_bar (547,)
                !rear_bar    #type normal_bar (720,)
$voice 1
                ?clef        #type F
                ?key         #type sharp 3
                ?time        #type 3/4
                !note        #pitch 'D (580,)
                             #duration 2
                             #stem down ((575,-12),(575,16))
                !note        #pitch 'E (654,)
                             #duration 4
                             #stem down ((649,-16),(649,16))
$bar 5
                @voice 1
                !front_bar   #type normal_bar (547,)
                !rear_bar    #type normal_bar (720,)
$voice 1
                ?clef        #type F
                ?key         #type sharp 3
                ?time        #type 3/4
                !rest        #duration 1 (636,)
$measure 9
                @bar 5
                @positon left_end
                !bracket     #type large
                             #bar 1-5 (-8,)
$bar 1
                @voice 1
                !front_bar   #type normal_bar (0,)
                             #long
$voice 1
```

```
              !clef          #type G
              ?time          #type 3/4
              !rest          #duration 4 (82,)
              !rest          #duration 4 (108,)
              !note          #pitch D (134,)
                             #duration 8
                             #stem up ((139,12),(139,36))
                             #beam 0 1 (139,12)
                             #tuplet 3 up begin (130,-3)
                             #slur down begin (133,43)
              !note          #pitch ,A (148,)
                             #duration 8
                             #stem up ((153,14),(153,48))
                             #beam 1 1 (171,16) (139,12)
                             #tuplet 3 up cont
                             #slur down cont
              !note          #pitch ,F (166,)
                             #duration 8
                             #stem up ((171,16),(171,56))
                             #beam 1 0 (171,16)
                             #tuplet 3 up cont
                             #slur down cont
$bar 2
              @voice 1
              !front_bar     #type normal_bar (0,)
                             #long
$voice 1
              !clef          #type G
              !key           #type sharp 3
              ?time          #type 3/4
              !note          #pitch B (85,)
                             #duration 8
                             #stem down ((80,16),(80,43))
                             #beam 0 1 (80,39)
                             #slur up cont
              !note          #pitch 'D (105,)
                             #duration 8
                             #stem down ((100,8),(100,37))
                             #beam 1 0 (100,33)
                             #slur up cont
              !note          #pitch 'F (125,)
                             #duration 4
                             #stem down ((120,0),(120,28))
                             #slur up end   (122,-8)
              !rest          #duration 4 (147,)
$bar 3
              @voice 1
              !front_bar     #type normal_bar (0,)
                             #long
$voice 1
              !clef          #type G
              !key           #type sharp 3
              ?time          #type 3/4
              !note          #pitch F (94,)
                             #duration 2
                             #stem up ((100,0),(100,28))
                             #slur down end   (90,31)
                             #slur up end   (91,39)
              !rest          #duration 4 (145,)
$bar 4
              @voice 1
```

```
              !front_bar        #type normal_bar (0,)
                                #long
$voice 1
              !clef             #type F
              !key              #type sharp 3
              ?time             #type 3/4
              !note             #pitch 'D (94,)
                                #duration 2
                                #stem down ((89,-12),(89,16))
                                #slur up end   (91,-16)
              !rest             #duration 4 (145,)
$bar 5
              @voice 1
              !front_bar        #type normal_bar (0,)
$voice 1
              !clef             #type F
              !key              #type sharp 3
              ?time             #type 3/4
              !rest             #duration 1 (123,)
$measure 10
              @bar 5
$bar 1
              @voice 1
              !front_bar        #type normal_bar (187,)
$voice 1
              ?clef             #type G
              ?time             #type 3/4
              !note             #pitch ,A (221,)
                                #duration 8
                                #stem up ((226,2),(226,48))
                                #beam 0 1 (226,2)
                                #slur down end   (221,57)
              !note             #pitch F (263,)
                                #duration 8
                                #expr staccato down (263,36)
                                #stem up ((268,-6),(268,28))
                                #beam 1 1 (341,-20) (226,2)
              !note             #pitch 'D (314,)
                                #duration 8
                                #expr staccato down (314,20)
                                #stem up ((319,-16),(319,8))
                                #beam 1 1 (341,-20) (226,2)
              !note             #pitch 'F (336,)
                                #duration 8
                                #expr staccato down (336,12)
                                #stem up ((341,-20),(341,0))
                                #beam 1 0 (341,-20)
              !note             #pitch D (238,)
                                #duration 8
                                #expr staccato down (238,44)
                                #stem up ((243,-1),(243,36))
                                #beam 1 1 (341,-20) (226,2)
              !note             #pitch A (290,)
                                #duration 8
                                #expr staccato down (290,28)
                                #stem up ((295,-11),(295,20))
                                #beam 1 1 (341,-20) (226,2)
$bar 2
              @voice 1
              !front_bar        #type normal_bar (187,)
$voice 1
```

```
                ?clef              #type G
                ?key               #type sharp 3
                ?time              #type 3/4
                !rest              #duration 1 (281,)
$bar 3
                @voice 1
                !front_bar         #type normal_bar (187,)
$voice 1
                ?clef              #type G
                ?key               #type sharp 3
                ?time              #type 3/4
                !rest              #duration 1 (283,)
$bar 4
                @voice 1
                !front_bar         #type normal_bar (187,)
$voice 1
                ?clef              #type F
                ?key               #type sharp 3
                ?time              #type 3/4
                !rest              #duration 1 (284,)
$bar 5
                @voice 1
                !front_bar         #type normal_bar (187,)
$voice 1
                ?clef              #type F
                ?key               #type sharp 3
                ?time              #type 3/4
                !rest              #duration 1 (286,)
$measure 11
                @bar 5
$bar 1
                @voice 1
                !front_bar         #type normal_bar (363,)
$voice 1
                ?clef              #type G
                ?time              #type 3/4
                !note              #pitch 'A (392,)
                                   #duration 8
                                   #stem down ((387,-8),(387,24))
                                   #beam 0 1 (387,20)
                                   #slur up begin (388,-17)
                !note              #pitch 'G (420,)
                                   #duration 8
                                   #stem down ((415,-4),(415,26))
                                   #beam 1 1 (523,28) (387,20)
                                   #slur up cont
                !note              #pitch 'F (446,)
                                   #duration 8
                                   #stem down ((441,0),(441,27))
                                   #beam 1 1 (523,28) (387,20)
                                   #slur up cont
                !note              #pitch 'E (476,)
                                   #duration 8
                                   #stem down ((471,4),(471,29))
                                   #beam 1 1 (523,28) (387,20)
                                   #slur up cont
                !note              #pitch 'F (504,)
                                   #duration 8
                                   #stem down ((499,0),(499,31))
                                   #beam 1 1 (523,28) (387,20)
                                   #slur up cont
```

```
            !note        #pitch 'D (528,)
                         #duration 8
                         #stem down ((523,8),(523,32))
                         #beam 1 0 (523,28)
                         #slur up end   (524,-12)
$bar 2
            @voice 1
            !front_bar   #type normal_bar (363,)
$voice 1
            ?clef        #type G
            ?key         #type sharp 3
            ?time        #type 3/4
            !rest        #duration 1 (458,)
$bar 3
            @voice 1
            !front_bar   #type normal_bar (363,)
$voice 1
            ?clef        #type G
            ?key         #type sharp 3
            ?time        #type 3/4
            !rest        #duration 1 (459,)
$bar 4
            @voice 1
            !front_bar   #type normal_bar (363,)
$voice 1
            ?clef        #type F
            ?key         #type sharp 3
            ?time        #type 3/4
            !rest        #duration 1 (460,)
$bar 5
            @voice 1
            !front_bar   #type normal_bar (363,)
$voice 1
            ?clef        #type F
            ?key         #type sharp 3
            ?time        #type 3/4
            !rest        #duration 1 (461,)
$measure 12
            @bar 5
$bar 1
            @voice 1
            !front_bar   #type normal_bar (547,)
$voice 1
            ?clef        #type G
            ?time        #type 3/4
            !note        #pitch 'C (574,)
                         #duration 2
                         #stem down ((569,12),(569,40))
                         #slur up begin (571,4)
            !note        #pitch 'E (602,)
                         #duration 8
                         #stem down ((597,4),(597,32))
                         #beam 0 1 (597,28)
                         #slur up cont
            !note        #pitch 'D (636,)
                         #duration 8
                         #stem down ((631,8),(631,36))
                         #beam 1 0 (631,32)
                         #slur up end   (634,-1)
$bar 2
            @voice 1
```

```
                  !front_bar        #type normal_bar (547,)
$voice 1
                  ?clef             #type G
                  ?key              #type sharp 3
                  ?time             #type 3/4
                  !note             #pitch C (561,)
                                    #duration 8
                                    #stem up ((566,9),(566,40))
                                    #beam 0 1 (566,9)
                  !note             #pitch E (577,)
                                    #duration 8
                                    #stem up ((582,8),(582,32))
                                    #beam 1 1 (644,5) (566,9)
                  !note             #pitch C (590,)
                                    #duration 8
                                    #stem up ((595,8),(595,40))
                                    #beam 1 1 (644,5) (566,9)
                  !note             #pitch E (607,)
                                    #duration 8
                                    #stem up ((612,7),(612,32))
                                    #beam 1 1 (644,5) (566,9)
                  !note             #pitch D (622,)
                                    #duration 8
                                    #stem up ((627,6),(627,36))
                                    #beam 1 1 (644,5) (566,9)
                  !note             #pitch E (639,)
                                    #duration 8
                                    #stem up ((644,5),(644,32))
                                    #beam 1 0 (644,5)
$bar 3
                  @voice 1
                  !front_bar        #type normal_bar (547,)
$voice 1
                  ?clef             #type G
                  ?key              #type sharp 3
                  ?time             #type 3/4
                  !note             #pitch ,A (581,)
                                    #duration 2
                                    #stem up ((587,16),(587,48))
                                    #slur down cont
                  !note             #pitch ,sG (615,)
                                    #duration 4
                                    #stem up ((620,16),(620,52))
                                    #slur down cont
$bar 4
                  @voice 1
                  !front_bar        #type normal_bar (547,)
$voice 1
                  ?clef             #type F
                  ?key              #type sharp 3
                  ?time             #type 3/4
                  !note             #pitch C (573,)
                                    #duration 2.
                                    #stem up ((579,-8),(579,20))
                                    #tie down begin (570,28)
$bar 5
                  @voice 1
                  !front_bar        #type normal_bar (547,)
$voice 1
                  ?clef             #type F
                  ?key              #type sharp 3
```

```
            ?time          #type 3/4
            !note          #pitch ,E (567,)
                           #duration 4
                           #expr staccato down (567,52)
                           #stem up ((572,12),(572,40))
                           #slur begin (566,58)
            !note          #pitch ,E (593,)
                           #duration 4
                           #expr staccato down (593,52)
                           #stem up ((598,12),(598,40))
                           #slur cont
            !note          #pitch ,E (622,)
                           #duration 4
                           #expr staccato down (622,52)
                           #stem up ((627,12),(627,40))
                           #slur end   (623,58)
$measure 13
            @bar 5
$bar 1
            @voice 1
            !front_bar     #type normal_bar (652,)
            ?rear_bar      #type return_fromto (685,)
$voice 1
            ?clef          #type G
            ?time          #type 3/4
            !note          #pitch 'C (662,)
                           #duration 4
                           #stem down ((657,12),(657,40))
            !rest          #duration 4 (671,)
$bar 2
            @voice 1
            !front_bar     #type normal_bar (652,)
            ?rear_bar      #type return_fromto (685,)
$voice 1
            ?clef          #type G
            ?key           #type sharp 3
            ?time          #type 3/4
            !note          #pitch C (657,)
                           #duration 4
                           #stem up ((662,12),(662,40))
            !rest          #duration 4 (668,)
$bar 3
            @voice 1
            !front_bar     #type normal_bar (652,)
            ?rear_bar      #type return_fromto (685,)
$voice 1
            ?clef          #type G
            ?key           #type sharp 3
            ?time          #type 3/4
            !note          #pitch ,A (657,)
                           #duration 4
                           #stem up ((662,16),(662,48))
            !rest          #duration 4 (669,)
$bar 4
            @voice 1
            !front_bar     #type normal_bar (652,)
            ?rear_bar      #type return_fromto (685,)
$voice 1
            ?clef          #type F
            ?key           #type sharp 3
            ?time          #type 3/4
```

```
                  !note           #pitch E (663,)
                                  #duration 4
                                  #stem up ((668,-8),(668,12))
                                  #tie down end    (662,20)
                  !rest           #duration 4 (671,)
$bar 5
                  @voice 1
                  !front_bar      #type normal_bar (652,)
                  ?rear_bar       #type return_fromto (685,)
$voice 1
                  ?clef           #type F
                  ?key            #type sharp 3
                  ?time           #type 3/4
                  !note           #pitch ,A (661,)
                                  #duration 4
                                  #stem up ((666,0),(666,28))
                  !rest           #duration 4 (672,)
$measure 14
                  @bar 5
                  @postion right_end
$bar 1
                  @voice 1
                  !front_bar      #type return_fromto (685,)
                  !rear_bar       #type normal_bar (720,)
$voice 1
                  ?clef           #type G
                  ?time           #type 3/4
                  !rest           #duration 4 (707,)
$bar 2
                  @voice 1
                  !front_bar      #type return_fromto (685,)
                  !rear_bar       #type normal_bar (720,)
$voice 1
                  ?clef           #type G
                  ?key            #type sharp 3
                  ?time           #type 3/4
                  !note           #pitch E (699,)
                                  #duration 8
                                  #stem up ((704,3),(704,32))
                                  #beam 0 1 (704,3)
                  !note           #pitch G (713,)
                                  #duration 8
                                  #stem up ((718,-2),(718,24))
                                  #beam 1 0 (718,-2)
$bar 3
                  @voice 1
                  !front_bar      #type return_fromto (685,)
                  !rear_bar       #type normal_bar (720,)
$voice 1
                  ?clef           #type G
                  ?key            #type sharp 3
                  ?time           #type 3/4
                  !rest           #duration 4 (709,)
$bar 4
                  @voice 1
                  !front_bar      #type return_fromto (685,)
                  !rear_bar       #type normal_bar (720,)
$voice 1
                  ?clef           #type F
                  ?key            #type sharp 3
                  ?time           #type 3/4
                  !rest           #duration 4 (708,)
```

```
$bar 5
                @voice 1
                !front_bar       #type return_fromto (685,)
                !rear_bar        #type normal_bar (720,)
$voice 1
                ?clef            #type F
                ?key             #type sharp 3
                ?time            #type 3/4
                !rest            #duration 4 (709,)
$end
```

Example 32.1 *SMX* encoding of the first 12 bars of the second trio from Mozart's Clarinet Quintet.

32.3.2 The Telemann Aria

The next example encoded represents the second and third staves, and the first four bars of the Telemann aria. Slurs are intentionally omitted from this code (please refer to Example 32.1 for their encoding). Multiple parts are encoded as multiple *$voice* in this example. Some examples of invisible rest codes, which are used for keeping the time consistent, are shown in $voice 2.

```
$score
                @title           "Telemann aria"
                @size            A4
                @meter           dot
                @format          p2*d1
                @staff_width     32
                @staff_len       720
                @staff_location (45,65) (45,181)
$measure 1
                @bar 2
                @positon left_end
                !bracket         #type middle
                                 #bar 1-2 (-9,)
$bar 1
                @voice 2
                !front_bar       #type normal_bar (0,)
                                 #long
$voice 1
                !clef            #type G (20,)
                !key             #type sharp 2 (41,)
                !time            #type 3/8 (66,)
                !note            #pitch 'D (97,)
                                 #duration 8
                                 #stem up ((102,-11),(102,8))
                                 #beam 0 1 (102,-11)
                !note            #pitch A (126,)
                                 #duration 8
                                 #stem up ((131,-9),(131,20))
                                 #beam 1 1 (156,-8) (102,-11)
                !note            #pitch B (151,)
                                 #duration 8
                                 #stem up ((156,-8),(156,16))
```

```
                                       #beam 1 0 (156,-8)
$voice 2
              ?clef                    #type G
              ?key                     #type sharp 2
              ?time                    #type 3/8
              !note                    #pitch D (97,)
                                       #duration 8
                                       #stem down ((92,36),(92,54))
                                       #beam 0 1 (92,50)
              !note                    #pitch F (126,)
                                       #duration 8
                                       #stem down ((121,28),(121,51))
                                       #beam 1 1 (147,44) (92,50)
              !note                    #pitch G (152,)
                                       #duration 8
                                       #stem down ((147,24),(147,48))
                                       #beam 1 0 (147,44)
$bar 2
              @voice 2
              !front_bar               #type normal_bar (0,)
$voice 1
              !clef                    #type F (20,)
              !key                     #type sharp 2 (41,)
              !time                    #type 3/8 (66,)
              !rest                    #duration 1 (127,)
$voice 2
              ?clef                    #type F
              ?key                     #type sharp 2
              ?time                    #type 3/8
              ?rest                    #duration 1
$measure 2
              @bar 2
$bar 1
              @voice 2
              !front_bar               #type normal_bar (175,)
$voice 1
              ?clef                    #type G
              ?key                     #type sharp 2
              ?time                    #type 3/8
              !note                    #pitch F (205,)
                                       #duration 16.
                                       #stem up ((210,-6),(210,28))
                                       #beam 0 2 (210,-6) (210,-1)
              !note                    #pitch G (250,)
                                       #duration 32
                                       #stem up ((255,-5),(255,24))
                                       #beam 3 1 (321,-4) (255,0) (255,5) (210,-6)
              !note                    #pitch A (276,)
                                       #duration 8
                                       #stem up ((281,-5),(281,20))
                                       #beam 1 1 (321,-4) (210,-6)
              !note                    #pitch D (316,)
                                       #duration 8
                                       #stem up ((321,-4),(321,36))
                                       #beam 1 0 (321,-4)
$voice 2
              ?clef                    #type G
              ?key                     #type sharp 2
```

```
            ?time           #type 3/8
            !note           #pitch D (204,)
                            #duration 4
                            #stem down ((199,36),(199,56))
            !rest           #duration 8 (315,50)
$bar 2
            @voice 2
            !front_bar      #type normal_bar (175,)
$voice 1
            ?clef           #type F
            ?key            #type sharp 2
            ?time           #type 3/8
            !rest           #duration 1 (264,)
$voice 2
            ?clef           #type F
            ?key            #type sharp 2
            ?time           #type 3/8
            ?rest           #duration 1
$measure 3
            @bar 2
$bar 1
            @voice 2
            !front_bar      #type normal_bar (349,)
$voice 1
            ?clef           #type G
            ?key            #type sharp 2
            ?time           #type 3/8
            !note           #pitch 'F (375,)
                            #duration 8
                            #stem up ((380,-26),(380,0))
                            #beam 0 1 (380,-26)
            !note           #pitch 'G (419,)
                            #duration 16
                            #stem up ((424,-24),(424,-4))
                            #beam 1 2 (509,-21) (380,-26) (424,-19)
            !note           #pitch 'F (446,)
                            #duration 16
                            #stem up ((451,-23),(451,0))
                            #beam 2 2 (509,-21) (509,-16) (380,-26)  (424,-19)
            !note           #pitch 'E (476,)
                            #duration 16
                            #stem up ((481,-22),(481,4))
                            #beam 2 2 (509,-21) (509,-16) (380,-26)  (424,-19)
            !note           #pitch 'D (504,)
                            #duration 16
                            #stem up ((509,-21),(509,8))
                            #beam 2 0 (509,-21) (509,-16)
$voice 2
            ?clef           #type G
            ?key            #type sharp 2
            ?time           #type 3/8
            !note           #pitch A (375,)
                            #duration 8
                            #stem down ((370,20),(370,47))
                            #beam 0 1 (370,43)
            !note           #pitch A (419,)
                            #duration 8
                            #stem down ((414,20),(414,49))
```

```
                        #beam 1 1 (498,49) (370,43)
            !note        #pitch G (475,)
                        #duration 16
                        #stem down ((470,24),(470,52))
                        #beam 1 2 (498,49) (470,43)
                                   (370,43)
            !note        #pitch F (503,)
                        #duration 16
                        #stem down ((498,28),(498,53))
                        #beam 2 0 (498,44) (498,49)
$bar 2
            @voice 2
            !front_bar   #type normal_bar (349,)
$voice 1
            ?clef        #type F
            ?key         #type sharp 2
            ?time        #type 3/8
            !note        #pitch 'D (381,)
                        #duration 8
                        #stem up ((386,-36),(386,-12))
                        #beam 0 1 (386,-36)
            !note        #pitch 'E (437,)
                        #duration 8
                        #stem up ((442,-36),(442,-16))
                        #beam 1 1 (495,-36) (386,-36)
            !note        #pitch 'D (490,)
                        #duration 8
                        #stem up ((495,-36),(495,-12))
                        #beam 1 0 (495,-36)
$voice 2
            ?clef        #type F
            ?key         #type sharp 2
            ?time        #type 3/8
            !note        #pitch D (381,)
                        #duration 8
                        #stem down ((376,16),(376,44))
                        #beam 0 1 (376,40)
            !note        #pitch C (435,)
                        #duration 8
                        #stem down ((430,20),(430,44))
                        #beam 1 1 (484,40) (376,40)
            !note        #pitch D (489,)
                        #duration 8
                        #stem down ((484,16),(484,44))
                        #beam 1 0 (484,40)
$measure 4
            @bar 2
            @postion right_end
$bar 1
            @voice 2
            !front_bar   #type normal_bar (535,)
            !rear_bar    #type normal_bar (720,)
$voice 1
            ?clef        #type G
            ?key         #type sharp 2
            ?time        #type 3/8
            !note        #pitch 'C (563,)
                        #duration 16.
```

```
                                 #stem up ((568,-12),(568,12))
                                 #beam 0 2 (568,-12) (568,-7)
                                 #ornament trill up
                    !note        #pitch 'D (595,)
                                 #duration 32
                                 #stem up ((600,-12),(600,8))
                                 #beam 3 1 (680,-14) (600,-7) (600,-2) (568,-12)
                    !note        #pitch 'E (627,)
                                 #duration 8
                                 #stem up ((632,-13),(632,4))
                                 #beam 1 1 (680,-14) (568,-12)
                    !note        #pitch A (675,)
                                 #duration 8
                                 #stem up ((680,-14),(680,20))
                                 #beam 1 0 (680,-14)
$voice 2
                    ?clef        #type G
                    ?key         #type sharp 2
                    ?time        #type 3/8
                    !note        #pitch E (564,)
                                 #duration 4
                                 #stem down ((559,32),(559,52))
                    !note        #pitch C (674,)
                                 #duration 8
                                 #stem down ((669,40),(669,60))
$bar 2
                    @voice 2
                    !front_bar   #type normal_bar (535,)
                    !rear_bar    #type normal_bar (720,)
$voice 1
                    ?clef        #type F
                    ?key         #type sharp 2
                    ?time        #type 3/8
                    !note        #pitch A (573,)
                                 #duration 4
                                 #stem up ((578,-20),(578,0))
                    !rest        #duration 8 (665,)
$voice 2
                    ?clef        #type F
                    ?key         #type sharp 2
                    ?time        #type 3/8
                    !note        #pitch ,A (573,)
                                 #duration 4
                                 #stem down ((568,28),(568,48))
                    ?rest        #duration 8
$end
```

Example 32.2 *SMX* encoding of the first four bars of the first and second parts of the Telemann aria.

References

Matsushima, Toshiaki, Sadamu Ohteru, and Shuji Hashimoto. "An Integrated Music Information Processing System: PSB-er," *Proceedings of the International Computer Music Conference 1989*, pp. 191–198.

Matsushima, Toshiaki, Kuniaki Naoi, Sadamu Ohteru, Shuji Hashimoto, Kentaro Oka, Y. Ishii, H. Ueno, and T. Hashimasa. "A Musical Data Expression for Integrated Music Information Processing System: *SMX*," 3K-3, *Proceedings of the 36th Annual Information Processing System (IPS) Convention* [in Japanese]. Japan, March 1988.

SMX Manual, Version 1 [in Japanese]. Ohteru Laboratory, Waseda University, February 25, 1989.

Appendix 3
Code-Translation Programs

New code translations are often attempted, so information about them will not be complete. However, by listing those translations that currently exist, we can establish that code translation in general is a feasible goal with some practical history. Specific information about where to find the translation programs is given either in the relevant chapters of this book or is available from the chapter author.

In general, it is not helpful to translate from a code representing fewer attributes to one representing more and/or different attributes because the new data set may be inadequate for use with software requiring the newly acquired code. Thus the number of translations that would be optimum for practical use would be considerably fewer than the number of cells that appear in the following tables. Readers may, however, wish to add information to these tables as new translation programs appear.

The sectional organization used here follows the tripartite division of this work into (1) sound-related codes, (2) notation-based codes, and (3) codes for management, analysis, and interchange (MAI). Codes of each category are considered in relation to codes of each other category. Among sound-related codes, we distinguish here between direct MIDI data transfer (MIDI) and Standard MIDI Files (SMF). Other abbreviations should be obvious from chapter titles.

A3.1   Sound→Sound

	Output Codes					
Input Codes	MIDI	SMF	*Csound*	*MML*	NeXT *SF*	*RBC*
MIDI	—				yes	
SMF		—	yes		yes	Format 0
Csound	yes		—			
MML				—		
NeXT *ScoreFile*	yes	yes			—	
RB Conductor						—

Table A3.1 Translation from one sound-related code to another.

Since hundreds of sound-related codes are not covered here, the chart above gives a somewhat impoverished notion of what exists. For example, among those that are mentioned, the *NeXT ScoreFile* accepts *Common Music* data files and provides output to the NeXT sound-file format.

A3.2   Sound→Notation

	Output Codes							
Input Codes	*DARMS*	*CMN*	*M*TEX*	*PMS*	*SCORE*	*LIME*	*Nightingale*	Braille
MIDI	yes[1]	yes[2]			yes	yes	yes	yes[3]
SMF		yes	yes		yes[4]	yes	yes	
Csound		yes						
MML								
NeXT *SF*		yes						
RBC								

Table A3.2 Translation from a sound-related code to a notation code.

A large number of commercial sequencer programs capture raw MIDI data streams and attempt to convert them to notation. In many cases the range of music that can be fully and accurately rendered by this method is limited. Some highly competent systems for the interpretation of MIDI data do exist in programs marketed chiefly for their notational capabilities. Often, however, the data formats used internally by these programs are proprietary.

1. MIDI data can be accepted by a *DARMS*-based notation program (the *Note Processor*; see Chapter 12), but it is converted directly to an intermediate code for page representation rather than to *N-P DARMS*.

2. All answers in this column assume the use of *Common Music*.

3. Via *Goodfeel Braille Music Translator*.

4. Via a separate program, *MIDISCOREWRITE*.

A3.3   Sound→MAI

The cells in Table 3 are not blank by accident. Developers of sound-related software have not so far attempted any translations to codes used for the mainly academic tasks of musical data management and analysis, although the developers of the latter often have some provision for the capture of MIDI data.

	Output Codes						
Input Codes	*EsAC*	*P&E*	*Kern*	*MD*	*SMDL*	*NIFF*	*SMX*
MIDI			yes	yes		yes[5]	
SMF							
Csound							
MML							
NeXT *SF*							
RBC							

Table A3.3 Translation from a sound-related to an analytical or interchange code.

A3.4   Notation→Notation

Developers of notation software are understandably reluctant to facilitate migration from their own code to others. However, many read data in no-longer-used formats. For example, *LIME* reads files in the *OPAL* format (the *OPAL* representation is a predecessor of *LIME*'s *Tilia*). Many notation programs provide direct output to *PostScript* and *Encapsulated PostScript* files. *SCORE* and *Nightingale* both import data from the notation program *Finale* but in different ways: *SCORE* reads *Finale*'s output files in *EPS* format; *Nightingale* reads *Finale*'s *Enigma Transportable Files*.

5. Via the optical recognition program *MidiScan* (see Appendix 4 and the glossary).

Input Codes	Output Codes							
	DARMS	*CMN*	*M*TEX*	*PMS*	*SCORE*	*LIME*	*Nightingale*	Braille
DARMS	—							
CMN		—						
M*TEX			—					
PMS				—				
SCORE					—			
LIME						—		yes[6]
Nightingale							—	pending
Braille MN								—

Table A3.4 Translation from an one analysis or interchange code to another.

A3.5   Notation→Sound

Input Codes	Output Codes					
	MIDI	SMF	*Csound*	*MML*	NeXT *SF*	*RBC*
DARMS						
CMN						
M*TEX		yes				
PMS	yes					
SCORE	yes	yes[7]				
LIME	yes	yes				
Nightingale	yes	yes				
Braille MN						

Table A3.5 Translation from a notation code to a sound-related code.

---

6. Via *Goodfeel Braille Music Translator*.

7. Playback via another program, *MIDISCORE*.

The ready availability of MIDI devices has made it the obvious choice for sound realizations of notation files. With the increasing practice of embedding sound codes on microprocessors, the likelihood that translation to other codes will occur increases. *LIME* also provides output for *Kyma* audio-signal-processing systems.

A3.6   Notation→MAI

Input Codes	Output Codes						
	EsAC	*P&E*	*Kern*	*MD*	*SMDL*	*NIFF*	*SMX*
DARMS						intended	
CMN							
*M*TEX*							
PMS							
SCORE			yes[8]			intended	
LIME						intended	
Nightingale						intended	
Braille MN						intended[9]	

Table A3.6 Translation from codes for notation to those for analysis and interchange.

Notation codes have often been used for analysis, although they are rarely ideal for the purpose. Thus the likelihood is that over the longer term those wishing to analyze musical data will prefer to generate files in an appropriate format from the large quantity of data created for publishing projects.

8. Via an independent program by Andreas Kornstädt running under UNIX.

9. Via *GOODFEEL* and *LIME*.

A3.7   MAI→MAI

	Output Codes						
Input	EsAC	P&E	Kern	MD	SMDL	NIFF	SMX
EsAC	—		yes				
P&E		—	yes	yes[10]			
Kern			—			intended	
MD			yes[11]	—			
SMDL					—	intended	
NIFF					intended	—	
SMX							—

Table A3.7 Translation from one analytical or interchange code to another.

The incentive for translating from one logical code another is to form pools of data in a uniform format for large-scale research or production projects.

A3.8   MAI→Sound

An important value of sound output for analytical encodings is in error-checking. Some kinds of analysis also concern themselves chiefly with sound data.   Many traditional analytical tasks actually employ selective combinations of sound-related and notated attributes.

---

10. Via an independent program by Brent A. Field.

11. All three translations to *Kern* have been written by David Huron.

Input Codes	Output Codes					
	MIDI	SMF	*Csound*	*MML*	NeXT *SF*	*RBC*
EsAC	yes					
P&E						
Kern	yes					
MD	yes	yes				intended
SMDL						
NIFF		intended				
SMX						

Table A3.8 Translation from an analysis or interchange code to a sound-related one.

A3.9   MAI→Notation

Notational capabilities linked with analysis codes potentially serve multiple functions, including screen display of material under examination and the ability for capture and mark up exceprts of notated material (usually for export for descriptive writings). In fact, without such capabilities it is difficult to convey many kinds of analytical results.

If interchange codes are to serve the purpose of linking domains, then it is obvious that they must be able to support conversions to codes for both sound output (A3.8) and notation (A3.9).

Input	Output Codes							
	DARMS	CMN	M*TeX	PMS	SCORE	LIME	Nightingale	Braille
EsAC	yes[12]		yes[13]		yes[14]			
P&E	yes[15]				yes[16]			
Kern[17]								
MD	partial[18]				yes[19]			
SMDL								
NIFF								
SMX								yes

Table A3.9 Translation from an analysis or interchange code to a notation code.

A3.10 Summary

On balance it seems fair to say that, with the exception of hardware-based MIDI data transfers, most translation systems that exist today are unidirectional. The chief motivation for writing translation programs at the present time is for data import.

The quality and efficiency of translation programs between relatively detailed represensations may depend to some degree on whether the expertise of the author of the conversion software is primarily in the old code or the new one.

12. Conversions to canonical and *N-P DARMS* by Frans Wiering.

13. Independent program by Ulrich Franzke.

14. Independent program by Nigel Nettheim.

15. Independent conversion program to *N-P DARMS* by John Howard.

16. Independent conversion program to the *SCORE* ASCII format by John Howard.

17. Screen display of notation using *MUP* (see glossary).

18. Independent program by Brent A. Field converting to *N-P DARMS* for use with the *Note Processor*. What the first program (*MuseData*) handles by code (e.g., first and second endings), the *Note Processor* handles by user-placed graphics (e.g., horizontal lines to mark first and second endings).

19. Independent program by Walter B. Hewlett.

Appendix 4
Codes Supported by Optical Recognition Software

Programs for the optical recognition of musical information are in their infancy. Although quoted rates of correctly recognized objects are sometimes high, the time required for file correction of the raw "recognized" data may diminish the apparent value of this method of input.

Those who develop scanning software usually work at the disadvantage of having no control over code modification. At the present time, most programs for recognition provide output to only one code and operate on only one system. Increased breadth and competence can be expected to develop over the next several years.

Some scanning front-ends for codes considered in this book are mentioned below. More information about the scanning programs named here is provided in the glossary. The operating system on which the recognition software was developed is given in parentheses.

OUTPUT CODE (FOR SOUND)	PRODUCED BY OPTICAL RECOGNITION PROGRAM[1]
Standard MIDI File Format 1.0	*Cantor* by David Bainbridge (UNIX)
	MidiScan (*Windows*[2]) by Musitek
	Music Reader (DOS) by William McGee[3]
Expressive MIDI	*Automatic Music Score Recognizer* (UNIX)
Csound	*Cantor*

1. Named programs are reported and discussed in Eleanor Selfridge-Field, "Optical Recognition: Survey of Current Work," *Computing in Musicology* 9 (1993-94), 109–143. See also the accompanying articles by William McGee ("*Music Reader*: An Interactive Music Recognition System," 144–149), Nicholas P. Carter ("Music Score Recognition: Problems and Prospects," 150–156), and Eleanor Selfridge-Field ("How Practical is Music Recognition as in Input Method?", 157–166). Brief information about each named system is given in the glossary.

2. Files can be read by Macintosh, Atari, Amiga, and DOS operating systems.

3. With Paul Merkley, a musicologist specializing in medieval music, McGee has worked on the optical recognition of medieval cheironomic notation (an eighth-century notation which was not pitch-specific). The purpose of this program, briefly reported with an illustration in *Computing in Musicology* 6 (1990), 42–43, was to produce diastematic notation, in which pitch is specified but there is little allowance for the expression of nuance.

OUTPUT CODE (FOR NOTATION)	PRODUCED BY OPTICAL RECOGNITION PROGRAM
Braille Musical Notation	Program by Ohteru group, Waseda University[4]
DARMS (N-P)	Music Reader (DOS) by William McGee[5]
DARMS (A-R)	Program by Ichiro Fujinaga[6] (UNIX)
LIME/Tilia	Cantor
Nightingale	NoteScan (Macintosh) by Cindy Grande[7]
SCORE	Sight Reader (UNIX/DOS) by Nicholas P. Carter[8]

OUTPUT CODE (FOR INTERCHANGE)	PRODUCED BY OPTICAL RECOGNITION PROGRAM
NIFF	NoteScan
SMX	Program by Ohteru group, Waseda University

Many scanning programs have also been written to produce files in formats not discussed here. These include a program for the recognition of Greek Orthodox chant notation (Dimitris Giannelos, 1990) and one to output MOD files (*Score Analyzing Maestro* by Elisabeth C. Botha et al., 1993).

4. The representation used to facilitate the Braille output is shown in Walter B. Hewlett, "The Representation of Musical Information in Machine-Readable Form," *Directory of Computer Assisted Research in Musicology* [later called *Computing in Musicology*] 3 (1987). Professor Sadamu Ohteru is now retired. Further information on the work of the Ohteru group is also given in the report on optical recognition in *Computing in Musicology* 6 (1990), 40–41.

5. *Music Reader* also produces a "Brinkman *DARMS*" score representation (see Chapter 11).

6. A short report on this system is included in the report on optical recognition in *Computing in Musicology* 7 (1991), 112–113. For further information see Ichiro Fujinaga, "Optical Music Recognition using Projections," Master's thesis, McGill University, 1988; Ichiro Fujinaga, Bo Alphonce, and Bruce Pennycook, "Issues in the Design of an Optical Music Recognition System," *Proceedings of the International Computer Music Conference 1989* (San Francisco: CMA, 1989), 113–116; and Ichiro Fujinaga, Bo Alphonce, Bruce Pennycook, and Natalie Boisvert, "Optical Recognition of Musical Notation by Computer," *Computers in Music Research* 1 (1989), 161-164.

7. With outputs, written by different people, to various operating systems and file formats. For example, the translation to *Nightingale* was made by Charles Rose and that to *MusicPrinter Plus* by Gary Barber.

8. Experiments have included acquisition of parts from sixteenth-century partbooks and computerized republication of music printed in the early twentieth century.

Appendix 5
Proposed Musical Characters in Unicode (ISO/IEC 10646)
Perry Roland

With the rapid growth of the World-Wide Web in recent years, it has become increasingly clear that the 7-bit ASCII character encoding scheme is inadequate for multilingual text processing. The proposed scheme known as Unicode (ISO/IEC 10646) is an attempt to create a single, universal, international character-encoding standard that encompasses all the characters used for written communication, both modern and historic, including technical symbols.

The symbols of Western music notation are not currently included in the proposal. While these symbols are technically glyphs, treating them as characters would allow for compact storage and easy integration into running text, such as theoretical and pedagogical works, terminological dictionaries, bibliographic databases, and thematic catalogues.

Numerous other considerations favor the inclusion of a set of musical characters. Adoption of a standard group of character names would facilitate future pseudo-textual musical encoding systems that offer efficient storage and high parsability and portability. Even though page layout and formatting are beyond the scope of ISO/IEC 10646, the proposed characters could be used within higher-level protocols, i.e., music description languages and file formats for the representation of music and musical scores. Adoption of a standard character set would help alleviate the problem of the lack of a common nomenclature and method for encoding even the most basic elements of music.

A5.1   Character Set Description

The Western Musical Notation character set described here consists of 222 characters. This list is provisional, and further additions may be made. The characters listed are drawn primarily from Common Music Notation (CMN) and its antecedents, mensural notation and plainchant (or Gregorian) notation. In addition, commonly recognized additions to the CMN repertoire, such as quarter-tone accidentals, cluster noteheads, and shape-note noteheads, have also been included. Symbols were compiled from the sources cited in the References.

Because page layout and formatting are beyond the scope of ISO/IEC 10646, no attempt has been made to encode pitch. So, while the designation TREBLE CLEF stands for the corresponding symbol in a stream of data, in conveys nothing about its placement or interpretation in any particular context. Similarly, ISO guidelines exclude single symbols that relate to multiple characters (e.g., a beam or slur that relates to a group of eighth notes).

For the purpose of disseminating this proposal via the World-Wide Web [*http://poe.acc.virginia.edu/~pdr4h*], the character set has been divided into a series of arbitrary categories.

- accidentals
- analytical symbols
- articulations
- bar lines, repeats
- clefs
- dynamics
- Gregorian notation
- instrument-specific symbols
- mensural notation

- noteheads
- note values
- octave signs
- ornaments
- rests
- staves
- tablature symbols
- time signatures

These categories need not be maintained in the future. Keeping characters of similar function together, however, would make the character set easier to use.

A5.2   Processing

The proposed characters could be used within higher-level protocols, i.e., music description languages and file formats for the representation of music and musical scores. Collation of the character set is unnecessary. There is no intrinsic order of symbols.

It is anticipated that music characters will be processed and displayed in a manner similar to mathematical symbols. For example, several of the math tags proposed in the HTML 3.0 specification could be used to place music characters relative to each other.

A5.3   Specification

The proposed characters and character names are given below. The complete proposal may be seen on the World-Wide Web at *http://www.lib.virginia.edu/dmmc/Music/UnicodeMusic*. Comments and suggestions may be sent to Perry Roland, Digital Media and Music Center, Clemons Library, University of Virginia, Charlottesville, VA 22904; tel. (804) 924-7474; fax: (804) 924-7468; *pdr4h@virginia.edu*.

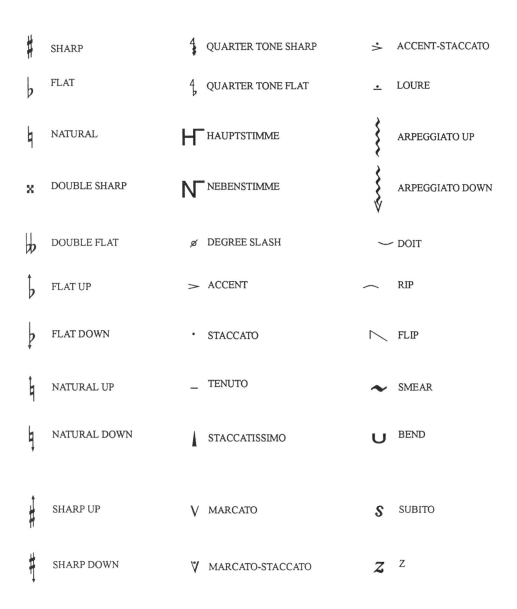

Figure A5.1 Proposed musical characters in Unicode.

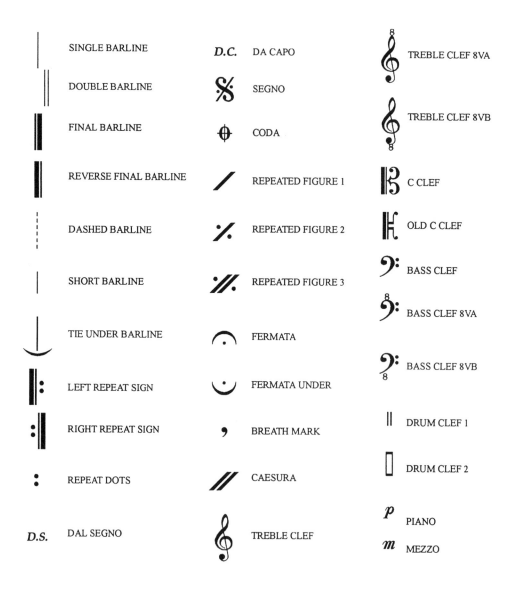

Figure A5.1, cont. Proposed musical characters in Unicode.

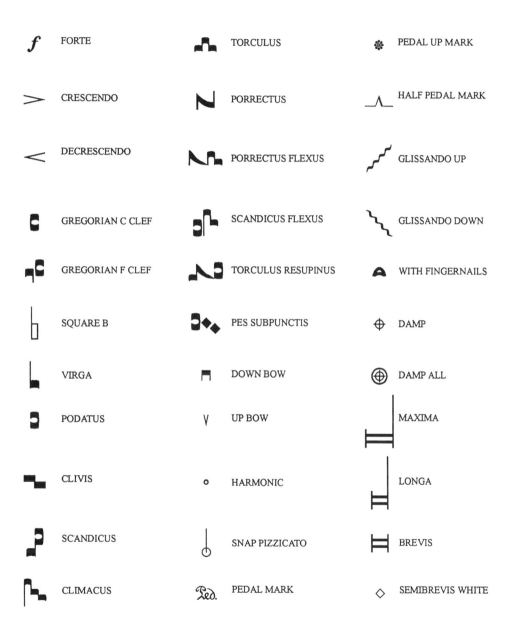

Figure A5.1, cont. Proposed musical characters in Unicode.

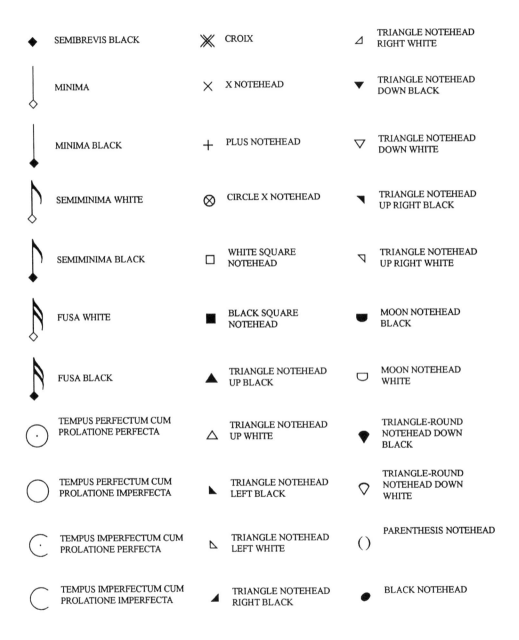

SEMIBREVIS BLACK	CROIX	TRIANGLE NOTEHEAD RIGHT WHITE
MINIMA	X NOTEHEAD	TRIANGLE NOTEHEAD DOWN BLACK
MINIMA BLACK	PLUS NOTEHEAD	TRIANGLE NOTEHEAD DOWN WHITE
SEMIMINIMA WHITE	CIRCLE X NOTEHEAD	TRIANGLE NOTEHEAD UP RIGHT BLACK
SEMIMINIMA BLACK	WHITE SQUARE NOTEHEAD	TRIANGLE NOTEHEAD UP RIGHT WHITE
FUSA WHITE	BLACK SQUARE NOTEHEAD	MOON NOTEHEAD BLACK
FUSA BLACK	TRIANGLE NOTEHEAD UP BLACK	MOON NOTEHEAD WHITE
TEMPUS PERFECTUM CUM PROLATIONE PERFECTA	TRIANGLE NOTEHEAD UP WHITE	TRIANGLE-ROUND NOTEHEAD DOWN BLACK
TEMPUS PERFECTUM CUM PROLATIONE IMPERFECTA	TRIANGLE NOTEHEAD LEFT BLACK	TRIANGLE-ROUND NOTEHEAD DOWN WHITE
TEMPUS IMPERFECTUM CUM PROLATIONE PERFECTA	TRIANGLE NOTEHEAD LEFT WHITE	PARENTHESIS NOTEHEAD
TEMPUS IMPERFECTUM CUM PROLATIONE IMPERFECTA	TRIANGLE NOTEHEAD RIGHT BLACK	BLACK NOTEHEAD

Figure A5.1, cont. Proposed musical characters in Unicode.

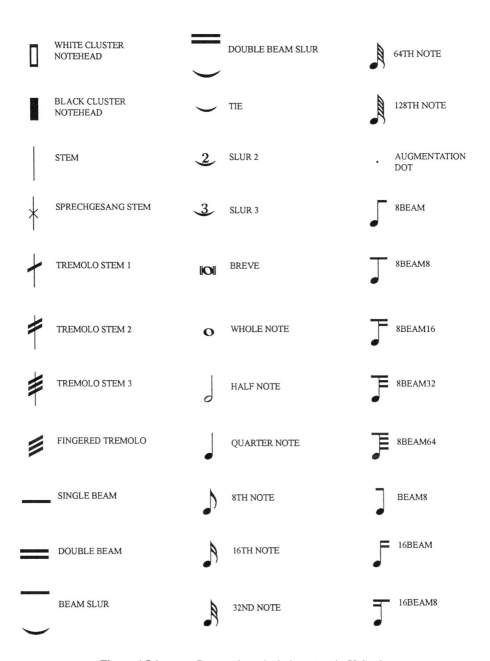

Figure A5.1, cont. Proposed musical characters in Unicode.

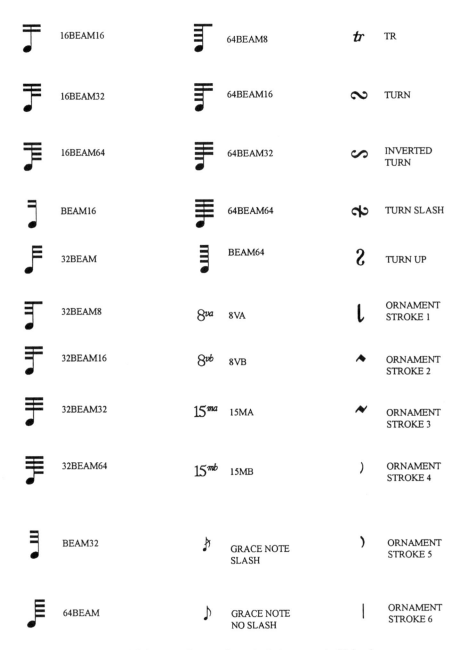

Figure A5.1, cont. Proposed musical characters in Unicode.

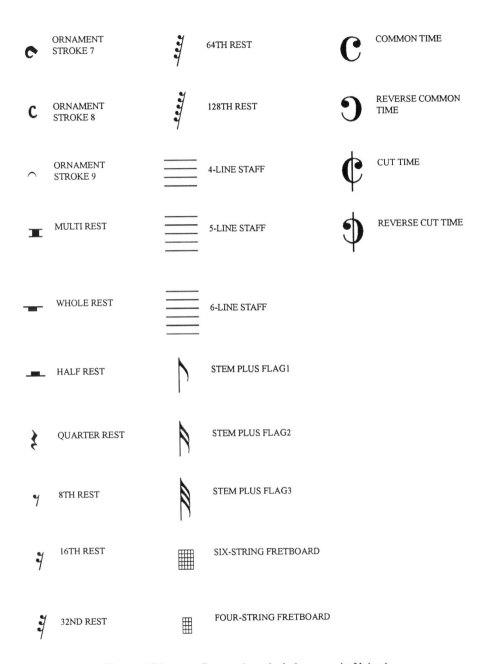

Figure A5.1, cont. Proposed musical characters in Unicode.

References

Balaban, Mira, et al. *Understanding Music with AI: Perspectives on Music Cognition.* Menlo Park: AAAI Press, 1992.

Gradual Sacrosanctae Romanae . . . . Paris: Desclie, 1961.

Heussenstamm, George. *Norton Manual of Music Notation.* New York: W. W. Norton, 1987.

Kennedy, Michael. *Oxford Dictionary of Music.* New York: Oxford University Press, 1985.

Ottman, Robert W. *Elementary Harmony: Theory and Practice.* 2nd edn. Englewood Cliffs: Prentice-Hall, 1970.

Randel, Don Michael, ed. *New Harvard Dictionary of Music.* Cambridge: Harvard University Press, 1986.

Rastall, Richard. *Notation of Western Music: An Introduction.* London: Dent, 1983.

Read, Gardner. *Music Notation: A Manual of Modern Practice.* Boston: Allyn and Bacon, 1964.

Stone, Kurt. *Music Notation in the Twentieth Century: A Practical Guidebook.* New York: W. W. Norton, 1980.

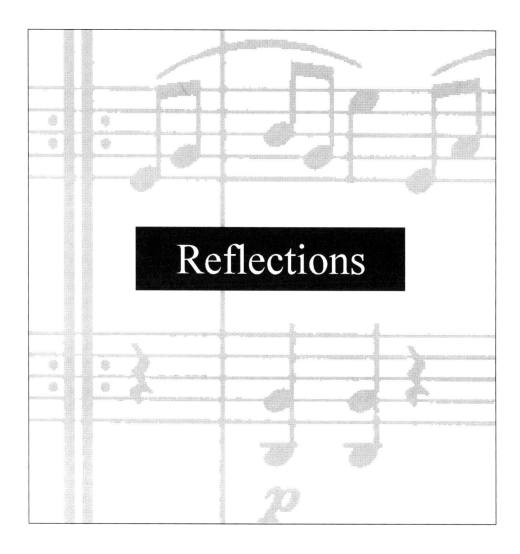

Reflections

33 Beyond Codes: Issues in Musical Representation

Eleanor Selfridge-Field

To enable readers to become familiar both with techniques used to represent musical information and with issues surrounding their end uses and interchange, we have tried to keep many things simple in this book. The six musical examples that are used are quotations, generally from much longer works with many complexities that are not explored here. Our aim is to provide a resource that is introductory.

Readers who intend to work with musical information will want to be aware of two factors of its treatment that affect the feasibility of music applications and the integrity of the data. These factors are the initial selection of attributes to represent music and the preservation of data modifications effected by the user. The transport of data between applications via an intermediary code is bound up with a third consideration—data generalization.

33.1 Representations as Attribute Selections

33.1.1 Feature Selection

Nothing differentiates one representation from another so much as the selection of specific attributes. Maps provide a useful analogy to representations of music (and particularly to musical scores) because they may assume many different appearances, each claiming to "represent" the same entity. Maps may be used to convey information that is physical (providing a rough analogy with sound), practical (providing a rough analogy with notation), or logical (to facilitate comprehension or analysis). Consider, by way of example, Figures 33.1a through 33.1f, in which we see six maps of the United States.

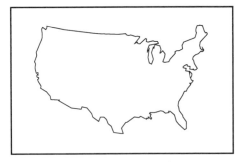

Figure 33.1a Country outline map.

Figure 33.1b State outline map.

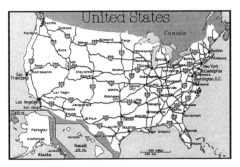

Figure 33.1c Highway map.

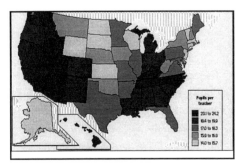

Figure 33.1d Pupil-teacher ratio map.

Figure 33.1e Topographical map.

Figure 33.1f Time-zone map.

Figures 33.1a–f. Six maps of the United States showing diverse selections of attributes and methods for representing them.

Map 1 (Figure 33.1a) merely provides an outline of the entity. It is not a complete representation of the United States for several reasons. Among them, it includes only the 48 contiguous states. It does not wholly represent "physical" information, since the northern and southern boundaries are not entirely defined by the meeting of land and sea. Map 1 is more useful as a symbol of the whole than as an accurate representation of the entity.

Map 2 (Figure 33.1b) shows outlines of all 50 states, so in a geopolitical sense it is more complete, but it does not show Hawaii and Alaska in geographically correct relationships to the continental U.S. The states are not named, so it is not very useful for didactic purposes. The "physical" outlines of the states essentially constitute "logical" information that helps to define political and administrative sub-entities. They are visible only in the context of maps, just as beams, let us say, are visible (and meaningful) only in the context of scores.

Map 3 (Figure 33.1c) has a functional purpose: it indicates the major highways that link various major cities within the U.S. It is vastly incomplete, since a great many other highways and cities can be found in the U.S. Cities are political and administrative entities that are represented symbolically here by their names. A road map can be considered a "logical" representation with respect to the geometrical portrayal of space, but essentially it represents a "physical" presence. In their functionality, key numbers in MIDI data are somewhat like the highway numbers shown here.

In this and the remaining maps Alaska and Hawaii are represented in inserts, and in Map 3 highway information for them is lacking, so their inclusion is gratuitous. However, it is instructive to compare these inserts with the positions of Alaska and Hawaii in Figure Map 2 (Figure 33.1b), where they might be said to exist in "real" (i.e., measurable) space (by analogy with "real" time).

Map 4 (Figure 33.1d) gives analytical information based on data that are not shown. Here the attribute of variable shading is used to bin the states according to a predetermined statistical ranking system. The state outlines are again "logical," but the main purpose of the map is to facilitate performance comparisons. In this sense the nature of the information is more akin to a recording of music than a machine-processable representation: it shows an end result in a format designed to facilitate rapid comprehension. It is not useful for any purpose other than the one for which it is designed. Task-specific codes are loosely analogous.

Map 5 (Figure 33.1e), a topographical map, describes physical surfaces, much as detailed encodings account for all parameters of sound relevant to a particular application. The attribute of altitude is conveyed not by specific heights for every point but on a continuum which is binned into sectors, each represented by a different shade. Binning is much less practical in the representation of notational information than it is in map making, but it does occur. MIDI note numbers, for example, might be considered "binned" information along a continuum in which enharmonic detail is lost. Conversely, information about duration may be said to be unbinned in MIDI data, while being binned (in relation to the temporal idiosyncrasies of performance) in notation.

Map 6 (Figure 33.1f) superimposes one set of logical information (time zones) on top of another (state boundaries). As in Map 3 some city names are given, but necessarily selectively. What is most striking about Map 6 is its treatment of "context": the time zones shown extend into Canada, whereas in Maps 3–5 one might be led to the fallacious conclusion that Canada lacks highways, schools, and a topography. Contextual information is similarly important in representations of music, because many details will be incorrectly interpreted without it. The sound domain is full of examples, such as room acoustics, tuning systems, and so forth.

33.1.2 Feature Relationships

In large measure, all systems for representing music are selective in some way, just as all maps are selective in the information they provide. The privileging of one domain may be as essential as it is practical: a "complete" representation of all domains simultaneously, requiring the same kind of superimposition as we can imagine in these maps, could easily produce an unintelligible mass of detail.

A word about the presence or absence of cumulative and/or hierarchical methods of organization is in order here. While Map 2 contains all the information in Map 1, most other hypothetical connections between these maps diverge. The boundary information shown in Map 2 is incorporated in Maps 4 and 6 but not in Maps 3 and 5, which incorporate the outline given in Map 1. If we were to superimpose any two maps from the set 3–6 on each other, the visual result would be incomprehensible and the logical result would be meaningless. Drivers may want information on time zones or altitude changes but knowledge of pupil-teacher ratios will not serve their immediate purposes, for example.

While it is often convenient for analytical purposes to view music as hierarchical in nature, it is only within the bounds of certain specific attributes that musical information can be thought of as being hierarchical. There may be a progression of detail in the encoding of diatonic, chromatic, and enharmonic pitch information (as in *EsAC*, MIDI, and *MuseData*), for example, but attribute classes are frequently not orderable between domains. One cannot necessarily generate enharmonically correct notation from sound-frequency data, no matter how refined, any more easily than one can generate a topographical map from the attributes present in a highway map: the necessary information is simply not there.

Feature or attribute selection is the single most important aspect of a scheme for representing music. No matter how elegant the design or how numerous the attributes included, if one attribute essential for a particular purpose is not present, the representation cannot be used for the intended application.

Attribute absence is the single most significant problem that confronts those wishing to devise interchange codes. Just as there is no way to generate a time-zone map from a highway map without collating new information, there is no way to retrieve, let us say, information about timbral synthesis from a score representation or information about stem direction from a MIDI transcription.

33.2   One Representation, Multiple File Formats

Amid all the theorizing that goes on about code translations, it is too little acknowledged that multiple data sets may be used in the progressive phases of a single application and that in consequence the attributes available from one stage to the next are not necessarily uniform.

Input data formats that are translated to an "intermediate" file structures have become the norm for notation programs. Originally this transformation accommodated machine constraints: computers processed only numbers, not ASCII code, and information reduced to numbers saved disk space and processing time. Hardware and operating-system constraints have been greatly diminished, but the redefinition of input code to data suited for storage and processing remains.

Although many considerations related to hardware, operating systems, and software could be cited as contributory, a little noted reason for preserving separate input and intermediate data sets is that raw musical materials (that is, the data files as they previously existed) and edited ones can be differentiated. Music is, after all, a sphere of endeavor in which expression and creativity are highly valued. Much of the appeal of music software resides in its ability to enable the user to make modifications. Modifications are not normally saved to input files, however.

The Center for Computer Assisted Research in the Humanities has made several attempts to translate musical information archived in its extensive databases to output formats intended to work with a variety of programs for sound, notation, and analysis. One student who worked on several exploratory programs left a progress report which contains penetrating observations for anyone attempting to translate from one musical code to another. It cites two reasons why a program-in-progress "does not translate everything perfectly." The description begins as follows:

> One [reason] is related to the interpretation of the code [by the applications program]. Some aspects of symbol placement must be left up to the program [to whose data format the translation is being made], for *in theory* it should handle page layout from its own code. However, because this is computationally difficult, the program relies on user interaction for much of the layout. With a mouse, symbols can be moved to a user-specified location. This information is then stored in a file which is "intermediate." The intermediate file subsumes the information provided by the input code.[1]

It is not uncommon for users of notation applications to discover that data entered by mouse-click is incorporated in a machine-processable intermediate file but not in a humanly-comprehensible input file. Thus input codes may not be a good starting point for intra-domain (e.g., notation → notation) translations. In some circumstances, user-supplied data may become, in relation to file formats, orphaned data. Users of sound applications may discover that their changes go directly from a buffer to an output device but cannot be stored at all. They may discover, in short, that their creative improvements are not represented in saved files, even though the data skeleton to which they appeared to be inextricably attached are saved.

Programs that support notation, data management, and code interchange usually also provide conversion to several image-file formats for printing.[2] Among these, *Encapsulated PostScript* is currently the most popular. As representations, output files will normally include all the information found in an intermediate file, but intermediate files do not always include all the information in an input file. A recent approach to data conversion has been to reverse *.EPS* files produced as output by one program to the intermediate (i.e., editable) file format of another.[3] This obviates the problem of working with protected intermediate codes.

---

1. Memo written by Brent A. Field, August 13, 1993.

2. For documentation of these (especially *EPS, GIF, IFF, JPEG, MPEG,* Microsoft RIFF, and TIFF) see James D. Murray and William van Ryper, *Encyclopedia of Graphics File Formats* (Sebastopol, CA: O'Reilly and Associates, Inc., 1994).

3. e.g., *SCORE*'s ability to read *EPS* files produced by *Finale*.

Input codes are not always the best codes to use in data translation. For many notation applications, translation to and from intermediate files (also called internal representations or parametric files) may be more useful. In his remarks in the *A-R DARMS* chapter, Thomas Hall suggests concentration on intermediate files in discussions of data interchange. This might be coupled with generalization of procedures that occur in all applications programs of a similar kind. The obstacles here are not technical. Many intermediate code structures, even though easily decodable within the applications they serve, are unavailable by virtue of legal protection.

33.3   Generalized Representations

Interchange codes proceed on the premise that generalized representations can facilitate efficient data exchange. No one involved in musical data interchange has ever claimed 100 per cent accuracy of data transfer, but it is efficient for programmers to work with only one code, or at the most two (an interchange code and an application code), since they must be familiar with countless intricacies of each one.

It is not so clear that restriction to one or two codes is similarly beneficial to users. They require consistency of data content across applications and optimum performance in diverse circumstances. Generalization comes at a price. This is the other obstacle to complete translation cited in the memo referred to above:

> One goal of mathematics is to generalize real-world processes. To generalize is to algorithmically compress the process of mapping the elements of an input domain to an output domain. Unfortunately, music doesn't lend itself to algorithmic compression. Some aspects of musical interpretation are highly compressible algorithmically, but others require unique handling. This means that tasks involving a large degree of musical interpretation will be more complex to carry out computationally.
>
> Complexity is the nemesis of computer applications. The more complex an algorithm is, the more likely it is to break down and the greater will be the amount of time that programmers will need to handle the not-so-compressible parts of the algorithm. Only under special conditions, in which the input domain is limited to a finite number of elements, could a music translation program work 100 per cent of the time.

In relation to representations grounded in attribute selection, generalized representations serve as a filter that will remove some attributes from any system of representation. This is why, over time, straight code-to-code translations may prove to be the most viable course for music applications requiring complete fidelity of derived data to original data.

33.4   Data Generalization vs. Attribute Specification

In a proposal for musical data interchange made in 1987 by Llorenç Balsach, the originator of a music notation program called *la mà de guido* [*Guido's Hand*], it was suggested that musical data interchange might be handled in a variable manner. Interchange protocols might address several possible levels of detail, with each level subsuming the attributes represented at the previous level. At the lowest level, only "note" information would be provided; at the next level information about modifying signs (accidentals, ornaments, articulations, etc.) would be given; at the highest level, notes, their signs, and their positions would be represented. MIDI data could be exchanged with Level-0 information. Some notation codes could be interchanged using Level-1 information. Information for pages already laid out would be exchanged using Level 2.

This is an idea that has never been put into practice, but it has the potential to make the absence of information about particular attributes a virtue rather than a vice. This scheme was conceptualized only for detailed print-to-print interchange and fairly general print-to-sound information. Within that realm of applications, it seems more practical than codes that attempt complete generalization to serve all application domains.

Undoubtedly there are many other approaches to the task of data interchange. The one thing that is absolutely clear is that everyone involved in applications capable of handling large amounts of data is eager for the day when large quantities of data that can be used in an entirely portable way will be available. We hope this handbook will further that goal.

34   Afterword: Guidelines for New Codes

David Halperin[1]

Do you really need to invent a new code? The answer is: probably not. As the preceding chapters demonstrate, codes which have already been developed answer, collectively, to a wide range of demands, from simple statistical counts to complex cognitive procedures. Taking the time to examine them can save a lot of trouble. Even if a code has to be modified to meet specific needs, this will be easier than constructing a new code from scratch. Some of these codes are, in their present form, the result of many years of refinement in the light of accumulated experience in using them.

Most codes now in use are in the public domain, and most of their authors willingly share their experience and labors. Indeed, one of the purposes of this *Handbook* is to make a variety of codes and some of their uses known to the scholar who is contemplating a computer-assisted research project.

Here we offer some "guidelines" (explicitly not "instructions" or "rules") for those who see justification in inventing new codes. The great variety of codes already in use, as attested by other chapters of this book, and the seemingly infinite variety of possible codes make it desirable to examine the problems and the options involved in establishing a code for research purposes. It should be made clear that we are not dealing in this context with codes which are meant primarily for printing or for sound reproduction but rather with those intended primarily for archiving or analysis.

---

1. This response to the *Handbook* is provided by David Halperin on behalf of the Study Group on Musical Data and Computer Applications of the International Musicological Society. Dr. Halperin's expertise spans a number of repertories from ancient to modern. He has been an active user of a number of codes for a variety of sophisticated purposes, chiefly in analysis and notation. The opinions he expresses are therefore well informed, but they are his own.

34.1 Choosing an Appropriate Code

It will be obvious that no one code is best for all cases. There are three main reasons for this:

- The music under scrutiny and its notated sources will determine, at least to some extent, just what features or parameters should be encoded, and the atomic unit measures of these parameters.

- The aims of the investigation or analysis will similarly contribute their own priorities and constraints.

- The language to be used for programming the manipulation of the encoded materials will influence the code's formal characteristics.

A brief elaboration will help to clarify these points.

34.1.1 The Nature of the Music

With regard to the first, ethnic repertories (e.g., Basque *txistu* [= fife] tunes) invite a code radically different from one appropriate to Wagner's *Tristan*: one is (except for tabor drumming) an unaccompanied instrumental melody, the other orchestral with voices and text. The scales used are different. The improvisatory and interpretive natures of their performance differ. The social functions of these repertories are dissimilar.

If we wished to encode a fourteenth-century Gregorian antiphonal, a seventeenth-century French lute tablature, a *Lied* by Schubert, and a quartet by Alois Haba, these are tasks which have intrinsic differences (even though we may think of them all as music). The written sources are themselves codes, and quite different ones. Our task is to encode the written sources, not the (sounding) "music."

34.1.2 The Nature of the Question

An examination of the harmonic language of Goudimel's homophonic psalm settings and an examination of chromatic voice-leading in Gesualdo's madrigals will both be based on common Western notation (CWN), but harmony is not simply a by-product of a number of melodies, nor is melody just an outcome of harmony.

34.1.3 The Nature of the Programming Language

Almost any standard programming language can be used for almost any task, but each language has its own set of primitive data types, primitive or built-in commands, methods and conventions of file handling, dependence (or independence) on operating systems and even hardware.

FORTRAN's basic units are real numbers; the language excels in extensive and demanding mathematical calculations. In Lisp the basic unit is the list. Pascal, BASIC, and many other procedural languages are single-character-oriented, while SNOBOL (and its offspring SPITBOL) and ICON treat strings of characters as units. Programming in a database language (*dBase*, *FoxPro*, and the like) consists mainly of manipulating and sorting *records* (a record is analogous to a library catalog card) and their *fields* (a field might designate height on a staff, a stem direction, or any other single parameter).

Since programming makes heavy demands on budgets of human and financial resources, the code and the programming language should be matched, preferably *a priori*. A code such as Helmut Schaffrath's *EsAC* lends itself to SNOBOL programming, while John Stinson's *Scribe* is suited to a database language like *FoxPro*.

Examples of Lisp programs can be found in David Cope's books *Computers and Musical Style* and *Experiments in Musical Intelligence*;[2] examples of programs written in Pascal can be seen in Alexander Brinkman's *Pascal Programming for Music Research*;[3] Dorothy Gross's dissertation[4] contains the SNOBOL programs for her research. (All three of these works are landmark studies in the use of musical information for academic purposes.)

34.2 Interpretive vs. Value-Neutral Encoding

Although most encoders aim to provide value-neutral representations and to leave interpretation to the end user, this is not always practical and in certain situations it may not be possible.

2. Vols. 6 and 12 of The Computer Music and Digital Audio Series, gen. ed. John Strawn (Madison, WI: A-R Editions, Inc., and Oxford University Press, 1991 and 1996).

3. Chicago: University of Chicago Press, 1990.

4. Dorothy Susan Gross, "A Set of Computer Programs to Aid in Music Analysis," Ph.D. dissertation, Indiana University, 1975. Facs., UMI 75-23,464.

The four physical-acoustical parameters of a steady-state sound are pitch, loudness, duration, and timbre. To these may be added the contextual parameter of onset time.

These parameters cannot be immediately encoded from notation for a variety of reasons:

- Timbre is not quantifiable, except by use of an infinite series (an indication such as "oboe" or "flageolette tone" does not, in itself, show timbre).

- Pitch, loudness, duration, and onset time are musically relevant only when relative—i.e., when they are referred to another musical sound.

- Many features of most notations give these in ambiguous (or not presently understood) fashion (e.g., durations in lute tablatures or CWN appoggiaturas).

Steady-state notes are idealizations rarely realized and indeed rarely sought in performance, but most notations assume them, using additional signs, words or assumptions for indicating changes during the duration of the note.

These considerations, among others, lead us to two techniques:

- encoding the written signs rather than the musical sounds;

- applying some well-chosen steps of pre-analysis or interpretation, based on extra-graphical knowledge of the musical language and notation conventions.

The first of these techniques enables us to distinguish between a *scandicus* and a *salicus* (used in early chant notation) on identical pitches, or requires that we invent a code-sign for a *Pralltriller* without explicitly defining the quasi-steady-state notes it represents. The second technique could lead to encoding a melody's pitches as a chain of melodic intervals, or (to take a trivial example) to encode a written F as an F♯ when the key signature is D Major, or even to apply rules of *musica ficta* to alter the written notes.

In general, interpretation of written signs is best left to the programming stage of the research and not imposed at the encoding stage. A certain amount of pre-analysis is inevitable, but it should be done consciously and be kept to a minimum, and should—except perhaps in the simplest cases—be explicitly documented (as should the entire code).

What is "simple" depends in part on the orientation of the code—whether it focusses on the graphic form of the source or is music-theoretically oriented. For a code which registers a "quarter note on the first line of a staff (at whose beginning there is a G clef on the second line)," it is "simple" to ignore slight deviations from the norm in the vertical placement of the black oval. For another code, it is "simple" to take that quarter note to be an E. A third encoder might see that the quarter note is part of a triplet, and encode its duration as 1/6 rather than 1/4 (of something).

34.3   Single- or Multiple-Pass Encoding

The question of single- vs. multi-pass encoding arises because we are trying to encode a two-dimensional score into a one-dimensional string of characters.

In single-pass encoding, each point in time is visited once at most. In multiple-pass encoding, each homogeneous component (a single voice, a vocal text, a chronological list of time signatures, etc.) is completely encoded (within the bounds of a logical section, which may be the whole piece) before moving on to another component. Single-pass encoding entails the use of identifiers or position assignments to enable the extraction of individual components, while multiple-pass encoding demands there be a means for synchronization of the components.

Most codes give global information—titles, time and key signatures, sources, etc.—before beginning to encode the sound representations. This is a trivial example of the multiple-pass approach; it may also be an example of a hybrid code: headers as in multiple-pass, body in single-pass codes.

The choice should be made while considering the music to be encoded. A five-voice organ fugue would probably use multiple passes, but a Skryabin piano sonata or a lute tablature probably would not, because the interrelationship of parts makes any kind of meaningful parsing difficult.

With vocal texts the considerations can be more complicated. In general, it is preferable to attach each syllable of the text to the first note to which it is sung. This may not be possible if, say, the text underlay is not unequivocal or even not specified in the source. If polyphonic music is to be encoded, a hybrid approach will probably be best: encode each voice separately (multiple-pass), but attach text syllables to the pertinent notes in each voice (single-pass).

34.4   Providing Editorial Additions, Emendations and Remarks

Differentiation of editorial content from authorial content is always desirable. Editorial additions, emendations, and remarks can occupy a separate file or be included in the code. The logical place for a suggested emendation, an expression of doubt, a comment, etc., is of course along with the item to which it refers—an unclear clef sign or a dubious note, for example. When editorial matter is so placed, it is imperative, and in accordance with good editorial practice, that it be marked as not being in the source. Separate files serve for global editorial matter, such as dimensions of a manuscript, performance history, alternative instrumentation, text translations, collations with other sources, string tunings, and the like.

34.5   Naming Code Elements

Until there is a completely reliable method for converting a scanned score into a code which is amenable to analysis, part of the menial work of the researcher will be the encoding process itself—typing the code equivalents of the musical score at the computer keyboard. This makes errors almost inevitable. One of the first programs written should be an error detector, which can check for proper code syntax, disallowed and misplaced symbols, correct total time values of measures, etc.

Obviously it will be useful to construct the code so that it invites accuracy, or at least discourages error. One way of doing this is to use code symbols which have mnemonic value. To use 8 to represent a quarter-note duration or + for a flat sign would be counter-intuitive, but other less obvious perversities have been perpetrated.

It is also helpful to use different subsets of signs for different parameters of an element. If 2 means the second scale degree (pitch), and 2 means a half note (duration), and 2 also means double dotting (duration again), then it is all too easy to type 124 when 241 or some other permutation of the digits is meant. But something like 2Q. is both less liable to error and more easily found if it is wrongly typed.

While modern storage devices and compression algorithms have made conciseness less of an issue than it once was, there are still the factors of typing effort and tedium to be considered. Thus an expression such as quarter-note would not be a good choice for the code representing a quarter note, even though it is certainly mnemonic and would not be confused with another encoded feature.

For codes with some degree of complexity, it will be useful to separate, at some levels of the hierarchy, the encoded elements and/or their individual parameters into fields—whether by fixed spacing or with the insertion of delimiters. The use of a standard database can help here, but most codes which are not to be manipulated by a database programming language depend on new lines (for records) and space characters (for delimiting fields) for this purpose.

34.6   Providing Secondary Parameters of Notes and Chords

Besides the signs which indicate the acoustical parameters of a steady-state sound listed previously, we often encounter secondary signs in the score which are attached to a note or chord. These can include arpeggiation signs, articulation marks, fingerings, ornaments, and the like. Such marks should always be attached to the note or chord to which they apply, even if the code is in general a multiple-pass one.

When they apply to a number of consecutive notes or chords, the usual solution is to attach something meaning, for example, "crescendo starts here," "*col legno,*" or "red color" to the beginning note of the range and its terminal counterpart ("end crescendo," "*arco,*" "black") to the last one. If the range is not precisely defined in the source, or if its limits are not coincident with notes, either one must guess those limits (adding appropriate remarks) or adopt some other, less explicit, strategy.

34.7   Providing Documentation: With, Within, and Without

Explicit and accurate identification of the sources should always be included with the encoded music. Don't merely call your file "New_Hall" and cite folio numbers with each piece; take a minute to write within the encoded file itself an explicit notation that will not become detached from the data (e.g., "New Hall ms. [ed. Elvis Parsley, Llareggub: Scripsit Books, 1666 B.C.]"). In other words, when the encoded material travels, as it probably will, through space and/or time, it goes with all the information the user or reader needs for its identification.

Every code should be thoroughly, permanently, and externally documented, with nothing taken for granted. It is all too easy to assume that "obviously, – means flat and + means sharp." This is natural but not necessarily obvious (maybe the signs indicate quarter-tones). B does not mean the same thing to a researcher in Heidelberg as it does to his colleague in Harristown. What is mnemonic to the encoder today may not be so to someone else—or even to the original encoder several years from now. It is a mistake to assume that because a code is simple it requires no documentation.

This documentation or code book will serve a triple purpose. Before encoding, it will help make it possible to see that the code decided upon is systematic and to avoid duplication of codes for different items. While encoding, it will serve as a reference for the codes being used (which may be changed when unforeseen problems arise).

After encoding, it will be a permanent record, which can be referred to in proofreading, in comparing codes, and in writing studies concerning the research results. It will also be an enormous help to third parties, should they become interested in the methodology employed.

Glossary

Edmund Correia, Jr., Eleanor Selfridge-Field, et al.[1]

> This glossary provides short entries on (1) some codes that, although not in vigorous current use, contain important concepts not necessarily absorbed in currently used systems; (2) specialized terminology that occurs in one or more chapters; (3) specialized terminology from the fields of both music and computer science that may not be familiar to those grounded exclusively in one field; (4) programs in use in the fields of music or computer music which, for a variety of reasons, lie outside the scope of this book; and (5) substantial repositories of encoded musical materials. Resources for further information are cited where appropriate.

Adagio is a musical code developed by Roger Dannenberg of Carnegie Mellon University (Department of Computer Science) as part of the *CMU Toolkit*. Pitch and octave representation are the same as in *MuseData* code and duration representation is roughly the same as in *DARMS* (Q = quarter, E = eighth, etc.).

AIFF. The Audio Interchange File Format (AIFF) was devised by Apple Computer, Inc., as a method for storing sampled sounds. It has gained substantial use across computer platforms, and is the standard format used by Silicon Graphics workstations. The specification is available from various ftp sites. A conversion utility called *SOX* (*SOund eXchange*) from the WAV format to AIFF is available from the World-Wide Web site *http://www.spies.com/Sox/*.

Alberti bass. A patterned bass consisting of alternating chordal tones (e.g., in such diatonic sequences as 1, 5, 3, 5 and –5, 3, 1, 3). It was especially prevalent in

---

1. Numerous individual contributors are cited after the entries they have provided.

Italian and Austrian keyboard works of the middle and later eighteenth century, including those of Alberti (who was not its inventor) and Mozart.

ALMA. An encoding language developed in the Sixties by Murray J. Gould and George W. Longman. It influenced the development of other early codes for music and was used in the early work of Donncha Ó Maidín. This has now been absorbed into an object-oriented approach to music representation called *Mscore*. FURTHER INFORMATION: Donncha Seán Ó Maidín, "A Programmer's Environment for Music Analysis," Ph.D. thesis, National University of Ireland, 1995.

Alpha/TIMES. An integrated input and analysis system developed in the mid-Eighties for the Apple Macintosh III line by Christoph Schnell. *TIMES* stands for *Totally Integrated Musicological Environment System*. An unusual input method (voice-recognition device with light pen) permitted accurate reproduction of non-common notation, including neumes. Conversion to *DARMS* code was supported. FURTHER INFORMATION: Schnell, Christoph. *Ein System zur computergestützten Forschung in den Geisteswissenschaften: Konzeption, Implementierung, Anwendungsbeispiele* (Bern: Peter Lang, 1989 [ISBN 3-261-04197-8]).

Amadeus. Amadeus Music Software, designed by Kurt Maas to run on Atari computers, uses a proprietary data format consisting principally of ASCII files. Music of arbitrary complexity may be represented. See especially *Computing in Musicology* 7 (1991), 156.

ANTOC. The *ANTOC* code for folksongs was invented in the early Eighties by Wolfram Steinbeck at the Rheinische Friedrich-Wilhelms-Universität in Bonn, Germany. The record structure provides four fields for identification of the work; four fields for specification of meter, key, tonality, and octave; and four fields for monophonic input. Of these the most complex is the representation of duration, which supports seven meters and 12 rhythmic values. *ANTOC* is described in Steinbeck's article "Struktur und Ähnlichkeit: Methoden automatisiertes Melodienanalyse" (*Kieler Schriften zur Musikwissenschaft*, 25), 394–395. FURTHER INFORMATION: Musikwissenschaftliches Seminar, Am Hof 34, D-53113 Bonn, Germany; tel. +49 0228/73-7581.

(Wolfram Steinbeck)

ANSI Z39. The ANSI/NISO Z39.2 specification defines procedures for bibliographic information interchange. The ANSI/NISO Z39.50 specifications for information retrieval (Information Retrieval Application Service Definition and Protocol Specification for Open Systems Interconnection) are available through the World-Wide Web site of the Library of Congress Z39.50 Maintenance Agency home page at *http://lcweb.loc.gov/z3950/agency.html*.

(John Howard)

ASCII. ASCII is the most commonly used method of assigning a binary representation to the letters and punctuation signs used in English. ASCII also assigns binary codes to common text-management functions such as line feeds and carriage returns. *Lower-ASCII* assignments (in the range 1..127) are common to almost all text-management software, while *upper-ASCII* assignments (in the range 128..255) are used in arbitrary ways by different vendors. Upper ASCII characters are commonly used to represent diacritical marks, alphabetic characters, and punctuation marks in languages other than English.

Musical (and other) codes that use only lower ASCII characters in their representation should be interpretable by any system; those that also use upper ASCII characters may perform unpredictably if used on a system other than the one used in development. Systems that are based on graphic images may not have an underlying ASCII representation.

AU. Audio file format used on workstations manufactured by Sun, NeXT, and DEC and for some Internet data transfers. See also μ-law (under letter M).

Automatic Music Score Recognizer. A UNIX-based optical recognition system for music developed in the early Nineties at Leeds University by Kia-Chuan Ng and Roger D. Boyle. Output is to the *Expressive MIDI* file format. FURTHER INFORMATION: *Computing in Musicology* 9 (1993-94), 121ff.

Berlioz. A set of programs (*ca*. 1990) by Dominique Montel and Frédéric Magiera to create music notation on the Macintosh. It utilized an entirely graphic system of input.

Binary number. Binary numbers are expressed in a base-2 representation. The rightmost numeral indicates the number of 1s, the penultimate numeral the number of 2s, the antepenultimate numeral the number of 4s, and so forth through the places for 8s, 16s, 32s (for "32-bit code"), and 64s (for "64-bit code"). They can be interpreted at the machine level as "on" and "off" switches.

The largest decimal (base-10) number that can be represented in a seven-bit binary code is 127; the largest decimal number in an eight-bit binary representation is 255. The decimal number 8 would be represented in binary notation as 1000 [($\mathbf{1}$ x 8) + ($\mathbf{0}$ x 4) + ($\mathbf{0}$ x 2) + ($\mathbf{0}$ x 1)]; the decimal number 53 would be represented as 110101 [($\mathbf{1}$ x 32) + ($\mathbf{1}$ x 16) + ($\mathbf{0}$ x 8) + ($\mathbf{1}$ x 4) + ($\mathbf{0}$ x 2) + ($\mathbf{1}$ x 1)].

Calliope. *Calliope* is a graphically-oriented program for music printing that has been under development on various UNIX platforms for several years. The developer is William Clocksin. *Calliope* does not encode music. The input is supported entirely by graphics images; the internally stored "score" is represented by a complex data structure.

Calliope was intended for producing performance editions of early music (up to *ca.* 1640) and has numerous provisions for figured bass, lute tablature, chant notation, multiple verses (for strophic vocal music), etc. It does not handle features such as grace notes, double stops, piano chord notation, or multiple parts on one staff. Examples appeared in *Computing in Musicology* 9 (1993-4), 218–222. FURTHER INFORMATION: William F. Clocksin, Computer Laboratory, University of Cambridge, New Museum Site, Pembroke Street, Cambridge CB2 3QG, UK; *William.Clocksin@cl.cam.ac.uk*.

CD-I (Compact-Disk Interactive). An offshoot of the IFF file exchange protocol adapted for music files read by compact disks. (It was originally called CD-I IFF). A file contains a single image, a single sound, or any combination of data allowed by the IFF protocol.

Cent. Fine unit of pitch representing 1/100th of a semitone. There are 1200 cents in an octave.

cmusic. A language for the synthesis of electronic scores based on the general principles of *Music V* but implemented in C to run under UNIX. It was written by F. Richard Moore in 1980 at the University of California at San Diego. A large number of *unit generators*, written elsewhere to extend synthesis functions, are available at multiple sites (e.g., from the World-Wide Web site *http://www.mathuab.edu/home/xin/cmusic.html*). FURTHER INFORMATION: A manual for *cmusic* is appended to F. Richard Moore, *Elements of Computer Music* (Englewood Cliffs, NJ: Prentice Hall, 1990), pp. 490–546.

Cochlear coordinate. For a given frequency input, the point of maximum excitation along the basilar membrane (measured in millimeters from the apex of the cochlea). For example, a pure tone of 440 Hz causes the basilar membrane to show a peak excitation roughly 9.4 mm from the apex. Hence 9.4 is the cochlear coordinate corresponding to 440 Hz.   *(David Huron)*

Common Lisp Music (*CLM*) is a set of Lisp extensions for sound synthesis and signal processing that descends from the *Music V* family. It was written primarily by Bill Schottstaedt at Stanford University. It is often used in conjunction with *Common Music (CM)* and *Common Music Notation (CMN)*; the latter is discussed in its own chapter. *CLM* has its own home page on the World-Wide Web (*http://ccrma-www.stanford.edu/CCRMA/Software/clm/clm.html*). Links are provided to a *CLM* tutorial, a *CM* tutorial, and Guy Steele's online manual for Common Lisp. *CLM* is also described by Schottstaedt in "Machine Tongues VII: CLM: Music V Meets Common Lisp," Computer Music Journal 18/2 (1994), 30-37.

Common Music (*CM*), written by Heinrich Taube, is an object-oriented composition environment which provides a control language for composers who wish to generate compositions from a model of their own design. It is based on a top-down approach stressing structures and patterns and is implemented in Common Lisp on a large number of platforms, including in particular the NeXT and Macintosh. *Common Music* can be used in conjunction with such music-representation schemes as *cmusic*, *Csound*, *Common Music Notation*, MIDI, and the *NeXT Music Kit*. It is a successor to *PLA* [see listing below]. A text-based editor called *Stella* is used with *Common Music*. Source-code is available from *ccrma-ftp.stanford.edu:/pub/Lisp/* and *ftp.zkm.de:/pub/cm/*. A description is available from the World-Wide Web (*http://ccrma-www.stanford.edu/CCRMA/Software/cm/cm.html*). FURTHER INFORMATION: Heinrich Taube, "*Common Music*: A Music Composition Language in Common Lisp and CLOS," *Computer Music Journal* 15/2 (1991), 21–32.

Critical bandwidth. A region of interaction or interference in the peripheral auditory system. In the middle range of hearing, a critical band corresponds to the interval of about three semitones.   (*David Huron*)

Dai Nippon Music Processor. This dedicated hardware system for the production of musical scores was developed in the late Eighties. Input is alphanumeric. Output files can be sent to MIDI instruments, to *PostScript* printers, to a Digiset typesetter, or to the *Standard Music Expression (SMX)* file format used in music research at Waseda University. Kentaro Oka, the author of a recent article on the use of Standard Generalized Markup Language for music documents [*cf. Computing in Musicology* 7 (1991), 20], is the current manager. FURTHER INFORMATION: Dai Nippon Printing Co., Ltd., CTS Division, 1-1 Ichigaya-kagacho 1-chome, Shinjuku-ku, Tokyo 162-01, Japan; fax +81 03/3266-4199.

Dal Molin Musicomp. Armando Dal Molin spent a lifetime in the effort of making music printing more efficient. This system accommodated a great number of changes in technology between the late Thirties and the late Eighties. His semi-automatic music printing system, recently in use by Belwin Mills, generated more than 500,000 pages of printed music. His internal code was shown in *Computing in Musicology* 3 (1987), 17.

d.p.i. Dots per inch.

Enigma Transportable File Format. *Enigma* transportable files are text files in a proprietary format used by *Finale*, a popular music printing program for the Macintosh and *Windows* environments, written in its original version (1987) by Phil Farrand. *ETF* files provide upward- and cross-platform compatibility for different versions of *Finale*.

Coda Music Technology, the owner and distributor of this program, offers several music fonts—*Petrucci* for conventional notation, *Rameau* for subscripted chord names and basso continuo figures, *Seville* for guitar tablature, and *Newport* for jazz and percussion notation. *Finale* also provides some support for mensural notation. *Finale ETF* files can be read and edited by *Nightingale* and *Finale* output files in *EPS* format can be read and edited by *FinalSCORE*, a special version of *SCORE*.

The company specifically requested that the *ETF* format *not* be documented in this publication. An overview of its original file organization can be gleaned from its first patent application—U.S. #4,960,031—together with additions and amendments described in subsequent filings. FURTHER INFORMATION: Coda Music Technology, 6210 Bury Drive, Eden Prairie, MN 55346-1718; (800) 843-2066; technical support line (612) 937-9703; fax (612) 937-9760.

Euterpe. Several unrelated programs have used this name. (1) A procedural computer music language developed by Stephen Smoliar in 1971, in which instructions for notes and sound synthesis were combined to form a score file. FURTHER INFORMATION: Stephen Smoliar, "Process Structuring and Music Theory," *Journal of Music Theory* XVIII/2 (1974), 308–336, and "Music Programs: An Approach to Music Theory through Computational Linguistics," *Journal of Music Theory* 20/1 (1976), 105–132.

(2) A printing system developed by Michel Wallet in the late Eighties for the Macintosh. It attempted to provide integrated support for encoding, printing, and analysis. It was particularly oriented toward some special repertories including lute tablature (based on previous work by Bernard Stepien) and Byzantine music with text underlay in Cyrillic characters. FURTHER INFORMATION: *Computing in Musicology* 7 (1991), 62-63.

Extended Standard MIDI File Format (***ESM***). In this scheme of extensions to a Standard MIDI File, an ID number for research applications (7EH) has been introduced. The intention is to provide both performance and score information. It is also possible to supplement existing information. An example of a Standard MIDI File containing a series of SysEx messages is shown below:

HEX CODE	MEANING
. . .	
00H	Delta time
90H 4DH 4CH	Note_On Event
00H	Delta time
F0H **7EH**	**Sys_Ex Start**
07H 09H	Dynamic: f
3FH 02H	Coordinates (optional)
00H	Separation
06H 03H	Articulation: v

05H 02H	Coordinates (optional)
F7H	SysEx_End
. . .	

Another manner of extension is provided by the introduction of dummy events (90H 00H 00H), which are used to represent rests and other kinds of information that are not attributes of single Note_On events. Dynamics and articulation as well as part separation and combination are some of the areas that can be covered in this way.

The development of this system, which originated in 1992, continues at the University of Cologne and nearby locales. Retrieval software running on Microsoft *Windows* is under development. FURTHER INFORMATION: Peer Sitter, Universität zu Köln, Musikwissenschaftliches Facultät, D-50923 Köln, Germany; tel. +49 (0)221 270 3802; fax +49 (0)221 470 4964; *alm05@rs1.rrz.Uni-Koeln.DE.*   (*Peer Sitter*)

FASTCODE. An encoding language developed in the early Seventies by Thomas Hall at Princeton University for white mensural notation of the fifteenth and sixteenth centuries. This code supported note values from the *semifusa* (the equivalent of sixteenth notes) through the perfect *maxima* (the equivalent of twelve semibreves) and could accommodate time changes local to one voice. It was used to encode several hundred works by Lassus and other composers of the period. Some results of the use of the code are reported in Thomas Hall, "Some Computer Aids for the Preparation of Critical Editions of Renaissance Music," *Tijdshrift van de vereniging voor Nederlandse Muzekgeschiednis* XXV/1 (1975); and Harold Powers, "Tonal Types and Modal Categories," *Journal of the American Musicological Society* XXXIV (1981).

Finale. Popular transcription and notation program for the Macintosh and *Windows* operating systems. An archived electronic discussion may be joined by sending mail to *LISTSERV@SHSU.edu.* See ENIGMA TRANSPORTABLE FILE FORMAT.

Floating-point number. A number containing a decimal point. Inside the computer, floating-point numbers must be processed differently from integers.

FTP (also ftp). File transfer protocol. Of the many ways that exist for transferring files from one physical site to another, this UNIX-based procedure is one of the most reliable and widely used.

Goodfeel Braille Music Translator. A program to automate production of Braille musical scores; also its data format. The original version is a DOS-based one; *Windows* and Macintosh versions are planned. Version 1.0 will convert the Standard MIDI and *LIME Tilia* file formats into Braille music output. This output conforms to the standards provided by the music committee of the Braille Authority of North America. FURTHER INFORMATION: William R. McCann, Dancing Dots Braille Music Technology, 130 Hampden Road, 3rd Flr., Upper Darby, PA 19082-3110; (610) 352-7607; fax (610) 352-4582; *mccann@netaccess.com*; *http://www.netaxs.com/~ddots*.

Grand staff. The grand staff, used for the notation of keyboard music, combines two staves (usually for treble [or G; 𝄞] and bass [or F; 𝄢] clefs) to show the separation of hands. The "missing line" between the treble and bass staves belongs to Middle C. The moveable C-clef sign indicates, conversely, where Middle C falls on a single staff.

Graphics file formats. The scaling of notation, the integration of musical examples in text files, and the interchange of music printing files between programs are three capabilities that depend, in many computer environments, on the ability to export notation files via a recognized graphics file format to external programs. Many such formats are in use. Among the most common are *Encapsulated PostScript* (*EPS*), which creates files for a *PostScript* printer; CompuServe's *Graphics Interchange Format* (*GIF*), used often on the World-Wide Web; Hewlett-Packard Graphics Language (HPGL); *PC Paintbrush* format (*PCX*); and Tagged Image File Format (TIFF). Microsoft's Resource Interchange File Format (RIFF) accommodates both graphics and sound files of particular kinds.

Graphire Music Press. A music-notation typesetting system by Alan Talbot combining line-art graphics, page layout, and notation expert systems. It has special features for various modern notations, commercial copying (show music), handbell music, and other special repertories. Accepts MIDI input; produces *PostScript* output. FURTHER INFORMATION: Graphire Corp., 4 Harvest Lane, PO Box 838, Wilder, VT 05088-0838; *info@graphire.com*; *http://www.sover.net/~graphire*.

hertz (Hz). Unit of frequency in cycles per second.

Hewlett's Base-40 System of notated pitch representation employs 35 names and five null positions (separating C/D, D/E, F/G, G/A, and A/B) to create a numbering system that produces complementary intervals and supports the invertible arithmetic familiar to music theorists. Thus, the difference (12) between the tones of the major third C–E (3, 15), when added to the difference (28) between the tones of the minor sixth E–C (15, 43) produces the sum of 40. A series of larger numbers can also be used for this purpose.

This facility is valuable in analytical and notational applications and less cumbersome than binomial procedures (involving pitch name and octave number) that have been proposed for the same purposes. This system was developed by Walter B. Hewlett in 1986 and has been in regular use at CCARH and among several user communities.

Hexadecimal representation. Hexadecimal code is a base-16 numeric representation scheme in which the ciphers 0..9 stand for the decimal numbers 1..10 and the letters A..F stand for the decimal numbers 11..16. In hexadecimal notation, the rightmost cipher counts 1s, the penultimate cipher counts 16s, and the antepenultimate cipher counts 256s. Thus the decimal number 320 would be indicated as 140 [(**1** x 256) + (**4** x 16) + (**0** x 1)].

Hexadecimal numbers can be organized either with the most significant digit on the left (e.g., on the Macintosh and on Sun workstations) or on the right (e.g., VAX mainframes and IBM PCs). In addition, the nomenclature may vary from the processing order, and the individual bits described in technical documentation may be labelled 0..7 or 1..8, etc.

HPGL. Hewlett-Packard Graphics Language.

IFF. The Interchange File Format originally developed for the Amiga microcomputer. The protocol provided for four file types—rasterized pictures, animations, musical scores, and sampled audio. These file types were "wrapped" in a uniform syntax. Some progeny are AIFF, RIFF, and CD-I.

IML-MIR. *IML*, an *Intermediary Musical Language* to represent common musical notation and accompanying text on punched cards, and *MIR*, a programming language for *Musical Information Retrieval*, were both developed at Princeton University in the Sixties. *MIR* was designed so that any music-theoretical question—i.e. any question whose answer is computable from the internal evidence of musical notation as represented in *IML*—could be posed as an *MIR* program. The answer could be obtained automatically by running the program.

The musical repertory for which *IML* and *MIR* were originally developed was that of the masses of Josquin des Prez printed in the Vereniging voor Nederlandse Muziekgeschiednis edition and related compositions. *MIR*'s capabilities were designed to transcend the more or less trivial calculation of elemental statistics by allowing structural concepts to be encoded as subroutines. *(Michael Kassler)*

Interactive Music System (IMS). This multi-faceted system, developed by Lippold Haken and others at the University of Illinois from the early 1970's until its work was subsumed by *LIME* [see Chapter 20], originated on the PLATO system and used an alphanumeric encoding language called *OPAL*. FURTHER INFORMATION: CERL Music Group, University of Illinois, 103 S. Mathews #252, Urbana, IL 61801-2977; tel. (217) 333-0766.

Java MIDI. MIDI support for the Java programming language used for World-Wide Web applications requires platform-dependent ("native") code. An open Standard MIDI Object and free access to the necessary native-code libraries is being promoted by Michael St. Hippolyte through the Web site *http://www.interport.net/~mash/ javamidi.html*. As of July 1996, Java MIDI was not yet able to support system-exclusive messages, built-in sequencing, or the Standard MIDI File format.

JavaTime. An audio *applet* designed to work as a World-Wide Web "little application" written in the Java programming language. The file *javatime.zip* can be downloaded from *http://www.pcmag.com*.

la mà de guido [*Guido's Hand*]. This music printing software for IBM PC, developed in Spain by Llorenç Balsach, used an alphanumeric input system based on a redefined QWERTY keyboard. It has also been marketed as an input system for *SCORE*.

Balsach devised an interchange code for certain other notation programs, including *SCORE*, in 1988. As this hexadecimal code was designed, there would be three levels of detail: Grade 0 would provide note information only, Grade 1 would provide information about notes and their signs (accidentals, ornaments, articulations, etc.), and Grade 2 would describe notes, their signs, and their positions. MIDI data could be exchanged with Level 0 information; some notation codes could be interchanged using Grade 1; information for pages already laid out would be exchanged using Grade 2. FURTHER INFORMATION: Llorenç Balsach, La mà de guido, Apartat 22, Ctra. de Parts 2, 08200 Sabadell (Barcelona), Spain; tel. +34 3/725-7052.   (*Llorenç Balsach*)

LazyCode. See *Musicode-A*.

Linear decomposition mode. Musical textures that can be interpreted to consist of variable numbers of voice tracks sharing a common staff can be represented more conveniently in linear decomposition mode than in a strict track-by-track representation. Some typical contents in which linear decomposition is useful include the keyboard preludes and other genres that imitate the arpeggiation of plucked string instruments, such as the lute. The term and the concept were originated by *DARMS* designers (see Chapter 12) in the early Seventies. As a procedure, linear decomposition has also been employed to represent multiple verses of text under a melody and basso continuo figures under a basso continuo part.

MDI. *Music Descriptor Instructions*, developed by Laurie Spiegel in the early Eighties, was designed to extend telecommunications protocols to accommodate music, image, and text. Attributes supported included voice, pitch, tuning, scale, chord, key signature, tempo, duration, volume, mixture, and so forth. The system was tested by three Canadian firms in 1984-85, after which development ceased. Software to represent music within the North American Presentation Level Protocol Syntax (NAPLPS) had previously been developed. Corollaries were an Audio Description Instruction (ADI) set and a speech descriptor instruction (SDI) set. FURTHER INFORMATION: 175 Duane St., New York, NY 10013; fax (212) 966-7176; *spiegel@amanda.dorsai.org*.   (*Laurie Spiegel*)

Mel. The psychoacoustic unit of subjective pitch. A sound subjectively judged to be *n* times higher than a 1-mel tone is defined as *n* mels. For example, where one pitch is judged to be "twice as high" as another pitch, the number of mels also doubles. The reference point for such judgments is a 1000 mel tone—defined as a 1000 Hz pure tone having a loudness level of 40 phons. Anyone who knows that an octave represents a doubling of frequency finds the mel scale counter-intuitive. However, naive listeners reliably make judgments of this sort. The mel scale has been shown to correlate well with cochlear coordinates.   (*David Huron*)

MelAnaly. *MelAnaly* is a system designed by J. Marshall Bevil for the comparative analysis of melodic relationships within ballad and fiddle-tune repertories. Its development can be traced to 1981. Pitch, duration, and stress are encoded as ASCII text and converted to numeric codes. The three-place pitch codes indicate pitch class (units), chromatic alteration or the lack thereof (tens), and octave species (hundreds). Duration codes represent lengths in terms of sixteenth notes (1–16), unmeasured grace notes (.1), and fermatas (100). Stress codes stand for primary and secondary stressed and unstressed beats, afterbeats, and the subdivisions of each of these, in both single-note and triplet configuration.

The codes form numeric arrays that represent the primary cells, or main mnemonic anchor points, and the melodic contour that is encoded at three successively complex levels (elemental, broad details, specific details). FURTHER INFORMATION: J. Marshall Bevil, 7918 Millbrook Drive, Coppercreek, Wheatstone Village, Houston, TX 77095; tel. (713) 859-5965.   (*J. Marshall Bevil*)

MELCODE. *MELCODE* was devised for use in pedagogical software for melodic dictation designed by Gary Wittlich, Eric Isaacson, and others at Indiana University in 1987. It was intended to meet the need for a simple representation of short melodic fragments that would require a minimal amount of interpretation on the part of an application program, particularly with respect to the display of beamed groups of notes. *MELCODE* uses three- and four-place integers. The function of the code is dependent (with a few exceptions) on the digit in the 100s place.

Rhythmic patterns are encoded in the form $n2xx$, where n is the size of a (possibly) beamed notational grouping (n = 0 for a rest), and xx is an arbitrary index to a particular pattern of durations stored in a table and used as a template for the drawing of a melodic figure on the screen. For example, `0206` encodes an eighth rest, `1204` a quarter note, `2201` a dotted-eighth/sixteenth-note pattern, and `6200` six beamed sixteenth notes.

The rhythmic-pattern code is followed by an appropriate number of pitch codes. Pitch is encoded using Alexander Brinkman's continuous binary representation, which represents pitches in the format *OPcN*, where *O* is the octave, *Pc* is the pitch class number (C = 0, C# = 1, ... , B = 11), and *N* is the name class (C = 0, D = 1, ... , B = 6). For example, C# above Middle C is represented as `4010`. Provisions exist in a similar format for meter, tempo, bar lines, and ties. Key signatures are not encoded because melodies are stored in a natural key (C Major or A Minor) and transposed at random to an appropriate register in the dictation drill.   (*Eric Isaacson*)

Meta. The *Meta* code, developed by Jonathan Berger and Paul Bercovitz at Yale University in 1994, represents Schenkerian middle-ground structures in functional tonal works, performance interpretations, information about articulation and phrasing, and other analytical constructs for audio playback and compositional purposes. It also facilitates pattern searching, comparison, and manipulation. Data can be converted from MIDI. The code exists in ANSI C, Lisp, and partially in Haskell.   (*Jonathan Berger*)

Metric representations. Musical meter can have several strata of accentual information. The common model—in which a whole note can be divided into two halves and each half into two quarters—portrays all subdivisions as binary. Metric signatures that suggest such an arrangement include 2/2, 2/4, 4/4, and 4/8. The most common entirely ternary arrangement is represented by 9/8 meter, in which there are three beats and each beat is subdivided into three "eighths." Compound meters are those in which one level is binary and another ternary. In 3/4 meter, for example, the first-order division is ternary and the second-order division is binary. In 6/8 the first-order division is binary, the second-order division ternary.

Most representation systems covered in this book make provision for all of these situations. However, in the classical instrumental and vocal repertories accentual "modulations" on the local level are common, and systems that wish to provide a foundation for the encoding of such material must offer a way of dealing with these irregularities.

MIDI. Musical Instrumental Digital Interface. See the glossary entry on *Extended MIDI* (for research applications) as well as Chapters 2-6 and Appendices 1 and 2 of the main text.

MidiScan. Commercial optical recognition program offered by Musitek Technologies (Ojai, CA). Output is to the Standard MIDI File Format. Support of the *NIFF* format is intended. FURTHER INFORMATION: *Computing in Musicology* 9 (1996), 129ff. Contact information is provided at the end of the *NIFF* chapter.

MidiShare. A real-time multi-tasking MIDI operating system for the development of musical applications. Based on a client-server model, it includes an event manager, a time manager, a task manager, and a communication manager. Runs on Apple Macintosh and Atari computers with interfaces for ThinkC and Common Lisp. Supports the Standard MIDI File Format. *MidiShare* is a public-domain product. FURTHER INFORMATION: GRAME Research Laboratory, 6 quai Jean Moulin BP 1185, 69202 Lyon Cedex 01, France; *grame@rd.grame.fr*.

MOD. An audio file format developed for Atari computers and subsequently used by some sound cards. MIDI data is contained in the files.

MODE and *SMOKE*. The *Musical Object Development System* (*MODE*), a software system, and the *Smallmusic Object Kernel* (*SMOKE*), a companion representation system, were designed by Stephen Pope for composition, performance, and analysis in the *SmallTalk* environment. *MODE* provides a music representation language, schedulers and drivers, user interface components, and built-in applications for editing and browsing. *SMOKE* aims to provide a description language that supports abstractions and generalizations that form the foundations of music theory and composition. FURTHER INFORMATION: Stephen Pope, "*MODE* and *SMOKE*," *Computing in Musicology* 8 (1992), 130–132; "The *Smallmusic* Object Kernel: A Music Representation, Description Language, and Interchange Format," *Proceedings of the 1992 Computer Music Conference* (San Francisco: ICMA, 1993), 106–109; "Machine Tongues XV: Three Packages for Software Sound Synthesis," *Computer Music Journal* 17/2 (1993), 23–54.

µ-law (pron. "mu-law"). Digital audio encoding scheme originally developed for compression of speech. Resulting files are normally saved with the extension .AU. In addition to being used with UNIX workstations from most vendors, µ-law data transfer methods are well suited to modems, for which reason this method of encoding is used for audio files used by World-Wide Web applications written in the Java language.

MUP. A music printing program written by John Ark and William Krauss. *MUP* produces *Postscript* output from ASCII text descriptions. Like *M*TEX*, *MUP* is a text-formatter that is especially suited to automatic layout of notation without requiring user interaction. Outputs can be printed or displayed using a *Postscript* viewer. *MUP* is written in C and can be implemented on systems supporting a C compiler. FURTHER INFORMATION: Arkkra Enterprises, PO Box 315, Warrenville, IL 60555; *http://www. arkkra.com.*

MusE (formerly *A-R Music Engraver*). A commercial program for music typesetting which employs the A-R dialect of *DARMS*. The software has been written principally by Thomas Hall. The current implementation is on UNIX. A music notation library of multiple text fonts created by Mergenthaler are cross-licensed and available for use with the program. FURTHER INFORMATION: A-R Editions, Inc., 801 Deming Way, Madison, WI 53717; tel. (608) 836-9000; fax (608) 831-8200.

Music V (5). The most enduring version of a series of languages for the electronic generation of musical scores. It was developed in FORTRAN at Bell Labs by Max V. Mathews. The earliest version was devised in 1957 as input to a compiler. Numerous attributes of sound (especially frequency, vibrato, and dynamics) were specified. A specification could be given for each sample point. The main components of the file were sound specification statements and a note list. The note list was time-ordered.

Music V, developed in the late Sixties, improved on its predecessor by providing more global sound-control features, the possibility of representing note patterns as well as individual notes, and in supporting simulation of performance nuance (with crescendos, diminuendos, retards, etc.).

In *Music V*, the leftmost parameters are required and trailing parameters are optional. The required parameters for a note event are a function generator, a two-byte instrument code, a start time, a duration code, an amplitude code (multiple amplitude codes for the same event are possible), and a frequency code. Specific codes for instruments and amplitude vary from one dialect to another. In Example G1 we show an oversimplified representation of the first two bars in "classic" *Music V* of the clarinet part of the Mozart trio example used throughout this book.

In more articulate scores, variable instrument numbers and operating codes could be given as initial parameters. Periodic and random amplitude changes were prescribed in parameters following the required ones. The sounds generated could be changed for each score event. Wave forms and envelopes could be elaborated in sub-routines. The generation of sound required conversion from digital to analog signals.

Music V, which is known in several dialects, is the foundation of a number of representations still in use. These include the internal file format of *SCORE*, which substitutes spatial placement parameters for time-ordered ones, and more recent formats used by Mathews in the development of his conducting tool, *The Radio Baton* [compare

GEN2 3 0.0 2 1 1 0 .5 0 .25 0	This statement defines an instrument. Here a wave-form table for the clarinet is set up. GEN2 calls an oscillator subroutine. The parameters are (1) an operation code [3 = generate function], (2) an action time, (3) an instrument number, (4) a table number, and (5–10) the relative amplitudes of harmonics 1..6.
NOT 1 2 0.0 .5 1 440	These statements cause notes to be played. The initial parameters are (1) an operation code [1 = play note], (2) an instrument number, (3) a start-of-action time, (4) event duration, (5) an absolute amplitude for the event, and (6) event frequency (Hz). These parameters may be followed by a variable number of user-defined parameters (not shown).
NOT 1 2 0.5 .5 2 554	
NOT 1 2 1.0 .5 3 660	
NOT 1 2 1.5 .5 4 554	
NOT 1 2 2.0 1.0 5 880	
NOT 1 2 3.0 .5 3 660	
NOT 1 2 3.5 .5 2 554	
NOT 1 2 4.0 .5 2 494	
NOT 1 2 4.5 .5 4 588	
NOT 1 2 5.0 1.0 5 740	

Example G1 Music V representation of Bars 1 and 2 of the *Clarinet* part of the Mozart trio.

this entry with the code shown in the *Radio Baton* chapter]. *Music V* was also influential in the development of *Csound* and a number of other sound-generation languages. In its basic differentiation of global parameters and note events it also prefigures the Standard MIDI File. Earlier variants of *Music IV* and *V* included *MUSIC4BF*, *MUSIC10*, *MUSIC11*, *MUSIC360*, and *cmusic*; most were adapted to specific mainframe computers. With only minor changes, the code itself was highly portable. FURTHER INFORMATION: M. V. Mathews, Joan E. Miller, F. R. Moore, and J. C. Risset, "Music V Manual" appended to Max V. Mathews, *The Technology of Computer Music* (Cambridge: MIT Press, 1969), pp. 113–188.

Music Engraver (also known as *HB Music Engraver*). A printing program for the Apple Macintosh which utilized alphanumeric input obtained by redefining the QWERTY keyboard.

Music Publisher. A program developed by Trevor Richards for the Apple Macintosh which required the use of a separate "presto pad" for input.

Music Reader. A DOS-based optical recognition program written in Ottawa and Montreal by William McGee and Paul Merkley in the early Nineties. Output to *NP DARMS* and the Standard MIDI File Format are supported. Applications to early chant repertories have also been explored. FURTHER INFORMATION: William F. McGee, "*Music Reader*: An Interactive Optical Music Recognition System," *Computing in Musicology* 9 (1993-94), 146–151; *mcgee@citr.ee.mcgill.ca*.

MUSICA. A language for music encoding used at the University of Padua. Alphanumeric system completed in 1981. Described in *Interface* **11**/1, 1–27.

Musicode-A. This code, developed by Ann K. Blombach at The Ohio State University for use in computer-assisted music analysis, was used most intensively from approximately 1974 until 1988. It has been used primarily for the encoding of Bach chorales and 12-tone works by Krenek, Schoenberg, and Webern). The music is encoded one voice at a time, and the information for each voice includes the name of the instrument or voice, clef, key signature, time signature, pitches, durations, rests, bar lines, double bar lines, change of time signature or key signature within the composition, and repeat signs. A tone-row field is available for twelve-tone music. *Lazycode*, developed by Tom Whitney (also at The Ohio State University), allows the user to enter an abbreviated version of the required musical information, which is then translated into standard *Musicode-A* format. FURTHER INFORMATION: Ann K. Blombach, The Ohio State University, School of Music—Weigel Hall, 1866 College Road, Columbus, OH 43210-1170; tel. (614) 292-4652, 292-1102; e-mail: *ablombac@magnus.acs.ohio-state.edu*.

MUSIKODE is an alphanumerical code used in the MUSIKUS system at the University of Oslo. It was developed in the early Seventies by Tor Sverre Lande and Petter Henriksen to provide a flexible code, de-emphasizing notation, for the interpretation and analysis of music. The MUSIKUS project, a collaboration between the Departments of Informatics and Music, is now a part of the Norwegian Network for Technology and Acoustics in Music (*NoTAM*).

    The design paradigm of *MUSIKODE* was to leaf through a composition in the same way as a score is read or played: events were entered linearly along a time axis. The notion of parts was essential, but these could be different from those of a musical score. A musical part, e.g., *Violin 1* in an ensemble, could, for example, consist of a grouping of several parts (one for pitch and duration, one for phrasing, one for dynamics, one for bowing, etc.).

For analytical purposes, vocal music of the late Renaissance/early Baroque, Romantic *Lieder*, Norwegian (and Lapp/Sami) folk music, English and Norwegian hymns, children's songs and music of Valen, Schoenberg, and Webern were encoded. The design of the external code was limited by the possibilities of the teletype-style terminals of the Seventies. The internal code, which was stored in a block data structure, is still used in analytical programs. An example appears below:

External *MUSIKODE*:

```
Fartein Valen [ HVAD EST DU DOG SKIOEN  "T6:4"
[SOPRAN_  6(u*5 - ^h / ^(e. - e`:2 - a) - d*2 - f:2 - ^h`:2 /
^h`. - c:2 - d`:2 - c`:2 - e`*2 - (d=. - e=:2):2 /
e. - ^(f':2 - h`. - f=:2 - 1c - (e` - f' - d):3 / ] ]
```

Internal *MUSIKODE*:

```
HVAD EST DU DOG SKIOEN"T6:4"[4684]%SOPRAN_152$ALT_102$TENOR_41
$BASS_117$$T6:4"6U*5:4-5H:4/"5E*3:8-5E`:8-5A:4-6D:2-6F:8-5H`:8
/"5H`*3:8-6C:8-6D`:8-6C`:8-6E`:2 6D*3:16-6E:16/"6E*3:8-5F':8-5
H`*3:8-5F:8-6C:4-5E`:12-5F':12-5D:12/
```

Examples G2a-c The beginning of the soprano part of "Hvad est du dog Skioen" by Fartein Valen and its external and internal *Musikode* encodings.

FURTHER INFORMATION: *NoTAM*'s home page on the World-Wide Web is *http://www.notam.uio.no/index-e.html*. Enquiries may also be addressed to Arvid O. Vollsnes, Department of Music, University of Oslo, PO Box 1017, Blindern, 0315 Oslo, Norway; tel. +47 22/85 47 60; fax: +47 22/85 47 63; *arvid@ifi.uio.no;* or to Tor Sverre Lande, Department of Informatics, University of Oslo; *bassen@ifi.uio.no.*   (*Arvid Vollsnes*)

MusiKrafters. A line of software by Robert Fruehwald for musical excerpts and unusual notations for the Apple Macintosh; it was developed in the late Eighties. Its shape-note and tablature capabilities could be incorporated in musical information management programs.

MUSTRAN. *MUSTRAN*, developed by Jerome Wenker at Indiana University from 1962-3 over several years, was one of the first comprehensive music description codes. Almost a quarter-century before MIDI, it ambidexterously supported both sound and graphical information. *MUSTRAN* was designed for folksong transcription and analysis but it has been used extensively for the printing and analysis of polyphonic repertories. In 1984 *MUSTRAN* was converted from a (Univac, IBM, and CDC) mainframe code to a (DOS) PC code. The code was written in a fully portable version of FORTRAN.

The basic component of *MUSTRAN* consisted of a translator which reads music encoded in a mnemonic, humanly oriented alphanumeric code and translates it into an internal machine-oriented notation. In this mnemonic representation, pitch is designated by letter (A. .G), duration by the reciprocals of standard *musical binary notation* [i.e., 2 = half note, 4 = quarter note, etc.]. A back-slash (\) indicates a bar line. Like other codes that originated when memory was scarce, *MUSTRAN* assumes a one-octave span for each clef and indicates the octave only for those notes which exceed it.

The code contains all symbols of common music notation used from the Middle Ages to about 1950 plus all symbols developed for use in folk music and ethnomusicology. In addition, codes have been added to aid in music printing by completely controlling the definition needed for a fully determined music printing process. Internally, pitches can be defined in equal increments of 1/256th of a semitone (about .39 cents) covering the range from about 16 CPS to 25,000 CPS. Durations include the Large, etc., symbols from the Middle Ages down to 1/256th of a whole note (and the internal notation allows values of 1/4 of that). Complete operatic scores could be encoded including all musical markings (bowing, slurs, etc.).

A large number of utility programs to select, sort, combine, rearrange, and otherwise manage the translated data were written. A set of analysis programs will perform most of the standard music analysis techniques developed by ethnomusicologists and folklorists for the analysis of single-voice music. An extensive set of subroutines makes the development of any form of music processing relatively simple.

One utility program[2] will read translated (binary) *MUSTRAN* data and write symbolic *MUSTRAN* data. By replacing the first part of the program with a syntax analysis program for a second notation, this program could convert a second music notation into *MUSTRAN*. Conversely, by replacing the last part of the program, it would be possible to create a program which would read *MUSTRAN* notation (after translation using a pre-existing program that needs no changes) and generate source notation for a second language.

---

2. Of less than 200 lines.

RELATED READINGS: Donald Alvin Byrd, "Music Notation by Computer," Ph.D. dissertation, Indiana University, 1984; Dorothy Susan Gross, "A Set of Computer Programs to Aid in Music Analysis," Ph.D. dissertation, Indiana University, 1975; Jerome S. Wenker, "A Computer-Aided Analysis of Anglo-Canadian Folktunes," 2 vols., Ph.D. dissertation, Indiana University, 1978; Wittlich, Gary E., John W. Schaffer, and Larry R. Babb. *Microcomputers and Music* (Englewood Cliffs, NJ: Prentice-Hall, 1986), pp. 22–24.

(Jerome Wenker)

NotaFile. The *NotaFile* format was designed by Chris Sansom (London, 1992-93) for the interchange of notational information, particularly between sequencers with transcription facilities and scoring programs. All elements represented are considered to be *position events*; some of these have durations, while others do not.

The file organization resembles that of a Standard MIDI File, with a header chunk and a music chunk. Hexadecimal notation is used. The designer intended this format as a complement to the MIDI file format. Many elements of notation supported by the *NotaFile* (*.NFL*) format address deficiencies of MIDI— enharmonic notation, articulation, and text markup (rehearsal marks, structure marks, expression marks, text fonts, unusual noteheads, etc.). In addition *NotaFile* supports quarter-tone representation, such that for each letter name there are nine possible inflections, e.g., C, C♮, C♭, C♯, C♭♭, C♯♯, C quarter-tone ♭, C quarter-tone ♯, C three-quarter-tone ♭, and C three-quarter-tone ♯. FURTHER INFORMATION: DataMusic, 57 Cricketfield Road, London E5 8NR, UK; fax +44 081/985-5268.

(Chris Samson)

NoteAbility. A graphical notation package developed by Keith Hamel for the *NeXTStep* operating system. Provides a library and *TIFF* and *EPS* graphics. Accepts MIDI data. FURTHER INFORMATION (*NoteWriter* and *NoteAbility*): Opus 1 Music Inc., 449 E. 37th Avenue, Vancouver, B.C., Canada V5W 1E8; fax (604) 321-1107; *opusone@unixg.ucb.ca*.

NoteScan. Optical recognition program by Cindy Grande with implementations on the Macintosh and Windows platforms via two programs from Musicware—*Nightingale* and *Music Printer Plus* respectively. Output to *NIFF* is intended. FURTHER INFORMATION: See *Computing in Musicology* 9 (1993-94), 124ff.

NoteWriter. A notation program for the Macintosh (*ca.* 1991) by Keith Hamel. It was the heir to Hamel's *MusScribe* (*ca.* 1988). It has been used to typeset examples of *avant-garde* and popular music and graphically complex analyses. Its representation is entirely graphical. *QuickScrawl* mode permits users to draw freehand. The system is described in "A General-Purpose Object-Oriented System for Musical Graphics," *Proceedings of the*

International Computer Music Conference 1989 (San Francisco: CMA, 1989), pp.
260–263.

Number-line systems of representation. Number-line systems of notated pitch
representation form a class of solutions to the problem of assuring the correct
interpretation of notated accidentals of arbitrary complexity. In all cases the number line
gives values for all the notes that may be encountered within one octave. For the diatonic
scale, this number is 7 (C, D, E, F, G, A, B); for the chromatic scale, it is 12 (all white
and black keys of the piano).

It is in the representation of accidentals that various options occur. If every black note
assumes two names (e.g., C♯ and D♭), then the base number of named tones per octave
is 17.[3] If, however, the named pitches B♯, C♭, E♯, and F♭ (all falling on white notes)
are permitted, then the number rises to 21—three spellings for each white note.

To deal with the possibility of double sharps and flats, more ample numbers are
required. The note we call D can conceivably be spelled as C♯♯ or as E♭♭. Although
some of the possibilities are rarely used, a system assignment provides each white note
with five possible names. See also HEWLETT'S BASE-40 SYSTEM.

Octave folding.   The base-12 pitch-class representation of sounding pitches in the
chromatic octave may be folded into six by setting a binary switch. The motivation to
concoct such representations has largely disappeared with improvements in the availability
of computer memory.

Phon.   Loudness perceptions depend on frequency (mid-frequency tones sound louder
than high or low tones of equivalent energy). The phon is the unit of loudness level that
compensates for differences in frequency. A tone is said to have a loudness level of n
phons when it is perceived as having an equivalent loudness to a 1000 Hz tone of n
decibels.   (*David Huron*)

Pitch classes.   Pitch classes are used as a system of nomenclature for the twelve (piano)
keys of the even-tempered octave that overrides enharmonic notation.   C♯ and D♭ are
both rendered as 2, G♯ and A♭ as 9, and so forth.   Pitch class sets are widely used as
an organizing principle in the composition and analysis of post-tonal music. These sets
are easily derived and manipulated in computer applications. They map readily onto MIDI

---

3. One system we looked at had a base of 16 (a convenient number in hexadecimal code), which was
achieved by assuming that the notes G♯ and A♭ would never occur. At the time the program was dealing
with a simple repertory of children's songs.

key numbers. Like MIDI, however, they suppress information required for notational and analytical applications in tonal music. See also HEWLETT'S BASE-40 SYSTEM.

Pitch nomenclature. Many systems are in use for the identification of pitches. Usage of pitch names (A..G) is highly consistent; the diversity occurs in octave specification. Music history and theory books often employ the Helmholtz system (1862), in which Middle C is c': the Cs of the piano, from left to right, are C', C, c, c', c'', c''', and c''''. An earlier representation (Robert Smith, 1748) looks similar but shifts the values by one octave: Middle C is c; the Cs of the piano, from left to right, are CCC, CC, C, c, c', c'', and c'''.

Many computer applications employ the International Standards Organization (formerly called "U.S. scientific") system, in which Middle C is C4; the keys of the piano, from left to right, are C1, C2, C3, C4, C5, C6, C7, and C8. In MIDI documentation Middle C is variously given the note number 48, 60, or 72 [60 is used in this book]. Prior to the advent of electronic keyboards, keyboard manufacturers used a variety of other key-number systems; among them equations of Middle C with the numbers 40 (representing its position among the piano keys 1..88) and 48 were common. For comparisons, see Figure G1 below.

FREQUENCY	PITCH NAME AND OCTAVE DESIGNATION		KEY NO.
(Hertz[4])	Helmholz	"Standard"	MIDI
4186.0	c''''	C 8	108
2039.0	c'''	C 7	96
1046.5	c''	C 6	84
523.3	c''	C 5	72
261.6	**c'**	**C 4**	**60** (Middle C)
130.8	c	C 3	48
65.4	C	C 2	36
32.7	C,	C 1	24

Figure G1 Pitch specifications, according to various systems of nomenclature, for all of the C's on the piano keyboard. The top note is represented on the first row.

PLA. *PLA* is a language for music composition developed by Bill Schottstaedt and used until 1990, particularly at Stanford University. *PLA* has been succeeded by *CMN*, which

4. Vibrations (cycles) per second.

is described in a separate chapter. FURTHER INFORMATION: Bill Schottstaedt, "*PLA*: A Composer's Idea of a Language," *Computer Music Journal* 7/1 (1986), 11–20.

PLAINSONG. The *PLAINSONG* series of programs supported transcription, analysis, and printing of black square neumatic notation on a four-line staff with C, F, D, or G clefs. It was developed in the early Nineties by Catherine Harbor and Andy Reid for IBM PCs. The work is described in Catherine Harbor, "*PLAINSONG*—A Program for the Study of Chant in Neumatic Notation," *Computers in Music Research Conference Handbook* (Belfast: The Queen's University, 1991), pp. 24–25.

The Portable Musicwriter. A method for printing musical examples, developed by Cecil Effinger, a recognized pioneer in music printing technology, which required a specially adapted IBM Wheelwriter. Music was represented alphanumerically; features such as slurs were added by hand.

Quantization. In the capture of information played on a MIDI keyboard, quantization refers to the regularization of durations to conform to a single measure of elapsed time and to fill up, but not exceed, "beat" boundaries. The small deviations from an established pulse that normally occur in individual performance, while being insignificant to the ear, may produce unsatisfactory results in graphical expression if the data are not quantized. Quantization is thus particularly important for the proper performance of notation programs that depend on data originating on an electronic keyboard.

QuickTime. The native method for storage of audio and video information on the Macintosh platform. Audio data is encoded in eight-bit samples.

QWERTY keyboard. The normal computer keyboard for text entry. Letters on the second row from the top begin Q, W, E, R, T, Y, ...

RULLE. *RULLE* is an environment to facilitate experiments concerned with (unwritten) rules for musical performance. Written by Anders Friberg in 1986, it is implemented in Common Lisp on the Macintosh. The *RULLE* music format is designed specifically for easy use in a Lisp environment. The music is organized in voices, each consisting of a note-list. A note can have several pitches but only one duration. A new voice starts with the voice name (v1..v16).

Pitch names require a tone name (G) and inflection (#) and an octave number (0..9). Durations ("notevalues") are specified as inverse binary numbers (8, 16, 32, etc.). Optional parameters, or "properties" as they are called here, include differentiation of written and sounding duration, pitch deviation, amplitude, vibrato frequency, vibrato amplitude, and so forth. The name of the property must be a Lisp atom and the value can be any valid Lisp expression. Tuplets, slurs, meter, tempo, bars, key signature, modality (major, minor), MIDI channel and program numbers, and phrase and sub-phrase markers are all supported. Chords and chordal analysis are also supported. In performance, these properties may be altered by the rules. There is no provision for articulation information, since it is assumed that almost all articulation will be actualized in different ways by performers. Approximately 150 works, from the Baroque era to the twentieth century, have been encoded in the *RULLE* music format. There are facilities for translating to and from Standard MIDI files. FURTHER INFORMATION: Anders Friberg, "Generative Rules for Music Performance: A Formal Description of a Rule System," *Computer Music Journal* 15/2 (1991), 56–71. Address enquiries to Anders Friberg, Royal Institute of Technology, Dept. of Speech Communication and Music Acoustics, Box 700 14, S-100 44 Stockholm, Sweden; tel. +46 8/790 7876; fax +46 8/790 7554; *anders@speech.kth.se.*

(Anders Friberg)

Schenkerian analysis. A reductionist method of analysis invented by Heinrich Schenker in early twentieth-century Germany; popular predominantly in the U.S. in recent decades. Schenkerian analysis seeks to explicate the "underlying" essential pitch structures (the *Urlinie*) of musical works as confirmed by broad harmonic changes. The details of an actual musical text are regarded as superficial. Schenkerian analysis is often accompanied by elaborate diagrams of *foreground, middleground,* and *background* notes. In computer software the reproduction of these charts is a significantly different technical task from the study of the musical thinking that Schenkerian analysis claims to represent. On the latter activity, see Stephen Smoliar, "A Computer Aid for Schenkerian Analysis," *Computer Music Journal* IV/2 (1980), 41–59. Recently Jonathan Berger has called attention (in not-yet-published work) to parallels between noise reduction in sound engineering and Schenkerian analytical procedures.

Score Analyzing Maestro. An optical recognition program under development at the University of Pretoria, South Africa, for Elizabeth C. Botha and her students. Output is to sound-file formats including MIDI and MOD. FURTHER INFORMATION: *Computing in Musicology* 9 (1993-94), 126ff.; by FTP from *ftp.ee.up.ac.za.*

SCRIBE. SCRIBE is a program developed in the Eighties to support the encoding in facsimile of various medieval and Renaissance notations. The program was designed for the DOS platform but will run on Macintosh computers under simulation. In particular it supports common neumes (through mnemonic codes such as L for *longa*, PD for *podatus*, CL for *clivis*, etc.), ligatures, and colored (red, black, and void) notation. Encoded data may be displayed either in square notation or in modern stemless noteheads with slurs indicating ligation. *SCRIBE*'s emphasis is on monophonic music but it has also been used to produce elegant scores in "colored" mensural notation. Examples of the printing capabilities were shown (in black and white) in *Computing in Musicology* 4 (1988), 100–101, and 6 (1990), 25, 34. The program was developed by Brian Parrish and John Stinson in conjunction with the creation of a large database of fourteenth-century music.

The *SCRIBE* database holds 4,564 items of Dominican chant, encoded form an early fourteenth-century set of antiphonals and graduals now in Perugia, Italy, checked against contemporary Dominican sources now in Bologna, London, Rome, and Melbourne as well as standard printed editions of the text (Dominican breviaries and missals, Hesbert's *Corpus antiphonalium officii*, the *Graduate Triplex*, and the *Liber Usualis*). By their common use of Hesbert's numbering of liturgical texts, the *SCRIBE* database can be easily related to other large chant projects such as *Cantus*, CAO-ECE, and ICCU.[5]

This database can be searched for any text string (liturgical texts have been entered complete, with abbreviations expanded and spelling normalized), any sequence of note-shapes, and any series of pitches at every transposition. Searches can be limited to specific manuscripts, liturgical offices and genres; to items selected by the user; to the beginning or ending of works, or the search can be made of the whole database in any position. FURTHER INFORMATION: John Stinson, Music Department, La Trobe University, Bundoora 3083, Australia; fax +61 3/4791700; *MUSJS@lure.latrobe.edu.au*.

(John Stinson)

SGML. *Standard Generalized Markup Language* (*SGML*) is a generic markup technique to facilitate preservation of document structure when material is interchanged between diverse hardware and/or software environments. By differentiating style elements (e.g., font sizes used to distinguish chapter titles and subheadings) from document content, each publisher can maintain a house style while avoiding the tedious task of remarking text every time it is moved from one platform to another. *SGML*, which is not related to music *per se*, is the parent of *Standard Music Description Language* (*SMDL*), *HyperText Markup Language* (*HTML*), and a number of other schemes for the markup of documents containing typographically complex material.

Sibelius. Highly competent music printing program developed in the UK for the Acorn computer line. The program is machine-dependent. Transportable files are written to the

---

5. These are all database projects concerned with information on liturgical works of the Roman Catholic church in the Middle Ages and their surviving musical sources. The files can generally be used with standard database and word-processing programs. Information on *CANTUS* (chants of the Divine Office) is available from the gopher server at */Other/North America/USA/Washington, D.C./The Catholic University of America/Special Resources/ABOUT_CANTUS* and from Ruth Steiner (*steiner@cua.edu*).

EPS and MIDI formats. MIDI files can also be imported. FURTHER INFORMATION: Sibelius Software, 4 Bailey Mews, Auckland Road, Cambridge CB5 8DR, UK; +44 223/302765.

Sight Reader. An optical recognition program by Nicholas Carter. Originally UNIX-based, a PC version has also been written. Output is to the *SCORE* internal format. FURTHER INFORMATION: Nicholas P. Carter, "Music Score Recognition: Problems and Prospects," *Computing in Musicology* 9 (1993-94), 152–158; also pp. 141–142 *et passim*.

Sone. The psychoacoustic unit of subjective loudness. A sound subjectively judged to be *n* times louder than that of a 1-sone sound is defined as *n* sones. For example, where one sound is judged to be twice as loud as another sound, the number of sones also doubles. The reference point for such judgments is defined as 40 phons. Hence, a sound of 40 sones is defined as the subjective loudness evoked by a 40-phon sound. (*David Huron*)

Sound-file formats. Sound files are hardware-specific, and for this reason a great number of them lack any intelligent representation of music. Some were designed primarily for sound effects. Some conversion utilities are mentioned under listings of individual formats. See AIFF, AU, MOD, WAV, etc.

Spectral centroid. The geometric mean frequency for some complex tone or sonority weighted by amplitude. Two equal-amplitude frequencies of 500 Hz and 1000 Hz would have a spectral centroid of 750 Hz. Spectral centroid is correlated with timbre or tone color. High spectral centroids tend to be perceived as sounding "bright."

(*David Huron*)

Stella. A representation system designed by Heinrich Taube to facilitate the creation and editing of algorithmic compositions. It differentiates two object classes—events and collections (of events). Events may contain sub-objects, but these will be edited collectively as the event level. FURTHER INFORMATION: "*Stella*: Persistent Score Representation and Score Editing," *Computer Music Journal*, 17/4 (1993), 38–50. See also *Common Music*.

Strophic text. Text set out in verses. Each line of text and its associated music forms a strophe. When multiple verses of text are set to the same music, the number of syllables per strophe may vary from verse to verse.

Structured Musical Language (***SML***). A top-down approach to music representation based on programming structures used in Pascal. FURTHER INFORMATION: Ronald E. Prather and R. Stephen Elliott, "*SML*: A Structured Musical Language," *Computers and the Humanities*, 22/2 (1988), 137–151.

Style brisé. A style of notation used in the seventeenth and eighteenth centuries to represent the staggered entries of individual notes in an arpeggio or rapidly played scale. While these individuals notes were represented horizontally in the order in which they were played, they were represented not with exact times values but instead by "whole notes," with "slurs" to show their groupings.

SYMCAT. The *SYMCAT* code was developed by Jan La Rue with David Cannata for storage and search of more than 16,000 incipits of eighteenth-century symphonies. The incipit code typically reproduces the note names (in upper-case letters) of about ten pitches at the beginning of the first violin part, without regard to duration or pitch class. This identifies the work sufficiently to distinguish it for many research purposes. More than two repetitions of a pitch are reduced to numbers. Accurate results for similarity searches are facilitated by encoding incipits with grace notes twice: once without the grace notes and once with grace notes represented by lower-case letters. FURTHER INFORMATION: Jan La Rue, *A Catalogue of 18th-Century Symphonies* (Bloomington: Indiana University Press, 1988) and Jan La Rue and David Cannata, "An Ancient Crisis in Music Bibliography: The Need for Incipits," *Notes: The Journal of the American Music Library Association* 50/2 (1993), 502–518.   *(Jan La Rue)*

Synclavier Music Engraving System. Now extinct, the *Synclavier Music Engraving System* offered by New England Digital (Lebanon, NH) produced musical notation of high quality both from a stand-alone workstation and as an adjunct to their larger audio and music processing systems. Several less common notations, including shape notes and guitar tablature, were supported; *PostScript* files were produced. Some of the expertise has now migrated to the Graphire music engraving system developed by Alan Talbot.

Tablature codes. A number of codes for various kinds of tablature (systems of notation used by fretted instruments) have been devised. Among these are the following:

> **ERATTO**, a system of automatic transcription and analysis of German lute tablatures developed in the Seventies and Eighties by Hélène Charnassé (ERATTO, Paris) and Bernard Stepien (Ottawa). Output to Wallet's *Euterpe* (see above) was facilitated. The program was also adapted to use in converting French guitar tablatures to keyboard notation by Denise Derrien-Peden and her coworkers. FURTHER INFORMATION: ERATTO, C.N.R.S., 27 rue Paul Bert, F-94200 Ivry-sur-Seine, France; tel. +33 49/60-40-45; fax: +33 49/60-40-80; or *derrien@ensth-bretagne.fr.* See also *Computing in Musicology* 7 (1991), 60-64.

Tab, a UNIX typesetting program for French and Italian lute tablature developed by Wayne Cripps. The files are in ASCII. Input may be given in either a vertical string, with carriage returns separating events, or a horizontal string, with commas used as delimiters. Examples are given in *Computing in Musicology* 9 (1993-4), 226–227. FURTHER INFORMATION: PO Box 677, Hanover, NH 03755; e-mail: *wbc@huey. dartmouth.edu.*

TabCode, a method of representing lute tablatures of the sixteenth through eighteenth centuries. It was devised by Tim Crawford in 1992 to run on the Macintosh platform. Conventional notation can be supplied through the scoring program *Nightingale*. *TabCode* supports a range of tablature styles and offers the ability to specify diverse numbers of strings (4, 5, 6) and tuning systems (e.g., English/French cittern or baroque guitar). See Crawford's "*TabCode* for Lute Repertories," *Computing in Musicology* 7 (1991), 57–59.

TEI. The *Text Encoding Initiative* (*TEI*) is a set of extensions to *SGML* designed to facilitate markup of scholarly apparatus and other typographical details of text documents. It is unrelated to the computer manipulation of musical information *per se* but has been proposed for use in the encoding of music theory treatises, in which, typically, passages of text and music are interleaved.

Teletau. *Teletau* was an encoding system used during the Seventies and Eighties in Italy, principally at the National Research Center (CNUCE) in Pisa and at the Florence Conservatory. Pitch was represented by letter, duration by number. The system, developed by Pietro Grossi, was based on an ASCII representation that was used to support sound applications. A library of 800 works was encoded; a number of programs for the analysis and modelling of music were written by Lelio Camilleri (now at the Bologna Conservatory). An example of its representation is given in *Computing in Musicology* 3 (1987), 22.

Terpsichore. *Terpsichore* is a system for the electronic performance of complex musical scores. It was developed at the Center for Computational Sonology at the University of Padua in the mid-Eighties by Giovanni B. Dibiasi and Mario A. Piccinelli. *Terpsichore* utilizes a special language to transcribe the instrumental parts of a score. Additional "parts" containing agogic, dynamic, accentual, and articulatory information enable the user to select various options for performance. *Terpsichore* is especially useful for the performance of difficult and/or rarely executed scores and for sound-tracks. FURTHER INFORMATION: Centro di Sonologia Computazionale, Via Gradenigo 6/A, 35131 Padova, Italy; fax +39 049/828.76.99.   (*Giovanni Dibiasi*)

THEME, The Music Editor. This commercial notation program by Mark Lambert, developed for the IBM PC, captured alphanumeric data from an input system using a redefined QWERTY keyboard (see *Computing in Musicology* 4 [1988], 48).

TMF. The Time-Stamped MIDI Data File Format (TMF) developed at the University of Helsinki by Kai Lassfolk and Tio Lehtinen in 1987 was designed to facilitate the standardized representation of music and other timed events in a sequential file. Based on MIDI protocol V1.0, TMF could accommodate changes of tempo, key signature, and instrumentation.

TML. The *Thesaurus Musicarum Latinarum* (*TML*) is a large database of Latin writings on music theory from roughly 600 to 1600 A.D. It has been designed and managed by Thomas Mathiesen at Indiana University. Although the *TML* consists principally of text, musical examples are captured graphically in *GIF* files and also encoded with ASCII characters in such a way that "texts" can be searched for the occurrence of the names of specific graphic objects (note shapes, rests, ligatures, commensuration signs, clefs, and miscellaneous features). An extensive description and the music codes used are given in *Computing in Musicology* 9 (1993-4), 33–48. FURTHER INFORMATION: School of Music, Indiana University, Bloomington, IN 47405; (812) 855-5471; e-mail: *Mathiese@UCS. Indiana.edu.*

Toppan Scan-Note System. The Toppan system, developed in the Eighties, originated in Aarhus, Denmark, where it was developed by Mogens Kjaer. It is a proprietary system for music printing that accepts electronic keyboard input; it has produced music of professional quality for major music publishers. FURTHER INFORMATION: Toppan International Group, Iwanami Shoten Annex Bldg. 2-3-1, Kanda Jimbocho, Chiyoda-ku, Tokyo 101, Japan.

Twelve Tone Strings (*TTS*). A procedural music-description language proposed in the Eighties by Mira Balaban. *TTS* is based on abstract data types and emphasizes "operations that have direct musical meaning." It attempts to provide a junction where the specific provisions for diverse applications can intersect, rather than to accommodate fully a representation for all conceivable specifics. FURTHER INFORMATION: Mira Balaban, "The *TTS* Language for Music Description," State University of New York at Albany, School of Computer Science, Technical Report 86-18, pp. 1–23.

Tuning systems. Western musical instruments have used the equal-tempered 12-tone scale since the early eighteenth century. Numerous non-equal temperaments for the 12-tone scale were in use previously. Contemporary composition explores divisions of the octave into more than 12 tones; quarter-tone systems have been numerous and smaller divisions of the octave range are also known.[6]

USMARC format. MARC format has been implemented and is maintained as a national standard in the United States by the Machine-Readable Bibliographic Information Committee (MARBI) of the American Library Association. The standard is described in "USMARC Specifications of Record Structure, Character Sets, Tapes" (Washington: Library of Congress Cataloguing Distribution Service, 1990). Specific implementation of data elements is described in "USMARC Format for Bibliographic Data: Including Guidelines for Content Designation" (Washington: Library of Congress Cataloging Distribution Service, 199-). See also ANSI Z39.50. (*John Howard*)

VOC. File format used by the Sound Blaster sound card for sound effects.

WAM. A descriptive code, whose acronym consists of Mozart's initials, was invented by Jane Perry-Camp to represent diplomatic information (particularly unusual markings) found in autograph manuscripts of the composer. The codes are now coupled with graphic images stored in a relational database. The purpose of storing the codes is to establish the source filiation for copies and editions of Mozart's music. FURTHER INFORMATION: Jane Perry-Camp, School of Music, Florida State University, Tallahassee, FL 32306; e-mail: *perrycp@fsu.bitnet*. (*Jane Perry-Camp*)

WAV. File format used by Windows products for sound effects. Uncompressed digital audio data is stored in the files. A conversion utility called *SOX* (*Sound eXchange*) from the WAV format to AIFF is available from the World-Wide Web site *http://www.spies.com/Sox/*.

WAVany. A DOS-based audio-file conversion utility available as shareware from *bill@solaria.hac.com*. It converts such formats as AU, IFF, and VOC to WAV.

WOLFGANG. An academically oriented music processor, developed by Etienne Darbellay for IBM PC compatibles. It was awarded the Swiss Prize for Technology for 1990. *WOLFGANG* used an alphanumeric encoding system and had the ability to represent and reproduce plainchant, mensural notation (black and white, with ligatures), and the unmeasured *style brisé*. It also supported automatic reduction to a two-stave

---

6. This book makes no effort to deal with the representation of diverse tuning systems either in notation or in data representation. In relation to MIDI readers may wish to consult Carter Scholz, "A Proposed Extension to the MIDI Specification Concerning Tuning," *Computer Music Journal* 15/1 (1991), 49–54.

transcription of up to five voices and permitted the creation of polylingual scores requiring Arabic, Cyrillic, and Gothic (as well as Roman) characters.

WWW. World-Wide Web. An Internet interface that enables users to access, view, and download text, sound, and graphics documents from servers at multiple locations. Documents may be invisibly linked to a single home page. Platform-specific formatting is avoided through the use of the generalized *HyperText Markup Language* (*HTML*).

ZIPI. The ZIPI musical interface language extends MIDI concepts to provide greater control of certain aspects of sound, particularly within a computer network environment. At this writing, ZIPI is still in beta-test at the Center for New Music and Audio Technologies (CNMAT) at the University of California at Berkeley. It has been jointly developed by David Wessel and Matthew Wright of CNMAT and by Keith McMillen of Zeta Music Systems of Berkeley.

ZIPI's *Music Parameter Description Language* (*MPDL*) is organized hierarchically into 63 "families," each accommodating 127 "instruments." This language provides synthesizer control parameters for articulation, pitch name, frequency (Hz), loudness, amplitude, brightness, three-dimensional timbre space, and a host of other sound and spatialization variables. Its controller measurement parameters permit selection of such physical variables (related principally to the guitar) as pick pressure, fingerboard position, fingerboard pressure, and so forth.

ZIPI's data layer link enables devices on a ZIPI network to be synchronized to within 50 μsec. Because of its network and hardware orientations, ZIPI is message- and address-intensive. There are two message classes: those specifying a note number and those addressing an entire channel. An overriding concern of ZIPI's developers has been to avoid the MIDI equation of synthesizer key number with pitch name and frequency. For example, ZIPI can control pitch bends that do not involve key action but affect pitch frequency.

FURTHER INFORMATION: Center for New Music and Audio Technology (CNMAT), University of California at Berkeley, 1750 Arch St., Berkeley, CA 94720; *Matt@cnmat. berkeley.edu*; or Zeta Music Systems, 2560 Ninth St., Berkeley, CA 94710; *McMillen @cnmat.berkeley.edu*. See also the Winter 1994 (18/4) issue of the *Computer Music Journal*, which contains a series of six articles on ZIPI.

Contributors

David Bainbridge is in the Department of Computer Science, University of Waikato, Private Bag 3105, Hamilton, New Zealand; *D.Bainbridge@cs.waikato.ac.nz*.

Ulf Berggren is in the Department of Musicology, University of Uppsala, Övre Slottsgatan 6, 753 10 Uppsala, Sweden; tel.: +46 18/13-80-76; fax: Fax: +46 18/12-09-54; *Ulf.Berggren@musik.uu.se*.

Roger D. Boyle is in the Division of Artificial Intelligence, School of Computer Studies. The University of Leeds, Leeds LS2 9JT, UK; *roger@scs.leeds.ac.uk*.

Donald Byrd is the founder of Advanced Music Notation Systems, Inc., 57 South St., Williamsburg, MA 01096; *dbyrd@crocker.net*.

David Cooper is in the Department of Music, The University of Leeds, Leeds LS2 9JT, UK; *d.g.cooper@leeds.ac.uk*.

Edmund Correia, Jr., is at the Center for Computer Assisted Research in the Humanities, The Knoll, Stanford University, Stanford, CA 94305-8180; tel.: +1 (650) 723-7139, X304.

David Cottle is at the Waterford School, Sandy, UT 84093; tel.: +1 (801) 572-1780; fax: +1 (801) 572-1787; *dmcottle@tmcbucs.byu.edu*.

Tim Crawford is attached to both the Music Department and the Research Unit in Humanities Computing, King's College, Strand, London WC2R 2LS, England, UK; tel.: +44 171/836-5454 x3528; fax: +44 171/873-2326; *t.crawford@kcl.ac.uk*.

J. Stephen Dydo is the founder of Thoughtprocessors, 56 Bayley Avenue, Yonkers, NY 10705; tel. and fax: +1 (914) 969-2663; *Steve@voyetra.com*.

Brent A. Field is in the Department of Neuroscience, 1227 University of Oregon, Eugene, OR 97403-1227; *bfield@darkwing.uoregon.edu.*

Roger Firman is at the Royal National Institute for the Blind, 224 Great Portland Street, London W1N 6AA, England, UK; *100565.1227@compuserve.com.*

John Gibson can be reached at 1509 Chesapeake St., Charlottesville, VA 22902; *jgg9c @virginia.edu.*

Cindy Grande, NIFF Technical Coordinator, is at Grande Software, 19004 37th Avenue S., Seattle, WA 98188; tel.: +1 (206) 244-3411; +1 (206) 439-9828; fax: +1 (206) 824-2612; *72723.1272@compuserve.com.*

Lippold Haken is at the CERL Sound Group, Electrical and Computer Engineering, University of Illinois, 1406 W. Green St., Urbana, IL 61801; tel.: +1 (217) 244-6686; *l-haken@uiuc.edu.*

Thomas Hall is at A-R Editions, Inc., 801 Deming Way, Madison, WI 53717.

David Halperin is in the Department of Musicology, Tel-Aviv University, Ramat-Aviv, 69978; Israel; +972 3/5450332; *ambros@vm.tau.ac.il.*

Philip Hazel is at 33 Metcalfe Road, Cambridge CB4 2DB, England, UK; tel.: +44 1223/365518; *P.Hazel@ucs.cam.ac.uk.*

Walter B. Hewlett is the director of the Center for Computer Assisted Research in the Humanities, Braun Music Center #129, Stanford University, Stanford, CA 94305-3076; tel.: +1 (650) 725-9240; fax: +1 (650) 725-9290.

John Howard is the head of the Eda Kuhn Loeb Music Library and the Director of the U.S. RISM Office, both located in the Music Building, Harvard University, Cambridge, MA 02138; *howard@rism.harvard.edu.*

David Huron is at Conrad Grebel College, University of Waterloo, Waterloo, Ontario; N2L 3G6 Canada; tel.: +1 (519) 885-0220, X247; fax: +1 (519) 885-0014; *dhuron @watserv1.uwaterloo.ca.*

Werner Icking is at the German National Research Center for Information Technology (GMD—Forschungszentrum Informationstechnik GmbH), D-53754 Sankt Augustin, Germany; *Werner.Icking@gmd.de*.

David Jaffe is at the Center for Computer Research in Music and Acoustics, The Knoll, Stanford University, Stanford, CA 94305-8180; tel.: +1 (650) 723-4971; fax: +1 (650) 723-8468; *david@jaffe.com*.

Bettye Krolick is at 724 Powderhorn Drive, Fort Collins, CO 80526; tel.: +1 (970) 226-2062; fax: +1 (970) 225-0952.

Max V. Mathews is at the Center for Computer Research in Music and Acoustics, The Knoll, Stanford University, Stanford, CA 94305-8180; tel: +1 (650) 723-4971; fax: +1 (650) 723-8468; *mvm@ccrma.stanford.edu*.

Toshiaki Matsushima is a member of the Faculty of Science, Toho University, 2-2-1 Miyama, Funabashi-shi, Chiba-ken, 274 Japan; tel.: +81 474/72-8237; fax: +81 474/75-1855; *matusima@is.sci.toho-u.ac.jp*.

Steven R. Newcomb is the founder of TechnoTeacher, Inc., PO Box 23795, Rochester, NY 14692-3795; +1 (716) 389-0961; fax+1 (716) 389-0960; *srn@techno.com*.

Kia-Chuan Ng is in the Division of Artificial Intelligence, School of Computer Studies, The University of Leeds, Leeds LS2 9JT, UK; *kia@scs.leeds.ac.uk*.

Kjell E. Nordli (Slettelokka 8A, 0597 Oslo, Norway) works for Norwegian Television (*kjelle@tvnorge.no*).

Sile O'Modhrain is at the Center for Computer Research in Music and Acoustics, The Knoll, Stanford University, Stanford, CA 94305-8180; *sile@ccrma.stanford.edu*.

Perry Roland is at the Digital Media and Music Center, Clemons Library, University of Virginia, Charlottesville, VA 22904; tel.: +1 (804) 924-7474; fax: +1 (804) 924-7468; *pdr4h@poe.acc.virginia.edu*.

Helmut Schaffrath† formerly taught at the Gesamthochschule für Musik, Essen University, Essen, Germany; enquiries about his work may be directed to **Ewa Dahlig**, Helmut Schaffrath Laboratory of Computer Aided Research in Musicology, Istytut Sztuki PAN, ul. Długa 16/29, 00-950 Warszawa skr. 994, Poland; fax: +48 22/31-31/49; *eda@plearn.edu.pl.*

Bill Schottstaedt is at the Center for Computer Research in Music and Acoustics, The Knoll, Stanford University, Stanford, CA 94305-8180; tel.: +1 (650) 723-4971; fax: +1 (650) 723-8468; *bil@ccrma.stanford.edu.*

Eleanor Selfridge-Field is at the Center for Computer Assisted Research in the Humanities, Braun Music Center, Stanford University, Stanford, CA 94305-3076, USA; tel.: +1 (650) 725-9240; fax: +1 (650) 725-9290; *esf@ccrma.stanford.edu.*

Peer Sitter has conducted his research at the Musikwissenschaftliches Institut, Universität zu Köln, Albertus-Magnus Platz, D-50923 Köln, Germany; *alm05@rs1.rrz.Uni-Koeln.de.*

Donald Sloan is at the Music Department, Ashland University, Ashland, OH 44805; tel.: +1 (419) 289-5113; *dsloan@ashland.edu.*

Leland Smith is the director of the San Andreas Press, PO Box 60247, Palo Alto, CA 94306; tel. and fax: +1 (650) 856-9394.

Andranick Tanguiane is at Fern Universität, Feithstrasse 140, 58084 Hagen, Germany; tel.: +49 2331/987-2615; fax: +40 2331/987-313.

Lynn M. Trowbridge can be reached at 4029 Autumn Court, Fairfax, VA 22030; tel.: +1 (202) 874-9491; fax: +1 (202) 874-9669; *tbridge@erols.com.*

Frans Wiering is in the Department of Humanities Computing, Utrecht University, Achter de Dom 22–24, NL 3512 JP Utrecht, The Netherlands; tel.: +31 30/253-6335; fax: +31 30/253-9221; *frans.wiering@ruu.let.nl.*

Addresses for contributors to the glossary are given with the relevant entries.

Index